Criminology

This book is dedicated to my mother, Gladys Jones (1922–2001)

Criminology

Third edition

Stephen Jones

Senior Lecturer in Law, University of Bristol

OXFORD

UNIVERSITY PRESS

Great Clarendon Street, Oxford ox2 6dp

Oxford University Press is a department of the University of Oxford.
It furthers the University's objective of excellence in research, scholarship,
and education by publishing worldwide in

Oxford New York

Auckland Cape Town Dar es Salaam Hong Kong Karachi
Kuala Lumpur Madrid Melbourne Mexico City Nairobi
New Delhi Shanghai Taipei Toronto

With offices in

Argentina Austria Brazil Chile Czech Republic France Greece
Guatemala Hungary Italy Japan Poland Portugal Singapore
South Korea Switzerland Thailand Turkey Ukraine Vietnam

Oxford is a registered trade mark of Oxford University Press
in the UK and in certain other countries

Published in the United States
by Oxford University Press Inc., New York

First published 1998
Second edition 2001

British Library Cataloguing in Publication Data

Data available

Library of Congress Cataloging in Publication Data

Data available

Typeset by RefineCatch Limited, Bungay, Suffolk
Printed in Great Britain

on acid-free paper by
Ashford Colour Press Ltd, Gosport, Hampshire

ISBN 0–19–928238–2 (Pbk.)   978–0–19–928238–8 (Pbk.)

1 3 5 7 9 10 8 6 4 2

Preface to the first edition

I must confess to having experienced a certain amount of discomfort in writing this book. Perhaps this came from my split personality. The half of me that is a law teacher has no problem in producing a textbook. The half of me that is a criminology teacher knows that *real* criminologists do not write textbooks and are reluctant to recommend their use to students. Textbooks, after all, are never detailed enough or cover all the arguments. It is far better to have a well-stocked library which, together with a carefully operated short-loan system, should be capable of meeting the students' needs.

The problem with this is that my experience of teaching criminology to undergraduates has taught me that they like the idea of having some sort of a textbook. It seems to provide a sense of security. With the increase in course assessment nowadays, I suspect that we tutors are making ever greater demands on our students. We would be delighted if they found the time to read all the references from the original sources that we set, but there are still only twenty-four hours in a day. Perhaps the references can be read in the vacation when there is more time but, for now, the students need to know where they are going. Hence this book.

The word criminology, in an academic context, is used in two different ways. The narrower usage is confined to the theoretical aspects, such as what determines the content of the criminal law and why some people act in such a way as to break the rules. The wider usage covers these considerations and also includes studies of sentencing and penology. This book is based on the narrower usage. This reflects developments at my own university (and, I suspect, at others) where modularisation has created a trend towards shorter courses.

The book is divided into three main parts. The first considers issues relating to the definition, measurement, portrayal and control of the phenomenon we call crime. The second looks at various explanations of crime which are predominantly based on societal influences. The third looks at some explanations of crime which mainly involve either biological or psychological influences, or both. The fact that much of the sociological analysis comes from America does not indicate some anti-British bias; it is simply a reflection of where a substantial amount of the research has been conducted, especially in the first half of the century. This occurred because not only were (and are) there extensive differences among individuals in America on account of widespread immigration, but because American culture has come to reflect the country's pioneering spirit and to exalt in its individuality. Hopefully, readers will be able to judge for themselves whether the cultural differences between the two countries (which some may feel are diminishing by the day) render the American literature less relevant. The biological and psychological material in the final part of the book is more likely to include British work: the medical sciences have never completely relinquished a hold on the study of crime in this country.

The inclusion of this last part may cause surprise to some people. Psychological explanations of crime have become distinctly unfashionable among criminologists, particularly as they embody what is perhaps the criminologist's most reviled notion: determinism. As will become apparent throughout this book, one of the commonest objections raised during the past thirty years to 'traditional' explanations of crime is that they deny individual actors 'freedom of choice'. However, this is a sweeping assertion, which should be treated with a certain amount of caution. Moreover, some sociologists appear to have an aversion to matters psychological and refuse even to contemplate the possibility that such issues could be relevant to anti-social behaviour. I have tried throughout to be open-minded. I do not provide 'the answers' at the end, but I hope I have asked the right questions.

Nor do I apologise for the fact that the approach (although, hopefully, not the contents) adopted in this book is basically a traditional one, using the conventional categories within the discipline and with a liberal sprinkling of references to 'the causes' of crime. My teaching experience suggests that such an approach is still fundamentally valid, and is more readily understood by undergraduate students. It also provides a good base for those who wish to progress further into the subject. In any case, as the difficulties with the traditional approach are raised in the text, students will become aware of them.

Some people may think the title *Criminology* to be somewhat grand for such a modest work. Indeed, a well-known criminologist colleague of mine was surprised by the brevity of the title and suggested that, in the best tradition of social scientific publications, I should follow the word 'Criminology' with a colon and then a suitably snappy subtitle. Unfortunately, I have been unable to think of one, so *Criminology* it remains. (In fact, the title became a 'working description' used in dealings with Butterworths, and then somehow found its way into their promotional literature!).

It is customary at this point to thank people who have provided assistance in the creation of this book, while at the same time assuming total responsibility for any blunders that it may contain. Thanks are due to Naomi Bull, Claire Hall, Katherine Rose Hall, Pat Hammond, Filomena Jones and Richard Jones. Yet, above all I owe a debt of gratitude to my students, who have sustained me over many years. They have been a source of inspiration, frustration and even humour (especially the one who wrote in an examination about 'rods and mockers'). If each of them were to buy a copy of this book, it would probably top the best-sellers list.

Stephen Jones
Tel Aviv, November 1997

Preface to the second edition

I am very pleased that the response to the first edition of *Criminology* has led to the publishers asking me to produce a new version some three years later. On the basis that I must have done something right last time, I have not changed the structure of the book, but have confined myself to updating the material and expanding one or two areas. Although the number of references has increased to the extent that the bibliography now forms a sizeable part of the book, many journals (as well as Home Office and other government publications) are increasingly available on-line in university and college libraries. I have also made some minor alterations: for example, readers will be relieved to discover that they are no longer required to contemplate the perplexing notion of 'pubic transport'.

Having looked again at the preface to the first edition, I find that I still agree with the views I expressed at that time, and there is no need to repeat them here. I should like to add the names of Sue Pettit, the University's Law Librarian, Vanessa Mortiaux and my colleagues Janine Griffiths-Baker and Sam Lewis to the list of people who have assisted in the preparation of this book.

Stephen Jones
Helsinki, May 2001

Preface to the third edition

As I write, it is increasingly apparent that a general election is immi-
nent in the UK. The strongest possible indicator of this is present—
politicians are vying to assure the public that they will take the tough-
est stance on crime. There is a widespread assumption that the only
way to prevent future offending is by imposing more severe punishments. Predictably, few politicians have raised the issue of why people
commit crimes in the first place.

Despite this depressing background, it is encouraging that students
are choosing to study criminology and related courses in increasing
numbers. I hope that the new edition of this book can continue to
help meet the growing need for a basic text in the subject. There have
been no changes to the structure of the book, but new material has
been added throughout and some areas expanded. My belief that it is
important for students to have a grounding in the traditional criminological theories has been strengthened by the renewed interest in the
several of the older writers, such as Robert K Merton.

In the preface to the second edition, I pointed out that government
publications and many journals are available on-line in university and
college libraries. Four years later, this is now even more likely to be
the case, and I hope this will provide some compensation for the
increased length of the bibliography.

Finally, I am very grateful to Oxford University Press for being
prepared to add this work to their already impressive list of criminology
publications.

Stephen Jones
La Rochelle, February 2005

Contents

Introduction: the origins and development of criminology

Writings about crime can be found from the earliest times. Sometimes they were in the form of novels and on other occasions they were accounts, such as the consequences of deprivation in slums and the evils of drink. Yet, such writers did not think of themselves as criminologists. They wrote from a variety of perspectives: religion, medicine and, in particular, a growing concern about the governance of the country that arose from increasing urbanisation. The term 'criminology' emerged at the end of the nineteenth century because a group of theorists laid claim to systematic knowledge as to the nature of criminal behaviour, its causes and solutions. Prior to this, commentaries on crime largely arose out of other enterprises. How was it that criminology came to develop as a specialist science of the criminal?

At the beginning of the nineteenth century, the administration of criminal justice in most European countries had been influenced by the views of several writers whose approach, although differing in certain respects, has come to be referred to as 'classicism'. The main exponent is generally agreed to be Cesare Beccaria, who set out his ideas in the book *On Crimes and Punishments* (1764). These were later taken up in England by the philosopher Jeremy Bentham. The basic view as to the organisation of society adopted by the classicists was influenced by the social contract theories of Hobbes and Rousseau. Individuals agree to join together to form a society, and there is a consensus within the society for the private ownership of property and the protection of its members from harm. People freely enter into a 'social contract' with the state to maintain this consensus. Part of this 'contract' gives the state the power to punish criminals. Punishment should not be arbitrary or excessive, but proportionate to the harm caused. Individuals are rational beings and are therefore considered responsible for their own actions. The classical approach to criminal justice was described by the American criminologist George Vold (1958) as:

> An exact scale of punishments for equal acts without reference to the
> nature of the individual involved and with no attention to the question
> of special circumstances under which the act came about.

In practice, this approach was modified—mitigating factors were
allowed in the determination of punishment—but during the nineteenth century, classicism had to confront the challenge of a new
set of writers, who came to be known as positivists. Their theories
developed as a result of growing scientific discoveries and, in particular, Darwin's theory of evolution, which was published in 1859. For
the positivists, scientific method was of paramount importance: techniques claimed to be successful in the study of the physical world were
said to be equally important in the study of humans and society in
general. In relation to crime, this initially came to include considerable reliance on the newly-emerging criminal statistics. Scientific
objectivity was crucial; the reasons for the existence of particular rules
in society were less important than the measurement of how they
operated. Free will was seen at best as of secondary importance: positivism suggested that a person's behaviour was influenced—or even
determined—by constitutional or structural forces over which the
person has no direct control.

The Italian criminologist Enrico Ferri (1895) provided a good illustration of how the strongest adherents to this position approached
their task:

> Just as in a given volume of water, at a given temperature, we find the
> solution of a fixed quantity of any chemical substance, not an atom more
> or less, so in a given social environment, in certain defined physical con-
> ditions of the individual, we find the commission of a fixed number of
> crimes.

Another Italian, Cesare Lombroso, is often described as the 'father' of
positivist criminology. Indeed, it was he who used the phrase 'scuola
positiva'—positive school. Lombroso was a doctor and his interest in
criminology arose out of his general exploration of anthropological
'types', ranging from the genius to the insane. His examination of
criminals led him to conclude that their constitutional peculiarities
held the key to the whole 'criminal problem'. It could be said that
criminology was 'born' as a discipline with Lombroso's work, at least
in parts of continental Europe. However, there has always been considerable resistance from officialdom in Britain and elsewhere to the
idea that criminology is a 'specialised' body of academic knowledge,
probably because of the clear implications for the politically sensitive

areas of criminal justice and penal policy. The study of criminology has, therefore, developed in distinctive ways in different countries. For example, in Italy it arose out of the study of anthropology; in the USA it grew out of forensic medicine and early sociology; and in Britain it emerged from forensic medicine and psychiatry.

The development of criminology in Britain

From the 1860s, medical people such as Maudsley worked within the court and prison systems to try to identify insane or 'feeble-minded' offenders. This was very much an 'establishment' activity; indeed, it had to be, for practitioners to retain any professional credibility and be taken seriously by judges and prison administrators. There was no real questioning that the normal course of the law and sentencing should apply for the vast majority of offenders. The distinction being made was between law and medicine or, in effect, between the prison and the asylum. More theoretically-minded criminologists, such as Havelock Ellis (1890), who tried to encourage the study of criminal anthropology in Britain, were destined to remain outside establishment circles. It is significant that Ellis was looked down on as having no experience as a practitioner. In fact, it was he who, in promoting the ideas of Lombroso, introduced the word 'criminology' into the English language (Garland 1988).

Following the end of World War I and the return of large numbers of shell-shocked and mentally disturbed men to Britain—some of whom would eventually end up in prison—a greater interest in psychiatry began to develop. It was also around this time that Sigmund Freud was writing about his theories of psychoanalysis (see Chapter 16). Soon, doctors such as Hamblin Smith (the first Briton to describe himself as a 'criminologist') were using psychological tests on prisoners and publishing their results in clinical periodicals. They eventually formed the Institute for the Scientific Treatment of Delinquency in 1932.

The first university lectures in 'Criminology' in Britain were given to postgraduate medical students at Birmingham in 1921. W Norwood East's books *An Introduction to Forensic Psychiatry in the Criminal Courts* (1927) and *The Medical Aspects of Crime* (1936) exemplify the interest that was being expressed by psychiatrists in the 'individual criminal personality'. East himself was a former prison medical officer who had trained in psychiatry. Nevertheless, moves away from a clinical approach to crime in Britain had already started. In 1913, Charles

Goring published *The English Convict: a Statistical Study* (see Chapter 14). By the use of copious amounts of data Goring refuted Lombroso's assertion that there was a 'criminal type': instead, he claimed that physical 'anomalies' were simply extreme forms of characteristic that could be found in everyone. Goring's conclusions—essentially a more sophisticated form of Lombroso's ideas—were already becoming unfashionable in the USA and Britain at the time of the book's publication. However, it was his use of statistics that set his work apart from Lombroso's essentially impressionistic study.

Of even greater significance for the development of the sociological study of crime in Britain was Cyril Burt's book *The Young Delinquent* (1925). Burt, an educational psychologist, was responsible for making psychological assessments of schoolchildren in London with behavioural problems, whether or not they had been convicted of any crime. The book itself is an analysis of 400 schoolchildren (problem cases and a control group) and utilised a wide range of statistical techniques and psychological measurements as well as social enquiries. The main significance of this work is that the different disciplines called upon, the variety of approaches adopted, and even the extension of the study beyond those formally convicted of a criminal offence, all pointed to the need for an independent discipline of criminology, with wide-ranging experts rather than narrow medical or psychological practitioners (Garland 1988).

Within a decade of the publication of *The Young Delinquent*, developments were occurring, which would establish criminology as an academic discipline in its own right in Britain. Curiously, it was three European immigrants escaping from Hitler who individually emerged at the forefront of the academic study of criminology in universities: Hermann Mannheim at the LSE, Max Grunhut at Oxford and Leon Radzinowicz at Cambridge. Post-war politics saw a broadly consensual view towards criminal justice policy. The belief existed that governments could directly influence social development and, in relation to crime, there was a conviction that appropriately directed policies could bring about a real reduction in delinquent behaviour (Morris 1988). With this in mind, the Institute of Criminology was established by the Home Office at Cambridge University in 1960 to study possible directions for penal policy. The brief was not for grand theorising but, as Radzinowicz wrote (1961), it was for:

> . . . descriptive, analytical accounts of the state of crime, of the various classes of offenders, of the enforcement of the criminal law and of the effectiveness of various measures of penal treatment.

For much of the 1950s, psychoanalysis (with particular reference to juvenile delinquency) was still the predominant academic interest in British criminology, as can be seen from articles in the *British Journal of Delinquency* (now *Criminology*), which started in 1950. However, studies of English cities by people such as Mays (1954) and Morris (1957) showed that criminologists were beginning to adopt a more sociological approach, and a major blow to psychoanalysis was dealt by Barbara Wootton's book *Social Science and Social Pathology* (1959). This was a wide-ranging review of:

> the contributions which the social sciences have made towards the understanding, and thereby also towards the prevention and cure, of the social problems associated with unacceptable forms of deviant behaviour.

The development of criminology in the USA

Meanwhile, developments in the USA had taken a different course, indeed one which was eventually to have a significant effect on British criminology. The influence of forensic medicine in the early years of the twentieth century, which had taken such a grip in Britain, soon came to be replaced in the USA by that of sociology. American academics were already aware of the work of Europeans such as Weber and Durkheim, but it was the establishment of the first ever American sociology department at the new University of Chicago in 1892 which provided the immediate direction for American criminology. The sociological study of crime now became pre-eminent. At first, in keeping with the work of writers such as WI Thomas and GH Mead, interest was shown in the area of socialisation. Chicago, with its massive influx of immigrants from a variety of cultural backgrounds, provided an ideal setting for detailed empirical studies of how these people managed to live together. The testing of hypotheses, including proneness to criminal behaviour (based on recorded convictions), and analyses of individuals' environmental and social experiences, became the standard tools of positivist criminology. Studies of criminals' physical or mental constitution still continued and these formed the basis of the first criminology textbook—appropriately entitled *Criminology*—by Maurice F Parmalee in 1918. However, such an approach was on the wane and increasingly becoming secondary to the sociological enterprise.

It was not until the late 1930s that the influence of European sociology of law really came to the fore in American criminology, when the work of people such as Thorsten Sellin and Edwin Lemert emphasised the importance of social structure and social institutions. Edwin Sutherland's work on 'white-collar crime' brought together the interactionism of Mead and the ecological approach of the Chicago researchers, but the emphasis was still on the criminal rather than the crime. This led neatly into the politics of 'Cold War' America during the 1950s, when 'functionalist' analyses of those who broke the rules ruled out any fundamental challenge to 'the system'. The work of Parsons is generally taken as exemplifying this approach. Little was heard of the more critical approach of writers such as Tannenbaum and Lemert during that period, a fact which Sumner (1994) considered may have been due to the political witch-hunts of Senator Joe McCarthy.

Nevertheless, by the end of the decade positivist criminology—both psychological and sociological—was coming under challenge from two directions. The first was from the so-called 'labelling' theorists who, basing their arguments on interactionism, argued that criminology takes a precise socio-political problem as its subject matter, and that 'crimes' and 'criminals' are the data of criminology. The data, therefore, is defined not by criminologists, but by the authorities. This meant that, for example, the earlier functionalist criminologists had taken an uncritical view of their data. They were, in effect, accused of scientific prostitution as they had ignored the value-laden nature of their enterprise. The emphasis, therefore, should not be on crimes as defined by the state but on deviance, and deviance itself was but a label. In what has become one of the best-known quotations in criminology, Howard Becker (1963) stated that:

> Deviance is not a quality of the act the person commits, but rather a consequence of the appreciation by others of rules and sanctions to an offender.

Sociologists of deviance focused more on the processes through which behaviour comes to be labelled crime, or persons labelled criminal. Such appellations are contested and contestable categories.

Britain's radical contribution

The other challenge to positivism centred on the questions of who has the power to apply the labels and then make them stick. Radical criminology disputed the consensual view of society which had been assumed by positivists, particularly during the 1950s. In the USA, this challenge first took the form of 'conflict theories', which were based on the view that different groups within a society are in constant competition for power. In Britain, however, a result of the growing interest in the interactionist approach was the setting up of the National Deviancy Symposium in 1968. This in turn led to the publication in 1973 of one of the most influential books in British criminology, *The New Criminology*. The authors, adopting a Marxist analysis, claimed that the development of a crime-free society was possible. It could be argued that neo-Marxist criminology is this country's most significant contribution to criminological theory and it is still alive, despite a change in the political and academic climate. However, it has lost some of its former adherents to other 'radical' criminologies, such as post-modernism.

The past thirty years

It was inevitable that the election of right-wing governments on both sides of the Atlantic at the end of the 1970s would lead to a reduction in political interest in the aetiology (cause) of crime. Instead, the political agenda since the 1980s has concentrated more on crime prevention and harsher punishment. Indeterminate sentencing—whereby a release date from prison was not fixed by the sentencer—had been increasingly common in the USA during the previous decade. This resulted in an academic-led backlash demanding greater 'justice' (by which was meant equality) in sentencing. The movement was subsequently taken up by some British academics and eventually the government, even though no such extreme sentencing practices had ever been adopted in this country. Several former radical criminological theorists, such as a co-author of *The New Criminology*, Jock Young, were now advocating a 'Left Realist' approach to criminology. This view, which directly influenced Labour Party policy on criminal justice, involved placing the victim and the local community at centre stage in the debate about crime. By the 1980s it seemed that, for the first time in the post-war era, party political considerations had taken a stranglehold on British criminology. However, by the end of the 1990s the second part of Tony Blair's earlier promise that a Labour Government would be 'Tough on crime, tough on the causes of crime' seemed empty rhetoric in his bid to convince the electorate that Labour would deliver on the first.

The rest of the book contains a more detailed consideration of this outline. Any student of history nowadays will realise that the emergence of different themes and the interrelationship between particular events cannot fully be appreciated from such a traditionally compartmentalised and linear view of the past. Unfortunately, a lack of space precludes the fuller analysis which the history of criminology merits. It is hoped that the references throughout the book will enable readers to gain a greater insight into the riches that such a study has to offer.

Where does this leave the study of criminology in Britain today? It could reasonably be claimed that criminology has been an academic discipline in its own right since the establishment of the first postgraduate course at the new Institute of Criminology at Cambridge University in 1961. However, it was during the next two decades that the subject really proliferated in higher education (Rock 1988). As, until fairly recently, this was generally at postgraduate level, most teachers, writers and researchers in the area have initially studied another academic subject, such as sociology, social administration, law or psychology. This diversity of background and approach is to be welcomed because it has provided a rich variety of theories and criticisms which makes criminology such a fascinating subject to study. The only people likely to be disappointed are those in search of the 'easy answer'.

Part 1

Crime and crime control: alternative discourses

1

The development of crime and crime control as social phenomena: the role of the police

Background

It is important to realise at the outset that what is nowadays thought of as a 'criminal justice system' is a development of modern history. For centuries English law was based on a system of tribal justice with an emphasis on retaliation—the 'blood-feud'. It was only around the eighth century that changes in Anglo-Saxon society saw a shift in autonomy from the family to kings and clerics, but even then societal problems were viewed as primarily existing between individuals, and compensation became the normal way of settling disputes. The number of kingdoms was reducing before the 1066 Conquest and the process was completed by the ensuing Norman kings who centralised administration of the country's affairs, including the dispensation of justice. Minor misdemeanours were still considered in the local community, but in the reign of Henry II (1154–89) the idea of 'the King's Peace' emerged, breaches of which were punishable in the Royal Courts. This is the earliest point in British history when it is sensible to refer to 'crime'.

It has never been possible completely to disentangle crime from crime control. The long political instability from the fifteenth century to the 'Glorious Revolution' of 1688 occurred without any standing army or police force. Enforcement of criminal law had, to some extent, been laid at the feet of justices of the peace, whose original function much more closely resembled that of witness than judge. However, justices, also known as magistrates, came to play a key role in crime control by the eighteenth century.

The most significant development in 'crime control' in England between the Middle Ages and the eighteenth century was the increased involvement of the state in problems which had initially been dealt with at a local, and more informal, level. Despite the developing concept of 'the King's peace', until the seventeenth century most small communities in England were self-policing, and local custom and opinion played an important role in ascertaining how to deal with criminals. The focus first shifted from the local manorial courts in the sixteenth century to the ecclesiastical courts in the seventeenth century. These courts had jurisdiction over all matters relating to the church as well as the enforcement of sexual morality. The idea of crime at this stage seems to have been closely related to sin, and even at the start of the eighteenth century there were still campaigns against drunkards, swearers and people who worked on the Sabbath. However, during the first half of that century, crime became increasingly separated from ideas of sin; more offences were being brought to the attention of the royal judges and the magistracy began to grow in importance.

Some historians (for example, Hay *et al.* 1975) have maintained that the change of emphasis away from sin was driven by the perception of the gentry that they needed to protect their land and goods. At the same time, it is argued, there was a particular type of crime developing among the ordinary people in rural areas with the intention of preserving customary rights, such as smuggling, poaching and collecting firewood. Until the eighteenth century, such activities had caused little concern to landowners. Where such customary rights appeared to be particularly under threat, so-called riots (probably more akin to modern demonstrations) would sometimes occur (Thompson 1975). Another area of crime which was increasingly troubling the rich was forgery. With the growth of financial and banking concerns in London, it was felt that strong action was necessary against all types of fraud. Between 1812 and 1818 almost twice the number of people were executed for forgery than for murder in London and Middlesex (Emsley 2005).

Early policing

By the eighteenth century the Assize system, under which the royal judges periodically visited the principal towns to try the most important criminal cases, was well established. County quarter sessions dealt with the middle ranking range of offences. The least serious crimes were considered by the petty sessions, a monthly meeting of local justices of the peace which also handled matters of local government. Established as long ago as 1361, justices reached the zenith of their power and influence during this period, and appointment to the magistracy was considered a mark of considerable social and political prestige among the gentry. For a century or more, justices of the peace were, in effect, both administrators and judges throughout rural England. The novelist Henry Fielding (author of *Tom Jones*) was for a while the Bow Street magistrate and wrote about his work, including his *Enquiry into the Causes of the Late Increase of Robbers* (1751).

The work of the justices of the peace was supported by the parish constables. These unpaid individuals would typically be reasonably wealthy farmers, artisans or tradesmen, who had been elected to the position by their neighbours for a year. Prosecutions were brought by private individuals. During the pressure for professional policing in the early nineteenth century, it became commonplace to portray parish constables as being lazy and incompetent. However, it seems that this was not always the case, at least in the seventeenth century (Wrightson 1980). Many parish constables were prepared to pay deputies, and several of these remained in office sufficiently long for them to acquire a reasonable level of expertise. In the urban areas, including London, there was greater use of night 'watchmen'. It was in the capital that Henry Fielding, together with his half-brother Sir John, created a group of half a dozen 'thief-takers', who came to be known as the 'Bow Street Runners'. Supported by government funds, the Fieldings operated as 'trading justices' charging modest fees to individuals who wanted efficient enforcement of the law in particular instances. The Runners also started an experiment of night patrols in the main routes into London. The 1828 Select Committee enquiring into policing in metropolitan London heard many compliments about the work of watchmen, most of whom were former soldiers (Emsley 2005).

Nevertheless, the attitude towards crime control towards the end of the eighteenth century had changed quite considerably from that found at the beginning. In the early years, there was little by way of crime detection; most routine crimes were dealt with on a local and relatively informal basis with courts used as a last resort; and the 'bloody code' of capital punishment, with its accompanying crowds, provided a useful deterrent against committing the most serious crimes. The system worked because everyone knew their place in the social order. However, considerable changes occurred throughout the century. By the end, there had been a clear move by the propertied classes towards private policing and protection societies. The turmoil in continental Europe, which culminated in the French Revolution, came to be feared by both the aristocracy and the rapidly emerging middle class of traders in Britain. The 1780 Gordon Riots in London were untypical, but served to reinforce these fears. The population of London almost doubled during this period. The growing industrial revolution led to massive shifts of population from the country to the towns. The urban setting only served to highlight and, indeed, widen the gap between the rich and the poor. There was less scope for the tolerance of minor acts of offending that had occurred in the countryside.

Creation of the 'new police'

This, then, was the background to the growing clamour among London merchants for a more efficient form of policing. Between 1795 and 1800 the reformer Jeremy Bentham (see Chapter 5) and Patrick Colquhoun formulated plans for reforming London's metro-politan police system. Colquhoun had estimated that there were 10,000 thieves, prostitutes and other criminals who stole over half a million pounds worth of goods annually from London's docks. Their proposals bore some fruit with the creation of Britain's first profes-sional police force, the Thames River Police, in 1798. The new force was given wide-ranging powers, including one of stopping and searching without a warrant anyone suspected of handling stolen goods. This was subject to much criticism as being repugnant to the spirit of English government.

The catalyst to substantial change, however, was the appointment of Robert Peel as Home Secretary in 1822. Peel, who had previously organised policing in Ireland, had already stated that he viewed the creation of a police force to prevent crime as being of paramount importance. Having appointed some uniformed constables at Bow Street in 1822, Peel went on to establish a Parliamentary Select Com-mittee in 1828 to consider the question of policing. As the committee largely comprised men sympathetic to his views, it was no surprise that it recommended the creation of a police force in London. In any case, there were already 450 paid police officers patrolling metropolitan London. Peel cited figures in the Parliamentary debate to indicate rising crime, and the Metropolitan Police Act 1829 was passed with little difficulty, creating seventeen police divisions, each staffed by 165 uniformed officers. One of the two commissioners, Charles Rowan, was an army colonel and many of the senior officers had a military background (Rawlings 1999). The first uniformed police force in America was formed in Boston a few years later in 1838.

Peel's use of statistics was somewhat misleading. Crime figures, first published in England in 1810, had been collected since 1805. However, these only consisted of the number of people committed for trial (as opposed to the number of people who had been convicted of crimes). This figure had increased from 5,000 a year at the beginning of the century, to around 15,000 a year in 1820 and nearly 20,000 in 1830. Nevertheless, it is arguable that other reforms in the criminal justice system could have been largely responsible for this. The problems with criminal statistics, which are considered in Chapter 3, had not become apparent at this early stage of their use.

The Metropolitan Police, and subsequently the other newly-created forces, were primarily charged with the prevention (as opposed to the detection) of crime. This made assessment of the force's efficiency difficult to gauge, and there is evidence that the force responded to pressure for results by arresting disproportionate numbers of drunks and vagrants. It is not even clear if they were initially more successful than the parish constables and watchmen who had preceded them. The police reacted to the prevailing view that 'crime' meant public disorder and street crime. During the nineteenth century the working class spent much of their leisure time on and around the street. For this reason alone, they were more likely to come into contact with the police, and the situation would be intensified if they took part in public demonstrations and marches. In the poorer areas of London and towns such as Liverpool, Salford and Merthyr, the local police were heavily involved in dealing with cases of assault, disorderly conduct and drunkenness, and there were still, in practical terms, 'no-go' areas (Morris 1989). Prostitutes, vagrants and gypsies were also targeted. Superintendents appearing before Parliamentary Select Committees on the Police between 1834 and 1853 recounted the extraordinary success of the Metropolitan Police in nearly every riot after the Reform Crisis. However, this was exaggerated, and was certainly not the case in the countryside where police numbers remained small (Jones 1982).

It would be wrong to assume that the creation of Peel's 'new police' was a natural development of the alleged shortcomings of the eighteenth century policing arrangements or the reforms of the Fieldings. Centralisation of institutions such as the police was still widely associated with the absolute monarchies of continental Europe. Historians generally agree that it was the rapid urbanization during the industrial revolution which led to the creation of the Metropolitan, and subsequently other, police forces. Where historians differ, however, is in their analysis of the particular consequences of this urbanisation which enabled the creation of these forces at that particular time. The traditional view was that the existing structure of law enforcement was so inefficient and corrupt that it was incapable of dealing with the increased crime that occurred in the newly-expanding towns and cities. Peel himself offered this view in the 1829 Parliamentary debate.

Other historians have provided a different explanation. They have pointed out that London already had extensive slums before its rapid expansion, and that the real reason for the creation of the police was that the growth of capitalism required tighter social relations between the different classes. Minor rioting, previously seen as normal, came to be considered more seriously (Taylor 1997). In addition, any inefficiency on the part of the local constables was greatly to the advantage of the aristocracy as it left them in near-total control. The new industrialists, for their part, feared that areas of 'looseness' (such as the keeping of perks), which had previously characterised the relationship between the controllers and the controlled, could undermine the success of their enterprise.

In the opinion of Reiner (2000), the views of both sides in this debate have been overstated. It is unlikely that the fear of severe public disorder could have been invoked as a justification for the 'new police' for very long. Although France had just undergone a revolution and there was fear of Chartism at home, many parts of England and Wales were slow to create their own police force after being empowered to do so by a series of statutes. The Municipal Corporations Act 1835 required boroughs to create a watch committee which should establish and supervise their own police force. The recommendation of the Royal Commission on Constabulary (1836–39) that a national police force be created was not acted upon: the Rural Constabulary Act 1839 (and the amending legislation of 1840) significantly left it to benches of magistrates to establish county constabularies if they so wished. Some counties took this course but, as late as the 1840s, efforts were still being made in some areas to improve the old parish constable system by appointing professional superintendents to train them. In 1842 there were campaigns against the new police in various parts of the country on the grounds of expense and inefficiency, and the Lancashire Constabulary was reduced in size by about a third.

Indeed, the new police were never as popular as the traditional view maintained. The aristocracy were afraid of losing their influence, the middle class feared the additional expense, and working class concern was based on police opposition to their traditional street recreation and growing involvement in industrial and political reform.

On the other hand, it is possible to exaggerate the cosiness between the landowners and the poor: Hay (1975), for instance, has suggested that the reaction to poaching could be very severe. Moreover, although the poor resented police incursion into their recreational and political activities, records indicate that working-class victims were not averse to using the police when the need arose to prosecute the offenders. Change was slow, even after the 1839 legislation. Where police forces were established, many of the former local constables were initially retained, although a considerable number of them did not last long in the job as a result of drunkenness and general inefficiency.

A measure of standardisation eventually arrived in the form of the County and Borough Police Act 1856. It became obligatory for all boroughs and counties to set up structured police forces rather than to try to improve the parish system, and a national inspectorate was established. Central government was to contribute a quarter of the cost of pay and clothing. (This was increased to half in 1874.) This piece of legislation did not have an easy passage and had to be introduced into Parliament three times before finally becoming law. Some boroughs had never complied with the 1835 legislation and, at the time the 1856 Act was passed, only about half the counties had appointed paid officers. The original bill of 1854 proposed that a number of borough and county forces be merged and that the Home Secretary draw up standard regulations. The hostility this provoked was so strong that the clauses were dropped from the 1856 version. In the end, 226 police forces emerged, some with only a single constable. The efficiency of the forces was measured by three new Inspectors of Constabulary, who had to submit a report to Parliament every year.

Nevertheless, the desire for local policing was as strong as ever, and borough and county police forces continued to exist side by side until the mergers of the past 40 years. Some areas were still employing parish constables into the twentieth century.

The ultimate acceptance of the 1856 proposals may have been facilitated by the ending of the transportation of convicts overseas and the return of the British army after the Crimean War. It was feared these events would result in an increased amount of lawlessness on the streets. However, it is probable that, whatever underlying factors are identified by historians, the development of the 'new police' was inevitable at some stage in the nineteenth century. The arrival of large numbers of people in towns and cities resulted in a growing complexity in everyday life that was bound to lead to stronger and more professional social control.

The fears of the aristocracy that they would lose control of policing eventually proved correct. The chief constables, fearing corruption and inefficiency at local level, wanted more control themselves. In the boroughs the growing middle class had some influence on police activities through the watch committees that were created. However, the middle class initially had less control over county forces where magistrates remained influential until the end of the century. Central government was also gaining more control. Working-class involvement was non-existent until they gained the franchise, and ever since then has been dependent on their willingness to become involved in local politics.

What sort of people joined the new police? Although the Metropolitan Police Commissioner and the chief constables in the county forces were chosen from the upper classes until World War II, the head constables in the borough forces and all the other ranks were selected from ordinary working men and given the opportunity to obtain promotion through their own efforts. The officers were expected to be physically fit for what was a rigorous job and there was a high turnover of staff—a significant number were dismissed for drunkenness on duty. Forces adopted different recruitment policies: some would discriminate against local people for fear of favouritism; others would be unwilling to take on former soldiers. Police officers soon began to develop their own culture, inevitably based on male toughness and physical prowess. Women police were introduced by some forces during World War I. They were not given the power of arrest, and many forces dispensed with their services at the end of hostilities. The role of women in the police was largely segregated from that of men until the 1970s. They were generally confined to looking after female and juvenile offenders and victims. 'Real' policing was seen as men's work.

Central control or autonomy?

After the 1856 legislation there were basically three different types of police force in England and Wales: the Metropolitan Police in London; borough (city) police forces; and county forces. Each type had its own different structure. The Commissioner (chief constable) of the Metropolitan Police has always been directly responsible to the Home Secretary. The borough forces were obliged by the Municipal Corporations Act 1835 to create 'watch committees', which themselves had to appoint head constables and their officers. The chief constables of county forces were appointed by police committees, but this had to be approved by the Home Secretary.

These differences raised their own distinctive problems. On numerous occasions up to the present day, complaints have been made that

Commissioners of the Metropolitan Police are the only chief police officers in England and Wales who are not—at least, in theory—accountable to the local population. The justification most commonly offered has been that the Metropolitan Police has unique functions of national (rather than local) importance, such as protecting the government and the monarch. The implication that the control of such a body could not be left to the vagaries of local (and, perhaps, radical) opinion is clear, and was actually enunciated in 1888 (Evans 1889). Watch committees, on the other hand, had complete control over the appointment of their police officers and the operation of the force, and this could sometimes result in head constables being directed to carry out policies with which they disagreed. The chief constables of county forces found themselves somewhere in between. They increasingly came to be appointed from former military officers and were therefore often of the same class as the local magistrates. After the establishment of county councils in 1888, the chief constables were responsible to committees comprising an equal number of magistrates and elected councillors. Suggestions that accountability should have been to the county councillors only were disregarded, once again on the basis of what might happen if socialists or radicals were to gain control of the council. This was an issue that was to recur a hundred years later.

Nevertheless, the increasing hold of government—both at central and local level—over the population during the second half of the nineteenth century made the growth of centralised control over the operation of policing inevitable. The provision of funding from central government in 1856 and its increase in 1874 only served to cement this process. In return, the Home Office gained a significant foothold in local policing with the power of inspection. At the end of World War I central funding was increased to half the cost of running the entire force. Gradually, head and chief constables, with support from the civil service, began to bypass local control. In the period before World War I, industrial unrest led the Home Secretary, Winston Churchill, to deploy both troops and the police around the country to deal with striking miners, railway workers and dockers. The view later suggested by some historians—that the actions of the police were not politically influenced—can be seen as clearly erroneous by even a casual look at their involvement in industrial relations disputes during this period. Churchill proposed the appointment of police reserves but, although this did not lead to opposition in the counties, some borough forces resisted it on the basis of further central intrusion into their domain.

The outbreak of war itself resulted in more cooperation between police, public and government, particularly as there were many rumours of spies and saboteurs. However, relations were not always easy between the growing Labour movement and the police: the Russian Revolution in 1917 and the ensuing demonstrations in support caused particular friction. Police officers, faced with far more work during the war years, formed their own union in 1913, but strike action in Birmingham and Liverpool in 1919 led to its abolition and a prohibition on police strikes (Reynolds and Judge 1968). The Desborough Committee, which subsequently considered the whole affair, made recommendations as to police pay and conditions which served to create even greater uniformity of practice among the existing forces.

The report of the Royal Commission on Police Powers and Procedure in 1929 claimed that 'The police of this country have never been recognised, either by law or tradition, as a force distinct from the general body of citizens'. To what extent did this reflect the legal position? Were constables purely the servants of their local authorities, or did they have a wider duty to uphold the law? The question was answered the following year in the case *Fisher v Oldham Corpn* [1930] 2 KB 364, when it was held that a wrongfully-arrested man could not sue the Corporation as the employer of the arresting officer. This remained a controversial case for many years, but it helped to support the argument that police officers can make operational decisions without interference from local politicians.

As a result of the level of cooperation among different police forces during World War II, the new Labour government decided that there could be some amalgamations and the number of forces was reduced from 181 to 131. The 1950s was a relatively quiet time in policing—indeed it was the period that gave rise to the stereotyped view of the benign British 'bobby' (after Sir Robert Peel) as exemplified in the long-running TV series *Dixon of Dock Green*. This was a period of consensus between the main political parties on most social issues, including criminal justice. However, events after the 1960s were to change this state of affairs significantly.

Policing from the 1960s

During the late 1950s one or two scandals (minor by modern standards) occurred surrounding individual police officers, and the resultant controversy led to the Home Secretary's establishing of a Royal Commission on the Police (Oliver 1987). The report affirmed the traditional view that a police officer's authority is 'original, not delegated and exercised at his own discretion by virtue of his office'. The question of creating a national police force was considered, but it was agreed (with one dissenter) to maintain the existing arrangements. The inquiry included a national survey of public opinion of the police. It emerged that 83 per cent of those interviewed held the police in very high esteem.

The 1960s also saw the beginning of sociological research into police and policing in Britain, with Banton's pioneering empirical study in 1964. Subsequent work took on a more ideological slant, reflecting the significant changes taking place in British criminology around that period (see Chapter 2). Comparisons with American literature showed a common finding—the importance of police discretion at street level. It emerged that the exercise of this discretion is largely influenced by police culture, which has changed little since its emergence around the turn of the century. Although the police are formally subject to a highly complex set of laws and regulations, participant observation and other research has revealed that the reality of policing involves an element of rule-ignoring, rule-bending and the application of the 'Ways and Means Act' (Reiner 2000). Villains—and even the general public—are apparently divisible in police eyes into a range of categories stereotyped in accordance with police 'macho' culture, which predictably includes racist and sexist values. Indeed, the report into the death of the black teenager Stephen Lawrence described the Metropolitan Police as 'institutionally racist' (Macpherson 1999). Many police officers find it hard to come to terms with anyone who is 'different', for whatever reason.

This research began to appear at a time when the exercise of authority in society came under widespread challenge not only, as previously, in the form of industrial disputes but, for the first time, from a young generation of politically aware middle-class students—a group which hitherto had acted deferentially towards the police and to whom the police had responded in like manner. Indeed, for the first hundred years or so of its existence, the police service had little contact with middle-class offenders; but this changed with the arrival of the motor car. There was also a new generation of adolescent blacks; the children of the West Indians that Conservative governments had encouraged to come to Britain in the 1950s to provide cheap labour. However, the cheap labour market was now in decline, the young blacks could find no work, and they tended to hang around on the streets—just as the unemployed poor had done in the 'rookeries' of mid-nineteenth century London.

Public order problems arising from demonstrations against the Vietnam War and the miners' strikes of 1972 and 1974 saw local police forces establish public order units to deal with such incidents. The Public Support Unit system enabled mutual help to be provided by forces when disturbances erupted. For the first time different police forces—once so fiercely independent—were prepared to cooperate on a widespread and formally structured basis. After the election of the Conservative Party in 1979 on a 'law and order' ticket, further serious outbreaks of public disorder soon put this to the test. Inner-city riots in 1979 and 1980, followed a few years later by mass picketing arising from miners' and printers' disputes, resulted in carefully coordinated joint operations among police forces. They also led to the use of riot shields, CS gas, and a general adoption of paramilitary policing techniques. A new form of crime control had emerged in a manner that could not have been envisaged some twenty years earlier. This has, not surprisingly, proved controversial, especially when used in wholly inappropriate cases, such as against the (predominantly) middle-aged and elderly women who demonstrated against the export of live lambs at Brightlingsea, Essex, in 1995. By 2000, the British Crime Survey (see Chapter 3) found that only 20 per cent of respondents felt that their local police did a very good job (Sims and Myhill 2001).

Police accountability

The 1930 decision in *Fisher v Oldham Corpn* determined that police officers are not merely servants but possess legal powers in their own right. This was reiterated by Lord Denning in *R v Metropolitan Police Commissioner, ex p. Blackburn* [1968] 2 QB 136:

> No Minister of the Crown can tell [a constable] that he must, or must not, keep observation on this place or that; or that he must, or must not, prosecute this man or that one. Nor can any police authority tell him so . . . He is answerable to the law alone.

For the purpose of accountability, police operations can be divided between those of individual officers in their routine work, and those reflecting the overall policy of the force on aspects such as policing priorities, targets and methods. In practice, these two categories are interrelated. Officers react to instructions from their superiors and the overall policy of a force is likely to be judged by what it actually does rather than from any formal statement of objectives.

(a) Individual accountability

As the police are 'answerable to the law alone', it follows that officers have no immunity; they can be sued in the civil courts just as any other individual can be. In many cases this would not amount to much more than a token gesture, as police officers are generally not wealthy individuals. However, in a reversal of the position established in *Fisher v Oldham Corpn*, the Police Act 1964 stipulated that police authorities can be held vicariously liable for the wrongful actions of constables in the course of their employment. In recent years, there have been several well-publicised cases, many against the Metropolitan Police Commissioner, arising from assaults against, and even the death of, suspects held in police custody.

The routine activities of police officers are nowadays regulated by statutory law, in particular the Police and Criminal Evidence Act 1984 (PACE). This Act, which replaced an assortment of common law and statutory (sometimes local) provisions, was designed to create a legal framework to protect the rights of suspects. PACE is accompanied by a series of detailed Codes of Practice to which the police are required to conform. Breach of a Code provision does not in itself amount to a criminal offence, but it can lead to disciplinary action and—perhaps more importantly—affect the admissibility in court of any evidence obtained as a result. One of the main safeguards introduced by PACE was the requirement that contemporaneous written records be made of the exercise of certain police powers, together with the reasons for their use.

Civil libertarian critics of PACE were initially suspicious of the level of discretion provided in the Act, both to the police in carrying out its requirements (phrases such as 'reasonably practicable to do so' occur on several occasions) and to the courts in deciding whether to take account of any breaches. However, nowadays it is the police who complain the loudest as a result of the greatly increased amount of paperwork they have to complete. It seems that suspects have benefited from PACE's safeguards in some respects. Far more of them are able to have access to a solicitor than previously (Morgan *et al.* 1990) and courts are more prepared to exclude illegally obtained evidence than they were under the old arrangements (Feldman 1990). However, as Sanders and Young (2000) have pointed out, these safeguards will be of little value to those pleading guilty, who form a clear majority of defendants in court.

It therefore remains the case—and perhaps is inevitable—that the police have a considerable advantage in the investigation process, which will always be adversarial in nature.

Few police officers are convicted of crimes; their actions are more likely to be challenged under the complaints procedure. In 2003/04 there were only fifty-five convictions for non-traffic offences compared with 15,885 cases of complaint (Cotton 2004). The Police Act 1964 created a national scheme whereby complaints could be made against the police. They were investigated internally except in particularly serious cases, where officers from another force would be brought in, or where there was a possibility of criminal proceedings, in which case the papers were sent to the Director of Public Prosecutions (DPP). The fact that the procedure contained no independent element led to much criticism and it was replaced by the Police Complaints Board in 1976. This in turn did not satisfy the critics as its membership comprised 'safe' appointments and it had no independent powers of investigation; the cases it had to deal with were presented by the police themselves. Very few findings against the police were arrived at, and the Board was itself replaced by the Police Complaints Authority (PCA) established under PACE.

The main difference was that the PCA was required to supervise a police investigation into allegations of serious injury or death resulting from police abuse, and was further permitted to do so in any other case which it felt was in the public interest. A senior PCA member authorised the appointment of investigating officers and then monitored the inquiry and examined the evidence. At the conclusion, the PCA referred the case to the Crown Prosecution Service if it considered there was evidence that an officer had committed an offence.

However, research into the functioning of the PCA indicated that, although it was capable of providing effective supervision on some occasions, it failed to inspire confidence in complainants, the police or the general public. In the 2000 British Crime Survey, 64 per cent of the respondents who complained about the police were unhappy with the way the police dealt with their grievance. The main reason given by those who did not make a complaint was that they saw no benefit in doing so (Sims and Myhill 2001). Fewer than 8 per cent of the complaints considered by the PCA between 1985 and 1994 led to an officer being disciplined (Home Office 1995).

The PCA itself admitted that it was often hampered by lack of evidence (PCA 1995). Even senior police officers considered that the situation was unsatisfactory. In October 1997 Sir Paul Condon, the Metropolitan Police Commissioner, said he was unable to sack the small number of corrupt officers in his force because of the disciplinary process. Many dissatisfied members of the public simply avoided the process altogether, and there was an increase in the number of civil actions brought against police forces. These usually ended in an out-of-court settlement with no admission of liability and no apparent action taken against the offending officer. Settlements and damages paid by the Metropolitan Police in civil cases increased from £471,000 in 1991 to £2,309,000 in 1998/99 (Newburn and Reiner 2004).

The Police Reform Act 2002 replaced the PCA by a new body, the Independent Police Complaints Commission (IPCC). It has been in operation since April 2004. A wider range of people can now make complaints against all levels of police officers, special constables and civilian employees. The categories of case where investigation is mandatory has been extended. Independent investigation teams comprise both police officers and non-police officers. The IPCC has the discretion to present or observe cases it investigated and those investigated by the police. In disciplinary cases, one of the three panel members will be independent of the police.

(b) Force accountability

The tripartite system of police accountability (chief constable—police authority—Home Secretary) which had existed since the nineteenth century was basically retained in the Police Act 1964. (The Metropolitan Police and the City of London Police retained their own individual structures.) Chief constables were to undertake the direction and control of their force; police authorities were responsible for providing an 'adequate and efficient' force; and the Home Secretary was to oversee policing throughout the whole country. Police authorities had the power to appoint chief constables and could retire them on grounds of inefficiency. However, all such major decisions had to be approved by the Home Secretary, who continued to hold the purse strings by allocating half the budget of each force. Provincial police authorities were to comprise two-thirds local councillors and one-third magistrates. They could ask their chief constable to submit a report following the policing of a particular event, but this could be refused if the chief constable considered that it would not be in the public interest to do so.

Although subject to academic criticism on the ground that the police authority merely served to rubber-stamp the wishes of the chief constable (Brogden 1977), the system appeared to function without much public attention until a series of events in the 1980s. During this period, radical left-wing councils were elected in several major cities and their police authorities began to challenge some of the policies of the chief constables, particularly in relation to public order and industrial disputes. The use of paramilitary policing methods at inner city riots in places like Toxteth, Liverpool (Loveday 1985) and the 1984–5 miners' dispute led to strong disagreements between some chief constables and their police authorities.

In 1988, the Northumbria Police Authority sought judicial review of the Home Secretary's decision to provide plastic bullets to forces where the police authority had refused to authorise their purchase by the chief constable. The Court of Appeal held that the Home Secretary, under both the Royal Prerogative and the Police Act 1964, has the power to take any action necessary to uphold the law, when acting on advice of a chief constable and HM Inspectorate of Constabulary (R v Secretary of State for the Home Department, ex p. Northumbria Police Authority [1989] QB 26). This important decision made it clear that, in practice, the opinion of the Home Secretary will always prevail over that of the police authority. Chief constables are unlikely to ignore the views of the Home Secretary, particularly if they are concerned about their future careers.

The question of police accountability came to the fore again at the end of the decade, but this time on the basis of financial rather than democratic criteria. In accordance with the growing 'managerialist' approach of the Conservative government, a number of detailed surveys were conducted into police effectiveness and efficiency. The problem appeared to be that, whereas the police budget had increased by 90 per cent over a decade, the clear-up rate had declined from 41 per cent to around 25 per cent. Such a presentation of statistics can be misleading (see Chapter 3) but, in political terms, it provides a great deal of ammunition for critics.

The Police and Magistrates' Courts Act 1994 (now consolidated with the 1964 Act in the Police Act 1996) resulted in a significant alteration to the tripartite structure. For the first time, a Metropolitan Police Authority was created for London. The original idea was that it would have the same composition as a provincial police authority but, following opposition from government backbench MPs, it is an unelected quango with its members appointed by the Home Secretary. There are smaller provincial police authorities limited to seventeen members and comprising eight councillors, three magistrates, five local people, and the chair, who is appointed by the other members. The Home Secretary is to set out national objectives and publish league tables to indicate performance. Chief constables are still in charge of the 'direction and control' of their force, as stipulated in the 1964 Act, but they must also act in accordance with their local policing plan which will outline objectives and expenditure. This will have been drawn up in conjunction with the police authority but, in practice, is likely to show the strong influence of the Home Secretary. The Police Reform Act 2002 has given the Home Office even greater powers to manage police performance through the introduction of a national Annual Policing Plan. Forces may also be required to take remedial action where they have been judged to be inefficient.

It is thus clear that police forces now have to operate in a more 'business-like' manner, and that their effectiveness will ultimately be judged by their success at solving crimes (Loveday 2000). Yet, this constitutes a restriction on other traditional police activities such as crime prevention (the main duty imposed on Peel's Metropolitan Police in 1829), keeping the peace and assisting in emergencies (Reiner 1994). Moreover, there is a large amount of evidence suggesting that not only would such a strong emphasis on crime detection be undesirable (for example, the Scarman Report into the 1981 Brixton riots), but also that the police have never been particularly good at it (see, for example, Morgan and Newburn 1997).

Thus, by the end of the twentieth century, the Home Secretary had assumed a level of power over police organisation and practice that would have been unthinkable at the beginning. The new police authorities, which are now directly responsible to central government, have a structure which makes it very difficult for them to be accountable to, or reflect the wishes of, their local communities (Leishman *et al.* 1996). It may even be that, with the emphasis now so strongly on quantifiable 'results', there will be a stronger temptation to break the rules, which could result in an increased number of wrongful convictions.

Conclusion

The British police has undergone an enormous transformation since its creation over a century and a half ago. This proposition may appear perfectly reasonable in the light of other major developments that have occurred during this period, but it is particularly significant that most of the important changes have taken place during the past forty years.

Sir Robert Peel established the Metropolitan Police in 1829 in the face of extensive political and social opposition, and the growth of provincial forces was relatively slow notwithstanding much encouragement from central government. There was a genuine fear of a centralised, paramilitary police force of the kind identified with eighteenth century continental Europe. In order to counter this unpopularity, considerable emphasis was placed on the police being fundamentally a local, unarmed civilian body of ordinary people from ordinary backgrounds. The British government had already shown that in other settings where public opinion was not so important—such as Ireland—it was prepared to engage in military-style policing (Palmer 1988). The development of the police during the nineteenth century was essentially part of the centralisation of government and administration that was taking place at both national and local level.

The peak of police popularity with the public was in the 1950s with the enduring image of the 'benign bobby on the beat'. At that stage, the British police had a level of support possibly higher than any other force in the world. That this is no longer the case can be seen from the 2000 International Crime Victimisation Survey of seventeen industrialised countries. In response to a question as to whether the police did a good job in controlling crime in their area, 89 per cent of Americans and 87 per cent of Canadians answered in the affirmative, compared with 72 per cent of the respondents in England and Wales (van Kesteren *et al.* 2001).

This situation began to change during the 1970s. A breakdown in social consensus, the reaction of the police to increased public disorder, and discriminatory policing against the growing ethnic minority communities all helped to make ever larger sections of the population antagonistic to the police. Even the middle-class support began to disintegrate when people read of police corruption and miscarriages of justice, such as the 'Guildford Four' and 'Birmingham Six' cases. More liberal individuals were concerned with the use of CS gas and riot shields. In fact, there has always been a degree of corruption among police officers: given the numbers employed and the temptations that come their way, it would be strange if it were otherwise. What has changed is the ease with which such corruption can be exposed.

Other supporters of the police, perhaps untroubled by civil liberties issues, still became increasingly disillusioned with the rise in the crime rate and the apparent inability of the police to deal with it. However, to some extent, this perception of police failure is unfair. Statistical measurements of crime nowadays manage to include incidents that previously fell through the net (see Chapter 3) and the increased police resources have still been insufficient to cover the additional demands (not to mention paperwork) with which they have to contend. Crime may be on the increase, but so is the police's public service role. The Association of Chief Police Officers (ACPO 1993) has estimated that, in any given day, only 18 per cent of calls to the police are for help concerning crime.

In accordance with its adherence to free-market economic principles, the Conservative government responded to this concern by introducing managerial and business practices into policing. The view was held that a properly and efficiently managed police force would be more successful in combating crime. Yet, this ignored a substantial body of research evidence which suggests that neither the resourcing of the police nor the policies they adopt has any significant influence on the overall level of crime. The police have always had a central role as peace-keepers and it is probably unrealistic to think that this can ever fundamentally change, notwithstanding alterations in management structure or the introduction of local plans. As Waddington (1983) put it:

> The police are the social equivalent of the AA or RAC patrolmen, who intervene when things go unpredictably wrong and secure a provisional solution.

It is likely, however, that further significant changes will be made to policing during the next few years, whether or not improvements in crime levels or detection rates occur. The Crime and Disorder Act 1998 encourages 'communitarian policing' in that different local agencies within the community must now cooperate to establish crime prevention policies. However, as Reiner (2000) has pointed out, the success of this initiative will depend on sufficient resources being made available—something which has yet to happen. The Police Reform Act 2002 allows chief constables to appoint 'community support officers' to patrol in the community with limited powers mainly aimed at dealing with antisocial behaviour. Although tradition may dictate that regional forces remain, the police will *de facto* become a far more centralised body and, in the style of continental Europe, specific functions may be hived off to separate units, perhaps cutting across force boundaries. An increase in electronic surveillance will probably further reduce beat policing. There is a possibility that certain police functions may be put out to private tender; there has already been a measure of civilianisation in police work. Any major increase in the level of public fear about crime may trigger whole communities into turning to private security firms to provide their policing. This, in turn, could lead to large organisations competing for the franchise to provide policing for a particular area. Although the police hierarchy was initially unhappy about the spread of private security, some chief constables have accepted its inevitability and there has been talk of working 'in partnership' (Blair 1999). However, rank-and-file officers remain to be convinced, and have expressed opposition to government proposals to employ private security guards in certain policing operations (Home Office 2001).

Although many people may view the privatisation of the police as a worrying development, it would not be that radical a departure from what has gone before. It would also be better than the vigilant-ism which could develop if policing were thought to be inadequate (Johnston 1996). It has already been shown that, before the devel-opment of professional forces in the nineteenth century, policing was carried out by local volunteers as part of the operation of what was, in effect, local government. Nowadays, there are several specialist bodies engaged in policing, such as the British Transport Police who deal with the railways. The idea that policing a society has to be carried out by a body known as the police organised along present lines has existed for only a small part of our history—the past century and a half. The police would be among the first to admit that everyone in society is involved in policing, be it through alert shop assistants, organised 'Neighbourhood Watch' schemes, or simply being observant in the street. Society is becoming both more complex and more fragmented every day and, although this does not necessarily require the struc-ture of the police to change, it certainly provides a justification for it to do so. The requirement of policing will always be there: the require-ment of the police in something resembling its present form may well not be.

2

Crime: definitions and conflicting images

Problems of definition and context

On the face of it, the subject matter of criminology should be self-evident. Both etymologically and in the largely unquestioning view of early positivists, it concerns the content and application of the criminal law of whatever society is under consideration. Such a definition has the advantage of precision: criminologists do not have to worry about the scope of their subject as the legislature and (in some countries) the judiciary have fixed it for them. Yet, such a definition is ultimately unsatisfactory for a number of reasons.

(1) It suggests that without the criminal law there would be no crime. As Michael and Adler (1933) put it:

> If crime is merely an instance of conduct which is proscribed by the criminal code, it follows that the criminal law is the formal cause of crime.

There would also be no crime unless the offender were apprehended and convicted. This view was held by the American criminologists Korn and McCorkle (1957) and later expressed by Jason Ditton in his book *Controlology* (1979): 'No "crime" has been committed (in law and logic) until a court finds—i.e. creates for all intents and purposes—guilty intent'. From this, Ditton concluded that there could be no 'dark figure' of unrecorded crime (see Chapter 3). However, not everyone who is known to have broken the criminal law is even prosecuted; an increasing proportion of offenders is cautioned. This definition of crime also appears to suffer from circularity: criminal law appears as both a response to crime and the formal definition of crime.

(2) It tells us nothing about why certain forms of behaviour are criminalised. It is sometimes said that crimes are 'immoral acts'. Unless the words crime and immorality mean the same, it is difficult

to agree with this statement. Many people equate morality with religious doctrine. Yet, it was shown in Chapter 1 that the equation of sin and crime had begun to decline as long ago as the eighteenth century. Nowadays, many sins are not criminal offences—indeed, avarice is encouraged in most societies—and it is possible to think of crimes which can only be described as sins in the most indirect of senses, if at all (for example, if a person's car number plate is the wrong colour). Likewise, many crimes—particularly so-called victim- less crimes—would not contravene a humanist code of morality based on not harming other people.

Inevitably, there are differing views about what should amount to a criminal offence among individuals in the same society. This is the point at which positivists usually draw the line and insist on confining themselves to the legal definitions, although even they must concede that, at the very least, this divergence indicates that the content of the criminal law is not set in stone.

It is also important to remember that it is rare for the physical-act component of a crime to be intrinsically 'wrong'. Killing can be lawful in certain circumstances: in self-defence, during a legally-declared state of war (but not during an act of 'terrorism'—see below) and as state execution. Cannabis, a drug widely used by doctors (and, allegedly, by Queen Victoria) during the nineteenth century, was available on prescription until 1971. Nowadays, a cannabis-based drug, THC, is used by doctors in Britain as part of treatment for cancer patients and, in America, to boost the appetite of AIDS sufferers. In 2001 it was estimated that 40 million people in the European Union used the drug. In April 2000 an Independent Inquiry established by the Police Foundation concluded that possession of cannabis should be decriminalised (Runciman 2000) and this view was later echoed by a former Lord Chief Justice, Lord Bingham (*The Spectator*, 25 May 2002). Following a recommendation in 2002 from the Advisory Council on the Misuse of Drugs, the drug's legal status was down- graded from Class B to Class C with the consequential reduction in the maximum penalty for possession.

(3) It fails to explain why the content of the criminal law can vary over a period of time. An Italian criminologist, Raffaele Garofalo (1914), tried to ascertain whether there were any crimes 'which at all times and in all places' would be considered as 'punishable acts'. He concluded that their existence could not be proved. Erich Goode and Nachman Ben-Yehuda (1994) provided an extreme yet graphic illustration of changing values from Central America:

Ancient Aztec priests cut open the chest of a human sacrifice and tore out his still-beating heart: in contemporary Mexico, the same act would be cause for arrest, prosecution, possibly commitment to a mental institution.

History is full of examples of individuals, ranging from Aristotle to the suffragette, Emmeline Pankhurst, and more recently Nelson Mandela, who at some point were condemned as criminals, but subsequently came to be considered as heroes.

The American jurist Roscoe Pound (1930) remarked at the end of the second decade of the century that 'Of one hundred thousand persons arrested . . . more than one half were held for violation of legal precepts which did not exist twenty-five years before'. No doubt, many of the crimes he had in mind were created during the Prohibition Era. This period of American history provides a useful illustration of how criminalization can occur—the crimes in question relating to alcohol and drug use.

Joseph Gusfield (1963) considered that Prohibition arose largely from pressure (particularly from rural Protestant interest groups) to reinforce respectable American middle-class values, together with the fact that brewing was predominantly controlled by Germans—'the enemy' during World War I. Becker (1963) argued that the Marijuana Tax Act 1937, which was enacted at a time when marijuana use was rare (and was only a criminal offence in sixteen states), resulted from a campaign by the commissioner of the Treasury Department's Federal Bureau of Narcotics, whom Becker referred to as a 'moral entre- preneur'. In Becker's view, the commissioner thought that this was an area which should be brought within the Bureau's jurisdiction, and was therefore happy to claim that the drug caused its users to lose control and commit crimes. Troy Duster (1970) considered that early efforts to criminalise drugs were reinforced by ethnic and racial preju- dices, as members of the Chinese, Mexican and black communities were considered (erroneously, according to Duster) to be the main users. Whereas the labour movement was able to wage an ultimately successful campaign against the prohibition of alcohol, there were no groups holding sufficient power and influence to do the same for drug users. David Musto (1973) agreed that the laws against marijuana were targeted at Mexican immigrants, who were widely identified with the drug, but claimed that this was because the cheaper labour they provided was undercutting the demands of the resident workers.

Richard A Berk and his colleagues (1977) classified changes made to the California penal code between 1955 and 1971. Although some criminal offences were abolished during this period, many new ones were created and at no time was there a net decline in the number of activities that were considered criminal. In Britain, suicide ceased to be a criminal offence in 1960 and abortion and homosexuality were to a large extent decriminalised in 1967. The Sexual Offences (Amendment) Act 2000 reduced the age of consent for certain homosexual acts from eighteen to sixteen. On the other hand, there is a growing number of provisions making smoking an offence in certain places, such as on the London Underground. Insider dealing in company shares, although long frowned upon, only became a criminal offence in 1980. It has been estimated that 661 new criminal offences were created between 1997 and 2003 (Cohen 2003).

(4) It fails to explain why, even at a given point in time, key differences can be observed within the same country, be they between different states in a federation such as the USA or between the three different legal systems that comprise the UK. The liberalising of the abortion law in England, Wales and Scotland as a result of the Abortion Act 1967 has never been extended to Northern Ireland. When homosexual acts committed in private between two consenting males aged twenty-one or over ceased to be criminal offences in England under the Sexual Offences Act 1967, the previous law remained unchanged in Scotland and Northern Ireland.

(5) It separates the criminal process from its social context. Some critics argue that a study of crime must include a consideration of why certain acts are criminalised and yet others are merely disapproved of (the smoking of cannabis and tobacco); why the criminal law is differentially enforced against various groups within society (young blacks and middle-aged whites); why some crimes are considered more important than others (social security fraud and tax fraud); and even whether those labelled as criminal consider that they have done anything 'wrong' (robbers and 'new age' trespassers).

Is it possible, therefore, to devise a more useful definition of crime for analytical purposes?

(a) Alternative definitions of 'criminal' behaviour

Because of the transitory nature of criminal law, some writers have argued that a better way should be sought to distinguish 'acceptable' from 'unacceptable' behaviour within a society. However, this has proved to be a much easier question to pose than to answer.

(i) Universal norms of conduct

American sociologists became aware of this problem in the earlier part of the twentieth century. Thorsten Sellin (1938) claimed that, if criminology were to be considered as a scientific discipline, criminologists should not allow parameters of the subject to be determined by legislators, who are non-scientists. Unfortunately, Sellin was unable to suggest a better alternative. He claimed that every group has its own standards of behaviour, which are not necessarily expressed in law. There are also norms which apply to all societies: universal categories 'transcending political and other boundaries, a necessity imposed by the logic of science'. The only problem was that Sellin was unable to suggest what these universal conduct norms are.

In later years other criminologists offered alternative approaches. Walter Reckless (1950) thought that crimes should be confined to illegal acts that have been reported to the police. Leslie Wilkins (1964) advocated a more scientific definition of crime. He considered the frequency with which various types of behaviour occurred in any particular society. This resulted in a continuum of different behaviours on which the most frequent were considered normal and the least frequent deviant. The main difficulty with this approach is that it does not explain why some infrequent acts are considered criminal and others are not.

In his work into the dubious—but often not strictly criminal—practices of the American business world, Edwin Sutherland (1949), who introduced the now famous term 'white-collar crime', thought that crime should be assessed according to notions of 'injury' and 'harm' to the state. One of the problems with this is that we are brought no nearer to a universal definition, as different states will have different ideas as to what is injurious. As Paul Tappan (1947) wrote:

> However desirable may be the concept of socially injurious conduct . . . it does not define what is injurious. It sets no standard. It does not discriminate cases but merely invites the subjective value-judgements of the investigator.

Indeed, because the business practices Sutherland described were, although dubious ethically, not always illegal, his publishers, fearing actions for libel, were not prepared to identify the companies concerned in print. (This was rectified in a later edition of the book in 1983.)

(ii) Fundamental human rights

An alternative approach could be to look for a definition based on violation of fundamental human rights. For example, Hermann and Julia Schwendinger argued in 1970 that criminal law should be based on the 'historically determined rights of individuals':

> If the terms imperialism, racism, sexism and poverty are abbreviated signs for theories of social relationships or social systems which cause the systematic abrogation of basic rights, then imperialism, racism, sexism and poverty can be called crimes.

The Schwendingers also advocated the extension of the criminal label to 'genocide and economic exploitation'. Cohen (1988) has taken issue with this, on the basis that bracketing the two devalued the impact of genocide, itself already a crime under international law. According to Cohen, it would be preferable to have a more restricted use of the concept of state crime: the scope of criminology could still be extended 'without our object of study becoming simply everything we might not like at the time'.

(iii) Deviance

In practice, the most enduring challenge to the traditional definition of crime has come from the sociological concept of deviance. This notion was popularised by American sociologists in the 1950s and was adopted by a younger, more radical generation of British criminologists a decade later in an attempt to break away from the positivist grip which they felt had taken hold of their discipline. The problem with the word 'deviant' is that its definition is far wider than the type of behaviour that is ever likely to be criminalised. Deviant behaviour is literally any conduct that differs from the prevailing norms of the reference group. For example, undergraduates (and, perhaps nowadays, lecturers) wearing suits in their classes would be considered as deviant by their peers. Yet, this is about as far removed as possible from the sort of rule-breaking that interests criminologists. The term seems to have stuck, however, and 'crime' and 'deviance' are often used in the literature almost interchangeably.

John Hagan (1994) has argued that behaviour which is 'different' or disapproved of can be classified into one of four categories on a continuum. At one extreme is 'consensus crimes': occurrences which have consistently been considered as seriously criminal over the centuries throughout Western societies. Examples include murder, rape, robbery and kidnapping. Lower down the scale is 'conflict crimes'. These are controversial in the sense that they are not supported by all the members of society. This category includes public order offences, crimes involving drugs, abortion and euthanasia. After this comes the borderline category of 'social deviations'. Hagan described such acts as not amounting to criminal offences, but worthy of official attention: he gave as examples the control of the mentally disordered and provisions for supervising disorderly juveniles. The final category on the continuum—at the opposite extreme to consensus crimes—is 'social diversions'. These are ubiquitous and are portrayed as mere fashions of appearance, speech and play. Hagan considered that such activities could range from talking to plants to 'streaking'.

With the possible exception of consensus crimes, the contents of these categories can change and a particular type of behaviour could, for example, easily move from being a social deviation to a conflict crime—or vice versa. For instance, drug use has changed from being a social diversion and then deviation at the beginning of the twentieth century to the conflict crime it is today.

(iv) Disorder and anti-social behaviour

While most attempts to re-define 'criminal' behaviour have been made by academics, a recent effort has come from 'New Labour'. This has involved adopting the terms 'disorder' and, in particular, 'anti-social behaviour' in an extension of the conduct which should be criminalised by the state. At first glance, this move might seem rather strange, as most criminal behaviour is (or should be) 'antisocial' by definition, and any such behaviour in a public place is likely to involve 'disorder'. However, in naming a statute the Crime *and* Disorder Act 1998 (emphasis added), the government showed that it considered the two words to have different meanings. This Act introduced the 'anti-social behaviour order', which can be made by magistrates. 'Anti-social behaviour' is defined as a person's acting 'in a manner that caused or was likely to cause harassment, alarm or distress to one or more persons not of the same household as himself'. The scope of the order (which has been subsequently extended) includes the banning of named individuals (usually the young) from specified places (usually city centres or shopping malls). The government could simply have chosen to criminalise this sort of behaviour, but instead decided to deal with it by way of a *civil* order, the need for which is determined on the *civil* law standard of proof—'the balance of probabilities'—rather than the criminal law standard of 'beyond reasonable doubt'. However, the breach of an anti-social behaviour order incurs criminal liability. This has led critics to claim that police and local authority officials have been given 'a vast power to create a new breed of outcasts and outlaws' (Ashworth *et al.* 1998).

(v) Crime—or 'social harm'?

It has recently been suggested that the traditional concept of crime should be replaced by that of 'social harm' (Hillyard *et al.* 2004). Whether people are the victims of 'crimes', 'mistakes' or 'accidents', they still suffer. Crimes amount to only a small percentage of the harms that are experienced throughout life but, because of their special status, they receive far more attention. For example, the authors state that 'the volume of preventable deaths is thousands of times greater than the number of deaths which are labelled as homicides'. In their view, it makes no sense to distinguish criminal harms from any other type of harm.

(b) Crime is in the eye of the beholder

Traditional explanations of crime assume that society is based on a consensus of values and that the criminal law reflects that consensus. However, other explanations deny the existence of such a consensus and suggest that societies comprise individuals and groups, each with their own values and interests. People learn to react—either positively or negatively—to the behaviour of others. Crime, therefore, is not a fixed given, but the consequence of a process which involves the legislature, the offender, the police, the lawyers and the courts, all of whom can have a significant input into the end result—the establishment of 'a crime'. It is not the behaviour itself which constitutes crime (the example of killing has already been given), but the attribution of the criminal 'label' to it by others. One of the best known comments in criminological writing is Howard Becker's statement that deviance is only a consequence of the application by other people of rules and sanctions to an individual (see Introduction).

Whereas a traditional explanation of crime is based on the existence of the criminal law, an alternative view suggests that, without a reaction by particular elements in society (usually people in positions of power), crime does not effectively exist. In one sense, society is responsible for 'crime' even if it is not responsible for criminal behaviour.

Nils Christie (2004) has said of crime:

> It is like a sponge. The term can absorb a lot of acts—and people—when external circumstances make that useful. But it can also be brought to

reduce its content, whenever suitable for those with a hand on the sponge.

If crime is viewed as having no independent existence, a whole new range of considerations opens up. In addition to asking why some forms of antisocial behaviour are criminalised while others are not, one can also look in more detail at why certain individuals are more likely to emerge from the criminal justice process as labelled offenders, and what purpose is served by stigmatising people in this way. These questions are considered in more detail in Chapter 9; but it may be noted at this stage that one of the main objections raised to the 'labelling' approach to crime is that its main tenets only really apply to 'fringe' areas of criminality, and that it is disingenuous to argue, for example, that the act of killing a person would not, in the vast majority of cases, be universally condemned as wrong.

(c) Crime as protecting the interests of the powerful

One assertion is that many criminal offences are created as a result of pressure from powerful groups who see their interests being threatened. Before the development of the nation state, many of the transgressions which are now classified as crimes were dealt with either as a matter of civil compensation between offender and victim or by the religious courts. Gradually, however, the emerging dominant groups in societies saw criminal law as a means whereby any challenge to their powerful position could be punished.

This is well illustrated in the study by William Chambliss (1964) of the vagrancy laws. After the Black Death had wiped out about half the population of England in the fourteenth century, there was a chronic labour shortage and a consequential sharp increase in wages. Feudal landowners were already experiencing difficulties as they were obliged to sell their serfs into freedom to raise money for the Crusades. Religious houses had customarily provided assistance for the poor and the sick. In 1349 a crime of vagrancy was created, which made it an offence to give money to any person who was unemployed while being of sound mind and body. Such people would have to work for any landowner calling upon their services at the wage level paid before the Black Death. These laws fell into disuse once the labour market had been filled, but were revived in the sixteenth century both as a means of encouraging employment and reducing the risk of the theft of goods carried by road.

Even the crime of theft, which is common to virtually all 'developed' societies, can be subjected to this analysis. Before the 'Carrier's Case' in 1473, it was not a crime to steal property that one had been given to look after. The defendant had been hired to move goods to a particular location, but instead took them for his own use. For a crime to have occurred there was a requirement that the taking of the goods involved an element of trespass '*vi et armis*' (by force and arms). A minority of the judges considered that, as the goods had been handed over to the defendant, this was not satisfied. However, the majority created the fiction of a trespass by stating that the goods had been removed from their bales. Thus, conduct which had previously given rise only to civil liability now constituted a criminal offence. In a famous analysis of the case, Jerome Hall (1935) considered that the decision was made as the growing mercantile class required protection from employee theft.

Theft has proved a difficult notion for the Australian Aborigines and other indigenous communities who traditionally had no concept of the ownership of goods, and for whom all property was communal. In some societies it was considered impossible to own land, as land was something one had a relationship with. This of course, was never likely to survive the conquest of such territories by Europeans, for whom the ownership of goods and land is a crucial part of their lives (Bottomley *et al.* 1991).

This sort of analysis portrays crime as a result of a political process, whereby people in positions of power are able to impose their will on everyone else. It is similar to the labelling position, which sees crime as a consequence of the social interaction between different individuals or groups; here, certain individuals or groups have obtained sufficient power to impose their will on others. A Marxist analysis locates the centre of power specifically in those who control the means of production. Some feminists would locate the centre of power in the male domination of the vital organs of society. Crime based on such a conflict approach not only challenges the consensus view of society, but maintains that it has no objective reality other than as a state-defined political entity. In capitalist societies, crime deflects the attention of the lower classes from the cause of their condition. This type of account provides justification for the criminologist's interest in why certain activities are criminalised, whereas others are more or less officially ignored. In this respect, the application of the Schwendingers' definition of crime (above) provides an interesting contrast to the approach almost universally adopted in 'developed' societies. Pollution would become a major target of state action, and 'ethnic cleansing' would result in more than the appearance of a token soldier or two in an international court of law.

Although some writers are unwilling to separate the existence from the enforcement of the criminal law, it is arguable that such a distinction is possible. It is surely undeniable that Judaeo-Christian morality has been influential in forming the content of our criminal law. Some present crimes (as opposed to the physical acts that are required for their commission), such as murder and causing grievous bodily harm with intent, are likely to be abhorrent in any type of society. Measures will be taken to try to prevent such acts occurring, and it is unlikely that these will be differentially applied in accordance with the perpetrator's status. However, crimes of homicide are, thankfully, still comparatively rare in Britain, and it is far easier to argue that theft is a good example of a long-established criminal offence that is clearly prosecuted on a discriminatory basis. For example, it is interesting to compare the official reaction to the theft of unofficial 'perks' available to middle-class office personnel (such as stationery) with that given to shoplifting by the poor.

Conflicting images of crime

It should therefore be apparent that there are conflicting images of crime. In the next two chapters a closer view is taken of the information from which these images are formed. Consideration will now be given to what some of these conflicting images are.

(a) Autonomous behaviour v structural forces

This is essentially an argument, which is as old as the discipline of criminology itself, between classical free-will notions of individual responsibility and positivist arguments suggesting that individuals are largely shaped by constitutional or environmental factors outside their direct control. Put simply—or simplistically—one could ask whether the crime problem is 'evil or bad people' or 'deprivation and unemployment'. The development of the classical and positivist 'schools' is discussed in Chapter 5.

(b) Rich law v poor law

(i) White-collar crime

This term was introduced by the American sociologist Edwin Sutherland in his presidential address to the American Sociological Society in 1939 (Sutherland 1940). Sutherland realised that crime was generally described as being committed by lower-class individuals and that explanations of their criminality emphasised poverty and individual personality defects. However, as it was obvious that there was little, if any, connection between poverty and white-collar crime, and as psychological explanations could not account for fraudulent company executives, Sutherland argued that traditional explanations were inadequate for such cases.

Sutherland defined white-collar crimes as criminal behaviour committed by upper-class individuals in the course of their employment which 'differs from the criminal behaviour of the lower socio-economic class principally in the administrative procedures which are used in dealing with the offenders'. He went on to add that, although the financial cost of such crimes was far greater than that of offences which were usually considered as constituting the 'crime problem', the real damage was that caused to social relations in the breakdown of trust that resulted. Sutherland considered that most offences, including white-collar crime, could be brought about by what he termed 'differential association'. (This is discussed more fully in Chapter 6.) In outline, this suggests that individuals are subject to influences both in favour of law-abiding behaviour and in favour of law-violating behaviour, and that criminals are those people who have been subject to stronger law-violating influences. This means that people who work in organisations where criminal practices are common are likely to engage in such activities themselves. Sutherland considered that the collapse of civilised standards in American business was the consequence of the replacement of small family businesses by monopolistic corporations.

There are several weaknesses in Sutherland's definition of white-collar crime. One which has been highlighted by many writers is that it does not distinguish between people who commit crimes on behalf of an organisation and those who commit crimes from within an organisation but against its interests. Nowadays, this division is routinely adopted. For example, Clinard and Quinney (1973) have divided white-collar crime into 'occupational crime', which is committed by employees at work, and 'corporate crime', which covers offences committed by company officials as well as those perpetrated by the company itself. Sutherland's definition places considerable emphasis on 'high status' offenders. Yet, he used as an example an account given by one of his students of the tricks the student was encouraged to employ when selling shoes.

A far higher proportion of the working population is nowadays employed in white-collar occupations than when Sutherland used the term half a century ago. Thousands of middle-class people, working in relatively low-level office jobs, seize the opportunity to practise embezzlement and fraud. Weisburd *et al.* (1991) have suggested that this has arisen as ordinary people have far greater access to the formerly restricted world of 'paper fraud' as a result of the use of computers in the banking and finance world: as the authors put it, 'lying and cheating are truly the weapons available to us all'. Their own analysis of a sample of convicted white-collar offenders in US federal courts illustrates the variability of the category. Weisburd *et al.* discovered that 80 per cent of the offenders were white, 79 per cent were employed at the time of the offence, 15 per cent were women, and a third had an ownership interest in the companies for which they worked. More than a third had a prior criminal record and almost a third had previously been arrested.

However, it remains the case that some right-wing American criminologists still consider that crime is what is reported in the official statistics, and that there is no reason to go beyond this and concern themselves with white-collar or corporate offending. Hirschi and Gottfredson (1989) dismiss white-collar offenders as a pointless category and claim that there is no reason to distinguish such offenders from any others. In their controversial book *The Bell Curve* (1994), Richard J Herrnstein and Charles Murray devote much space to explaining why crime is committed by people of low intelligence. There is no discussion whatsoever of business crime.

(ii) Tax avoiders—or benefit scroungers?

In her books *Rich Law, Poor Law* (1989) and *Poverty, Crime and Punishment* (1997), Dee Cook has shown the completely different responses of the authorities to tax evasion and social security fraud. Only the very worst cases of tax evasion reach the courts. Most are dealt with by means of out-of-court financial settlements, often arrived at with professional advisers in comfy, well-furnished offices. In contrast, social security fraudsters, usually for much smaller amounts, are labelled 'scroungers' and are vigorously pursued through the courts.

Cook argued that society's attitude to social welfare is a legacy of the 1834 Poor Law, which effectively drew distinctions between the 'deserving' poor (the aged, the sick and children) who should be entitled to relief, and the 'undeserving' poor (the idle and unemployed) who should not be. The basic tenets of the 1834 Law—those of 'less eligibility' and the 'workhouse test'—still exist today, although the latter is now manifested in various modern types of work test and 'job schemes'. Although they may well help people to find employment, they are also designed to weed out the 'scroungers'. 'Less eligibility' still survives in the incentives for the unemployed to take up low-paid (often part-time) jobs, which are appropriate to their status of being at the end of the queue when it comes to help. Welfare recipients are viewed as 'takers', so the state is entitled to impose strict measures against those who break the benefit rules. Tax payers, on the other hand, are viewed as 'givers', so any disciplinary action taken against them should be far less severe. Tax evasion is often seen by those who practise it as a 'game'. Yet, both types of fraud—tax or benefit—involve making false statements of personal circumstances to the financial detriment of the state. In this respect, the essence of the two offences is the same.

In recent years, both Conservative and Labour governments have sought to target social security fraud. During the early 1990s the annual number of prosecutions doubled to around 10,000. In August 1996 a free-phone 'fraud hotline' was introduced in Britain for people to report anyone who they think is illegally claiming state benefit. The scheme was called 'Beat-a-Cheat'. It is notable that no such encouragement is given to the reporting of people who are illegally failing to pay tax. A belief had grown up in government circles that there was a series of highly sophisticated 'fraud networks' which were responsible for much of this loss. However, this view was questioned by a Policy Studies Institute report for the Department of Social Security (Great Britain, DSS 1997). This showed that most individuals, while realising their actions were wrong, considered that fraudulent claiming was simply the lesser of two evils where the other was turning to 'real crime' in order to provide for their family. There have also been suggestions in reports from the National Audit Office that there is a large underpayment of benefit to claimants who are entitled to it, which could even exceed the cost of overpayments (National Audit Office 1991–2). For example, it has been estimated that one million pensioners are failing to claim all the benefits to which they are entitled.

In 2000, the Grabiner Report on the Informal Economy was published (Grabiner 2000). Although the report estimated that the cost of people working while 'signing on' could be around half a billion pounds a year, it also recognised that there is a substantial amount of tax fraud, and recommended that a new criminal offence should be created of fraudulently evading income tax. Needless to say, the government's response to the report chose to emphasise the defrauding of the benefit system (HM Treasury News Release, 9 March 2000). The Inland Revenue is unwilling to estimate the level of tax fraud, but it is generally believed to be at least £3 billion a year. In contrast, the Department of Work and Pensions' website *Targeting Benefit Fraud* estimates that social security fraud costs the country £2 billion each year.

There are signs that efforts against tax fraud are becoming less successful. The number of convictions declined throughout the 1990s and only 183 were obtained between 1998–9 and 2001–2 (National Audit Office 2002–3b). In 2001–2 over 11,000 people were convicted of benefit fraud (National Audit Office 2002–3a). The situation regarding indirect taxation appears to be even worse. The National Audit Office has estimated that HM Customs and Excise lost £11.9 billion in 2002–3 through 'fraud and error' in VAT payments. Once again, informal resolution of the 'problem' is the preferred course of action, although even then the number of 'civil evasion penalties' (agreements to pay a fine) fell from 898 in 1997–8 to 276 in 2002–3, a year in which there were just 86 completed prosecutions resulting in 69 convictions (National Audit Office 2003–4).

(c) Corporate crime v street crime

Corporate crime does not receive much discussion in the mass media unless there has been fraud on a massive scale. Examples include: the collapse of the investment managers Barlow Clowes in 1988, leaving 17,000 small investors owed a total of £200 million; the Guinness–Distillers affair of 1990; the disclosure in 1991 that the late Robert Maxwell had appropriated £500 million from his employees' pension funds; and the collapse of Asil Nadir's 'Polly Peck' empire in 1993 with the disappearance of £450 million. Nadir subsequently 'jumped' bail and fled the country.

The late 1980s saw a series of large-scale 'disasters' involving companies and organisations. Thirty-one people died when a fire broke out at Kings Cross underground station in 1987. There were three major incidents in 1988 alone: the Piper Alpha oil rig explosion (which killed 168 people), the Clapham Junction train crash (thirty-five dead) and the overturning of the 'Herald of Free Enterprise' ferry (188 dead). In 1989, there was the disaster at Hillsborough football ground (ninety-six dead) and the sinking of the *Marchioness* pleasure craft. In contrast, the 1990s were relatively quiet, but there were serious rail accidents at Southall in 1997 (seven dead) and Paddington in 1999 (thirty-one dead).

The only successful prosecutions in these cases concerned health and safety matters; there were no convictions for manslaughter.

Injuries and deaths at the workplace are not uncommon. Health and Safety Executive (HSE) reports indicate that every year around 200 employees are fatally injured and 28,000 suffer major injuries from accidents at work. It has been estimated that 70 per cent of these deaths resulted from management failure. Research by Slapper (1999) suggested that 60 per cent of them were attributable to 'corner-cutting' to save money rather than ignorance about safety. The Trades Union Congress considers that the deteriorating industrial safety record has resulted from increasing deregulation. In recent years, the HSE has claimed that in around three-quarters of cases, lives could have been saved if the management had taken more positive action. Employees may also suffer from foreseeable diseases such as cancer or asbestosis. Box (1983) has estimated a ratio of 7:1 concerning deaths from occupational accidents and illnesses in proportion to deaths recorded as homicides.

Over the past twenty years or so, the operation of business has become far more complex and, with the growing exposure to low-cost production in the Third World, far more competitive. Greater competition has itself led to pressure for deregulation and an opening up of markets. Medium-sized and even small businesses have been turned into corporations with stock market quotations. The ownership of businesses has substantially shifted from one or two individuals, who would formerly have controlled much of the operation, to multinational conglomerates with extra layers of management. The growth of the Internet and 'e-commerce' has also increased the opportunities for fraud.

Given that it is now impossible to deny that such offences occur on a large scale, why are there not more prosecutions in cases of corporate crime? Different explanations have been put forward. Such crimes are not always particularly visible unless they end in spectacular financial crashes or human tragedies, as in the examples mentioned above. The prosecution of most offences is reliant on evidence from victims and witnesses, but many business crimes are never as transparent as, for example, robbery. The police may have to take on a proactive role which is time-consuming and expensive (Braithwaite *et al.* 1987). Victims (for example, individual shareholders) may not become aware of their financial loss. The symptoms of diseases such as asbestosis or cancer, which can result from prolonged unsafe working conditions, may take years to develop and then, if the victim is elderly, there will always be problems in pinpointing the exact cause.

Some frauds are genuinely complex and the Serious Fraud Office (SFO) is reluctant to prosecute if there is little chance of obtaining a conviction. The SFO has itself been criticised for a number of unsuccessful (and expensive) prosecutions in high-profile cases, such as that of Kevin and Ian Maxwell in 1996. Company executives in the 'Herald of Free Enterprise' case could not be prosecuted because it was impossible to identify senior individuals who had a direct influence on the operation of the ship. This was another consequence of the intricate and impersonal structure of present-day large corporations. These are the sort of arguments that persuaded Clarke (1990) to argue that it is preferable to encourage errant companies to comply with the law rather than to prosecute them.

Why do companies and their executives resort to white-collar crime? Several of the explanations that are considered in this book—such as anomie or opportunity theory—could be applicable. A radical view would suggest that, when companies find difficulties in making profits by lawful methods, they will have few qualms about resorting to unlawful means (Box 1983). Pressure to make savings of costs can lead to the cutting of corners in health and safety matters. In the 1970s the Ford Motor Company in America proceeded with the manufacture and sale of the Pinto model even though they knew that, because of an important design fault, it was dangerous (Swigert and Farrell 1980). It has been estimated that, as a result of this, Ford were responsible for between 500 and 900 deaths (Dowie 1988). In 2000, it was alleged that Ford may have contributed to a number of blown tyres on its 'Explorer' model by rejecting design changes when the vehicle went into production. Some of the accidents resulted in fatalities (*The Times*, 25 August 2000). It could also be argued that the entrepreneurial nature of capitalism—so much to the fore in the 1980s—is not that remote from some of the more enterprizing schemes of corporate fraud that have been devised in recent years. On the other hand, Braithwaite (1985) has shown how American pharmaceutical companies, by being prepared to abide by the law in obtaining authorization for their products, are virtually guaranteed highly profitable markets in countries which cannot afford to conduct their own drug testing.

Crime on the streets—as opposed to 'in the suites'—tends to be viewed completely differently. The term 'mugging' was introduced by the British press from the USA in the 1970s to describe relatively minor street robberies such as handbag-snatching. (A robbery is technically a theft which is brought about by the use or even threat of violence.) This led to a general 'moral panic' which came to be reflected in longer custodial sentences. The police take a hard line against any kind of street disturbance, be it a robbery or a May Day anti-capitalism demonstration. Is this simply because such behaviour is so visible, or is it that concentrating on it will divert attention from the more institutionalised illegal practices of the powerful?

It is interesting to note that many 'rich' people who approve of CCTV surveillance of the 'poor' as a means of deterring disorder in public places are horrified by the use of 'speed cameras' to monitor their own illegal behaviour.

Public disorder and street crime tend to be the preserve of young men, and this leads to proclamations that the youth of today is 'out of control' or that there has been a general deterioration in standards of behaviour amongst the young. Yet, this is not a new phenomenon. Adelaide Johnson (1959) cited a 6,000-year-old inscription of an Egyptian priest, which claimed 'Our earth is degenerate . . . children no longer obey their parents'. While it is the case that conventions governing behaviour in general are far less strict than they were fifty years ago, there is a danger in painting too rosy a picture of a typical urban street scene in the past. Although the homicide rate has risen since the late 1960s, the figure of around 1.5 killings per 100,000 of the population is still one of the lowest in the world, and estimates have put the corresponding figure as high as 15 in the thirteenth century (Given 1977).

Geoffrey Pearson's book *Hooligan* (1983) provides a graphic illustration of how 'moral panics' concerning predominantly young people have occurred for well over a hundred years. In 1862 a panic arose when a member of parliament, Hugh Pilkington, was attacked and 'garrotted' (a partial strangulation for the purpose of robbery) when walking from the Houses of Parliament to the Reform Club. Other such incidents were reported (and duly exaggerated) in the press and the Security from Violence Act was passed, which imposed corporal punishment for such crimes. The antics of the Hooligan family in London introduced the word into the vocabulary at the beginning of the twentieth century. The razor gangs of the 1940s, as illustrated in Graham Greene's novel *Brighton Rock*, show that the war years were not as tranquil at home as the propaganda led people to believe: Steve Chibnall (1977) has pointed out that there was a 250 per cent increase in the number of adolescents sent to prison between 1939 and 1947.

A panic over the import of 'horror comics' led to the now forgotten Children and Young Persons (Harmful Publications) Act 1955. Damage was caused to cinemas by exuberant 'teddy boys' during showings of *Rock around the Clock*. The 1960s is remembered for clashes between scooter and motor-bike gangs ('mods' and 'rockers') at southern sea-side resorts. More recent examples have included 'lager louts' and 'joy riders'. The 'mugging' scare of the 1970s (Hall *et al.* 1978) seemed like a rerun of the garrotting panic. In short, popular youth culture seems always to have been associated with over-exuberance and, where this spills over to the streets, the police have not been slow to react.

Walklate (2004) illustrated this point well:

> . . . what makes the often rude, and belligerent *behaviour* of the old boys' network of the House of Commons all that different from the lads who shout, whistle and jostle, hanging about on the street corner? The reply has to be that in behavioural terms, very little . . . what differs, of course, is their public and political *acceptability* (emphasis in original).

Hirschi and Gottfredson (1983) have stated that '[o]ne of the few facts agreed on in criminology is the age distribution of crime'. This assertion has regularly been supported by official figures: the 2003 Criminal Statistics show that the peak age for offending is eighteen for males and fifteen for females. However, it is arguable that the criminal justice system operates in such a way as to exaggerate the amount of crime committed by young offenders and minimise the recorded levels of offending by older people. Overall, the young are subject to greater surveillance and this may give rise to a 'self-fulfilling prophecy': if resources are targeted at one particular group, it is more likely that what is being sought will be found. Young people spend more time in public places and often commit crimes in groups. Research suggests that members of groups are more likely to be identified and detected than individual offenders (Hirschi and Gottfredson 1983). As far as older offenders are concerned, they will constitute the white-collar criminals and perpetrators of sexual abuse and domestic violence who do not appear in the statistics. Moreover, even where a crime has been exposed, prosecution may be less likely with the increasing age of the suspect. Farrington and Burrows (1993) found evidence that shop owners are less likely to call the police if elderly offenders are involved.

Further light is thrown on this issue by a consideration of self-report studies. In the Cambridge Study in Delinquent Development, which is described in Chapter 3, Farrington (1989) found that the commission of certain offences, such as theft of vehicles, declined sharply with age.

On the other hand, some offences, such as theft from work, showed an increase. A similar finding was reached from the self-report questionnaires administered as part of the British Crime Survey (Mayhew and Elliott 1990). The overall conclusion, therefore, is that young people seem to be heavily represented in the more visible types of offending that are usually recorded in official statistics, and older people commit a significant number of offences of the type that are less likely to come to the attention of the authorities.

(d) Terrorism v justifiable state action

Nowadays, politicians go to considerable lengths to describe terrorists as being no different from common criminals. It was not always thus. In the nineteenth century, Britain obtained a reputation for being a safe haven for political 'agitators' and refugees from the turmoils of continental Europe. Although, not surprisingly, the same courteous treatment was not extended to Irish independence fighters at that time, there was at least a serious political debate as to whether they should be treated differently from other offenders in prison. However, the situation had changed by the end of World War I (Ingraham 1979). This may have been a reaction to the increased number of anti-colonial movements growing up around the world, or it may have been because of a belief that, with the growth of democracy, there was less justification for terrorist action. 'Political criminals' thus became 'terrorists', reviled by governments throughout the world.

'Terrorism' is an emotive word, designed to emphasise the extreme fear caused by apparently indiscriminate violent actions of individuals and groups claiming to be operating on behalf of some particular cause. It was first used to describe the 'reign of terror' perpetrated during the French Revolution (de Than and Shorts 2004). Since the attacks on New York and Washington on 11 September 2001, terrorism has risen to the top of the political agenda in the Western world.

Despite this, there is no single agreed definition of the term. In the UK, the Terrorism Act 2000 refers to actions 'designed to influence the government or to intimidate the public or a section of the public' where they are 'for the purpose of advancing a political, religious or ideological cause'.

Sometimes terrorist activities are funded by states ('state-sponsored terrorism') and the finger is often pointed by the West at countries such as Iran and Syria. Yet, there is considerable hypocrisy here, as many Western countries have themselves supported terrorist organisations when it has suited their purpose to do so. In this respect, the biggest hypocrite is the USA, who in the climate of the Cold War backed many right-wing movements, such as the Contras in Nicaragua (Chomsky 1988) and UNITA in Angola, often with considerable bloodshed and loss of life. Israel also uses a large amount of anti-terrorist rhetoric, conveniently forgetting that the Israeli state came into existence on the back of terrorism (Rokach 1986). One of the actions of the Jewish organisation, Irgun Zvai Leumi, was to blow up without warning the King David Hotel in Jerusalem in July 1946. Over ninety people were killed, many of them British. The leader of Irgun, Menachem Begin, was sought by the British as a terrorist and a murderer. Later, he became prime minister of Israel and was awarded the Nobel Peace Prize in 1978. One person's 'terrorist' is another person's 'freedom fighter'. Perhaps the best example of such 'rehabilitation' is Nelson Mandela who, having been imprisoned by the South African government for more than a quarter of a century, became the country's president within five years of being released.

The term terrorism is generally thought to be inapplicable to 'normal' military engagements when a declared state of war exists under international law. After World War II, the International Military Tribunal at Nuremberg (1947) created two new war crimes: 'crimes against peace' covers the planning, preparation, initiation or waging of aggressive war, or a war in flagrant and unjustified violation of international law; 'crimes against humanity' includes 'murder . . . and other inhumane acts committed against any civilian population before or during the war . . . whether or not in violation of the domestic law of the country in question'. There was clearly no difficulty in deciding that the Nazi regime had committed both these international crimes over and over again. Yet, what about the Allies' saturation bombing of German cities such as Dresden, or the Americans' dropping two atomic bombs on Japan? Or, some twenty years later, the Americans' use of napalm bombs to defoliate large areas of Vietnam?

Attempts have been made to prosecute contemporary politicians for war crimes. Ariel Sharon of Israel faced charges under a wide-ranging Belgian law in relation to his role in the massacre of Palestinian refugees by Christian militiamen in Beirut in 1982. However, in 2003 the Belgian parliament, which had been subject to diplomatic pressure, drastically amended the law to ensure that the case was simply passed back to Israel.

The point being made here is to re-emphasise that killing is not always considered unlawful. Terrorist acts are criminal offences, but the same acts are not considered as such when they are carried out by governments. The notorious 'death on the rock' incident in Gibraltar where the Government claimed that British soldiers were justified in shooting unarmed IRA suspects is held out by some as another example of this. It is also alleged that apparently unlawful killings carried out by the British army in Northern Ireland have gone unpunished. When it is politically expedient, the label of 'terrorist' can be quietly forgotten.

Conclusion

Hopefully, it has been shown in this chapter that, although both in common parlance and media portrayals the definition of crime is generally treated as non-problematic, this is in fact far from the case. The constantly changing content of the criminal law emphasises that, in many respects, crime is not only a very common, but also a very ordinary event. A brief moment's reflection will reveal that most people commit crimes nearly every day of their lives. Everyone who drives a motor vehicle commits crimes, whether by exceeding the speed limit, parking illegally, or making a simple error in some manoeuvre. It has been estimated that three out of every four employees steal from their employers. Many people, having discovered that they have been given too much change in a shop, fail to rectify the error; or, having found a valuable item in the street, fail to hand it in to the police; or make unauthorised telephone calls from work. Yet, these same people may be among the first to condemn, for example, social security 'cheats'.

Nevertheless, the evidence shows that only a relatively small number of people become persistently serious offenders. On the basis of a continuing research study (known as a 'longitudinal study') of a large sample of people, a 2001 Home Office Report claimed that a third of all males (but only 9 per cent of females) born in 1953 had obtained at least one conviction for a criminal offence (excluding minor ones) before the age of forty-six. However, the same study also indicated that two-thirds of the court appearances were made by a quarter of the sample, or 8 per cent of the male population (Prime *et al.* 2001). Although, in one sense, it appears that these are the people who create the 'real problem of crime', some will still continue to point to the activities of white-collar offenders as providing a greater threat to society.

3
The statistics on crime and their meaning

Many people might agree with Benjamin Disraeli's view that there are 'lies, damned lies and statistics'. However, statistical information is still disseminated by politicians and the mass media and cited in discussion as if it represented an accurate reflection of the phenomenon under consideration. This is just as true with crime statistics as with any other, and they are often referred to by the media as if they provide a true measurement of crime. Yet, it is now increasingly accepted that criminal statistics provide a deficient guide to both the level of crime and trends in criminal behaviour.

Although Jeremy Bentham had advocated the collection of national crime statistics in England in 1778, this did not happen until the following century. 'Crimes made known to the police' were included in the Judicial Statistics for the first time in 1856. Prison statistics were not published until 1910. Nowadays, the main compilation of crime figures is found in the annual 'Criminal Statistics England and Wales' first published in 1876, which contains data derived from police and court records throughout England and Wales. This report, which is accompanied by several supplementary volumes, is published by the Home Office. Regular bulletins and interim reports are also issued. There has been a massive increase in the amount of statistical information promulgated about crime in the last few years. This reflects in part the greater sophistication in statistical techniques, but is mostly a consequence of the growing political interest in the criminal justice system and an accompanying call for greater accountability and openness.

There are certain facts that appear incontrovertible from all measurements of crime in England and Wales. Until 1995, the number of crimes recorded had steadily increased since records began, with the largest rise being in the 1980s. However, since 1995 there has been an overall decline—as much as 39 per cent, according to the British Crime Survey (BCS). The great majority of offences consist of crimes against property and about half the recorded offences involve theft or handling stolen goods. Over 80 per cent of all crimes are committed by men.

Court statistics

As these are concerned with the formal dealings of the courts, they are not subject to so many of the inaccuracies that affect the police statistics. It is, however, important to appreciate what is and is not being counted. The court statistics list the appearances of offenders in court and not merely individual offenders. Moreover, the statistics do not count the charges; a single appearance may include more than one charge. If a conviction was based on more than one charge, the offence recorded is the one for which the heaviest sentence was passed. If the sentences were the same, the one recorded is the one with the highest possible sentence.

The main court tables are the ones which show the end results of appearances before the magistrates' courts and the Crown Court. These tables contain a breakdown of the courts' sentences from the choices available to them. Clearly, it would be meaningless to compare crude totals; at the very least the totals should be in percentages of the overall number of convictions. Even then there are problems in comparing the severity with which courts deal with different types of offence. For example, the statistics may suggest that one type of crime is likely to attract a more severe sentence than another. Yet, the figures do not distinguish between first offenders and those with previous convictions. Property offenders are more likely to have previous convictions than violent offenders, and this probably accounts for the fact that the former group often appears to have been dealt with fairly severely, given the offence charged.

Problems can also arise when comparing the sentencing policies of courts between different years. The introduction of a new sentence, or abolition of an existing one, can render comparisons between adjacent years meaningless. This is particularly important to bear in mind when looking at sentencing since the mid-1960s, as many new forms of punishment have been introduced during this period. There can also be distortion as a result of changes in the percentages of persons sentenced who have criminal records or who have asked for other offences not charged to be taken into consideration (TIC) in order 'to wipe the slate clean'. In addition, 'moral panics' over a particular offence, such as 'mugging' or football violence, can lead to a temporary increase in sentencing levels before a reversion to the usual.

Police statistics

Nevertheless, it is the police statistics which receive the most publicity. It is crucial to realise at the outset that they provide an incomplete and even inaccurate picture of offences known to the police. The statistics record what are deemed to be 'notifiable' offences—those which the police have to list in returns to the Home Office. Two groups of offences, involving firearms and homicides, are given specially detailed consideration in the Criminal Statistics: homicide reports, for instance, record the method of killing and the relationship of the victim to the suspect. However, these are the only types of crime for which information provided by all police forces about the surrounding circumstances of the offences is formally recorded. The only information provided for most offenders is their 'sex' and 'age group'.

For procedural purposes, criminal offences are divided into three categories. 'Indictable offences', which include serious crimes such as murder, manslaughter, robbery and rape, can only be tried before a jury at the Crown Court. 'Summary offences', such as minor motoring crimes, can only be tried by magistrates. In between is the category of 'offences triable either way'. Offenders charged with these crimes can be tried either by magistrates or at the Crown Court.

Notifiable offences comprise most indictable and triable-either-way crimes and a few summary offences. There are no detailed records of summary offences, although the Criminal Statistics notes the number convicted or formally cautioned. This vastly exceeds the equivalent number for notifiable offences. The Home Office sometimes changes the list of notifiable offences. Criminal damage of £20 or less was not counted before 1977, but is now notifiable. This in itself immediately increased the overall recorded crime level by about 7 per cent. On 1 April 1998, several other offences became notifiable, including assault on a constable and common assault. It has been suggested that the large percentage increase in recorded incidents of these crimes in the twelve months to September 2000 may have resulted from greater police attention being given to them (Povey and colleagues 2001).

Comparisons between different years can be problematic if new criminal offences have been introduced or the definitions of existing ones amended. For example, the enactment of the Theft Act 1968 made it very difficult to compare levels of property offences before and after that period, and the Misuse of Drugs Act 1971 made important changes to the definitions of drugs offences. Even monetary inflation can have a significant effect. Rohrer (1982) has pointed out that this largely accounted for an increase in acts of criminal damage exceeding £20 in value, which were recorded notifiable offences, from 17,000 in 1969 to 124,000 in 1977. Another example, given by Walker (1995), is the Criminal Justice Act 1982 which designated gross indecency with a child and trafficking in controlled drugs as notifiable offences. Statistics for one year can even be altered several years later. Following the enquiry into the poisonings carried out by Dr Harold Shipman, a further 200 cases were reclassified as murders. Many of these had originally been recorded as strokes or heart attacks.

(a) Reporting crime

A crucial factor that can affect the recorded level of crime is the extent to which members of the public are prepared to report incidents to the police. Crime surveys have gone some way towards shedding light on what is referred to as 'the dark figure of crime'—the amount of crime that never comes to the police's attention. Taken together, the BCS reports suggest that only about half of all known crime is brought to the attention of the police.

Why do individuals choose not to report crimes? Many offences appear trivial to victims: few people are going to bother to tell the police that their car radio aerial has been snapped off. Lack of seriousness was the commonest reason given for lack of reporting in the 2003–4 BCS. The next most common reasons were the belief that there was no loss and that the police would or could do nothing about it. Some people may be deterred by fear of initimidation or reprisals by the offender, or the offender's family and friends (Tarling *et al.* 2000). People may be unaware that a crime has been committed: motoring offences, for example, take place all the time, but many non-drivers may not realise this. The crime may not involve an apparent 'victim', or any such individual may have been fully compliant in what occurred, such as in the commission of various types of drug offence. Child victims and other people who lack power or status in society may find it practically very difficult to report crimes against them. (It is significant that the level of child abuse brought to the attention of society has dramatically increased since the introduction of the freephone 'Childline' service.) Minor acts of public disorder committed by members of the university rugby club may be less likely to be reported than similar acts committed by local 'yobs'. Some people, such as victims of sexual offences or racial intimidation (Shah and Pease 1992), may be embarrassed, or feel that the police will not take their complaint seriously. In an analysis of BCS data, MacDonald (2001) found a significant relationship between people's failure to report crimes and dislike of the police.

There may be cultural expectations that women accept physical and sexual abuse without complaint. Choudry (1996) found that Pakistani women in London are under strong pressure to succeed in their marriages, and that failure would lead to dishonour both for them and their families. These women generally live with their husband's relatives, who are likely to support him in any dispute and condone any violent behaviour towards his wife.

However, there is no reason to suspect that the level of unreported crime is constant, and changes can have a significant impact on the crime statistics. Some of the apparent increase may be due to a greater readiness on the part of the public to report crimes. The fact that police forces now treat victims of sexual offences with greater sensitivity has resulted in more people coming forward and a corresponding increase in the number of such crimes made known to the police. Variations can also occur through economic factors. MacDonald (2001) found that the unemployed are far less likely to report property offences to the police than those who have a job.

The growth of property and contents insurance has similarly inflated the levels of recorded burglaries and criminal damage cases. It is usually a condition of making such an insurance claim that the police have been informed of the crime. The 1996 BCS found an increase in the number of bicycle thefts since the previous report; yet during the same period the number of such thefts recorded by the police had declined. It appears that fewer people had their bicycles insured in 1995 and, of those who did, a smaller number than usual made claims. In the 1996 report, most of the crime victims who had not reported to the police said they would have done so if they had made an insurance claim. It is possible that the greater number of people who now have a telephone may also be a contributory factor.

Bottomley and Pease (1986) pointed out that, while the number of recorded burglaries increased by half between 1971 and 1981, General Household Surveys conducted during that period indicated that there had been virtually no change at all. They suggested that the increased reporting may have been partly due to the growing popularity of household contents insurance policies providing for the replacement of used items with new ones, with the consequential incentive to making fraudulent claims. There is also a possibility that, in an increasingly 'rights-conscious' society, more people may be prepared to report incidents in general, and that there may be less antagonism to the police in certain areas than there was in the past (however, Sparks, Genn and Dodd (1977) found no evidence in their London victim survey that this was a significant factor).

(b) Recording crime

Not all offences are recorded in the police statistics. Some crimes are dealt with by organisations other than the police; for example, tax evasion by the Inland Revenue, and both VAT fraud and smuggling by the Customs and Excise. These offences will only appear in official criminal records if they are subsequently brought to court, and it was shown in Chapter 2 that this is by no means certain to happen. There is also the vital question of the discretion that exists at different stages of police work. The patrol officer may decide to administer an on-the-spot informal caution, although this is not so likely for notifiable offences. Formal cautions, administered at the police station, are shown in the criminal statistics but, as they are included in the totals of convictions, any significant increase in cautioning for notifiable offences may give the impression of a major increase in crime. As formal cautions should only follow an admission of guilt, it may seem that this is not a problem. However, people may be induced to confess to something they have not done if promised a caution in return and, as Pearson (1983) has indicated, there is clear evidence that the increased use of formal cautioning (especially for juveniles) since the 1970s has led to 'net widening'—the inclusion of people in official records who previously would have been dealt with informally and 'off the record'.

Members of the public, who alert the police to over 80 per cent of reported crime (Bottomley and Pease 1986), may be disbelieved or no action taken on their reports for a variety of reasons, including making the force's 'clear-up' rate look better, or because the offence is considered to be trivial, or because it occurred a long time ago (Bottomley and Coleman 1981). The police may believe that the reporter has concocted the story. It may be apparent that there is insufficient evidence to take the matter any further, or that a dispute has been settled to the satisfaction of both parties. Police forces vary in the extent to which they record reported incidents as crimes. For example, in 1998–9 the Avon and Somerset police recorded an identical number of incidents and crimes for sexual offences, which indicates that all such incidents were recorded as crimes. However, in the adjacent Gloucestershire force there were more sex crimes reported than incidents, which suggests that not all incidents were recorded

(Home Office 2000). In Scotland, the Lothian and Borders police halved its reported crime figures by recording some incidents as 'suspicious occurrences' and downgrading a number of serious attacks to 'minor assaults' (*The Times*, 22 November 2002).

There are also several situations when a crime is recorded as having been cleared up even though there has been no conviction. If a person is charged or summonsed for an offence, it is treated as cleared up. The same result ensues in several instances when there is not even a charge: for example, where the alleged offender is under the age of criminal responsibility (which is ten); the victim cannot or will not give evidence; or the offence has been admitted and 'taken into consideration' (TIC) by a sentencing court (see below). An offence for which the offender has been cautioned is also treated as cleared up, although a caution should only be administered to offenders who admit their guilt.

The whole question of 'clear-up rates' is problematic. Some commentators have used them as a percentage of crimes made known to the police to suggest an index of the force's efficiency. Yet, some types of offence are much easier to clear up than others; for example, personal violence and murder where, contrary to common belief, the assailant is usually known to the victim. Also, far more police resources are likely to be utilised in serious cases. Some incidents, such as shoplifting, may initially seem to have a very high clear-up rate, but this is because shoplifting is not usually reported to the police unless the offender has been caught. Shoplifting is theft and, given its frequency, the reporting practices of different shops could have a marked effect on the recorded levels of that offence in the police statistics.

Using comparisons with the BCS, Mayhew *et al.* (1993) considered that between 1981 and 1991 there was a decrease in the police's recording of acquisitive crimes, but an increase in the recording of offences of violence and vandalism. Although it is possible that offences not recorded are predominantly trivial, other factors may be involved. For example, the police have been under pressure in recent years to take assaults on women and members of ethnic minorities more seriously.

Police officers must still pay close attention to questions of their efficiency, and there have been suggestions that figures may sometimes be presented in such a way as to show their performance in a better light. In 1986, PC Ron Walker presented evidence to the Police Complaints Authority and *The Observer* newspaper indicating that the Kent police had been persuading offenders to admit to hundreds of offences which they had not committed or which, in some cases, had not even occurred. The offender would be promised some benefit (such as the removal of any objection to bail) in return for having these offences taken into consideration on sentencing, with the risk of little if any increased punishment. A subsequent enquiry upheld Walker's claims. More recent evidence has suggested that this practice is still continuing, and it appears that manipulation of the statistics is now occurring to help satisfy the requirements imposed on police forces by the Police Act 1996, whereby their efficiency is now measured in terms of clear-up rate (see Chapter 2). In 1997, an investigation was launched into allegations by a retired police superintendent that Nottinghamshire Constabulary had routinely managed to improve its 'success' rate by downgrading the offence charged (for example, from burglary to criminal damage) and exaggerating the number of offences taken into consideration (*The Independent*, 30 April 1997).

In September 1994 the Home Secretary, Michael Howard, announced a 5.5 per cent drop in recorded crime—the largest for forty years. However, senior police officers subsequently conceded that much of this decline resulted from their forces' classifying certain incidents so as make them non-notifiable (for example, actual bodily harm could become a common assault), or even 'no crimes' on the grounds of triviality. The offences covered by the BCS increased by 2 per cent between 1993 and 1995 (Mirrlees-Black *et al.* 1996).

Another aspect of discretion concerns the targeting by police forces of particular areas or types of offence. If the police decide to concentrate their resources on a specific part of a city which is 'known' to produce a lot of crime, there is a good chance that there will be an increase in the overall number of crimes they discover. This is especially likely with so-called victimless crimes such as drug possession. Increases in Customs checks during the 1980s were at least in part responsible for the massive increase in recorded drug trafficking during that period. The police may also lose interest in certain types of illegal activity that they believe the public are not so concerned about. Some forces adopt this approach to soliciting by prostitutes, unless there are complaints from local residents, or the activity is accompanied by other forms of illegality. Lea and Young (1984) have suggested that the massive rise between 1958 and 1963 in the number of convictions in Manchester for importuning men for homosexuality was really a consequence of targeting by the Chief Constable, rather than a result of any real increase in the level of offending. The main categorisation of notifiable offences in the police statistics is into different types of crime. These are divided into broad categories: offences of violence; sexual offences; robbery; burglary; theft and handling stolen goods; fraud and forgery; criminal damage; and other notifiable offences. Most of these could include a wide range of criminal behaviour, but each typically contains only one or two subdivisions. For example, 'violence' could range from murder to assault occasioning actual bodily harm (which often involves bruising or less severe cases of broken bones), and it is the latter which comprises the vast majority of cases in this category. 'Fraud' could range from a major financial swindle to the use of a stolen credit card. It is, therefore, clear that superficial comparisons between these groups would provide very misleading impressions. The same would be true for any attempt to spot trends over a period of time, as they might have been caused by changes for one particular crime. For instance, recorded offences of violence have greatly increased in recent years, but the rise has been far greater for the less serious forms of assault than it has for murder.

The apparently low figures for recorded cases of fraud are especially misleading. Many frauds are dealt with by non-police agencies such as Customs and Excise. In addition, fraud cases provide a good example of the danger of assessing the importance or magnitude of a particular crime, simply by counting the number of times it occurs. If one assessed the importance of property offences on the basis of the value of the property, fraud cases would vastly exceed every other category. The value of the alleged fraud in any one of the celebrated cases (such as Guinness, Maxwell, or Polly Peck) was greater than that of all the goods stolen in thefts and burglaries in a year (Levi 1993).

A second main classification found in the police statistics is that, where appropriate, the data is broken down for each of the forty-three forces in England and Wales. Some attempt is made to compensate for the different size of populations covered by police forces by expressing the 'crime rate' for each offence per 100,000 of the population. However, no analysis is provided to reflect the different types of region covered by each force: the West Midlands force area, for example, is hardly comparable with that covered by the Dyfed-Powys police. Nor are the figures for each force broken down to distinguish between different parts of the area: residents of rural Somerset appear to suffer from a fairly high crime rate until it is appreciated that the figures include those for Bristol. Not surprisingly, forces which cover predominantly urban environments have higher crime rates in every category than those in mainly rural areas.

Some of the problems with police statistics are indicated by a study of Nottinghamshire. By the 1980s it had become apparent that Nottinghamshire regularly had the highest recorded crime rate of all the police forces. This seemed particularly strange when it was further noted that the rate was significantly higher than for adjacent forces, such as Leicestershire and Staffordshire, which have a very similar urban–rural mix. Farrington and Dowds (1985) carried out a study to ascertain whether the citizens of Nottinghamshire really did commit more crimes than anywhere else, or whether their police adopted different recording practices. They concluded that, although there was a slightly higher crime rate than in neighbouring counties, 'between two-thirds and three-quarters of the difference in crime rates . . . reflected differences in police reactions to crime'.

(c) The counting rules

There are also problems with the counting of offences. One such difficulty arises when someone commits a chain of offences—say, with a credit card—in one evening. Formerly, there was considerable variation among police forces as to how this should be recorded. Following the recommendations of the Perks Committee (1967), the Home Office established a set of rules. These were subsequently revised. If several offences were committed 'in one incident', only the most serious would be counted unless the offences were violent or of a sexual nature, in which case the rule became 'one offence for each victim'. The rules also stated that just one offence would be counted if a continuous series of offences was only possible because of a special relationship between offender and victim—for example, between a violent man and his partner.

With the exception of murder, if an offender was charged with one offence, but only convicted of a less serious one, the original offence charged would still be the one recorded.

Different interpretations of these rules were possible, and anecdotal evidence suggested that variations existed among police forces. It is important to remember that, although such counting rules are arbitrary, they have a major effect on the way that the level of crime is portrayed. Monica Walker (1995) has pointed out various distortions that can result from this. The fact that different counting rules applied to violent and property offences meant that crimes of violence appeared as 'over-represented' in relation to crimes against property. As a person who was dealt with for several offences at the same time only appeared once in the statistics, whereas repeat offenders throughout the year made a separate appearance for each incident, men—who are more likely to be repeat offenders—were recorded disproportionately to women.

However, in 1998 the counting rules were revised again. The practice of only recording the most serious in a chain of crimes was abolished and replaced by the principle of 'one crime per victim'. This change had a considerable inflationary effect on the first set of crime figures to which it applied (Povey and Prime 1999).

In 2000, the Home Office published a discussion document suggesting changes that could be made to the ways in which the police statistics are recorded and presented to the public (Home Office 2000). The document pointed out that the present system 'would still seem familiar to statisticians from the nineteenth century'. It cited approvingly a comment made by the journalist Simon Jenkins that the current statistics make 'what is measurable important, not what is important measurable'. A survey of practitioners in the criminal justice system revealed that the two most important changes felt necessary were the provision of more detailed information and greater contextual analysis. The discussion document proposed that the best way of achieving these aims would be to make greater use of information technology. Instead of a reliance being made on the fairly crude statistical data supplied by the police, the problems that need addressing should first be defined and then the information required to address them should be readily available. This could, for example, include changing the current procedure-based list of notifiable offences.

The discussion document made a large number of recommendations. The recording (either as an 'incident' or a 'call for service') of every crime-related matter brought to the attention of the police was suggested. Eventually, all police data should be collected and stored electronically. It was envisaged that patrol officers could use either hand-held computers or forms that could later be scanned on to a computer. The views of victims should play a far greater role in the collection of crime data and they should be informed of developments in the case. Victims' assessment of the suspect's motives should be recorded. The sort of contextual information currently provided for homicides should also be available for non-fatal crimes of violence.

In an attempt to make counting practices more consistent, the National Crime Recording Standard (NCRS) was introduced in all police forces in April 2002. Recording should now be based more on the victim's perception of a crime having taken place rather than the police's satisfying themselves of the fact. The Standard contains three basic principles. First, all reports of incidents, from whatever source and whether crime-related or not, should be registered by the police.

Second, the incident should be recorded as a crime (a notifiable offence) if, on the balance of probability, the circumstances as reported amount to a crime in law, and there is no credible evidence to the contrary. Third, a crime should remain recorded unless there is additional verifiable evidence to disprove that it occurred.

A predictable consequence of this change has been an increase in the percentage of reported crimes recorded by the police. An analysis of data from the 2003–4 BCS suggested that the police recorded about 74 per cent of the crimes covered by the Survey that were reported to them—an increase from 62 per cent in 2001–2. This probably accounts for the fact that the number of crimes recorded by the police in 2003–4 showed a 1 per cent increase over the previous year, whereas the BCS found a decrease of 5 per cent in the number of crimes disclosed to researchers (Dodd *et al.* 2004). However, a review by the Audit Commission of crime recording practices during 2003 and 2004 found that only seventeen of the forty-three police forces in England and Wales had fully complied with the NCRS (Audit Commission 2004).

In spite of these changes, the police statistics remain a record of decisions that have been made about people in the criminal justice system rather than an indicator of the actual amount of crime that has occurred (Kitsuse and Cicourel 1963). Malcolm Young (1991) has suggested that during the 1950s and 1960s the police did not have a strong incentive to report large amounts of crime: there was no political pressure to do so and no extra resources would be likely to result. The lack of incentive still remains, but nowadays it is because of meeting performance targets and a greater interest by the government in reflecting the concerns of victims.

Victim surveys

The growing appreciation of the shortcomings of police statistics, coupled with an increasing curiosity about the extent of the 'dark figure' of crime, served to fuel the interest of researchers in 'victim surveys'. The results of three surveys carried out in the USA under the sponsorship of the President's Commission on Law Enforcement and Administration of Justice were published in 1967. The best known was the survey conducted by the National Opinion Research Centre. It found that victimisation was significantly greater than the officially recorded rate: for example, there were five times the number of rapes and eight times the number of assaults. Subsequently, the National

Crime Survey (now called the National Crime Victimization Survey) was introduced in 1972 and has reported regularly ever since. It started with three separate elements: city surveys, commercial surveys, and the National Crime Panel. Only the last of these remains today. It comprises a nationwide representative sample of addresses, where all the occupants aged twelve or over are regularly interviewed on their experience of victimisation.

In Britain, Sparks, Genn and Dodd conducted a victim survey in London (1977). Three different samples were taken from each of three London boroughs. Two of the samples were of known victims from official records and the third was a random sample of residents. The researchers also wanted to find out people's attitudes to crime and the criminal justice system. Their results were sufficiently impressive for the Home Office to become interested, and its Research and Planning Unit was instructed to institute the British Crime Survey (BCS). The first report was in 1982 and further reports have appeared in 1984, 1988, 1992, and then at two-year intervals. From 2001, the BCS has been conducted annually. Various modifications to the methodology have occurred over the years: for instance, the first three reports drew their samples from the electoral register. However, it became apparent that many lower income groups had not bothered to register to vote, a phenomenon that probably increased after the introduction of the community charge (poll tax). Since 1992, the BCS has used the Postcode Address File. The original sample of 10,000 in 1982 was increased to 40,000 in 2001. This contains 'boost samples' of 3,000 non-white respondents and 1,500 sixteen to twenty-four year-olds to increase their representation above what would otherwise occur. In the latest report, interviews were conducted with people aged sixteen or over in the sample throughout England and Wales (Scotland, which was originally included, has had its own survey since 1993).

The victimisation questions in all the reports have been broadly the same. Respondents are now asked if they have been the victim of one of a range of crimes in the previous twelve months (originally, it was during the last calendar year). Anyone answering in the affirmative is asked to complete a form for each incident up to a maximum of six. All the respondents have to complete a demographic questionnaire and a follow-up questionnaire. The BCS is increasingly being used to measure other factors, such as attitudes to the criminal justice system.

The survey divided crimes into 'personal offences' (assaults, robberies, thefts from the person, other personal thefts, and sexual offences) and 'household offences' (car thefts, bicycle thefts, other thefts and vandalism of household property, and domestic burglary). Household offences can have more than one victim. It is important to note that only about three-quarters of these categories are the same as those used in the police statistics, and the statistics cover a number of offences not raised in the BCS, such as theft from a shop, fraud, and burglary at commercial premises. The BCS findings cannot, therefore, be used as a replacement for the police statistics, but as a more reliable indicator for the offences to which it applies.

What, then, has the BCS discovered? In short, the 1982 report found twice as many burglaries, five times as much wounding, twelve times as much theft from the person, and thirteen times as much criminal damage as recorded in the official statistics. The number of robberies reported has consistently been low—just 2 per cent of respondents in the 2003–4 survey—and this increases the dangers of making generalisations from relatively small numbers. The only category for which the figures are generally similar was for theft of motor cars which, given the financial implications, was to be expected.

The overall ratio was four times as much crime recorded by the 1982 BCS than for comparable offences in the police statistics. There has always been a discrepancy between the two sets of figures, but the gap has been narrowing in recent years as the police are now recording a higher percentage of crimes reported to them. The difference would be much greater if, for example, fraud were included in the BCS, as this is a crime which is distinctly under-recorded in the annual figures. In the Sparks, Genn and Dodd survey, the ratio was eleven to one, but this had included categories such as 'miscellaneous theft' which were not found in the BCS.

The general message that came out of the first BCS report was that, although there appears to be far more crime than is officially recorded, most of the extra crime is petty. The unreported crimes usually involved much lower levels of harm than those reported to the police. Other interesting points have also emerged. A comparison of the 1982 and 1996 reports suggests that the increase in crime was at a slower rate than that suggested in the police statistics. This is to some extent caused by the greater readiness to report certain crimes to the police, which was mentioned above. The basic differences between the frequency of offences shown in the police statistics and in the BCS surveys are broadly the same. Both sets of figures are strongly influenced by thefts of or from motor vehicles, and violent offences form a relatively small part of the totals. Criminal damage provides the exception—the BCS level was seven times higher than the level recorded in the police statistics.

The main advantage of the BCS is that it measures both reported and unreported crime and is not affected by changes in the patterns of reporting offences to the police. It also notes information about circumstances surrounding the commission of the crime and victims' attitudes, which the police do not collect. On the other hand, the BCS is only concerned with certain types of crime. As it is based on a household survey, it does not measure fraud or any other crime against commercial or public sector establishments. Nor does it measure victimless crimes, such as drug use or consensual sexual offences, or crimes where the victim is unavailable for interview. The BCS does not include victims under the age of sixteen and is not designed to provide an indication of victimisation in particular small localities: police data, however, are broken down into forty-three police areas. It will also undercount crimes where the victim knew the offender and, therefore, may not consider that a 'real crime' has been committed. Yet, in this respect the BCS data will still be superior to that of the police, who are likely to undercount such crimes even more.

The definition of crime may also have been another point of difference between the BCS and the police records. The BCS has adopted a formal definition of crime; any incident which appears technically to amount to a crime is recorded. The police, on the other hand, only recorded incidents which they considered to be supported by evidence and which, in their view, deserved to be dealt with by the criminal justice system. For example, the victim way not wish the police to proceed. All this could have resulted in the BCS figures being inflated by the inclusion of a number of trivial incidents. However, since the introduction of the NCRS in April 2002, this is less likely to be a problem as the police are now also required to consider the legal definition of crime.

There is also, of course, a strong possibility that a person being questioned will have an inaccurate recall of events during the previous twelve months. Research carried out both in this country (Sparks *et al.* 1977) and in the USA (Skogan 1986) has identified certain factors that can inhibit or prevent accurate answers. A respondent may make up an offence, not realise that an incident comes within the scope of a question, forget a relevant incident, or recall an earlier incident as having occurred within the reference period or consider that a recent incident fell outside the period. This last phenomenon is known as 'telescoping' and can involve the shifting of events in the memory either forwards or backwards in time: Sparks *et al.* considered that the two would be likely to cancel each other out. Where subjects are asked about offences which are known to have been reported to the police, minor crimes such as vandalism and theft are less likely to be recalled. The general conclusion is that, as the forgetting of incidents will be a greater distorting factor than the imagining of them or confusion as to when they occurred, victim surveys are likely to underestimate rather than exaggerate the amount of crime that has taken place.

Another possible distortion in victim surveys arises from the finding that well-educated people are more likely to report being victimised, particularly from violent crime. Sparks (1981) suggested that this may be because such individuals are better equipped to conceptualise and verbalise their thoughts to interviewers. Hough (1986) agreed with this, and added that the educated middle class may also have lower thresholds of tolerance to threatening and aggressive behaviour.

The BCS findings have been subject to a series of strong criticisms from several writers who, in some cases, have reinforced their arguments with their own small-scale victim surveys within local communities. The first BCS report in particular placed considerable emphasis on the unlikelihood of a 'statistically average' person being the victim of a crime: a robbery once every five centuries; an assault resulting in any injury once every century; a family car to be taken once every sixty years; and a burglary in the home once every forty years (Hough and Mayhew 1983). The overall impression given (despite the phrase 'statistically average') was that much fear of crime is irrational and that young men on the streets, who generally express the least fear of crime, are more likely to be victims of crime than women in their homes, who are likely to express the greatest fear. This was seized on by 'Left Realist' critics such as Jock Young, who claimed that the BCS had failed to show how victimisation is unequally distributed among the population (see Chapter 11). This is slightly unfair to the BCS, which had shown that occupants of council houses were more likely to be victims of burglary than owner-occupiers. The latest reports have confirmed earlier ones in revealing that Afro-Caribbeans and Asians were at greater risk than whites for a range of crimes, although this can usually be attributed to demographic factors. Indeed, in the 2002/3 report the higher risk disappears when allowance is made for the fact that these ethnic minority groups contain a higher proportion of younger people (Salisbury and Upton 2004).

Nevertheless, these points were given much greater emphasis by a number of local victim surveys which showed that certain residents of inner city deprived areas were far more likely to be the victims of certain crimes than the general impression (if not the precise wording) given by the BCS. The first Islington Crime Survey (Jones *et al.* 1986) showed that a third of all the households in that area of London contained people who had been victims of burglary, robbery or sexual assault during the previous year, and that young white women were twenty-nine times more likely to be victims of assault than white women over forty-five. Young criticised the implications of the BCS that much fear of crime is irrational by pointing out that some people are much better able to withstand the impact of crime than others, and that it is misleading to talk of criminal events as 'random' because crime 'occurs in particular hierarchies of power'.

This point has been taken up by several writers in relation to women. The BCS researchers have conceded that, particularly in the earlier reports, they have not been particularly successful in illuminating the 'dark figure' of sexual crimes and domestic violence against women. The 1982 and 1984 reports each contained only one report for rape—and they were both for attempts. Since the 1994 report, the subjects have been able to respond to cards asking questions about sexual victimisation by the use of laptop computers; this was extended to questions on domestic violence in the 1996 report. Designers of the local crime surveys drafted particularly sensitive questions to cover such offences and more specific training was provided for the interviewers. The consequences can be seen in the first Islington survey where much higher levels of sexual assault were reported and over 20 per cent of all assaults were described as 'domestic'—a rate far greater than that reported in the BCS. Other surveys have also shown high levels of actual or threatened sexual violence against women. Painter (1991), who questioned 1,000 married women, claimed that '1 in 4 women have been raped at some time by some man'. Painter's survey was based on the legal definition of rape and included a significant proportion of wives raped by husbands. Other researchers (such as Hanmer and Saunders 1984) broadened their enquiry to use such non-criminal terms as 'harassment'. They would no doubt claim that this provided a more realistic picture of the problem faced by women, but it does make it more difficult to compare the findings with those of the BCS, which generally adheres to legal definitions of crimes.

The BCS and other crime surveys have shown that far more crime is committed than is made known to the police. Even the surveys themselves do not completely expose the 'dark figure'. It could be argued that any crimes which are not revealed either to the police or to a sympathetic researcher can hardly be of sufficient importance to be considered realistically as 'crimes'. However, although this may be true for 'unemotional' incidents of minor vandalism, it would be an unrealistic assumption for domestic and sexual offences. Both the official crime statistics and the BCS place a limit on the number of instances of the same crime that will be recorded. Moreover, not only do the crime statistics fail to give us an accurate picture of the quantity of crime, but they also fail to provide us with an account of how much crime is processed by the courts. Because of a range of factors including the requirements of evidence and the availability of resources, many reported offences are never proceeded with. In 2003, about 335,100 people were found guilty of indictable offences and 150,700 were cautioned: in the same year there were about 5,935,000 offences recorded by the police. Only about 2 per cent of known crimes result in a conviction. There is plenty of hard information about this population and a stereotypical offender emerges: male; late teens; several previous convictions; left school at sixteen; unskilled or partly skilled. There is also a disproportionate chance (compared with the general population) that the offender will be from an ethnic minority group and will at some point have been in local authority care.

Self-report surveys

Is there any evidence that offenders whose crimes have not come to the attention of the authorities show markedly different characteristics to those who have been convicted? The other side of the coin, so to speak, to a victim survey is a self-report study, where people are asked to disclose their offending behaviour. Self-report studies have been around for at least as long as victim studies, but they have never been as popular with researchers (at least, in Britain) because of the perceived high level of under-reporting. Most of the research, which dates from the 1940s, has been conducted in America. Many people were startled by the claim of American sociologists Short and Nye in 1958 that middle-class children were just as likely as lower-class children to engage in delinquent acts, despite the predominance of the latter in the courtroom. However, this had been, and continued to be a common finding in self-report studies. The implication widely drawn was that there must be routine class bias on the part of the police and prosecutors against lower-class individuals. This, in turn, fuelled the concern of a range of American sociologists, including those who were interested in labelling theory (see Chapter 9) and conflict theory (see Chapter 10). Hirschi's influential control theory (1969), which is considered in Chapter 12, is based on such a study.

The growing mass of contradictory self-report studies was analysed by John Braithwaite in 1979. He concluded that, not only do lower-class juveniles commit more crime than those from the middle class, but they also commit more of the type of crime that is typically dealt with by the police. This second point is also true for lower-class adults in comparison to middle-class adults. However, as Braithwaite conceded, the offences involved in the studies he considered were predominantly 'street' crimes such as burglary and car crime, and did not extend to offences committed in the more private worlds of the home or the office—areas where the middle class would be more likely to be represented. Another analysis of the research by Rutter and Giller (1983) found that, although 82 per cent of their juvenile sample admitted breaking windows in empty houses ('street crime'), 70 per cent said they had stolen from a shop and practically everyone admitted to some offending. Adolescent middle-class children interviewed in Edinburgh were also prepared to admit to a wide range of offending (Anderson *et al.* 1994).

The early self-report studies in particular suffered from a number of factors tending to unreliability. Some of these have already been identified in relation to victim surveys: for example, individuals may have forgotten particular incidents or be prone to exaggeration. Most of the research has centred on juvenile delinquency at the expense of adult crime and has consequently revealed only relatively minor offences. Overlapping categories could result in the same incident being counted twice. The samples have often been unsatisfactory: in the earlier studies they were often drawn from schools in rural areas or small towns. It is likely that the most delinquent members of society rarely featured in the sampling—for instance, they may have either been truanting or suspended from school. This in itself could partly explain the higher than expected levels of middle-class offending among juvenile respondents. Another factor is that the American studies found that children from wealthier families were more likely to report trivial vandalism cases that would be unlikely to result in a charge (Gold 1970).

The National Youth Survey, developed in America during the 1980s, is said by some to have eradicated many of the methodological problems found in the earlier research (Elliott and Huizinga 1989). This is a longitudinal survey of a representative sample of boys aged eleven to seventeen and is based on households rather than schools. The Survey has consistently shown higher levels of self-reported delinquency by lower-class and ethnic minority groups. On the other hand, white-collar offenders, who are generally accepted as being under-represented in official statistics, are still highly unlikely to feature in self-report studies, however sophisticated.

One of the best-known uses of a self-report study in Britain has been as part of the Cambridge Study in Delinquent Development. In this project 411 males from a working-class area of London were first approached in 1961–2 when aged eight and nine. They have subsequently been contacted by the researchers about their involvement in delinquency on various occasions. This type of ongoing research into the same sample is known as a longitudinal study. Self-report questionnaires have been issued on each occasion and the researchers have also checked the subjects' criminal records. By the age of thirty-two nearly all the sample admitted to having committed at least one of the ten offences on the list, whereas only a third had been convicted of any of the offences (Farrington 1989).

In 1992–3 the Home Office conducted the first Youth Lifestyles Survey, which was the largest self-report offending study conducted in England and Wales (Graham and Bowling 1995). The Survey was repeated in 1998–9 (Flood-Page *et al.* 2000). On this occasion 4,848 people aged from twelve to thirty and living in private households were asked if they had ever committed any of twenty-seven crimes. The list included four types of fraud—tax evasion, benefit fraud and making false expenses and insurance claims. Almost half (57 per cent of men and 37 per cent of women) admitted committing at least one of the offences. However, the researchers not surprisingly chose to concentrate on the twelve months prior to interview. The figures were then considerably lower: 19 per cent of men and 11 per cent of women. About half of these people had committed only one or two offences during this period.

One problem with household surveys is that they do not include people living in institutions such as prisons. This means that their samples are unlikely to include the most serious offenders.

The Home Office has recently published the results of the 2003 Crime and Justice Survey, the first national self-report study to include older people (Budd *et al.* 2005). Once again, this was a household survey which concentrated on a fixed number of crimes, but the age range was from ten to sixty-five and the questioning covered not only the previous twelve months but also whether the respondents had committed at least one of the 'core' offences at least once in their life. The results confirmed earlier findings that offending is more widespread than many people believe and is most frequent amongst teenagers. However, the findings also demonstrate the problems surrounding the accuracy of this approach. It is difficult to believe that only 28 per cent of people have ever stolen anything unrelated to vehicles. Given the extent of domestic violence, it is even harder to believe that 92 per cent of all assaults by males were against other males.

A telling criticism of all types of survey is that their very nature makes them 'event-orientated'. The emphasis on counting, which places limits on the number of any type of incident recorded, tends to undervalue the ongoing nature and general impact of certain forms of victimisation, particularly involving violence and sexual abuse. For many victims, crime cannot be partitioned into discrete events; it is a continuing part of their daily lives (Genn 1988). One way of trying to reflect this would be by greater use of participant observation, where the researcher is able to spend more time with the subject (be it victim or offender) and build up some kind of rapport which could provide a far more meaningful account of the experience under consideration.

International crime comparisons

(a) Official data

There are considerable problems in comparing the official crime stat-istics of different countries. The difficulties inherent in the compil-ation of any criminal statistics, which are discussed above, will apply in varying degrees in all jurisdictions. In addition, there will be differ-ences in legal definitions which make it very doubtful whether like can ever truly be compared with like (Zimring and Hawkins 1997). The International Criminal Police Organization (INTERPOL), which has produced comprehensive statistics for more than eighty countries, adopts its own broad definitional categories in an attempt to over-come this problem. The United Nations Crime and Justice Informa-tion Network also publishes wide-ranging international statistics.

Archer and Gartner (1984) have claimed that the only reliable use of such figures is to note the apparent trends in criminal behaviour for each country, on the assumption that any distorting features in the compilation (such as political interference) are likely to remain rea-sonably consistent over the years. The Home Office publishes infor-mation about crime in EU and other selected countries (Barclay and Tavares 2003). Some researchers are prepared to accept the validity of comparative data on homicide rates on the basis that, as most inci-dents are recorded, the statistics are far less likely to be subject to the usual inaccuracies. However, this premise seems rather dubious: there may well be political reasons for not recording homicides in some countries.

(b) The International Crime Victims Survey

Another way of obtaining comparative international data is by administering a victims survey. The International Crime Victims Survey, which first reported in 1989, has now published information on more than fifty countries. The fourth and latest of its reports was based on data compiled in seventeen industrialised countries in 2000 (van Kesteren *et al.* 2001). Interviewing was generally conducted by telephone. As the questions were formulated by researchers, there was less danger of the findings being corrupted by different legal definitions. However, the usual problems associated with victim surveys can still apply. In the category of 'assaults and threats', respondents were asked the question: 'have you over the past five years been personally attacked or threatened by someone in a way that really frightened you . . .?' In reply, the England and Wales sample revealed 12.4 incidents per hundred of the population; Australia 11.2; Scotland 10.3; Canada 8.5; and Northern Ireland 4.3. This question typifies a problem in such surveys: in an attempt to avoid legal terminology, it is imprecise and could be interpreted in different ways. (For example, is it the attack or the threat that has to be really frightening—or both?)

The International Crime Victims Survey received extensive coverage in the British media as it claimed that, on the basis of victims' reports, crime rates in England and Wales were higher than in any other European country or the USA. The comparison with the USA seemed particularly startling, as it has a far higher recorded homicide rate than England and Wales (Barclay and Tavares 2003, although see Zimring and Hawkins 1997). Together with Australia, England and Wales came ahead of The Netherlands, a country not hitherto regarded as a particularly unsafe place in which to live. It is possible that, for whatever reasons, the British, Dutch and Australians have become more sensitised to crime than the citizens of countries which feature lower down the table.

(c) The International Study of Self-Reported Delinquency

This survey has developed since the late 1980s as a means of investigating self-reported delinquency in a number of countries for a range of crimes committed by young people aged fourteen to twenty-one (Junger-Tas *et al.* 2003). Most of the problems concerning self-report studies which are discussed above also apply here, in particular the concentration on youthful offending. Although it might be thought that the main purpose of such a survey would be to make cross-national comparisons, the organisers themselves urge extreme caution in so doing. Only five of the countries used national random samples; the other six obtained their data from big cities, three of which based their findings on school samples. There were also differences in the methods used to collect the information.

Conclusion

Given all the problems identified with the crime statistics, can they still be said to have any value? Some critics have gone so far as to dismiss them as totally useless, but this seems excessively harsh. The requirement when looking at these statistics is to remember their limitations and *consider them for what they are*. On that basis, some utility can be found. Bottomley and Pease (1986) have identified several advantages. For example, the crime statistics, with all their failings, can provide an antidote to wildly inaccurate views about crime expressed in general conversation. They can also provide information about the workings of the police forces, such as their different rates of cautioning.

Another—at first glance, surprising—source of support for the crime statistics comes from certain radical criminologists. Miles and Irvine (1981) argued that, despite their statistical shortcomings, the crime figures are valuable as they provide an insight into the class-based structure of the criminal justice system. The very fact that the poor and the ethnic minorities feature so prominently among those prosecuted and imprisoned by the authorities is compelling evidence not of their greater criminality, but of their lack of power within society.

Nevertheless, despite the widespread realization of their shortcomings, crime statistics are still invoked by the popular press and certain politicians as an accurate barometer reading of the pressure of crime. Even in the serious newspapers, it is sometimes necessary to search carefully to find caveats warning of their unreliability. The government is very keen on league tables and performance targets—the signs are that this is likely to increase, and police efficiency will come under even greater scrutiny. Although there are problems with simply looking at the totals of officially recorded crime, perhaps the most dangerous conclusions are those which some people choose to draw from changes in the figures. These changes can just as easily reflect variations in the operation of the criminal justice system—for example, as a result of police targeting or discretion—as they can fluctuations in the level of criminality.

4

The media and 'law and order'

It is still the case that most of the information that people in Britain receive about crime is second-hand. Everybody is a victim of crime; even those individuals who are fortunate enough not to suffer from petty acts of theft or vandalism pay for the consequences of crime through increased taxes or insurance premiums. However, as relatively few people are victims of serious crime, images of offending which are formed in the minds of the majority largely come from reports and discussions in the mass media. Indeed, with growing urbanisation, it is increasingly necessary to rely on the media to find out what has been happening in one's own neighbourhood. In this chapter, consideration will be given to whether the mass media's reporting of crime has a significant impact on people's daily lives and their attitudes to 'law and order' issues. There is also a body of research evidence which suggests that media portrayals of violent crime may inspire some people to engage in 'copycat' incidents. This will be considered in Chapter 16.

'The media' is a term increasingly found in popular usage and refers to the common forms of mass communication—newspapers, books, magazines, TV and radio. In terms of conveying current information and discussion to a large audience, the most effective forms are newspapers, TV and, to a lesser extent, radio: these collectively come to the attention of the vast majority of the population.

Legal constraints on the media

An initial distinction must be made between broadcasting and the press. The Royal Charter which established the BBC requires impartiality in the reporting of news and political matters, and the maintenance of good taste and decency. This is now stipulated in the 'BBC Licence and Agreement' (1996). Similar requirements are made of independent broadcasting under section 6 of the Broadcasting Act

1990. The press, however, is under no such legal obligation. Generally, the written media can publish more or less what it wants, subject to the law of libel and a number of specific prohibitions. These include the Contempt of Court Act 1981, which *inter alia* prohibits jurors from discussing the case even after its conclusion; provisions under the Official Secrets Act 1989 prohibiting the publication of allegedly 'sensitive' information; and other provisions, such as the Sexual Offences (Amendment) Act 1976 which prevents the press from disclosing information about the victims of certain sexual offences, on the basis that such coverage could cause them hardship or embarrassment. Restrictions on revealing the identity of juvenile offenders have existed since the 1930s, although these can be waived in particularly serious cases (for example, following the murder of James Bulger in 1994). It has been suggested that the level of anonymity should be reduced in order to 'shame' young offenders into stopping their criminality (see Chapter 9).

In 1990, the Newspaper Publishers' Association and the Newspaper Society published a Code of Practice and established a Press Complaints Commission (which replaced the Press Council) to adjudicate on alleged breaches of the Code. Most of its members have strong links with the media, and the Commission cannot insist on the publication of a correction, a right of reply by an aggrieved party, or an award of compensation. In short, the Commission cannot penalise its members in any way.

Sources of the media's information on crime

(a) The police

Unlike some other journalists, it is rare for crime reporters to have witnessed the stories about which they proceed to write. Nowadays, there are many different sources of information on crime available to the media. It does not seem surprising that the police still provide the bulk of the material, as they have the greatest involvement with crime and criminals. Although individual officers are still prepared to brief their chosen journalists, after the appointment of Sir Robert Mark as Commissioner of the Metropolitan Police the days when the press were dependent on carefully-prepared briefings or unofficial tip-offs from Scotland Yard were numbered, and a much more open and professional approach was adopted, including regular press conferences (Schlesinger and Tumber 1994). Nevertheless, sensational crime reporting has existed in Britain since the nineteenth century, and in the early days the writers were reliant on official court reports rather than information from the police. It was only when popular journalism became more widespread in the first part of the twentieth century that the growing demand for crime stories necessitated a more productive source—and the police were the ideal providers.

It is arguable that this position of influence has been exploited by the police to control the supply and slant of information. Schlesinger and Tumber (1994) suggested that manipulation of the news media has now become an integral part of policing. They cited television programmes such as *Crimestoppers* and *Crimewatch UK*, where the police have complete control over the provision of information and the usages to which it is put:

> Without the active cooperation of the police, no programme such as *Crimewatch* could exist. It is plain that control over access is decisive, and that is where power ultimately lies.

Regular viewers of these programmes will be well aware that they concentrate on homicides and other offences against the person to the exclusion of the far less spectacular frauds and crimes involving property. In 2000, a firm of Bristol estate agents which sponsored the local *Crimestoppers* programme ('leading the fight against crime') had to pay £10,000 in fines and costs for providing false descriptions of two homes (*Bristol Evening Post*, 29 March 2000).

(b) Other sources of information

Earlier accounts of the media and crime, such as those of Chibnall (1977) and Hall *et al.* (1978), tended to emphasise the role of the police in reflecting the apparent general political consensus in filtering the information it provided to the press. However, later studies, while not doubting the importance of the police in this respect, have shown that other organisations can have a significant input. These bodies include the Home Office, the legal profession, the Prison Officers Association, penal pressure groups, and even academics. The Home Office Press Office, which is a unit of the Communication Directorate, will sometimes 'call in the appropriate people (that is, journalists) for an appropriate subject' (Schlesinger and Tumber 1994), hold press conferences, and generally operate by way of the 'lobby' system of off-the-record briefings. The Head of Information deals with the Home Secretary's relations with the media, and each of the Home Office junior ministers is assigned a press officer. The Law Society, which represents solicitors, has been particularly active in objecting to criminal justice legislation in recent years.

Pressure groups in particular work very hard to ensure that their views are not ignored. They are more likely to receive publicity if they are perceived as 'establishment' bodies, such as the Howard League for Penal Reform, Liberty or the National Association for the Care and Resettlement of Offenders. Given the variety of interests reflected, it is hardly surprising that the slant of the information can vary quite considerably. The police and the Home Office are the main and most influential sources of information on crime. Nevertheless, Ericson *et al.* (1989) have shown the important role played by unofficial pressure groups in Canada, and the research by Schlesinger and Tumber (1994) suggests that they can be very influential in this country as well.

Selection of crime news

Clearly, the journalist and editor play the pivotal role as to how a story is formulated and presented in a newspaper. Theirs has been described as the role of 'gatekeeper' in the news process (White 1950). They select their stories on a mainly subjective basis, although in accordance with their newspaper's 'agenda' (see below), and thus hold considerable power.

Several writers have considered the journalistic criteria applied in the selection of crime stories. Galtung and Ruge (1973) listed the qualities they thought make a story more likely to be reported. These include: the unambiguity of a story; its unexpectedness; its unpredictability; a reference to the negative; the size of the event; its meaningfulness within the culture; and its reference to elite persons. In his book *Law and Order News* (1977) Steve Chibnall listed eight criteria or 'professional imperatives' which 'act as implicit guides to the construction of news stories'.

1 *Immediacy* The story must relate to the present and be instantly reportable. There is no place for a consideration of long-term patterns or historical context. Stories which cannot be easily fitted into this formula are likely to be ignored. The lengthy, but extremely important, fraud trial involving Kevin and Ian Maxwell in 1995–6 soon disappeared to a few lines in the business pages as it became more complicated.

2 *Dramatisation* Reports must emphasise action and drama so as to

capture the attention of the audience immediately. This leads to banner headlines, which often promise more than the text of the story can deliver. The headline 'Wolfman broke free by using toothpaste' (*Today*, 16 May 1991) provides a good illustration of this. The story only concerned a prisoner with a bizarre nickname who managed to facilitate his escape with a little lubrication.

As Chibnall pointed out, one finds far less coverage in the popular press of domestic violence, breaches of health and safety at work provisions, or pollution, as such incidents generally lack the dramatic impact that journalists are seeking, although far more prevalent than the crimes that are reported.

3 *Personalisation* Individuals involved in stories will receive far more attention than the issues. Ideally, there will be an innocent victim; victimless crimes receive relatively little attention. The victim, the offender and the offender's family will be the subject of in-depth reporting, particularly if any of them are well-known 'personalities' (Graber 1980). In homicide cases, it is now routine to see news conferences on television featuring understandably distraught relatives of the victim. Newspaper editors sometimes come close to being prosecuted for contempt of court for publishing stories that could be prejudicial to the defendant during the trial. Examples include the trial of Rosemary West in 1995 and the collapse of the 1997 trial of escaped inmates from Whitemoor prison. Although such prosecutions are uncommon, in 2004 the *Daily Star* was fined £60,000 for revealing the identities of two footballers who were facing allegations of rape (*The Times*, 25 November 2004).

4 *Simplification* Issues are presented in an overly simple way by the press. Chibnall recalled that a former editor of the *Daily Express* once defined a bad news item as 'a story that cannot be absorbed on the first time of reading'. Events are portrayed as black or white, often ignoring the inherent complexities of human behaviour and relationships. Explanations for crime and deviance are unusual (Marsh 1991). When they occur, they generally ignore criticisms of the social structure and concentrate on individual pathology or intoxication— particularly for crimes of violence. Accounts of crimes can omit key facts. Most violence takes place between individuals who already knew each other, but press reporting seems keen to support the popular stereotype of a stranger–stranger attack.

5 *Titillation* The *News of the World* established many years ago that 'sex sells', and now most popular newspapers give particular prominence

to reports of sexual offences, particularly if well-known people were involved. Photographs will enhance the story, although on other pages the same newspaper may well be censorious of immorality and 'the permissive society'. This illustrates an interesting paradox about the media's reporting of crime: the same edition of a tabloid newspaper can both show photographs of nude women and castigate minor acts of immorality. In 2000, the *News of the World* ran a high-profile campaign to 'name and shame' convicted paedophiles without apparently making any adjustment to its usual high content of sex stories.

6 *Conventionalism* Events, however unusual, must be placed in a conventional context. Readers must be able to feel familiar with the story's setting. This results in new developments having to be described in established terms; for example, 'new age travellers' were initially referred to as 'hippy convoys', the term 'hippy' being familiar to journalists and their readers from the 'flower-power' era of the 1960s.

7 *Structured Access* Stories are often reinforced by 'experts' in a particular field, such as politicians, criminal justice professionals or criminology lecturers. Ericson *et al.* (1991) have pointed out that, in the vast majority of cases, these experts never provide any evidence to support their claims. On television, academics are usually interviewed seated in front of rows of books. Such views are used to give weight to the particular side of the argument that is being presented and usually represent the 'official' or 'acceptably critical' view. Certain Conservative MPs are regularly sought out for an instant quote on their entirely predictable 'hardline' views on law and order. The pressure group 'Justice for Women' is routinely approached by journalists who want a quote to the effect that a sex offender has been given too light a sentence. (It is interesting that journalists very rarely approach anyone to offer the view that a sentence is too severe.) Members of the public can be asked for their reactions to events which have already been formulated by these experts.

Support for this can be found in an American study by Gitlin (1980) of the relationship between a student anti-Vietnam war group and the national news media. Gitlin showed how, to obtain any credibility, the group had to put forward authoritative individuals to speak on its behalf. This had the effect, for a while, of making celebrities out of previously unknown individuals.

8 *Novelty* Events that are unusual or original are likely to attract the readers' interest, and journalists sometimes indulge in speculation

to create a new 'angle' on a story, often without any supporting evidence.

Yvonne Jewkes (2004) has offered a list of twelve features which are important in the reporting of crime. It includes several of Chibnall's 'professional imperatives' plus some others such as 'spectacle or graphic injury' and 'children'. The former reflects the greater ability that journalists now have to present high-quality photographic images to support their stories. The latter illustrates the point that the involvement of children in crime—whether as perpetrators or victims—has become particularly newsworthy since the murder of the Liverpool toddler James Bulger by two ten-year-old boys in 1993.

Women's criminality is often dealt with differently from that of men. As statistics suggest that women commit far fewer crimes, it is perhaps not surprising that offending is portrayed in the mass media as a predominantly male activity (Sacco 1995).

When stories of female crime do appear, the incidents are more likely to be portrayed by the press as being due to illness or mental imbalance. In a study of the reporting of violent crime in four British newspapers, Naylor (2001) found that women's violence was more likely to be reported as emotional or irrational than that of men. On the other hand, there is a competing benchmark by which women have to be measured—that of the good wife and mother. Any failure to fulfil these sex-role expectations or, indeed, any suggestion of cruelty to children will result in a woman being vilified by the popular press. The question of release from a life sentence of the so-called 'Moors Murderer', Myra Hindley, provides a good illustration of this. Although Hindley's crimes involved complicity in the torture and murder of children, it is likely that cases of similar gravity could be found where male offenders have eventually been released from prison. Hindley's crimes undoubtedly attracted greater opprobrium because she was a woman. In a 1997 MORI opinion poll, 23 per cent of the people who thought she should not be freed said it was because she is 'a woman who killed a child' (*The Guardian*, 29 October 1997). As certain newspapers conducted a long campaign against her ever being released, no politician was likely to risk the wrath of the tabloid press by taking such an action. At the time of her death in November 2002, it appeared that, as a result of a European Court of Human Rights ruling, the Home Secretary might lose the power to overrule the Parole Board if it recommended a killer's release. According to one newspaper report, the police had formed a plan to cover this eventuality whereby they would have charged Hindley as a result of her confession in prison to murdering two other children (*The Independent*, 19 November 2002).

An even more bizarre illustration of the press's treatment of female offenders can be seen in the hysteria surrounding the conviction of Maxine Carr, the girlfriend of the 'Soham murderer' Ian Huntley. Carr was sentenced to forty-two months in prison for perverting the course of justice—providing Huntley with a false alibi for the time of the killing. She was not even charged with being an accessory to the murder of the two young girls. However, her vilification at the hands of the tabloid press was so great that on release from prison she was advised by the police to wear a bullet-proof vest, and an injunction was taken out preventing the media from revealing details of her new identity. As Beatrix Campbell's damning commentary put it, 'Myra is dead, long live Maxine' (*The Independent*, 16 May 2004).

The content of crime news

Several researchers have analysed the content of crime news in Britain and the USA. The older studies have generally found lower levels of crime reporting than the more recent ones. Bob Roshier (1973) looked at the prevalence of crime news in English local and national newspapers. The more popular newspapers reported more crime stories: the *News of the World* led the way with about 11 per cent of its news space, and the average for all the papers was about 4 per cent. Roshier also discovered that, over a three-year period, the more serious crimes such as murder, robbery, crimes against old people and drugs-related crimes were over-reported. There was an excessive emphasis on offenders who were caught by the police, convicted in court and sentenced. Such a picture gives the impression that criminals are more likely to be caught than is actually the case, and Roshier indeed found that newspaper readers overestimate the amount of crime solved.

Ditton and Duffy (1983) considered the content of crime news in the Strathclyde region of Scotland and compared their findings with the official statistics for that area. The purpose of the research was to discover if newspaper coverage of crime was selective and if any selection resulted in distortion. Four daily and two Sunday newspapers were studied for one month in 1981 and the news reports were compared to the crimes made known to the police during that period and the court cases that took place. The newspapers devoted an average of 6.5 per cent of their news space to the reporting of crime.

The results revealed a high degree of selectivity. Although nearly

48,000 offences were made known to the police or recorded as court proceedings during the particular month, only 120 were reported in the papers. The finding that court cases were twice as likely to be reported was in keeping with Roshier's research. Such cases were allotted 1.3 times as much space as crimes made known to the police and placed an unrealistic emphasis on the successful capture and conviction of offenders. Ditton and Duffy concluded that an 'over-emphasis on crimes of violence is an almost universal finding' and, furthermore, they discovered 'an additional and noticeable over-reporting of crimes involving sex'. Crimes involving dishonesty and minor assaults were found to be reported broadly in proportion to the official statistics, and motoring offences were found to be consistently under-reported.

Research carried out by Susan Smith (1984) into the contents of local Birmingham newspapers supported Ditton and Duffy's findings that the provincial press tends to distort the official picture of crime. Offences of violence were found to be heavily over-reported in comparison to their actual occurrence, with such offences accounting for less than 6 per cent of known crimes, yet occupying over half the space that the papers devoted to crime. In contrast, theft and burglary, which accounted for about 84 per cent of recorded cases, covered only about 4 per cent of the column space devoted to crime news. Violent and sexual crimes were consistently over-reported, and the press were prone to link crime with issues of race. Smith noted that less 'exciting' crimes were played down, even though members of the public were more likely to be victims of them.

Soothill and Walby (1991) studied the reporting of sex offences in the British press. Between 1951 and 1985 there was an almost four-fold increase in the number of rape trials. However, during the same period the number of such cases reported in the press increased by five and a half times from twenty-eight to 154. In a study of sex crime reporting in the Northern Ireland press, Greer (2003) found a substantial increase in coverage between 1985 and 1997. Williams and Dickinson (1993) analysed crime reporting in ten national newspapers for four weeks from 19 June 1989. They discovered that, on average, nearly 13 per cent of news stories referred to incidents involving crime. The tabloid press contained far more crime stories than the serious newspapers: *The Sun* devoted 30 per cent of its reporting to such stories, whereas the figure for *The Guardian* was 5 per cent. Williams and Dickinson also found that 64.5 per cent of the space allocated to crime reporting contained stories dealing with personal violence. Research by Cumberbatch *et al.* (1995) showed that broadcast news paid even greater attention to crime reports than most news-papers. Independent Radio News carried the most stories of all (21 per cent of total output), and Sky News (18 per cent) had the highest figure for television. Stories concerning death accounted for 53 per cent of all crime reports on Sky News and over 40 per cent of such items on most BBC Radio stations. Reiner *et al.* (2001) looked at a random sample of issues of *The Times* and the *Daily Mirror* for each year between 1945 and 1991. They found that the proportion of stories about crime increased in both papers from under 10 per cent in the 1940s to 21 per cent by the end of the period.

The emphasis on, and typification of, violent and dramatic crimes is not confined to the British press. Doris Graber (1980) compared the number of street crimes recorded by the Chicago police with the coverage of similar crimes in the *Chicago Tribune*. She discovered that murders, which accounted for 0.2 per cent of all crimes recorded by the police, comprised over a quarter of all crimes mentioned in the newspaper. Yet, non-violent offences, such as theft and car theft, which constituted 47 per cent of crimes recorded by the police, only comprised 4 per cent of crimes mentioned in the *Tribune*. Hickman Barlow *et al.* (1995) carried out a thorough content analysis of the American magazine *Time* over a five-year period. They discovered that violent crime was heavily over-reported in comparison to its actual occurrence, whereas property crimes were consistently under-reported. Ericson *et al.* (1991) found an emphasis on violence in the reporting of the Toronto mass media, although their analysis was based on a wide definition of deviance rather than the more usual, but narrower one of crime.

Marsh (1991) conducted a comparative analysis of crime reporting in the USA between 1960 and 1988, and fourteen other countries between 1965 and 1987. He found remarkable similarity in the types of crime reported, with an over-representation of violent crime. There was also a general failure to consider possible causes and a suggestion that the police and courts are far more effective at dealing with crime than is actually the case.

Although there is a clear over-representation of sex and violent crimes in the press, Stephenson-Burton (1995) has warned against the assumption that white-collar crime goes entirely unreported. Using information from the Serious Fraud Office, she calculated the number of articles on white-collar crime appearing in the national daily papers in July 1992: The *Financial Times* contained 125 articles; the *Daily Star* contained none. The other newspapers appeared in a ranking that most people would imagine, with the serious papers

featuring substantially more stories than the popular ones. Not surprisingly, when the popular press did discuss white-collar crime, great
reliance was still placed on Chibnall's 'professional imperatives':
stories were presented in a sensational and personalised way.

Such 'content analysis' has been the commonest way of studying
crime reporting by the mass media. However, the objectivity which
some have claimed as its greatest strength must be viewed with a
certain amount of caution. The research typically involves contrasting
media representations of crime with the official picture, usually as
represented by the criminal statistics. Yet, as Sparks (1992) has pointed
out, there must be some reason for undertaking such an exercise, and
it is usually an assumption that the media's exaggerated portrayal of
crime will increase fear in the community, and that this is undesirable. In other words, although this kind of research can provide many
valuable insights, it should be remembered that it is constructed on
certain assumptions which are subjectively held. Moreover, it was
shown in the previous chapter that the official criminal statistics are
an unreliable indicator of the real level of crime.

Individuals who are suspected of committing crimes are dealt with
in a distinctive way by the popular press. In addition to the legal
restrictions which circumscribe the media's treatment of individuals,
the Press Complaints Commission has a code of practice which is
designed to curb excessive intrusion into individuals' personal lives.
However, it is still possible for the media to use symbolism and imagery
which, although not amounting to an infringement of the law, can
create fear and prejudice among the general public.

A media agenda?

The ideological background to much press reporting of crime appears
as the triumph of law and order against evil, and a reinforcement of
the status quo and the consensus in society. Words such as 'sickness',
'disease' and 'moral decline' are freely used. Newspaper headlines
seek to engage the nation in the 'hunt' for the criminal or the cry for
severe punishment following arrest and trial (Frayn 1973). The suspect not only assumes responsibility for the actual crimes committed,
but also becomes a scapegoat for society's ills.

Do newspapers have an additional agenda to that of upholding
'right' over 'wrong'? A radical viewpoint would suggest an answer in
the affirmative. In Britain most of the newspapers are owned by
extremely wealthy individuals or groups who have an obvious interest

in maintaining the type of society that enabled them to amass their fortune. Any sort of threat to that society, be it through political, criminal or any other deeds, has to be resisted. Editors are installed who will carry out their proprietor's wishes and support the status quo. In terms of national politics, this has generally resulted in backing the Conservative Party, which has traditionally emphasised the need for discipline, control, and law and order. However, most newspapers supported the Labour Party in the 1997 general election, realising that little, if any, threat to the status quo was offered by 'New Labour' and correctly predicting that, in any event, the party would form the next government with a considerable majority. A change of proprietor can lead to a change of political stance: the formerly pro-Conservative *Express* became a supporter of the Labour Party following the paper's acquisition by Lord Hollick, but then reverted to its former stance following the paper's acquisition by Richard Desmond.

The situation now is that only the *Financial Times, The Guardian* and *The Independent* among the national daily papers provide balanced reporting of crime. Even the traditionally Labour-supporting *Mirror* has adopted a hard-line stance towards crime, which is becoming indistinguishable from that of *The Sun* and the *Daily Mail*. Nowadays, *The Times* and *The Daily Telegraph*—formerly serious newspapers—are filled with reports of lurid cases. Research by Hough *et al.* (1988) showed that readers of quality newspapers were more likely to have lenient views about crime and punishment than readers of other newspapers. This applied even after factors such as age, sex and social class had been taken into account. However, the combined sales of *The Independent, The Guardian* and the *Financial Times* is under a million copies a day, whereas the combined daily sales total of all national papers is around 13 million.

The picture remains the same when wider aspects of the criminal justice system are considered. Police officers and policing are rarely subject to criticism in the popular press, unless there is clear evidence of police corruption or their impropriety has some sexual overtones, such as harassment of women police officers by their male colleagues. This is hardly surprising: as the police are still a major source (both official and unofficial) of news on crime, journalists are reluctant to offend them, and a favourable representation of the police by the media assists in supporting the status quo in society. There is some force behind the view of Hall *et al.* (1978) that the media image of the police is misleading, complacent and uncritical.

Without fundamentally disagreeing with these arguments, Schlesinger and Tumber (1994) have pointed out that the economic constraints under which the press operate cannot be overlooked. Newspaper publishing is like any other business; it has to make a profit. At present, sensational and distorted crime reporting helps to sell newspapers because the public, in the absence of any other easily-accessible information, has become sensitised to it and is prepared to accept it at face value. Suppose, however, that for some reason the public became sick and tired of reading about crime and deviance. It is inconceivable that the editors of the tabloid press would not be instructed by their proprietors—whatever their ideological position—to change the content of their papers accordingly. This is not a completely far-fetched notion. Following the death of Diana, Princess of Wales, in August 1997, when apparently trying to evade intrusive photographers, the general public reaction led to a severe reduction in the number of photographs of the Royal Family published in the British press.

The media's presentation of the courts and sentencing contains an inherent contradiction. Newspaper reporting consistently portrays the courts as ineffective in securing sufficient numbers of convictions of the guilty and failing to pass sufficiently harsh sentences on those who have been convicted. Yet, because the press concentrates on cases that have come to court rather than reporting on crimes that have not been solved, the public is given the misleading impression that the chances of being apprehended, tried and sentenced for an offence are higher than is really the case. Reporting typically concentrates on sentences which appear on the lenient side; little, if any, reference is made to the fact that Britain sends a higher proportion of its population to prison, and for longer periods, than almost any other European country.

The portrayal of a typical crime by the media as involving violence and brutality has now been adopted by television as a form of entertainment. From its inception, television has shown 'cops and robbers' programmes, but these have changed over the years from the benevolent bobby of the legendary *Dixon of Dock Green* era in the 1950s to the more violent and 'realistic' portrayals which are nowadays churned out by American film companies. Perhaps present-day audiences are able to distinguish between fact and fiction, although it appears that many American television viewers considered the nightly reports of the OJ Simpson trial to be good entertainment (Bondebjerg 1996). Another development has been the emergence of programmes such as *Crimewatch UK*, where visual reconstruction of horrific crimes are presented allegedly in the name of crime detection, but really as entertainment. This popular programme, which has attracted almost twice the audience of the main BBC evening news, still continues to be shown, despite numerous criticisms, including one from the Report of the Working Group on the Fear of Crime (Home Office 1989), chaired by TV executive Michael Grade, that it unnecessarily increases the public's fear of crime. Indeed, the Grade Committee commissioned a survey of elderly people in Brighton which showed that:

> Most fears stemmed not from direct or personal experience of crime but from mediated experiences received through the press.

In September 2002, BBC 1 devoted a whole evening's programmes to the theme 'Cracking Crime'. The Home Secretary, having originally commented that this would 'frighten everybody to death', eventually agreed to participate (*The Times*, 6 September 2002). The first offering was entitled 'Don't Have Nightmares'.

The foregoing analysis of the significance of the news media in determining both the form and substance of the crime stories which are served up to the population should indicate that the depiction sometimes adopted of news sources, such as the police, as 'primary definers' (Hall *et al.* 1978) and the mass media as simply passive 'secondary definers', is an over-simplification. Apart from any 'agenda' a newspaper may have, the association between journalists and their sources, and even the journalistic discretion arising from the choice of sources, makes the whole relationship more complex than at first appears to be the case.

The implications of the media's portrayal of crime

If the above observations had no relevance either to the incidence of crime or to the ways in which people view and react to crime, then their significance would be largely confined to the sociology of journalism. However, there is a considerable body of evidence which suggests that the media's reporting of crime has very real consequences for many people in society.

(a) Deviance amplification

This expression was first used by Leslie Wilkins (1964). Society describes members of a group as deviant and isolates them. The group, thus alienated, proceeds to develop further its own norms and values which society then perceives as even more deviant than before. The social reaction against the group increases, the group becomes more isolated, engages in even more deviant activity, and the whole cycle begins to repeat itself in an ever-increasing spiral of deviance and crime. The central problem is that each input of information into the spiral is distorted. The role of the media is crucial in this process in its publicising of the group's increasing violence. Therefore, according to this notion, the media can be responsible for an increase in crime. In his book *The Drugtakers* (1971), Jock Young described how this process served to increase the cannabis use of 'bohemian' subcultures in the Notting Hill area of London. The media would amplify such acts until there was 'a translation of stereotypes into actuality, of fantasy into reality'. Young considered that deviance amplification would have been far less likely in small-scale societies, as there was a varied source of information and it would have been far more difficult for individual identity to be reduced to a single characteristic, such as deviance. However, in larger societies lack of direct information about deviants leads to increased reliance on the mass media as a source of such information. The need to maintain circulation results in the media's playing on 'normative worries' of large sections of the population.

Deviance amplification is very difficult to test empirically and, in any case, seems only to apply to the more borderline areas of deviance which came to preoccupy both British and American criminologists in the mid-1960s. The theory does not make it clear why certain deviant activities come to be amplified rather than others, or how the amplification comes to stop.

(b) Moral panic

This term, which is related to the idea of deviance amplification, was first used by Jock Young (1971) in relation to drug taking, but was given wider prominence when adopted by Stanley Cohen in his book *Folk Devils and Moral Panics* (1972). Cohen carried out empirical research into the gathering of working-class youths from the East End of London at the seaside town of Clacton, Essex, over the Easter bank holiday weekend in 1964. Such excursions had quite a history, and a decade earlier concerns had been expressed at similar gatherings of 'teddy boys'. At this particular weekend, the weather was bad, the youths became bored, and minor acts of vandalism occurred. This subsequently became front page news in the national press with the claim that Clacton had been terrorised by rampaging groups of 'mods' (scooter riders) and 'rockers' (motor-bike riders). In fact, such individuals were in a clear minority among the young people present and any rivalry was more likely to have been based on the area from which they came than the mode of transport that they used. Cohen considered that the most typical criminal offence that occurred was not criminal damage, but threatening behaviour.

However, deviance amplification then set in. The media reaction led to intensified policing which, in turn, resulted in more arrests and apparently vindicated the original press reporting. The emphasis in the press on the differences between mods and rockers only served to polarise the two groups, and further clashes on subsequent bank holidays were now really based on rivalry between them. This caused increasingly hostile press coverage and the spiral had been set in motion. As Cohen put it, 'The Mods and Rockers didn't become news because they were new; they were presented as new to justify their creation as news'.

A similar reaction was recorded in America by Hunter Thompson (1966) in relation to incidents involving 'Hell's Angels'.

Cohen considered why all this occurred in the mid-1960s. This was a period of considerable social change, when even working-class youth came to have more money to spend and the dawn of 'the permissive society' thrust young people enjoying themselves into the forefront of public attention. Cohen argued that the unease amongst the older generation required a scapegoat and that the over-exuberance of the youth at Clacton cast them in the role of 'folk devils'.

Clearly, when politicians, judges and newspaper editors view such a threat in the same way, this can lead to a moral panic, with resulting changes in social and legal policy (Goode and Ben-Yehuda 1994). Around the time of the publication of Cohen's book, the term 'mugging' was introduced from America by the British press (there is technically no such crime as 'mugging') to describe relatively minor street robberies, typically involving handbag-snatching. This was represented as a new type of crime (which it was not) and a moral panic ensued, whereby people were led to believe that the British streets were as unsafe as those of New York when it came to street robbery. Mugging also took on racial overtones as it was portrayed in the tabloid press as being perpetrated almost entirely by black youths, whom Hall *et al.* referred to as 'a false enemy'. In their book *Policing the Crisis* (1978) they pointed out how these problems were first and foremost defined by the press as acts of lawbreaking, with practically no consideration given to the possible underlying causes such as poverty or racial inequality. The authors analysed thirteen months' worth of the press coverage of mugging from August 1972. They concluded that the press had sensitised the public's reaction to mugging to such an extent that it ceased to be 'a particular kind of robbery occurring on British streets' and became a reflection of a 'general social crisis and rising crime'. Sentencing levels increased for a while, although there is no evidence that this had any impact on the rate of offending.

Goode and Ben-Yehuda (1994) have provided an interesting illustration of how politicians and the media can help to create a moral panic and then allow it to diffuse, in their analysis of the American 'war against drugs' started by President Nixon in the 1970s. Between 1969 and 1974 the allocation of the federal budget dedicated to drug abuse was increased nearly ten times. Amid the accompanying rhetoric, a Gallup Poll in 1973 revealed that 20 per cent of the American public considered drug abuse as the number-one problem in the country. However, when Nixon left office in 1974 the campaign began to fade. By the middle of the decade, only 2 per cent to 3 per cent considered it to be the main problem. The analysis by Jenkins (1998) of the various moral panics relating to child molestation, which occurred in the USA at intervals of about thirty-five years throughout the twentieth century, has shown that their timing was related to a number of factors, such as the level of fear in society, the sense of family stability, and even the size of the current generation of children.

In recent years there has been a series of media-led moral panics. Shortly after the mugging scare, attention turned to football hooliganism. Rowdy behaviour at football matches is as old as the game itself (indeed, it was at its worst in the inter-village challenges before the rules of the game were standardised in the nineteenth century: see Pearson 1983). Football hooliganism was alive and kicking in the 1960s, but it was only a decade later that the press caught up with it. Various well-publicised incidents in the 1980s resulted in the Football (Offences) Act 1991, where a new criminal offence of going on to the playing area without reasonable excuse was created. Yet, even the press reporting of football hooliganism is taken at face value; it is describing the actions of, at most, a few hundred individuals throughout the whole of Britain acting in a number of relatively small groups. This hardly seems to amount to a major challenge to society 'as we know it'.

Other pieces of hasty, and sometimes ill-conceived legislation have occurred as a result of moral panics. In 1991, two particular laws were enacted which illustrate this. The Dangerous Dogs Act resulted from a few cases where children were attacked by dogs, and the awkwardly-named Aggravated Vehicle Taking Act was passed following extensive newspaper publicity of 'joy riding' by teenage boys on a few housing estates. In 1996, the House of Commons Home Affairs Select

Committee recommended that significant changes should be made to ease the restrictions of the Dangerous Dogs Act, and in 1997 the Dangerous Dogs (Amendment) Act was passed. This gives magistrates more discretion over whether to order the destruction of a dog. The fact that such incidents rarely make the news nowadays does not appear to be a consequence of any decrease in their frequency. Similar panics have occurred in relation to 'hippy convoys' (new age travellers) and 'raves'. Specific criminal offences designed to minimise the impact of these phenomena were created in the Criminal Justice and Public Order Act 1994.

Occasionally, sensational claims of unusual criminal activity are made which subsequently prove to be spurious. In the late 1980s and early 1990s stories of the satanic ritual abuse of children in England and Scotland began to emerge. An official enquiry found no evidence to justify the allegations (La Fontaine 1998). Between 1983 and 1993 newspapers reported stories about 'horse ripping'—the sadistic mutilation of horses. More than 160 incidents were alleged to have occurred throughout the country. The Hampshire police force launched 'Operation Mountbatten' to investigate the phenomenon, but no successful prosecutions have ever resulted. In 2001, the International League for the Protection of Horses declared that, although there may have been isolated incidents of such attacks, the vast majority of cases resulted from horses being involved in accidents and then aggravating their wounds, or even being attacked by other animals after their death (*The Guardian*, 23 April 2001).

(c) Public perception of crime

Jock Young (1974) thought that the media can affect public opinion in one of three ways: by mass manipulation, by a commercial 'laissez-faire', or by the 'consensual paradigm'. Mass manipulation theorists see the public as a gullible body who are open to political manipulation. Given the right-wing slant of most British newspapers, this view is most commonly held by those on the left. In contrast, the commercial '*laissez-faire*' view maintains that individual's attitudes have already been formed, and that they select newspapers which provide the best reinforcement of them. Those who believe that the media portrays a 'consensual paradigm' consider that readers are infrequently presented with competing arguments and that, in general, people form opinions as a result of what the media tells them, rather than as a result of any direct experience.

In her Birmingham research, Susan Smith (1984) found that 52 per cent of her sample obtained most of their information about crime from the media; about 36 per cent obtained it from hearsay or the alleged experiences of friends and neighbours; about 3 per cent from their own experience; and about 1 per cent from the police. The study indicated that people who obtained most of their information from media reports were more inclined to think that local crime predominantly consisted of violence, and the same group, when asked to comment on crime in general, made greater reference to violent and personal incidents. The area covered by the survey was portrayed in the local papers as being particularly prone to crime, and those who relied on the papers as their principal source of information on crime were more likely to believe this than others. Smith also discovered a similar pattern when she questioned 117 representatives from voluntary organisations about their views on the level of crime in different parts of Birmingham. More recently, the annual report *British Social Attitudes* found the public believed that 52 per cent of crimes involve violence, when the true figure is 22 per cent (National Centre for Social Research 2003).

A 1986 survey of 1,249 people over 18 in England and Wales (Hough *et al.* 1988) revealed that, when asked about their main source of information about crime, 48 per cent said newspapers or magazines and 43 per cent television or radio. Only 1 per cent mentioned their own experience as a main source. Most people were exposed to the news media: 78 per cent of the sample read a daily paper five or six times a week and 82 per cent watched the news on television every day. The research of Williams and Dickinson (1993) also confirmed that most people base their idea of the risk of being a victim of crime on information they have received from the press and television. This was the case even after the respondents had been matched with controls for socio-economic status, sex and age. On the other hand, the authors of the Second Islington Crime Survey Report (Crawford *et al.* 1990) considered that media coverage of crime is only a reinforcement of what the local population already knows.

Such is the power of the media's portrayal of crime that even politicians cannot afford to ignore it. In a study of how national crime prevention policy was decided in England and Wales between 1979 and 1997, Koch (1998) quoted a senior Home office official as saying 'It is rarely based on research but on what is thought by the individual minister to be popular to *The Sun* readers'.

(d) Effect on attitudes and behaviour

The balance of the evidence, therefore, seems to support the contention that the public as a whole forms its opinions on crime from what it reads in the papers and sees on television. Given the 'agenda' of the popular press and the emphasis placed by television on visual and dramatic crimes in programmes like *Crimewatch UK*, it is perhaps not surprising that many people—particularly women and the elderly—are reluctant to leave their homes, especially at night. In research by the IBA into the impact of their *Crimestoppers* programme, a third of the respondents remarked that it 'made them feel more cautious about going out alone in the dark or that other people had probably also become more afraid of crime as a result of watching the programme' (Wober and Gunter 1990). In 2000, it was reported that government ministers were becoming increasingly concerned that an unjustifiable fear of crime was being caused by TV programmes such as *Crimewatch UK* and *The Bill* (*The Guardian*, 7 November 2000). More than half the women interviewed in a study commissioned by the Broadcasting Standards Council considered that television and the tabloid press increased their fear of crime, with a third saying that such reports made them 'feel afraid'. Attempts by programme presenters to reassure viewers that the crimes were untypical were sometimes met with derision. There was much scepticism about police effectiveness in solving crimes. Only half the sample said they would be willing to report crimes, and only a quarter said that their confidence in the police had been increased by watching *Crimewatch UK* (Schlesinger *et al.* 1991). Although the British Crime Survey has not included any questions relating to the mass media and crime, in an analysis of anxiety about crime arising from the 1994 'sweep', Hough (1995) suggested that media reporting may not have much effect on the fear of crime.

Nevertheless, it would be dangerous to consider fear of crime as a phenomenon that is universally and evenly created by the mass media. It is clear that some individuals and groups are far more prone to fear than others: age, sex, class, area of residence and level of education are all obvious factors which can influence a person's reaction. It may be that simply discussing crime can increase people's fear of it. The Home Office reduced its publication of recorded crime figures from three months to six months because of the effect it considered that quarterly bulletins were having on fear of crime (Home Office 2000). However, a perception of the likelihood of being a victim of crime is far more likely to result from sensational and unbalanced reporting.

The British Crime Survey has indicated that most street offences are committed by and against young adult men, although critics such as 'Left Realists' have pointed out that this is hardly any comfort for the unfortunate victims who do not fall into this category. In addition, if women and the elderly have been reduced to keeping off the streets, one would hardly expect them to feature prominently in the statistics on street crimes. It seems that, through its reporting of crime, the media has played at least some role in influencing the daily activities of a significant part of the population.

Another unfortunate consequence of the media's obsession with sexual offences has been an apparent rise in the number of vigilante attacks. Although no newspaper editor would be stupid enough openly to advocate such behaviour, some of them have come very close to doing so. Stories are reported in such a way as to suggest that the guilty receive little more than a 'slap on the wrist' and that 'something should be done about it'. The anti-paedophile campaign run by the *News of the World* in the summer of 2000, which involved publishing photographs of a whole range of convicted sex offenders, is now recognised by senior police officers as being responsible for witch-hunts culminating in a series of 'revenge' attacks, which resulted in at least two suicides and a murder (*The Independent*, 22 February 2002).

It is also clear that the 'hard line' generally taken by the public in this country towards crime and the treatment of criminals is a consequence of the media's portrayal of serious violence as typical of crime as a whole. In particular, because of the attention paid by the popular press to an apparently lenient sentence (but very rarely to an apparently severe one), the public appears to be under the impression that sentencing levels are lower than they actually are. Using data from the 1996 British Crime Survey, Hough and Roberts (1998) discovered that people thought that the courts were more lenient to burglars than is really the case, and that the overall view on the appropriate punishment for burglars was broadly in line with practice. Those individuals who are most afraid of crime tend to call for heavier sentences than others. This is supported in a study by O'Connell and Whelan (1996), who found that older people and women tend to be more punitive than other sections of society. Nevertheless, Hough and Roberts also found that the victims of crime were no more punitive than anyone else. As they commented:

The most likely reason for public misperceptions is that information about sentencing comes largely from the media, and news values militate against balanced coverage. Erratic court sentences make news; sensible ones do not. As a result large parts of the population are exposed to a steady stream of misleading stories about sentencing incompetence.

A similar situation exists in other countries. Doob and Roberts (1988) pointed out that, although in Canada between 80 per cent and 90 per cent of people convicted of robbery are sent to prison, in a 1983 poll 86 per cent of Canadians underestimated this figure, including 76 per cent who gave large underestimates. Doob and Roberts referred to four separate studies they had conducted into people's reactions into reports of sentencing hearings:

> In all of the studies that compared different newspaper accounts of the same sentencing hearing, the reaction to the sentence depended on the account that was read . . . in all cases, the reactions to at least one of the newspaper accounts differed from the reactions to the court-based documents.

(e) Effect on sentencers

It is obvious that judges and magistrates cannot ignore public opinion when passing sentence. However, there are crucial issues of: (a) where they obtain their knowledge of public opinion; and (b) what weight they should give to it. There have been many reported cases of judges being pilloried in the press for imposing punishments that newspaper editors considered too lenient.

A study by Hough *et al.* (2003) has shown that the two main reasons for the 71 per cent increase in the prison population between 1991 and 2003 were that sentencers imposed longer sentences for serious crimes, and that they were more likely to imprison people who ten years earlier would have received a community penalty or even a fine. Part of the research involved interviewing five members of the senior judiciary. All of them stated that the increased severity in sentencing was partly a response to media pressure.

Conclusion

Although the police and various pressure groups are generally successful in their endeavours to influence both the provision and form of information about crime, it is now clear that the situation is more complicated than a straightforward demand–supply model between such sources and the news media (Ericson *et al.* 1989). The selection and reporting of news stories is ultimately carried out in accordance with the newspaper's 'agenda'. As Ericson *et al.* (1991) suggested:

> Deployed stereotypically, explanations of deviance in the news are political. They impute motives, whether noble or blameworthy, which in turn bear justifications and excuses for deviant behaviour with specific control implications.

The popular press often uses phrases such as 'public opinion is shocked by' or 'the public demands that'. However, editors and journalists have no direct line to public opinion, and it seems that often it is they who are the creators of the opinion and not the reflectors of it. (The increasing recourse in the tabloid press to an unrepresentative telephone poll—which always occurs after the story has been reported—does not affect this.) Even the BBC and independent broadcasting stations are increasingly following the lead of the popular press in the selection of stories, although their requirement of impartiality means that the reporting is usually more balanced.

The inter-relationship between the mass media and crime is a complicated one, but there does seem to be clear evidence that the attitudes of many people to crime are influenced to some extent by what they read in the papers or see on television. The speed with which politicians have reacted in recent years—often in poorly-prepared legislation—to the 'crime scares' reported in the press suggests that they themselves recognise this fact. There is a counter view, associated with some Left Realists, which claims that people select their newspapers and their TV viewing in accordance with their existing attitudes. Yet, how did these attitudes come to be formed in the first place? As most people are not the victims of serious crime, the obvious alternative source of information is conversation. However, questions then arise as to how the other person's opinions were reached. Even rumours have to start somewhere.

Part 2

Sociological explanations of crime

5

The classical and positivist traditions

In the Introduction, reference was made to these two major themes in the formation of criminological thinking, and it is now time to consider them in greater detail. This is not simply an excursion into history for its own sake: the tension between these two traditions has existed since the development of positivism in the nineteenth century, and is still of considerable importance in present-day debates about crime and 'law and order'.

Pre-Enlightenment Europe

It is common to single out France as typifying all that was bad with the administration of the criminal law in pre-eighteenth century Europe. It was the excesses of French society which stimulated writers such as Charles Montesquieu, Jean Jacques Rousseau and Francoise-Marie de Voltaire, and led to that crowning point of European (and, perhaps, world) history, the French Revolution. Yet, France only provided an extreme example of what passed as criminal 'justice' throughout most of Europe.

The evils of the 'ancien regime' are well-documented. The power of the sovereign—'the divine right of kings'—church and aristocracy was so overwhelming that individual rights as perceived nowadays were virtually non-existent. There were crimes against religion, such as atheism, and against the state, including the mere criticising of its actions. Criminal offences were poorly defined and judges exercised arbitrary powers to punish acts that were not legally defined as crimes. In court there were no formal rules of procedure and no legal representation was permitted. Confessions were frequently obtained by torture, and then repeated to obtain the names of accomplices. Punishments, which had changed little since the days of the Roman Empire, included breaking on the wheel, burning alive, mutilation and branding. They were applied unequally—sometimes in accordance with local custom—and the aristocracy were exempt from some of the most degrading forms. The judges were able to increase or reduce sentences, even where they were fixed by law. Superstition and cruelty were rife.

It was generally believed that crime was the consequence of evil. In some cases, it was assumed that the Devil or demons had taken over individuals and directed them to perform wicked acts (Mair 1969). Otherwise, people whose faith in God was insufficiently strong might have yielded to temptation and made a pact with the Devil. Humans were seen as both being controlled by external forces and creators of their own destiny—a dichotomy which has remained central to explanations of crime up to the present day (Einstadter and Henry 1995).

The classical school

The growing number of writers questioning this situation throughout the eighteenth century, while varying somewhat in their detailed pre-scriptions for change, were in general agreement as to the funda-mental reforms that were needed. They looked back to the 'classical' era for guidance: to the writings of Plato, Aristotle and Cicero, rather than to the religious texts of St Augustine and St Thomas Aquinas, which gave the power to punish wrongdoers to an absolute monarch ruling under the Divine Right—the direct inheritance of power from God. Reason and common sense should replace superstition and arbi-trariness. People's actions were not guided by supernatural forces, but resulted from a rational calculation which balanced the benefits against the cost. The corruption and inefficiency of the institutions of state must be rectified. Authority should be open to question. The starting point for dealing with this was an appeal to 'natural law'.

In the state of nature all individuals were born free. It was only the development of society that made them dependent on others and, therefore, limited their freedom. Under social contract theory, indi-viduals were deemed to have contracted to form a society, within which everyone would have to give up part of their freedom in order to obtain the wider benefits of collective living.

The freedom of individuals in a society was thus constrained by the requirement to respect the similar freedom of others, and it was necessary for this freedom to be protected by law. Nevertheless, laws were inevitably restrictive of individual freedom and should be kept to a bare minimum. People should be able to do what they wanted, so long as it was not proscribed by law. However, in situations which were governed by the law, the 'rule of law' must always apply. There should be equality before the law but, although in the state of nature everyone was born equal, this did not mean there had to be equality of wealth or status in a society.

Eighteenth-century writers were certainly not suggesting a fundamental challenge to the existing social arrangements. After all, they were part of a privileged class who had prospered from their position in society. However, the very fact that such inequalities were inevitable rendered impartiality in the law and the legal system all the more important. Nor did such inequalities in rank or property justify slavery—everyone at least was equal in being a human. Montesquieu's *The Spirit of Laws* (1748), which advocated the separation of legislative, executive and judicial branches of government, was published in the midst of a growing freedom of expression in art, architecture and music—a period that came to be known as the 'Enlightenment'. This book, which rejected torture and other abuses, was a significant prelude to what has become known as 'the classical school'.

(a) Cesare Beccaria

The Frenchmen Montesquieu and Voltaire were just two such writers calling for equality before the law and an end to arbitrary punishment during the first half of the eighteenth century. Similar views were being independently expressed in Austria and Germany at the same time. However, the greatest impact was made by a hitherto little-known Italian university professor, Cesare Bonesana, Marchese di Beccaria, in his book *Of Crimes and Punishments* (1764). Beccaria never published anything else of any significance, and it has even been suggested that he was used as a front by the real authors, who were already in trouble with the authorities (Paolucci 1963). In any event, fearing accusations that he was a revolutionary (which he strongly denied in the Introduction), Beccaria at first published the book anonymously. It was initially condemned in France and Italy and in 1766 by the Catholic church. Nevertheless, the book was welcomed by so-called 'enlightened despots' such as Frederick the Great of Prussia and Empress Catherine of Russia, and was soon translated into French (with a preface by Voltaire) and then English.

Like the social contract theorists, Beccaria considered that people have agreed to sacrifice a portion of their own freedom of action 'so that [they] might enjoy the rest of it in peace and safety'. It is important to realise that Beccaria viewed the social contract as a fundamentally selfish idea, which was not primarily designed to benefit one's fellow citizens. For Beccaria, there should be as little law as possible. Prohibiting an action was likely to increase rather than decrease crime. The criminal law should not simply uphold moral values for their own sake, but should furnish the requirements of a particular society. Criminal offences should be clearly defined; there should be no retrospective legislation or scope for judicial interpretation or discretion. From this it followed that there should be a written code of the whole criminal law. In accordance with the social contract, individuals could then see how far their freedoms were being protected.

A substantial portion of Beccaria's book was devoted to discussing the administration of criminal justice. At every stage the rights of the accused must be fully protected. Torture should be prohibited, as it 'is an infallible means for absolving robust scoundrels and for condemning innocent persons who happen to be weak'. Suspects should be tried by their peers: if there were a difference in class, half the jury should be selected from the class of the suspect and the other half from the class of the victim. The presumption of innocence should be paramount.

Beccaria went on to claim that punishment should be proportionate to the harm done to society; it should not exceed that which was necessary to ensure that the criminal did not re-offend. As far as possible, punishments should be visible. The purpose of punishment should be to deter, in a general rather than an individual sense. Beccaria was opposed to the punishment of transportation, as its lack of visibility meant it would have no deterrent effect. There should be no place for exemplary punishments or attempts to reform individuals. Punishments should not try to reflect the sinfulness of the act; that is a matter for God. Nor should they be too severe: as Beccaria pointed out:

> The severity of punishment of itself emboldens men to commit the very wrongs it is supposed to prevent; they are driven to commit additional crimes to avoid the punishment for a single one.

There must be a certainty of punishment and it should be imposed promptly. The certainty of a moderate punishment would have a greater impact than the mere possibility of a more severe one. Moderate punishments would also carry a greater deterrent element because they would be easier to enforce. The prevention of crime was more important than its punishment, and this necessitated that laws should be simple and clear. However Beccaria, together with other writers of the period, did not envisage the creation of a body charged with the control of crime such as a police force. At the time, such bodies were rightly viewed as little more than royal spies, and were anathema to most people. For Beccaria, the prevention of crime would follow from the adoption of his other recommendations, in particular the swift and consistent imposition of punishment.

Beccaria's dislike of the death penalty, although in part emotional, was also fuelled by his belief that the duration of a punishment was of greater significance than its intensity. Whereas execution provided a degrading but brief punishment, long-term imprisonment was imagined by Beccaria as having a greater deterrent effect. Execution could create martyrdom. Beccaria also objected to capital punishment on the basis that individuals would never have entered a social contract which allowed other people to kill them. The death penalty was totally abolished in Tuscany and, for a while, in Austria, and became more sparingly used in other countries. However, Beccaria was not opposed to corporal punishment and considered it to be an appropriate way of dealing with violent offenders. Thefts should normally be punished by fines but poor people, whose position would be exacerbated by a financial penalty, should be placed in temporary servitude.

The impact of Beccaria's book was immediate. Its spirit is evident in both the American Declaration of Independence and the Declaration of the Rights of Man in France. An American Attorney-General, William Bradford, commented in 1793:

> We perceive . . . that the severity of our criminal law (that is, the old criminal law inherited from England) is an exotic plant, and not the native growth of Pennsylvania . . . as soon as the principles of Beccaria were disseminated, they found a soil that was prepared to receive them.

In France some changes were made to the criminal process as a result of Beccaria's views: 'preparatory' torture was abolished in 1780 and 'preliminary' torture in 1788. However, such changes could never have been sufficient to prevent the French Revolution.

(b) Jeremy Bentham

Britain had not experienced the worst excesses of continental criminal procedure and the accused was relatively well protected. Torture was practically unknown by the eighteenth century. Yet, although it had one of the lowest rates of violent crime, Britain still had one of the highest rates of capital punishment in Europe. Between 1688 and 1820 the number of capital statutes increased from fifty to 200. Beccaria's work provided great encouragement for opponents of the death penalty in Britain, such as Jeremy Bentham (1748–1832). Bentham, who acknowledged his debt to Beccaria, applied his utilitarianism—'the greatest happiness of the greatest number'—to most aspects of life and society, including the criminal justice system. He wrote that:

> Nature has placed mankind under the governance of two sovereign masters, pain and pleasure . . . [T]hey govern us in all we do, in all we say, in all we think: every effort we can make to throw off our subjection will serve but to demonstrate and confirm it (1789).

Bentham formulated a sort of moral calculus to predict if a given person would commit a particular crime. It was based on the premise that every human act has first been evaluated in terms of whether it will cause pleasure or pain. Examples of pleasure are skill, benevolence and piety: examples of pain are desire, disappointment and hunger or thirst. The logical way to deter or prevent crime was, therefore, to ensure that the amount of pain derived from the forbidden activity was greater than the amount of pleasure.

Utility demanded that the same principle be applied to punishment: it could only be justified on the basis of prevention and should only impose a level of pain just in excess of the amount of pleasure that might be derived from the crime. Criminals would be deterred from crime if they calculated that the pain would exceed the pleasure. These thoughts were set out in the book *Introduction to the Principles of Morals and Legislation* (1789). For Bentham, human activity could be subject to this 'felicity calculus'. He argued that, if hanging people's effigies could have the same preventive effect as hanging people themselves, then it would be cruel and unnecessary to carry out real executions.

Some writers have maintained that there is an important difference between Beccaria and Bentham in their approaches to crime and punishment. For instance, Hart (1983) considered that, whereas Beccaria's idea of utility was limited by considerations of the dignity of the individual, Bentham was prepared to sacrifice such a notion if this would benefit the greater good of the population in general. Certainly Bentham was favourably disposed towards the use of imprisonment, and wrote extensively about prison design and regimes. However, Roshier (1989) has argued that this important distinction between the rights of the individual and the happiness of the greatest number is not clearly shown by a close comparison of the views of these two classical writers. Bentham was prepared to countenance the use of torture if it resulted in obtaining information which would prevent a greater harm, but Beccaria's opposition to torture was not so much based on its cruelty as on its lack of value in obtaining confessions. Beccaria was prepared to accept corporal punishment, and even his opposition to the death penalty was founded on its lack of effectiveness. It may be that, for Beccaria, any constraints on the severity of punishments which were not wholly explicable on utilitarian grounds were based on his idea of the social contract: that no-one could be taken to have agreed to the possibility of receiving excessively harsh punishment.

It would be inaccurate to consider reformers such as Beccaria and Bentham as 'criminologists' in anything like the current usage of the term. The particular significance of these authors arises from the fact that they were prepared to apply notions of reason and free will to an area—crime and justice—which had previously been governed by religious determinism. However, the price of the emphasis they placed on the contents and procedure of the criminal law was any proper consideration of why people offended in the first place. In particular, Bentham's felicity calculus was based on a remarkably simplistic assessment of human nature. Gilbert Geis (1960) has criticised Bentham's work on the grounds of 'its total failure to consider criminals as human beings, as live, complicated, variegated personalities'.

Nevertheless, reforms in the administration of criminal justice did ensue. The use of capital punishment declined significantly in Britain throughout the nineteenth century. By 1838, only eight criminal offences carried the death penalty. In that year six offenders were executed, which was a decrease from fifty-nine ten years earlier and ninety-two twenty years earlier (Radzinowicz and Hood 1986). In 1833, Commissioners were appointed to draw up a criminal code. They worked for fifteen years and produced thirteen reports, the content of which was considerably influenced by the writings of Beccaria and Bentham. One of the most significant features of their proposals was to reduce judicial discretion in sentencing. However, their efforts were perceived as pointing towards the abolition of the common law, and this perhaps indicates why their ideas were ultimately doomed to failure. The Code Napoleon was held up by some as an example of what could be achieved. Yet, opponents claimed that not only would such a development be against English political and legal traditions, but codification in France and Germany had served the purpose of unifying the legal structures of different provinces—a problem which did not exist in England. It was therefore inevitable that the draft bill introduced in 1848 would be unsuccessful. One further attempt was made when in 1878 the government entrusted the task to a Royal Commission led by Sir James Fitzjames Stephen. However, the

Criminal Code (Indictable Offences) Bill also failed, largely on the ground that it did not include lesser, summary offences. England has never subsequently acquired a criminal code.

(c) Problems with classicism

After the French Revolution in 1789, Beccaria's proposals were used as the foundation for the Revolutionary Code of 1791. The level of punishment was related to the precise nature of the offence to such an extent that the only function left for the judge was the determination of guilt or innocence. The number of offences for which capital punishment was available was reduced from more than 100 to thirty-two. The problem, however, was that, although Beccaria had envisaged that punishments should be applied equally where the crimes themselves were similar, he had ignored the fact that the criminals themselves might be particularly dissimilar. In other words, under the classical system, the punishment would depend entirely on the offence and not at all on the individual circumstances of the offender. Children were to be treated in the same way as adults, the mentally ill the same as the sane, and first offenders the same as recidivists. In his enthusiasm to punish only in proportion to the amount of harm caused, Beccaria had not even distinguished between crimes committed intentionally and those caused by accident. The feelings of injustice created by such an approach could only have served to weaken the deterrent effect, which was such a crucial aspect of Beccaria's approach.

The neoclassical school

An attempt was made to incorporate some of Beccaria's proposals in Article VIII of the 'Declaration of the Rights of Man and the Citizen' passed by the revolutionary National Assembly of France in 1789. However, it was not until the French Code of 1791 that the legislature systematically tried to put his ideas into practice. Napoleon's Code of 1810 combined principled alterations to the 1791 Code with changes resulting from political expediency. An element of discretion in punishment was reintroduced. Fixed punishments were replaced by stated maximum and minimum sentences. The prerogative of mercy was re-established. On the other hand, the death penalty was extended to offences considered dangerous to the state. Punishments in general became more severe. In a revision of the Code in 1819, greater allowance was made for the exercise of discretion by judges.

This combination of the classical theory of free will and individual responsibility with considerations of age, mental state and mitigating circumstances provided a compromise which is often referred to as the neoclassical school. It has now come to provide the basis of the criminal justice systems of most industrialised countries in the world. However, neoclassicism represented a refinement of, and not a complete break with, the classicism that had developed during the previous century. Human beings were still considered as being guided by reason, as having free will and freedom of choice, and therefore able to be considered both morally and legally responsible for their actions. Classical theory was attractive to rulers as its social contract basis emphasised that, as everyone had a stake in society, it was in everyone's interests to obey the law. Crime was portrayed as an irrational act which, because it is concentrated in the lower classes, suggested that they contain a sizeable proportion of irrational people.

What social contract theory did not do was to question whether particular laws were just. The political and social status quo was unquestioningly accepted by the writers, who themselves were from privileged backgrounds. There was no recognition of the possibility that the disadvantaged position of the lower classes might have something to do with their criminality. Nor did the fact that some people could obtain far greater benefits from the social contract than others have any impact on these writers. After all, if crime is based on a lack of rationality, however temporary, why is it not spread more equally among the different strata in society?

Beccaria, although often described as a social contract theorist, appears to have taken a more critical position towards the structure of society. He was aware that the law could cause considerable hardship to the poor: 'The majority of laws are nothing but privileges, that is, a tribute paid by all to the convenience of some few'. One sociologist, Lynn McDonald (1976), has even argued that Beccaria could be described as a conflict theorist (see Chapter 10).

The classical and neoclassical schools replaced the earlier view that criminals were simply the objects of supernatural forces, and claimed that humans are intelligent, rational beings who are responsible for their own decisions. Classicism also resulted in extensive reforms to the criminal justice system. Yet, 100 years on from the publication of Beccaria's seminal work, crime did not appear to have diminished significantly throughout Europe. Suspicion of the idea that crime could inevitably be reduced by the threat or imposition of punishment was further fuelled by growing scientific advances which suggested that human behaviour was perhaps not entirely governed by reason after all. Classicism itself had emphasised practical measures for crime control, as opposed to pure retribution. The development of neoclassicism showed that, at least in some cases, people's behaviour could be determined, as opposed to resulting from the exercise of a rational choice. These factors eased the transition into the positivist study of criminology.

The positivist school

The first half of the nineteenth century saw the beginning of a rapid growth in scientific knowledge and the consequential adoption of scientific method to investigate the properties of every type of phenomenon. Inevitably, this extended to include the very nature of humanity itself, and a growing scepticism began to envelop religion and philosophy. In 1826, the philosopher Auguste Comte expounded the 'law of three states'. He claimed that the history of civilisation had developed through three stages: the theological, the metaphysical and the positive. In the first of these, people ascribed goodness, evil or change either to divine or demonological intervention. In the second stage, abstract notions such as 'ideas' and 'forces' replaced the supernatural as the explanation of causation. It was only when people reached the third stage—the positive state—that they dispensed with theological and metaphysical explanations and turned to scientific descriptions of causation. The question 'why?' was replaced by the question 'how?' and, for Comte, the answer should be sought by the use of simple mathematical calculations.

Comte is widely considered as having laid the foundations of what has come to be known as sociology (he referred to it as 'social physics') by his exposition of positivism. He thought that social science could solve the problems that were arising from the massive social upheaval resulting from both the French Revolution and, more generally, the Industrial Revolution. The application of principles from the natural sciences to the study of human behaviour also had clear policy implications: social change could develop gradually without the need for revolution.

All the doubts surrounding earlier explanations seemed to be confirmed by the publication of the book *On the Origin of Species* by Charles Darwin (1809–82) in 1859. Darwin considered that evolution occurs by natural selection which results from the survival of the fittest species and the fittest members within each species. In 1871, his book *The Descent of Man* was published. In this, he provided evidence that humans had evolved from animals and were simply a more highly-developed form. Once the possibility of this break in the link to divinity had entered people's minds, the application of scientific method to study human behaviour became far more acceptable, at least in intellectual circles. If animal behaviour was neither influenced by a deity nor controlled by reason, why should human behaviour be any different?

The social implications of Darwinism were profound. The idea of 'the survival of the fittest' suggested that governments should not take steps to interfere with the course of nature by introducing policies to protect the weaker members of society. There was no point in facilitating the continuation of inferior stock which was manifested, according to social Darwinists, in the poor, the idle and the immoral.

Two distinct approaches to the study of humans began to develop. One was the study of behaviour within society which, in relation to crime, involved an analysis of the social factors that appeared to be related to law-breaking. These studies are among the very first recorded examples of the sociological investigation of crime. The other involved a study of the biological or constitutional features of convicted criminals to see if they could be distinguished from 'normal' members of the population. Although it is clear that these two channels of enquiry are not mutually exclusive, they were at first considered as such.

(a) Quetelet and Guerry

Very little information about crime was systematically collected before the nineteenth century. France was the first country to see the publication of official criminal statistics in 1827 and other countries soon followed. Piers Beirne (1993) has suggested that this was in part motivated by a desire in post-revolutionary France to keep a closer watch on its citizens, and a fear of the 'dangerous classes' by the growing middle class. A Belgian astronomer and mathematician, Adolphe Quetelet, and a French lawyer, André-Michel Guerry, at about the same time began to analyse the French crime figures over a period of years. Both men investigated the level of offending in relation to age, sex, race, educational attainment, profession, and even the weather! They compared different regions of the country. Their main findings (reached independently) showed that the annual levels of recorded crime for most offences stayed about the same. In addition, the contributions to the crime figures of different groups within society—such as the young and the old—living under different social conditions remained similar from year to year.

Quetelet and Guerry also discovered that some general beliefs about crime were not born out by their investigations: for example, some of the poorest areas of France had the lowest crime levels. Yet, it could now be shown that, in general terms, differences in rates of offending correlated with variations in social conditions and demography. Quetelet commented that 'society prepares the crime and the guilty [person] is only the instrument by which it is accomplished'.

By modern standards, some of Quetelet and Guerry's conclusions might be difficult to sustain and their attempts to predict crime appear somewhat naive. However, the important point was that a breakthrough had been made: by the meticulous analysis of copious amounts of data, crime could clearly be viewed as a social and environmental phenomenon. All of this seemed some way removed from the classical notions of free will and rationality. In 1864, Guerry wrote that:

> The time has gone by when we could claim to regulate society by laws established solely on metaphysical theories and a sort of ideal type which was thought to conform to absolute justice. Laws are not made for men in the abstract, for humanity in general, but for real men placed in precisely determined conditions.

Similar studies were being conducted in other countries. In Britain, several important presentations on crime were given by members of the Statistical Society of London in the mid-nineteenth century. In 1839, one Rawson W Rawson gave a paper entitled 'An Inquiry into the Statistics of Crime in England and Wales'. Rawson examined the judicial statistics (records of court proceedings) for the years 1835–9. Based on census data from 1831, he divided the counties of England and Wales into four groups: agricultural, manufacturing, mining, and metropolitan (near London). Not surprisingly, Rawson found that crime was most common in large towns and least common in rural areas. However, in arriving at this conclusion, he ruled out climatic and regional ethnic differences and argued that 'the employments of the people' would relate to their criminality. In 1848–9, Joseph Fletcher, using a modified version of Rawson's division of the counties, investigated the relationship between education and crime. He concluded that 'a Christian education' would not in itself prevent crime and that idleness was a major causal factor.

In 1856, John Glyde, another member of the Statistical Society of London, read a paper to the British Association in Glasgow entitled 'The Localities of Crime in Suffolk'. The most interesting conclusion to emerge from Glyde's study was that the 'ratio of criminals to population' was not that much higher in the large towns than in the countryside. This may be attributable to the political unrest which could be found among East Anglian agricultural workers at the time (Morris 1957).

(b) Cesare Lombroso

The second main approach to the study of crime that developed during this period was based on research into the physical characteristics of criminals. This has become indelibly linked with the work of the Italian professor Cesare Lombroso (1835–1909), although it appears that many of the findings which are now associated with him had derived from the work of others, not least Charles Darwin. Lombroso's theories are discussed in greater detail in Chapter 14. He obtained a degree in medicine at the University of Pavia in 1858, exactly 100 years after Beccaria graduated from the same institution. At that point the similarity between them ends. In his best-known book *The Criminal Man* (1876), which was published only five years after Darwin's work *The Descent of Man*, Lombroso argued that criminals are biologically reversions to an earlier stage of evolution and are thus more primitive than law-abiding individuals. He termed them 'atavistic' and claimed that research showed them to possess physical anomalies such as unusually-shaped jaws, ears and noses; excessively long arms; and an abundance of wrinkles. In short, they would possess something of an ape-like appearance.

History has not altogether been kind to Lombroso: his views on atavistic man are often dropped into criminology courses for light relief before the next substantial topic is discussed. Yet, this area formed only a relatively small part of Lombroso's criminological writings, and by the time of his death he was prepared to concede a far greater role for social and environmental influences than he had been in his youth. The final edition of *The Criminal Man* at 1903 pages was almost eight times the length of the first, and much of the extra length resulted from the addition of environmental rather than biological material. In any event, the study of anthropology had significantly progressed in the half century that Lombroso had been studying the subject, and by the early twentieth century few people believed in the straightforward linear progression of evolution which had been suggested by writers such as Darwin. Lombroso's legacy as being known as the founder of the positivist school ('scuola positiva') is not without justification.

Why did Lombroso's work receive so much more contemporary

attention than that of Quetelet or Guerry? It is possible that their accounts provided too great a challenge to the social arrangements at the time, whereas Lombroso's notion of the 'born criminal' enabled offenders to be bracketed off as a separate category and not in any sense seen as a consequence of society's failings.

(c) Enrico Ferri

Lombroso's positivist explanation of crime was carried forward by two other Italians, his pupil Enrico Ferri and Raffaele Garofalo. Ferri (1856–1928) was a socialist who placed greater emphasis on political, economic and social factors than his teacher. In his best-known work *Criminal Sociology* (1881), Ferri argued that crime is caused by a variety of factors which he classified as: (1) physical, including race, geographical location and climate; (2) anthropological, such as age, sex, biological and psychological condition; and (3) social, by which he meant nature of the government, economic conditions, religion and general customs. Ferri thought that crime prevention was more important than punishment, and considered that the state could do much to reduce crime: birth control, inexpensive houses, better street lighting, provisions for public recreation and freedom of marriage and divorce are examples of steps that should be taken. Many of these ideas are among the least that would be expected from governments nowadays, but they were very advanced for the late nineteenth century. Ferri left academic life for a while and concentrated on politics. He returned as a criminal law professor in Rome in 1904 and, after World War I, was asked to draft a new Italian Criminal Code.

Article 18 of the draft exemplified Ferri's positivist views on social and legal responsibility. Social responsibility referred to the individual's responsibility towards society and the state. Legal responsibility did not refer to the imposition of a judgement on the offender's moral guilt, but simply to ascertaining whether the offender had carried out the forbidden act. If this were proved to be the case, measures should be taken not to punish the offender by way of retribution, but to restrain the offender from committing further offences. These would take into account the offender's physical and mental state, together with social circumstances. Ferri and his supporters considered that it was wrong that all but the totally insane should be considered criminally responsible and punished accordingly. Criminal responsibility should be based on the needs of society, and be concerned with the possible danger to the community rather than the guilt of the offender. However, in 1922, the year after Ferri had completed his draft, Mussolini took power in Italy, and Ferri's proposals were rejected by the Italian parliament.

(d) Raffaele Garofalo

The third of the major Italian positivists was Raffaele Garofalo (1852–1934). Like his compatriots, Garofalo rejected the doctrine of free will and considered that crime could only be properly studied by the use of scientific methodology. In his book *Criminology* (one of the first recorded uses of the word), which was published in 1885, Garofalo attempted to construct a universal sociological definition of crime. To be considered as universal, the crimes must be such that no society could ever tolerate them. Garofalo termed these 'natural crimes'. To qualify, acts must violate the two basic moral sentiments of pity (revulsion against the voluntary infliction of suffering on others) and probity (respect for the property rights of others). Other crimes, which Garofalo described as 'police crimes', were less important. They were acts which did not offend these basic moral sentiments, but happened to be given the label of crime at a particular time.

Having obtained experience of the criminal justice system as a judge of the Court of Criminal Appeal in Naples, Garofalo heavily criticised the idea of penal proportionality on the basis that there were far too many factors to consider and that it was impossible to say which were the most important. The dangerousness of offenders and the likelihood of their continuing as criminals should be the key elements in deciding what to do with them. In assessing this, the nature of the offence should be one of a number of factors to be taken into account. It should not be considered in isolation, but as a part of the overall personality of offenders and the likelihood of their continuing in their criminal behaviour. The idea of punishment should be irrelevant and in its place should be measures of 'social defence' against the perceived state of danger.

These positivist theories did not necessarily imply the gentle treatment of offenders. Lombroso considered that 'born' murderers should be executed and sex offenders castrated. Garofalo thought that the death penalty should be used for offenders whose crimes resulted from a 'permanent psychological anomaly which renders the subject forever incapable of social life'.

Evaluation

Both the classical and positivist traditions in criminology view the main purpose of the criminal justice system as being to control crime. However, the ways in which this should be achieved are set out in fundamentally different terms.

Broadly speaking, the classical approach considers that individuals are free and rational decision makers who are motivated by self-interest. People are likely to break the rules for their own advantage if they think they can get away with it. It is, therefore, to their advantage to enter a social contract with their fellow citizens to protect themselves from what they all agree would be harmful. According to Beccaria, the appreciation of what is harmful and how best to deal with it will come to those people who apply rational thought to the situation. What emerges will be taken as the consensual view. It will be necessary for the criminal justice system to uphold this consensus by the use of threats and deterrents. The importance of the content of the law is in contrast to the position of the positive approach, in which it becomes a secondary consideration in the quest for the cause(s) of crime and the most suitable forms of treatment.

According to the early positivists, this concentration on free will and the rights of offenders had been responsible for the increase in crime throughout the first part of the nineteenth century. Darwin's conclusion that humans are descended from apes led positivists to think that the principles of scientific research which had been successfully applied to the material and animal world could also be relevant to the study of humans. Jeffery (1960) has suggested that positivism can be distinguished from classicism by three key features:

(1) *Determinism*. Crime is viewed as behaviour which is caused by biological, psychological or social factors. Crime does not, therefore, result from rational decisions made by offenders.

(2) *Differentiation*. Criminals differ from non-criminals in their biological or psychological make-up, or in terms of their values. Indeed, it is an essential requirement of positivist theories of crime causation that they can establish the existence of 'types' of people who are likely to commit crimes. These types can be based on biology, personality or values.

(3) *Pathology*. Not only are criminals different from non-criminals, but there is also something 'wrong' with them, which cannot simply be described as a variation of normality. This has to be

attended to by the application of psychological or sociological mechanisms.

The first extreme manifestations of biological positivist criminology are certainly not without their inconsistencies and, in places, absurdities. Yet, they have also served as a catalyst for some extremely important developments in the study of crime. The individual became the focus of attention: as van Hamel (quoted in Radzinowicz 1966) put it: 'The classical school exhorts men to study justice; the positivist school exhorts justice to study men'. The individual criminal—as opposed to the content of the criminal law—became the focus of attention from many different directions. In addition to sociology, psychiatry was a newly-developing discipline which, together with psychology and anthropology, was apparently able to shed some light on criminal behaviour. The rise of positivism was accompanied by the rise of professions and a growth in the number of 'experts', such as doctors, psychiatrists and teachers. The growth of biological or constitutional explanations of crime spurred on writers who were convinced that a study of social factors would be more productive. Although biological positivism is open to the charge that, in locating the causes of criminal or anti-social behaviour firmly within the individual, it frees society from responsibility for the crimes committed within it, the researchers would probably have claimed that this was hardly their fault.

From the beginning of the twentieth century, criminology began to emerge as an academic discipline in its own right, especially in the USA and continental Europe, and a growing number of periodicals came to be published. Positivist criminologists were at first unhappy with basing their research on the legal definition of crime because it is variable over time and between different countries (see Chapter 2). Efforts were made to find a universal definition of crime, and the early biological positivists were attracted by Garofalo's notion of 'natural crime', which is considered above. Perhaps inevitably, this and every other 'universal' definition has been found wanting. Garland (1985) has suggested that one reason why the early biological positivists wanted to formulate a theory of the causes of crime which had nothing to do with the existing criminal law was a desire to establish themselves as the new generation of penal experts. In this respect, they hoped to replace the old profession of lawyers.

As with all historical developments, there is a danger of assuming that one school of thought—positivism—suddenly and neatly replaced another—classicism—almost overnight, and that the former vanished without trace. In fact, the neoclassical developments in the criminal justice system have never disappeared and have remained the underlying basis of Western criminal procedure up until the present day. The impact of positivism was more on considerations of why people commit crimes and, to a lesser extent, of what society should do with offenders. Indeed, it is arguable that the development of positivism needed the background of classicism. Most early positivist research was based on samples of convicted offenders. The fact that their convictions were the culmination of a rational and structured criminal justice process could only serve to enhance the scientific status of any research into their criminality. To some extent, the preoccupation with science during the nineteenth century held up the broader intellectual ferment that had developed during the previous century.

However, a cloud on the criminological horizon could perhaps be detected from the fact that both Ferri and Garofalo had little difficulty in accommodating the fascism of Mussolini when he took power in Italy. Ferri, originally a socialist, became attracted to fascism because it represented the authority of the state against unfettered individualism. This illustrates the argument that positivist theories fit well into totalitarian regimes, as positivism assumes superior knowledge on the part of 'experts'. On the basis of their 'scientific' knowledge, they can decide why people have committed crimes and prescribe treatment for them without their consent and without paying any regard to the views of the public as a whole.

The classical and positivist approaches: later developments

Just as classicism was the prevailing basis of criminological and penological thought for about a hundred years following the publication of Beccaria's *On Crimes and Punishments*, positivism then formed the interest of most criminologists for the next hundred years. Garland (1985) has commented that, during the final quarter of the nineteenth century, positivist criminology:

> . . . developed from the idiosyncratic concern of a few individuals into a programme of investigation and social action which attracted support throughout the whole of Europe and North America.

Positivism brought with it the scope for empirical research, which was essentially designed to discover differences between 'criminals' and 'non-criminals'—the major assumption being that such differences would exist. This has led to copious research projects resulting in a far wider range of theories of criminality than was possible adopting a classical approach.

Nevertheless, by the 1960s there was a change in the social climate throughout Western societies. America was affected by the growing civil rights and women's liberation movements. In both America and Britain there was opposition to the war in Vietnam and a growing revulsion with the technology which had produced the napalm bomb and the threat of nuclear war. The spread of the 'hippie culture' involved an increasing use of drugs. There was a heightened sense of freedom and openness and an accompanying questioning of rules and conventions. With this background, positivist criminology not only looked conservative, but the suggestion that protesters against war and the infringement of civil rights had 'something wrong with them' came to be viewed as insulting. The spirit of this period required human action to be seen as willed and voluntary, not determined by pathological or social considerations. A more radical political stance provided a target for human action: the oppressive state or—for the even more radical—the capitalist system.

The 'sickness' analogy used by positivist explanations of offending also seemed to relate largely to working-class street crime and, in particular, to offences of violence. However, by the 1960s there was a growing awareness not only of the existence of business and corporate crime, but also of state action such as the creation of pollution. Although Sutherland's theory of differential association had suggested that white-collar offending could be learned (see Chapter 6), many people felt that traditional positivist explanations could not provide an adequate explanation for such occurrences.

The theoretical perspective of crime that particularly flourished during this period was interactionism, which is discussed in Chapter 9. In some respects this suggested a return to classicism: the voluntary nature of human behaviour and the emphasis on the crime rather than the criminal are key components of this approach. However, the 1960s version emerged as 'labelling theory' which seemed to possess certain positivist characteristics, particularly in the consequences of the application of the label. In 1969, Hirschi's control theory (see Chapter 12) showed some influence of classicism: people are viewed as rational and self-seeking, and therefore conform because it is in their interests to do so. However, Hirschi did not consider the possible significance of the criminal justice system in controlling crime. He also shared the positivists' rejection of deterrence as a relevant factor in offending.

There was a parallel change of thinking in relation to the operation of the criminal justice and penal systems. Just as the growth of positivism had been encouraged by the perceived lack of success of classically-based criminal justice systems in reducing the level of crime, by the 1970s there was a growing feeling among criminologists and politicians that a 'treatment' orientated approach was failing to work. Many states in the USA had adopted indeterminate prison terms as part of their sentencing systems. An individual's release date was assessed by panels of experts in accordance with successful treatment criteria, rather than being fixed by judges in accordance with the gravity of the offence (Frankel 1973). This is a perfect illustration of the positivist versus the classical approach. The positivist (indeterminate sentencing) approach was seen as secretive, inconsistent, undemocratic and ultimately—in terms of recidivism—unsuccessful. The classical (fixed sentencing) approach was increasingly favoured as consistent and democratic, in that sentences were openly announced by publicly-appointed officials (judges).

Significantly, there was a change in the political climate in both the USA and Britain. The right-wing administrations of Ronald Reagan and Margaret Thatcher were, in both social and economic terms, far more attracted to eighteenth century liberalism and personal responsibility than the state interventionist approach of the twentieth century. The utilitarian or treatment model of sentencing in the USA was replaced by a 'just desert' approach which is clearly based on classical principles. Pettit and Braithwaite (1993) considered that the approach has four basic principles:

(1) no-one other than a person found guilty of a crime should be punished for it;

(2) anyone found guilty of a crime must be punished for it;

(3) punishment must not exceed a degree commensurate or proportional to the nature or gravity of the offence and culpability of the criminal;

(4) punishment must not be less than a degree commensurate or proportional to the nature or gravity of the offence and culpability of the criminal.

In the USA, the judicial role in the sentencing process has now been considerably reduced, as closely-detailed sentencing guidelines have been formulated (Parent 1988). The English criminal justice system has never moved to either of the extreme positions seen in the USA, although the Criminal Justice Act 1991 did try to point sentencers in the direction of a 'just deserts' or retributive approach.

Conclusion

In summary, therefore, it can be said that both the classical and positivist traditions are still relevant in the study of crime and the practice
of the criminal justice system. However, each approach has its own
discrete areas of influence. Empirical research based on positivist
techniques still predominates in studies of the aetiology and epidemiology of crime, methods of crime prevention, and the efficacy of different types of sentence. However, at the end of the twentieth
century, positivism had not achieved the breakthrough that once
looked possible in terms of sentencing. Increased levels of crime, both
real and imagined, and the election of right-wing governments have
largely shifted the spotlight from the offender to the offence. A neoclassical approach to punishment remains firmly in place, with the
only remaining area of debate being the extent to which individual
characteristics should be influential.

6

Crime and the environment

In the previous chapter it was shown how Adolphe Quetelet and André-Michel Guerry pioneered the collection of crime data in France and Belgium during the 1820s. Theirs were the first significant efforts to study both the environments in which crimes occurred and the areas in which the criminals lived. Guerry in particular utilised maps to aid his research. This type of study was to establish a tradition which began to take hold throughout Europe before entering its best known period in the hands of the Chicago Ecologists.

The Victorian slum

Before the Industrial Revolution had progressed very far, the level of poverty and degradation which had rapidly developed in European inner city areas was becoming increasingly apparent to a number of observers. The accounts provided by these writers were generally unsystematic, based on observation and oral recollection. Yet, they provided a fascinating and worthwhile account of deprivation, arguably just as valuable as the later more sophisticated offerings of sociologists.

The ills of society, including crime and disorder, were perceived as emanating from the 'dangerous' classes. They were considered as vicious and depraved and, after the writings of Charles Darwin (see Chapter 5), it became easier even for educated opinion to portray them as a race apart. At any time they might break out into political revolt, as they had in France. Indeed, it was in that country where some of the earliest efforts were made to assess the lifestyle of such people. These forays were far removed from the more sophisticated statistical measurements of Quetelet and Guerry, and involved the writers providing a general impression, after going to look at the slum areas for themselves. Fregier (1840), a former policeman in Paris, was already well-acquainted with the slums of that city when he embarked on a study of the lifestyle found there. He noted that it was almost impossible to distinguish actual criminals from the general mass of the poor and depraved. Nevertheless, he was convinced that any defects in morality could be attributed to the appalling conditions in which they had to live.

The demographer GC Holland, in his book *Vital Statistics of Sheffield* (1843), commented on the association between a poverty environment and crime:

> Among the numerous causes . . . producing crime and immorality, the following deserve particular notice. The crowding together of the working classes in narrow streets, filthy lanes, alleys and yards, is a serious evil and one which has hitherto increased in all manufacturing towns. The poor are not resident in these places from choice, but from necessity.

In *The Condition of the Working Class in England* (1845), Frederick Engels used newspapers, pamphlets and individual accounts to supplement his own observations in compiling a view of working-class life in Manchester. He concluded that blame for the deprivation and crime he saw all around him lay at the feet of the middle and upper classes in their ruthless exploitation of the workers within capitalism. Violence or 'conflictual' crime could be explained as a form of retaliation against 'the bourgeoisie and their henchmen'. Such crime could also be committed against members of the working class: Engels appears to have seen an irony in this within the capitalist system:

> This war of all against all . . . it is only the logical sequel of the principle involved in free competition.

Theft or robbery were viewed as arising from grim economic necessity. Engels attributed the sexual immorality and drunkenness among the workers to a lack of moral training and to being the only pleasures that were left to them. All these problems were more prevalent in the population of unemployed or casual workers, whom Marx termed the 'lumpenproletariat'.

Therefore, crime could be egotistical and against the interests of the working class, as with much petty theft; or it could be political but reactionary, such as smashing machinery or burning haystacks; or it could be political but progressive, such as taking part in a banned march or demonstration.

The main contribution of the English journalist Henry Mayhew (1812–87) to Victorian ethnography was his four-part work *London Labour and the London Poor*, published as a book in 1862. The study, written in a journalistic style, is not specifically a criminological text, but more a social survey of London. It is rich in local detail and includes vivid accounts of the 'rookeries' or slum areas inhabited by criminals. Mayhew preferred to travel around London talking to people than to indulge in statistical analyses in the manner of Rawson and Fletcher (see Chapter 5). He was not prepared to attribute crime purely to urbanisation and poverty or immorality. Nor was he attracted by the increasingly popular view—soon to find a wide audience through the work of Lombroso—that the shape of a person's head or other physical attributes could be causal factors. Mayhew considered that crime resulted because children were born into families where anti-social attitudes and lifestyles already existed. They would then grow up effectively unsocialised, unable to conform to 'civilised habits', and become street urchins. Mayhew noticed that certain areas of London appeared to be responsible for more crime than others. According to Morris (1957), such an observation 'marks him out clearly as an ancestor of the ecologists of the twentieth century'.

The work *Life and Labour of the People in London* (1902–3) by Charles Booth ran to no fewer than seventeen volumes. Again, much ethnographic detail is evident in Booth's analysis, which he too was more prepared to attribute to social conditions than individual pathology.

It was as a result of such writings that concern began to shift from what has been termed 'the criminal theme into the social theme' and then from the dangerous classes to the entire working class. The views of Lombroso (see Chapter 5) were still influential, particularly in Europe, but already a new interest in the prevalence of crime in particular social conditions was beginning to emerge. Perhaps it is not surprising that, with massive immigration into centres of vast industrial growth, such studies found their main impetus in the USA.

The Chicago School and social disorganisation

It has already been noted that criminology began to develop as a separate discipline at the beginning of the twentieth century from two separate strands: one from clinical medicine, heavily influenced by the constitutional theories of Lombroso, and the other from the development of sociology, particularly in the USA and particularly at the University of Chicago.

The city of Chicago provides a classic illustration of the rapid urban expansion that was occurring in the USA at the turn of the century. In 1860, the population was about 110,000. By 1880, it stood at half a million, and it then doubled to one million during the next ten years. By 1910, the population had doubled again to two million. Much of the increase was a result of mass immigration from Europe, particularly from Ireland, Italy and east Europe, as well as black families from the south seeking a better life for themselves in the northern states. The newcomers had been poor in their native land and were destined to start life in America in the same manner. Wages were very low and a twelve-hour day, six days a week in unsafe factories was the norm (Palen 1981). This vast melting pot of different cultures provided an almost unique opportunity for the conducting of empirical research on how families from such varied backgrounds managed to co-exist, and no-one was better placed for this task than the members of the first ever Department of Sociology (1892) at the University of Chicago. Indeed, the Department had been given funds for this very purpose.

It is clear that the work of the 'Chicago School' was a development of the writings of Emile Durkheim (see Chapter 7), which depicted crime as a social product and the level of criminality as representing the extent of social integration. Another influential strand of thought was the interactionism of GH Mead (see Chapter 9). The end result was a sociological study of crime in which social action was considered as an intentioned and sometimes creative response to the prevailing social conditions, rather than an analysis based on psychiatry or statistical evaluation.

Among the earlier Chicago researchers into the growth of the city, one of the most eminent was Robert E Park, a former crime reporter who sent graduate students on to the streets of Chicago with instructions to 'tell it like it is'. Their detailed findings emphasised the petty nature of much crime and delinquency, and appeared to support Durkheim's view that such incidents were not a serious threat to the stability of society. Drawing on the biological concept of plant ecology, Park and Ernest W Burgess formulated an analogous notion of 'human ecology'. This was later defined by Morris (1957) as 'the relationships which exist between people who share a common habitat, or local territory, and which are distinctly related to the character of the territory itself'.

Central to the idea of human ecology was the 'zonal hypothesis', as illustrated in Burgess's analysis of Chicago (1925). This divided the city into five concentric zones, which resemble the rings formed on the surface of still water after a stone has been thrown in. The innermost zone was the central business district, known then and now as 'The Loop'. The next zone outwards was the 'zone of transition', a deteriorating area where factories, poorer residences and the 'red-light district' could be found. Beyond this was zone three, which contained the homes of ordinary working people (many of whom had 'escaped' from zone two), and zones four and five, with increasingly affluent homes reaching out into suburbia. The hypothesis was that new immigrants would initially settle into the zone of transition and then, if they became more prosperous, move further out towards zone five. If the city was growing considerably, areas which had been in zones three or four could find themselves becoming part of the zone of transition with a corresponding deterioration. In short, the concentric growth of the city occurred through what has been termed 'invasion, dominance and succession'. The Chicago researchers considered that, in the longer term, once the different ethnic groups settled down and became established in a suitable area, their crime rates would start to diminish.

The aptly-named zone of transition was therefore a highly volatile area—an area lacking in social integration. There was a constant throughput of immigrants from different cultures, all striving to make something for themselves, and whose children in particular had divided loyalties between their old world and their new home. It was a zone of disorder and potential criminality.

The best-known application of the Chicago School's urban sociology in relation to crime is found in Clifford Shaw and Henry McKay's *Social Factors in Juvenile Delinquency* (1931), the findings of which were later expanded in their book *Juvenile Delinquency and Urban Areas* (1942). Shaw and McKay plotted the rates of male delinquency in Chicago between 1900 and 1933 with the help of three different types of map. 'Spot' maps showed where all the arrested juveniles lived; 'rate' maps showed the percentage of juveniles with arrest records; and 'zone' maps showed the delinquency rates for each of the five zones identified in the concentric model. Shaw and McKay supported this with an in-depth study of the life histories of the delinquents. They found that areas with high rates of delinquency were characterised by a decreasing population; a high percentage of 'negro' and 'foreign-born' families; a high percentage of families receiving welfare payments; a low level of home ownership; and low rental values. There were also high rates of adult criminality, infant mortality, mental disorder, tuberculosis and truancy.

Applying the zonal hypothesis to their data, Shaw and McKay found that the habitats of juvenile delinquents were usually more prevalent in inner city areas, that the social problems declined with increasing distance from the city centre, and that this picture remained true over a considerable period of time. As one set of immigrant groups moved into the transitional zone and another set moved away to an outer zone, delinquency rates remained the highest in the transitional zone, but failed to increase in the outer zone into which the former residents of the transitional zone had moved. Although the transitional zone was also economically deprived, Shaw and McKay did not consider this to be the primary factor in the breakdown of the social structure. Instead, they attributed the problems to 'social disorganisation' or, to use an ecological term, disturbance of the 'biotic balance'. This referred to the general instability arising from the constant changing of the population and its heterogeneity, competing forces of different cultures, and of legitimate and illegitimate activities. In contrast, the outer areas of the city were integrated and stable.

'Social disorganisation' is one of the more enduring concepts of the Chicago ecological tradition and was later adopted by Cloward and Ohlin in their analysis of differential opportunities (see Chapter 8). It was based on three variables: poverty, residential mobility, and racial heterogeneity. Poor communities encourage social disorganisation because they do not have adequate resources to deal with their problems. The high level of mobility among the area's residents causes anonymity and no sense of community is thus able to develop. The decline of social control through the absence of common values allows a pattern of delinquent behaviour to develop, which can be handed down from one generation to the next through 'cultural transmission'.

Urban crime, therefore, was portrayed as resulting from the failure of the inner city environment to encourage proper integration and a sense of community for its different cultures. At a practical level, lack of adequate facilities certainly had a part to play in this.

The work of Shaw and McKay in particular remained influential for many years, perhaps as its welfarism was seen by many powerful Americans as an antidote to the growing interest in communism. However, there are several problems with the approach adopted by the Chicago sociologists. The main criticism has been reserved for the ecological metaphor itself. Shaw and McKay did not make so much use of this, but other Chicago authors likened the city to the lungs or digestive system of the body, or transportation routes to the arteries of a living organism. Population movements within a particular area would be compared with the migration of animals and insects. It is interesting to speculate on how much credence the Chicago researchers really gave to social ecology; perhaps they considered that the adoption of a 'scientific' basis for their study would give it greater credibility. WS Robinson (1950) pointed out the so-called 'ecological fallacy': the fact that the economic resources of communities are found to be associated with their crime rates does not automatically mean that the same relationship will be found at an individual level. In addition, the data used by the researchers was based on official police and court statistics, and it is shown in Chapter 3 how unreliable this information can be. Furthermore, the term 'social disorganisa-tion' begs the question of what amounts to social organisation and in whose terms it is defined.

It has also been suggested that the layout of cities does not just 'happen'—nowadays there are many legal and planning restrictions that have to be complied with before a person can move on to land. Even the layout of Chicago was largely planned (Suttles 1972). This was well-illustrated in the study by Terence Morris of criminal areas in Croydon (1957). Morris showed that the Chicago 'concentric zones' theory was inapplicable in Croydon because of the development of council estates on the outer edges of the town which became areas of high delinquency. On the other hand, this could be seen as providing an illustration of what can result from interference in the natural 'ecological' process. The theory as propounded by some writers can be tautologous: crime is viewed as an indicator of social disorganisation, but also as its consequence. Nor was it always accurate to describe the slum areas as 'disorganised'. Participant observation by the Chicago researchers themselves revealed that high levels of organisation were possible, as shown in Thrasher's *The Gang* (1927) and Whyte's *Street Corner Society* (1943). Some critics (for example, Snodgrass 1976) have maintained that the idea of social disorganisation largely ignores the distribution of power in society. As Snodgrass wrote of the Chicago sociologists:

> Instead of turning inward to find the causes of delinquency exclusively in local traditions, families, play groups and gangs, their interpretation might have turned outward to show political, economic and historical forces at work.

Of course, as any devotee of Hollywood is aware, much of the power in Chicago during this period was exercised by gangsters, so perhaps it is not surprising that the Chicago ecologists chose to concentrate on juvenile delinquency (Sumner 1994).

Valier (2003) has argued that the analysis of social disorganisation put forward by the Chicago sociologists can only be applicable to the special circumstances found in the USA during that period. Immigrants were expected to assimilate into American culture in due course, becoming 'nationals' rather than 'foreigners'. Nowadays, this distinction is far from clear-cut. The widespread migration through-out Europe and elsewhere is experienced quite differently—by both the migrants and the societies they enter—than a century ago. Many ethnic groups are increasingly keen to maintain their own identity.

Attempts to replicate Shaw and McKay's research have led to mixed findings. Lander's study in Baltimore (1954), which was based on official statistics, found an association between social disorganisation and delinquency. In a study of Merseyside (Hirschfield and Bowers 1997), which was based on convictions, cautions and calls to the police, it was discovered that disadvantaged areas lacking social cohe-sion experienced significantly higher levels of crime than similarly disadvantaged areas with higher levels of cohesion. However, where measures of self-reported delinquency have been used, the conclu-sions are not so supportive. A study of youth gangs in Chicago by Johnstone (1983) found that, although the opportunity to form a gang was created by the local environment, the decision to do so was primarily affected by social and institutional attachments. This con-clusion was also reached by Fagan *et al.* (1986) who, having inter-viewed violent offenders in four American cities, stated that social and economic conditions could amplify the processes that led to delin-quency. However, most adolescents living in deprived conditions avoided the predictable consequences of becoming involved in such processes.

Evaluation

By the 1960s it seemed that many criminologists had lost interest in the detailed tenets of 'Chicago ecology', which by then appeared to belong to a bygone age and have little relevance to the modern city. Nevertheless, the Chicago School has left distinct and important legacies for criminology. On their journeys between the central busi-ness district and their homes in the suburbs, commuters would have to pass through the zone of transition and could hardly have failed to recognise the overcrowded and decayed nature of the area and the fact that life appeared to be lived largely on the streets. A strong and lasting image of chaos is likely to have been formed in the minds of the middle class, and this could have been the seed which grew into the now common view which almost inexorably links crime and disorder with the inner city.

A further important legacy has been the development of the Chicago School's methodology based on the collection and analysis of empir-ical data. This has proved vital for positivist criminological research and is still widely in use at the present day, as typified by the work of the Home Office's Research and Statistics Directorate. However, the Chicago researchers also engaged in what Matza (1969) called 'appreciative sociology'—a technique which allows people to tell their own stories. This approach is probably more valued now than it was then. In addition, despite the spread of empiricism to other investigations into the aetiology of crime, together with the growth of interest in more abstract criminological theory, a broad-based study of environmental criminology has continued to occupy researchers, and this is now increasingly coming to the attention of policy makers and academics alike.

Chicago continues to be used as a centre for research by environmental criminologists. Bursik and Grasmick (1993) have claimed that research supports Shaw and McKay's account of varying rates of crime in different residential areas. However, Shaw and McKay had failed to consider the relationship between each neighbourhood and the exercise of social control by the agents of wider society. Bursik and Grasmick argued that the solution was to combine the idea of social disorganisation with control theory (see Chapter 12). The resulting 'systemic theory of neighbourhood organisation' suggests that the exercise of social control in particular areas operates at three levels. At the 'primary level' individuals are socialised by family and friends against committing deviant acts. The second 'parochial' level involves the application of control by local groups, such as schools and voluntary organisations. The final 'public level' is provided by agencies from outside the area, either in the form of funding local projects or in the exercise of control through policing. Bursik and Grasmick emphasised that these three levels of control can only operate successfully in neighbourhoods which have acquired a degree of stability. A particular difficulty is that this necessitates a degree of homogeneity within these communities which, particularly nowadays, may be increasingly hard to find (Wilson 1996).

Post-war developments in Britain

The end of World War II heralded the beginning of a massive new housing programme in Britain. It seemed at the time that the Luftwaffe's bombing of major industrial cities might have had some benefits after all in the destruction of the slum housing areas that had often grown up around the targeted industrial areas. A good opportunity was also presented to clear other slum areas. Council-owned housing estates began to appear either on the edge of the 'zone of transition' or further away on the outskirts of the city. Also, throughout the 1950s many new towns were created. Moving the working classes away from what had come to be identified as their 'dangerous' habitat appeared to many to be an excellent piece of social policy. Indeed, for a decade until the late 1950s, relatively little association was made in Britain between criminality and specific areas of towns and cities such as the zone of transition. Of course, crime— and particularly juvenile crime—was still seen as a problem, but attention was now being focused more on 'working-class values' and 'youth culture' as underlying causes. One notable exception to this was Terence Morris's book *The Criminal Area* (1957), referred to above, where the author attempted to apply the Chicago School's zonal hypothesis to Croydon.

However, by the end of the decade certain changes had started to take place which, in due course, were to result in the inner city being viewed as a centre of crime and disorder. In contrast to the previous outwards expansion from the city, a proliferation of high-rise flats began to occur in more central areas. Although it did not take the residents very long to realise that this accommodation, with its lack of amenities and sense of community, was far from satisfactory, it took some time before local authorities and the wider public realised that these areas were associated with an extensive range of social problems (see below). The population of inner city areas increasingly comprised elderly people, who had lived there all their lives and had no wish to move away, and the young who could not afford anything better. In between there was a void created by the absence of established family units.

By the 1960s the young male occupants of inner city high-rise flats were developing their own culture on the streets. The situation was further exacerbated, as an increasing number of these youths were the children of Afro-Caribbean immigrants, who had been encouraged to come to Britain during the 1950s when there was practically full employment to work as unskilled labour in the more menial jobs, such as public transport. However, the supply of work had started to dry up by the 1960s. As ever, it was the 'incomers' who were blamed, and with the addition of a large measure of racial prejudice, a dangerous brew was created. Race riots had already occurred in the Notting Hill area of London in 1958.

The 1970s saw the start of a strong economic recession throughout the world. One consequence of this in Britain was that there was less money for local councils to spend on inner city refurbishment. This grew even worse in the following decade when the Conservative government made further swingeing cutbacks in the funding of local authorities. The consequence was that high-rise blocks that were already inadequate began to crumble, in some cases literally, around their tenants' feet. Under the model of the Chicago sociologists, the zone of transition had been so-called because most of its residents had been merely passing through; their upward social mobility had eventually taken them away from the centre towards the suburbs. This had often been the case in British cities too, but by the 1970s any such mobility had become a pipe dream for many inner city residents, who seemed increasingly trapped in their environment.

The growth of modern environmental criminology

An interest in the relationship between crime and the environment had begun to develop in wider circles during the 1970s. Recorded crime figures had started to increase sharply, the mugging panic was under way (see Chapter 4), and crime was increasingly being attributed to young disaffected males who lived on inner city high-rise estates. In the eyes of many, this was born out by the serious riots which erupted in several inner city areas, such as Brixton, Toxteth and St Paul's, in the early 1980s. At the same time, there was a growing dissatisfaction among both academics and politicians with the frustrating search for 'the cause' of crime within the individual, and a gradual rightwards shift in political opinion (culminating in the election of a Conservative government in 1979) rendered any serious questioning of the fundamental structure and organisation of society off-limits. In addition, the feminist movement's concern with victimisation became allied with the newly-developing 'Left Realism' (see Chapter 11). The result of all this was that far more interest began to be shown in the offence than the offender.

In America, Cohen and Felson (1979) set out an elaborated version of opportunity theory which they called 'routine activities theory'. People satisfy their basic needs through routine activities, such as work, shopping and leisure. Such activities determine where people can be found and what they are doing at any particular time. Crimes against both people and property require the convergence of three factors: a motivated offender, an appropriate target, and the absence of a custodian or guardian. The second and third of these are especially dependent on patterns of routine activities. In this theory, emphasis is placed on the day-to-day activities of both potential victims and those who can naturally offer surveillance, such as neighbours. Changes in social life over a period of years or in different communities can have significant consequences for offending in general. For example, if homes are left unoccupied for lengthier periods than before through changing work patterns, there is likely to be an increase in crimes involving residential properties. Nor is this only applicable to property offences; the routine activities of possible victims of violence in public must be considered. With the decline in public transport, people are more likely to walk alone in dark streets at night and are therefore at greater risk of crime. This leads to avoidance techniques being adopted, particularly by women—either they walk in pairs, or they avoid certain areas of the city. Cohen and Felson were able to show that changes in the patterns of crime in the USA during the 1960s were significantly predictable from changes in routine activities, such as people living alone, the number of working married women, and even the size and weight of consumer items.

The Chicago sociologists had looked at the areas where the delinquents lived and not the localities where their offences took place. Routine activities theory suggested that these were not necessarily the same. Other research has supported this view.

Certain criminal offences tend to be concentrated in particular urban areas. In a study of Sheffield conducted by Baldwin and Bottoms (1976), 24 per cent of offences recorded by the police were committed within a half-mile radius of the city centre. Wikström (1991), also working from official figures, found a similar pattern in Stockholm, particularly in relation to violence, vandalism and car thefts.

Patricia and Paul Brantingham (1981) suggested that, once offenders had decided to commit a crime, its location was likely to be an area which they knew well. This view has been supported by subsequent research findings. Rengert and Wasilchick (2000) interviewed imprisoned burglars in Philadelphia. They were asked to rate each area in their county for familiarity and as a potential burglary site. Not only was there a strong correlation between the two, but neither included the most affluent areas on the edge of the county (nor, indeed, the poorest areas through their lack of target attractiveness). The inmates were also asked to provide details of their daily journeys to work or for recreation. It was discovered that the burglaries they had committed were clustered around these familiar routes. Therefore, just as Cohen and Felson (1979) showed the importance of the routine activities of victims, researchers such as Rengert and Wasilchick have indicated the significance of the routine activities of offenders. In England, Wiles and Costello (2000) also found that most offenders chose to commit crimes in their own neighbourhood, or at least areas with which they were familiar.

In their study of Merseyside, Hirschfield and Bowers (1997) found that the rates of burglary and assault in affluent areas were significantly higher when the areas are adjoined by disadvantaged areas than when they are adjacent to other affluent areas. On the other hand, disadvantaged areas surrounded by affluent areas did not have significantly higher crime rates than disadvantaged areas in general. This provides further support for the opportunity and target attractiveness hypotheses.

Some critics of environmental explanations of crime have argued that offending takes place because of risk factors peculiar to the offender rather than any special characteristics of the locality. However, on the basis of information from the longitudinal Pittsburgh Youth Study, Wikström and Loeber (2000) found that people who did not in other respects appear to be at a high risk of offending would become so if they lived in a run-down area with a substantial amount of public housing.

Effect on social policy—USA

Have any efforts been made to apply these findings to the development of social policy? In their writings Shaw and McKay considered that delinquency and social problems could be reduced through the development of greater social stability within the city. In 1932 Clifford Shaw himself set up twenty-two neighbourhood delinquency crisis intervention centres in six Chicago districts with a view to providing support and fostering a sense of community. Participants in the 'Chicago Area Project' were encouraged to prevent their own delinquency by expressing law-abiding behaviour as a means of achieving status, such as intervening to prevent other youths from breaking the law. To this end, the centres were staffed by local individuals rather than professional social workers. There was an improvement in recreational facilities and general physical appearance within the twenty-two areas. The Project's staff would mediate on behalf of juveniles in trouble and a counselling service was provided.

In the twenty-five years of the Project's existence before Shaw's death no evaluation was made of the effect on juvenile delinquency, although in an assessment fifty years later Schlossman *et al.* (1984) were prepared to attribute some reduction in recorded crime to it. Snodgrass (1976) summarised the Project as designed to impart

American middle-class values to slum residents in the hope that this would reduce the problems that were so common in such areas. Although the Project led to the creation of many community programmes during the 1960s, Walter Miller's evaluation of a similar scheme in Boston in 1962 found no significant reduction in delinquency.

Richard Taub *et al.* (1984) have reported a more recent attempt to provide stability in Chicago. The University, with help from both the government and the private sector, had put large sums of money into its local area in an effort to prevent decay. University employees were provided with low-cost mortgages to stay in the area; private security was provided; extra buses were laid on; and telephones placed at crucial points to promote a feeling of security. As a result the area, which with a 41 per cent black population might have seen a 'white flight', was racially stable and had increasing property values, despite a high crime rate.

The American criminologists James Q Wilson and George Kelling set out their 'broken windows' theory in an article published in 1982. This stated that any signs of disorder—such as broken windows, graffiti or litter—would weaken the informal processes of social control within a community. Residents would be more likely to stay indoors and show little interest in what was happening on the streets. Drug dealers and prostitutes might move into the area, which would start to fall into even greater decay. On the other hand, the prosecution of 'quality of life' crimes would clear the area of such undesirables and send out a clear message that no type of crime would be tolerated. Practical ideas as to how the 'broken windows' can be 'fixed' have been suggested by Kelling and Coles (1996). In a review of American research, Wesley Skogan subsequently found evidence to support this hypothesis (Skogan 1986). Disorder reduced the extent to which the local community could exercise control over its own affairs and crime might increase as a consequence of this. More recently, findings from a longitudinal study in Baltimore conducted by Taylor (2001) have provided further support. However, Taylor pointed out that disorder was not wholly responsible for the changes that occurred, and that other social factors had to be considered as well.

The 'broken windows' argument impressed certain American politicians, particularly the Mayor of New York City, Rudolph Giuliani. His supporters claimed that Giuliani's policy of 'zero tolerance', with its 25 per cent increase in the levels of arrest (and, therefore, fingerprinting), led to the first occasion that New York's annual murder rate fell below 1,000 after 1968, and more than a halving of that rate during the 1990s. Figures released by the NYPD showed that between June 1996 and June 1997 the murder rate fell by 30 per cent from 529 to 371. Assaults, rapes, robberies, burglaries and car thefts declined by 13 per cent in the same period. According to the FBI, New York City was at that time only number 144 in America's top 189 most dangerous cities.

At face value, these are extremely impressive statistics. However, critics have claimed that the fall in crime may have been caused by factors other than the 'zero tolerance' approach. There has been a demographic shift in American population, with a reduction in the number of young males—the group most likely to commit violent crime. Wars between rival drug gangs have been decreasing for some time, with many of the leaders now in prison. Reduction of crime has occurred throughout the USA; there have been dramatic falls in the murder rate in 125 American cities. Changes in policing may be responsible for much of this decline. For example, in New York, local precinct commanders are required to explain the level of crime in their area, and the measures they are taking to deal with it, at weekly strategy meetings with senior officers (Bratton, with Knobler 1998). A further problem is that much of the 'zero tolerance' policing in New York City appears to have involved illegal actions on the part of the police, and as a result the City found itself facing a multi-million dollar civil rights lawsuit (*The New York Times*, 11 January 2001).

Effects on social policy—Britain

The Home Office Research Unit (now called Research and Statistics Directorate) was established in 1957 to undertake a 'scientific' study of crime. In the 1970s, the Unit came under the leadership of Ronald Clarke and began to work on ideas to reduce the opportunity for crime or, as it came to be called, 'situational crime prevention'. This approach sees crime as the outcome of instant decisions and choices, and concentrates on these proximate causes rather than more fundamental sociological or psychological explanations. Situational crime prevention does not apply to 'career criminals', who will create their own opportunities where necessary; but as Hough *et al.* (1980) stated:

> Much crime is best understood as rational action performed by fairly ordinary people acting under particular pressures and exposed to specific opportunities and situational inducements.

Opportunity is a key factor: offending levels can be reduced by taking practical steps to reduce the opportunity for criminal behaviour. Other considerations are also relevant, such as target attractiveness and the level of surveillance. Ekblom and Tilley (2000) thought that the resources available to the offender are particularly important. These comprise resources for avoiding the commission of crime, such as the possession of certain personal skills, as well as the resources needed to commit a crime, such as a willingness to take risks, a knowledge of the appropriate techniques, and the tools for the job.

Early research showed many examples of benefits which were attributed to situational crime prevention. McNees *et al.* (1976) found that, whereas the introduction of signs in a department store stating that shoplifting is a crime led to a modest decrease in theft, identifying frequently stolen items by means of stars and signs almost entirely eliminated it. The level of vandalism at London Underground stations could be reduced by the introduction of closed-circuit television cameras (Burrows 1979). In 1983, Clarke noted that public telephones in the street were more likely to be vandalised than those in pubs and launderettes. A small-scale study discovered a sharp reduction in the number of burglaries recorded after the well-publicised introduction of property marking in three Welsh communities (Laycock 1985). In a review of the findings of eight studies from both the USA and Britain, Farrington and Welsh (2002) found a reduction in crime following the introduction of improved street lighting.

Situational crime prevention has its critics. It is, perhaps, the ultimate consideration of the offence rather than the offender. Tonry (2004) has claimed that it is likely to increase the fear of crime, and Crawford (2000) considered that it 'institutionalises suspicion and mistrust'. The use of anti-social behaviour orders (see Chapter 2), the exclusion of young people from shopping malls, and the enclosure of (usually wealthy) areas are examples of ways in which concern about the risk of crime can be used to widen the divide between the haves and the have-nots. Proponents claim that the approach only relates to 'opportunist' crime but, although most people are presented with the opportunity to commit murder at some point in their life, very few take it. Making the commission of crime more difficult in one setting may only displace it to another. For example, Mayhew *et al.* (1980) discovered that, following a requirement that steering locks be fitted to all new cars in 1971, the theft of older cars increased. However, the researchers considered that displacement was more likely for professional crime than for chance, opportunistic offending. Clarke (1980) pointed to a non-displaced reduction in telephone kiosk vandalism following their redesign. From interviews with burglars, Bennett

(1986) found that their choice of targets was not always based on the criteria suggested in crime prevention and Neighbourhood Watch schemes.

Having interviewed 341 imprisoned commercial robbers, Gill (2000) discovered evidence of several difficulties with standard situational crime prevention measures. The problem of displacement was confirmed; many robbers would simply avoid premises fitted with security devices. In some cases, the use of screens and cameras encouraged robbers to act violently in smashing them up. If cameras were present, robbers would be more likely to cover their faces, which increased fear among staff and customers. Cameras could lull staff into a false sense of security and encourage management to remove safety screens. Gill suggested that screens have also been abandoned as many customers dislike them, and some may even avoid premises adopting what are perceived as heavy-handed and impersonal security devices.

The costs of 'target hardening' can be considerable and do not always relate to the type of street crime that seems to cause the public the most concern (Trasler 1986). In 1999, the government announced it was to spend £170 million on fitting surveillance cameras in urban centres over a three-year period. It has been estimated that Britain contains 10 per cent of the world's CCTV cameras (*The Times*, 30 April 2004). However, research has suggested that such devices do not necessarily reduce violent crime, and may instead drive incidents behind closed doors, particularly into pubs and clubs (Sivarajasingam and Shepherd, 1999). Indeed, such elaborate measures are not necessarily more effective than simple ones. Researchers from South Bank University, London (Sarno 1996), studied the effect of introducing closed-circuit cameras in Sutton. Although crime fell by 13 per cent in the area where the cameras were installed, it fell by 30 per cent throughout the borough as a whole. The researchers concluded that simpler methods such as locking multi-storey car parks at night and providing security staff with pagers had been more effective in reducing the overall crime rate in the area. The installation of CCTV in Glasgow was followed not only by an increase in recorded crime, but also a lack of any increase in feelings of safety among the population (Ditton 2000). A review by the crime reduction charity NACRO of the recent research into the effectiveness of CCTV in reducing crime queried whether its low level of effectiveness justified the vast expense involved (Armitage 2002). Having looked at the provision of CCTV surveillance in six different locations, Goold (2004) concluded that it made little difference to the organisation and practices of the police. In a study of CCTV projects for the Home Office, Gill and Spriggs (2005) found that only two out of thirteen showed a statistically significant reduction in crime when compared with control areas.

The involvement of the community in crime prevention in the form of Neighbourhood Watch schemes has greatly escalated since their introduction in 1983. In recent years the interest in these schemes may not be wholly unrelated to the lower insurance premiums generally available to residents in areas which they cover. However, research on the efficacy of Neighbourhood Watch schemes has been inconclusive. Husain (1988) observed two areas before and after the introduction of Neighbourhood Watch schemes, as well as an adjoining area to see if, as often alleged, there was any displacement of crime from the Neighbourhood Watch areas. Although he did not find displacement, he concluded that there was no overall decline in the level of crime. On the other hand, Pease (1992) found a reduction in burglaries in both the Neighbourhood Watch area and the surrounding area.

Another researcher whose work has been adopted by policy makers is Alice Coleman (1985). Her claims that the design of an area can have an impact on anti-social behaviour found favour with many people, including Margaret Thatcher and the Metropolitan Police Commissioner. Indeed, the £43 million spent on improving the condition of seven housing estates around England after 1988 was largely a consequence of Mrs Thatcher's interest in Alice Coleman's writings. Coleman argued that council estates and high-rise flats are generally characterless and therefore unlikely to encourage the residents to be concerned with the upkeep and appearance of the area. Little, if any, surveillance was provided and there were plenty of easy escape routes. In this respect, Coleman was influenced by Oscar Newman (1972), who had found that, in New York housing estates, crime rates varied in relation to the height and position of buildings. Those which had 'semi-public' entrances or contained thoroughfares that were neither the concern of any particular occupier, nor regularly used were most at risk of crime. Newman suggested that the creation of 'defensible space', over which individuals could exercise some sort of proprietary interest, could help to reduce the opportunities for crime. However, other researchers (Wilson 1980) have found that social factors such as the age and structure of the resident families are also important in determining the level of crime.

Coleman recommended that multi-storey flats should not be built and that, as far as possible, each dwelling or set of dwellings should have its own entrance and garden. Several London boroughs have turned to her for advice, and she has been able to point to some impressive results. The crime rate at the Lisson Green estate was halved following the removal of walkways. At the Lea View estate the crime rate plummeted after many of her suggestions were incorporated. On the other hand, Coleman reported that there was no such reduction at a similar estate where none of her suggestions were implemented.

However, the British evidence has not been wholly supportive, as can be seen from the conclusions of two reports for the Joseph Rowntree Foundation. Osborn and Shaftoe (1995) claimed that many of the advantages initially gained by expensive refurbishment and redesigning of council estates were relatively short-lived and that levels of crime started to pick up again. Power and Tunstall (1997) analysed thirteen riots and violent disturbances which occurred on various housing estates in the early 1990s. Twelve of the estates largely comprised houses with gardens rather than flats, thus emphasising that high-rise blocks are not a necessary requirement for the fermenting of social unrest. Most of the inhabitants were white and the rioters were typically males aged between ten and thirty. Power and Tunstall found that the main problems arose from an unstable family life and poor economic prospects. The existence of empty properties and abandoned land encouraged vandalism and arson among youths with few outlets for constructive leisure activities. There was very little feeling of community among the inhabitants of the estates. In the opinion of the authors, resources had erroneously been concentrated on buildings rather than on creating training and work opportunities. They considered that the provision of local centres to deal with problems would help to reduce tension and foster a feeling of community.

Politicians expressed interest in the dramatic reduction in street crime apparently resulting from Mayor Giuliani's New York campaign, referred to above. In 1995, while in opposition, Jack Straw pledged that a Labour government would 'reclaim the streets from the aggressive begging of winos, addicts and squeegee merchants [an American term for unwelcome washers of car windscreens]'. The Metropolitan Police conducted a six-week experiment of 'zero tolerance' in Kings Cross, London, an area which was notorious for drug-dealing and prostitution. An extra twenty-five officers were deployed on high-profile foot patrols and instructions were given that no law-breaking or threatening situations were to be tolerated. There was an immediate sharp increase in the number of arrests, but this soon fell back to more normal levels. The police claimed that the crime rate dropped significantly during this period and that there was no evidence of displacement on to adjacent neighbourhoods (*The Independent*,

8 January 1997). However, 'zero tolerance' policing has also experienced problems in Britain. Its adoption in Middlesbrough was described in a report by a Treasury barrister as '[having] brought few if any rewards in the number of crimes detected, the amount of stolen property recovered or the number of suspects prosecuted' (*The Guardian*, 23 June 2000).

Conclusion

How important is the environmental aspect of criminology? The main criticisms levelled at the work of the Chicago sociologists have been considered above. Even at the time, doubts were expressed about such notions as the zonal hypothesis and, although there has been some support, most subsequent researchers have been unable to replicate their findings. In England, writers such as Morris (1957) and Rex and Moore (1967) have shown that there is little that is 'natural' in the development of housing, and that a combination of local government policies and class considerations has been more influential. On the other hand, the idea that deprivation and crime can remain linked to a particular area has received recent support from a study by Dorling *et al.* (2001), which revealed that the spacial patterns of social deprivation in London have changed little since Charles Booth's survey at the turn of the nineteenth century.

Indeed, so much has changed in Western society that, at times, the picture of urban life painted by the Chicago sociologists looks barely recognisable, notwithstanding the decay and poverty that can still be found in cities. To a large extent the urban–rural divide has broken down, with extensive modern out-of-town business parks and retail developments reflecting a shift of population from the cities into the countryside. One important consequence of this has been the breakdown of local communities—whether urban or rural—and the institutions which they fostered, such as the church. The growth in car ownership, which increased in Britain by 50 per cent between 1976 and 1996, means that it is not only the perpetrators of organised crime who can quickly move their ill-gotten gains over a considerable distance. Even traditional physical demarcations within the city have broken down. Computer technology, now available to the moderately poor, has opened up a whole new world of communication: as Jock Young (2003) has pointed out, 'virtual communities set up by the mass media easily transcend physical demarcations'. Although America experienced a higher level of immigration in the 1990s than in the first three decades of the twentieth century, these new arrivals will have found a very different life to that which they would have faced in the days of Shaw and McKay.

However, in a wider respect, the writings of the Chicago sociologists have been extremely influential. They provided the first significant break with the pathological approach which had hitherto been the mainstay of criminological study. Theirs was the first systematic sociological approach to crime. Their key reliance on empiricism, although subsequently derided, is still much in evidence today. The Chicago School was also significant in that it saw the beginning of a viewpoint which has continued to the present day, whereby crime and disorder are associated with particular localities.

What of their successors? As there has been a declining interest in the aetiology of crime, and governments have become more concerned about crime prevention, the environmental aspect has returned to the forefront of attention and research has led to some clear benefits. Both official statistics and victim studies make it clear that certain types of crime are far more prevalent in urban than in rural areas. Yet, this finding raises more questions than it answers. Does it necessarily follow that this imbalance is explicable by characteristics of the area rather than characteristics of people who live in the area? What about other crimes, such as fraud and sexual abuse, which are now clearly recognised to be at least equally as common in more affluent areas? Environmental criminology as a positivist approach is open to the charge of being deterministic in that individual choice and free will are considered to be far less relevant than the dominant impact of structural and areal forces. Newman's work on 'defensible space' has been criticised for largely ignoring social factors and he himself has conceded that the evidence does not always support his claims (Reppetto 1974).

Finally, it has been suggested that the interface between crime and the environment as it has been traditionally understood is problematic. Anthony Giddens (1989) claimed that it is impossible to study the modern city without considering the transformation in society brought about by the development of capitalism. Previously, the main division between urban and rural areas was in the density of dwellings; most people still worked on the land. Capitalism, however, made all aspects of life into saleable commodities: not only the workers' time and the products of their toil, but also the space in which they live and work. Therefore, rather than simply concentrate on the physical characteristics of a particular area, the urban sociologist or criminologist should consider the occupation of space in routine social practices over a period of time. Matters such as housing policy and budgetary conflicts between local and central government thus take on a role of crucial importance.

Postscript: differential association — the interactionist link

By the 1940s the writings of the first wave of Chicago sociologists were starting to decrease and, in any event, had already been subjected to some of the criticisms outlined above, not least of which was that they seemed excessively deterministic. Whereas the work of earlier writers such as Park and Burgess had concentrated on the effects of competition and succession in socially disorganised areas, the later Chicago researchers shifted the emphasis from culture conflict to consideration of the wider social structure. In 1938, the book *Brothers in Crime*, written by a leading member of the Chicago School, Clifford Shaw, noted that, because parents and neighbours tend to show approval of unlawful behaviour, many delinquents grow up in a world where delinquency is considered an accepted form of conduct. The following year a more developed version of this thesis appeared in Edwin Sutherland's book *Principles of Criminology*. It was called differential association.

Sutherland, himself a former professor at the University of Chicago, had first put forward an outline of his theory in 1924, although it was only fully elaborated in his 1939 book. Differential association claims to show how delinquent practices came to be 'culturally transmitted' (to use Shaw and McKay's term) from one individual to another, and that coming into contact with delinquents is a necessary but not sufficient condition of becoming delinquent oneself. Apart from his Chicago background, Sutherland was also clearly influenced by the book *The Laws of Imitation* (1890) written by a French social psychologist, Gabriel Tarde. At a time when the writings of Lombroso were enjoying popularity (see Chapter 14), Tarde argued that criminal behaviour is learned from environmental influences rather than being inherited. He formulated three laws of imitation: human beings imitate each other in proportion to the extent to which they live in close contact; generally, the inferior person imitates the superior person; and when two mutually exclusive 'fashions' occur simultaneously, one will come to replace the other. Tarde offered the replacement of knives by firearms in violent crime as an example of the third law.

The idea of differential association was developed by Sutherland largely in conjunction with his writing on white-collar crime. In many respects, differential association is a learning theory (see Chapter 16), but it is considered here as it provided an important bridge between the essentially positivistic Chicago School and the growing influence of writers from symbolic interactionist and subcultural perspectives.

The theory was set out in a list of numbered propositions. Criminal behaviour is learned in interaction with others especially in 'intimate personal settings' (that is, not through reading or watching films; television was not available when the theory was first propounded). All the social and psychological mechanisms which apply to learning in general apply here. In this respect, Sutherland was also influenced by the symbolic interactionist theories of George Herbert Mead, who was at the University of Chicago when Sutherland was a doctoral student there (see Chapter 9). The learning includes not only techniques of committing crime, but the direction of drives, motives, attitudes and definitions of the law.

The key statement of differential association is that a person who is exposed to 'an excess of definitions favourable to violation of the law over definitions unfavourable to violation of the law' is likely to become a criminal. The likelihood is determined by variations in the frequency, duration, priority and intensity of the associations. For example, police officers do not generally turn to crime because their associations with law-abiding individuals are far more numerous and stronger than their frequent dealings with criminals. 'Priority' suggests that associations made in early childhood are likely to have a greater impact than those created in later life. Sutherland was prepared to accept that there are differences in individual disposition to criminality, but maintained that these were only relevant in that they might affect the chances of a person's exposure to different associations. An individual cannot inherit a propensity to criminal behaviour as, in accordance with the tenets of Mead's symbolic interactionism, human behaviour only has meaning in a particular cultural setting. The theory also claims that, while crime is an expression of needs and values, it cannot be explained by those needs and values. The desire for a high income may be widespread: some people work hard to try to attain it, whereas others steal.

Unlike Shaw and McKay, who had confined their attentions to the delinquency of slum dwellers, Sutherland and his colleagues applied their theory to several areas, including his own notion of white-collar crime and professional crime. Sutherland claimed that individuals became white-collar criminals because of their absorbtion in a business process which considers illegal practices as acceptable. In 1949, he wrote:

> The data which are at hand suggests that white-collar crime has its gen-
> esis in the same general processes as other criminal behavior, namely,
> differential association . . . Businessmen are not only in contact with def-
> initions which are favorable to white-collar crime but they are also isol-
> ated from and protected against definitions which are unfavorable to
> such crime.

Furthermore, people who criticise the world of business usually carry little weight and, as Sutherland pointed out, may be dismissed as communists or socialists.

The main strength of the theory of differential association at the time of its exposition was that it showed that crime was not just a product of poverty, but could occur in the most routine settings, ranging from the Chicago slum to the largest business operation. The earlier Chicago School explanations had tended to concentrate on juvenile delinquency and had portrayed the world of the criminal as inevitably discrete and set aside from mainstream culture.

In the first two versions of the theory in 1924 and 1939, Sutherland wrote that culture conflict was an underlying cause of differential association and, therefore, criminal behaviour. This reflected his opinion that various groups in society differed in their views as to what constituted appropriate behaviour, and that culture conflict was the clearest indicator of the social disorganisation within society. However, this reference to conflict was omitted from later versions of the theory, and in his writings on white-collar crime Sutherland offered no fundamental criticism of the American capitalist system. (For a consideration of conflict theory, see Chapter 10.)

Evaluation of differential association

Some critics have argued that the theory of differential association is difficult to test empirically; indeed, Sutherland's collaborator, Cressey, conceded this in 1960. Nevertheless, other researchers have tried. Their findings have been mixed.

Reiss and Rhodes (1964) concluded that, although boys generally chose friends with a similar involvement in delinquency to themselves, working-class youths did so far more frequently than middle-class youths, who were more likely to make associations with less serious offenders. However, Reiss and Rhodes could not show that the delinquents learned the specific techniques of committing crimes as a result of relationships with friends. This finding was later supported by Farrington (1982) in the Cambridge Study in Delinquent Development (see Chapter 3). In formulating his control theory (see Chapter 12), Hirschi (1969) discovered from his research that, although boys with little commitment to conventional society generally had delinquent friends, there was no evidence that they were influenced by them.

On the other hand, Clinard and Abbott (1973) found support for differential association in several developing countries. Tittle *et al.* (1986) claimed that the theory does not require the imitation of particular techniques or the learning of criminal attitudes: rather, differential associations are formed by the learning of motivations to engage in crime.

Combining the theory with Becker's (1963) writing on marijuana, Orcutt (1987) attempted to predict the use of the drug among college students. They were asked to estimate how many of their four closest friends smoked marijuana at least once a month. Orcutt found that students with negative views of marijuana usage usually avoided the drug even if their friends used it. Those with positive views about marijuana were likely to smoke it themselves if at least one of their four closest friends did so. Among the students with a neutral attitude towards marijuana usage, students almost never smoked the drug if none of their closest friends did so. However, one in four of this group used the drug if one of their friends did, and this rose to one in two where two or more friends were users. Orcutt considered that this finding was broadly in line with exposure to an excess of definitions favourable to breaking the law (that is, smoking marijuana).

In defining their concept of a 'subculture of violence', Wolfgang and Ferracuti (1967) have also utilised the idea of differential association. They claimed that, in the poor neighbourhoods where such subcultures can be found, people learn favourable attitudes towards violence through 'a process of differential learning, association or identification'. Consequently, violence is not necessarily considered as unlawful behaviour and many apparently trivial acts are met with a violent response. The individuals who perpetrate these attacks may not experience any feelings of guilt.

Recent years have seen a revival of interest in the theory and the research findings have been generally supportive of it. McCarthy (1996) found clear evidence of what he termed 'tutelage' in methods of criminality among homeless youths in Toronto. Using data from a longitudinal study, Haynie (2002) discovered that the proportion of delinquent friends in a person's network had a strong positive effect on the person's subsequent delinquency—indeed, stronger than the absolute level of the friends' delinquency. Hochstetler *et al.* (2002) found that the attitudes and behaviour of friends were significant factors in a person's offending, irrespective of the person's own attitudes, or whether the friends were present when the offence occurred.

Attempts have been made to reformulate differential association in terms of psychological concepts of learning (see Chapter 16). Daniel Glaser (1956) set out a variation of learning theory called 'differential identification'. This claimed that the degree of identity with a person (either real or fictional) is the vital element in determining whether that person's behaviour patterns are learned. For example, a well-known footballer may be a much stronger influence than an individual whom the learner meets every day. Ronald L Akers (1973) has integrated the theory with operant conditioning and imitation. He considered that Sutherland's 'intimate personal groups' provide an individual's major source of reinforcement. 'Definitions' are the meanings given to behaviour which may be directly reinforced. Such positive reinforcement either defines deviant behaviour as permissible, or serves to neutralise 'definitions unfavourable to law violation' by negatively reinforcing pronouncements that are avoiding others' disapproval. Deviance, therefore, is seen as a result not of an excess of definitions favouring deviance, but of differential positive reinforcement of one set of values over another.

Akers *et al.* (1979) tested this theory in relation to adolescent self-reported drug and alcohol use. They found that a large part of the variation in the use of these substances could be accounted for by differential reinforcement. A stronger test was carried out by Andrews (1980). He conducted a series of experimental studies in prisons and among probation officers, which examined the effects of exposure to criminal and anti-criminal patterns and the effect of intimate personal groups on criminal attitudes and behaviour. It was shown that anti-criminal learning by prisoners could be linked to differential exposure to criminal and anti-criminal patterns which had been organised within a group counselling programme. In addition, re-offending rates and changes in attitude on the part of probationers could be related to the skills of the probation officers.

The theory of differential association was initially very popular. However, one of its biggest drawbacks is that it was the culmination of Sutherland's search for a single-factor, all-embracing sociological explanation of crime. Sutherland was strongly opposed to the psychological explanations that were prevalent in his day (Gaylord and Galliher 1988). Strictly speaking, differential association cannot explain the origins of criminal behaviour: if it did not exist beforehand it could not be learned by anyone else. Nor is the theory of general application. For example, it cannot properly explain crimes of passion, many sexual offences, or the not uncommon phenomenon of the loner—the solitary offender who never mixes with other people. There is also the 'chicken and egg' problem: delinquent associations may be the result rather than the cause of criminal behaviour (Tittle *et al.* 1986). Although it is set out in a series of linked propositions, the theory has an inherent vagueness: for instance, there is no detailed explanation as to how learning takes place. This was the issue that was confronted by writers such as Glaser and Akers, and it may be that their development of the theory has provided it with a greater coherence.

7

Poverty, anomie and strain

Because a large number of the crimes recorded in official statistics were committed by people who do not have much money, there is a common and understandable belief that poverty can be a significant factor underlying offending. In this chapter, consideration will first be given to the research evidence connecting crime with poverty and unemployment. Thereafter, a wider view will be taken of the ways in which the structuring of society can create pressures on individuals to break the law.

Crime and poverty

From the earliest times people have sought to equate crime with poverty. If this belief is correct, there should be more crime in areas where more poor people live and at times when overall levels of poverty are higher. It was not until the development of national crime statistics in the nineteenth century that any evaluation could be made of this widely-held view. The first proper analysis of the level of crime in Europe was carried out on the 1827 French statistics by Guerry (see Chapter 6). He discovered that the richest part of France had a higher rate of offences against property, but only about half the amount of violent crime. Nevertheless, there were poor people living in the wealthy areas, and Guerry concluded that poverty in itself did not cause property crime, but that the greater wealth simply provided more opportunity to steal. At about the same time, the Belgian Adolphe Quetelet was making a detailed study of crime in France, Belgium and Holland. He also considered that opportunity could be relevant in explaining the higher crime levels in wealthy cities, and pointed out that the considerable inequalities between rich and poor in the same area could serve to increase temptation. In contrast, the regions that were generally poor had relatively little crime, as long as the inhabitants had enough to live on.

In more recent years similar attempts have been made to assess whether areas with greater numbers of poor people experience higher levels of crime. The results have been varied. Ehrlich (1974) discovered a positive correlation between the rates of property crimes and the percentage of homes receiving half the average income in American states for 1940, 1950 and 1960. However, Jacobs (1981) could find no connection between levels of burglary, robbery and theft, and people living below the poverty line. There is stronger evidence of a relationship between crime and 'structural poverty', which is an assessment based on income, one-parent families, poor education and high infant mortality rates (Messner 1983).

Crime and unemployment

Unemployment is sometimes considered to be a gauge of economic conditions, as it generally increases in times of depression and declines during boom periods. There is certainly a feeling among the public that unemployment and crime are related. In a MORI/Readers Digest opinion poll conducted in January 1994, 71 per cent of those surveyed considered that unemployment was a major cause of crime. However, on closer investigation the situation is not so straightforward.

The underlying assumption that unemployment levels can more or less be equated with the experience of poverty is questionable. There is no standard definition of poverty in Britain, and it is likely that there are people who would generally be classed as poor who are in employment, and that there are many unemployed people whom no-one would consider to be poor. Moreover, unemployment is experienced in different ways by different individuals (Lea and Young 1993). Most of the research in this area has involved comparing aggregate unemployment levels, either national or regional, with official crime statistics. This immediately raises major methodological problems. The unemployment rate shares many of the drawbacks of the official crime rate. Both are reflections of counting practices which happen to have been adopted at a particular time.

Indeed, the Conservative government in the 1980s was frequently under attack from the opposition parties for making changes to the methods of calculating the unemployment level. The present system excludes people under eighteen, many single parents, and anyone working for at least sixteen hours a week. Both can be affected by legislation: the Social Security Act 1986 effectively removed the status of unemployed from those under eighteen. In short, both provide considerable underestimates of the true position.

It is also dangerous to assume that because both unemployment and crime levels are high the two are necessarily linked. This mistake could be made because of the assumption that it *makes sense* for them to be connected—a fact born out by the 1994 opinion poll. Both have increased significantly during the past twenty-five years, but so have many other social phenomena that no-one would think of linking to crime (Tarling 1982). It must also be remembered that unemployment is often associated with other factors frequently related to offending such as age, educational attainment and class.

Nevertheless, many studies have sought to reach conclusions by connecting aggregate unemployment levels and crime. Glaser and Rice (1959) discovered that, during periods of high unemployment, recorded levels of crime increased for adult crime and decreased for juvenile delinquency. They speculated that this latter finding might result from parents' being able to spend more time with their children. Other research has indicated a connection between unemployment and juvenile delinquency as well, especially as job prospects for young adults are likely to be bleak during such periods (Calvin 1981). It may be, as Steven Box (1987) suggested, that this relationship appears stronger than it really is because unemployed juveniles are more likely to be arrested by the police. However, in reviews of the evidence, neither Box himself nor Tarling in an earlier study (1982) could find a consistent connection between crime and unemployment. Box went on to submit that the *belief* that unemployment causes crime could itself be responsible for an increase in recorded offending. If the public expect a rise in crime, this could generate more fear which could then result in more crime being reported and the police using greater surveillance.

More recent research has reached differing conclusions. Dickinson (1993) found a correlation between the unemployment rates of young males and domestic burglary committed by the same age group. Yet, in an analysis of increased rates of unemployment and recorded crime at police force level, Orme (1994) was unable to find a significant relationship between the two. In a study of regional conviction rates for five theft-related offences in England and Wales between 1979 and 1993, Witt *et al.* (1998) discovered that an areal growth in unemployment was positively correlated with four of the five crimes. The relationship was strongest for long-term unemployment: between 1983 and 1993 a 1 per cent rise in that rate resulted in an increase in recorded crime of between 5 per cent and 10 per cent.

There was little relationship with the short-term unemployment rate, which suggests that the duration of unemployment is a significant factor in the level of crime.

It has been suggested that specific alterations to government policy impacting on economic incentives have had a direct influence on the levels of crime. Machin and Marie (2004) looked at this question in relation to the introduction of the Jobseekers Allowance in the UK in October 1996. The resulting changes included a reduction in the length of contribution-based unemployment insurance from twelve to six months and a 20 per cent lower benefit rate for claimants aged under twenty-five. Machin and Marie discovered a higher increase in crime rates in areas where more people were affected by this policy change. These were also the areas where people were most likely to drop off the unemployment register without entering work, education or training, or claiming other benefits. Hansen and Machin (2002) studied the recorded levels of four different types of crime both before and after the introduction of the minimum wage in the UK in April 1999. Their hypothesis was that increased pay might have an impact on those who were on the borderline of legitimate work and illegitimate activities. The researchers found relative crime reductions in areas of the country where a greater proportion of workers had benefited from the introduction of the minimum wage.

A more accurate way to look for a connection between unemployment and crime would be to consider offenders on an individual basis. However, very few studies of this type have been attempted. There are several variables that could influence both crime and unemployment and it would be important to create a properly matched control group. Alternatively, the same individuals could be monitored in a longitudinal study. This method was used in the Cambridge Study in Delinquent Development (see Chapter 3). Farrington *et al.* (1986) studied differences in their subjects' offending during periods of employment and unemployment. They found that the commission of property offences—whether self-reported or officially recorded—was more likely during periods of unemployment.

Economic inequality

It is necessary at this stage to distinguish between poverty and economic inequality. Poverty is defined in different ways by different organisations but, broadly, it relates to the deficiency of material items that are necessary for a minimum level of existence. Economic inequality, on the other hand, involves a comparison of the levels of material possessions between different groups in a society. There are countries where there is relatively little poverty, but enormous inequalities of wealth. Conversely, there are very poor countries where there is little inequality of wealth. An analysis by the Institute of Fiscal Studies (Goodman *et al.* 1997) showed that the UK had become 'massively' more unequal than it had been just twenty years earlier. The income of the bottom 5 per cent of earners hardly changed between 1983 and 1993, whereas the income of the top 5 per cent of earners increased by nearly a half. The combined income of the top 10 per cent of earners was equal to that of the lower half of all earners. A study of the 2001 Census data has shown that the gap between rich and poor is continuing to widen (Dorling and Thomas 2004).

The question, therefore, arises as to whether there is a correlation between inequality of income and levels of crime. Stack (1984) argued that, as the gap between rich and poor grows, increasing crime is likely, especially by those who consider that existing political structures will not improve their position. According to this theory, a general increase in the standard of living, which has occurred in most Western societies during this century, would not deal with this problem; it is a person's relative position to others which is significant. Box (1987) considered that this explanation accounts for increasing crime rates in periods of recession, especially among the young, women and members of ethnic minorities, who feel that their chances of closing the wealth gap are particularly poor at such a time. He assessed sixteen studies on crime and economic inequality which had been conducted between 1974 and 1985. Eleven of the studies showed a correlation between economic inequality and crime. In the study conducted by Witt *et al.* (1998), three of the theft-related offences were positively correlated with an increase in earnings inequality.

John Hagan (1994) has sought to analyse the impact of inequality on crime in America by what he calls 'a new sociology of crime and disrepute'. Since the late 1970s, socially and economically disadvantaged communities have been deprived of capital resources. In the past, members of such communities had still been able to attain a measure of upward social mobility. If this failed, they could always fall back on the underground economy, involving activities such as vice and racketeering. Nowadays, however, the general economic climate and the run-down state of America's cities makes this extremely difficult. The underground economy has become much more competitive and serious violence has taken over the world of drugs and vice. Meanwhile, at the opposite end of the social and economic scale, the massive diversion of investment to the business world and the better-off has created the opportunity for such people to take advantage of the poor by both disreputable and illegal means.

Conclusion

There are problems underlying the view that crime may be directly linked with absolute poverty. Apart from the obvious point that many poor people throughout the world would rather go hungry than steal, the research evidence does not provide much support for such a connection. Moreover, according to Spicker (2002), the view that poverty in Britain is a continuing condition found in a particular group is erroneous; it is usually temporary and most people are subject to it at some time in their life. It is also now widely recognised that a great deal of acquisitive crime is committed by wealthy, white-collar offenders (see Chapter 2). A stronger link appears to exist between crime and unemployment. However, there is significant support for a relationship between crime and economic inequality. This should not come as a surprise: Quetelet and Guerry arrived at a similar conclusion over 150 years ago. What needs to be considered further is whether the connection is purely a result of attempts to reduce the gap in wealth, or whether such disparities cause a disruption to the social order and lead to certain individuals suffering from some form of strain.

Functionalism and anomie

For a twenty-year period leading up to the 1960s, when it came under attack from more radical theorists, functionalism was generally accepted as a major item in sociological discourse. The essence of functionalism is that there is a consensus of core values within a society which corresponds to the needs of its members, and it is the task of institutions such as the family and the school to socialise individuals to conform to those values. The concern of sociologists is seen as the study of why some people violate these commonly-held values. Society is viewed as a functioning entity comprising many parts, each of which interrelates with and supports the others. As crime is a part of society, it therefore becomes conceivable that crime and deviance could also serve a function.

(a) Emile Durkheim

The writer who is primarily associated with this last proposition is the French sociologist Emile Durkheim (1858–1917). Durkheim wrote at a time of considerable social change, not only in France but throughout the whole Western world. It was now becoming acceptable to challenge previously-held assumptions: what had formerly been accepted as right suddenly became questionable. This applied to most spheres of life, including religion. Durkheim did not denigrate religion as Marx had done, but considered that all such influences were subservient to the collective sentiment or soul of a society. Cesare Lombroso (see Chapters 5 and 14) had rejected the classical notion of free will in favour of a determinism based on individual pathology. Writing some twenty years after Lombroso, Durkheim suggested a different form of determinism. The focus of his studies was on how the organisation of society can drive people towards breaking its rules.

Durkheim considered that the fundamental problem facing Western society was the rise of the cult of the individual. This came at the expense of a people's attachment to society and the development of social solidarity. The situation was exacerbated by the decline in the power of religion and the growth of industrial capitalism. The collective sentiment of society was becoming secular and individualistic, and the values that were now necessary for a stable society—such as individual dignity and social justice—were at odds with the values of obedience and discipline which were required by capitalist enterprise. Industry, rather than being a means to an end, had become the end in itself. Durkheim, however, considered that it was the role of government to regulate the affairs of the state in such a way that wealth creation and social stability could be maintained without compromising the integrity of the individual.

Although many of Durkheim's views on crime can be found in his work on suicide, they have subsequently been adopted by criminologists as being of more general application. Durkheim thought that some crime is normal in society and, furthermore, that it would be impossible to imagine a society without crime. What makes a society, as opposed to a group of individuals, is a sharing of basic values, which in turn necessitates rules to encourage compliance with these values. However, it is inconceivable that everyone will subscribe to the rules and so dissensus is inevitable. Rule-breaking will result and some of this will infringe the criminal law. A society without crime is a utopian fantasy:

> Imagine a society of saints, a perfect cloister of exemplary individuals. Crimes, properly so called, will there be unknown; but faults which appear venial to the layman will create there the same scandal that the ordinary offence does in ordinary consciousnesses.

The term 'anomie', which is derived from the Greek *a-nomos* and means 'lawless', was used by Durkheim in two different senses. In his doctoral thesis, published as *The Division of Labour in Society* (1893), Durkheim stated that anomie resulted in the transition from early 'mechanical' or pre-industrial societies to industrial 'organic' societies. Mechanical societies were groupings where the members followed the same customs and religion and tended to their own needs. There was little division of labour outside the family unit and the similarity among the members encouraged group cohesion. In contrast, industrialised organic societies are more heterogeneous in terms of wealth, religious beliefs and ethnicity, and have a highly developed division of labour involving more elaborate and specialised forms of work.

Each type of society is characterised by a particular form of collective consciousness. This refers to the set of beliefs which is common to the whole society and acts as a powerful force in shaping the way it behaves. In a society largely based on mechanical solidarity, this takes the form of strict conformity and uniformity of culture. On the other hand, in an organic society the members are associated through structural interdependence rather than shared life experiences. Durkheim considered that all societies are at some stage between being mechanical or organic; no society is entirely one or the other. Primitive societies have some form of division of labour and industrialised societies require a degree of uniformity among their members.

For Durkheim, crime in mechanical states is functional to society in three important respects. As deviant behaviour can lead to exclusion from the group, individual members are obliged to abandon their own interests to maintain group solidarity. This also makes the identification of offenders relatively simple. The second function of crime is to reaffirm the group's collectivity through the punishment of criminals. Punishment is not about deterrence, rehabilitation or retribution; its sole aim is to reinforce social solidarity. Through the punishment of offenders, not only are society's moral boundaries set out, but allegiance to them by the rest of society is strengthened. Just as a young child can be seen proudly to proclaim its own obedience when a sibling or friend is rebuked, adults gain an enhanced moral commitment on hearing of the wrongdoings of others.

The third function of crime is the constant testing of the boundaries of tolerance; this will lead to a continuing evaluation of society's norms. Crime can, therefore, play a positive role in social change. Durkheim referred in this respect to Socrates, who was condemned as a criminal by the Athenians. Other examples of 'deviants', such as Jesus Christ, Mahatma Gandhi and Martin Luther King, could be cited. In Kai Erikson's book *Wayward Puritans* (1966), which analysed the Salem witchcraft trials in Massachusetts, the public trial and expulsion of a dissident group who had refused to follow the elders in an early puritan sect is analysed as being functionally necessary to maintain the unity of the group. As Erikson stated:

> ... when these people come together to express their outrage over the offense and to bear witness against the offender, they develop a tighter bond of solidarity than existed earlier.

This last function may at first sight appear to be incompatible with the second. Does deviance help to promote social stability through the punishment of offenders, or does it prepare the way for social change through the testing of society's boundaries? The view of Ben-Yehuda (1985) on this 'double bind' is that it can do either, but whichever consequence results will depend on the sort of deviant behaviour involved and the type of society it occurs in.

Although the division of labour in a mechanical society will be minimal on account of its rudimentary nature, in an organic society the industrial growth is likely to happen so quickly that abnormal divisions of labour can result. The legal structure of society will then be unable to control dealings between the various social groups. This abnormal division of labour can take three forms: the coincidence of a financial crisis and industrial unrest; the 'forced' division of labour which prevents workers taking up jobs commensurate with their abilities; and the alienation of workers from each other and their jobs. The last of these forms was referred to by Durkheim as 'anomic'. In a reversal of the views of Marx, class conflict and industrial turmoil were seen as symptoms and not causes of anomie. Such disruption can clearly lead to criminal behaviour, which will no longer be functional to the existence of society.

Durkheim's second usage of the term anomie—and the one which has gained more attention—was in his book *Suicide* (1897). This was based on a study of French suicide statistics from the mid-nineteenth century. Sociology was still a very young academic discipline, and Durkheim, in a search for credibility, perhaps felt that it would be better to base his analysis on the official reports of a commonly-known phenomenon. (His own brother had also committed suicide.)

Durkheim distinguished four different types of suicide, which he claimed are causally related to the strength of social integration and social regulation in a society. Broadly speaking, Durkheim related excessive strength to 'mechanical' societies and excessive weakness to 'organic' societies. 'Altruistic' suicides result where the individual is over-integrated into the group and thus lacks a separate identity. Japanese 'kamikaze' pilots in World War II and Muslims prepared to sacrifice themselves in a 'holy war' provide examples of this category. 'Fatalistic' suicides occur where there is excessive social regulation, but Durkheim only referred to these in a footnote as he considered them rare in modern societies. Slavery was given as an example and perhaps the long prison sentences that are more common nowadays sometimes result in this type of suicide. 'Egoistic' suicides result from excessive individualism, where individuals lack the support of family, workmates or the community. Durkheim illustrated this by claiming a higher suicide rate among Protestants than Catholics (Protestantism is arguably the less integrating of its members) and among unmarried than married mothers. However, he claimed there is a reduction in this type of suicide during times of political crisis:

> Great social disturbances and great popular wars rouse collective senti-
> ments, stimulate partisan spirit and patriotism and . . . at least temporarily
> cause a stronger integration of society.

Durkheim claimed to have found evidence of this in a declining suicide rate during the great social upheavals in France in 1830, 1848 and 1870.

The final category of suicide is termed 'anomic'. These suicides result from the disturbances caused by major changes in economic conditions resulting in a weakening of the forces of regulation in everyday life (which is in itself an almost inevitable consequence of an organic society). It is important to note that rapidly enhanced economic prospects are just as likely to increase the suicide rate as rapidly diminishing ones. Durkheim found the lowest suicide rates in some of the poorest areas of Europe. Sudden economic upheaval can reduce the degree of societal regulation which normally settles the limits of individual aspiration and, as individuals lack adequate internal self-restraint mechanisms, a state of anomie or normlessness will result. Indeed, anomic suicides could result from any major upheaval: Durkheim also found higher suicide rates during wars and revolutions. Nothing is any longer considered impossible, and excessive (that is, no longer 'normal') levels of not only suicide but also crime will result.

Durkheim did not subscribe to the Marxist theories which were becoming popular at the time. He considered that societies' problems were not simply a question of class or reducing the wealth of some in order to redistribute it to others. What is necessary is to recreate what Durkheim referred to as the 'moral constitution' of society.

There have been many criticisms of Durkheim's views. Official statistics must be treated with a great deal of caution, and it is hardly surprising that a nineteenth century compilation of figures for such a difficult phenomenon as suicide has given rise to considerable scepticism. As Atkinson (1978) noted, the process of categorising a death as a suicide cannot be an objective one, but depends instead on coroners' applying their common sense ideas of suicide to the information presented to them. Moreover, Durkheim assumed that all crime rates would fluctuate in the same way as the suicide rates on which he based his analysis. However, McDonald (1982) has claimed that crime rates in general did not increase in France during the periods of upheaval identified by Durkheim. Indeed, there is more than a mere suggestion that Durkheim was prepared to make 'the facts' (which, in the form of official statistics, to him were an absolute given) fit the theory. Douglas (1967) highlighted this in relation to Durkheim's explanation of the differential suicide rates of Catholics and Protestants, and McDonald asserted that crime rates were available to Durkheim and other researchers of the day, but they chose to ignore them.

In relation to the functional value of crime, it has also been argued (Roshier 1977) that it is the functional aspect of the ideas that is important and not the fact that they happened to be promoted by crime. For example, in the case of Socrates, it was not the fact that he was adjudged a criminal that made his ideas so important. Prostitution, which often involves the commission of a crime, can be seen as functional to society (Davis 1937), but this does not arise from its criminal status.

Nevertheless, Durkheim, who taught the first sociology course at a French university, remains a pivotal figure in sociology and criminology. He realised that crime is a contemporary social construct rather than a set of universal values or the reflection of some intrinsic evil. This theme was not popularised by criminologists until almost seventy years later in labelling theory. Durkheim appreciated that deviants and criminals can, in fact, be in the vanguard of social reform. He saw the contradiction between the constant search for profit and the need to control morality within a society. He appreciated the importance of scientific analysis and research, and the shortcomings in his own methodology were probably not sufficiently extensive to detract significantly from his own theories.

Perhaps Durkheim's most important contribution to the development of criminology was that he successfully challenged the prevailing orthodoxy of individual pathology, as found in the writings of his contemporary, Lombroso. As Taylor *et al.* (1973) put it, Durkheim made the crucial break with 'analytical individualism'. Instead, he established a fully sociological explanation of crime, which was to be taken up in the USA, at first by the Chicago School (see Chapter 6) and then by Robert Merton.

(b) Merton, anomie and strain

The American sociologist Robert Merton adopted the broad concept of anomie and used it not to develop Durkheim's writings, but as a means of new theorising. Merton first presented his theory, which was partly based on empirical research, in an essay 'Social Structure and Anomie' in 1938. This was the year that saw Sutherland's theory of differential association and the play *Brothers in Crime* by George Bernard Shaw, which pointed out the similarities between delinquents and non-delinquents. It is important to appreciate the different settings in which Durkheim and Merton were writing. Whereas both lived in the midst of considerable economic inequality, Durkheim lived in a Europe still under the influence of the aristocracy and privilege. Merton, on the other hand, lived in the midst of 'The American Dream' where, in the post-Depression era, hard work and enterprise could (allegedly) bring countless rewards, and where progression from a log cabin to the White House was seriously claimed to be a possibility.

Although, for Durkheim, the condition of anomie only arose exceptionally when weak social regulation was unable to restrain people's aspirations during economic turmoil, for Merton it was an ever-present feature in American society. However, Merton did not attribute anomie to poor regulation. He considered that it resulted from the lack of a structured and legitimate means for most people in society to attain what was indiscriminately held out to all as the ultimate goal—material wealth. Not everyone will be able to attain such wealth, but everyone is expected to try, or risk being called 'lazy' or 'unambitious'. The goal of acquiring wealth in the USA is portrayed as not just another aspiration: perhaps more than in any other country, it is equated with personal value and social status. For Merton, anomie is:

. . . conceived as a breakdown in the cultural structure, occurring particularly when there is an acute disjunction between cultural norms and goals and the social structured capacities of members of the group to act in accord with them.

Durkheim had described anomie in terms of society's inability to regulate the natural appetites of its members. Merton, however, thought that these appetites were not necessarily 'natural', but were 'culturally induced'. He was acutely aware of the growth of advertising which accompanied the development of mass production of consumer goods in the period between the two World Wars. The growth of such a 'free market' economy required heavy and sustained consumer purchasing. Merton's anomie theory is sometimes referred to as 'strain theory' to indicate the strain which drives people into committing deviant acts.

Merton assumed that in American society there was an overriding cultural goal of material success; an unequal availability of permissible means to attain such a goal; and the consequent utilisation of alternative deviant means. He considered that people can react in five different ways to the challenge of 'The American Dream'. The particular form of reaction will depend on the strength of the individual's commitment to the challenge and the availability of institutionalised means to pursue it. The institutionalised means are based on the 'Protestant ethic' of hard work, education, honesty and deferred gratification. The antithesis to this involves 'get rich quick' notions, including fraud or force. Merton pointed out that, as some people are never likely to achieve the goals of a culture, it is important for the society that there is an element of enjoyment involved in adhering to the institutionalised means—in simply 'taking part'. However, where the goal becomes unduly emphasised—as the goal of material wealth is in America—and it becomes apparent that it can be attained without using institutionalised means, then the acceptability of the means themselves will be increasingly questioned.

The five modes of reaction are as follows:

(i) Conformity

This, of course, does not involve deviance. It arises when an individual accepts the ultimate goal of material wealth and the institutionally provided means of attaining it. Conforming individuals will continue to try to obtain wealth through middle-class legitimate means even when they are not succeeding. Apart from dictatorships, societies could not function unless a majority of their members adopted at least a broadly conformist approach in their daily activities.

Merton considered that this was the reaction of most Americans, and accounted for the crime rates not being any higher. However, Merton was basing this view on official crime statistics and it is nowadays accepted that crime is committed by a much wider range of the population than appears in official records.

(ii) Innovation

This deals with an area which has traditionally been the prime focus for criminologists. Here, the ultimate goal of material wealth is accepted, but the institutionally available means are rejected, presumably—on Merton's analysis—because they are considered inadequate. Merton thought that it is among the lower social classes that legitimate means for achieving financial success are most restricted, and that this explains why the poor commit the most crimes. On the other hand, people working in business may also devise new forms of fraud and other types of white-collar crime, and Merton began his section on 'innovation' with a discussion of white-collar offences. He noted that this is the situation which classical writers considered would occur naturally unless controlled by punishment: individuals choosing the most efficient ways of attaining their desires (see Chapter 5). However, Merton considered that such a state would only occur when cultural goals are so strongly emphasised that the norms disintegrate.

(iii) Ritualism

Merton himself admitted that 'deviant' is not the most appropriate way to describe this form of reaction. This refers to situations when individuals do not reject, but lose sight of 'the end' (material wealth) and concentrate on 'the means'. Merton described it thus: 'The original purposes are forgotten and close adherence to institutionally prescribed conduct becomes a matter of ritual'. Such people will not be disappointed if they fail to achieve society's goals as they have effectively abandoned them. A good example is officials in a large-scale bureaucracy who claim that there is nothing in the rules which allows them to act in an obviously beneficial way. Merton himself referred to another type—'the frightened employee'. Ritualism can be seen as a typically lower middle-class reaction, resulting from over-socialisation accompanied by restricted opportunity for advancement. Such people have achieved a small degree of success by adhering to institutionalised means, but they have no hope or expectation of achieving anything more, and are afraid of losing what they already have. They do not open themselves up to the possibility of failure.

(iv) Retreatism

This category comprises people who, because of internalised pressure or their own conscience, reject both the ultimate goal and the means of achieving it. Merton emphasised that such rejection does not necessarily mean that such people are not committed to the culture: the commitment may be strong, but there may be no prospect of achieving success. The tramp, vagrant or addict drops out of society, but does not attempt to create anything new in its place. Retreatists are 'in society, but not of it'. Any crimes they commit will probably be for the purpose of self-preservation, whether through drugs or food.

(v) Rebellion

This involves the less common situation where not only are the ultimate goal and prescribed means of achieving it rejected, but a new goal and new means are substituted. This form of reaction would cover both people who withdraw from society for spiritual reasons (perhaps to meditate) and revolutionaries although, as Laurie Taylor (1971) has pointed out, many terrorist groups publicly announce their dissent, but still try to avoid criminal sanctions. As Merton himself stated, 'the rebel, revolutionary, non-conformist, heretic or renegade of an earlier day is often the cultural hero of today'.

These 'adaptations' (to use Merton's term) are not descriptions of personality types, but accounts of how people may react under the strain of anomie. The different reactions are not mutually exclusive. For example, an obsessive bureaucrat (ritualist) may also steal money from an employer (innovator), and periodically indulge in an alcoholic binge (retreatist). Nor is the theory simply confined to criminals and drop-outs. Merton himself noted how the over-emphasis on originality in scientific research caused some scientists, who were unable to achieve this, to react by being selective with evidence (and sometimes fabricating it), making false charges of plagiarism and being excessively secretive.

These adaptations do not necessarily involve criminality. The innovator is clearly the most likely offender but, if the innovation involves some new variety of business 'sharp practice', the conduct may not amount to a criminal offence until the legislature or the courts make it so. The ritualist is so bound to society's norms that crime is not going to occur. The retreatist may only commit the sort of crimes which result from 'dropping out', such as vagrancy or drunkenness. Rebellion may also involve criminal activity involving bombings and killings.

(c) Durkheim and Merton

What are the essential differences between the notion of anomie as used by Durkheim and Merton? They both wrote about a condition in a society which would lead to a collapse in the control of its members' desires, and result in their having aspirations which were unattainable. Otherwise, the two approaches are different. Durkheim saw anomie as created by sudden changes in a society, whereas Merton viewed the condition as being always present. For Durkheim, anomie afflicts a whole society: for Merton, anomie usually applies to disadvantaged members of the lower classes. Durkheim considered that individuals' wants arise as part of human nature and are therefore static. A higher level of anomie must consequently be the result of a decline in the efficiency of social regulation. Merton, however, thought that it is society that determines what individuals want, and it is the inability of people to attain these goals that causes anomie, rather than the weakness of social regulation. For Merton, society encourages—or even demands—excessive aspirations whereas, for Durkheim, a properly-regulated society would provide an effective curb on excessive aspirations. Merton saw the pressure to commit crime arising from the social structure rather than human nature. It is the structural imbalance within a society which results in lower-class individuals committing more crimes than those in the upper-class. However, Merton also considered that Durkheim had paid insufficient regard to the significance of the subjective element as a factor in social action. Messner and Rosenfeld (see below) have argued that their theory combines Durkheim's interest in the regulatory function of social institutions with Merton's emphasis on the anomic consequences of the undue emphasis on goals over means.

(d) Evaluation of Merton's theory

Following its adaptation by Cloward and Ohlin (Pfohl 1985), Merton's theory was popular during the late 1950s and early 1960s. Many criminologists at that time probably agreed with the view of Clinard (1964) that Merton's theory was 'the most influential single formulation in the sociology of deviance in the last twenty-five years'. Nevertheless, within a decade it had fallen out of fashion. This was largely because of the growing popularity of control theory, which is very critical of explanations of crime based on strain (see Chapter 12). However, more recently theories relating to anomie and strain have been enjoying something of a renaissance.

There have been a number of criticisms of Merton's theory, some more convincing than others. One of the commonest has been objections to the assumption that there is a consensus in America (and, by extension, in other highly-developed capitalist societies) that everyone is pursuing an ultimate goal of material wealth. It is claimed that this view overlooks the reality of a pluralism, both ethnic and otherwise, which precludes such a sweeping generalisation. For example, Edwin Lemert (1964) doubted if any contemporary society subscribes to such a single set of values. There is, however, some support for the proposition that most Americans aspire to middle-class status (Erlanger 1980). Moreover, it is arguable that sharing a particular goal does not necessarily imply a general consensus. Historically, much strife has been generated by opposing parties competing for the same goal (for example, land), and it is conceivable that 'the rich man in his castle and the poor man at his gate' may have nothing in common other than their desire for money.

It has also been suggested that the theory is deficient in that it underplays the issue of power in society. This point is strikingly made in Laurie Taylor's well-known comparison of Mertonian anomie with individuals playing a fruit machine, which is rigged so that the same people keep winning (1971):

> The deprived ones then either resort to using foreign coins or magnets to increase their chance of winning (Innovation) or play on mindlessly (Ritualism), give up the game (Retreatism) or propose a new game altogether (Rebellion). But in this analysis nobody appears to ask who put the machine there in the first place and who takes the profits.

It is not clear, however, why any failure by Merton to give greater emphasis to the power of American big business should detract from his theory. It may have benefited in clarity from such an exposition, but it hardly seems significantly weakened by its omission. Merton made it perfectly clear that he did not consider that a direct relationship between poverty and crime is inevitable, although he appreciated that there is a strong correlation between the two in America. It was probably this that caused Gottfredson and Hirschi (1990) to assert that Merton's concept of anomie and Sutherland's views on white-collar crime are incompatible. Yet, as Merton himself has pointed out (Merton 1997), there is nothing in the theory which specifically excludes its application to white-collar crime. Box (1983), for example, considered that it provides a particularly good explanation. Passas (1990) has argued that white-collar crime can be viewed as an 'innovative' response by sections of the business world to the 'strain' of having to maintain profit levels in a difficult economic climate. Waring *et al.* (1995), by slightly modifying Merton's typology of adaptations to include situational circumstances, found that anomie theory was relevant to their study of a group of convicted white-collar offenders.

On the basis of official statistics, Merton assumed that most crime is committed by the lower classes, as they are subject to the greatest strain. However, there is some evidence that, contrary to the predictions of anomie theory, high aspirations among working-class youth tend to correlate inversely with later delinquency (Elliott and Voss 1974). In addition, the unreliability of official statistics is now generally recognised (see Chapter 3). The modern realisation that crime, in the form of middle-class and white-collar offending, is more widely distributed than the statistics suggest is used as a criticism of anomie (for example, Box 1971, Taylor *et al.* 1973). Yet, even allowing for the fact that much crime is committed at the top end of the social scale, it is still possible to argue that the pressure is greatest at the bottom. Moreover, if the view were taken that the powerful in society create definitions of criminal offences for their own advantage, it would hardly be surprising to discover that offending behaviour was more common among the less successful members of society, even if this is exaggerated by the inherent biases of the criminal justice system (Reiner 1984).

Other criticisms have been made of the theory. Lemert (1964) argued that Merton's anomie ignores the impact of social control on the commission of deviant acts (for details of Lemert's notion of labelling, see Chapter 9). Lindesmith and Gagnon (1964), in a consideration of addiction, were concerned that anomie theory provides no indication as to what form of addiction will be adopted by a retreatist. Nor is it clear how one can determine whether a case of addiction has resulted from anomie or has led to anomie. Merton did not deal with the situation where results exceed expectations, such as in the case of the pools or lottery winner. Nor does the theory seem directly applicable to group crime or juvenile delinquency, or explain why many juvenile delinquents abandon their criminal lifestyle on reaching adulthood (Hirschi 1969). However, unlike a number of other criminologists, Merton never claimed that his theory was all-embracing: 'anomie is designed to account for some, not all, forms of deviant behaviour customarily described as criminal or delinquent'.

Although Merton's theory of anomie was set out in terms of economic strain, it has recently been suggested by Parnaby and Sacco (2004) that it is flexible enough to encompass the relationship between deviant behaviour and the acquisition of celebrity status. The authors provided examples for each of Merton's deviant 'adaptations' to illustrate this. For 'innovation', Parnaby and Sacco referred to the gangster Al Capone, who sought not only material success, but also the notoriety that would result from the achievements of the uneducated son of immigrant parents. Another example they gave is the 'tagging' of graffiti artists and the social recognition this activity bestows within the subculture. 'Ritualists', who have to 'scale down' their ambitions, could include an aspiring actress who abandons her dreams of Hollywood success for a career in pornographic films. For 'rebellion', the authors suggested a different sort of relationship—the accomplishment of fame as an *unintended* consequence of the challenge to the social system. Anti-globalisation protests were offered as an example. Finally, Parnaby and Sacco viewed the relationship between celebrity and 'retreatism' in terms of a person's shunning public recognition, perhaps in the style of a millionaire benefactor, although the authors pointed out the paradox that such reticence often has the opposite effect to that desired.

(e) Empirical support

Research has been carried out into the theory. An early attempt was made by Lander (1954) in a study of juvenile delinquency in Baltimore between 1939 and 1942. Although Lander claimed that 'delinquency was essentially related to the instability or anomie of [the] area', there is a distinct note of circularity in his argument, as the same predictors were used to measure both anomie and offending. With Merton's approval, Leo Srole (1956) devised a scale of 'anomia' to measure how individuals experience anomie as a psychological state. Though generally ignored as a research tool, the scale was utilised by Sparks *et al.* (1977) in their London victim survey. The term was also used by Dahrendorf in his 1985 Hamlyn Lecture on 'Law and Order'.

In a study of 730 American adolescents, Brennan and Huizinga (1975) found that anomie, peer pressure and negative labelling were significant factors underlying self-reported delinquency. The research of Cernkovich and Giordano (1979) showed that both male and female delinquents have a greater sense of blocked opportunity than male and female non-delinquents. According to a study by Farnworth and Leiber (1989), there is stronger evidence of a relationship between anomie and crime if education is substituted for occupation. Menard (1995) concluded that earlier tests had been inadequate and that, with the use of proper techniques, anomie theory has much stronger support.

Hannon and Defronzo (1998) looked at the relationship between resource deprivation and crime rates in 406 large metropolitan counties in the USA. They discovered that high levels of welfare assistance reduced the strength of the otherwise positive relationship between the size of the disadvantaged population and the amount of crime. The researchers interpreted these findings as supportive of anomie theory, in that welfare provision allows the recipients to obtain culturally defined goals through legal means and thus reduces frustration and strain. They also thought their results supported the argument of Messner and Rosenfeld (see below) that welfare not only reduces anomie by removing a total reliance on market forces, but also increases the social control function of non-economic bodies.

Early developments of anomie theory

The most significant development of Merton's theory of anomie was made by Richard Cloward and Lloyd E Ohlin in their book *Delinquency and Opportunity* (1960). However, as their analysis also incorporated a view of subcultures, it is considered in Chapter 8. It is worth noting that Merton subsequently agreed with the authors' view that the consideration of illegitimate opportunity, which provided the basis of the book, was an appropriate modification of his anomie theory.

In his book *The Social System* (1951), Talcott Parsons stated that the concept of deviance was 'inherent in and central to the whole conception of social action and hence of social systems'. Parsons provided an early extension of Merton's theory, incorporating an interactionist dimension. Merton had only referred to the strain between goals and institutionalised means, but Parsons's scheme utilised other forms, such as the strain resulting when individuals are unable to form a relationship with a member of the opposite sex, or feel they are unable to live up to other people's expectations. Robert Dubin (1959) also modified Merton's scheme by dividing 'institutional means' into 'institutional norms', which represent the boundaries between prescribed and proscribed behaviour, and 'means' which represent the actual behaviour of people in a particular setting. In other words, Dubin sought to distinguish between the norms and values to which people refer in making choices from alternatives, and what people actually do in practice.

Merton's anomie theory received a further reassessment in an essay by Albert Cohen (1965), who had already made a major contribution to the sociology of deviance in his discussion of delinquent sub-cultures. Cohen also criticised Merton's theory for paying insufficient regard to role theory. In his view, anomie theory ignores the insights into cultural transmission provided by the Chicago School and the writings on interactionism. Instead, it seems individualistic and static, concentrating on initial states and outcomes.

More recent developments of anomie theory

(a) Agnew's general strain theory

In the 1970s, attempts were made to shift the focus of strain theory from Merton's consideration of longer-term aspirations to the more immediate wants of young people, such as popularity with their peers, good results at school and sporting success. The expectation was that strain could be produced by a failure to achieve these short-term goals. This would have helped to explain the problem of middle-class delinquency. However, no strong empirical support for this approach was forthcoming at that time (Elliott and Voss 1974).

Nevertheless, the idea that Merton's strain theory had been too restricted in its sources of strain and could, therefore, be usefully extended has led to an interesting development by Robert Agnew (1992). For Agnew, strain is more prevalent than just a divergence between aspirations and expectations. In a 'general strain theory', he has identified three particular types of strain. The first, strain arising from a failure to achieve desired goals or goods, includes the areas covered by writers such as Merton and Albert Cohen (see Chapter 8), but also covers strain when a personal expectation (not only economic) does not materialise; this includes strain resulting from an unjust decision. Agnew's second type of strain is caused by the removal of positively valued stimuli and the presentation of negatively valued stimuli. Examples of this include: the loss of a friend as a result of an argument, or through death; moving to a new neighbourhood; and poor relations with parents, teachers or others. The third type of strain occurs from negative stimuli such as physical pain, punishment, embarrassment or some form of psychological trauma.

Any of these forms of strain is likely to be reflected in emotions such as fear, disappointment and, in particular, anger, and may give rise to criminal activity such as drug use or some form of vengeful reaction. Strain can vary in its effects on delinquency according to its intensiveness, duration and proximity in time. Everyone feels disappointment and anger, and people cope with these emotions in a variety of ways, most of which do not involve the commission of a criminal offence. Agnew considered that some individuals have higher levels of aggressiveness than others. Aggressive individuals are irritable, impulsive, have a low tolerance of adversity, are prone to blame their problems on others, and are more likely to respond to their difficulties with criminal behaviour. Associating with delinquent peers can also increase the likelihood of a delinquent adaptation. Criminal acts can be instrumental (trying to regain what has been lost, or obtain what has hitherto been unobtainable), retaliatory (hitting back at the source of the strain), or escapist (seeking comfort from the unpleasant states of anger and strain).

Agnew (1992) was keen to distinguish his strain theory from other criminological theories. Whereas in control theory (see Chapter 12) delinquency can occur through the absence of positive relationships with others, in general strain theory delinquency can occur because of negative relationships with others. Indeed, for Agnew, the presence of negative relationships will be a far stronger predictor of delinquency than the absence of positive ones.

In the first empirical study of the theory, Agnew and White (1992) found that four of the eight measures of strain they used were significantly related to delinquency. Utilising measures to test several different types of strain, Paternoster and Mazerolle (1994) were able in a longitudinal study to assess variations in the intensity and duration of strain in a national American sample of youth aged from eleven to seventeen. They discovered that four out of five measures of general strain (neighbourhood problems, negative life events, school or peer hassles, and negative relations with adults) had a significant effect on delinquency. They also found that having 'conventional moral beliefs' and obtaining good results at school were effective inhibitors to involvement in criminal behaviour. Strain was shown to have an indirect effect on delinquency by weakening conventional social control and increasing ties to delinquent peers. Using Agnew's analysis, Hoffmann and Su (1997) discovered that stressful life events have a similar impact on levels of delinquency and drug use among both males and females. In a longitudinal study, Hoffmann and Miller (1998) found a relationship between strain and delinquency in the final year of a three-year period.

General strain theory has continued to be the subject of extensive testing. Aseltine *et al.* (2000) found that various types of strain were significantly related to interpersonal aggression, but not to marijuana use. Agnew *et al.* (2002) concluded that juveniles with high levels of emotionality and low levels of constraint were most likely to react to strain by committing delinquent acts. Using a distinction between 'situation-based' and 'trait-based' anger, Mazerolle *et al.* (2003) discovered that the former had a much stronger link with deviance.

Most of the research has been based on white Americans. However, in a study of African-American adults Jang and Johnson (2003) found a relationship between negative emotions and deviance, although this was much weaker when the subjects reported high levels of religiosity.

Support for extending general strain theory even further has come from research by Hagan and McCarthy (1997) into delinquency by young people who have left home and are living on the 'mean streets'. The adverse conditions they experience can lead to crime, both directly and indirectly. Such people have typically grown up in poor families, lacking either one or both biological parents. The strain they have encountered, which often involved physical and sexual abuse, has driven them on to the streets. Once there, they have to resort to crimes such as theft and prostitution in order to survive.

(b) 'Crime and the American Dream'

In their book *Crime and the American Dream* (1994) Steven Messner and Richard Rosenfeld sought to explain why the USA has a higher level of serious crime than any other industrial nation. Having decided that biological accounts (see Chapter 14) cannot alone account for such a discrepancy, they concluded that there must be something distinctive about the very essence of American society. Messner and Rosenfeld identified as central to their explanation the role played by Merton's notion of the 'American Dream'. They defined this as 'a commitment to the goal of material success, to be pursued by everyone in society, under conditions of open, individual competition'. However, according to Messner and Rosenfeld, criminologists have given too much attention to Merton's theory as a social-psychological explanation of criminality based on individual strain, at the expense of viewing it as a wider theory of social organisation. This is in spite of the fact that Merton himself has sought to emphasise the variations in rates of criminal behaviour (Merton 1968). One consequence of this is that criminologists have generally ignored Merton's criticisms of the anomic tendencies in American society.

In addition, Messner and Rosenfeld considered Merton's analysis to be deficient as it did not emphasise what is different in the structure of

American society from those of other countries: namely, the fact that the wielding of economic power is paramount over other important institutions of society such as the political system, the family and the school. Indeed, the relationship between these four institutions is crucial and there needs to be a proper balance between them for societies to function properly. However, the 'American Dream' places such a strong emphasis on monetary success that this goal overwhelms all others. As Orrù (1990) put it, 'money is literally, in this context, a *currency* for measuring achievement'. It is always possible to have more money and, in the words of Merton, 'in the American Dream there is no final stopping point'. For example, whereas in America education is seen as a way of obtaining a better job, in other developed countries it is one of a range of influences which develops values and beliefs. As Messner and Rosenfeld pointed out, the real value (as opposed to the rhetoric) accorded to family life in America can be seen in the inferior status accorded to those who are most heavily involved in its maintenance—women.

Messner and Rosenfeld suggested that the rising crime levels in countries which have started to embrace the market economy, such as Russia, may be explained by their theory. They also feared that the reduction of political controls on the market is likely to lead to increased crime: '. . . cutbacks in the welfare state could be viewed as tipping the institutional balance of power toward the economy and away from the polity' (Rosenfeld and Messner 1997).

Savolainen (2000) discovered that countries which use the provision of welfare to protect their citizens from the problems created by market forces have lower levels of homicide than those with high levels of poverty. However, relative deprivation alone could not account for this finding, as the gap between the rich and the poor was not as significant as the size of the economically marginalised population. Savolainen concluded that this showed a negative interaction between economic inequality and the strength of the welfare state, and was thus supportive of Messner and Rosenfeld's theory.

(c) 'The Exclusive Society'

In his book *The Exclusive Society* (1999) Jock Young invoked Merton's anomie theory in his explanation of how rising crime rates have resulted from a growing tendency over the past thirty years for societies to exclude more of their members. During the period between the end of World War II and the 1970s, society was intolerant of diversity in general and tried to make everyone, whether 'criminals' or 'deviants', fit into the same lifestyle. According to Young, diversity and difference are nowadays not problematic; they can be tolerated as part of the general growth in consumerism (as exemplified in the increasing number of restaurants providing exotic food). The real problem is 'the difficult and the dangerous' who, although they are *culturally* included (as having embraced the values of society), are nevertheless *structurally* excluded. Merton's analysis is pertinent here. All members of society are involved in the call to consumption, whether through the media, the market place or schooling. Through modern communications, the 'American Dream' now has a far greater reach than ever before. Nevertheless, it is inevitable that many will remain excluded.

Conclusion

Durkheim's methodology was clearly defective and, although this does not destroy the basis of his theory of anomie, plenty of ammunition is thereby provided for its detractors. Merton's writings can also be criticised for their reliance on official crime statistics and their failure to embrace interactionist theory. Both writers provided positivist explanations of criminality where the individual's actions are largely controlled by outside forces, and freedom of choice becomes very much a secondary consideration.

Nevertheless, strain theory remains one of the few sociological explanations of crime that concentrates on negative relations with other people and accounts for a rising rate of offending in increasingly prosperous societies. It is easy to imagine that, whatever the impact made by advertising in 1930s America when Merton first set out his account of anomie, it is considerably greater nowadays on both sides of the Atlantic—and the same can be said for the crime rate, official or real. Of course, it would be dangerous to rely completely on such a simple cause and effect model, but it can at least provide a justification for anomie theory to be taken rather more seriously. As the poor are more likely to come into contact with the rich through the breakdown of social divisions, the wealth that is there to be obtained is even more apparent than ever.

It is also possible to argue (although he did not do so) that Merton's version of anomie explains why women have traditionally committed less crime than men. For women, dominant culture has held out domesticity as the ultimate goal rather than material wealth. This has begun to change during the past thirty years and female crime has also increased. Merton's anomie has an appeal for some because it is based on an optimistic view of human nature, particularly when compared with other explanations such as control theory (see Chapter 12). Individuals are viewed as fundamentally good and conforming, and people only break the rules when they are unable to attain what society is encouraging them to attain.

Merton's theory of anomie has gradually come to be reappraised. Many criminologists now consider the theory to be a 'middle range concept', which means that they view it not as a comprehensive explanation of crime, but as a flexible notion which is open to elaboration and analysis on different levels. Indeed, Merton himself has in recent years described his theory as an 'evolving paradigm' (1995). This has allowed different writers to emphasise different aspects of anomie (See Adler and Laufer (eds) 1995 and Passas and Agnew (eds) 1997). Whereas Agnew has concentrated on extending consideration of the social-psychological impact of strain on individuals, Messner and Rosenfeld have preferred to highlight the macro or societal impact of excessive concentration on the 'American Dream'. It may not be a coincidence that this renewed interest in anomie has coincided with a reduction in welfare expenditure and an increasing gap between rich and poor in many parts of the industrialised world. Economic and social upheaval has also resulted in some eastern European countries following the break up of the USSR. It seems likely, therefore, that further new interpretations of strain theory will follow.

8
Subcultural theories

Merton's anomie theory indicated several possible forms of reaction by individuals who had suffered from the strain of being unable to attain society's ultimate goal (in America, material wealth) by the institutionalised means made available to them: typically regular, productive work. For some, the reaction could involve engaging in deviant or criminal behaviour. Merton's approach was adopted and modified by other sociologists and criminologists who were interested in studying the behaviour of groups—usually of young people—within a society, which deviate from or totally reject the views of the majority. Such groups are referred to by sociologists as subcultures.

The use of the term 'subculture' has largely centred on juvenile delinquent gangs. Although Spergel's study of the literature found references to 'organised gangs' in seventeenth-century London (1995), most of the research has been conducted in America. In some respects this restriction has been unfortunate: subculture is a sociological concept that has a wide application, and the relationship with the emotive topic of gangs has in many ways proved to be counterproductive. Nevertheless, by the 1950s juvenile delinquency was considered a major social problem in America. The loosening of the parental shackles on children and the greater affluence that came with the growing prosperity of the post-war era was reflected in the popularity of film icons such as James Dean (*Rebel Without a Cause*) and Marlon Brando (*The Wild One*), as well as the growth of rock and roll.

Even before World War II, researchers from the Chicago School (see Chapter 6) had been describing subcultures in terms of gangs growing out of social disorganisation and a lack of cohesion in the slum. Perhaps the best-known of these accounts was provided by Frederick Thrasher.

Frederick M Thrasher

In his classic impressionistic study of 1,313 Chicago juvenile gangs, Thrasher (1927) divided them into four types: the diffuse gang, which had loose leadership and little solidarity; the solidified gang, which had a high degree of loyalty; the conventionalised gang, which was similar to an athletics club; and the criminal gang, whose members were the most likely to become career offenders. Thrasher described delinquent gang activity as fundamentally the over-exuberant action of youth in deprived areas. Some of their activities could be seen as a substitute for the recreational activities of the more privileged; for example, taking boats on the river. The boys might steal what they did not actually have, such as alcohol and cigarettes, or fight to protect what they considered to be theirs, such as girls or territory. Thrasher viewed delinquency as a normal progression from a childhood search for excitement in a frustrating and limiting environment. He adopted what Matza (1969) later termed an 'appreciative' stance, which brought him closer to the gang in understanding and sympathy. However, although 'The Gang' makes vivid reading in the best Chicago School tradition, as a study of criminality its impact is somewhat lessened on the realisation that the research is generally uncritical of the accounts given. Moreover, it is difficult to attribute delinquency to deprivation alone, as Thrasher suggested.

William F Whyte

In his book *Street Corner Society* (1943) Whyte showed that it was easier for the resident of a slum to achieve upward social mobility by excelling in a racket, such as bookmaking, than by conventional means. Whyte lived for three and a half years in an Italian slum, which he referred to as 'Cornerville', situated in 'Eastern City'. Utilising parts of Sutherland's differential association theory (see Chapter 6), Whyte considered the extent to which the members of gangs in the area formed attachments to law breakers rather than to law abiders such as school teachers. He discovered that pre-delinquent youths who avoided significant attachments with positive role models were likely instead to create them with law violators. Whyte did not describe the gangs in terms of social disorganisation, as the earlier Chicago theorists had. On the contrary, he found that their existence was based on mutual support and cooperation. However, the problem was that their organisation did not mesh with that of the wider society.

Albert K Cohen

Cohen criticised Merton's anomie theory for seemingly being inapplicable both to juvenile and group crime. His own attempt to explain these phenomena is set out in his book *Delinquent Boys: the Culture of the Gang* (1955). Cohen had been a student of both Merton and Sutherland, and his work shows the influence of these writers. He thought that juvenile delinquency was 'a major practical problem of every sizeable American community', and was concerned that existing theory failed to account adequately for the non-acquisitive nature and apparent lack of purpose of much of this delinquency. Cohen saw many working-class boys (whom he referred to as 'corner boys', an expression borrowed from Whyte) as being propelled into a delinquent subculture to retrieve their self-esteem which had been destroyed by middle-class institutions, especially the school.

According to Cohen, most boys who have been socialised in lower-class families are inadequately prepared to perform successfully in a middle-class school setting. He drew a distinction between achieved status, which is obtained among one's own peers, and ascribed status, which one gains from the social position of one's family. Achieved status is usually earned at school. However, the school rewards and punishes for acceptable or unacceptable performance in accordance with middle-class values such as ambition, constructive use of leisure, cultivation of skills, individual responsibility (as opposed to the typical lower-class notion of shared family obligations) and postponement of immediate gratification for long-term gain.

Cohen described the application of these values as a 'middle class measuring rod' against which all children are judged in institutions run by middle-class individuals. Although everyone is measured against this standard, not everyone is adequately equipped to attain it, particularly working-class children. They are less likely to have grown up in an educationally stimulating environment and are thus more likely to have restricted aspirations. Having received disapproval, rejection and punishment, and lacking both ascribed and achieved status, they may consequentially suffer what Cohen called 'the problem of status deprivation'.

When working-class children encounter this 'middle class measuring rod', they are likely to react in one of three ways. The clever ones may seek upward social mobility through 'the college boy' solution. The less able may become what Cohen referred to as 'stable corner boys'. They will continue to conform to middle-class values without much success and will accept a position of low status among their peers. Others will seek the delinquent solution.

This occurs because, to some extent, the children will have come to share this evaluation of themselves. As a result of the mass media, they will be aware of the prevalence of middle-class values in society, and will have realised that, through upward mobility, some lower-class people are able to be successful. They are also likely to have partly accepted the middle-class measuring rod as providing a legitimate—or even superior—set of values. The children will thus suffer from feelings of low esteem and guilt, and experience a 'reaction formation'. This is a psychological term borrowed from Freud (see Chapter 16), whereby the formerly desired middle-class values are now turned on their head and held in contempt. A shared solution will evolve— the delinquent subculture—which will take the place of middle-class values and norms.

In contrast to Merton's emphasis on the individual's desire for monetary gain, Cohen described the subculture's activities as non-utilitarian, malicious and negativistic, with an emphasis on group autonomy. They are non-utilitarian, because stolen goods are often thrown away; malicious, because burglary is often accompanied by vandalism; and negativistic, because much of the behaviour appears to be in total opposition to generally accepted values. The subculture is formed to deal with both an external and an internal enemy: the agents of the middle class and the internal feelings of inadequacy. What the delinquent does is right according to the standards of the subculture because it is wrong according to the standards of the school. Merton's victims of strain make individual responses: Cohen's seek a collective solution. Even juveniles whose level of discontent is such that, if left to themselves, they would be unlikely to resort to delinquency, can be enticed by the attractions of the gang, with its offer of excitement and comradeship.

Cohen's theory is particularly relevant to schooling. It assumes that lower-class children perform worse at school than middle-class children, and that this is a result of the conflict between the dominant middle-class values of the school and the values of lower-class youth. The theory also supports several regular findings in official criminal statistics: lower-class youths commit more offences than middle-class; boys commit more offences than girls; and crime rates are higher in urban than in rural areas.

The theory is not without support in Britain. In his book *Social Relations in a Secondary School* (1967), David Hargreaves described how he carried out research while working as a teacher in an English secondary-modern school. It was clear that there was little opportunity of educational advancement for its working-class pupils, many of whom were engaged in delinquency. By their final year of schooling, Hargreaves had identified two subcultures in the school, one 'academic', the other 'delinquescent'. The 'academic' boys in the top stream came from working-class families, but had still internalised middle-class values and were supportive of the school. The 'delinquescent' boys, although not necessarily delinquent at that stage, were also from a working-class background and were opposed to the middle-class values of the school. These lowest-stream boys had lost status on two counts: first, by failing the 'eleven plus' examination, and second by being negatively evaluated by teachers and placed in the 'D stream'. As a result of this, the boys sought a collective response, which occurred in the formation of a subculture which was anti-teacher and anti-school.

Although it has quite reasonably been suggested that it could be delinquency that leads to poor educational performance rather than (as asserted by Cohen) the other way round, Hargreaves was convinced that the negative evaluation by teachers was the crucial factor. While generally supportive of Cohen's theory, Hargreaves differed in one particular respect: he did not find evidence of Cohen's 'reaction formation'. The resentment caused by lack of status was sufficient to propel these boys into a subculture.

Several questions arise concerning this explanation of delinquency. Cohen himself did not make any policy recommendations in his book. Perhaps he felt that its conclusions spoke for themselves, or perhaps— in the repressive McCarthyite atmosphere of the early 1950s—he did not want to appear too radical and offer a direct critique of American culture. In case this appears a dramatic statement, the sense of the times can be seen in the fact that, for several years after its publication, a number of people considered *Delinquent Boys* to be subversive and encouraging of crime. Nevertheless, a consequence of this reticence is that it remains uncertain as to whether Cohen thought that working-class youths should try to alter their values, or that middle-class teachers should be instructed to alter their approach.

Cohen assumed that the actions of the gang members are non-utilitarian, malicious and negativistic, but other observations of gangs have shown that, from their own perspective, their conduct could be meaningful. This is significant because Cohen's description of the gangs forms part of his theoretical statement. Cohen has also been criticised for claiming that lower-class individuals generally aspire to middle-class status (Box 1971). Working-class boys may resent their low status, but that does not mean they consider their own culture to be inferior. It is not even clear that delinquent working-class youths are anti-middle class in their outlook (Downes 1966). Elliott *et al.* (1985) have also pointed out that there are longitudinal studies supporting the view that association with delinquents precedes, rather than follows, an increased involvement in criminal behaviour.

The whole question of the 'reaction formation' is problematic and, like many Freudian concepts, is difficult to test empirically. Box (1971) considered that there is no reaction formation in these cases because working-class boys do not internalise the status criteria of the school: it is more that they are unable to be indifferent to such criteria.

Walter B Miller

One writer who provided an explanation of subcultural delinquency in the tradition of Thrasher rather than Merton or Cohen was the cultural anthropologist Walter B Miller in his study *Lower Class Culture as a Generating Milieu of Gang Delinquency* (1958). A research team comprising seven social workers and directed by Miller spent three years with members of delinquent gangs in a town near Boston. Whereas Cohen had claimed that lower-class culture was a reaction to the dominant culture and an inversion of middle-class values, Miller considered that the culture had its own distinct 'focal concerns', and that lower-class delinquency, rather than being a counterculture, directly resulted from these concerns. Such delinquency was, therefore, not a reaction to middle-class values, but was directly in conflict with them. Indeed, Miller asserted that the pursuance of lower-class cultural practices would inevitably lead to the commission of certain crimes.

American lower-class culture, in Miller's view, was formed from a common adaptation of unsuccessful immigrants and blacks. In his study he was mainly concerned with the 'lowest' of the lower class. Miller analysed the life of this group as being based on a series of structural elements and a system of what he referred to as 'focal concerns'. Although similar to values, focal concerns are said to have the advantage of being directly observable in the subjects' behaviour. The main structural elements are a female-based household and a one-sex peer group. The female-based household reflects the fact that adult males play little part in the family and do not provide it with stable economic support. The one-sex peer group shows the importance that each sex gains from interacting with its own members. They can provide an emotional haven for both sexes. The focal concerns of lower-class culture are listed by Miller as trouble, toughness, smartness, excitement, fate and autonomy.

'Trouble' is what life gets you into, especially with officialdom. Miller considered that members of the lower class are particularly keen to avoid the complications resulting from interference by the authorities. Criminal or deviant behaviour is not in itself necessarily considered problematic and may conform to subcultural expectations; it is the ensuing consequences that are to be avoided. However, it is not only court appearances and punishment that lead to trouble. Truancy can cause meddling by school officials and cohabitation may result in the withdrawal of welfare benefits. There is an ambivalence here: a lower-class male can be considered as 'one of the lads' but, at the same time, a person denounced as always being in trouble.

'Toughness' refers to the emphasis on 'masculine values' and includes a complete rejection of anything feminine, including much middle-class behaviour and displays of emotion. Toughness is one of the causes of being in trouble. Where individuals stand on the scale between law-abiding and law-violating behaviour is crucial to their reputation. Miller thought that the emphasis on this focal concern is probably a reaction to the female-dominated household in which the boys grow up.

'Smartness' means the ability to con, outwit, hustle or manipulate events and people for one's own advantage with a maximum use of mental agility and a minimum of physical effort. Although formal educational achievements are treated with disdain by the lower class, being 'street-wise' is highly regarded.

'Excitement' is best reflected in a 'Saturday night on the town' scenario, with sex, gambling, alcohol and fighting. The routine lower-class life which occupies the week in between, whether it consists of 'hanging out' or working in a monotonous job, is dull and boring.

'Fate' refers to the belief of many lower-class individuals that their lives are determined by forces over which they have little if any control, rather than by education, work, saving or other aspects of deferred gratification which are favoured by the middle class. This is reflected in their love of gambling. Indeed, gambling performs key functions in the areas of fate, toughness, smartness and excitement.

'Autonomy', according to Miller, is treated with considerable ambivalence. Overtly, individuals complain about interference by others, such as the boss or the authorities. However, secretly they are gratified by the care that is being shown to them, perhaps by a comforting wife.

Miller's aim is to provide an explanation as to why boys go on to the streets and form juvenile gangs. A lower-class boy spends most of his early life in the company of women. During that period he is told that men, although desirable, are irresponsible and that, if he loves his mother, he will not grow up to be like other men. The adolescent street group is the means which enables the boy to escape from both the feminine domination and overcrowded conditions of his home and fulfil his male identity. In essence, the street group becomes a training ground for the lower-class boy. Miller commented:

> Since women serve as a primary object of identification during the pre-adolescent years, the almost obsessive lower-class concern with 'masculinity' probably resembles a type of compulsive reaction-formation.

The lives of the boys thus come to reflect the overtly masculine characteristics of adult society's 'focal concerns' with a particular intensity. Like Thrasher, Miller emphasised that much of the gang's behaviour is non-delinquent. However, the crucial difference between the two is that, whereas the behaviour of Thrasher's boys is influenced by a lack of facilities, Miller's boys are simply striving to be 'real men'.

Miller was not alone during this period in thinking that young American males grew up with a sex role identification problem. Talcott Parsons (1954) claimed that the role of fathers in the American family made it difficult for boys to develop their masculinity naturally. Occupational demands would keep the father preoccupied outside the home and leave the mother as the most important person in the family. Fathers would consequently be a poor role model for their sons. Parsons did not go so far as to claim that lack of identification with a male figure could be a direct cause of juvenile delinquency. Nevertheless, he did consider that it could result in 'a strong tendency for boyish behaviour to run in anti-social if not directly destructive directions, in striking contrast to that of pre-adolescent girls'.

Criticism

It is, perhaps, not surprising that Miller's theory has been subject to a number of criticisms. It has been claimed that the explanation is tautological in that the behaviour of individuals in a lower-class setting was observed to identify their focal concerns which, in turn, were then used to explain the behaviour (Whitehead and Lab 1990). A further objection is that the evidence does not bear out Miller's claim of lower-class homes dominated by women in the extreme form he sugg-ests. Hirschi (1969) has even denied the existence of lower-class culture along the lines depicted by Miller (see Chapter 12). Yet, matri-archal domination of a family is not unknown, even when there is a stable adult male presence. It can be found (albeit in a milder form than suggested by Miller) in some West Indian families, and research has indicated it exists among the very poorest Latin-American and American black families (Lewis 1959). Nowadays, the argument centres more on whether children can be properly brought up in one-parent (usually fatherless) families, many of which are very poor. Relatively high rates of delinquency can be found among the children of such families, but it is difficult to attribute this to the absence of a male figure. As with other positivist explanations of crime, one can also ask if the working class is as culturally insulated as Miller implied. Matza and Sykes (1961) have suggested that many of Miller's focal concerns are almost identical with middle-class goals.

Another problem for Miller's theory is that the past twenty years have seen a growth in the number of female gangs, something which was rare in the 1950s and for which Miller's theory cannot account. On the other hand, a subculture of violence among young males in the inner city was identified by Wolfgang and Ferracuti (1967). It is certainly possible that Miller's theory could explain the formation of some delinquent groups: the link between male consciousness and crime underlies so many studies of lower-class offending. Moreover, in contrast to some other subcultural theorists, Miller has the advan-tage of emphasising what lower-class street boys are 'for' rather than 'against'.

Richard A Cloward and Lloyd E Ohlin

Cohen's subcultural theory was to some extent based on the writings of Merton in that it incorporated the idea of strain, albeit strain result-ing from problems of status rather than from problems of material wealth. However, the subcultural theory that has greatest similarity to Mertonian anomie is the differential opportunity theory devised by Cloward and Ohlin, which is set out in their book *Delinquency and Opportunity* (1960). Cloward and Ohlin considered that Cohen had placed too much emphasis on the school as a key element in the creation of a subculture, and had failed to recognise the degree of specialisation that subcultures could take. They agreed with Merton's view that strain applies most strongly among the poorer members of society, but thought that his analysis had paid insufficient attention to the conditions that determine which form of adaptation an individual will make. In addition, Merton had failed to realise that strain can also lead to the creation of delinquent subcultures.

Cloward and Ohlin were also clearly influenced by the ideas concerning the cultural transmission of delinquent values, which originated in the work of the Chicago School and became prominent in Sutherland's theory of differential association (see Chapter 6). Rich people are in a position which gives them the opportunity to practise fraud: poor people, although unable to indulge in white-collar crime, still have acquaintances who can teach them how to steal or deal with stolen goods.

Delinquency and Opportunity addressed two main questions: why the structure of American culture results in some people failing and others becoming involved in delinquency; and why some of the latter fail yet again within the structure of the delinquent subculture. Like other strain theorists, Cloward and Ohlin started from the position that American society encourages its members to aspire to success, which in practice is measured by material wealth. People who obtain the necessary qualifications within this meritocracy will expect to obtain a high status job. However, there are not enough such jobs for everyone seemingly entitled to them. Cloward and Ohlin considered that it is the working class, even if reasonably well qualified, who are most likely to become the victims of this process. A key element in their theory is that such individuals had originally held middle-class aspirations, but now found themselves thwarted. Consequently, it is they who are the most likely to lose support for society's structure and norms. On the other hand, lower-class individuals who feel they have obtained a position in society commensurate with their status and ability will not suffer strain.

Cloward and Ohlin were, therefore, particularly concerned with able working-class boys who are encouraged to aspire to 'a better life', but who still fail and are embittered by the experience. These are the individuals who are the most likely to seek a collective solution in a delinquent subculture. Cloward and Ohlin used Sutherland's theory of differential association to analyse the different techniques available for learning criminal behaviour. They concluded that there are three types of subculture that can result: criminal, conflict or retreatist. Whichever form evolves will largely depend on the nature of the local neighbourhood.

The criminal subculture is found in more stable lower-class areas where juvenile delinquency can be integrated with adult crime. The aim of the young delinquent is to graduate to the successful adult criminal class. The adults use their authority to exercise control over the juveniles, and facilitate their activities by providing outlets for stolen goods. Local politicians may well tolerate the criminal behaviour in return for pay-offs, but this also ensures that the illegal behaviour is generally restricted to property offences. This is the stuff of countless Hollywood movies and TV series. In Britain it was epitomised by the 'control' of large parts of London by gangs such as the Krays and the Richardsons in the 1960s.

Where such opportunities are unavailable, such as in an area of recent immigration, conflict subcultures may be found. The emphasis here is on gaining what one lacks by coercion. There are no developed adult role models—either conventional or criminal—because of the transient nature of the population. The third type of subculture, the retreatist, exists for the 'double failures'. These are people who have neither criminal opportunities (perhaps they have been rejected by other gangs) nor the ability to compete in a conflict group. This is similar to Merton's retreatist adaptation. The members of this group are likely to retreat into the world of alcohol or drugs, or drop out. Other 'double failures' may manage to avoid the retreatist subculture by becoming 'corner boys'.

Thus, it can be seen that the subcultures of Miller, Cohen, and Cloward and Ohlin each involves different aspirations. Miller's boys (and his theory can only apply to boys) seek to assert their masculinity; Cohen's delinquents try to gain some status; and Cloward and Ohlin's delinquents pursue 'the American Dream' of material wealth. Although *Delinquency and Opportunity* was presented as an analysis of subcultures, Cloward and Ohlin considered that their theory provided a general framework for the study of deviance and crime (Cloward 1959).

Cloward and Ohlin's theory certainly had an impact on American juvenile justice policy in the early 1960s. The implication of their work was that, if legitimate opportunities for the underprivileged could be increased, delinquency would be reduced. After Robert Kennedy, then Attorney-General in his brother Jack's administration, had read their book, he invited Lloyd Ohlin to help him develop a new policy on juvenile delinquency. Cloward, meanwhile, was appointed research director of 'Mobilization for Youth' (MFY), which was charged to implement the new approach. The result was the Juvenile Delinquency Prevention and Control Act 1961 and a comprehensive programme to improve education, create jobs, and organise lower-class neighbourhoods into community action groups, similar to those found in Clifford Shaw's Chicago Area Project. This was later extended by President Johnson to include adults and became the basis of his 'War on Poverty'.

This was probably the pinnacle of a 'welfare' approach to delinquency in America and, in particular, it provided a notable (and rare) example of politicians endeavouring to implement the proposals of academic criminologists. However, the situation in America nowadays shows that the initiative was ultimately unsuccessful. Millions of dollars were spent, but the scheme was eventually abolished by President Nixon. What went wrong? Several reasons have been suggested. Unlike Shaw's Chicago Area Project, which had been content to provide better facilities for the deprived, the leaders of MFY thought that changes were needed in the political structures which created such inequalities. For a while, it seemed that the whole social and economic basis of American society was being challenged. Rent strikes against slum landlords and protests against welfare policies ensued. The inevitable direct confrontations with local politicians led to a smear campaign being launched against MFY leaders and several (including Cloward) resigned (Liska 1981). As the original idea of spending money on improving social structures had now been obstructed, it was spent on poor people instead. This resulted in short-term alleviation of the problems, but no long-term benefit (Rose 1972). In addition, when it came to employment initiatives, many American employers were reluctant to cooperate in the utilisation of a low-skill workforce in their businesses (Jones 1971).

Efforts in Britain during the 1960s to adopt a similar approach to juvenile delinquency were far more influenced—and ultimately thwarted—by changes of government. The election of a Labour government in 1964 was accompanied by the pamphlet *Crime; a Challenge to Us All* (Longford (ed) 1964). However, its main thrust of increased social work intervention into 'problem' families was unpopular and politically controversial. Some of these policies were enacted in the Children and Young Persons Act 1969 but, before the Act was fully operational, the Conservatives were returned to power. On their return to office in 1974, Labour lacked both the will and a sufficiently large Parliamentary majority to reintroduce the measures.

Delinquency and opportunity: criticisms

Cloward and Ohlin's theory has been subjected to a number of criticisms. Short and Strodtbeck (1965) claimed that delinquency cannot be compartmentalised in this manner; many offenders combine activities from each of the three categories, 'criminal', 'conflict' and 'retreatist'. According to Kornhauser (1978), the evidence shows that delinquents have both low aspirations and low expectations. Therefore, no strain can exist as there is a very small gap between what the boys aspire to and what they realistically expect to achieve. Bernard (1984), on the other hand, pointed out that Cloward and Ohlin only intended their theory to apply to a small number of extremely delinquent inner city gangs, and that the evidence in this respect is clearly supportive of their theory. Bernard conceded that the evidence does not support Cloward and Ohlin's classification of gangs into criminal, conflict or retreatist, but claimed that this is not fatal to the validity of the overall theory. He argued that many of the criticisms of strain theories in general concern cultural aspects of the delinquents' lifestyle. However, these aspects should always be considered as secondary to the structural considerations that are fundamentally responsible for creating the strain.

Evaluation of American subcultural theories

The writers considered so far have all sought to explain the formation of the delinquent street gang. The typical gang appears to resemble something out of the musical *West Side Story* with its own leader, strict hierarchy and clear set of norms. Yet, other writers in both the USA and Britain have questioned the extent to which crime takes place in such closely-defined groups. In his study of New York gangs, Lewis Yablonsky (1962) challenged earlier research such as Thrasher's, which had attributed a definite group structure to gangs, and claimed that the gangs he discovered were more in the nature of a 'near group' with imprecise boundaries. David Downes, in his book *The Delinquent Solution* (1966), which was based on a study of delinquency in east London, also found that groupings were much less rigid than described in the earlier American studies. However, John Braithwaite (1989) claimed that even individual crime is often made possible by a learning process which starts in loosely-formed groups. These provide support for crime, either by approval, or by the provision of information which serves to facilitate the offending.

There is also the assumption, particularly in the case of Cohen, that there is a range of working-class values that are fundamentally different from those adopted by the middle class. This is a sweeping generalisation which is questionable and, some believe, patronising. It appears, however, that writers such as Cohen and Miller are actually referring to the 'lower lower class'—what Marx had called the lump-enproletariat. These are people who are virtually unemployable and live off welfare benefits (Wilson 1987). They are quite different from poorly educated individuals in low paid jobs, but still in the mainstream of American culture. Brown (1985), who considered that Cohen's analysis was based on 'a two-class model comprised of the *really* lower class and of everyone else', found that violent offences were associated with affiliation to the underclass.

The subcultural theories of Cohen, and Cloward and Ohlin follow on from the writings of Merton. They are also called 'strain theories' because, in different ways, the authors describe delinquency as a reaction to the strains imposed by the unequal opportunities available to attain the goals held out by American society. The logic of this requires that, if realistic equality of opportunity were created, there would be no strain and therefore less crime. (These authors do not claim that their theories explain all crime.) Yet, equality of opportunity is not the same as equality of wealth. Perhaps more would succeed, but many would still fail. There is clear evidence of an increase in the gap between the richest and the poorest people in many Western societies. None of the strain theorists suggest a fundamental redistribution of wealth or breaking down of class divisions in society. All they seem to advocate is an equal opportunity to succeed or fail. Following the publication of Cloward and Ohlin's book, measures were introduced in the USA to deal with poverty at the bottom but, even if fully implemented, they would have done little to eradicate the inequalities and divisions that existed—and still exist—in that society.

David Matza

The whole notion of delinquent subcultures was strongly criticised by the American writer David Matza. He pointed out that the traditional theories predicted and explained too much crime: 'an embarrassment of riches which seemingly goes unmatched in the real world'. Such explanations portrayed offenders as being different from non-offenders in some essential way, often for biological or psychological reasons. Matza, however, sought to emphasise that juvenile delinquents are not all that different from other young people. For example, if—as claimed by some theorists—delinquents viewed their behaviour as morally correct, they would presumably show no feelings of shame when detected. Yet, the evidence suggests the contrary, and that juvenile delinquents often admire and respect law-abiding individuals. In addition, delinquents often draw a clear line between those individuals they may victimise and those they should not.

Matza therefore concluded that juvenile delinquents are at least partly committed to the dominant social order and that delinquency is a way of life for only a handful of individuals. Most of the time delinquents act conventionally. A lot of delinquency is mundane and usually occurs in the period between childhood and adulthood when peer group acceptance is considered important. This offers an explanation as to why most adolescents cease to be delinquents on reaching adulthood: itself a problematic phenomenon, when so many of the factors traditionally related to crime, such as poverty, strain or opportunity, are still present. The values of the delinquent are often those of the leisured classes—concern for excitement and adventure.

According to Matza and Sykes (1961), such concerns form part of a 'subterranean' value system within the dominant culture. They referred to Thorsten Veblen's observation as long ago as 1899 in his book *The Theory of the Leisure Class* that delinquents are simply conforming to the standards of the business world when they adopt the desire for 'big money' as part of their value system. The entrepreneurial traditions of American culture encourage excitement, adventure and risk. In middle-class society these values are confined to certain approved situations, but delinquents express them at inappropriate times. Later on, they are likely to revert to a more conventional lifestyle. Matza (1964) considered that most juvenile delinquents drift in and out of delinquency. In maintaining this, he also wished to emphasise the freedom of choice which an individual has in direct contrast to the strongly positivist approaches of writers such as Cohen and Cloward and Ohlin.

Matza also claimed that much delinquency is rendered acceptable to its perpetrators by justifications (or, as Matza called them, 'neutralizations') of criminal behaviour, which are seen as valid by the delinquent but not by society as a whole. In the eyes of the delinquent, these are similar to the sort of defences to crimes that can be raised in a court, such as accident, insanity and self-defence. However, according to Matza, they are prior justifications which enable delinquents— although realising the objective wrongfulness of their behaviour—to offend without any feelings of guilt. They are not merely excuses after the event. Matza pointed out that such justifications are reinforced by the culture of the juvenile court, which does not consider juveniles to be fully responsible for their crimes.

The techniques used by delinquents to 'neutralise' their behaviour were first described in an article by Matza and Gresham Sykes (Sykes

and Matza 1957). The writers asserted that juveniles become delinquent through learning these techniques rather than by learning a
value system in contradiction to that of the dominant society. There
are five main techniques, each of which can be summarised by a
typical comment. Thus, 'denial of responsibility' occurs where delinquents, adopting the language of experts, express themselves to be the
product of some other forces, as reflected in the comment 'I'm ill'.
'Denial of injury', which allows vandalism to be defined as mischief
and joy-riding as borrowing, can also be summed up in the statement
'They can afford it'. 'Denial of the victim' may suggest that it is the
victim who is really guilty or that revenge was in order: 'They had it
coming'. 'The condemnation of the condemners' seeks to shift the
focus on to those who are critical of the delinquent's action; thus
'Everybody is fiddling'. Finally, 'the appeal to higher loyalties' claims
that, when a conflict arose between the two, the demands of society
had to be subordinated to the demands of the delinquent's own peer
group, and is reflected in the comment 'I couldn't leave my friends'.
Sykes and Matza considered that these techniques form a vital
component of Sutherland's theory of differential association—his
definitions favourable to the violation of the law (see Chapter 6). As
differential association was originally devised to explain white-collar
crime, this illustrates the usefulness of the theory in its ability to use
the same logic to explain crime in both the upper and lower levels of
society.

It is necessary for this explanation that the techniques of neutralisation precede and, in a sense, account for delinquency. Yet, the
alternative view that these techniques are simply rationalisations or
excuses offered after the event (and, of course, they always have
to be after the event) is appealing. People who are more likely to
commit crimes are less likely to subscribe to society's values and so
are less in need of techniques of neutralisation. However, in a different context, Stanley Cohen (2001) has argued that states use
techniques of neutralisation similar to those of Sykes and Matza to
deal with blame from themselves and others for the use of torture
and murder.

There is some empirical support for Sykes and Matza's view. On the
basis of longitudinal data from the National Youth Survey, Agnew
(1994) concluded that their assumption about the temporal order of
crime and neutralisations was justified in relation to violent incidents.
In a study of forty-two car thieves, Copes (2003) found that those
who had more attachments to society were more likely to use neutralisations. On the other hand, an analysis of interviews with 137

apprehended shoplifters led Cromwell and Thurman (2003) to conclude that it was impossible to determine whether apparent neutralisations were genuinely held beliefs or mere excuses. The authors
agreed with Hirschi (1969) that an excuse in one situation may provide
a causal neutralization in another situation.

Matza's theory was popular in the mid-1960s at a time when the
'ordinary' nature of much deviancy was being emphasised; when an
increased interest in illicit drugs led to a questioning of the boundaries
of legal behaviour; and when the realisation that almost anyone could
be a part-time delinquent held a certain appeal. However, Matza did
not give a proper explanation for violent behaviour and is nowadays
considered to have had a somewhat romanticised view of crime. It is
clear that, while everyone engages in delinquency at some stage in
their life, there is a hard core that continues to commit serious
offences on a regular basis, sometimes even lasting into adulthood.

Moreover, throughout his writings Matza, in contrast to the positivist views of earlier subcultural theorists, has been at pains to emphasise
the element of choice that his adolescents have in deciding whether to
become delinquent. Yet, the 'drift into delinquency' he described itself
seems to be brought on by external circumstances over which the
delinquents have no real control.

Following the strong focus on American gangs in the 1950s and
1960s, academic interest waned for some time, even though the
number of gangs began to escalate considerably after that period
(Klein 1995). However, it is hardly surprising that the modern versions are in many ways unlike those observed in the 1950s. Nowadays, gangs operate among the growing underclass who inhabit the
run-down areas found in most of America's large cities. They are divided far more on racial grounds. Disputes over territory arise for economic reasons rather than as expressions of male machismo. In any
case, the traditional lower-class street 'playgrounds' of earlier generations have long since disappeared. There seems no indication of a
search for upward social mobility; material wealth is the name of the
game. Nevertheless, authors still note a search for, and pride in, local
identity (Sánchez-Jankowski 1991), which can be traced back at least
as far as Thrasher's study, and has been a theme found in much of the
subsequent research. The renewed focus on gangs that arose in the
1990s was in the context of alleged 'drug wars' and the belief that
gang activity had become significantly more violent. In September
1994, President Clinton declared a 'National Gang Violence Prevention Week' to highlight the increasing concern. In the following year,
the Office of Juvenile Justice and Delinquency Protection published

some data about juvenile gangs. The fact that only 6 per cent of serious violent crime was committed by juvenile groups put the issue into some perspective. The report also revealed that 92 per cent of group offenders were male and that about half were African-American (Snyder and Sickmund 1995).

Martín Sánchez-Jankowski (2003), who carried out participant observation in gangs between 1978 and 1989, has expressed the view that contemporary American gangs are strongly influenced by the social settings in which they operate. Although membership provides entertainment and a degree of status, most young people join gangs in order to obtain money, and will use whatever means are necessary (including violence) to this end. Any available opportunities for work will be in low-paying service industries and are therefore likely to be rejected. Sánchez-Jankowski agreed with the view of Thrasher that many gangs are akin to social clubs in the way they provide benefits and support for their members.

Subcultures: the British experience

British sociologists and criminologists did not turn their attention to subcultures to any great extent until the post-war era. This was certainly not because gangs did not exist in Britain before that time; Graham Greene's novel *Brighton Rock* (1938) provides a chilling account of the 'razor gangs' that used to operate in the South Coast resort during the 1930s. It was more that the study of crime was still strongly connected with psychiatry.

The first major analysis of subcultural tradition in Britain was carried out by John Barron Mays in Liverpool and reported in his book *Growing up in the City* (1954). Mays's work, which in its areal analysis and extensive interviewing owed much to the earlier approach of the Chicago School, portrayed juvenile delinquency as reflecting widespread deprivation and poverty; it was 'a normal aspect of growing up in the Liverpool slums'. Mays considered that the values of working-class culture, which were passed down from adult to child, were such that a certain level of delinquency would inevitably occur. However, although most of the eighty youths he studied had committed delinquent acts, the majority had desisted by the time they reached adulthood. (It is significant that, in accordance with the prevailing thrust of British criminology at the time, Mays was criticised in some quarters for not carrying out psychological testing on his delinquents.) There was no extensive discussion of the origin of these particular values:

Mays certainly did not suggest that they had arisen through opposition to those of the middle class. His conclusions, which are similar to those that Miller (1958) later reached, are considered nowadays to be over-predictive of working-class delinquency.

At about the same time, an unpublished (but subsequently widely-cited) study by Jephcott and Carter (1954) into a mining town the researchers called Radby found that there were two distinct types of working-class family. In one street, families were accepting of delinquency and several of their members had criminal records. However, in a nearby street families of the same socio-economic level did not accept delinquent values and almost none of its residents had criminal records. The research emphasised the important role played by the family in the transmission of cultural values.

Terence Morris (1957) sought to apply the Chicago School's 'zonal hypothesis' to Croydon in an attempt to explain delinquency, but ultimately concluded that both social class and the existence of council estates on the edge of the town, to which 'problem families' were allocated, were more accurate indicators (see Chapter 6). However, the most significant contribution of the period was the book *The Delinquent Solution* (1966) by David Downes. Based on a study of subcultural delinquency in the Stepney and Poplar areas of east London, Downes's research compared the North American experience with his own findings. Downes discovered that his working-class boys had no desire to become middle class; indeed, in some ways, they celebrated their working-class status. They felt that school was a waste of time and left as soon as possible. The boys' response was a 'dissociation' rather than a reaction formation. Some would take up a 'dead-end' job, whereas others would spend most of their time on the street, where they would seek the excitement they could not find in school or work. Because of the extra time on their hands, the boys wanted even more from leisure than their employed counterparts, but they did not have the financial means to pursue legitimate recreational activities. Inevitably, given these frustrations and the amount of time they spent on the street, they came into contact with criminal activity. This was not 'rebellion' or 'retreatism', nor was there any organised gang structure. As Downes put it, 'The self-image of the Poplar boy . . . was that of the hooligan not the criminal'. Indeed, evidence on both sides of the Atlantic suggests that most juvenile crime is committed by groups of two or three offenders rather than by organised gangs (Zimring 1981).

To some extent, Downes incorporated the idea of 'subterranean values' put forward by Matza and Sykes. However, he did not accept their view that middle-class youths are involved in delinquent activity to the same extent as the working class.

The 1970s saw a flourishing of subcultural research in Britain. A few early studies reflected the 'hippie' ethos of the late 1960s in their consideration of the use of soft drugs (for example, Young 1971). Before long, however, the analysis reverted to the more usual subjects. James Patrick's book *A Glasgow Gang Observed* (1973) described a situation more redolent of the earlier American studies than most other British research: there are accounts of distinct membership roles and territorial disputes. However, Patrick himself emphasised that Glasgow had a long-established tradition of such activity. In one of the leading studies of the period, Howard Parker (*View from the Boys*, 1974) turned the attention once again on Liverpool. He showed how the theft of car radios proved a highly profitable activity which enabled the youths to enjoy themselves for a while before they settled down and married, or ended up in prison.

Two key studies of the period considered the problems of schooling. In his book *Learning to Labour* (1977), Paul Willis described research he had conducted in a Midlands secondary school as to why a group of working-class youths ('the Lads') formed a subculture in opposition to formal educational values and the boys who subscribed to them ('the Ear'oles'). Willis studied the Lads during their last year in school and their first year at work. Albert Cohen had described such behaviour as delinquent, but Willis thought this conclusion to be too simplistic. For him, the Lads' rejection of middle-class values provided a sort of preparation for the values of the shop floor or manual labour culture, which was realistically all they were likely to attain. They were, in effect, substituting a more realistic form of socialisation. In a later study of bike boys and hippies, Willis (1978) viewed the formation of such subcultures as a means of trying to restore a working-class cultural cohesion which had been considerably eroded in the post-war era.

A similar situation can be seen in Paul Corrigan's book *Schooling the Smash Street Kids* (1979), which was based on his research into why young people at school in Sunderland played around or truanted. Corrigan saw this behaviour as a form of resistance to compulsory schooling from individuals who realised that the formal system had little to offer them.

Although Downes (1966) did not believe that descriptions of gangs by writers such as Cohen or Cloward and Ohlin had much application to Britain, behaviour involving theft, violence and drugs—the basis of Cloward and Ohlin's tripartite analysis—seems to feature prominently in many of the British studies. Parker's description of car radio theft in Liverpool suggests an established criminal structure whereby youths stole the radios and passed them on to older men to dispose of. This could be described as similar to Cloward and Ohlin's 'criminal sub-culture'. The situation concerning 'retreatist' subcultures, however, is more confused. Unlike the position in the USA, drug use, whether individual or subcultural, was uncommon in Britain until the 1960s. 'Mods' took 'Purple Hearts' and there was a degree of cannabis usage among the young working class going into the 1970s. However, the subsequent use of hard drugs such as heroin has led to a fundamental challenge to the 'retreatist subculture' notion. Although it is the case that drug abuse does cause some individuals to 'retreat' into isolation-ist groups, research in Britain and the USA has also shown the highly organised side of both using and dealing in hard drugs—something to which the term 'retreatist' seems wholly inappropriate. In addition, the popularity of drugs such as 'Ecstasy' among the young working and middle class in the 1990s shows that it is possible to use drugs for short-term indulgence and still maintain a conventional lifestyle.

The British subcultural tradition is notable for having dealt with certain issues which have not really arisen in the USA. These include the greater significance of class and trade unionism in this country and the different experience of ethnic minority integration. In its evaluation of group delinquency as a working-class phenomenon, the British research perhaps owes more to Walter Miller's analysis of 'lower-class culture' than it does to the more conflict-orientated gangs described by other American writers such as Cohen, and Cloward and Ohlin.

In the 1970s, much of the work on gangs came from the University of Birmingham's Centre for Contemporary Cultural Studies. A good illustration of the importance of class can be seen in the writings of Phil Cohen on youth culture in the East End of London (1972). In considering the development of the 'Mod' and 'Skinhead' styles, Cohen maintained that the replacement of inner-city working-class housing areas by new estates had created fresh opportunities for some, while leaving others to the diminishing job opportunities caused by the running down of London's dockland. From the 1950s, the working class had become polarised by the replacement of trad-itional skilled work with automation and machinery. Many people from the so-called 'respectable' working class now took the 'upward option' into minor office jobs. The untrained, on the other hand, were increasingly forced into the 'downward option' of poorly paid, insecure work and—from the 1960s—increasingly long spells of unemployment. These generally comprised the individuals who were left behind in what remained of the old communities.

According to Phil Cohen, the conflicting lifestyles and prospects facing the adult working class had an impact on the form of culture adopted by their young. Aspirations of upward social mobility were reflected in 'Mod' culture, with its emphasis on style in general and Italian scooters in particular. In contrast, 'Skinheads', who adopted an appearance based on that of a manual labourer, clung to older traditions such as protecting territory. For Cohen, these subcultural reactions were not 'real' solutions, but were imaginary or 'magical' ones expressed in terms of style and other references to popular culture. Yet, magic does not always last for ever, and such flights of fantasy could at best only provide a temporary respite from the more desolate world in which the youths had to live.

Much of the writing from the Birmingham Centre suggested that youthful subcultural activity was a form of political reaction to the dominant culture from which such individuals considered themselves excluded. Expressions of dress and style were said to provide indications of this (Hall and Jefferson (eds) 1976). An interesting question then arises as to whether the political significance of such cultural statements is dependent on the individuals' having intended them to be viewed as such, or whether it is only necessary that others imbue them with this meaning.

Another issue which American writers have not had to contend with is that of gangs claiming allegiance to sports teams. In Britain, the sport in question has been football, and violence surrounding matches between professional teams has been in the news since the 1970s (although it is clear that 'football hooliganism' is as old as the game itself). Phil Cohen explained this on the basis of adherence to traditional working-class values which, for him, meant an adoption of the 'Skinhead' style. In more recent years, however, football gangs have taken to an ostentatious display of designer label clothing, especially Burberry. As more former 'hooligans' have offered accounts of their activities, it has become clear that the feeling of comradeship has been particularly important, alongside more common explanations such as the protection of territory and the display of macho values (see, for example, Chester 2003).

The racial aspects of subcultures have been less well covered. Stuart Hall *et al.* (1978) illustrated the racial stereotyping that occurred during the 'mugging' moral panic of the 1970s (see Chapter 4). In his book *Endless Pressure* (1979), Ken Pryce showed how lack of opportunity and racism among the black population of St Paul's, Bristol led—for some—to cultural reinforcement as provided by outlets such as reggae and—for others—to street crime.

After a period during the 1980s when there was relatively little British academic research into gangs, recent studies suggest that they are still, so to speak, alive and kicking. In a postal survey of all police in the UK, Stelfox (1998) received information about seventy-one gangs. Most were described as adult male with an average age between twenty-five and twenty-nine. Their structure was generally loose, with no clear leader. Most of the gangs engaged in a wide range of crimes. About two-thirds were white.

Three-quarters were said to be involved in drug dealing and 60 per cent to carry guns. The police considered that most of the gangs were violent.

Other research has found that gang members are generally younger than suggested in this study. In an ethnographic study of gangs in the Manchester area, Mares (2001) found that most of the members were under twenty-five and some were as young as ten. Whereas in the central area most of the gangs were Afro-Caribbean, in Salford they were generally white. Most of the gangs were involved in drug-dealing. Bullock and Tilley (2002) identified four major South Manchester gangs, with between twenty-six and sixty-seven members. The majority of the members were male and black. They committed a wide range of offences and generally carried weapons.

In another approach to obtaining information about gangs, people aged seventeen and over who had been arrested for drugs offences were interviewed about their involvement (Bennett and Holloway 2004). The researchers found that 15 per cent admitted to current or past gang membership. Around 95 per cent were male and most were white and under twenty-five. They were more likely than non-gang arrestees to have committed a range of property offences and significantly more likely to have committed robbery and to carry a weapon.

Girls and subcultures

As with virtually all other sociological explanations of crime before the late 1960s, the earlier subcultural theories were based on the assumption that crime is committed by males. The opportunity structures for teenage girls in working-class areas were never discussed. Yet, it does not inevitably follow from these theories—with the exception of Walter Miller's—that female cannot be substituted for male. The strain suffered by Albert Cohen's boys could just as easily be felt by girls, although Cohen himself assumed that this was not the case. He took the view that female delinquency was in accordance with sex-role expectations, such as theft of cosmetics or clothes. Cohen also considered that the relatively low levels of such delinquency were because most women valued marriage to a successful male far higher than making a career for themselves. Moreover, it is arguable that Matza's 'drift' explanation could apply equally to males or females. One reason, in addition to the prevailing gender assumptions of the time, may be that subcultures were viewed as largely synonymous with gangs, and that girls did not form gangs.

However, it is clear now that subcultural theory does apply to girls and there is evidence that girls do form gangs. Thrasher, who identified only six female gangs in his total of 1,313, considered that this low number resulted from the stronger parental supervision of girls and their general lack of aggressiveness. More recently, a study of American female gangs by Anne Campbell (1984) found that they were perfectly prepared to use violence to protect their territory. Angela McRobbie (1991) claimed that the typical female version of the male delinquent subculture is a 'culture of femininity' in which working-class girls, through adopting the distinctive modes of style and youth culture, develop an oppositional stance to school.

Joe-Laidler and Hunt (1997) identified two basic types of female gang organisation. The more common type, sometimes called an 'auxiliary' gang, is based on an affiliation to a male group. The men make the important decisions and try to control the women. The other type is the truly independent female gang, which is not subordinate to the males and establishes its own rules. The researchers interviewed sixty-five women from seven San Francisco female gangs. All the women, who were from poor families often with absent parents, claimed that the main benefit from gang membership was the sense of kinship. Patterns of violence were found to vary according to the organisation of the gang. Women in the auxiliary gangs were subject to more 'violence prone situations', largely because of their association with male gangs. The women in the independent gangs would generally only encounter violence in confrontations with members of other female gangs. However, women in both types of gang were far more likely to encounter violence from their boyfriends, who themselves were often gang members. Peterson *et al.* (2001) claimed that the sex composition of gangs—rather than the sex—was important in formulating their norms and activities. For example, youths in all-male and all or majority-female gangs reported less participation in delinquency than members of other types of gang.

On the other hand, recent research in Glasgow as part of the 'View from the Girls' project has found that very few girls (5 per cent) regularly engaged in violent activities and that groupings that could be described as gangs were extremely rare (Batchelor *et al.* 2001).

Conclusion

Cloward and Ohlin's theory can be viewed as a development of most sociological writing on crime that had preceded it. The work of the Chicago School had revealed the existence of subcultures and Sutherland had shown how delinquent values could be passed from one individual to another by ordinary learning processes. Durkheim's suggestion that crime could result from a severe disruption in the 'normal' order of society was specifically honed by Merton to the problems resulting from the differential ability to attain the ultimate goal of material wealth held out by American society. Cohen translated this into a lower-class group response to their inability to succeed in a middle-class society, and Cloward and Ohlin substituted Merton's desire for material wealth for Cohen's class frustration.

Yet, it can be argued that Durkheim remains the key figure here in that, whether strain is considered as an individual or group reaction, and whether the underlying desire is for money or middle-class status, there is still a basic assumption that these are simply functional issues within a society where everyone has to be allocated a place. In other words, there is a greater emphasis on the strain resulting from individuals not obtaining what they think they are entitled to, than from a fundamental appraisal of what they should actually be entitled to. Both strain theorists and their progeny, subcultural theorists, identified problems arising from the lack of an equal opportunity to succeed, but in a meritocratic society that rewards success there still has to be failure. Cloward and Ohlin placed a lot of emphasis on the point that many delinquents are just as talented as people who have obtained success in society, but they never considered the question—even more important now than forty years ago—of what society would do if these individuals had the skills and qualifications, but could still not find employment.

One unfortunate, but predictable consequence of the concentration by American writers on gangs is that a widespread assumption has grown up that the American subcultural literature has little, if any, application to Britain. To some extent, this is reinforced by the view of Downes (1966) that there were no such closely-structured entities to be found in east London. The more recent research of criminologists such as Phil Cohen has gone some way to shift the focus away from street gangs back on to subcultures, but the wider notion of strain theory seems relatively undeveloped in this country. Writers from the Birmingham Centre have argued that, whereas Cloward and Ohlin wrote of the problems arising from 'position-discontent', this was largely irrelevant to post-war subcultural development in Britain. In this country, the rigid division of society along class lines made such discontent seem inevitable and, therefore, hardly a source of strain. Instead, it is the demands of leisure and style which have been more influential in shaping the substance and form of the British sub-cultural experience.

9

Interactionism and phenomenology

In previous chapters, consideration has been given to certain positivist explanations of offending which, although varying among themselves, have contained common features. Crime is considered as a fixed, non-problematic entity, which is somehow 'out there' in society. As society itself is based on a general consensus of values, crimes must be committed by people who have something 'wrong' with them. The application of positivist research techniques can find out what this is by comparing 'criminals' with 'non-criminals'. In this chapter, two alternative hypotheses will be considered. The first, based on interactionism, is that crime is not an objective entity, but a consequence of social processes which occur in societies made up of different value systems, and in which particular individuals are able to influence both the actual and perceived status of others. The second, based on phenomenology, is that it is impossible to impose meaning on the behaviour of others and that the only function of a 'scientific' researcher can be to provide an adequate account of the meaning of behaviour for the actors themselves.

Interactionism

As the name suggests, interactionism refers to the processes by which people come to react to their own self-image, their view of others and their perception of how others see them, as well as the settings in which they meet or interact with others. For example, people might consider themselves as attractive, lazy or bad, and this assessment is likely to have been made—at least in part—as a result of responses from other people. All of these perceptions are fluid and individuals are making constant assessments and reassessments of themselves and each other. As these change, so do the individual's attitudes and actions. Albert Cohen (1966) stated that 'Everyone is continually engaged in a lifelong process of building, maintaining, or re-fashioning a self'. Interactionism is sometimes referred to as 'symbolic interactionism', as an individual's assessment of a person or situation is said to be built up from recognisable names or symbols. (A symbol is a means of referring to something else: for example, through a mode of dress or the wearing of a badge.) This was the term used by the main proponent of the theory, George Herbert Mead (1863–1931).

The notion of 'self' is fundamentally difficult. Circumstances are constantly changing and a continual reassessment of the self is necessary. Interactionists sometimes refer to the 'looking-glass self' to indicate that our self-image is what we see of ourselves reflected in those around us. Self is seen as a process rather than a structure. The use of language is also important. Individuals engage in role playing. People are usually aware of the likely effects of what they say and do, and so their words and deeds are fashioned to take account of the anticipated responses of others. This process most commonly takes place through the use of language, although facial expressions, body language, gestures and even one's choice of clothing can signify meaning. From an interactionist perspective, the re-evaluation of oneself is just as significant as a re-evaluation by others. However, interactionists have tended to concentrate more on the public meaning and interpretation of behaviour, including deviant behaviour.

The first stage in human interaction is therefore one of defining the situation. Where the individuals share the same definitions, the process of communication should be straightforward, as they will be interpreting cues and symbols in the same way (Berger and Luckmann 1967). Sometimes there are misunderstandings: the world of humour is full of examples of two people holding a conversation where each has a different understanding of what they are talking about. Interactionists argue that it does not matter what the objective facts of a situation are: its social reality is how it is defined by the participants.

In criminological study, the roots of interactionism go back to the ethnography of the Chicago School (Mead was at the University when Sutherland was a doctoral student there). One of its first applications to criminal activity can be seen in Frank Tannenbaum's book *Crime and the Community* (1923). In common with other Chicago researchers such as Thrasher, Tannenbaum noticed that many types of juvenile delinquency were a routine feature of adolescent street life. However, such acts might be perceived as a nuisance by the local community and result in the summoning of the police. This could begin a process whereby individuals come to be viewed differently, at first by others and then eventually by themselves. Tannenbaum considered that there is a gradual change of emphasis from defining the prohibited acts as evil to a more general definition of the individuals involved as evil. Once a person has been stigmatised as a criminal, the ratio of contacts with other people thus stigmatised and those considered law-abiding changes considerably. Tannenbaum referred to this process as 'the dramatisation of evil':

> The first dramatisation of 'evil' which separates the child out of his group for specialised treatment plays a greater role in making the criminal than perhaps any other experience . . . the process of making the criminal, therefore, is a process of tagging, defining, identifying, segregating, describing, emphasizing, making conscious and self-conscious; it becomes a way of stimulating, suggesting, emphasizing and evoking the very traits that are complained of.

Lonnie Athens (1997), who interviewed fifty-eight violent offenders in prison, provided an interactionist explanation of violence. Rejecting pathological accounts as ignoring situational factors, Athens argued that the key elements were the actors' self-image and the process by which they came to define themselves. He considered that there are four interpretations of situations made by the 'self' that can lead to violence: 'physically defensive', where the victim is perceived as intending to attack; 'frustrative', where the victim resists an order or encourages the offender to carry out an unwanted act; 'malefic', where the victim belittles the actor; and 'frustrative-malefic', which is a combination of the previous two categories.

A consideration of offenders' self-images resulted in three categories: 'violent' self-images arise where the actors are judged by others and see themselves as having a violent disposition; 'incipient violence' refers to the actors' tendency to make serious threats of violence; and 'non-violent'. The type of self-image will directly relate to the definition of a situation as warranting a violent intervention. For example, people with a violent self-image could define almost any situation as requiring violence on their part while, at the other end of the scale, offenders without a violent self-image would only use violence in physically defensive situations.

Heimer and Matsueda (1994) also found support for the significance of symbolic interactionism in the creation of the violent individual. Association with delinquent peers, exposure to delinquent attitudes and the appraisal by others as delinquent produced a greater self-reported involvement in delinquency than exposure to social disorganisation or poor control.

However, the influence of interactionist theory in criminology has become particularly identified with the writings of several American sociologists in the late 1950s and 1960s, who developed what has come to be known as 'labelling theory'. (This term is far from satisfactory, but it is so widely used in the literature that it will be adopted here.) Although little of what emerged was new—and could be traced back at least as far as Tannenbaum—the emphasis changed from a consideration of the ways in which definitions and meanings are developed by individuals and within groups to an analysis of the ways in which such definitions and meanings are imposed by members of other, more powerful groups.

The timing of this development was not fortuitous. It arose during a period when most aspects of Western society were affected by a greater openness, existing rules were challenged and long-standing customs and practices questioned. 'Bohemian' lifestyles emerged among certain sections of the population in the late 1950s (in America such individuals were said to belong to the 'beat' generation, and called 'beatniks'!) and extended into the 'flower power' era of the mid-1960s. Significantly, existing laws were flouted by the use of soft drugs, especially cannabis.

In criminology, this mood was reflected by a rejection of traditional positivist explanations, and particularly the functionalism of the 1950s, as being complacent and deterministic. A greater emphasis came to be placed on individual motivation. At the same time, the increasing contact between the police and middle-class 'hippies' or demonstrators led to a questioning of the role played by the criminal justice system in the ultimate formulation of 'crime'.

Perhaps the best-known writer in the labelling tradition is Howard S Becker. In his book *Outsiders* (1963), Becker considered the processes that are involved in ascribing that particular status to an individual. For this purpose, a definition of deviance had to be found. Becker rejected the statistical, as being too remote from rule-breaking, and the pathological, as locating the cause entirely within the individual. According to Becker, society itself creates deviance by making the rules, the breaking of which constitutes deviance, and by labelling the rule-breakers as deviants or outsiders. Therefore, an act is only deviant if other people respond to it as such. Once applied, the label of deviant overrides all other labels. Labelled individuals may come to associate with other people so labelled, perhaps because the general public refuses to mix with them or even because they are all imprisoned together. (Prisons are sometimes referred to as 'universities of crime'.) People released from prison may be unable to obtain legitimate work and may therefore return to crime as a living. The extent to which an act is considered deviant can change over time, and even vary in accordance with the individual who has committed the act—the rules can be applied unevenly. In fact, according to Becker, one cannot know for certain whether a particular act will be classified as deviant until other people have responded to it.

A development of this theme can be found in the writings of Edwin M Lemert. His work in this area considerably pre-dates that of Becker. Lemert's views were set out in his book *Social Pathology* (1951), but they gained a wider audience following the impact made by *Outsiders*, and were amplified in another book *Human Deviance, Social Problems and Social Control* (1967). Lemert considered that there are two important questions that have to be answered in the study of deviance: first, how deviant behaviour originates, and second, what are the consequences of labelling a person as deviant on the person's subsequent acts of deviation.

Lemert made a crucial distinction between 'primary deviation' and 'secondary deviation'. An act of primary deviation can occur in a wide variety of situations. The reasons why it occurs are not really important and will have little significance for the individual, as primary deviation does not result in self re-appraisal. Lemert described it as having 'only marginal implications for the psychic structure of the individual'. However, the way an act of primary deviation is responded to will be of central importance. If the act of primary deviation is labelled deviant by a person or institution with the authority to make the label stick (typically the courts), then acts of secondary deviation will occur as a way of dealing with the problems caused by the reaction to the primary deviation. Lemert thought that secondary deviance could serve to stabilise a pattern of deviant behaviour which, had it been left alone, might have been merely transitory. The emphasis here is very much on the actions of the labeller. An individual's personal and social attributes are only significant in that they may influence the way that other people respond to an act of primary deviation.

Lemert said of his theory:

> The distinction between primary and secondary deviation is deemed indispensable to a complete understanding of deviation in modern pluralistic society. Furthermore, it is held that the second research problem is pragmatically more pertinent for sociology than the first.

Lemert also highlighted how the social reaction to the act of primary deviance can itself result from rivalry or conflict between different groups involved in a power struggle:

Trivial or insignificant departures from social norms are stimuli for . . . 'storms of protest' and controversies. Closer inspections of these reactions often reveals that a political alignment within a community is seeking to embarrass the party in power, and has seized upon some otherwise unimportant deviant event . . . for this purpose.

Likewise, a government could seek to create a diversion to deflect from its own unpopularity. Many of the 'moral panics' which have arisen in Britain (and, no doubt, in other countries) in recent years could fit this analysis. The Conservative government of the 1980s was able to use 'law and order' issues to mask political and economic difficulties. In a similar context, the Falklands War has been referred to as Margaret Thatcher's 'Waterloo'.

The idea of secondary deviation could help to explain why, although almost everyone commits some criminal offences in their life, most people do not become persistent offenders. Few people could honestly say that, for example, they have never kept an excessive amount of change they have mistakenly been given in a shop or bought alcohol under age. It is virtually impossible to drive a car over an extended period of time without committing a crime. Figures from the Department of Environment and Transport in 1997 suggested that nearly three-quarters of drivers regularly break the 30 mph speed limit—and that is probably an underestimate. However, the rate of detection and prosecution of criminals is low, whether for motoring or other offences. The alternative argument is that it is those individuals who persistently re-offend who inevitably come to the attention of the police, and so recidivism precedes labelling rather than follows from it.

In his book *Becoming Deviant* (1969), David Matza set out four stages in the process of interaction between an individual and the formal social control agencies which lead to the attribution and adoption of the deviant label. He referred to the first as 'ban and transparency'. People whose behaviour has been 'banned' by the state will have difficulties in keeping their activities secret. They will start to worry that others will see through their efforts at concealment, and this anxiety will instil doubts about their real identity. The second stage is 'apprehension and labelling'. The deviant is processed by the criminal justice system and treated as a criminal. Any doubts about identity that the deviant may have held at the first stage will now be increased. For many deviants the process will stop here, but for others it will go on. Matza's third stage is 'exclusion'. The remaining vestiges of one's former identity are likely to disappear. Imprisonment will certainly confirm an individual's self-image as a criminal, and will continue to reinforce it on a daily basis. The fourth stage is 'post-prison stigmatisation and social rejection'. The family and community may be unwilling to welcome the deviant back. What Box (1981) referred to as an 'atrophy of interactional skills' may have occurred and a job will be hard to find. The police are likely to maintain a level of surveillance and will routinely approach the deviant when rounding up 'the usual suspects'. At Christmas 2000, police in Birmingham sent 'known villains' Christmas cards which read 'Thinking of you this Christmas and into the New Year'! (*The Guardian*, 15 December 2000). All this will help to confirm the deviant's identity as a criminal and may lead to further offending.

Another development of labelling theory is Leslie Wilkins's notion of 'deviance amplification', which he discussed in his book *Social Deviance* (1964). This has already been considered in Chapter 4, as the mass media can play a key role in its creation. The term may have belonged to Wilkins but, yet again, the idea was not new, as can be seen in the quotation from Tannenbaum. Wilkins sought to show how societal reaction can actually increase the amount of deviance that occurs. Most of the information people receive about deviance and crime is second-hand and has been processed by the informing agent, be it an individual or a part of the mass media. Wilkins described a spiral effect, whereby deviance is reported, stereotyped and then reacted to. If the reaction is hostile or punitive, the deviant or group of deviants will feel alienated, view themselves as even more deviant, join with others in a similar position, and engage in further acts of deviance. The whole process is likely to repeat itself and deviance amplification has occurred.

In their study of crimes committed by homeless young people in Toronto and Vancouver, Hagan and McCarthy (1997) found that those with a background of parental abuse were particularly likely to increase their involvement in crime following arrest and official sanctioning. The authors speculated that this may have resulted from the compounding of a sense of shame and embarrassment. It also emerged that male street youths with a parent who had been arrested were likely to offend more frequently following their own arrest than females in the same situation. Hagan and McCarthy suggested that the experience may have proved a greater deterrent for women.

(a) Evaluation

It is difficult to imagine nowadays the impact that Becker's statement—that deviance is not a quality of the act but a consequence of behaviour being ascribed the label of deviant—had in the early 1960s. On the face of it, it is a statement of the obvious, similar to 'an elephant is an animal which we choose to call an elephant'. Just as this statement tells us nothing about elephants, Becker's comment seems to say nothing about the essence of deviance. However, the point it was intended to convey was that one does not need to know anything about deviance, other than the fact that deviance is in the eye of the beholder. At a time when the mainstream explanations of crime and deviance were all positivist, this approach seemed like a breath of fresh air to the growing number of radicals who were increasingly questioning 'the system'.

Yet, it is this appeal to the spirit of the age that has been seized on by critics as being a major flaw in labelling theory. Its main thrust seems directed at behaviour which is on the margins of criminality, such as drug taking (an area previously studied by Becker), deviant sexual behaviour and victimless crimes (Schur 1965). Liazos (1972) referred to this as comprising a study of 'nuts, sluts and "preverts" ' (*sic*). There is almost an implication that the only people who oppose the behaviour are those in authority, and that it is the deviants who are the real victims. Becker, in particular, appears to have overlooked the fact that a deviant is not always the underdog: there are some nasty people out there committing some gruesome crimes. In this respect, labelling theory, with its emphasis on the reactions of powerful groups to deviance, provides a narrower focus than symbolic interactionism, which is interested in the reactions of all members of society.

For instance, how convincingly does labelling theory account for murder? It is clearly the case that killing can occur in situations which do not amount to criminal offences, for example in self-defence, by state execution, or in times of war. However, on other occasions the wrongfulness of killing is surely not dependent on its being labelled as such by the state. Taylor *et al.* (1973) suggested that labelling theorists were trying to divorce a physical act from its social meaning and that, on the whole, most people in a society are aware of what behaviour is considered deviant. Taylor *et al.* asserted that it *is* possible to say that deviance is a quality of the act if, following Weber, a distinction is made between *behaviour*, which refers to purely physical conduct (falling on the ground), and *action*, which includes the purely physical conduct, but also has a socially ascribed meaning (falling on the ground to score a try in rugby football).

Another problem concerns Lemert's distinction between primary and secondary deviation. Lemert considered that the reasons for an act of primary deviation are largely irrelevant, and that an act of secondary deviation is likely to be committed for entirely different reasons, based on the reaction of 'labellers' to the primary deviation. The category of primary deviation appears to be an attempt by Lemert to acknowledge that there are forms of behaviour which any group or society would recognise as deviant or criminal. Labelling or 'social reaction' theorists have offered a number of explanations as to why people might commit acts of primary deviation. An individual may belong to a minority group whose values are likely to result in violation of the rules of the dominant group. A person may have conflicting responsibilities and the adequate performance of one may lead to violations of the other. Someone may violate rules for personal gain and not expect to be caught. People may be unaware that they are violating rules at all (Gove (ed) 1980).

Yet, it is not clear if this distinction between primary and secondary deviation exists and, even if it does, why primary deviation should be considered unimportant. In the case of 'political' (such as 'terrorist') and organised crime, for example, it seems highly implausible. Such people may even welcome a deviant label: anti-road and other environmental protesters claim that they obtain extensive publicity through their illegal actions. Lemert's writings also raise the problem of 'hidden crime'. Many persistent offenders never come to the attention of the authorities and it is unlikely that few if any delinquents are apprehended after committing their first offence. However, symbolic interaction theory in itself would not recognise this difficulty: persons are able to reassess themselves as a result of an 'internal conversation' and without any input from other people. Becker acknowledged this in his discussion of 'secret deviance' (1963).

Labelling theory assumes that an individual's whole persona can be affected by being labelled a deviant or criminal. There is supposed to be an element of what Robert Merton (1948) referred to as 'self-fulfilling prophecy'—'a *false* definition of the situation evoking a new behavior which makes the original false conception come *true*'. To what extent is this the case? There is certainly evidence that some people are deterred from committing crimes by the shame and embarrassment that conviction would bring upon them and their families, although this is probably less so nowadays. Yet, does even this amount to a fundamental change in their whole idea of 'self'? Professional and 'political' criminals may truly lead a 'life of crime', but they form a very small proportion of convicted offenders. In contrast to Matza's notion of delinquents 'drifting' in and out of crime, labelling theory seems to polarise individuals as being normal or deviant.

The popularity of labelling theory in the 1960s was, in part, a result of the growing questioning of the positivist theories of the day which seemed to give individuals little if any choice of action and render them liable to forces beyond their control. However, labelling theory, particularly as reflected in the writings of Lemert, has itself been criticised for failing to allow for individual choice. Akers (1967) described this vividly:

> One sometimes gets the impression from reading this literature that people go about minding their own business, and then—'wham'—bad society comes along and slaps them with a stigmatised label. Forced into the role of deviant, the individual has little choice but to be deviant.

There is an element of overstatement in this, as labelling theorists never claimed that deviants had to be unaware that they were contravening the rules prior to being successfully labelled. Even those on the edges of criminality, such as users of soft drugs, generally know they are breaking the law. Nevertheless, the 'deterministic' critique can still be made. Although labelling theory appears to portray deviants as the unwilling recipients of the label, in some situations, such as joining a delinquent gang, the evidence suggests that deviants actively go out and seek the label. Moreover, even the choice apparently exercised by the stigmatised in the process of becoming a secondary deviant is arguably not a true choice: as Taylor *et al.* (1973) pointed out, it is the choice of a degraded individual with a limited range of options available.

Another drawback of labelling theory is that it is not easy to subject to empirical testing. Some interactionists would be unconcerned about this, especially if such testing involved the application of positivist research techniques. There is clearly a problem in trying to assess what factors have been significant in creating an individual's self-image. A further difficulty in any attempt to research the effects of labelling arises from the distinction between primary and secondary deviation. Whether researchers consider samples of convicted offenders or samples based on self-reported delinquency, the starting point is likely to be an act of secondary deviation. Using secondary deviation as a base from which to consider primary deviation is a reversal of the usual labelling process and is thus hardly satisfactory.

However, such difficulties have not deterred researchers from trying to evaluate labelling. An American study by Piliavin and Briar (1964) concluded that the disproportionately high level of stops and searches of black youths was prompted by widespread dislike of blacks by the police. Although the authors were convinced that this was an exercise based on racial discrimination which created a self-fulfilling prophecy and, effectively, secondary deviation, they also had to concede that the police actions could be justified on the basis of statistical information. West and Farrington (1977), in the longitudinal Cambridge Study in Delinquent Development (see Chapter 3), found that boys who were apprehended and then convicted of crimes became more delinquent than boys with an equally delinquent background, but who had managed to avoid apprehension. This conclusion has subsequently been supported in research by Bazemore (1985) and Palamara *et al.* (1986). Feldman (1977) considered that labelling theory is consistent with principles of operant learning (see Chapter 16) and therefore provides a useful account of the development of the delinquent role.

Research by Robert Sampson (1986) discovered that, even allowing for the seriousness of the criminal behaviour, the police are more likely to make arrests in poor rather than better-off areas. This finding raises a familiar problem for labelling theorists: does concentrating police resources in a particular area create a self-fulfilling prophecy, or is it simply an accurate appraisal of where most crime is taking place? An assessment of the research evidence by Tittle (1980), while revealing that offenders who were punished more severely had a greater likelihood of reoffending, also found that these offenders had previously been extensively involved in criminality.

Edwin Schur (1980) has claimed that critics such as Hirschi (1975), who say that empirical evidence is not supportive of labelling theory, have made the mistake of trying to evaluate the deviant's behaviour:

> Yet this is not at all its aim, which is instead to concentrate on the processes through which social *meanings* come to be attached to types of behaviour (and to individuals), and the consequences of such attachment. The central focus, then, is on *character-izations of behaviour* rather than on behaviour itself.

It has been claimed that all the emphasis in the literature is on the labelled, with very little attention devoted to the labellers. Presumably, a vital component of a successful labelling exercise is—to continue the metaphor—that the label should initially stick and then not readily drop off. For a person convicted of a criminal offence, the situation seems straightforward: the label is applied by a criminal court in the form of a sentence. However, in other respects—such as a consideration of why certain behaviour is criminalised at all, and who has the power to make a deviant label stick—labelling theorists are generally silent. No real attention is paid to why the label will stick to some people, but drop off others. There seems to be an assumption in the literature that people who define others as deviants must be in a more powerful position than the deviants themselves. This arises from a failure to distinguish between the reaction of, on the one hand, official agencies of social control and, on the other hand, that of other individuals or groups in society. Official policies can be viewed as emanating from whichever interest group or groups hold sufficient power to speak for a society at a particular time (see Chapter 10). However, not only may the policy itself result from a compromise, but it is quite possible that a majority of the population is opposed to it. To provide an illustration, many British governments have been elected with fewer votes than the combined number of votes of the opposition parties.

Finally, it may be questioned whether labelling is inevitably counterproductive. Although the efficacy of deterrence-based punishment has been challenged, it is still likely that many people are deterred from committing crimes because they fear the stigma associated with a conviction more than the actual punishment imposed. This is evidenced by the fact that minor, non-custodial punishments are often effective for first offenders. On this analysis, the real question to be asked is whether the labelling process creates more crime than it prevents.

Braithwaite (1989) has highlighted the problem of failing to delineate the limits of tolerance:

> If 'moral panic' over petty juvenile offending was anathema to liberal labelists, was moral apathy over some forms of sexual abuse of women and white-collar crime equally a cause for celebration?

(b) Policy implications

If labelling theory, particularly as propounded by Lemert, has any validity, two clear implications seem to follow. One is that the criminal law should intrude into people's lives as little as possible. The other is that, where it is absolutely necessary to invoke criminal sanctions, the manner in which the criminal justice system deals with a person who has been apprehended for the first time (although this person is unlikely to be a 'first offender') is of crucial importance. The system must somehow prevent the individual from feeling devalued or like a 'real criminal'.

The first of these could be achieved by limiting the number of criminal offences, or by using prosecution only as a last resort. Although the content of the criminal law does vary over time, the clear trend has been to create more offences. Edwin Schur (1965) argued that so-called 'victimless' crimes, such as drug use, actually serve to create more crime. For example, drug users have to steal or rob to support their habit. As America saw only too well in the 1920s, the prohibition of a desired commodity creates a profitable illegal market. This can also lead to the corruption of police officers who are bribed to turn their attentions elsewhere. There have been calls in Britain for a discussion of the whole issue of decriminalising 'soft' drugs such as cannabis (see Chapter 2).

The argument over prosecuting only as a last resort has usually centred on juveniles. In Britain, the policies of successive governments have been inconsistent in this respect. Until recently, there had been a consensus for more than sixty years that particular efforts should be made to prevent young offenders from exposure to the usual adult criminal justice process. Juvenile offenders are very likely to be cautioned—certainly far more so than adults—except for serious offences. Adults are also cautioned in greater numbers nowadays, although it may not be too cynical to suggest that this owes more to the need to save court costs than to avoid stigma. However, cautioning has been criticised as being unjust. There are differences in its use among the various police forces and evidence shows that it is less likely to be used for black people (Commission for Racial Equality 1992). It has also been suggested that cautioning leads to 'net-widening', or the inclusion of people within the criminal justice system (as formal cautions are recorded) who would previously have been dealt with informally (Cohen 1985).

The fact that court proceedings themselves can have a labelling or stigmatising effect was recognised by Harold Garfinkel (1956) in his well-known article 'Conditions of Successful Degradation Ceremonies'. In England and Wales a separate juvenile court (now called youth court) was established by the Children and Young Persons Act 1933. A list of special requirements was set out, governing matters such as the physical distancing of the court from adult courts, the layout of the court and the relative informality of the proceedings. Members of the public are not allowed to observe the court in session without special reason. In an attempt to protect juveniles from stigma, no information can generally be published which might identify them. There has always been a judicial discretion to waive the anonymity afforded to juveniles in courts and, starting with the case of the young killers of the Liverpool child, James Bulger, judges have done this in a growing number of high profile cases.

The government has now moved towards removing anonymity

from juvenile offenders in an attempt to shame them in the eyes of their peers and embarrass their parents into taking better care of them. The Serious Organised Crime and Police Bill 2004 contained a clause which would, in effect, provide a presumption in favour of identifying children and young persons who have been made the subject of an anti-social behaviour order.

Adults, on the other hand, have generally enjoyed no such protection. The only significant measure that has been taken to reduce their stigma has been the Rehabilitation of Offenders Act 1974. This allows job applicants to withhold information about previous convictions after a certain period of time (the length of which depends on the punishment imposed). However, the Act never applied to certain occupations, including the legal profession and employment with children, and its progressive tone has not been continued in other provisions. In fact, many people hold the view nowadays that stigmatising or shaming offenders is necessary as it is likely to deter them from re-offending (although there is no strong evidence to support this). Police forces write to men who are suspected of 'kerb-crawling', in the hope that their wives or partners will see the letters. Local newspapers publish lists of (wholly unnewsworthy) cases from the magistrates courts, including names, addresses and punishments imposed. For several years, American judges have been ordering offenders placed on probation to wear labels around their necks or place signs in their gardens proclaiming their guilt. As Pratt (2000) has pointed out, such shaming punishments are a return to the penality of the eighteenth century.

Following the murder of a little girl, Sarah Payne, in 2000, sections of the media in Britain began to focus on paedophiles. The *News of the World* promised to publish the names and addresses of thousands of convicted sex offenders (see Chapter 4). It was eventually persuaded to stop, but not before vigilante attacks had occurred throughout the country, including several cases involving mistaken identity (perhaps the most bizarre of these was against the home of a paediatrician living in South Wales). A police-run national register of convicted sex offenders had been established under the Sexual Offences Act 1997, and the newspaper was campaigning for a general public right of access to it. No such right has yet been given.

Vigilante action is not new, but there is a certain irony where it results directly from measures that have been introduced to reduce crime. The labelling process is alleged to be responsible for further offending, but it is usually envisaged that this will be crime committed by offenders and not against them.

There have even been suggestions that some individuals have harmed themselves as a result of being 'named and shamed'. In January 2001, the West Midlands Police projected sixty-feet high images of ten of the force's most-wanted criminals on to the side of its headquarters. Two of them were later found dead in mysterious circumstances. The Law Society called for the scheme to be abandoned (*The Guardian*, 8 November 2002).

The virtues of denunciatory punishment have been extolled since at least the nineteenth century (von Hirsch 1985) and, according to Garfinkel (1956), all societies employ a basically similar type of degradation ceremony. However, a more recent approach to crime has emerged which suggests that degradation can be harmful, and that what is needed is the successful reintegration of offenders into society.

(c) Reintegrative shaming

In his book *Crime, Shame and Reintegration* (1989), John Braithwaite undertook the daunting task of setting out a general theory of crime. He started by listing what he thought are the thirteen most consistent research findings about crime. These can be broadly condensed into the following statement: crime, which has been increasing in most Western societies since the end of World War II, is committed disproportionately by young, unmarried lower-class males who live in areas of high residential mobility in large cities; have performed badly at school; are on poor terms with their parents; and have criminal associates. Braithwaite then considered existing theories of crime and, although he found many of them valuable, concluded that they all have deficiencies which would spoil any claim to be a general theory.

Crime, according to Braithwaite, can be dealt with in one of two ways: either by stigmatisation, which is usually what happens at present, or by reintegrative shaming. He described shaming as:

> . . . all social processes of expressing disapproval which have the intention or effect of invoking remorse in the person being shamed and/or condemnation by others who become aware of the shaming.

Reintegrative shaming is shaming which is 'followed by gestures of reacceptance into the community of law-abiding citizens'. Whereas stigmatisation involves a denigration of the person, reintegrative shaming involves a denigration of the behaviour. Braithwaite saw it as the 'missing link in criminological theory' (Braithwaite 1995). He cautioned that reintegrative shaming is a powerful tool and should not be used lightly.

In their book *Not Just Deserts* Braithwaite and Pettit (1990) set out what they called a republican theory of criminal justice. By this, the authors were referring to a system within a society which balances the interests of all citizens, ensures political equality, and allows the participation of everyone in public life. These aims can be attained by the maximisation of 'dominion', a term which was used to refer to a collective concept of liberty: a sense of liberalism protected by law which historically preceded the 'free market' liberalism that developed in the nineteenth century. All members of a society must enjoy an equal amount of liberty for dominion to exist. Every criminal offence affects the dominion of the victim and society as a whole through the challenge to its collective security. The punishment of offenders also affects their dominion. A minimalist approach should be adopted to the criminal law and the criminal justice system: the key word in punishment should be parsimony. The purpose of the criminal justice system is to promote dominion for all. This would encourage progress towards a fully communitarian society, based on trust, loyalty and caring for others.

For Braithwaite and Pettit, reintegrative shaming, together with compensation and restitution where appropriate, is the best method of restoring dominion to society, victims and offenders. However, it is only suitable in the case of criminal offences that can be justified within a republican criminal justice system. Victimless crimes, for example, would be excluded.

Braithwaite likened reintegrative shaming to the 'family model', where punishment is administered within the framework of a loving family and then the child is 'welcomed back' again. Disapproval should be made clear, but a relationship of respect must still exist. Braithwaite also believed that the influence of the family accounts for the different offending rates between men and women, as adolescent girls in Western societies remain far more integrated within the family structure than adolescent boys. It also helps to explain why adult men, within the interdependency of a new family, are more likely to desist from crime. However, he went on to argue that reintegrative shaming can also apply to larger groups—what he called 'communitarian' societies. Braithwaite held out Japan as a classic example of where reintegrative shaming works. Japan has a particularly low crime rate for a modern, highly industrialised society and makes little use of imprisonment. It is part of the Japanese culture that wrongdoers are given every encouragement to admit their errors and ask for forgiveness. This appears to operate at all levels of society from the criminal up to the president of a corporation. On the other hand, stigmatising or non-communitarian societies, such as Britain and the USA, which have high rates of imprisonment, shame their offenders in a stigmatic way, making little or no attempt to reintegrate them into society. The resulting stigma and blocked opportunities can lead to the creation of subcultures, which provide an environment within which the learning of criminal techniques can take place.

According to Braithwaite, his theory explains the thirteen most consistent research findings better than any of the existing theories. He did not reject these theories outright, but considered that by the addition of one variable—reintegrative shaming—the leading explanations of crime could be synthesised into a new, stronger one.

Evaluation

Confronting the victim and making reparation for loss or damage would be key elements in any implementation of such an approach. In Britain, trial schemes centred on reparation were conducted in the late 1980s, but they were not given statutory recognition in the wide-ranging Criminal Justice Act 1991 and eventually lapsed (Marshall and Merry 1990). However, community conferences involving young offenders have been introduced in New Zealand and Australia. These involve the young persons, members of their family, police representatives, victims and their family. There has been some suggestion that victims feel pressurised into taking part and accepting outcomes that are far from ideal (Maxwell and Morris 1993). Concerns have grown in Australia as to whether the involvement of the police in the conciliation process is likely to emphasise stigmatisation over reintegration (Cunneen and White 1995), and Blagg (1997) has argued that reintegrative shaming is an inappropriate way of trying to reduce the over-representation of Aboriginal youths in custody. However, Braithwaite and Mugford (1994) have set out fourteen 'conditions of successful reintegration ceremonies' and claim that, if these are adhered to, they will provide a process to satisfy all parties and reintegrate an offender into the community.

Braithwaite (1995) has accepted the criticism of Scheff (Scheff and Retzinger 1991) that his original formulation should have given more prominence to pride as a complement to shame. The instillation of pride in being responsible, law-abiding and considerate of others could have a greater effect than shaming on the likelihood of a person's (re)turning to crime. Braithwaite considers that pride may be a particularly important emotion for the women's movement to develop, especially pride in being a woman in a patriarchal society.

One difficulty with Braithwaite's notion of reintegrative shaming is that it appears to place the emphasis on the actions of the shamer and the appropriate members of society (or the family), but has less to say about the impact of the shaming process on the offender. The whole event was portrayed by Braithwaite as a transaction in a single direction from the shamer to the offender. However, reintegration can presumably only be accomplished with the consent of the individual being shamed. As with other forms of labelling theory, Braithwaite seemed less interested in the initial or primary act of deviance.

Russell (1998) argued that the idea of reintegrative shaming is superficial. He contrasted it with the work of Norbert Elias (1994), whose view of civilising processes suggests that human emotions such as shame are complex and largely to be found in the unconscious mind. For this reason, Russell considered it unlikely that Braithwaite's approach would have any significant effect on offenders.

The theory of reintegrative shaming does not seem capable of distinguishing between feelings such as shame, guilt or repentance by the offender's reaction. Potter (1992) has pointed out that it is necessary to differentiate between mere compliance with what the group requires, which is not internalised, and conformity, which is internalised. For example, the directors of a negligent corporation may appear to be expressing extreme remorse for a particular incident, whereas, in truth, they may simply be acting out of self-interest and be more concerned with maintaining their level of business. Best (1990) has argued that Braithwaite gave examples of how shaming has worked for relatively small corporations in different countries, but has failed to consider whether the same degree of success would be likely with transnational corporations. Nor is there any discussion of the significance of power or how certain behaviours have come to be criminalised (Potter 1992).

It is, perhaps, not surprising that efforts to reintegrate offenders should concentrate on juveniles. Societies expect young people to show contrition and are not so concerned about any accompanying humiliation. 'Welcoming them back' into the community is also not so difficult. In effect, it is like dealing with a naughty child. Would such an approach be so easy to operate for adults? Fundamental changes would have to occur in the structure of society. Braithwaite frequently referred to the importance of the family model in effecting reintegrative shaming, but the family in Western society is nowadays a far less cohesive unit than he implied, and it may be unrealistic to expect a state to build its criminal justice policy around such a fading entity. There is also the potential difficulty of 'net-widening' (see above), which can result from intervening in the cases of children or other offenders who have not formally been found guilty in a court of law.

It seems rather optimistic of Braithwaite to believe that everyone will rally around the core values which he propounded for his republican society and accept that these values should be protected by the criminal law. While the values themselves—centring on his notion of dominion—would seem unobjectionable to many, Braithwaite appears to have overlooked the culture conflict which several writers have identified as being an inevitable consequence of the exercise of legal authority in a pluralistic society (for example, Sellin 1938). Reintegrative shaming assumes the existence of a society in which there is a broad consensus as to values and the acceptance of those values by the offender. However, if the offender feels alienated from society and is unrepentant, it is unlikely that reintegrative shaming can successfully take place: the offender may never have been integrated into society in the first place.

Braithwaite assumed that offenders whose crimes are not regarded as repugnant by a consensus within a society will not be susceptible to reintegrative shaming. He clearly had in mind 'victimless' crimes, and referred to drug use or homosexuality. For this reason, he considered that in 'the good society' crimes should be restricted to 'predatory offences against person and property'. However, Braithwaite could well find that more people think that cannabis use and even homosexuality should be criminalised than he imagines. A high level of consensus on the content of the criminal law may well be hard to achieve.

Russell (1998) was concerned about the scope for manipulation in the theory: 'What ideological forces are at work in the formation of notions of crime and criminality? What are offenders being reintegrated to, or, more pointedly, whose version of the "good" society and acceptable behaviour do we take as a guide?'

The Japanese system was held up by Braithwaite as providing a model in this respect, but Japan has a higher rate of juvenile crime than the USA (although this drops dramatically in the late teens). Currie (1985) suggested that Japan's low crime rate is due to its policy of full employment. There are also many oppressive aspects of Japanese society, and it has been argued that the pressures on suspects to confess to crime result in miscarriages of justice (Foote 1992). A survey of Japanese prosecutors by Johnson (2000) found only partial support for Braithwaite's theory. Although the vast majority considered that rehabilitating and reintegrating offenders was a major work objective, few thought that invoking the condemnation of the crime and the criminal was a significant part of their job.

In an interesting account of the importance of different locality-based groups within Japanese culture, Komiya (1999) showed how it would be wrong to assume that the notion of 'shame' as used in Japan could simply be adopted in the entirely different social world of Western countries.

However, it is arguable that such countries could profitably make some movement in the direction indicated by Braithwaite, and success with juvenile offenders would render possible difficulties with adults less important. Although Braithwaite predicted that reintegrative shaming would most likely be found in cultures particularly concerned with shame, Vagg (1998) found that Hong Kong, which fits this description, shows a high level of intolerance towards offenders.

Some empirical support for the advantages of reintegrative shaming was found in a study of Australian nursing home inspection teams (Makkai and Braithwaite 1994). It was discovered that nursing homes which were visited by a team embracing a reintegrative shaming ideology displayed an improved level of compliance for a period after the inspection. On the other hand, those homes which were visited by inspectors adopting a stigmatising attitude showed an approximately equal decline in the level of compliance over the same period. Hay (1998), who thought that Braithwaite's theory lacks clarity in certain key areas, questioned the relevance of such research to the workings of the criminal justice system. However, Young and Goold (1999) have reported positively on the workings of the Thames Valley Police's Restorative Cautioning Unit in Aylesbury, which they consider to have been clearly influenced by reintegrative shaming.

(d) Conclusion

In some respects, the creation of labelling theory did not do any favours to its much wider-ranging source, symbolic interactionism. Labelling came to be seen (fairly or otherwise) as a fairly mechanical process, subject to many of the old, familiar problems, such as determinism, which had inspired its proponents to look for a new approach to crime and deviance in the first place. One difficulty arose from the description of labelling as a 'theory' and, in a re-evaluation of his work, Becker (1974) was happy to refer to it as a 'perspective'. Nevertheless, labelling—theory or perspective—played a highly significant role in the development of criminology in the 1960s. Attention was shifted from the rule-breakers to the reaction of others in society.

Matza (1969) pointed out the irony that systems designed to enforce social control could be responsible for the creation of deviance. For the first time, the content of the criminal law came to be seen as problematic and not simply a fixed given.

In the light of subsequent developments, it seems rather quaint that the essentially liberal perspective of labelling was considered a radical perspective in the 1960s. This was largely in the context of what had gone before. The concentration on criminal justice processes was timely in the America of the late 1950s and early 1960s—the height of the Cold War—as it represented a move away from the strait-jacket of positivism, and yet did not initially provide a political challenge to the structure of American society.

However, this was soon to follow. The popularity of labelling theory led to considerations of power and the whole operation of the criminal justice system: who has the power to criminalise, and what factors influence the widespread use of discretion. Indeed, Lemert's discussion of secondary deviation had touched on these issues as long ago as 1951. Criminology was now being politicised, and labelling theory was in danger of being sidelined for devoting too much attention to the 'nuts, sluts and "perverts" ' view of deviance. Gouldner (1968) criticised labelling for its excessive reliance on 'man-on-his-back' rather than 'man-fighting-back'. Later, he referred to labelling theorists as 'the zookeepers of deviance' (1975), who wanted to keep their rare specimens behind bars and display them to the public. Labelling theory could also be said to have paid too much attention to the relatively low-level decision making of police officers, psychiatrists and social workers, while shying away from a critique of the real power structures within society. Yet, for others, the relative intimacy of such micro-studies provides one of labelling theory's greatest strengths. It allows an important shift of emphasis from studies of economic and cultural developments to the effects of political decision-making on individuals. Underlying labelling theory is an objection to excessive state interference, which can be traced back to writers such as Beccaria (see Chapter 5).

The influence of interactionism still remains, and Braithwaite's notion of 'reintegrative shaming' provides an attempt to use the power of societies to affect the self-perception of individuals more positively than by merely imposing stigma. However, one of the main difficulties with Braithwaite's theory is its practicability. It assumes a level of consensus among members of a society—and, crucially, a willingness to cooperate on the part of offenders—which may not exist in today's rapidly fragmenting world. What is commonly accepted as good child-rearing practice in the home might be more difficult to apply to adults in the courtroom.

Phenomenology and ethnomethodology

A further approach to the study of human behaviour that is not based on the individual pathology and determinism of positivist research can be found in phenomenology and ethnomethodology. Phenomenology is a German philosophy and ethnomethodology is an American sociological approach based on phenomenology which was developed during the 1950s by Harold Garfinkel. These are both difficult concepts to follow in the original literature, and an attempt will be made here to provide a simple (but, hopefully, not simplistic) outline.

In essence, phenomenology is a study of that which appears to be the case in the perception or consciousness of a particular person, and of how it came to be built up or constituted. Unlike some other philosophies, phenomenology considers that mind and action are intentional, not determined. Consciousness must always be consciousness about something: even if people are puzzled or confused, they are puzzled or confused about 'something'. An individual lives among these 'somethings': individuals can therefore be said to live in their mind. However, as individuals live together in a society, these 'somethings' are constantly changing. The way that the 'somethings' are received and dealt with by other people will affect the way in which individuals see the world.

There are said to be two 'imperatives' in the study of phenomenology: phenomenological description and phenomenological constitution. The former seeks to record the field of objectivities ('somethings') experienced by the subject. The latter shows how the phenomenon is built up and meanings are constructed by the subject. It is vital to realise that the constitution, or building up, of the phenomenon is dependent on its prior description. The test of a valid constitutive account is whether it would be possible to reproduce the same consequences and results using either the same or other actors.

Writers from a phenomenological perspective have not adopted a standard approach. It was Alfred Schutz who was to have the greatest influence on deviance theorists and, subsequently, ethnomethodologists. Schutz distinguished between two 'systems of relevances'. This phrase refers to the elements in a situation which individuals pick out as being relevant to their course of action. One system of relevances characterises individuals in their practical, daily commonsense activities, which Schutz called their 'natural attitude'. The other characterises individuals in their role as 'scientists'. In moving from a 'natural attitude' to a 'scientific attitude', social scientists would move from their own biographical situation within the world to a disinterested, or scientific observation of it. The 'natural attitude' is formed from commonsense notions based on taken-for-granted knowledge. However, scientific (or social scientific) concepts are referred to by Schutz as 'second-order constructs' (that is, constructs of the constructs made by the original actors). Scientists have their own 'taken-for-granted' knowledge, but this is quite separate from the values and beliefs of these individuals in their natural attitude. In short, social scientists should aspire to the scientific attitude when carrying out their work, but this will be far from easy to achieve.

Traditional criminology is governed by society's definitions and problems. In Schutz's terminology, the system of relevances is that of members of society and politicians in their natural attitudes. Criminology, therefore, adopts the public's commonsense definition of crime and the criminal as major social problems. Examples of this 'commonsense' definition, which is fuelled by the media, are that society is divided into criminals and non-criminals, and that the extent of crime is shown in the official statistics. However, a phenomenological perspective would be very different. The system of relevances would be based on an approach of subjective interpretation, rather than societal definitions of what the problem is. The validity of the sociologist's interpretations, or 'second order constructs', would depend on the extent to which they made sense to the actors whose experiences were being interpreted.

Ethnomethodology is not a theory, but a mechanism by which a group of sociologists, working from a phenomenological perspective, have attempted to show how members of society organise their daily lives and, in particular, how they make their often routine activities meaningful to themselves and significant to outsiders. Individuals generally act in such a way as to make their actions 'accountable', or 'observable-reportable' to others. In other words, people 'design their actions so as others may identify them as what they are' (Hester and Eglin 1992). However, the requirements of a society dictate that most of people's routine daily activities are not minutely explained or justified to those around them, but performed in a context which is taken for granted. Ethnomethodologists take nothing for granted: every action, however trivial it seems, is open to their analysis. They pay special attention to the creation and recognition of social action in particular settings. Indeed, the emphasis seems to be more on the actions or settings than on the participants themselves. Ethnomethodologists argue that, without an understanding of the real nature of what is commonly accepted as ordinary, no valid account can be offered of any human behaviour.

Harold Garfinkel (1967), the originator of ethnomethodology, was influenced by the view of Sellin (1938) that it is not the general principles of morality that are important in sociological research, but the conduct norms that individuals consider appropriate to social action in particular circumstances. Garfinkel used to tell his students to try acting atypically in routine daily situations—such as by pretending that members of their families were complete strangers—to provide evidence of how much is taken for granted in social interaction. (It is said that Garfinkel was unamused when his students tried this approach on him!)

The essence of ethnomethodology's perspective on the creation and enforcement of criminal law was stated by Hester and Eglin (1992):

> No definition of any rule, such as a criminal law, or of a concept, such as insanity, can stipulate all the cases or circumstances that may be counted as falling under it. The meaning of the rule or concept is open-ended. What the rule or concept means, then, depends on how good an argument, say, can be made for the applicability of the rule or concept to the case in question.

Studies into aspects of the criminal justice system have been carried out in this tradition. In his book *The Social Organization of Juvenile Justice* (1968), Aaron Cicourel showed that official indices of crime are a result of everyday contingencies faced and dealt with by agencies such as the police, courts and social workers. They do not reflect the real level of crime, but only that which has been handled and processed by the social organisation (actual rather than formal) of the control agencies. Cicourel described what lies behind the decision making process which produces the crime figures.

A similar study, although on a smaller scale, was conducted by David Sudnow (1965) into the plea bargaining process in an American public defender's office. Through what is known as 'participant observation'—a key research device for ethnomethodologists—Sudnow showed how the legal categories of criminal offences were routinely transformed into commonsense categories through which the participants (that is, the lawyers) negotiated the business of the organisation (that is, maximising the number of guilty pleas without causing embarrassment to the prosecutor). He referred to the resulting stereotyped categories as 'normal crimes'. They were normal because, however they came to be constructed by the lawyers to fit the category, they represented the emergent reality of the situation.

More recently, a further study of plea bargaining was conducted by Douglas Maynard (1984), based on tape recordings between lawyers in an area of California he called 'Garden City'. Maynard showed how both the prosecutor and the defending lawyer used attributes of the defendant such as age, sex, ethnic background, occupational and marital status, together with the circumstances of the case, to determine the offence which would be deemed to have taken place and the punishment that should be imposed. (In the USA, prosecutors can recommend a sentence to the judge.) Meaning was only given to any attribute in the context of its relationship with other attributes. (For example, the relevance of 'being employed' would have to be considered in the context of whether the defendant had a family.) It was also important to consider how the case would appear to the jury. Maynard considered that:

> To locate systematic features of the social process, however, we must look at participants' actual practices—at their methods—and not let the dominant methods of empirical social science presuppose the nature of the social world for us.

Meanwhile, in Britain Max Atkinson (1978) indicated the processes by which coroners come to classify particular deaths as suicides. Atkinson showed that, although the cues which coroners relate to in categorising a death as suicide are, in practice, similar to those adopted by experts, the views of the experts were themselves largely the same as those held by the person in the street. The label of suicide was only applied where the social characteristics of the deceased were consistent with the ideas of the person applying the label.

(a) Katz's 'Seductions of Crime'

A striking example of a work based, in part, on a phenomenological approach is Jack Katz's book *Seductions of Crime* (1988). Katz argued that the positivist explanations of traditional criminology have failed to explain criminal behaviour because of their concentration on 'background' social variables such as economic deprivation, class and ethnicity as causal elements. The theory which came in for particular criticism in this regard was Mertonian anomie, which Katz described as 'sentimental materialism'. Such positivist approaches have not portrayed the meaning of the behaviour as perceived by the individuals themselves. Katz claimed in his book that he had tried to capture 'the lived experience of criminality'. Without this insight, criminal behaviour could never be fully understood. He applied a phenomeno-logical analysis, in that he reversed the usual positivist mode of inquiry which considers the 'background' factors first, and instead placed far more emphasis on the 'foreground' factors: the actors' own professed motives or, as Katz referred to them, 'personal projects'. His data were gathered from case studies, ethnographies, journalistic and fictional stories.

In a series of colourful accounts, Katz depicted six categories of criminal: novice shoplifters; youthful 'badasses'; street elites (gangs); 'hardman' robbers 'doing stickup'; 'righteous' killers; and cold-blooded murderers. Each crime has its own distinctive thrills. What the criminals apparently have in common with other people is the need to be valued, to be considered of worth, and to avoid humili-ation. However, they go further through their desire to make these feelings practically real by creating 'magical environments'. Doing evil, according to Katz, is motivated by a search for moral transcend-ence—a sense of righteousness in the face of bored and chaotic lives. For example, the 'hardman' robber, in Katz's words, 'discovers, fan-tasises or manufactures an angle of moral superiority over the intended victim', whom he has made to look a fool. Novice shoplifters are said to experience 'sneaky thrills' (sometimes bordering on the orgasmic) in being able to achieve their enterprise in such a normal setting without apprehension. The obtaining of goods is of far less, if any, significance. Katz's consideration of the possible influence of background variables is fairly standard for all his types of offender. They are likely to be of little importance, as either many people in the alleged causal category do not commit the crime; or many people who commit the crime do not fit into the category; or many people in the category do commit the crime, but go for long periods without doing so.

Seductions of Crime contains many of the strengths and weaknesses of phenomenological analysis. Although Katz's account provides a vivid portrayal of motivational factors underlying certain types of crime, it seems inconceivable that the thrills and excitement he described can be present for all—or even a majority—of offenders. Indeed, Katz wondered why there are almost no participant accounts of white-collar crime, but did not pursue the issue. Accounts given by prostitutes do not suggest that they are seeking to create a 'magical environment'. Inevitably, emphasis is placed on understanding the complexity of individual behaviour—the actor's 'lived experience'—

rather than compiling any generalisable body of knowledge. Although this process is not very common in criminological research nowadays, it can prove very illuminating in specific cases. Yet, on several occasions Katz claimed that his 'foreground to background' approach would lead to a 'comprehensive' theory of crime. The data which have given rise to Katz's six categories of criminal appear to have been largely selected at random, and there is no attempt to study comparative samples. The accounts contained in the categories seem to resemble certain types of offender, but by no means cover the whole range of possibilities.

There is also the usual problem with the reliability of the offenders' accounts (although Katz did reject some wholly unbelievable claims, and gave more weight to those with some evidential support). For instance, the information on which Katz based his appraisal of shoplifters was gathered from self-report essays written by his own students, who were presumably familiar with the purpose of the enterprise. In a later book, *How Emotions Work*, Katz (1999) also used written student reports in a consideration of road rage in Los Angeles. Sánchez-Jankowski (2003) has pointed out that, in his desire to concentrate on the actor's emotions, Katz has largely ignored the calculation of the costs and benefits of criminal behaviour which people often make. Although Katz paid lip-service to the consideration of background variables, his overall treatment of them is generally inadequate. It is admittedly part of his thesis that social structural elements, such as class and ethnicity, should be removed from front-line consideration, but in practice they are so strongly denigrated in this account as to be effectively rendered worthless. It could be argued that, in this respect, Katz has 'thrown out the baby with the bath water'.

(b) Cultural criminology

Aspects of Katz's phenomenological approach have been included in what has come to be termed 'cultural criminology'. Human creativity and individualism, particularly as reflected in style and leisure, are seen as far more relevant to criminal behaviour than the current approaches of rational choice theory or positivism, which largely downplay or ignore motivation. The growth of the consumer culture has been accompanied by an increase in personal expression. Crime is recognised as holding its own attractions—'an existential pursuit of passion and excitement' (Hayward 2004). Where writers such as Ferrell *et al.* (2004) differ from Katz is that they are prepared to acknowledge the significance of 'background' factors such as poverty and inequality. However, they do not accept the traditional positivist view that such factors automatically translate into various forms of behaviour; it is the way they are individually experienced that matters. Poverty, for example, could be viewed as amounting to a form of exclusion from the material benefits of society which could lead to intense humiliation and a sense of injustice. Jock Young (2003) has commented on an approach that takes account of both Merton's anomie and Katz's phenomenology: 'It is Merton with energy, it is Katz with structure'.

(c) Evaluation

The popularity of ethnomethodological research into deviance reached its peak in the 1960s for similar reasons to those which brought interactionism into vogue at that time in the form of labelling theory. However, phenomenology could have no possible claim to provide an explanation as to why different groups of people commit deviant or criminal acts. This is one reason why it has been ignored by many criminologists, who have preferred to look for generalities and create typical models. Nevertheless, a phenomenological analysis could certainly be useful in challenging an explanation of a particular criminal act. Perhaps the main contribution of phenomenology has been to show that it is unwise simply to rely on formal structures and official definitions to make sense of what is happening in the world. As an existential philosophy, phenomenology is as far removed from determinism as it is possible to be. Yet, radical criminologists have levelled the same criticism at phenomenology that they have at labelling theory: that it ignores the significance of power in society. Sumner (1994) likened ethnomethodology to 'describing the flow of fluids in an engine without telling us about the vehicle, its normal functions and the direction it travels in'.

There are also other difficulties with phenomenology. The essential research method based in this approach is participant observation. This is by no means easy to carry out properly or to evaluate. In Schutz's terms, a valid phenomenological account involves the observer's adopting a 'scientific attitude'. This involves blocking out any preconceptions the observer may have of the phenomenon under scrutiny. What would be the situation if different observers were to provide different accounts? Garfinkel's (1967) suggestion that 'If the interpretation makes good sense, then that's what happened' does not overcome this problem. Schutz's view that 'second-order constructs of social science must be compatible with first class concepts of commonsense' would provide one basis for deciding between the two, but one which may not always be able to separate the accounts. Schutz considered that a valid account requires, in addition to subjective interpretation, logical consistency and what he termed 'the postulate of adequacy'. This raises the question of how adequacy is determined. Supposing an individual whose behaviour is being observed does not agree with the observer's analysis of it? Moreover, how do researchers know when they have said enough? How do they know when to stop?

Because of the subjectivist and relativist nature of phenomenology, and the critiques of such approaches by criminologists in more recent years, it is has not had a major impact on the study of crime and deviance since the 1970s. However, the research projects of Cicourel and Atkinson referred to above exemplify some of the gains that such an approach has provided. In the early 1960s, criminological orthodoxy did not question official statistics or formal processes: by the beginning of the twenty-first century no study of the subject could conceivably be undertaken without their unreliability being emphasised at an early stage.

10

Conflict, Marxist and radical theories of crime

In the long recorded history of human thought, two contrasting views of society have repeatedly been put forward. One is a consensus view, where it is claimed that society is based on a general consensus of values and that the state is operated in such a way as to protect this. If various groups hold different views on particular issues, the state will arbitrate in such a way as to represent the general interest. In criminology, this approach is most strongly represented in the functionalism of Emile Durkheim, and much criminological theory up to the 1960s was also based on the consensus view of society.

Nevertheless, labelling theorists, such as Howard Becker, raised as a central issue the question 'Who makes the rules and why?'. This reflected a contrasting, conflict view of society, which recognises that society includes groups with competing values and interests. This, too, has a long history stretching back to writers such as Plato and Aristotle, although renewed interest began to develop in the 1960s following the issues raised by labelling theory. Unlike the consensus view, a conflict approach claims that the state does not uphold the interests of society as a whole, but only those of the groups which are powerful enough to control it.

The best-known conflict theorist was Karl Marx, who argued that in capitalist societies the state is controlled by those who own the means of production. Consequently, the interests of the population as a whole could only be properly served if such ownership were assumed by the state. Marxist criminology, which has been set out by a number of writers particularly in the past twenty-five years, will be considered later in the chapter. First, attention will be given to several theorists who have adopted a conflict stance, but whose position does not depend on the overthrow of capitalism. There is some overlap between their views, but each writer has a distinctive explanation of the particular form that conflicting interests take.

Conflict theorists

(a) Thorsten Sellin

Although not the first writer to offer an analysis of crime and deviance from a non-Marxist conflict perspective (an interesting earlier example is a 1931 article by Louis Wirth), Thorsten Sellin's 1938 book *Culture Conflict and Crime* is widely accepted as one of the first definitive statements of that position. Sellin was critical of the positivist idea of science, and claimed that knowledge is an uncertain notion. There is, therefore, no basis for assuming that legal definitions of crime correspond with valid sociological accounts of different varieties of behaviour. What is required is a study of 'conduct norms'.

Sellin argued that 'conduct norms' are 'products of social life' which are found in different groups and cultures. This causes little difficulty in an elementary society. However, as a society grows bigger, there is a greater likelihood that these different norms will come into conflict. 'Primary culture conflicts' will then occur. These may be in the border areas between two different cultures, or as a result of colonisation, or as a consequence of migration, where the members of one group have moved into the territory of another. 'Secondary culture conflicts' occur when a single culture fragments into different subcultures, each with its own norms and values. The law will still reflect the norms of the dominant culture rather than any consensus among the individual members of the society. In Sellin's explanation, subcultural norms do not signify class-based frustration, but simply represent fundamentally different values held by particular groups.

Sellin's theory had a particular appeal in his own country, the USA, which had experienced massive immigration during the previous half century. In 1939 Sellin published an article in which he highlighted the relegation of the African-American to an inferior social caste with accompanying economic deprivation. During the next twenty-five years, the consequences of this were to come to the forefront of American political life.

(b) George Vold

Whereas Sellin's analysis was based on the conflict of behavioural norms among different subcultures, Vold's theory was centred on a conflict of interests. Vold (1958) started from the assumption that most people are group-orientated and that their lives are essentially tied up with group affiliation. Groups emerge when people have common interests or needs which can best be advanced through collective action. Unlike Sellin's subcultures, Vold's groups themselves are fluid, forming and then disappearing when there is no longer a particular interest to serve. Ultimately, individual members come to have a psychological rather than rational attachment to particular groups, and will be prepared to devote a great deal of effort to them. Groups come into conflict with each other and this only serves to strengthen the loyalty of their own members. Society comprises a series of groups with opposing interests which still manage to form a balance. Vold considered that politics is inevitably based on compromise: 'the principle of compromise from positions of strength operates at every stage of this conflict process'. There is a constant shifting of position, with individual groups changing the balance in the power equation. If the 'criminals' were successful in overthrowing the government, then the former national leaders themselves would become the 'criminals'. Vold's analysis was strictly based on logic and avoided questions of which group was 'right' and which was 'wrong'.

The conflict between these groups, with each constantly struggling to maintain or improve its position in the hierarchy, is essential in the normal running of society. It is especially visible in the legislative process, where some groups manage to have their interests enshrined in law at the expense of other groups. The 'winning' groups are not only more likely to obey the law than the losers, but will be particularly active in urging the police to enforce it. Crime can therefore be seen as the activity of minority power groups. Individual crime must be viewed as activity which is carried out for the ultimate benefit of the group.

According to Vold, much crime is committed by groups. Individuals come together for strength and support, and to protect themselves against the police, who are seen as the agents of the dominant group. For example, juvenile crime is usually directed against the rules of the adult world, which are upheld by the police. Such individuals do not see themselves as criminals; they consider their actions to be in support of the rightful claims of their group. Vold had noticed the growth in the occurrence of 'political' crimes throughout the 1950s, particularly involving the struggle between black civil rights activists and white supremacists. He pointed out how much political conflict involves what would otherwise be described as ordinary criminal offences. Another example is crime resulting from disputes between employers and trades unions. However, unlike some other theorists, Vold did not claim to be setting out a general theory of crime, and he conceded that certain forms of criminal activity, unrelated to any conflict, could not be explained by it.

(c) Ralf Dahrendorf

In 1958, the same year that Vold presented his theory, Dahrendorf published his first significant essay on conflict theory, which he later expanded (1959, 1968). Dahrendorf, who considered a consensus view of society to be utopian, claimed that in any given relationship members of a society had to be in one of two positions: a 'position of domination' or a 'position of subjection'. It is inevitable that members of society evaluate each other differently and conflict is bound to occur. An order of social status will emerge and norms will be developed to maintain this by the people who hold institutionalised power.

Dahrendorf rejected the Marxist approach of a simple bifurcation between the bourgeoisie and proletariat as being 'old-fashioned' and inapplicable to today's age. For example, the needs of unskilled and semi-skilled labourers may conflict with those of skilled labourers just as much as they conflict with the managers and the owners. In effect, Dahrendorf abandoned the Marxist notion of 'class' and substituted 'authority'.

Those who are in a position of domination will use sanctions wherever necessary to enforce the norms. The norms themselves can only be altered by the efforts of others to bring about change. There will, therefore, be a permanent readjustment because the inequality in society will provide the incentive to the disadvantaged to try to obtain power themselves. The 'permanent readjustment' will by definition ensure a constant state of conflict.

(d) Austin T Turk

Turk's conflict theory (1969) was clearly influenced by the writings of Dahrendorf. Seeking a general theory of criminalisation, Turk followed Dahrendorf in seeing society as comprising 'authorities' and 'subjects', and considering that a degree of conflict is inevitable. Social order is dependent upon the authorities' keeping a proper balance between consensus and coercion. Either too much or too little conflict in society is unhealthy. People will then become duly conditioned into roles as authorities or subjects. Turk claimed that:

> The stability of an authority relationship appears to depend far less upon subjects' conscious or unconscious belief in the rightness or legitimacy of

the rank order than upon their having been conditioned to accept as a fact that authorities must be reckoned with as such.

Turk made a distinction between cultural norms, which relate to the verbal formulation of values, and social norms, which concern actual behaviour. From the authorities' position, cultural norms represent the law as prescribed, and social norms the law as enforced. For the subjects, the cultural norms could be subcultural and the social norms will be individuals' actual behaviour. Authorities and subjects are constantly learning how to interact with each other in accordance with their respective positions. However, there is never total agreement on the lessons to be learned. Conflict will occur when there is a high degree of congruence between the cultural and social norms on the part of the authorities (that is, involving a positive law enforcement policy), and an equally high level of congruence between the different cultural norms held by the subjects and their action in support of those norms. In other words, there will be conflict when, as Turk put it, each side 'come(s) close to acting in accord with the way they talk'. Conflict is also more likely if either the authorities or the subjects are particularly well-organised or 'sophisticated': Turk used this term to refer to the ability to manipulate the other side without recourse to conflict. Almost by definition, the authorities are more organised and sophisticated than the subjects. For example, juvenile delinquents will inevitably come into conflict with authority because of their lack of organisation and sophistication. Turk considered that a person's age, sex and race will help to determine the extent to which the person accepts the norms of domination. A black youth is more likely to be in conflict with authority than an elderly white woman is.

Although other conflict theorists were clearly situated on the political left, Turk appears to have adopted a conservative stance against what he saw as the rising level of disorder in America:

> There are indications that some authorities are beginning to understand that such norm violations as juvenile misconduct, family disorganisations, indifference to hygiene, personality disorder, and lack of available work skills constitute insoluble problems until and unless a total, determined, attempt is made . . . to force people (impolitic phrasing!) into structures that lead to 'good'.

The transition

It was in the America of the late 1960s and early 1970s that conflict theory really flourished. The result of such major social upheavals as the war in Vietnam and the civil rights movement was an unprecedented fragmentation of interest groups representing almost every shade of opinion. Labelling theory had pointed towards the making and enforcement of rules, but it did not wholly confront issues of power. Conflict was abundant, and so was injustice. Suddenly, Vold's almost clinical analysis of conflict in morally neutral terms, and the continuation in this vein by Dahrendorf and Turk, seemed, to some people, inadequate to explain the ferment that was growing around them. It was left to writers such as Quinney and Chambliss to introduce a radical political element into the discussion.

(a) Richard Quinney 1

Quinney, a prolific writer, has modified his views on criminological theory in almost every book he has produced. In *Crime and Justice in Society* (1969) he adopted a position which reflected the writings of Turk and Chambliss. This was developed in *The Problem of Crime* (1970), where Quinney also introduced a more phenomenological perspective (see Chapter 9). In effectively rejecting positivism, he claimed that 'there is no reason to believe in the objective existence of anything'. Crime as an entity did not exist—it was simply a construction by other people. In his book *The Social Reality of Crime* (1970), Quinney argued that, whatever the physical reality may be, it was the *social* reality that mattered: the processes by which a collective meaning of crime came to be established and maintained.

Quinney expressed his 'social reality' in six propositions, each of which can be seen as originating in earlier criminological writings.

(1) 'Crime is a definition of human conduct that is created by authorized agents in politically organised society'. This is based on the interactionist perspective. Crime is not pathological, but simply behaviour defined as criminal by others.

(2) 'Criminal definitions describe behaviors that conflict with the interests of the segments of society that have the power to shape public policy'. This is similar to Vold's discussion of organised interest groups, but Quinney's notion of 'segments' includes groups with little, if any, organisation in defence of their own

interests, such as women and the poor. Whereas Vold excluded certain types of criminal activity, such as impulsive and irrational behaviour, from being the result of political conflict, Quinney's segments of society include every kind of behaviour and interest.

(3) 'Criminal definitions are applied by the segments of society that have the power to shape the enforcement and administration of criminal law'. This is self-explanatory: the power to administer and enforce the law will be in the hands of those who have the power to legislate.

(4) 'Behavior patterns are structured in segmentally organized society in relation to criminal definitions, and within this context persons engage in actions that have relative probabilities of being defined as criminal'. This proposition has been influenced by Sutherland's theory of differential association. Different segments adopt different systems of norms, each arising from the segment's own cultural background. The more power a segment has in the creation and enforcement of the law, the less likely it is that one of its members will be criminalised.

(5) 'Conceptions of crime are constructed and diffused in the segments of society by various means of communication'. Quinney here argued that the term 'crime' can either refer to individuals' personal experiences or to the definitions of reality that are provided through various means of communication, including the mass media. Politicians promote particular notions of crime to suit their own interests and, to this end, a supportive mass media is essential. Thus, there is a great deal of emphasis in the media on the crimes of the poor, such as benefit fraud, and relatively little concern with crimes of the rich, such as tax evasion, and crimes which particularly impinge on the poor, such as those concerning health and safety at work.

(6) 'The social reality of crime is constructed by the formulation and application of criminal definitions, the development of behavior patterns related to criminal definitions, and the construction of criminal conceptions'. This provides a summary of the earlier propositions. The reality of crime which is promulgated is that which is set out by the powerful segments in society. They claim that they are protecting the general interest, whereas in fact they are only protecting their own. People tend to accept these definitions of crime as applying to them, especially as they are reinforced so strongly by the media.

(b) William J Chambliss [1]

From his earliest writings, William Chambliss showed an interest in the role played by powerful groups in society. However, his form of conflict theory developed initially from the American tradition of legal realism rather than the work of Vold and Turk, who were more interested in the form that conflicts took. Chambliss (1964) studied the English vagrancy laws, which date back to the fourteenth century. He argued that feudal landlords used these laws as a means of making people work on their land. Labour was already in short supply, as landlords had to 'sell' serfs their freedom to raise money for wars and crusades. The final straw was the 50 per cent reduction in the population caused by the Black Death of 1348. Agricultural workers were now prohibited from moving from one county to another to seek higher wages. The Vagrancy Acts also made it an offence to give food or shelter to people defined as vagrants, and vagrants themselves could be imprisoned if they refused work offered by a landowner. The laws fell into disuse once there was sufficient labour available, but were revived in 1530 to support the interests of the growing mercantile class. Chambliss concluded that the only purpose of the Acts was to keep down the cost of labour.

In their book *Law, Order and Power* (1971), Chambliss and Seidman suggested that societies which are not highly stratified are better able to resolve disputes through reconciliation and compromise. However, it is when societies become more complex that reconciliation as a means of resolving disputes is replaced by a rule-enforcement approach. The questions of the particular rules to be enforced and who should be the targets then become of vital importance.

The authors studied the day-to-day working of the American criminal justice system to see whether a conflict or a consensus perspective provided a more accurate picture. In particular, they were interested in seeing if the role of the State in the operation of the system was value-free, as maintained by consensus theory, or if, as they put it, 'the power of the State is itself the principal prize' in accordance with conflict theory. They concluded that every step of the process could be better explained from a conflict perspective. Legislation is passed to serve particular groups rather than the public interest. As dissenting judgements in cases are often just as valid as the majority arguments, the decisions must be based on some other grounds which, according to Chambliss and Seidman, are the judges' personal values. These will inevitably reflect the interests of the rich over those of the poor because judges come from the more privileged sections of society. Promotion of judges to appellate level (where the important decisions are made) is to some extent influenced by politicians, so that any judge who has dealt inappropriately with individuals in positions of power is unlikely to be promoted. Moreover, there are additional impediments to poor people's being successful in the criminal justice system, such as the question of cost and the pressure to reduce the number of cases before the criminal courts. This means that only issues concerning the rich and powerful will receive proper consideration.

Chambliss and Seidman also looked at the role played by the police. It is in the interests of the police to cause as few problems for themselves as possible, particularly with the powerful sections of society from whom they obtain their funding. It therefore follows that the police are likely to concentrate on the weaker members of society and try to avoid prosecuting those in positions of power. Even within criminal organisations there are those who have influential contacts and should therefore be avoided. The authors arrived at a definition of the guiding 'rule of law':

> The rule is that discretion at every level . . . will be so exercised as to bring mainly those who are politically powerless (that is, the poor) into the purview of the law.

Therefore, the poor and ethnic minorities form a large part of the official criminal statistics not because they are more prone to behave in a criminal way, but because they lack the organisational resources to provide protection against prosecution.

Evaluation of conflict criminology

A criticism that has been levelled at many criminological theories is that they have failed to accommodate the significance of power in society. Conflict theories, which offer broadly similar explanations of criminal behaviour and the activities of law enforcement agencies, confront this issue directly. They play a similar role to labelling theories in that they emphasise how particular behaviour comes to be deemed criminal by the powerful. However, conflict theories also go further in offering explanations as to why people behave in a particular way, as well as accounting for variations in law enforcement practices. Nevertheless, these explanations are not without their own problems.

Conflict theories assume that it is only the interests of the powerful that are protected by criminal law. This seems odd when one considers traditional criminal offences, such as murder and rape, which protect all people from very serious harm. Conflict theorists would respond that there are many other types of harmful activity which have not been criminalised because of their threat to powerful interests. Examples of environmental pollution could be given, and some might point to the massive profitability (both to the manufacturers and the Inland Revenue) of cigarette production. However, as Braithwaite (1989) has pointed out, there are more laws that criminalise the behaviour of corporations than criminalise the behaviour of the poor. The criminal law in books is on the side of the working class. What differs is the enforcement of these laws by the police and other agencies: the criminal law in practice is heavily class-biased.

It is easy, reading conflict theories, to feel sympathy for the powerless in a society and assume that, if they were to obtain power, everything would become just and proper. Yet, all that such theories dictate is that they would now be the ones in power. This would not necessarily lead to any change in the level or type of crime; arguably, the same crimes would just be committed by different people. There seems to be an assumption that the formerly powerless would exercise power in a better manner than those they have displaced, but this would only follow if it is believed that those presently in power are 'bad' and that any replacement would inevitably be better. It should be remembered that the Nazis were a powerless group in Germany at the beginning of the 1930s.

The assumption of conflict theorists that individuals form themselves into interest groups or segments within society has also been questioned. The sociologist C Wright Mills pointed out that most American citizens do not belong to any organisation large enough to be politically significant. The same could be said of the British public. However, conflict theorists might respond that the groups do not need to be that structured or even visible to exist.

Conflict theorists also provided a power-based explanation for differential patterns of law enforcement. They cited in evidence the fact that the police appear to devote far more effort to low-level crime than to the crimes of the powerful. Police forces—particularly in America, but also in Britain—are under political pressure to deal with certain types of crime. Conflict theorists would maintain that these are inevitably the crimes of the poor and not the rich. The police, however, could argue that the crimes of the rich require far more time and, therefore, money to deal with and that, in times of diminishing resources, they have to concentrate on more visible crimes, which are usually the crimes of the poor. This is a problem which has confronted the Serious Fraud Office in Britain. In support, the police could cite evidence of what the public wants them to do, and the urgings of the popular press. Conflict theorists, however, could retort that both these forms of pressure are indirectly created by the powerful.

Nevertheless, power seems to be a strand running throughout much criminological theory. Lack of material wealth is a good indicator of lack of power, and explanations from the Chicago School onwards have highlighted this. After all, the immigrants did not move into the areas of Chicago occupied by the rich. The strain theories of Merton, and Cloward and Ohlin illustrated lack of opportunities which were clearly associated with lack of power. It has already been noted (in Chapter 8) how proposals to put Ohlin's ideas into effect were taken over and used by powerful interests for their own purposes. Labelling theory requires that the labeller is more powerful than the labelled.

Some of the difficulties arising from the assumption of a simple conflict perspective of crime can be seen in the study by Norrie and Adelman (1989) of criminalisation in Britain during the 1980s. On the face of it, key pieces of legislation were created in a 'divide and rule' strategy, driving a wedge between rich and poor, black and white, north and south. The Police and Criminal Evidence Act 1984 extended police powers of stop and search and detention, and increased police discretion. The Public Order Act 1986 also gave the police greater powers and, once again, increased discretion, this time in their ability to restrict demonstrations and marches. The Prevention of Terrorism (Temporary Provisions) Act 1984 extended the original legislation to include members and supporters of any organisation in the world which used 'violence for political ends'.

Norrie and Adelman suggested that there are two different explanations for these developments. The first claims that such legislation was necessary to support Margaret Thatcher's free-market economic and social policies. The mass unemployment and reduction of social service provision that resulted inevitably led to demonstrations, riots and strikes, which had to be suppressed. Such an explanation portrays a vivid picture of a freshly-arisen conflict between the powerful state and the working classes. However, Norrie and Adelman claimed that the second explanation is far more in keeping with the evidence. Ever since the middle of the nineteenth century, a section of the working class has formed a 'labour aristocracy': a group of skilled workers who benefited from being given enhanced responsibilities and greater rewards under capitalism. A consensus thus developed between the 'respectable' working class (and its representatives, the trades unions and the Labour Party) and the police and the state. The breakdown in this consensus started to develop in the 1970s, before the leadership of Margaret Thatcher. Therefore, on this analysis, the laws referred to above did not create a new conflict, but simply a harsher mechanism for dealing with the consequences of one which already existed.

Marxist criminology

Karl Marx (1818–83) wrote very little specifically on the topic of crime. His collaborator Frederick Engels was more forthcoming: his book *The Condition of the Working Class in England* is considered in Chapter 6. Marx's references to crime could be viewed as justifying its functionalist value in a capitalist society. However, many Marxist scholars consider the following to be irony:

> The criminal moreover produces the whole of the police and of criminal justice, constables, judges, hangmen, juries . . . Torture alone has given rise to the most ingenious mechanical inventions and employed many honourable craftsmen in the production of its instruments.

Nevertheless, it is possible to view crime within the overall context of Marx's view of history and social change.

Marxist criminology is essentially a more specific form of conflict theory. Whereas conflict theories assert that acts of the powerless which challenge the exercise of power (in a value-free sense) are criminalised, Marxist criminology claims that the power resulting from the exercise of capitalism is basically responsible for crime. Marx wrote in the period immediately following the turmoil of the Industrial Revolution. He was trying both to explain why the feudal system that had existed in Europe for hundreds of years had collapsed, and to predict what would happen next. Marx identified a conflict between the forces of production, meaning society's ability to produce material goods, and the social relations of production, which refers to the relationships between people, and includes the question of how what is produced is distributed. Although the forces of production had developed considerably throughout history, the social relations of feudalism had remained relatively fixed over the same period, and had come to hinder the further development of material production. They had to be replaced and the Industrial Revolution served this purpose.

Marx considered that the material forces of production would go on developing. As part of the new capitalist process, property and goods would increasingly be concentrated in the hands of fewer people as they took over the operations of their competitors, and the growth of mechanisation would lead to greater unemployment and lower wages. Society would therefore polarise into two groups, with a diminishing number of individuals becoming increasingly rich and a growing number of individuals increasingly poor. Eventually, this would become intolerable to the masses and there would be a revolution to establish common ownership of the means of production.

(a) Willem Bonger

One of the earliest writers to provide a Marxist explanation of crime was the Dutch criminologist Willem Bonger (1876–1940) in his book *Criminality and Economic Conditions* (1916). Bonger studied European crime rates from the late nineteenth and early twentieth centuries. He concluded that capitalism encourages egoism and greed rather than altruism. The advantages of the rich, the struggle of the middle class to make a living, and the deprivation of the poor all directed these groups towards egoism. Bonger echoed Durkheim in relating crime to egoism but, unlike him, he attributed the rise of individualism to capitalism. For Bonger, egoism could never be reduced by closer social integration, as it was society itself that caused the egoism. There is no reason why the lower levels of the working class in particular (whom Marx called the 'lumpenproletariat') should have altruistic feelings towards those in power. Crime is more prevalent among the lower classes because they have little, if any, security in their employment. Moreover, society, which has encouraged the poor to compete against each other for material gain, criminalises their greed and yet does nothing about the greed of the rich. The poor have been dehumanised by capitalism and, additionally, have not received adequate moral training, as the rich do not consider it necessary for industrial work. Bonger did not deny that there are inborn differences between individuals, which make some more liable to commit crimes than others, but still maintained that capitalism is the major driving force behind criminality.

Bonger attributed not only economic crimes to the growth of capitalism, but a range of others as well, with a perspective that was far ahead of its time. Soliciting, prostitution and rape occur because of the low economic status of women. Domestic violence and infanticide were explained along similar lines, and violence in general was blamed on the degradation of the individual and the military ethos of capitalist societies. Bonger noted the link between capitalism and the patriarchal society, and considered that the economic subjugation of women explains their lack of involvement in crime on a wider scale. However, he considered that, if this were eased, the level of female crime would increase. It is arguable that this prediction has been proved accurate.

After the work of Bonger, no significant Marxist criminology appeared until the 1970s. The route to Marxism for British criminologists was through interactionist theory. In the USA, the situation was different.

(b) Richard Quinney 2

American Marxist criminology was developed by Quinney out of his earlier conflict theory. In two books published in 1974, Quinney argued that the existing power base of society used traditional criminology, which he described as a 'cultural product', to reinforce the existing social reality wherever possible, and ignored traditional criminology when it became too challenging. Quinney now stated that his previous phenomenological approach had 'done little to provide or promote an alternative existence'. This conclusion led him into a Marxist stance in opposition to the existing system. Quinney claimed that the existing laws and legal structures were invalid, as they merely existed to serve the interests of the capitalist ruling class. In the process of exercising its domination over the working class, the ruling capitalist class itself committed crimes. In his book *Class, State, and Crime* (1977), Quinney divided these into crimes of 'control', which are committed by the police and other law-enforcement agencies; crimes of 'government', such as Watergate; and crimes of 'economic domination', such as pollution, economic exploitation, sexism and racism, which the ruling class manages to ensure are not even legally defined as offences. Working-class crimes were described by Quinney as taking place within the context of capitalist oppression. These include 'predatory' crimes, such as burglary, robbery and drug dealing, which arise from a need to survive; 'personal' crimes, such as murder and rape, which are committed by people who have been brutalised by capitalism; and 'defensive actions', such as industrial sabotage, which are committed by alienated workers.

For Quinney, criminal law is used by the ruling class to preserve the existing economic and social order. Crime control is in the hands of government agencies, representing the interests of the ruling class, and is exercised to maintain order and resist any challenge to the status quo. Quinney argued that existing laws and structures should be completely rejected and replaced by new 'social realities' based on a more equitable distribution of power, in which popular notions of right and justice should be substituted for traditional notions of law.

Perhaps it is not surprising that Quinney's theoretical perspective changed again in his later writings. In the second edition of *Class, State, and Crime* (1980), he concentrated more on the religious implications of socialism, and in his more recent work he has advocated 'peace-making criminology' (Pepinsky and Quinney 1991).

(c) William Chambliss 2

Like Quinney, Chambliss also moved towards Marxism from his earlier conflict perspective. One factor which undoubtedly influenced both these writers was the conservative 'backlash' to the liberal 1960s which followed the election of President Richard Nixon. In an important article in 1975, Chambliss argued that crime is only a reality when acts are defined as criminal to suit the ruling class, who themselves can break the law with impunity. The content of the criminal law will expand as the gap widens between the bourgeoisie and the proletariat. Echoing Marx's own (ironic) statement, Chambliss claimed that crime creates employment for law enforcers, criminologists and others. It also serves to divert the attentions of the lower class towards each other rather than against the oppressive economic system.

In his book *On the Take: from Petty Crooks to Presidents* (1978), Chambliss studied organised crime in Seattle. He devoted several years to participant observation in the city's bars, where he was eventually able to gain the confidence of a key operator. Many of the illegal goods and services on offer had at one time been available legitimately and the demand for them still existed. Politicians control the enforcement of the law, but they also need to generate vast sums of money to finance election campaigns. A combination of these factors made the cooperation between gangsters, politicians, police officers and the business world that Chambliss found in Seattle perfectly good financial sense. It is not surprising that the powerful interest groups in the legal system direct their attention towards the apprehension of the least powerful offenders, such as drug users and prostitutes. Racketeering is just a form of capitalism which, after all, Al Capone had referred to as 'the legitimate rackets' (Sutherland 1940).

Having analysed police practices in Washington DC, Chambliss (1995) claimed that the same unlawful acts would evoke a completely different response from the police, depending on whether they were committed in the slums or on the university campuses.

The assessment provided by Chambliss in these and other writings (for example, Block and Chambliss 1981) shows that he had moved away from the 'utopian' form of Marxism put forward by writers such as Taylor *et al.* (1973) (see below), which had suggested that a crime-free society is possible. Every society will contain contradictions to which crime will appear to some as a logical response. The problem with attempts to control crime is that, as there can be no fundamental questioning of the structured power base in society, only the symptoms are addressed.

A similar analysis emerged from Tony Platt's book *Street Crime—A View from the Left* (1978). Victim surveys reveal that American street crime is far more common than is suggested in the official records. Such incidents are not merely a by-product of capitalism; they are endemic to it. Most of the crimes are intra-class and intra-racial and many of them are not reported because of police corruption and incompetence. Much, though not all, of the crime is committed by the poor and unemployed, just as in nineteenth century Britain at the height of industrial capitalism. An organised and politicised working-class movement has developed, but there still remains a residual layer of the poor who resort to predatory street crime in a similar way to those observed by Frederick Engels in Manchester over a century earlier.

(d) Marxism and crime in Britain: 'The New Criminology'

The specific application of interactionist theory to crime and deviance, which became increasingly popular in America in the early 1960s, also had a considerable impact in Britain. A group of young sociologists, who were frustrated by the stranglehold of positivism over British criminology, established the National Deviancy Conference in 1968 (Cohen 1970). Several of its more radical members came to distance themselves from the relativism of interactionist theory and developed an interest in Marxism. Three of them, Ian Taylor, Paul Walton and Jock Young, set out their ideas in the book *The New Criminology* (1973). The authors claimed to be offering 'a full-blown Marxist theory of deviance'. Although it has subsequently been much criticised, this remains a seminal work and one of the most influential contributions by British academics to the field of criminology. Some of the arguments dealt with in the book were modified in a later collection of essays, *Critical Criminology* (1975).

Taylor *et al.* sought to create a Marxist-based explanation of how certain acts come to be described as deviant and the processes by which particular individuals are criminalised. This involved highlighting the role of the powerful in the creation and enforcement of law. The book emphasised rule making rather than rule breaking. Deviance and crime are simply diverse forms of behaviour which are criminalised by the powerful in society to protect their own interests. The authors asserted that they were espousing a 'normative criminology': by this they meant a socialist criminology based on the eradication of the inequalities that are inevitable under capitalism. Therefore, in a different form of society without the widespread inequalities that exist at present, and where human diversity could be tolerated, the power to criminalise would be unnecessary and a 'crime free' society would be possible. This could only be achieved by the development of class consciousness. Taylor *et al.* rejected all deterministic explanations of crime, and argued that human behaviour is willed and deviance is generally a chosen political form of action. Contrary to the view of Becker and other labelling theorists, they considered that deviance *is* a quality of the act a person commits. Consequently, they disagreed with the orthodox Marxist explanations of Engels and Bonger which, in viewing crime in terms of the 'dangerous classes' or lumpenproletariat, based their account on individual pathology.

There is, however, an irony in that the criticism of determinism that Taylor *et al.* levelled against traditional positivist criminology can also be made of them. A brief look at their explanation of crime is sufficient to reveal that individuals seem to be just as much under the influence of forces outside their control as they are when living in poor neighbourhoods or affected by anomie.

Some of the strongest critics of *The New Criminology* have been other Marxists. For example, Hirst (1975) argued that crime and deviance are inappropriate subjects for Marxist analysis, as this suggests that deviant behaviour is intrinsically different from non-deviant behaviour. Marx himself had little time for the subject of crime. He associated it with the 'lumpenproletariat', a parasitic body who had no part to play in production and would be useless in the revolution. This view, which Hirst and some other Marxists supported, seems to be too reliant on official crime statistics and overlooks the vast amount of crime that is committed by middle and upper-class individuals. Moreover, even Hirst was prepared to concede that crimes such as industrial sabotage can have a political motivation. In contrast to this passive depiction, however, Taylor *et al.* portrayed deviants as active in the political struggle. They considered that Marx's specific comments on crime were misleading and that criminal and deviant behaviour should be considered in the light of Marx's general theories.

In *Critical Criminology* (1975), Taylor *et al.* made some changes to their original position. They indicated that *The New Criminology* had conveyed 'an abstracted and individualistic idealism', which could never amount to more than a moral gesture. They admitted that they had been too concerned with 'expressive deviance' and the meaning that deviants give to their own actions. This 'romanticism' had led them to be neglectful of the role of the state. One of the authors, Jock Young, went even further and, in what he himself termed a 'confessional', repudiated much of what he had said two years earlier in *The New Criminology*. Young's position is considered in more detail in Chapter 11.

The years immediately following the publication of *The New Criminology* saw a large amount of criminological writing based on Marxism. Steven Spitzer (1975) developed the Marxist notion of 'surplus population' to argue that the criminalisation of much behaviour, and particularly the emphasis placed on street crime, was aimed at those parts of the population who are surplus to the labour market. Such chronically unemployed individuals, who are produced by, and yet not needed for, capitalism, usually feature prominently in the crime figures. David Greenberg (1976) suggested that the depictions by Taylor *et al.* of the ruling class as a single entity whose interests alone are reflected in legislation, and criminality as a political response to oppression, are simplistic. In fact, Marx never claimed that either the ruling class or the workers are organised into single cohesive groups. The term 'class' was used to signify shared interests resulting from the means of production and not to suggest that each class would inevitably organise itself to protect its interests. Moreover, in the earlier statements of Marxist criminology, research showing a widespread consensus on existing definitions of crime, indicating that it is the poor who are the most frequent victims of many types of crime, seems to have been ignored.

Subsequently, more sophisticated versions of Marxist criminology have appeared, with a closer historical analysis of how change in particular societies occurs. Some of these explanations are similar to the more traditional criminological theories. In his book *Crime and Capitalism* (1981), Greenberg sought to explain juvenile delinquency from a Marxist perspective, although with distinct overtones of strain theory. Many sociological explanations of crimes fail to deal adequately with the prominence of juveniles in the offending population, or account for their withdrawal from delinquent behaviour in their late teens. Starting from the Marxist view that class is defined according to one's position in the means of production, Greenberg argued that juveniles form a separate class, as they are excluded from economic activity while being required to undergo training for a future role in the system. They experience strain as they wish to participate in social activities with their friends, but they cannot finance their leisure. Compulsory education and laws prohibiting child labour may, therefore, help to explain why juvenile involvement in crime is much greater than in the nineteenth century, when children were sent out to work. Greenberg concluded that the capitalist economic system needs to be modified to take account of this strain if it wishes to reduce delinquency.

Schwendinger and Schwendinger (1985) claimed that the breakdown of family and community life caused by capitalism leads to adolescent street-corner subcultures, whose members commit serious property and violent offences. Middle-class youths, who have different outlets for their activities, are more likely to commit vandalism, vehicle violations and crimes related to drunkenness.

Some Marxist views of crime are similar to the traditional criminological position that criminal behaviour is normal learned behaviour: the rational response of individuals acting in accordance with their own economic interests in situations governed by the social structures of capitalism. Gordon (1973) argued that violent thefts and robberies should be viewed as a desperate means to make money resorted to by poor people who are unable to use more refined methods to steal. Furthermore, organised crime is a rational way of fulfilling a demand for illicit goods and services utilised by individuals denied access to legitimate business activities.

In Britain, Hall *et al.* have studied how the notion of 'mugging' came to be constructed. There is no such crime as mugging, and it appears to have been introduced into the British popular press from American journalism to describe a particular form of sudden street robbery. However, Hall *et al.* maintained that, once introduced, the term was taken up by the government and used to apply to street offences committed by young blacks. The authors contended that the government was facing a 'crisis in hegemony', and that the emphasis on the mugging scare was a deliberate ploy to divert attention from more serious problems such as economic difficulties, disparities of wealth and power, and the problems in Northern Ireland. Hall *et al.* did not deny that muggings were occurring, but argued that it suited the government to encourage the common stereotypes concerning the breakdown of law and order and the involvement of black youths in crime.

The book provides an interesting analysis of how powerful elites can create a moral panic to divert attention from the real difficulties. Unfortunately, it does not provide any strong evidence that this was what occurred with the mugging scare. Indeed, Waddington (1986) has suggested that there had been a gradual increase in the number of muggings before the 'moral panic' is said to have arisen. Nor is there any real discussion of when an understandable concern turns into a moral panic. The argument of Hall *et al.* also seems to contain a contradiction. The moral panic thesis seeks to exonerate black youths from any disproportionate involvement in crime, but the Marxist analysis portrays the same individuals as exploited members of the working class, whose resort to crime is therefore inevitable.

Some Marxists consider that the concepts of crime and deviance are no longer relevant. Steinart (1985) claimed that the notion of 'crime' had lost its meaning, as any impact the label might have had is now inseparable from its association with capitalism. Instead, Marxist criminology should focus on those who suffer the greatest harm—the proletariat—and advocate policies which have the effect of reducing harm without having to involve the criminal process. A prominent British Marxist criminologist, Colin Sumner, has claimed that what was formerly referred to as deviance should now be considered as 'social censure'. In his book *The Sociology of Deviance: an Obituary* (1994), Sumner concluded that the concept of deviance was based on a view of a society which no longer exists; the age of social democracy during the 1960s and 1970s which was presumed to be built around a general consensus. This may have always been a pretence but, according to Sumner, the pretence was finally abandoned during the Reagan–Thatcher years of the 1980s:

> Now, the ideological and political character of moral censures is so open to view, and the rulers' fear of their social divisiveness so minimal, that the concept of social deviance is revealed as a notion within the politics of social democracy.

Therefore, the term 'deviance' relates to an area of study and enquiry that has now simply dissolved into one of political ideology. According to Sumner, 'the consensus against which [deviance] was to be set [has] never materialised'. Instead, we now have 'censure', which does not merely follow a breaking of consensus-based rules, but is an ideological tool used to uphold and reinforce the capitalist system. Criminologists should concentrate on what Sumner (1990) has referred to as 'the negative categories of moral ideology' rather than the 'deviants' or offenders they produce.

Despite the challenge from post-modernist criminology (see below), criminological research from a Marxist perspective is still active. For example, Lynch (1987) has sought to use empirical research techniques to test whether there is any relationship between rates of crime and imprisonment, and Marx's notion of 'surplus value'. White and van der Velden (1995) have claimed that patterns of crime are related to particular social classes, as people's class and their relationship to the means of production affect their ability to organise economic and political resources. In essence, people's power and wealth can determine the type of crimes they commit.

(e) Evaluation of Marxist criminology

Broadly speaking, Marxist criminology is a conflict theory where there is only one type of conflict in issue—the inherent conflict of a capitalist society. Some writers from a Marxist perspective do not always make this distinction clear. For instance, the writings of historians such as Thompson (1975) and Hay (1975) provide strong evidence that the ruling class ensured that both the existence and enforcement of criminal laws protected their interests from the perceived threats of the lower orders. Yet, it is not apparent why this resulted from the set of economic arrangements which are called capitalism rather than from the simple exercise of authority by the powerful—the basis of conflict theories. Marxist analysis of criminal law does not always clarify the distinction between prohibitions which are essential for an organised existence, without which there could be no communal life, and prohibitions which are essential for existence under a particular economic system, such as capitalism. Is it not inevitable that human diversity will necessitate rules of conduct in any type of society? Who is to say whether an apparently anti-social or deviant act is 'political' or just plain greedy?

Early arguments from a Marxist perspective suggesting that a crime-free society is possible have predictably been criticised. More sophisticated explanations have subsequently emerged, but they all suggest that capitalism is a 'cause' of crime in the sense that, were social arrangements fundamentally different, crime would at least be significantly reduced and certain types of crime may even disappear. This seems, to say the least, implausible, as does the suggestion that much crime and delinquency is proto-revolutionary in its origins. This belief would hardly survive a close examination of working-class street subculture in large inner-city areas, where the ideology of far Right groups has had more impact than that of the Left (Robins and Cohen 1978). Indeed, one of the criticisms of Marxist criminology is the relative lack of attention paid to working-class and street crime. Moreover, when criminal organisations become powerful, they usually assume the characteristics of the most insatiable and predatory capitalist enterprise (Roshier 1989). Nor is it possible to claim that the activities of the powerful are never criminalised: there are many offences, including insider trading, which impose constraints on the excesses of capitalism. It often seems the case that the crimes of the rich and powerful are not prosecuted, but this can—at least in part— be explained by the enormous complexity and cost of pursuing fraud allegations against corporate enterprises.

A particular problem for Marxism is, of course, the seventy-year existence of the Soviet Union and the post-war experience of Eastern Europe. These countries can hardly be said to have been free of crime during this period. Some will no doubt argue that they were not true Marxist societies, and it is interesting that many of the emergent nations from the former Soviet bloc appear to have experienced increases in crime. Nevertheless, it remains the case that the major examples the world has seen of states claiming to be run on Marxist principles have been oppressive dictatorships.

There is also a difficulty with the differing crime rates found among societies that have fully embraced capitalism. In his study of crime in Switzerland, Clinard (1978) discovered a low level of working-class involvement in crime.

Greenberg (1981) has argued that the existence of crime in Marxist societies should not necessarily be seen as a denial of the validity of Marxism. He claimed that three alternative explanations are possible: that crime results from capitalist tendencies that still exist among sections of Marxist societies; that such societies still contain elements of inequality and exploitation on their way to developing into fully-fledged Marxist states; or that crime is a consequence of the inherent bureaucracy of such states, with officials determined to maintain their own privileges at the expense of the rights of the workers.

However, most criticisms of Marxist criminology still concentrate on the earlier, cruder forms and overlook the fact that more sophisticated versions have now emerged. The earlier form of Marxist criminology, as exemplified by Quinney (1974), is often referred to as 'instrumentalist'. This maintains that the people who are in positions of power in a society are either capitalists or identify with the aims and methods of capitalists. All law, therefore, is not only a reflection of the interests of the ruling class but, even if it is not immediately obvious, it must somehow benefit the ruling class. Otherwise, it would not have been created. As a camouflage, the law—both on paper and in practice—must be presented as neutral, and the importance of 'the rule of law' will be emphasised.

Towards the end of the 1970s, many Marxist criminologists began to turn from an 'instrumentalist' to a 'structuralist' approach. The problem they had to contend with was why so many people consider such apparently biased laws to be fair and just. In simple terms, instrumental Marxism portrays a sort of conspiracy among the few members of the capitalist elite, who are always able to intervene in any event to see that their interests are protected. However, Marxists such as Louis Althusser (1971), in rejecting the instrumentalists' approach, argued that the main purpose of a capitalist state is not to serve its short-term interests, but to protect class relations and take whatever steps are necessary to ensure that capitalism survives in the long term. There is a need for capitalism—which always creates tension—to exist in an ordered and quiet society, and this can only occur if the society has a proper, smoothly-functioning structure. The problem with the instrumentalist critique is that every law, however innocuous, is assumed to have been created to enable the capitalists to oppress the proletariat. Structuralists, however, admit that laws can be created to serve a variety of different interests, including those of the workers, in order to ward off any challenge to capitalism. Such an approach is necessary not only in the creation of criminal law, but also in its enforcement. On this analysis, it is not a fatal argument to Marxist criminology to indicate that most criminal offences and most police activity protect the workers as much as they protect anyone else.

At the beginning of the 1980s in Britain, most Marxist and radical criminological writing was in this vein, and there had been a gradual movement away from the 'utopian' approach associated with *The New Criminology*. However, as the decade progressed, a further split developed in radical criminology between 'Left Idealism', 'Left Realism' (which is considered further in Chapter 11) and 'post-modernism'.

Post-modern criminology

Post-modernist analysis is generally accepted as having derived from French writers in the late 1960s and 1970s. The disillusionment that followed the 1968 student protests in France and the later collapse of communist governments in Eastern Europe contributed to a growing disenchantment with Marxism, which was now considered to be an increasingly irrelevant remnant of the fading 'modern' era. This refers to the period from the eighteenth century 'Enlightenment' (see Chapter 5) until the late twentieth century (post-modernists do not agree on whether 'the post-modern era' has yet started). The modern era is portrayed as optimistically having attempted to make progress towards finding 'the truth' through seeking the answers to broad and abstract questions. The techniques used to this end were the application of rationality and scientific method. In its declining years, the characteristic features of the modern era are (or were) materialism and information technology at the expense of social relationships. There has been a shift from a manufacturing society to a service society where many goods are produced for their image rather than their usefulness. The late modern era can almost be summed up by the development of the computer notion of 'virtual reality'.

Modernism was also sustained by the belief that acquired knowledge could be systemised and both reflected in, and transmitted through, language. Post-modernists consider that this was always a flawed enterprise, the search for an illusion and, in any event, is now irrelevant. Whereas modernism sought to find a universality or a general order in social life, post-modernism maintains that there is a limitless number of 'orders', each of which can be related to micro or localised arrangements. The dichotomy between left and right, which has become such a familiar feature of social scientific thought, is seen as a classic illustration of misguided modernist thinking. Post-modernists are particularly hard on the left, with its apparently rigid analysis of the shortcomings of capitalism. Indeed, the disenchantment that developed amongst French radicals after 1968, which was fuelled by the broad political move to the right throughout the Western world in the 1980s, resulted in many former left-wing academics moving to embrace post-modernism. O'Reilly-Fleming (1996) has remarked that the collapse of the Soviet Bloc 'dealt a body blow to much of the Marxist underpinnings of a significant stream of radical criminological thought'.

Post-modernism questions what have been accepted as pivotal features of the provision of law under Enlightenment (or modern) thinking. Michel Foucault (1980) has described these as totality (law's application to the whole society), unity, civilisation, and the importance of 'the subject' (the bestowing of individual responsibility and legal liability on the citizen).

In contrast, post-modernists emphasise plurality over totality and individuality over unity. They are sceptical about modernism's claim to have developed civilisation, on account of its oppression of minority groups. Post-modernism rejects the claims of any theory to provide a foundation of knowledge; social life is instead characterised by diversity. In passing, it may be observed that there is an apparent difficulty here: as Alan Hunt (1991) commented 'In general, post-modernism announces the end of theory whilst paradoxically insinuating an alternative "non-theory theory"'.

Post-modernism was neatly summarised by Einstadter and Henry (1995):

> Indeed, post-modernism challenges the whole idea of how reality is conceived. It questions the superiority of 'science' as a mode of analysis and explanation (just as it questioned high art). It questions all attempts to reduce life to essences or causes. It questions any attempt by communities or individuals as 'experts' to prioritise their knowledge over the knowledge of others, and it asserts that no one can claim their knowledge is privileged.

What, then, do post-modernists offer in place of the old orthodoxies? At the political level, their rejection of modernist concepts of state power leads them to repudiate grand designs for change and to replace a macro analysis of social issues with a more localised and participatory approach. Traditional groupings such as left, right, political party and class are also rejected as representing entrenched power groups. Foucault's analysis of power (1980) is important here. Power is not simply a repressive device wielded by one individual or group at the expense of another; its usage can be far more subtle. Even a repressed group retains a certain amount of power. Foucault considered that power is far less centralised in society than Marxist and other critical theorists have assumed. There are extensive networks of power which can be found in almost any form of relationship, and are subject more to their own internal arrangements than to the restrictions of class, the practices of institutions or the repressive actions of states. Indeed, the state can only exercise power with the support of influential sections of society. At a local level, this can give rise to what Foucault termed 'an insurrection of subjugated knowledges'. In terms of criminological research, post-modernist studies have looked at local communities, informal justice and whether criminology can embrace feminism—or vice versa (Smart 1990). The approach post-modernists generally use is to 'deconstruct'. This involves the breaking down of the formal language and appearance of whatever is under analysis (for example, aspects of the law or the criminal justice system), and exposing the way it was created by revealing what lies just beneath the surface—the 'reality' of its operation. All forms of discourse, whether the printed word, verbal communications, film and television, or even gesture, are considered as 'text' which can also be deconstructed. Post-modernism replaces 'the individual' with 'the human subject'.

According to Hunt (1991), the environmentalist movement provides a good example of the appeal of post-modernist over modernist thought. It is ironic that what was originally viewed as the progress resulting from humans' ability to control nature through the application of science is nowadays seen instead as one of the greatest threats to their continued existence.

A number of criticisms have been levelled at post-modern criminology. Many of these have come from Marxists, whose overall impact in the intellectual world appears to have been reduced by the impact of post-modernism. This is to some extent because post-modernists have emphasised the plight of oppressed and minority groups— women, gays, blacks—which Marxists should have considered but, with their preoccupation with the practice of capitalism and the class structure, had largely failed to do. For post-modernists, capitalism and class are just examples of the categorisations of modernism which they see as being meaningless. Schwartz (1991) pointed out that, if the consequence of deconstruction is that categories can be no more than fictions, society loses the ability to challenge sexism, racism and classism. Lea (1998) has claimed that deconstruction could be a never-ending process and that the eventual stopping point will be arbitrary: in other words, a deconstruction can always be deconstructed.

One particular objection which has been raised to post-modernism at a practical level is that its fundamental rejection of macro-level politics, and its reliance on single issue campaigns at a local level, means that the disadvantaged in society will never be able to organise themselves sufficiently to obtain a significant level of empowerment. In reply, post-modernists may claim that attempts at such organisation have not been successful in the past, but this seems an unduly pessimistic, if not inaccurate, assessment.

A further area of contention is that some post-modernist writers, in their concentration on the current plurality of existences, completely disregard any historical context. They consider that, as only the present can be knowable, then only present experiences can be of any value. This is another point of departure from Marxism, which places considerable importance on the role of history. The stance has also been criticised in a telling analysis by Cohen (1993), on the basis that past atrocities, such as the Holocaust and the ethnic cleansing in the former Yugoslavia, would be of no particular significance in post-modern analysis. By way of illustration, Cohen referred to an article by a leading French post-modernist, Jean Baudrillard, entitled 'The Gulf War has not taken place'. In the piece, which was published shortly after most people assumed 'the war' had ended, the author relied on a post-modernist approach to writing and literature which assumes there can be no points of reference to distinguish historical from fictitious material. Therefore, if Baudrillard claimed that the war never occurred, then it never occurred in accordance with his own subjective 'reality'. For post-modernism, no opinion is invalid.

Peacemaking criminology

Another development in critical criminology has been the development of peacemaking criminology. This perspective in part sees crime as a result of the confrontational and sometimes violent ways in which societies are prone to react towards offenders, particularly with the growing emphasis on retribution and imprisonment. Peacemaking criminology rejects the notion that violence can be suppressed by the use of state violence. Instead, people should be reconnected with others and societies should seek to promote reconciliation and harmony (Pepinsky and Quinney 1991). Most people would agree with the sentiments behind these aims, but many—especially Marxists—also claim they are naive and utopian. Russell (2002) said of peacemaking criminology 'absent a class analysis rooted in historical materialism and a global critique of capitalism, it falls prey to pacifism, liberalism, and philosophical idealism'.

Constitutive criminology

In their book *Constitutive Criminology: beyond Postmodernism* (1996), Henry and Milovanovic sought to divide the post-modern perspective of crime between 'sceptical post-modernists' and 'affirmative post-modernists'. Although the radical deconstruction of the former was depicted as a useful analytical tool, it does not provide a constitutive approach as it ultimately portrays subjects in a passive role. 'Affirmative post-modernists' were described as those who adopt the authors' own approach of rejecting the sceptics' futile position, and engaging in a reconstruction where subjects are viewed more as creations of interaction and discourse. Constitutive theory was held out by Henry and Milovanovic as being a significant advance on both modernism and post-modernism. The authors, who considered that any excessive use of power amounts to a crime, rejected the employment of force or power to achieve social change, and advocated the promotion of peacemaking activities instead. Constitutive theory aims for total human freedom where no interest is privileged over another.

Marxist (as well as other modernist) critiques would yet again describe this approach as utopian, and claim that the material basis of industrialised societies cannot be overlooked in the desire to effect social change. Many people may share the view of Henry and Milovanovic that major harm is caused by 'excessive investors' in the organisation of society. However, as Thomson (1998) put it, 'The usual answer to obliging the powerful to accept social change is to subject them to counter-power'.

Conclusion

Marxist criminology only developed as an area of intellectual interest in Britain and the USA in the early 1970s. In Britain, it first came to be strongly associated with the book *The New Criminology*, and criticisms of a Marxist perspective on crime have sometimes amounted to little more than an evaluation of that work. This is unfair: *The New Criminology*, which was described by Sumner (1994) as essentially an anarchist text, was more a product of a fermenting British criminology scene which had discovered interactionism and wanted to use it to attack 'the system'. More recent Marxist criminology, both in Britain and the USA, has shown a greater sophistication and has resulted in several penetrating analyses of the criminal justice system.

However, Marxist criminology, if not Marxism itself, still has to contend with the fundamental argument that the criminal law is not the most effective means of social control available to present-day capitalists. Industrial disputes could be viewed as a significant form of threat to capitalism. Yet, the emasculation of trade unionism by the Thatcher government during the 1980s resulted more from an extension of the civil law and the growth of fear resulting from mass unemployment than from the use of police powers to maintain public order. It is probably the case that the system of ownership and disposition of estates, which dates back to the feudal system, has been of the greatest significance in creating the current socio-economic arrangements in Western societies. The law of trusts has been more influential than the law of crime in ensuring the continuance of capitalism.

In addition, the realisation by writers such as Platt that most crime is intra-class and intra-racial appears to have been lost on some Marxists. Throughout the 1980s, it became increasingly apparent that members of local communities were more concerned with protecting the integrity of their body and their property (even if this did involve increased levels of policing) from attacks by their neighbours than fulfilling a role in a proletarian struggle against the powerful upper classes. Such individual acts of crime and deviance pose little threat to the maintenance of capitalism, but they could be—sometimes literally—a matter of life or death to those at the other end of the social divide. It was from these beginnings that the idea of Left Realism began to emerge.

11
Realist criminology

Realist criminology is a phenomenon which appeared, under different names, in Britain and the USA during the 1980s. Just as with the re-emergence of interactionism and the development of the 'new criminologies' in the 1960s, realist criminology owes much to the political background of the day: what is sometimes referred to as the 'Reagan–Thatcher Decade', with right-wing governments in both countries. In such a climate, it is hardly surprising that little interest was shown in considerations of why people commit crimes, but great interest was shown in doing something about it.

However, the new impetus did not come only from the political right. From the late 1970s, the impact of feminism grew considerably in criminology and this resulted in, first, a growing awareness of the extent of female victimisation, and subsequently a greater concern with victims in general. The 'reality' which now came to the fore was the reality of crime in people's everyday lives. Criminologists had, for more than two decades, been making various claims: that crime is a political construct; that crimes are often the poor 'getting their own back' on the rich; that rising crime figures are only a result of different counting techniques; and that society should not forget the import-ance of business crime. Meanwhile, the victims in deprived inner-city areas were facing a different 'reality' every day, with their lives blighted by muggings, sexual assaults and burglaries.

Out of this, two 'realisms' have emerged: a 'Right Realism' and a 'Left Realism'. The 'realism' they have in common is a belief that official statistics, now supported by victim surveys, correctly show that crime is increasing; a belief that the lives of communities are adversely affected by this; a belief that 'something should be done about it'; a belief that theorising unrelated to any immediate practical benefit is pointless; and a belief that resources should only be utilised on a cost-effective basis.

Right Realism

Right Realism, sometimes referred to as 'Neo-Conservatism' or 'The New Right', is more prominent in the USA than in Britain. It is not in itself a discrete theory, but an overall conservative view of crime which arose largely in opposition to the strain and labelling theories which had dominated criminological discourse during the previous two decades. A down-turn in the world economy in the mid-1970s resulted in right-wing governments being elected in both the USA and Britain. Right Realism has come to be particularly associated with the writings of James Q Wilson, a former policy adviser to Ronald Reagan. The right-wing stance that underlies all Wilson's criminological writings is shown in two main themes: criminal law is defined by the state and its composition is non-problematic; and 'street crime' (including burglary) is by far the most important area to study.

Such writers reject the commonly-held view that an expansion of welfare provision could significantly reduce the crime rate. They point to the fact that, although such expansion occurred in America during the 1960s, the crime rate still continued to increase. The 'realist' tag results from their belief that governments should set themselves achievable targets in dealing with crime. More wide-ranging changes in society's structure would lead to a greater reduction in crime, but this would be at the cost of certain fundamental freedoms, which is something the Right Realists are not prepared to contemplate.

In their book *Crime and Human Nature* (1985), Wilson and the psychologist Richard Herrnstein attempted to construct a bio-social approach to crime, which also adopted classical notions of free will. For them, crime does not result from social factors; it is based on individual choice. The fact that anti-social conduct is chosen results from general permissiveness and dependency on welfare benefits. Wilson and Herrnstein utilised the body-type theories of writers such as William H Sheldon together with more recent research on genetics (see Chapter 14) to account for a predisposition to crime. The social-psychological aspects were drawn from writers on learning theory such as Eysenck and Trasler (see Chapter 16), with their particular emphasis on socialisation in the family. Wilson and Herrnstein considered that an interaction between constitutional factors and social conditioning can affect the way in which certain people balance, on the one hand, the attraction of rewards and, on the other hand, the pull of their conditioned conscience. As effective social conditioning can only take place in a nuclear family, Wilson and Herrnstein were disapproving of single parent families.

For Wilson and Herrnstein, constitutional factors predispose certain individuals towards offending and then the quality of their socialisation will ultimately determine whether they turn to crime. Individuals will weigh the possible gains of crime against the potential punishments. Crime is increasing because of a general deterioration in the quality of socialisation, coupled with the attraction of even greater rewards from criminal activity as a result of an increasingly prosperous society. However, it is not the structure of society that is to blame for this.

Having set out their views on the causes of crime, Wilson and Herrnstein did not proceed to advocate the implementation of any particular policies specifically directed at them. The technology does not exist to deal with an individual's biological make-up. Nor are there any obvious practical solutions to the problem of deficient socialisation. To a large extent, this is seen as an inevitable consequence of the freedom that all Americans cherish. Instead, Wilson and Herrnstein argued that pragmatism should be adopted and that particular problems should be dealt with as they arise. This is essentially what makes their right-wing approach a 'realist' one. The police should not proceed against drug dealers or addicts (whose involvement in crime is so great that they are beyond help), but instead go after first-time users. Not only may such people still be deterred, but they are also the more visible signs of the problem and thus more likely to undermine the stability of the neighbourhood.

This emphasis on 'visible' crime shows that protecting the integrity of both an individual's body and personal possessions from direct attack is considered to be by far the most important role of the criminal justice system. The more 'libertarian' versions of Right Realism do not see a need for victimless crimes, as they amount to an unwarranted extension of government intervention. There is no great interest in state or corporate crime. More traditional right-wing criminology is interested in the upholding of Christian moral values for their own sake, but this seems to have been of declining influence since the rise of the Right Realists.

Writing with George Kelling (1982 and 1989), Wilson suggested that much can be achieved by making the police revert to their traditional role of maintaining order on the streets. A failure to do this gives an impression of the breakdown of law and order within a community. This generates fear and increases the likelihood of parts of the neighbourhood turning into no-go areas. However, if the residents are aware that control is being maintained, they are more likely to take a pride in their community and be on the look-out for crime. The function of the police, therefore, is not so much to react to specific criminal events, but to help create an atmosphere in which crime is unable to prosper. Drunkenness, soliciting and brawls are examples of behaviour which, although not constituting the most serious criminal offences, have a deleterious effect on the character of the neighbourhood (see also Kelling and Coles 1996).

Wilson and Kelling also considered that the police should be allowed to deal with potentially disruptive behaviour giving cause for concern, which perhaps has not been regarded as criminal in a strict sense. Examples include dispersing groups of 'undesirable persons' congregating on street corners and dealing with excessive noise. Traditionally, many police officers performed such a role before they took to patrol cars and, some people argue, became constrained by liberal attacks alleging abuse of their power. The restoration of law and order should be concentrated in those areas where it has not completely broken down, but appears in danger of doing so. Wilson and Kelling felt that it would be a waste of scarce resources to throw money at hopeless causes.

It is possible to see clearly the effects of such an approach in current American and British criminal justice policy. A 'law and order' stance has been adopted, which in practice translates into increasingly severe punishments and a rejection of attempts to use penal dispositions as a means of treatment or reform. In both countries there has been talk of adopting a policy of 'zero tolerance' in efforts to reduce crime (see Chapter 6).

Evaluation

Criminologists may have some difficulty in agreeing among themselves as to what are the key determinants underlying criminal behaviour, but few of them have much difficulty in finding objections to the approach of James Q Wilson and his collaborators. Right Realism appeals to a fundamental populism which, as typically expressed in the tabloid press (see Chapter 4), portrays crimes as simple events which can be dealt with by simplistic solutions. However, research evidence is either not provided or, as in the case of Lombroso, is almost literally incredible. Gibbs (1985) criticised Wilson and Herrnstein's approach for being based on a lack of precision in their terminology, which creates obstacles in subjecting their theory to empirical research.

Right Realism is heavily influenced by classical theory, and many of the criticisms made of that approach in Chapter 5 are also applicable here. The analysis of Right Realists ignores virtually all socio-economic influences on the way people live and, in particular, the high levels of inequality found in most industrial societies. Issues of power, class, gender and race are overlooked. On a more specific level, writers such as Wilson are, therefore, unable to explain different crime rates in different American cities; differences which appear to be linked to variations in levels of deprivation, racism and unemployment (Currie 1991). Even if one were prepared to accept Wilson's controversial attempt to rehabilitate Lombrosian views of 'the criminal man', he does not support it with any new evidence, and it is still bizarre that Wilson can overlook the large body of research conducted over decades which relates crime to social factors. It has also been suggested that Wilson and Herrnstein were selective in the research they chose to cite in support of their propositions (Kamin 1985).

Wilson's own prescription is also open to question. There are considerable problems in relying on official statistics (see Chapter 3). His total concentration on street crime, while 'realist' in acknowledging its significance, is at the expense of any consideration of the crimes of the powerful which, in financial terms, are infinitely more important than public order offences. Wilson appears only to be interested in highly visible criminal behaviour. On this basis, burglary is bracketed with street crime, and white-collar crime does not concern him, as most people are unaware that they are victims of it. The content of the criminal law is unquestioned and, presumably, is considered to reflect a general consensus within society.

Although Wilson and Kelling's 'broken windows' study in New York claimed that smartening up a neighbourhood led to a reduction in crime, research in this country by Matthews (1992) could not find clear evidence of a relationship between delinquency and urban decline. All the indicators suggest that factors such as lack of investment and inadequate facilities are more relevant to the deterioration of a neighbourhood. Even if Wilson and Kelling's hypothesis were correct, it is likely that criminal and anti-social activities would be displaced to adjacent, more run-down areas which, according to them, should not be targeted by the police as they are already beyond help. This does not appear to worry Wilson and his colleagues too much; it is the fault of the residents of these areas for allowing them to fall into this state in the first place.

There are also problems with Wilson and Kelling's reliance on informal control mechanisms and, in particular, the idea that the police should be allowed to go beyond the strict limits of the criminal law in their efforts to maintain order on the streets. The authors justified this extension of police powers by their central argument that disorder increases fear of crime. This causes the local inhabitants to stay at home, fail to carry out important surveillance activity, and generally take less interest in their neighbourhood. However, Kinsey *et al.* (1986) have argued that such an approach would not only make it difficult to assess police efficiency accurately, but would also increase the scope for discriminatory and arbitrary practices, and make police accountability very difficult. Wilson has shown no great interest in ideas such as 'due process', and appears to view curbs on police power (such as were introduced in Britain in the Police and Criminal Evidence Act 1984) as a hindrance to their ability to maintain order in communities effectively.

Wilson stated that American society has become too permissive, and that American courts are too lenient in their punishment of crime. Repeat offenders are a major problem and should be given a lengthy prison sentence to reflect both the seriousness of their crime and to protect the public from them. This has already been introduced in the USA with the now infamous 'Three strikes and they're out' baseball metaphor whereby, in certain cases, multiple offenders can be imprisoned for life. However, as Currie (1991) has pointed out, the USA has a higher rate of imprisonment than practically any other industrialised country. It also has a higher rate of crime. Moreover, as the rate of imprisonment increased during the 1980s, so did the level of crime. The USA is also unusual among Western democracies in its retention of the death penalty.

Left Realism

Right Realist criminology was almost entirely a development of the USA. This reflects the greater academic respectability that right-wing theories in general have always gained in America. Left Realism is mostly associated with British criminologists such as Jock Young, John Lea, Richard Kinsey and Roger Matthews. It is generally said to have emerged during the 1980s. However, its origins can be seen as far back as 1975 when Jock Young, a co-author of the influential radical 1973 text *The New Criminology*, published a chapter in a follow-up book, *Critical Criminology*, entitled 'Working-Class Criminology'. Young's abrupt shift from a Marxist stance is discussed in Chapter 10. To the surprise of many on the left, he now expressed the view that 'it is unrealistic to suggest that the problem of crimes like mugging is merely the problem of mis-categorisation and concomitant moral panics'.

Left Realism arose in part as a reaction to radical or 'Left Idealist' criminology, which seemed to academics such as Young to be growing increasingly irrelevant to the political climate of Margaret Thatcher's Britain. Left Idealism was still obsessed with the issues of the 1970s: the criminalisation of deviant behaviour, the labelling of offenders by powerful elites, the romanticising of crime as a political act, and the utopian dream of a crime-free society (see Chapter 10). In the view of Left Realists, this is what had allowed the right to seize the initiative in the law and order debate. As some Left Idealists questioned whether crime really had increased, they were not minded to propose any solutions to deal with it. However, Left Realists believe that not only has crime increased, but it has increased to a greater extent than revealed even in the British Crime Survey. On the streets, people are aware of this and their complaints are regularly brought to the attention of 'middle England' through the pages of the tabloid press. Ordinary people do not share the Marxist obsession with the crimes of the powerful; they are far more concerned with what is happening in their own everyday lives. Such incidents are not necessarily the moral panics previously described by criminologists. Left Realism has sought to position itself between the 'law and order' policies of the right and the apparent indifference to the consequences of crime shown by the far left.

On the other hand, Left Realists consider that Left Idealists, in their search for an ideal society, have failed to address the very real problem of crime being encountered on a daily basis, particularly by poor and disadvantaged people living in run-down inner city areas. Left Realists have expressed a concern to 'take crime seriously'. It is clear that working-class people—especially women—are the main victims of working-class crime. For Left Realists, there are no 'sacred cows'. They do not see offenders as victims of society, and are quite prepared to accept that young black working-class youths commit large numbers of crimes against both black and white working-class people. This has led to accusations of racism from some radical criminologists (Lowman and MacLean 1992). Most criminological writings—radical or otherwise—have concentrated on only one part of the criminal justice process, such as the behaviour of the offender, or the police, or perhaps the reaction of the victim, or of society as a whole. For Left Realists, however, all these different aspects must be combined into a study of the entire system.

Jock Young considered that a crime should be defined in terms of the interaction between four distinct elements: an offender; a victim; agencies of formal control (usually the police); and the informal control exercised by the general public. Young referred to this as 'the square of crime'. Another Left Realist, Richard Kinsey, managed to create a pentagon by subdividing informal control into 'the public' and 'the city' (Anderson *et al.* 1991). Young stated that levels of crime are a result of changes at all four corners: changes in behaviour; changes in the operation of social control; changes in the definitions of what should be treated as a crime; and consequently, changes in the number of victims. Criminology has generally restricted itself to considering the behaviour of offenders and the operation of social control but, if the public come to view an illegal act as unimportant (for example, bigamy in the absence of deceit), then the police do not bother about it and it does not appear in the crime statistics. In contrast, if there is considerable public concern about a crime, it will feature more prominently in the crime statistics even though it might be decreasing (this could be true of certain sexual offences). Society's level of tolerance is constantly shifting and crime control agencies are not always able—or willing—to react accordingly.

In their more recent writings, Left Realists have paid greater attention to the causes of crime. Young has highlighted the problem for criminology resulting from the fact that crime levels can be seen to have increased during periods of both affluence and recession. Left Realists consider that the fundamental cause of crime is the feeling of relative deprivation (see Chapter 7). This can occur anywhere within the social structure, although in the conditions found in most Western societies at present, it is likely to be strongest among the poor. However, it is certainly not an inevitable outcome of poverty; crime levels were far lower during the Depression in the 1930s. Nowadays, areas with high crime rates do not have sufficient social solidarity to protect the inhabitants from the effects of deprivation.

Left Realists also say that relative deprivation can explain non-economic crime, as it can lead to violence by people of all social classes. In essence, this arises where people consider that resources have been distributed unfairly, and take action in an attempt to remedy the perceived injustice. This is not portrayed as a determined outcome; an element of choice is still involved. However, it is more likely to be exercised in present-day circumstances of largely unrestrained '*laissez-faire*' capitalism, with its emphasis on individualism. According to Left Realists, relative deprivation in Britain has been the particular fate of Afro-Caribbeans. These people see themselves as cut off from mainstream society and have developed their own street culture. They have been isolated from centres of power and have played little part in the political process or trades unionism. Left Realists consider that subcultural theory has a role to play here, in that individuals come together in groups to seek shared solutions to common problems and to gain mutual reinforcement. These are likely to be male gatherings and therefore will promote 'macho' and patriarchal values. Merton's anomie theory is also acknowledged as being significant. People who have grown up in the interventionist economies of the post-war era have been encouraged to feel an entitlement to certain basic provisions, not least of which is a job. Indeed, Afro-Caribbean immigrants were enticed to this country with the promise of employment. When job opportunities dry up, the resultant strain may lead to crime. The use of violence, as exemplified in the inner-city riots of the early 1980s, is seen by Left Realists as a measure of last resort.

Concern is expressed by Left Realists at the inclination, which was arguably established in the British Crime Surveys of 1982 and 1984, to dismiss the fear of crime among certain groups in society as being irrational on the basis of the (apparently) low risk of their being victimised. This typically highlights the fact that women and elderly people, whose fear tends to be the greatest, are far less likely to be victims than young men, among whom the fear of crime is usually the least. Apart from making the obvious point that those who fear crime the most are likely to take the strongest precautions against it (such as remaining behind locked doors), Left Realists have argued that such measurements of risk are misleading because they combine low-risk and high-risk groups. Instead, steps should be taken to examine why crime tends to be committed predominantly against women, the poor and ethnic minorities living in certain inner-city areas. Such people often feel the effects of crime more severely than others, as they lack the resources—both financial and otherwise—to deal with their loss or harm. Moreover, women are often the victims of crimes, such as sexual attacks or domestic violence, which they are reluctant to report to the police and which are unlikely to be revealed in any but the most sensitive of victim surveys. Considering that the methodology used in the early reports of the British Crime Survey was inadequate to deal with such sensitive issues of victimisation, Left Realists conducted their own surveys, such as the Merseyside Crime Survey (Kinsey 1984) and the two Islington Crime Surveys (Jones et al. 1986, Crawford et al. 1990). These revealed far higher levels of these crimes than were officially recorded. Left Realists have therefore suggested that measures of risk should be replaced by measures of impact.

In sharp contrast to the view of Right Realists such as Wilson, Left Realists consider that justice should always be more important than control of crime. In any case, if the police were to behave in such a way as to antagonise the public, it would be highly detrimental for social control. Not only would the young working class and ethnic minorities feel even further alienated and perhaps be pushed over the edge into crime, but the general cooperation of the public, on which the police are so reliant, would start to disappear. It is crucial for Left Realists that the police are fully responsible to the local community (Kinsey, Lea and Young 1986). The replacement of consensus policing by the confrontational use of 'swamp' procedures and paramilitary methods has obscured the distinction between offenders and non-offenders and resulted in whole communities feeling under attack (Lea and Young 1982). Indeed, the problems of heavy-handed policing were identified by Lord Scarman in his report on the Brixton riots (1981). For Left Realists, the growing moves to privatise aspects of crime prevention are unlikely to be successful, as such schemes will lack public involvement and are likely to be targeted on the 'better' areas where they have the greatest chances of success.

One development of Left Realism in the 1980s, which would have been unthinkable only a decade or so earlier, was the involvement of left-wing criminologists in the development of programmes aimed at crime prevention. Previously, such individuals would have criticised this sort of action as correctionalist. Yet, now Left Realists have put forward practical proposals, inter alia, to design streets so as to deter prostitutes and kerb-crawlers (Matthews 1986), and improve street lighting (Painter 1989).

Evaluation

Radical criminologists have criticised Left Realists for 'selling out' to stereotypical, populist and 'common sense' notions of crime which portray it as some sort of unified entity. Although there has more recently been some Left Realist consideration of corporate and white-collar crime (Pearce and Tombs 1992), it seems to have taken very much second place to an analysis of working-class crime. This serves to reinforce the image conveyed by the powerful of what is the real crime problem. Left Realists have placed considerable emphasis on the potentially debilitating nature of fear of crime. For instance, in the second Islington Crime Survey (Crawford et al. 1990) almost two-thirds of the respondents said that fear of crime prevented their going out.

However, it is arguably misleading for Left Realists to assert that much fear of crime is, indeed, rational. It may be *understandable*, but society could take steps to deal with fear—which admittedly is a real problem—without having wrongly to concede that it is based on a true foundation. As Sparks (1992) has pointed out, it is inappropriate to consider fear purely in terms of rationality. The ability of survey respondents to make an accurate estimation of risk will be governed by their fear of crime, which itself will be indicative of a range of factors relating to their personality. Most people have no means of making a reliable assessment of the risk of crime in their neighbourhood. The information they receive is usually second-hand and probably based on sensationalised reporting in the local press (Williams and Dickinson 1993).

There is certainly evidence that fear of crime exists. The 2000 International Crime Victimisation Survey showed that the citizens of England and Wales topped the list of seventeen industrialised countries for the number of security devices installed, with 69 per cent claiming to have special door locks and 34 per cent burglar alarms (van Kesteren *et al.* 2001).

The Australian criminologist Rob White (1996) has claimed that fear of crime has been sold as a commodity in the form of locks, surveillance cameras and private security services. This has a particular impact on the poor, for whom economic insecurity is a fact of life. In reality, white-collar and corporate crime is far more damaging to society. However, as White commented:

> The structural vulnerability of various strata and groups within the working class (such as the elderly, ethnic minorities and women) means that campaigns promising more coercive safety measures will have a strong resonance.

In any event, some feminist writers consider that the question whether fear of crime is rational is irrelevant to women. Walklate (2004) stated that rationality in this context is a male construction; women must be considered to have 'expert' knowledge on the subject. Even local victim surveys, which are still based on measuring incidents, cannot assess the routine, underlying threat to security that characterises the lives of many women (Stanko 1987). Nevertheless, Walklate (1997) has pointed out that, in addition to considering fear from the point of view of gender, risk-taking should also be viewed as being attractive to both men and women. It is important not to overlook the fact that men also suffer as victims.

Hulsman (1986) has argued that members of the working class

suffer a whole range of hardships in their lives that are unrelated to crime, such as poverty, housing problems and matrimonial difficulties. The people who are affected do not distinguish between these and the problems that result from crime, and it is unnecessary for criminologists to do so. Brown and Hogg (1992) considered that:

> The most fundamental problem in the realist theory, programme and methodology lies in the diminution of concern with the concept of crime itself.

The willingness to accept whatever happens to be defined as criminal at the time leaves Left Realists open to the charge of being 'of the moment': the field of study is restricted to the content of the criminal law at a particular instant. This appears to be a return to arguments which many people thought had been settled some time ago (see Chapter 2). Whereas Marxist and labelling theories have emphasised the contextual nature of crime, Left Realists have restated the centrality of the concept of crime to the debate. Their view, if accepted, would arguably remove many of the supposed advances in criminological theory in the past forty years.

Left Realist theories of crime are largely based on small-scale victim surveys conducted in inner-city areas. Several of these were commissioned by local authorities, who perhaps had their own agendas, and there may be some people who doubt whether the research was completely independent. These surveys were able to probe with a degree of intimacy which is not generally possible in the more common national forms of inquiry. The researchers were thus able to elicit information on sensitive issues, such as domestic violence and sexual attacks. Their findings have a personal, localised feel which seems to place much emphasis on poverty, class and victimisation. There are both advantages and disadvantages in this approach. Is this a theory of crime for deprived inner city areas or for the whole country? As Mugford and O'Malley (1991) stated:

> Arguably, the advocacy of inner-city victims, and an ill-concealed contempt shown for 'suburban souls', constitutes a narrow platform for a socialist strategy dealing with crime.

Left Realists appear to listen very carefully to their victims' accounts and accept that they constitute the reality of crime, but then impose a structural analysis on what they hear without any apparent reference back to their sources. Thus, the much-heralded 'empowerment' of victims only operates at the level of providing information.

Critics such as Alison Young (1996) consider that Left Realism gives the victim far too central a role, making the offender little more than a peripheral figure. This is largely because victims are to have the crucial function of galvanising the local community. Their experience becomes the basis of the whole criminal justice system.

The way in which the community is policed is of considerable importance for Left Realists. Because it is vital that the method of policing is supported by the local community, there needs to be: accountability at local level; legal control of police powers; a limit to the exercise of discretion (which is often perceived by the public as unfair); and community involvement in determining policing priorities. Apart from the inevitable opposition of the police to many of these points, there are other problems. The removal of discretion from policing is impossible: discretion in the criminal justice system is like a bubble which, if pushed down at one point, will reappear somewhere else. Much police–public interaction at street level is sufficiently private to be beyond the scope of legal controls. If the police were subject to greater restrictions, they might not be able to deal adequately with serious offences. At times, Left Realists appear to be arguing for a minimalist approach to policing, but that might not be what members of the local community want. In addition, as Pearce and Tombs (1992) have indicated, it would be highly unlikely to prove an effective way of dealing with white-collar crime.

Moreover, the assumption that more consistent and community-sensitive policing would lead to a greater acceptance of the police seems naive. Although the police do rely on the public for the provision of information about crime, much of what they receive is provided by informants in return for inducements.

The local democracy which Left Realists consider should underpin the provision of policing (Michalowski 1983) might not work to the advantage of the community as a whole. Given the well-known degree of apathy in local politics, it is possible that more organised and vocal groups would dominate, and that some of the sensitive issues identified in the victim surveys would continue to receive little attention. Left Realism's aim of empowering the local community might also be assuming an appreciation of the patterns of offending in the area which do not exist. If the local community were rallied around the notion of 'popular justice', it might lead to pressure for excessively punitive measures to be taken. In August 2000, the behaviour of a group claiming to be representative of a local community in Portsmouth led to vigilante actions against suspected paedophiles in the area.

It may be that many converts to Left Realism have been unable to discard the antipathy towards the police which was an inevitable component of their former, more radical stance. The emphasis placed by Left Realist criminologists on police accountability could be a relic of the battles fought in the 1980s between certain left-wing local councils (of which some Left Realists were members) and their chief constables over the use of paramilitary methods in policing riots and industrial disputes. Whether this is now (or, indeed, was) an issue for the people whose cause Left Realists are claiming to champion is another matter.

Left Realists have criticised other criminologists for concentrating excessively on certain aspects of the criminal justice system rather than providing an account of the whole picture. Yet, in its concentration on the experiences of victims in urban communities, Left Realists lay themselves open to precisely the same charge. Issues such as the prevention and detection of crime and the decision to prosecute are relatively unexplored. Such matters do not, perhaps, lend themselves so readily to local determination, and this may reveal a flaw in the decentralist argument. Moreover, an emphasis on crime as perceived at the community level is likely to result in a heavy concentration on street offences. Recognising the importance of such events is a central feature of Realist criminology, both Right and Left (although not for the same reasons). Yet, there is a real danger that this might prove to be at the expense of less visible crimes involving corporate or environmental issues. Working-class people also have their lives affected by pollution.

More recently, Left Realists have claimed that identifying possible causes of crime is one of their most important tasks. Given the earlier writings of some of the theory's leading protagonists, such as Jock Young, a purely positivist explanation was never likely to be forthcoming. What emerges is the notion of 'relative deprivation'. This approach has the advantages of locating the causes of crime within the social structure (unlike Right Realism) and providing an account which does not attribute crime directly to poverty or unemployment (which would not be sustainable by the evidence). Yet, there are still difficulties. Why should certain individuals experiencing the problems of relative deprivation choose crime? One possible answer is that they wish to improve their economic circumstances. However, attempts to explain non-economic crimes, such as crimes of violence, through the idea of relative deprivation seem unconvincing. Any objective measurement of relative deprivation would acknowledge its positivist credentials. It also considerably over-predicts the level of crime. Relative deprivation is said to be a form of discontent felt by certain individuals. As such, it is impossible to validate or invalidate the theory.

Furthermore, it is not made clear how Left Realism's emphasis on addressing problems of total deprivation within a community would in itself solve problems of relative deprivation, which arguably need to be dealt with by far more fundamental changes in the structure of society.

Emphasis is placed on the subcultural solution, which such discontented individuals seek in order to obtain mutual support. While this is a possible reaction from a group of individuals within the small neighbourhoods on which Left Realists have usually concentrated, it is unlikely that the evidence from wider society would support such a proposition.

Conclusion

Realist criminology represents a shift from ideology to a pragmatic concern for dealing with the problem of crime. What the 'problem' actually is depends on a person's political standpoint. For Right Realists such as Wilson, it is the breakdown of public order on the streets. Visibility becomes the vital issue—what goes on behind closed doors seems almost not to matter. For Left Realists such as Young, the problem is also found in deprived inner-city areas. This time, however, the focus switches to the poor as victims. Interest is certainly shown in what is happening behind the curtains, particularly as it reveals domestic violence, which hitherto has not been brought to public attention.

Right Realist criminology has received little academic support in Britain, where greater attention has been paid to Left Realism. There are several reasons for the growth in this interest. The rise of 'Thatcherism' in the 1980s inspired some on the left to try to put their ideas into practice in local government. Certain councils, such as Islington and Liverpool, were prepared to hire sympathetic criminologists to research into crime in their areas. The writings of the Left Realists soon came to be reflected in the official policy of the Labour Party in opposition. Also, by this time, the rise of feminism had spread to academic criminology. Writers such as Carol Smart (1976) had criticised radical criminologists for romanticising crime and overlooking the widespread victimisation of women. Left Realism thus helped to prevent the alienation of feminist criminologists from the left's interest in crime. In addition, the increasing sophistication of victim surveys enabled Left Realists to demonstrate that there are real problems of crime in working-class communities, which hitherto had not been revealed by traditional forms of measurement.

Left Realism is not the first approach to crime to be very much a reflection of the prevailing climate; the renewed interest in interactionism in the 1960s could be explained on the same ground. Yet, does Left Realism add anything new to criminological theory? Rock (1992), describing it as the criminology that has come in from the cold, considered that Left Realism comprises a combination of anomie, subcultural and control theories from a leftist slant. Left Realism could, perhaps, best be described as a repackaging of existing theories to suit what its proponents consider to be a post-ideological age.

Postscript: victims

If Left Realism were to have played no other role in the development of criminology, it would be remembered, together with feminism, for helping to place victims on both the criminological and political agendas. In one sense, everyone is a victim of crime, whether it be through increased local authority spending, or through higher insurance premiums, or through the limiting of areas into which people are prepared to venture at night. For many years the policies of successive governments seemed to emphasise this aspect rather than the effect that crimes had on individual victims. Crime was primarily viewed as an attack against society as a whole, and the main thrust of government policy was in trying to reduce its level.

Criminology was unable to devote much attention to victims because of its propensity to ascribe that status to offenders, whether as a result of individual pathology or societal forces. The direct victims of offenders were simply presumed to exist and were rarely discussed, except in the context of their absence: should 'victimless crimes', such as homosexuality or drug-taking, be criminal offences at all? Marxist and radical theorists viewed crime as a political act in reaction to the forces of capitalism. The term 'victimology' appears first to have been used in the 1940s by American writers who concentrated particularly on aspects of the victim's lifestyle which might be said to encourage or facilitate crime. For example, Hans von Hentig (1948), whose work had no empirical basis, considered that the law posited an arbitrary division between offender and victim which was often unjustified. In advocating an interactionist approach, von Hentig pointed out that victims often initiate incidents by making the first move in a violent confrontation. Certain people, therefore, are victim-prone. This view was supported by Marvin E Wolfgang in his book *Patterns in Criminal Homicide* (1958). Based on an examination of 588 homicides in Philadelphia, Wolfgang's research found that in 26 per cent of the cases the victim had made the first use of physical violence.

However, the approach to victims began to change during the 1960s when victim surveys started to be developed in America. Although they were primarily aimed at determining the level of hidden or unreported crime, the surveys also revealed the impact that victim-isation had on a vast number of individuals. Thus by 1971, when Menachem Amir's book *Patterns of Forcible Rape* suggested (on the basis of police reports) that 19 per cent of rapes were victim-precipitated, there was a strong adverse reaction from feminists. They were able to point to the evidence that many rapes are unreported, and argued that the level of emotional devastation caused by such incidents made it inappropriate to suggest that they were self-induced (Morris 1987). Curtis (1974) found evidence of victim-precipitation in only 4 per cent of rapes, although he claimed it was a factor in 11 per cent of robberies, 14 per cent of aggravated assaults and 22 per cent of homicides.

Fattah (1979) tried to rescue the idea of victim precipitation from the notion of blame that was increasingly accompanying it by suggest-ing that it is perfectly legitimate to consider what may be a complex interactional process between offender and victim. However, such an argument was by then going against the tide of academic opinion.

The early writers have been criticised for creating an impression that there are two types of victim: innocent and blameworthy. The innocent victim, who is fully deserving of sympathy, is typified by an elderly lady or child who has been mugged. Such people are con-sidered 'helpless' and in need of society's protection. The blame-worthy victim, who is less deserving of sympathy, includes the woman whose demeanour or dress suggests that she was 'asking for it', as well as the drunken victim of an assault received during a fight (Walklate 1989). There is also an expectation that women should try to fight back: this was highlighted in a notorious case in 1999 when an Italian court decided that a woman could not have been raped as her jeans were too tight to have been removed without her cooperation (*The Times*, 12 February 1999).

This view of victim culpability is reflected throughout society in several ways. The part played by the victim in the crime may affect the level of sentence passed on the offender. The Criminal Injuries Com-pensation Scheme, which was established in 1964, has always made a distinction between deserving and undeserving victims. People who were considered to have provoked offences, or had failed to report the crime to the police, or were even related to offenders, were originally excluded from the Scheme's ambit. Financial incentives are offered by insurance companies to policy holders who take certain precautions to reduce the risk of being victimised. Female students in universities and colleges are warned about the dangers of walking alone at night. Does this mean that such people will be partly to blame for any misfortune that befalls them and cannot be considered as victims?

This is not to say that victims' behaviour never plays any part in precipitating criminal offences. A study of the series of events leading up to assaults and homicides has shown that victim retaliation can be a significant factor (Felson and Steadman 1983). At the beginning of the twenty-first century, if people living in urban areas of the Western world go out of their homes leaving all the windows open, there is a reasonable chance that they will become the victims of burglary. The issue, which usually becomes entangled with considerations of blame, involves asking what was reasonable behaviour in the circumstances. Yet, this itself raises the question: reasonable in whose eyes? Feminists have claimed that some writers on crime precipitation wrongly equate the ability of wholly different types of victim to exercise power and influence the outcome of a situation (Walklate 2004). It would be totally unrealistic, for example, to consider the behaviour of home-owners leaving all their windows open in the same terms as female victims of sexual assaults.

The concept of victim precipitation did not appear to some people to provide an adequate explanation for the fact that many individuals are persistently victimised. It was, therefore, developed into a consideration of victims' lifestyle in the book *Victims of Personal Crime* (1978) by Hindelang, Gottfredson and Garofalo. Based on an analysis of data from surveys conducted by the Bureau of the Census in eight American cities in 1972, the authors set out a series of propositions, all of which could be tested empirically. They discovered that the probability of being a victim of a personal crime is related to the amount of time people spend in public places, particularly at night; the extent to which the victim shares demographic characteristics with the offender; and the amount of time the victim spends with non-family members. This type of analysis proved to be the forerunner of the much larger-scale victim surveys which have subsequently become so popular.

Victim surveys 'came of age' in Britain with the publication of the first British Crime Survey (BCS) in 1982. Subsequent 'sweeps' have

ironed out shortcomings in the original report, and localised surveys—for example in Islington and on Merseyside—have pointed the
way to the provision of more detailed and intimate information. This
has been particularly useful in relation to sexual and domestic assaults
against women, which were considerably under-represented in the
early BCS reports.

The information provided by the BCS concerning the groups of
people who are most likely to be victimised does not provide any great
surprises. Single young males (16–29) who have been drinking and
are either on the streets, or using public transport in inner-city areas at
night, are more prone to be victims of assault. On the other hand,
female victims of mugging tend to be older and married. Burglaries
are more common in flats or end of terrace houses (particularly if
owned by the council) which lack security devices and are situated in
inner-city areas. Vehicles are more likely to be taken if their owners
(also living in inner-city council properties) park them on the street at
night. People in paid employment are three times more likely to be
victimised than non-workers, and students are five times more likely
to be victimised than other people. Workers are more likely to be
victimised at their place of employment, presumably because there is
less surveillance. Racial minority groups are more likely to be victimised than whites. They are also more likely to live in identified high-
crime areas. The BCS has also suggested that Afro-Caribbeans are
more likely to be victimised by other Afro-Caribbeans. This may be
true for more serious and visible crimes, but there is other evidence
suggesting that blacks and Asians receive racial harassment from
whites which is certainly not reported to the police, and may not have
been mentioned to researchers.

The earlier victim surveys did not enquire into child victimisation,
and there is not a great deal of empirical evidence on the extent of
child physical or sexual abuse. Research in San Francisco by Russell
(1984) found that 31 per cent of her subjects reported being victims of
some form of sexual abuse outside the family, and 16 per cent within
the family. Given the embarrassment involved in making this sort of
revelation, it is likely that the true figures were even higher. Some
estimates have suggested that, within the family setting, about 90 per
cent of the victims are female and nearly all the offenders are male.
Children are also affected by other offences committed against them,
particularly bullying.

Findings from the BCS claiming that the people who fear crime the
most are often least likely to be victims have been criticised by Left
Realists, partly on the ground that those with the greatest fear are

particularly likely to take precautionary measures. In the 1982 BCS, 1 per cent of males aged sixteen to thirty felt 'very unsafe' on the street, whereas 7.7 per cent of that age group reported being victims of street crime. The corresponding figures for women were 16 per cent feeling very unsafe, and 2.8 per cent of the age group actually being victimised. It is also the case that the BCS findings can mask considerable local and regional variations.

On the other hand, research by Ditton *et al.* (1999) found that, rather than a *fear* of violent crime, a much stronger emotion experienced by people was *anger* about it. In a survey of around 1,600 people in the Strathclyde region of Scotland, 55 per cent of the respondents claimed to be angry about assault some or all of the time, compared with 27 per cent who reported being afraid. There was no significant difference in the responses of victims and non-victims.

A further consequence of the growing fear of crime is an increase in the level of parental restriction placed on the activities of their children. Nowadays, they are increasingly driven by car both to and from school and to see their friends. Play in the street and other open spaces has declined, and children may suffer from being unable to explore the world around them (Furedi 2001). A report by the Mental Health Foundation (1999) claimed that such a reduction in 'risk-taking' activities could lead to a lack of self-confidence and an increase in psychological problems among the young. The Royal Society for the Prevention of Accidents has suggested that an inability to make a proper assessment of risk could at least partly account for the 50 per cent increase in drownings among the under-fifteens in 1999 (*The Guardian*, 4 October 2000).

As a result of victim surveys, Left Realism and feminist criminology, victims have been placed firmly on the criminological agenda. More significantly, they have also come to be a major item in 'law and order' politics. In America the victims' organisation, NOVA, is a right-wing body which has become associated with a more punitive approach to offenders, including support for the death penalty. Its British equivalent, Victim Support (formerly NAVSS), has avoided political lobbying and concentrated on securing practical help for victims.

Nevertheless, the plight of victims is an issue which has become very important to the main political parties in Britain. As Rock (1990) has pointed out, the public relations advantages of providing support for victims are considerable, and an appearance of 'doing something' for the victims of crime may help to offset the impression of having failed to prevent the crime occurring in the first place. The Labour

Party's support for high-profile confrontations which resulted in considerable public disorder during the 1980s (such as the printers' and miners' disputes) enabled the Conservative government to portray them as being anti-police and 'soft' on crime. However, the Conservatives had not hitherto been prominent in advocating a better deal for victims. The typical deprived inhabitant of an inner-city area is unlikely to be a natural Tory voter. When grass roots opinion (and Left Realist writings) began to make an impression on Labour Party policy, the Conservatives could not afford to be left behind. The result was that victims began to feature more prominently in the law and order rhetoric of the 1980s. Financial backing was given to Victim Support, and in 1990 the Home Office announced a 'Victims Charter'; this was updated in 1996 (Home Office 1996). It sets out basic standards as to what victims have a right to expect from the criminal justice system, including information about the progress of the case against the accused.

However, not everyone has given an unreserved welcome to the increased focus being placed on victims. Sumner (1994), in arguing that the sociology of moral censures should replace the sociology of deviance, offered political correctness and the 'politics of victimism' as examples of the increasingly censorious world in which we live. He quoted the American writer CJ Sykes (1992):

> Now enshrined in law and jurisprudence, victimism is reshaping the fabric of society, including employment policies, criminal justice, education, urban politics ... A community of interdependent citizens has been displaced by a society of resentful, competing, and self-interested individuals who have dressed their private annoyances in the garb of victimism.

In many American states, Australia and Canada, victims are allowed to make a statement as part of the trial process, which may include suggesting the punishment they would like imposed on the offender. Such 'victim impact statements' are encouraged by Declaration 6 of the United Nations' Charter of Victim Rights, which states that the relevant judicial and administrative processes should:

> (6b) [allow] the views and concerns of the victims to be presented and considered at appropriate stages of the proceedings where their personal interests are affected, without prejudice to the accused and consistent with the relevant criminal justice system.

The use of victim impact statements is controversial. Their proponents claim that one of the main aims is to increase victims' satisfaction with the criminal justice system (Erez 1999). However, critics argue that the process introduces an undesirable subjective element into the sentencing process which encourages vindictiveness and more severe sentencing (Ashworth 1993). It could also be detrimental to some victims to encourage them to re-live experiences that they would prefer to forget.

The police may also have their own reasons for taking care of crime victims. In 1982, the Thames Valley Police were heavily criticised for their treatment of rape victims as portrayed in a documentary television series. Subsequently, there has been considerable public and political pressure for the police to act more sensitively in dealing with victims. The performance targets to which the police are increasingly subject inevitably require a reduction in recorded crime. In order to secure convictions, the police usually need the cooperation of victims. It is therefore arguable that the police need to look after victims in order to improve their reliability as complainants and witnesses (Miers 1992).

The status of victim in the criminal justice system relates to discrete criminal offences. An alternative view is that this is a meaningless approach because victimisation is a continual feature of many people's daily lives—especially those of women, inhabitants of deprived inner-city areas, and members of ethnic minority groups. Governments are reluctant to face up to this, as the major shifts in social policy required would necessitate the expenditure of vast sums of money. As a result, the inevitable problems are left to the criminal justice system, which addresses them at the level of particular breaches of the law caused by individual defendants.

Even the statuses of 'offender' and 'victim' are not as clear-cut as the criminal justice system requires. Although the earlier emphasis given by some writers to victim precipitation was misleading, it remains the case that some people, who could quite reasonably be described as victims, were not wholly innocent bystanders when certain crimes—such as assault—were committed against them. Also, the growing emphasis on victimisation enables many offenders to claim that, through abuse or other problems in their early lives, they themselves should be considered as victims (Lamb 1996). In 1998, the government announced that teenage female prostitutes should be treated by police and prosecutors as victims rather than offenders, as they are likely to have been sexually abused (Department of Health 1998). As many other offenders, both male and female, also suffered abuse in their childhood, such consideration should perhaps also be extended to them.

Certain groups are so keen to impose the label of victim on particular individuals that the question arises whether someone can be a victim of a crime without being aware of it. Two issues which illustrate this problem are 'date rape' and recovered memory loss. It has been suggested that, although there is at present no separate offence of date rape, such incidents should be distinguished from the stereotypical attack perpetrated by a stranger. A Home Office report showed that the percentage of rapes by offenders unknown to the victim decreased from 30 per cent in 1985 to 12 per cent in 1996. This coincided with a decline in the conviction rate for rape from 24 per cent to 9 per cent. The report stated that consideration should be given to 'grading' the offence of rape to allow for different levels of seriousness (Harris and Grace 1999). However, many women strongly oppose this view, and claim that serious victimisation occurs in all types of rape. The new definition of rape in the Sexual Offences Act 2003 (see Chapter 17) has not divided it into different categories

Recovered memory loss involves the use of hypnosis and other techniques by therapists who suspect that their clients have repressed memories of childhood abuse. Many psychologists are sceptical about such claims (Loftus and Ketcham 1994). The Royal College of Psychiatrists commissioned a report, but refused to publish the findings because of a division amongst its members. The report found a high probability that 'recovered memory therapy' is ineffective (Brandon *et al.* 1998).

Best (1999) argued that groups seeking to extend the definition of victimisation have strongly influenced the creation (or, at least, redefinition) of certain criminal offences. The American example he used was 'stalking', which he considered has now come to be identified almost entirely with battered women being followed by their former partners.

There may also be a problem concerning victims' self-perception. It has been suggested that such people increasingly join groups and define themselves 'only in terms of their claims to special identity and suffering' (Cohen 1996). From an interactionist perspective, this could have a significant effect on people's sense of identity and value. It may also help to encourage what some see as the growing 'medicalisation' of victimology (Best 1999). Even the adoption of the correct terminology may become important. Many writers and campaigners have replaced the word 'victim' with 'survivor'. Best considered that, as this approach has been borrowed from discussions of the Holocaust, some people may think the term is inappropriate to describe victimisation resulting from more routine criminal offences.

In addition to the argument that Western society appears to be moving towards the position where 'we are all victims now', there is a further problem for the study of crime and criminology. Since the 1980s successive governments have claimed that victims have been neglected at the expense of offenders. Even if this were a true reflection of the state of academic interest, it is hardly an accurate portrayal of government action, which for many years largely ignored both. It would be most unfortunate—and, arguably, counterproductive—if the growing interest in the victim proved to be at the cost of demonising the offender. Some people have argued that both could be helped by being brought together, particularly where the crime was not particularly serious. Experimental schemes in victim-offender mediation have produced a high level of approval among the participants (Parliamentary All Party Penal Affairs Group 1996). Even in situations where this is undesirable or impossible, the dangers of placing offenders 'beyond the pale' (which are considered in Chapter 9) must be borne in mind. Of course victims must be helped—but it would surely be preferable if there were far less need to do so.

12
Theories of control

The significance of control in the operation of society has been recognised by philosophers and writers for many centuries. Aristotle considered that the most heinous crimes were committed through indulgence, and classical theorists such as Hobbes viewed fear as an essential feature in the maintenance of a law-abiding society. Utilitarian philosophers thought that individuals apply rational analysis to decisions as to whether a proposed course of action would cause more pleasure than pain. Control is an aspect of most theories of crime and deviance. Durkheim considered that lack of regulation could lead to anomic suicide. Shaw and McKay's notion of 'social disorganisation' was based on the assumption that crime was related to poor social control. In labelling theory, it is the differential use of control that creates secondary deviation. Nor does control only feature in sociological explanations of crime. Learning theorists such as Hans Eysenck stressed the importance of social conditioning in child-rearing techniques (see Chapter 16), and even Freud's analysis of personality development emphasised the importance of parental control in the early years of life.

With such a long and varied history, it may seem surprising that control has not, until comparatively recently, been studied in its own right as a significant causal feature of crime and deviance. There are several possible reasons for this. One may be that criminologists were reluctant to research into ideas that so clearly support discipline and regulation, particularly in the liberal climate of the early 1960s. Another may be that the pathological undertones of the theory were unappealing to the sociologists who had largely come to replace the psychologists in the forefront of criminological writing. Furthermore, perhaps the importance of control was thought to accord with general common sense, and criminologists, in attempting to provide a mystique in order to have their discipline taken more seriously, preferred to concentrate on less obvious phenomena.

However, a number of theorists have written specifically from a control perspective. Most of them have attributed crime and deviance to a weakness in the level of control exercised over, or by, offenders. More recently, an alternative control-based explanation has been put forward: that offenders themselves either have too much control over events, or do not have the opportunity to exercise sufficient control over their own lives.

Early social control theories

Albert J Reiss (1951) studied the court records of 1,100 white male youths on probation to see if any factors provided an accurate prediction of the revoking of their probation licence. He found that revocation occurred more often when the juvenile had been diagnosed by a psychiatrist as having a weak ego or superego (these Freudian terms are considered in Chapter 16) and intensive psychotherapy or in-patient treatment had been recommended. Revocation also occurred more when the youths had been missing school or were described by teachers as having behavioural problems. Reiss claimed that this showed that the juveniles had weak 'personal controls' in that they could not resist satisfying their wants in socially disapproved ways. Although fundamentally based on Freudian concepts, Reiss's views were presented from a sociological perspective, and provided one of the very first statements of a control theory. Nevertheless, his methodology was dubious, being based on the uncritical acceptance of psychiatric reports without any confirmatory evidence. Reiss's views are now of little more than historical interest.

Jackson Toby (1957) claimed that all youths are tempted to break the law, but some will risk far more than others by giving in to such temptation. For example, boys who are doing well at school will risk not only punishment for their crime, but also endangering their future career prospects. They have a high 'stake in conformity'. However, boys who do not perform well at school have far less to lose and, therefore, less incentive to resist temptation. If such boys are surrounded by others with a low stake in conformity, they will obtain peer group support and crime rates might, therefore, rise higher than would be expected from a study of the individuals alone. On the other hand, individual youths with a low stake in conformity might not turn to crime if they fail to gain support from other youths in their area. Toby also acknowledged the roles played by the family and the community in shaping the form of adjustment made at school. Briar and Piliavin (1965) later presented a similar theory, with the additional notion of 'situational inducements' as a new motivating factor.

Toby's plea that, despite the importance of the school, the significance of the home should not be overlooked as a vital element in the control process was taken up by F Ivan Nye (1958), who attributed most delinquent behaviour to inadequate social control. He used 'social control' in a broad sense to embrace direct controls imposed by restrictions and punishments by such people as parents, teachers and the police; indirect control arising from identification with parents and non-criminals; the internal control of conscience; and the availability of legitimate outlets to satisfy needs. Nye administered a questionnaire to 780 schoolchildren in Washington state which contained a list of questions designed to evince information about their family life and measure their rate of delinquency. He rated their responses in such a way as to put the top quarter into the 'most delinquent' group and the remainder into the 'least delinquent' group. The youths in the 'most delinquent' group were likely to be rejecting and critical of their parents; to have parents whom they considered to be bad-tempered, difficult to please and rejecting; and to have more money than is usual at their age. On the other hand, youths in the 'least delinquent' group had a close relationship with their parents and approved of their disciplinary techniques; were the oldest or only child; came from a small family; and were regular church attenders.

Nye's empirical findings appear impressive, but closer analysis shows that they are of dubious value in relation to delinquency. His sample did not include any children from large cities, and the numbers drawn from ethnic minorities or from foreign-born parents were negligible. Only two of the types of behaviour mentioned in his questionnaire were illegal. Youths who were more prepared to disclose their criminal and anti-social activities might also be more willing to disclose unfavourable aspects of their home life. In short, Nye's study seems more about the effect of family relationships on the anti-social and petty-criminal behaviour of generally non-delinquent boys.

Walter C Reckless (1961) synthesised a number of existing criminological theories into what he termed a 'containment theory'. Reckless was not proposing a theory of crime causation; he acknowledged that there was already a wide variety of such theories in existence. Nevertheless, he considered that the sum of these theories was better than the individual parts in providing a general theory of crime. He argued that everyone is subject to various forces, some of which propel people towards crime, and others which restrain them from it. The forces pressurising towards crime include what Reckless termed 'social pressures': lack of opportunities, poor living conditions and low status; 'social pulls' enticing people away from conventional lifestyles, such as delinquent companions; and internal 'pushes', including aggression and hostility. Reckless provided examples of such forces, but did not offer specific definitions. What is important to consider is why everyone does not succumb to these forces. This is because, in opposition, there are other forces which serve to contain any movement towards crime. Reckless divided these into forces of 'outer containment', including family cohesion and consistent discipline, and 'inner containment', such as a strong superego (a Freudian notion: see Chapter 16), a sense of responsibility, and self-control. Reckless thought that inner containments in particular are of vital importance in controlling behaviour.

The idea of containment theory arose from various studies that Reckless and others carried out into law-abiding boys living in areas of high crime. He claimed that a high degree of inner containment in particular provides a good shield from delinquency. However, later research has not found a strong correlation between inner containment and crime, and Reckless's methodology has been criticised (for example, Orcutt 1970). Clarence Schrag (1971), for example, pointed out that the placement of variables in particular categories seemed either arbitrary or too vague to be of use. It is hardly surprising to find that 'bad companions' are listed as a force pulling towards delinquency and 'supportive relationships' as one militating against it!

Travis Hirschi and social control

Control theory has come to be most closely associated with Travis Hirschi. In his book *Causes of Delinquency* (1969), Hirschi claimed that it is unnecessary to explain why people commit delinquent acts:

> Delinquency is not caused by beliefs that require delinquency but is rather made possible by the absence of effective beliefs that forbid delinquency.

The pertinent question, therefore, is why people do *not* commit delinquent acts. Unlike classical theorists such as Hobbes, Hirschi did not view crime as the expression of free will, but simply as normal behaviour. Hirschi argued that people who are tightly bonded to social groups such as the family and the school are less likely to commit criminal offences. Provided there is normative consensus, a weakening or breaking of social bonds will reduce a person's likelihood of obeying the rules. Hirschi listed four key interrelated elements in the creation and maintenance of this bond.

The first and most important element is 'attachment', in the form of sensitivity to, and affection for, 'conventional others'. Hirschi considered this to be the main component required to internalise norms and values. It appears to be similar to Nye's notion of internal and indirect controls. For most people, the strongest attachments are formed with members of their family. Criminologists who are sympathetic to Hirschi's theory, such as Cernkovich and Giordano (1987), think that attachments to family and school are the best predictors of conformity. The second element is 'commitment'. This relates to the amount of commitment that delinquents have to conventional society and the consequent level of risk that they take by committing crimes. If people do not make these commitments, or consider them unimportant, they are more likely to turn to delinquency. This element is similar to Toby's 'stake in conformity'.

The third element is 'involvement' in conventional activities, and reflects the idea that keeping occupied leaves less time for criminal activity. The fourth and final element in the social bond is 'belief'. Whereas Sykes and Matza (1957) had maintained that delinquents subscribe to conventional morality, but use 'techniques of neutralization' so they can commit criminal acts without feelings of guilt (see Chapter 8), Hirschi argued that not everyone is equally committed to obeying society's rules. 'Belief' refers to the acceptance of this commitment. As these beliefs are not necessarily strongly-held convictions, they need to be continually reinforced by society. For example, some individuals may believe that they should not smoke because society frowns upon it and it annoys people, even though they themselves cannot see any fundamental objection to the practice.

Hirschi, like Nye before him, administered a self-report questionnaire to test his theory. His sample comprised 3,605 high school boys aged twelve to seventeen from an area outside San Francisco. There were various questions relating to family, school and friends, and others covering six different types of delinquency. Three of these involved thefts of different values and three related to joy-riding, vandalism and assault. Hirschi also referred to school and police records. In his view, the commission of any two of these offences would amount to 'serious delinquency'. Hirschi found that there was no significant relationship between reported crime and class, except a slightly higher tendency to delinquency among children from the very poorest families. The racial differences in self-reported crime were insignificant, although there was a considerable difference in the rates of arrest. Hirschi felt that these findings could not be reconciled with strain theories, which are largely reliant on class.

The four elements making up the 'social bond' were then analysed. Hirschi discovered that boys who had a closer attachment to their parents were less likely to report involvement in crime, and that this held true regardless of race, class or the criminal activity of their friends. This finding is inconsistent with subcultural theory, which emphasises the importance of peer groups, but is compatible with control theory. The youths who reported more crimes also performed worse and had more disciplinary problems at school. Hirschi argued that this finding was inconsistent with theories such as Albert Cohen's (see Chapter 8), where it was assumed that the boys cared about being successful at school: Hirschi's delinquent boys were manifestly not interested in school at all. Both the ambitions for, and expectations of, educational success and employment are lower for delinquents than for non-delinquents, and so they have less commitment to conformity, and risk relatively little by engaging in crime. Again, Hirschi pointed out that this finding is contrary to strain theory, which predicts that delinquents will come from people with high ambition, but whose opportunities for advancement are structurally blocked.

For his third element—involvement in conventional activities—Hirschi's findings did not fit neatly into his control theory, as the boys who worked, had girlfriends, watched television and read books were more likely to report involvement in crime. However, it also emerged that being bored, spending little time on homework and hanging around with friends were also strongly correlated with delinquency. The final element—belief in the rules of society—was tested by a statement in Hirschi's questionnaire, 'It is alright to get around the law if you can get away with it', with which the respondents were asked to agree or disagree. A strong correlation was found between reported criminality and agreement with this statement. Hirschi considered that this finding ran counter to the underlying basis of Sykes and Matza's techniques of neutralisation, and suggested that these techniques were used after the illegal act and were really just excuses. He also discovered that religious beliefs had hardly any effect on levels of delinquency.

The basis of Hirschi's research has been replicated in many other North American studies, particularly involving juvenile offenders. (For examples, see Hindelang 1973, Poole and Regoli 1979, Wiatrowski *et al.* 1981, Lasley 1988.) The applicability of the theory to adult offenders is far less clear from the evidence, although it could be maintained that adult crime is just a continuation of juvenile delinquency.

Gottfredson and Hirschi's individual control theory

More recently, Hirschi has turned his attention from general social control theory to a consideration of facets pertaining to the individual which are amenable to control. Individual, self-control is a development from social control theory, as low self-control is considered to originate from deficient training in early childhood. Individual control theory is set out in the book *A General Theory of Crime* (1990) by Michael Gottfredson and Hirschi. The authors criticised existing theories for not paying attention to certain key facts of crime which are consistently revealed by empirical research. One is that crime typically involves the obtaining of short-term gratification, often in the form of small amounts of money or excitement. This is at the expense of long-term planning or consideration of negative consequences such as punishment. Crime—including white-collar crime—is unsystematic and unplanned, and of no real advantage to offenders. Most criminal acts 'are trivial and mundane affairs that result in little gain'. They are part of a wider personal irresponsibility which includes behaviour such as speeding in cars, proneness to accidents, smoking and casual sexual relationships. Consequently, criminals have often failed at school, at work and in their marriages, all of which require planning and the delay of gratification. A further consistent finding from research is that people who show behavioural problems in early childhood usually grow up to become offenders.

Gottfredson and Hirschi claimed that their theory can account for all 'acts of force or fraud undertaken in pursuit of self-interest'. The theory itself hinges on two basic features: the lack of individual self-control, which is the main factor, and the opportunity to commit a crime. Given such an opportunity, a person with low self-control is more likely to offend than a person with high self-control.

As with previous versions of control theory, Gottfredson and Hirschi provided very specific definitions for the seemingly ordinary terms they use. For them, lack of self-control is found in individuals who prefer quick solutions over protracted consideration, generally lack perseverance, and are prepared to take risks. Gottfredson and Hirschi proceeded from this to attribute other characteristics to these individuals, such as insensitivity, selfishness, and preferring physical to mental endeavour. These traits, which arise at an early age and never completely disappear, exist in people who find it very hard to withstand the temptation to commit crimes. This was used by the authors as evidence of the inapplicability of sociological variables. The traits which result in low self-control will last into adult life. Although Gottfredson and Hirschi accepted that rates of offending diminish with age, they argued that the lack of self-control still exists, but is now manifested in other activities, such as heavy drinking, a bad employment record, a failed marriage, or an increased possibility of being involved in road traffic accidents. In Canadian research Keane *et al.* (1993) claimed to have found a relationship between low self-control and driving under the influence of alcohol.

Gottfredson and Hirschi therefore considered that, as the cause of crime—poor self-control—is the same at every age, there is no need for longitudinal studies of delinquent 'development'. Sampson (1992) has pointed out that it seems strange for the authors to dismiss longitudinal studies when the data provided by such research is necessary to justify their assertions regarding the lack of change over the course of people's lives. Moreover, Sampson and Laub (1993) have been able to use a longitudinal study to show that bonds arising in adulthood from a stable job or a steady marriage can redirect offenders into a law-abiding lifestyle.

The failure adequately to explain the reduction of crime with age is seen as a weakness in the theory by some critics, although Tittle (1991) suggested that the authors should have portrayed it as a consequence of diminishing opportunity. The lower rate of female crime is attributed not to women's greater self-control, but to more intimate socialisation by their families in early childhood and the relative lack of criminal opportunities compared with men. As with older people, women are more likely to show any lack of self-control in other, non-criminal ways.

Gottfredson and Hirschi were keen to emphasise that poor socialisation is not a result of innate differences between individuals, although they did concede that such differences can affect the quality of the socialisation. In general, however, everyone can be properly socialised, although for some the socialisation provided is inadequate. The level of self-control is shaped by the external factor of socialisation but, once this has been provided, it is internalised by individuals and becomes part of their personality.

Socialisation primarily takes place within the close family group. If it is inadequate, no later exposure to the influences of friends or school can properly repair the damage, as individuals with poor self-control will experience considerable difficulty in making the necessary learning adjustments. The authors claim that bad parenting can only be an *indirect* cause of crime as it results in low levels of self-control, which itself provides a *direct* cause. However, findings from a representative sample of a national American survey of adolescents has shown a stronger relationship between parental efficacy and delinquent behaviour than between self-control and such behaviour (Perrone *et al.* 2004).

In their book, Gottfredson and Hirschi did not provide much detail about the second aspect of their theory, the availability of an opportunity to commit the crime. They did, however, comment that the opportunity must involve a low risk of being detected. Yet, this appears to create a contradiction when it is remembered that their definition of low self-control includes the preparedness to take risks! In a later article, Hirschi and Gottfredson (1993) provided an example—drink-driving—to illustrate what they meant by opportunity. The availability of both alcohol and a car are obvious requirements for the commission of this offence. However, if alcohol were unavailable at the relevant time, even people with low self-control would lack the opportunity to carry it out. Opportunity is, therefore, a structural consideration, but one which still is only relevant because of the individual's own actions. This provides support for the point made by Barlow (1991) that Gottfredson and Hirschi's control theory pays little more than lip service to social structure and is really concerned with poor socialisation alone.

On the face of it, there is some similarity between Gottfredson and Hirschi's control theory and the social learning theories of writers such as Albert Bandura (see Chapter 16). The common features include the role of the family in the learning of behaviour and the individual choice to commit offences. However, unlike Gottfredson and Hirschi, social learning theorists believe that people have different levels of motivation, which can be affected by the continued learning process that lasts throughout their lives. Some learning theorists would also allow for other ways of acquiring motivation, such as through the experiencing of strain. However, Gottfredson and Hirschi considered that low self-control is formed at a young age and cannot be significantly changed by future events.

Gottfredson and Hirschi did not accept that sociological variables can be significant in explaining the causes of crime. For them, the only importance of the social factors which other writers consider are relevant to criminal behaviour is in the development of self-control. They have also denied that class is related to crime. Yet, their theory appears to predict a strong correlation between the two. The denial of the relevance of sociological variables involves a rejection of Hirschi's earlier theory of social control. Moreover, it enables Gottfredson and Hirschi to reach some surprising conclusions, including the total lack of significance of poverty or unemployment among American blacks:

> It seems to us that research on racial differences [in American crime rates] should focus on differential child rearing practices and abandon the fruitless effort to ascribe such differences to culture or strain.

One critic of control theory, Elliott Currie (1985), has referred to the refusal of Gottfredson and Hirschi to accept that structural conditions such as poverty can affect the quality of parenting—and thus the level of self-control—as 'the fallacy of autonomy'.

Given the scope claimed for the general theory of crime, it is hardly surprising that it has been subject to extensive comment and analysis. Grasmick *et al.* (1993) subjected the theory to empirical testing and found a degree of support for it. However, they also discovered that opportunity was at least as strong a factor as low self-control in accounting for delinquency. The authors concluded that the theory would provide a better account of low self-control if it considered additional factors, such as strain theory, which could help to explain the unequal drive to commit offences. Gottfredson and Hirschi dismissed this suggestion and maintained their assertion that there are no deterministic elements in their theory: crime has the same appeal for everyone. In their view, Grasmick *et al.* did not find a stronger relationship between low self-control and crime because they had used a self-report questionnaire (which, interestingly, was a form of methodology adopted by Hirschi for measuring self-control in his 1969 book) instead of the more appropriate technique of direct observation (Hirschi and Gottfredson 1993).

Nevertheless, it is this reliance on direct observation that has caused critics such as Akers (1991) to criticise Gottfredson and Hirschi's theory for being tautologous. Akers argued that the criminal behaviour observed by Gottfredson and Hirschi was used both as the subject of their study and then evidence that their theory is correct. Their response (Hirschi and Gottfredson 1993) was that they did not use criminal behaviour as a mark of low self-control, but instead measured behaviour such as smoking, drinking, watching too much television, and experiencing difficulty in relationships with others. As none of this behaviour is criminal, Gottfredson and Hirschi considered that their theory remains intact. In passing, it may be noted that Arneklev *et al.* (1993) were unable to find a strong correlation between lack of self-control and smoking.

Geis (2000) has pointed out the ideological nature of Gottfredson and Hirschi's 'general theory', particularly when one looks at the non-criminal acts (such as 'disease', which the authors assume one can be blamed for catching) they include alongside crimes. He asks—perhaps frivolously—why they have not included an arguably common form of lack of self-control in America: overeating.

In a meta-analysis of twenty-one studies published in the ten years following the publication of Gottfredson and Hirschi's book, Pratt and Cullen (2000) found that there was fairly strong statistical support for a relationship between low self-control and crime. However, the authors claimed that Gottfredson and Hirschi's position still fell short of meriting the title 'a general theory of crime'. Marcus (2004) has claimed that most of the empirical research into this question must be considered suspect, as a proper definition of 'self-control' has rarely been formulated.

Because of the political unwillingness to embrace the fundamental changes in society seemingly required by many sociological explanations of crime, and the growing pressure to reduce levels of offending, many Western governments have embraced the 'opportunity' aspect of control theory. (Embracing the self-control aspect would be too controversial, as was shown in the failure of the Conservative government's 1993 'Back to Basics' campaign for 'Victorian values'.) This 'situational' crime prevention theory is reflected not only in schemes to reduce the opportunity for offending, but also to increase the likelihood of detection and apprehension. It is shown in measures such as greater surveillance in public places and on public transport, including the use of closed-circuit television (CCTV), and the construction of new buildings which have been designed in such a way as to reduce the opportunities for offending. Under the leadership of Ronald Clarke, the Home Office Research and Planning Unit set up a Crime Prevention Unit in 1983 and commissioned a series of small research projects into practical ways of reducing crime. The idea was popular, particularly with politicians. Criminals could be portrayed as making conscious and rational choices, rather than as debased individuals propelled into crime through the pressures of an unequal and unjust society. Situational crime prevention and the problems arising from it are discussed in Chapter 6.

However, it seems clear that Gottfredson and Hirschi did not consider that the opportunity requirement was a central component of their theory. The ways in which individuals come to be exposed to different criminal opportunities remain largely unexplored. The authors appear to have considered that motivation, involving the self-interested pursuit of pleasure and avoidance of pain, is of greater significance. Yet, it is arguable that this view ignores the ways in which motivation and opportunity can be interrelated, for example when wealthy and powerful interests try to shape the actual content of the law (Yeager 1994).

Hagan's power control theory

In his book *Structural Criminology* (1989), John Hagan set out a theory of 'power-control'. The term relates to how the balance of power between parents influences the type and substance of the parenting that is provided and, consequently, the likelihood that their children will turn to crime. Following on from his earlier work (see Chapter 13), Hagan argued that patriarchal families exercise more control over female than male children. Girls growing up in such households will perceive a greater risk of being caught and punished. Daughters are socialised into domesticity, whereas sons are encouraged to prepare for their role of providers by being more adventurous and taking risks. Hagan agreed with Gottfredson and Hirschi's view that a preparedness to take risks makes delinquency more likely. However, in families where there is a more balanced relationship between the parents, with the mothers assuming similar levels of power, daughters are given greater freedom and are therefore more likely to engage in risk-taking activities themselves. According to Hagan, this trend towards egalitarianism between parents explains the convergence between male and female crime rates in recent years.

In a major test of Hagan's theory conducted by Blackwell (2000), 350 adults from Oklahoma City were questioned about the authority exercised by their mothers and fathers when they were growing up. Whereas Hagan and several other researchers had only considered the perceived threat of formal legal sanctions, Blackwell's study included the risk of shame and embarrassment—informal sanctions which some writers have claimed are particularly likely to be relevant to female decision-making (for example, Naffine 1987). The results supported Hagan's argument in that, among people brought up in more patriarchal households, the women perceived much stronger threats of legal sanctions than the men, and this was reduced by variables in parental control. There were no differences between the sexes in the perceived threat of embarrassment in the more patriarchal house-holds, and in less patriarchal homes females perceived lower threats of embarrassment than men. Blackwell speculated that this latter finding may have resulted from the greater role that men play in child-rearing in such homes and the consequential greater desire of sons to please their fathers. However, females reported higher perceived threats of shame in all types of household.

Hagan's original explanation was open to the criticism that the increased participation of women in the workplace since the second half of the twentieth century could not adequately explain the continuing (if reduced) gap between male and female delinquency. In a revised version of the theory, based on data obtained from Toronto and Berlin, Hagan *et al.* (2004) have now claimed that, where patriarchy has ceased within the family unit, its vestiges may simply have moved to a male delinquent subculture.

Control theory in Britain

Control theory has also been considered, albeit to a lesser extent, by British writers. In his book *Deviance, Reality and Society* (1971), Steven Box attempted to construct an explanation of crime and deviance which was based on control theory, but which dealt with what he considered to be its greatest drawbacks. Box was concerned as to why ethnicity and class have such a weak correlation with crime in the American self-report studies, and yet such a strong one in official statistics. He decided that this could be explained by labelling theory. In labelling terminology, self-report studies reveal primary deviation whereas the official statistics show secondary deviation—the crimes committed by the poor and ethnic minorities, who have been unable to extricate themselves from the official process following their acts of primary deviation. Once officially labelled, any hold that the conventional world has over them will be further loosened, and so control mechanisms will become increasingly ineffective.

Box was also keen to develop a control theory which recognised the importance of motivation. He considered that the choice to commit a criminal act is based on both the ability and the will to do so. The ability depends on the following factors:

- *Secrecy.* Box thought that deterrence theory, although initially ignored by Hirschi, is relevant here. If individuals consider that they would be unable to hide their criminal behaviour, then they have been deterred.

- *Skills.* Individuals must have the necessary ability to carry out the crime.

- *Supply.* They must also have the necessary equipment, such as a weapon.

- *Social support.* Individuals must think that they have the support of any social groups to which they belong.

- *Symbolic support.* Although no support may, in fact, be forthcoming from peers, individuals may be aware of alternative sources, such as the mass media, or they may resort to Sykes and Matza's 'techniques of neutralization' (see Chapter 9) to justify their behaviour to themselves.

Given the ability of individuals to offend, Box then proceeded to consider what factors could help to provide the desire. His conclusion was broadly along the lines of the 'subterranean values' suggested by Matza and Sykes (1961). People enjoy taking risks, and the thrill may be enhanced because the activity is unlawful or disapproved of. The term 'macho values' is sometimes used nowadays to describe this sort of attitude. Matza and Sykes had pointed out that these values are found in all sections of society and are certainly not peculiar to the lower classes. The problem for the poor, however, is that through lack of money they do not have the legitimate outlets for these activities which are available to the better-off.

Wilson and Herbert (1978) conducted research into fifty-six socially deprived families in Birmingham. The families were selected for possessing certain characteristics, such as having at least five children, both parents being present, and living in old housing in a deprived inner-city area. Wilson and Herbert devised an index of 'chaperonage' to measure the extent to which the parents protected the safety of their children. Factors such as escorting the children to and from school, allowing them to play in the streets, and whether they were told to come in at a particular time at night were among those assessed. Wilson and Herbert found that low chaperonage was strongly linked to high delinquency. Their findings seem to provide support for control theory, although in a later article Harriet Wilson (1980) was at some pains to point out that the poverty and deprivation in which these families lived could not be ignored:

> The essential point of our findings is the very close association of lax parenting methods with severe social handicap . . . If these factors are ignored, and parental laxness is seen instead as an 'attitude' which by education or by punitive measures can be shifted, then our findings are being misinterpreted. It is the position of the most disadvantaged groups in society, and not the individual, which needs improvement in the first place.

In his book *Controlling Crime: the Classical Perspective in Criminology*

(1989), Bob Roshier set out a version of control theory which he called 'postclassical'. He started from the assumption that both social and economic differences between societies have a much greater effect on crime rates than differences between individuals, and will therefore be a more productive source for obtaining an understanding of the frequency and control of crime. Variations in control exercised by incentives and disincentives are also far more important in accounting for differences in criminal behaviour than are variations between individuals. An important proviso is that the constraints must be accepted as being necessary for the attainment of some greater benefit and should operate fairly. Unlike the positivist view, people are not considered to be 'good' or 'bad': they can be either at different times. Like classicism (see Chapter 5), the postclassical perspective views crime as a problem of conformity: it is more likely to occur if conformity fails to satisfy our basic needs. However, unlike other control theorists, Roshier was prepared to view conformity as problematic. As he put it:

> . . . conformity is only 'good' to the extent that we regard the rules as 'good'. That is, crime and conformity are ultimately moral and not technical issues.

In a development of Hirschi's four control elements, Roshier suggested no fewer than seven human 'needs' which amount to sources of control, as their satisfaction can provide an incentive to conform and the threat of their removal can be used to deflect individuals from criminality.

(1) *Affection.* This provides one of the earliest and most powerful sources of control in a person's life. Practically everyone wants affection and the fear of losing it is a key factor which ensures that most people conform. As Roshier commented, 'the loss or gradual erosion of ties of affection is . . . a liberator of our criminality; never to have experienced them is perhaps the greatest liberator of all'. On the other hand, the mere existence of ties of affection does not guarantee conformity: the people whose affection is required must themselves be disapproving of criminality.

(2) *Status.* This also involves concern about other people's feelings for us, but the other people are likely to be more distant and the feelings are different: respect, admiration or even fear. Roshier included self-esteem in his definition of status. It is a less reliable form of control than affection, as people may attain status through anti-social behaviour. There can also be a tension

between affection and status. For example, the desire for a reputation of masculinity can inhibit the bonds of affection.

(3) *Stimulation.* Everyone is stimulated by something, be it work, leisure pursuits or friends. Stimulation can be gained through direct experience or vicariously as a spectator. Crime can be a source of stimulation—either directly or vicariously. Punishment has traditionally been used to reduce stimulation, ranging from children being sent to their room through to prisoners' being placed in solitary confinement.

(4) *Autonomy.* Most people value individual autonomy and there is evidence that its routine denial to young people can be a factor in their resorting to crime. Indeed, society uses imprisonment, which involves a major withdrawal of autonomy, in an attempt to control crime. It is therefore apparent that people should be provided with the ability to exercise control over significant parts of their lives. If this does not happen, they might turn to crime as a form of self-expression.

(5) *Security.* This relates to people's need to feel free from the experience or threat of physical discomfort or injury. Corporal and capital punishment were formerly the methods used by the penal system to ensure compliance. Nowadays, this is achieved by the removal of the comfort and safety of the home through imprisonment, or by the confiscation of the money which provides comfort in the form of a fine.

(6) *Money.* This can bring status, autonomy and security, and can also increase stimulation. Money is therefore a vital element for both conformity and control. The desire to acquire more of it is a common stimulus to crime, but it can also be used for control purposes by means of a fine or confiscation order.

(7) *Belief.* Roshier adopted a definition of this element which is similar to the one used by Hirschi. Individuals are more likely to conform if they believe in the rules that are imposed on them. Belief does not ensure obedience to the rules any more than disbelief automatically leads to their breach, but it provides an important impetus. Roshier considered that belief enables people to accept short-term constraints in the expectation of some long-term personal advantage.

Evaluation

In his book *Causes of Delinquency* Hirschi wrote:

> With respect to their logical framework, [other] theories are superior to control theory, and, if they were as adequate empirically as control theory, we should not hesitate to advocate their adoption in preference to control theory.

This telling passage indicates the trump card which control theorists claim to have up their sleeve: the strength of empirical support for their theories. Yet, how supportive is the research evidence? The telling criticisms of Nye's self-report questionnaire in Washington state have already been mentioned. Similar problems exist with Hirschi's San Francisco methodology, and his questionnaire has been used by other researchers. It is now widely accepted that Hirschi's final sample contained very few serious delinquents (Bernard 1984). He obtained information from 73.5 per cent of his original sample. The greatest source of loss was absence of permission from parents—probably the parents of the most delinquent children. Moreover, the openness (or ability to recollect) of his subjects seems to be in serious doubt. Over half of the sample claimed to have committed none of the offences listed, which included theft of under \$2 and any type of criminal damage. The utter implausibility of this provides a strong illustration of the shortcomings of self-report questionnaires (see Chapter 3). These drawbacks might not seem so damning, were it not for the centrality of empirical evidence for control theorists. Gottfredson and Hirschi have been accused by Polk (1991) of ignoring copious amounts of empirical research data which did not fit into their 'general theory'.

The empirical shortcomings are not the only criticisms faced by control theorists. It seems that, for them, the nature of crimes and the characteristics of offenders are of no real significance. The other main sociological explanations of crime, although varying in a number of respects, do at least seek to explain the character of the delinquent behaviour and the relationship between this and the circumstances of the offender. Control theory, on the other hand, stops short with the assumption that everyone would commit crimes if they were not prevented in some way. In criminological terms, the question shifts from 'Why did they do it?' to 'Why did they not do it?'. The rationality of behaviour is assumed; there is no scope for enquiring how people come to make sense of the world around them. Important questions about criminal behaviour remain unconsidered. There is also the possibility that delinquency leads to a weakening of the social bonds rather than the other way round. Nearly all empirical tests of control theory have relied on cross-sectional rather than longitudinal data. Agnew (1985), who carried out a longitudinal study of high school boys, found little support for the theory.

A further problem is that control theory assumes all good parents should be trying to teach stereotypical middle-class values to their children. However, many people have argued in different ways that what these values have come to represent—such as schooling and unquestioning loyalty to 'the organisation' (Whyte 1957)—are more related to the problem than the cure.

Control theory seems unable to explain adequately the crimes of the powerful. Is there really no difference worthy of consideration between the minor vandal and the fraudulent company director? According to Box (1981), such crimes 'are not even touched by the notions of stake in conformity, attachment to significant others, or beliefs in conventional morality'. Gottfredson and Hirschi's view of white-collar crime seems particularly implausible. Much white-collar crime is not 'trivial and mundane', but involves a large amount of planning. Gottfredson and Hirschi considered that sociologists are wrong to portray it as costing the state billions of dollars a year, or as being a form of crime that is particularly different from any other. As the authors' thesis is that criminals do not specialise in any one type of crime, they presumably envisage that corrupt company directors could equally commit burglary or rape. A surprising willingness to accept official statistics at face value also enabled Gottfredson and Hirschi to conclude that blacks are more likely to commit white-collar crime than whites in the USA, as they have a higher arrest rate.

In a study of sentences in eight federal district courts, Benson and Moore (1992) found that most of the white-collar offenders had significantly different offence patterns from those of the other offenders. The white-collar offenders were less likely to have been arrested, to have alcohol or drug-related problems, or to have performed badly at school. In general, white-collar offenders also committed far fewer offences.

Perhaps control theory is better suited to explaining periodic juvenile delinquency than habitual or career criminality. Certainly, the bulk of the research supporting Hirschi's original theory involved young people. On the other hand, how does a 'general theory' of crime based on control explain sexual offences? According to control theory, the feminist writers who consider that all men are potential rapists may have a point after all.

Control theory has also been criticised for over-predicting the amount of crime. A significant number of poorly-socialised individuals do not become persistent offenders (Elliott *et al.* 1979). If social bonds are related to behaviour, it is clearly necessary to understand the nature of such bonds. Yet, Hirschi did not state how bonds come to be broken or, indeed, how they fail to be created in the first place. His theory does not make clear exactly what it is that socially-bonded individuals do that restrains delinquency. There is plenty of evidence that loving parents who have strong attachments with their children do not always effectively use those attachments as a form of social control. The spoilt child can cause as much trouble as the neglected child. Hirschi can also be criticised for adopting a single dimensional approach (strong–weak) to bonding, when other dimensions— qualitative and quantitative—could have also been considered (Colvin and Pauly 1983).

Conclusion

Control theory became popular, particularly with right-wing politicians, as it seems to provide a 'common-sense' approach to dealing with crime which reinforces the traditional role of the family and does not fundamentally challenge the structure of the state. It appeals to some criminologists because it lacks the determinism of many other theories and appears to revert to classical free-will notions of behaviour. This may explain why Hirschi's book received much more attention than the earlier offerings of writers such as Nye and Reckless. By the end of the 1960s, a reaction was building up against what were seen as the liberal policies of that decade, and the political climate had become more receptive to criminologists who wished to concentrate on individual offenders rather than wider society.

However, while classical criminology concentrates on legal penalties as a deterrent, control theory is more dependent on social constraints. It is also attractive to those members of the general public who are unwilling to accept excuses, as it does not provide a pathological explanation for offenders' behaviour. The nearest the theory comes to challenging political orthodoxy is the implication that crime could be reduced if the state took a more interventionist role in the support of family life and the bringing-up of children. Such a move could involve political difficulties, but a step has been taken in this direction by section 8 of the Crime and Disorder Act 1998, which, in certain situations, enables parents to be punished for the crimes of their children: punishment, in effect, for not bringing-up their children properly.

Control theory has considerable drawbacks. Its strongest advocate, Hirschi, has conceded that the theory derives its strength entirely from its empirical support, and yet there are methodological problems with much of the evidence. Control theory over-predicts delinquency and relegates motivation to a matter of minor significance. The content of the criminal law and the maintenance of social order are considered to be non-problematic. Some people may feel that the application of the theory in 'situational crime control' could lead inexorably to an Orwellian society.

Control theory has always been more popular in the USA than in Europe. This may be because Europeans tend to equate 'control' with 'state control' and, on account of their recent history, contemplate a strengthening of this with a degree of concern. Americans, however, are more likely to view control in terms of the relationship between individuals and their adjacent surroundings.

Postscript: Tittle's control balance

A different use of the concept of control can be found in Charles Tittle's book *Control Balance: toward a General Theory of Deviance* (1995). Tittle defined deviance as 'any behaviour that the majority of a given group regards as unacceptable or that typically evokes a collective response of a negative type'. Having rejected existing theories as deficient, he concentrated on four causal factors.

'Control' is a restriction on behavioural options. 'Deviant motivation' results from situational influences and factors such as a desire for autonomy and the 'control ratio'. This is the amount of control one is able to exercise relative to the amount of control one experiences. Individuals who, in accordance with their status or personal strengths, are able to exert more control over other people than other people exert over them are said to have a 'control surplus'. Correspondingly, individuals of low status who have little opportunity to control others, but who themselves are subject to considerable control, have a 'control deficit'. For deviant motivation to exist, individuals who enjoy a control surplus must be motivated to extend it, and individuals who experience a control deficit must be motivated to try to eliminate it. The third causal factor, 'constraint', or the likelihood that there will be controlling actions, is a consequence of the control ratio, the seriousness of a particular act and the chance of discovery. The final factor, 'opportunities', refers to situations where deviance is a possibility.

The main element of Tittle's thesis is the idea of the 'control ratio'. Tittle has suggested that an imbalance, either of surplus or of deficit, can lead to crime. For this to happen, the four causal elements must coincide. There must first be motivation which is fired by provocation, and then there must be a lack of constraint coupled with an opportunity to offend. The provocation could be in the form of a challenge, an insult, or perhaps even some unwelcome observation about the control deficit (or surplus). It may at first appear strange that someone with a control surplus should be open to provocation in this way. Tittle argued that individuals with a control surplus are likely to find that other people subordinate themselves to them, and that powerful individuals are generally happy to take advantage of this. In due course, any initial gratitude will disappear and the subordination will come to be expected. Any challenge to it may then be taken as a provocation to crime. In addition, Tittle claimed that excessive domination by those individuals with a control surplus may itself cause the dominated to retaliate by way of crime or deviance.

Three different levels of imbalance were initially described by Tittle for both control surplus and control deficit. Individuals who exercise only slightly more control than that to which they are subject were said to be practising exploitation. Tittle considered this to be the most common form of crime for those enjoying a control surplus. It included extortion, bribery and price-fixing. Those whose control surplus is slightly greater were said to plunder. This would encompass the destruction of forests and rivers and the creation of environmental pollution. When extreme control surplus is enjoyed, Tittle referred to the resulting form of deviance as decadence. The Emperor Nero and the American tycoon Howard Hughes were offered as examples.

Mild forms of control deficit were described by Tittle as predation. This covered what most people would think of as typical crimes—stealing and acts of violence. A medium level of control deficit was said to be reflected in defiance. Deviant acts in protest at the level of control imposed came into this category, as did 'escapist' deviant acts, which Tittle listed as 'alcoholism, drug abuse, suicide, family desertion, mental illness or counterculture involvement'. Finally, in the most extreme form of control deficit, Tittle identified submissive deviance as being the usual reaction. People here are so oppressed that they are too scared to involve themselves in either predation or defiance. Tittle claimed that black Americans during the period of slavery were more likely to manifest submission or defiance than predation.

Following emancipation, predation became more common as the level of white control reduced.

In a revision of the theory, Tittle (2004) has heeded the advice of Braithwaite (1997) who had argued that it would be preferable to base it on the simpler notion that everyone is seeking more control. Tittle has admitted that the differences among the categories of deviance were imprecise and should be collapsed. There is now one continuum of 'control balance desirability' and people with either control surpluses or control deficits can resort to similar forms of deviance, especially in the middle of the range. Tittle has also accepted Braithwaite's suggestion that 'submissiveness' should be considered a special, non-deviant category.

Other criticisms have been made of the theory. Savelsberg (1996) has questioned whether desire for autonomy is the universal human condition Tittle assumed it to be. Singer (1997) considered that the psychological issues inherent in the notion of control would be difficult to measure. Curry (1998) raised the broader question of whether it is necessary to look for a general theory of criminal behaviour. In his view, such a quest is destined to prove unsuccessful.

Jack Katz's book *Seductions of Crime*, which is considered in Chapter 9, is important in Tittle's theory. Although Katz's phenomenological approach did not allow for generalisations, Tittle concluded that Katz's criminals found crime attractive because it put them in control. Katz himself had referred to the desire of violent offenders to humiliate their victims. This can also be seen at the societal level: perhaps societies with large control imbalances are more humiliating than those with smaller control imbalances. Braithwaite (1997) has pointed out that, at the end of World War I, the Allies made the mistake of burdening Germany with emotional and material humiliation. This made it possible for Hitler to develop a sizeable control surplus which led to an attempt at world domination and the Holocaust.

Tittle's theory of control balance seems able to meet some of the recurring objections that are raised to general theories of crime and deviance. It manages to include an element of rational choice, a consideration of the factors which influence that choice, a study of motivation, and an acceptance that human emotions play an important role. The theory assumes that most people are trying to maximise their freedom from control and that, in certain circumstances, they will indulge in deviant behaviour to achieve this. It is also able to account for both 'suite' crimes arising from greed (control surplus) and 'street' crimes arising from need (control deficit). The fact that the very young and the very old do not expect to have any significant control over anything can explain their low levels of deviance in comparison to people in their teens and early twenties—the peak period of offending—who want to establish their independence. As young people also spend more time in public places, they are likely to be subject to greater levels of provocation and have more opportunities for predatory crimes. The theory can also account for that universal phenomenon, higher rates of offending by men than women. Because the traditional male role has involved their exercising control over their family and territory, men care more about the loss of control than women do.

13

Gender and crime

It is only in the past quarter of a century that extensive consideration has been given to the different roles played by men and women in the commission of crime. Feminist writers first highlighted the fact that most criminologists, in assuming that crime is a male phenomenon, had largely ignored female crime. If it was discussed at all, the focus was on the biological given of *sex* (male–female) rather than the social construction of *gender* (male role–female role). In recent years, a number of writers have started to consider the part that different assumptions of male gender roles—'masculinities'—play in the commission of crime.

The extent of female crime

Different explanations have been offered for the earlier neglect of women's crime. One reason may be that official criminal statistics have routinely shown that women are convicted of crimes to a far lesser extent than men. Most offences are technically capable of being committed by either sex: women can even be convicted of sexual offences such as rape as an accomplice. The 2003 Criminal Statistics for England and Wales showed that, of everyone found guilty of, or cautioned for, indictable offences, 81 per cent were males and 19 per cent were females. This imbalance has been fairly consistent for many years, although it appears that the gap was much closer in previous centuries. In an analysis of cases tried at the Old Bailey between 1687 and 1912, Feeley and Little (1991) discovered that about 45 per cent of the defendants were female. Zedner (1991) has noted that female crime declined at a faster rate than male crime in the nineteenth century. An analysis by Tarling (1993) found that the ratio of male to female crime fell from 7.1:1 in 1955 to 5.2:1 in 1975, only to remain steady thereafter. Soothill *et al.* (2002) have estimated that 35 per cent of males born in 1958 will have had a criminal conviction by the age of thirty-five; for women the figure is 9 per cent. In the 1998–99 Youth Lifestyles Survey (see Chapter 3) 11 per cent of women aged twelve to thirty admitted to offending during the previous twelve months compared with 26 per cent of men (Flood-Page *et al.* 2000). The 2003 Crime and Justice Survey, which covered the much wider age range of ten to sixty-five (see Chapter 3), found that the corresponding figures were about 7 per cent for women and 13 per cent for men (Budd *et al.* 2005).

This pattern seems to be similar throughout the world. American statistics show that women constituted 23 per cent of those arrested for criminal offences in 2003 (FBI 2004). Harvey *et al.* (1992) cited United Nations survey data revealing that, in all member states between 1975 and 1985, 'men greatly outnumbered women among those suspected, apprehended, prosecuted, convicted, and imprisoned'.

The UN report's additional finding that women are usually convicted of less serious offences than men is supported by other evidence. In the 2003 Criminal Statistics for England and Wales, 32 per cent of males and 54 per cent of females convicted of, or cautioned for, an indictable offence had committed the crime of theft or handling stolen goods. For males, the next most frequent crimes were drug offences (22 per cent) and violence against the person (14 per cent): for females, they were drug offences and violence against the person (both 12 per cent). The peak age of offending in the 2003 Statistics was eighteen for males and fifteen for females. Using data from 1990, Tarling (1993) indicated that the ratio between men and women for convictions and cautions was 105:1 for sexual offences and 3:1 for theft and handling stolen goods. An analysis of the American Uniform Crime Reports for arrests for minor property crimes showed that female involvement had increased from an average of 17 per cent in the early 1960s to 27 per cent in the early 1970s and then to 35 per cent by the mid-1980s. Taking the same three points in time, the percentage of female arrests for most other types of crime had either increased slightly, remained the same, or declined (Steffensmeier and Allan 1991).

The problems with official statistics and the advantages of self-report and victim studies are considered in Chapter 3. Early self-report studies suggested that the statistics did not reveal the full extent of female crime. However, it later became apparent that the narrowing of the anticipated gap was because a large amount of petty offending had been reported. The 1998–99 Youth Lifestyles Survey (Flood-Page *et al.* 2000) showed that the crimes most frequently committed by girls under fifteen were criminal damage, shoplifting, buying stolen goods and fighting. The sixteen to twenty-one year-olds became increasingly involved in fraud and buying stolen goods, and these two offences predominated for women over twenty-one. For boys, fighting featured quite prominently, especially in the eighteen to twenty-one age bracket. The general picture was that, over the age of seventeen, male offenders outnumbered female offenders by a ratio of about 3:1. In the 2003 Crime and Justice Survey, the offences most frequently committed by women throughout their lives were theft and assault (Budd *et al.* 2005).

Although such studies show a narrower gap for some offences, the overall picture is still the same: men and women commit similar crimes but at different rates, and women appear to commit far fewer serious crimes, such as murder and robbery. Indeed, Box (1983) pointed out that women may even be over-represented in the criminal statistics because of their relative lack of involvement in organised and corporate crime, which is seldom recorded.

One question that arises from this is whether, broadly speaking, women commit crimes for different reasons than men. It may seem odd nowadays that the comparative rarity of female crime did not historically attract the curiosity of criminologists. The world of academic study (and many women may feel the world in general) has traditionally been the preserve of men, and it is only since the 1970s that women have come to be appointed in any significant numbers in higher education institutions (Heidensohn 1996). It is hardly surprising that this new wave of female criminologists became interested in the relative lack of literature on offending by women. What they found was not particularly to their liking.

Traditional criminology: biological and psychological explanations

Various explanations of female crime appeared during the nineteenth and early twentieth centuries. Many of these were written by journalists, such as Henry Mayhew (1861), and prison chaplains, such as Horsley (1887), and generally considered that the causes of both male and female crime were the same—moral weakness and poverty. Women were considered as being more at risk because of their greater purity (Zedner 1991).

(a) Cesare Lombroso

In the earliest form of what is now considered positivist criminological writing—the works of the Italian, Cesare Lombroso—women were certainly not overlooked. Together with his son-in-law, Guglielmo Ferrero, Lombroso wrote *The Female Offender* (1895). Lombroso, clearly influenced by the evolutionary theory of Charles Darwin, considered that criminals are atavistic throwbacks and that crime results from a reversion to their more primitive state. He thought that white males represent the most advanced form of evolution and that non-white females are the lowest form. Women stop growing too soon and are therefore the products of arrested development. Having studied the skulls and bones of women criminals and prostitutes, and looked at the life histories of both criminal and non-criminal women, Lombroso declared that any physical characteristics that were more common in the criminal group were atavistic, such as large hands, short stocky stature, and dark hair.

As he viewed women as a lower form of life than men, Lombroso was faced with the problem of explaining why females commit fewer crimes. He dealt with this in several ways. Natural selection will play a part: the 'worst' examples are so unattractive that they are unable to find partners and breed. Because of their inferior life form, women are better able to adapt to an unappealing environment than men. Women are also more prone to psychological disturbance on account of their smaller cerebral cortex. Moreover, some women turn to prostitution as an alternative to crime. According to Lombroso, the most distinctive aspect of female criminals is their similarity to men. The cranium is more similar in size to a man's and they possess more body hair. They lack a woman's usual passivity.

Lombroso's specific findings are not taken seriously nowadays, although feminist writers such as Smart (1976) considered that they have had a lasting effect on the study of women and crime. Even at the time, Kellor (1900) was unable to replicate Lombroso's findings, and thought that environmental and social factors were likely to be far more important. Lombroso's methodology was extremely suspect. His control group of Sicilians comprised small individuals, with dark hair and skin, and any physical stigmata they possessed would today be explained by the considerable poverty in which they lived. Sicilians were generally looked down on by other Italians as being lazy and unreliable. The use of photographs by Lombroso to analyse 'fallen women' was, in the words of Heidensohn (1996), 'as objective as an adjudication in a beauty contest'.

Lombroso is sometimes criticised as being racist, but such an observation misses the point. Writing at the time of the newly emerging Darwinism, this was simply one of the first—if least plausible—in a long line of positivist explanations of criminal behaviour. The methodological shortcomings which are so obvious now would not have appeared as such at the time. Nevertheless, Lombroso's theories have been significant in influencing more recent biological and physical explanations of women's crime.

(b) WI Thomas

The views of Lombroso were developed in the writings of William I Thomas. Although he accepted Lombroso's account of the evolutionary inferiority and passivity of women in general, he did not agree with Lombroso's theory that criminal women are more like men. In his book *The Unadjusted Girl* (1923), Thomas blamed female crime on the sexual freedom resulting from the removal of the traditional constraints on women. For Thomas, everyone has four main desires in life: desire for new experiences, for security, for response (including sexual response), and for recognition. Thomas considered that women have the greatest desire for response. Most women maintain their 'virtue' until marriage, but amoral women use their sexuality to obtain whatever they want. This results in promiscuity, prostitution and sometimes illegal activities; many of Thomas's case histories were based on non-criminal sexual behaviour. It is therefore crucial that such women are identified as soon as possible by welfare agencies and taught to see the error of their ways. Needless to say, this condition was predominantly associated with working-class women and no account whatsoever was taken of their economic circumstances. Indeed, the main focus of Thomas's study was lower-class immigrant American women. This sort of paternalist explanation of crime can, perhaps, be linked to the later prevalence of social work intervention in the lives of 'problem' families.

More recently, writers such as Freda Adler (1975) and Carol Smart (1976) have claimed that resistance to the emancipation of women in general was encouraged by Thomas's views, the clear implication of which is that women should be strictly controlled and that traditional female roles should be maintained. Smart (1976) also considered that Thomas's somewhat anecdotal treatment of his female subjects only served to encourage later writers to avoid structural considerations in dealing with women's crime, and resort to emotional and 'psycho-physiological' observations.

(c) Sigmund Freud

An explanation of female crime was also provided by Sigmund Freud (1925). His general theory of human personality development is explained in more detail in Chapter 16. Unlike Lombroso, Freud considered that everyone is born with the potential to be a criminal in that the basic human instincts, if uncontrolled, will lead to anti-social behaviour. Individuals who pass successfully through the various stages of personality development become balanced and law-abiding. For boys, this involves the successful resolution of the Oedipus complex, whereby their superego (or conscience) becomes properly formed through the relinquishing of sexual love for their mother.

This occurs because boys fear that their father will castrate them. As girls do not have a penis, they are unable to develop a conscience in this way, and will also retain a sexual desire for their father. (This is known as the Electra complex.) Moreover, girls feel resentful because of their defective sexual organs. To deal with this, they dress up and show off in order to attract men.

Freud also thought that, because of genetic differences, women are more passive than men. As women also have a strong wish for approval and affection, particularly from their father (or father figure), they do not generally perform acts which would incur male wrath, such as committing crimes. Freud agreed with Lombroso in one particular respect—that female criminals are rejecting passivity and trying to be like men. However, Freud considered that this aggressive stance results from their desire for a penis. They will not succeed in emulating men: indeed, the only way to overcome the feelings of penis envy is to give birth, which Freud saw as an adequate substitute.

Even psychologists who have subsequently embraced Freudian theory have been unhappy with the notion of the Oedipus complex and some have dissociated themselves from it. Freud wrote little specifically about crime, and his views on female criminality were not widely known until they were discussed by feminist criminologists in the 1970s. Whereas Lombroso based his explanation almost entirely on constitutional factors, Freud's approach, while acknowledging the possible impact of heredity, was primarily a psychological one. However, as with his predecessors who had written on female crime, he took no real notice of economic or social factors.

(d) Otto Pollak

The significance of female sexual behaviour is also a central feature in the book *The Criminality of Women* (1950) by Otto Pollak. Having considered official data from several countries, Pollak asserted that the real levels of female crime are similar to those of males. However, they appear lower because the crimes are under-reported and harder to detect, and because the police and prosecution authorities are less likely to proceed against women. Pollak offered abortion and shoplifting as common examples of such crimes. He attributed the lower visibility and detection of female crime to feminine cunning and deceit. The willingness to excuse or impose a light punishment on female offenders was put down to male chivalry. Pollak thought that women's ability to be deceitful is learned from pretending to enjoy sexual intercourse—women can fake an orgasm, but men cannot fake an erection—and concealing their monthly menstruation. Women are likely to be behind much of the crime that is committed by men. Where women themselves commit crimes, the offending is likely to be brought on by a psychological disorder, such as kleptomania (an urge to steal), or be of a sexual nature, such as prostitution.

Pollak's evidence for a higher level of female crime was largely drawn from domestic and low-level employment scenarios. His claim that female domestic servants frequently committed crimes against their employers was not supported by any substantial evidence. Nor was any real evidence offered for his assertion that women conceal their criminal activity more than men. Pollak's methodology now-adays appears hardly satisfactory: for example, he failed to take account of changes in the law against abortion in several of the countries he considered. Some of his illustrations—such as women's feigning pleasure during intercourse—seem extraordinary now, and should even have appeared as such in the late 1940s, when a woman's acquiescence in sexual activity was generally taken for granted. Moreover, this book appeared over half a century after Lombroso wrote about women, and at a time when, in America at least, sociology was already emphasising the significance of economic and social forces. Pollak, although a sociologist, inexplicably made no reference to contemporary authors such as Merton. Despite all this, the book gained a certain influence, largely because there was no other work dedicated to explaining female crime being produced at the time. Even as late as 1965 a leading figure in British criminology,

Hermann Mannheim, could write in terms not wholly dismissive of Lombroso and Ferrero and accept that 'many of Pollak's points may be valid'.

As Dorie Klein (1973) has indicated, there is an apparent contradiction in the writings of Freud, Thomas and Pollak. On the one hand, women were portrayed as cold and calculating: yet, on the other hand, they were also seen as emotional and the most appropriate people to care for children. Girls' sexual behaviour plays a central role in these explanations. It is significant that the literature on juvenile delinquency contains very little about the sexual behaviour of boys (Daly and Chesney-Lind 1988).

Studies of women's crime based on biological considerations are still carried out, generally with more sophisticated methodology than that used by the earlier writers, but with the occasional lapse. One such example is the research of Cowie, Cowie and Slater, published in their book *Delinquency in Girls* (1968). In methodological terms, the study started badly by considering a group of girls in a female approved school to be a representative sample of delinquents. The authors thought that boys are less able to cope with stress than girls because of their different biological structure. This accounts for the fact that boys commit more crimes than girls. However, some girls are born with masculine characteristics and will thus be prone to criminality. Cowie *et al.* concluded that female delinquency is more likely to involve sex-related offences than that of boys. No clear evidence was provided to justify these conclusions.

Various critics, such as Smart (1976), have pointed out that Cowie *et al.* are just further examples of theorists who have confused sex and gender. Cowie *et al.* described their delinquent girls as 'lumpish, uncouth and graceless', but they failed to consider how this could have arisen through environmental aspects, such as a poor diet, which have typically influenced the sort of people who are found in penal institutions.

Some writers have concluded that female crime is committed by women who have an increased level of male hormones. The thinking behind this stems from the observation that women generally appear less aggressive than men. The view is then taken that, where women do show aggression, it may be a result of hormonal changes. Money and Ernhardt (1972) considered that differences in the brains and the hormonal balance of men and women can account for disparities in the level of crime. However, the only available evidence comes from experiments on animals and there is always a problem in assuming that such findings can apply to humans. The opposing view is that variations in levels of aggression can be attributed to differences in socialisation.

It has also been suggested that women are more inclined to commit criminal offences during periods of hormonal disturbance, such as menstruation, pregnancy or during the menopause. Pollak (1950) put forward this idea, but did not provide any supporting evidence. Katharina Dalton (1961) found that almost 60 per cent of imprisoned women in her sample had committed their crimes in a sixteen-day period covering the hormonal changes resulting from menstruation. Apart from the fact that this is hardly an overwhelming figure, if it were taken to suggest a direct causal link, it would considerably over-predict the level of female crime. Although no link with crime has been conclusively proved, courts have been prepared to reduce sentences for female offenders (but not males) shown to be suffering from hormonal disturbance. There is no such general defence in criminal law, although women who kill their new-born babies may have a murder conviction reduced to manslaughter (Infanticide Act 1925; Marks and Kumar 1993; Wilczynski and Morris 1993), and any charge of murder can be reduced to manslaughter on the grounds of 'diminished responsibility' (Homicide Act 1957, section 2). Although there is a mandatory sentence of life imprisonment for murder, any lawful punishment can be imposed for manslaughter and a number of women who have killed in these circumstances have been placed on probation (Edwards 1988).

Feminist criminologists, while no doubt sympathetic to individual cases, are unhappy with this legal perpetuation of the idea that women are fundamentally 'mad not bad', particularly as similar allowances are seldom made for men. A good case in point is shoplifting. (This is not a legal category; it is simply the name given to theft in shops.) Although the statistics have consistently shown that this crime is committed more frequently by men, it has come to be particularly associated with women. Whereas Gibbens and Prince (1962) attributed shoplifting by lower-class boys to peer group pressure, women were considered to commit such acts because they were depressed, mean, resentful or wanted to 'keep up their appearance'. Campbell (1981) commented on the alleged sexual undertones to shoplifting: women are said to be sexually excited by the act, or have some masochistic desire for punishment. Yet, shoplifting appears to most people to be an act totally devoid of sexuality (although see the view of Katz (1988) in Chapter 9). Once again, analyses emphasising female participation in a crime have completely overlooked the social and economic factors which might lead abandoned, lonely and impoverished women—or men—to resort to such acts.

Various forms of post-traumatic stress syndrome are increasingly being invoked in defence of women who commit offences following some particularly disturbing event, often involving personal violence. Rape trauma syndrome has been discussed in some cases, but the most controversial form has been battered woman syndrome. This has been put forward by the defence in several well-publicised cases where women have killed their partners after being on the receiving end of physical abuse for long periods. If a jury accepts that a woman has responded to this kind of treatment in such a way as to satisfy the legal test of provocation (Homicide Act 1957, section 3), it can find her guilty of manslaughter rather than murder. Problems have arisen as lawyers have not always been able to fit cases of battered woman syndrome into existing legal categories (Nicolson and Sanghvi 1993). Some criminologists are also unhappy about the need to use psychological explanations to circumvent deficiencies in the law, and thus reinforce the stereotypical view of women as inferior beings (O'Donovan 1991).

Traditional criminology: sociological explanations

Although feminist criminologists have criticised traditional criminology for ignoring the issue of gender (see below) and leaving the question of female crime to be discussed by doctors and psychologists, such an assertion is not completely accurate. It is certainly the case that much criminological writing has been specifically related to male crime, which all the available evidence (other than the views of Pollak) suggested was far more prevalent. However, the use of the male pronoun was (and still is) common practice, and its use does not automatically indicate an intention to exclude women from the scope of the discussion. Leonard (1982) has attempted to show how certain sociological explanations of crime, such as labelling and radical theories, could be adapted to apply to women. Furthermore, some theories have specifically dealt with the issue of gender.

The studies of gangs in the Chicago ethnographic tradition by Thrasher and Whyte ruled out their coming into contact with many girl delinquents, whose closer supervision generally kept them away from the street corner groupings (see Chapter 8). However, in a later formulation of Sutherland's theory of differential association, Sutherland's collaborator, Donald Cressey (Sutherland and Cressey

1966), claimed that it is of equal application to both men and women. According to the theory, criminal behaviour is not an inborn characteristic, but is learned through interacting with other people in circumstances where criminal 'definitions' outweigh the effect of law-abiding 'definitions' (see Chapter 6). Sutherland had attributed the relative lack of criminal activity on the part of women to two factors. The first is their socialisation into a feminine role and the greater supervision which is exercised over them; this results in far less chance of their exposure to criminal definitions. The second is that girls are not taught to be aggressive, tough risk-takers; attributes that Sutherland considered necessary for a successful criminal. Thus, even though girls and boys grow up in the same deprived neighbourhood, females emerge as non-participants in the male contest to acquire power and wealth. This view is consistent with differential association theory, but it is shown in Chapter 6 that the theory itself is open to a number of criticisms which its extension to cover female crime does nothing to answer.

Theories based on strain may also apply to female offenders. Merton's use of the notion of anomie (see Chapter 7) to explain the actions taken by people who are unable to achieve 'the American Dream' of material wealth appears to be a description of male deviance. However, in recent years Merton (1997) has accepted that he should have considered the position of women. Elaine Player (1989) claimed that anomie theory provided an excellent explanation of female burglary and robbery. Albert Cohen's theory of delinquent subcultures also made specific reference to female crime, although hardly in a convincing manner. Whereas Cohen's lower-class boys suffer the strain of blocked educational opportunity, his girls are only interested in finding a steady relationship with a man and, if they suffer strain, it will be through a failure to achieve that goal. Cohen hardly endeared himself to feminist criminologists by stating that 'boys collect stamps and girls collect boys'. Any criminal behaviour will be related to sexual promiscuity or conduct designed to attract their male partner. Otherwise, women remain passive and are unlikely to act aggressively. Cloward and Ohlin were also dismissive of female criminality, as they considered that women would not experience the financial strains which confront men (see Chapter 8). However, the evidence is clearly contrary to this. Womens' involvement in the criminal justice system is far more likely to result from the commission of offences against property than any other crime, and the youthfulness of the perpetrators suggests that no partner is yet in contemplation.

In her book *Girl Delinquents* (1981), Anne Campbell took issue with Cohen's analysis of women's role in crime as mainly sexual in nature. She discovered female involvement in a wide variety of offences, although usually to a far lesser extent than for males. In a later work, Campbell (1984) found that girls were prepared to form gangs, although in other respects their aspirations were conventional; they wished to settle down and have a family. Pat Carlen (1988) discovered that over half her sample of women had been members of gangs which had engaged in anti-social and criminal behaviour.

Writers such as Sutherland, Cohen and Walter Miller (who is also considered in Chapter 8) were clearly influenced by the functionalist approach of Talcott Parsons (1937). For Parsons, children growing up in a family are socialised to learn specific roles. As it is women who bear children, their function is to be a caring one and their main duty is to look after the family and keep it together. The role of men is that of the bread-winner. Adherence to these roles is what ensures the proper functioning of the family and maintains the equilibrium of society. However, boys do not necessarily have a stable male role model to follow. They have learned that a feminine role model will not equip them to be 'real men', and so they learn to reject any behaviour perceived as feminine, such as kindness, gentleness and expressing their feelings. Instead, boys vigorously pursue what Parsons called 'compulsory masculinity', often to an exaggerated extent and sometimes involving anti-social behaviour. Such an account is said to provide the explanation of the greater involvement in delinquency by boys. Female offenders were usually only considered by functionalist theorists if they had deviated from their designated sex-role; this typically involved a discussion of prostitution and promiscuity. Women were not portrayed as aggressive or challenging, as that would be too far removed from their stereotypical role (Naffine 1987).

Bob Connell (1987) considered that there are three main advantages in adopting a sex-role approach to the study of gender differences. It replaces the biological explanation of sex differences in behaviour, which was so common in the early positivist accounts, with one based on learned expectations. Such an explanation also provides a way of integrating the effects of social structures into an understanding of personality. Finally, role theory offers a means of change: if people have suffered through the impact of socialisation, the process can in principle be changed for the better. At the same time, Connell appreciated that such an approach can have the disadvantage of minimising the impact of power in gender relations.

Interactionist theory ought, in principle, to be equally applicable to both males and females. Labelling theorists such as Becker were highly critical of earlier positivist approaches to crime (see Chapter 9). However, there has been relatively little research into the effects of applying a deviant label to women. In her book *The Booster and the Snitch* (1964), which studied shoplifters in Chicago, Mary Owen Cameron gave some consideration to gender. Having analysed the records of thefts by men and women, Cameron showed that many women shoplifters stole luxury items which they could not afford to buy. There was no evidence of any pathological factors underlying these thefts. James H Bryan (1966) was able to demonstrate that prostitutes learned their trade through a form of apprenticeship, and were driven by economic considerations rather than by some form of sexual deviation, as had been suggested by earlier writers.

Heidensohn (1996) has suggested that there are several reasons for the lack of sociological research into female crime up to the 1970s. There were very few women working in higher education institutions during this period. The male researchers appear to have been captivated by the appeal of the exaggerated masculine values shown by the street gangs they chose to study. Girls played a peripheral part in these and were rarely mentioned, let alone studied. In addition, according to Heidensohn, many male researchers were rather scared of tackling female criminality. It did not easily fit into prevailing functionalist explanations and, as a result of the lingering influence of Lombroso and Thomas, was still considered as essentially biological in origin. The 'normality' of male deviance was constantly emphasised, but the researchers could not bring themselves to make the same observations about women, who were expected to act in a 'feminine' way. Even labelling theorists found it difficult to break away from stereotypes and look beyond their deviant subjects to consider more structural issues relating to power and gender. Smart (1976) referred to 'the naive belief that femininity is the antithesis of criminality'.

Writers have become more prepared to link the idea of strain with a wider range of female crime. Box (1983) considered that the response of girls to blocked opportunity structures would be different from that of boys. As the girls have been socialised into internalising blame:

> ... [their] disorganised and spontaneous 'protests' are more likely to be channelled away from innovative criminal behaviour and into retreatist and self-defeatist adaptations.

Box (1987) also concluded from his study of American and British research into the relationship between crime and unemployment that the economic impact of the recession on women provided the best explanation of female crime. Carlen (1988), who conducted detailed interviews with thirty-nine convicted women, thought that financial need was usually the reason for their crimes. About 80 per cent admitted to being poor, although only half the sample mentioned their poverty as a relevant factor in their criminality. Many women, according to Carlen, find themselves in both a 'gender bind' and a 'class bind', and their restricted opportunities to make money result from a combination of the two. However, it remains the fact that most female property crimes are committed by teenage girls as opposed to older women, and there is also evidence that many young female delinquents obtain excitement from their criminal activities (Katz 1988).

Control theory, which shifts the focus from asking why people commit crimes to the question of why people conform (see Chapter 12), has also been invoked to explain the lower level of female criminality. Nye (1958) suggested that girls are subject to much more stringent socialisation than boys and are more heavily punished if they break the rules. Hirschi (1969), the best-known of the control theorists, appears to have set out his original theory in gender-neutral terms. However, he has been criticised by Naffine (1987) for slanting it towards males by ignoring the fact that women are by far the greater conformers of the two sexes, and invoking the traditional male role of provider as a model of what constitutes conformity. Hindelang (1973) replicated Hirschi's study, but with the specific inclusion of girls. He found that control theory accurately predicted criminality among both males and females, although with slightly greater accuracy for males. Hindelang concluded that women's conformity arises from their closer control within the home and their being denied the opportunity of going out to work.

The Canadian researchers Hagan *et al.* also found that the strongest forms of control were the informal ones used at home and that this explained the lower involvement of women in crime. Using Hirschi's self-report questionnaire, Hagan *et al.* carried out two studies into the relationship between gender and crime based on a blend of control and conflict theories. Using a sample of several hundred high school children in Toronto, their first study (1979) considered whether self-reported delinquency rates could be linked to differences in socialisation. They concluded that the girls were more likely to be the objects of informal social controls than the boys. The growth of industrialisation has confined the seat of informal control to the home, which has increasingly become the domain of women. Men, on the other hand, are far more likely to be subject to the formal control mechanisms of society as a whole. Even girls who grow up to assume a full-time career cannot escape from their early domestic socialisation. The findings of Hagan *et al.* supported their hypothesis that the strong controls experienced by girls at home would result in greater conformity. On the other hand, boys, who in the research defined risk-taking and delinquency in far more positive terms, are relatively undersocialised and thus more likely to get into trouble.

In their second study (1985), based on a similar sample of Toronto schoolchildren, Hagan *et al.* added the factor of class into the relationship between gender and control. The only correlation found between class and control was that the children of employers admitted to the highest rate of delinquency. However, once gender was introduced into the equation, the relationship between gender and common forms of crime weakened, with movement down the social scale. Hagan also found that the correlation between parental control and the level of delinquency was not uniform across all families; it was at its strongest in families where the father exercised more power than the mother. This typically occurred when the father worked away from the home, usually supervising others, while the mother assumed the role of the housewife. However, in egalitarian households, where both parents exercised a similar level of power, it was unlikely that the daughter would be subject to a greater level of control than the son.

Socialisation goes from mother to daughter in a perpetual cycle. Box (1981) intended that his version of control theory should apply equally to both sexes. Women are more likely to conform as they obtain greater support from their friends and are more able to see the risks involved in crime. Carlen (1988) thought that most working-class women are subject to dual controls: at work, where the necessity of a pay packet will discourage any temptation to crime; and at home, where they will be under the control of their parents or husband.

Heidensohn (1996) also considered that women are subject to stronger controls within the home environment. Girls grow up learning that they have to fulfil a caring role as wives and mothers. Even if women enter employment, they still have to devote a great deal of their time to domestic activities. Women typically have part-time or low-level jobs which discourage them from taking part in any activity that might endanger their employment. They are also controlled by the threat of violence, not only in the home but also on the street; this makes them stay indoors and out of harm's way. Women may also feel more restricted by the fear of gossip and stigma. Nevertheless, they can still be seen as making rational choices not to commit crime.

Much of the empirical testing of control theories in relation to female criminality has been conducted with girls, and the evaluation of delinquency has often included minor offences such as under-age drinking and truancy. The study of more serious offending by older women would be useful to determine whether earlier controls remain operative in later life.

Given their professed greater awareness of the effects of social structures, it is surprising that so little consideration was specifically given to female crime by the 'radical' theorists of the 1960s and 1970s. The labelling perspective in particular could have been a fruitful source of empirical research into various biases against women, but little of any significance emerged. The National Deviancy Conference was largely a male preserve (Sumner 1994). The call for a socialist state without the need to criminalise made in *The New Criminology* (Taylor *et al.* 1973) provided a critique of existing criminology without any discussion of gender. However, it was about this time that the first avowedly feminist literature on criminology began to emerge (Chesney-Lind 1973, Smart 1976).

Female emancipation

Following on from control theory, several writers have suggested that the greater involvement of women in crime is a direct result of the female 'emancipation' that has been taking place over the past thirty years. Once free of the greater level of control that used to restrict them, women have begun to behave in many respects more like men. This view was first propounded by two American writers, Freda Adler and Rita James Simon.

In her book *Sisters in Crime* (1975), Adler suggested that differences in rates of male and female crime were formerly attributable to the different roles each sex had to play. With the breakdown of those distinctions, women started to allow their competitive instincts to surface and began to commit crimes that used to be associated with men, such as assaults and robbery. Women have also gained greater opportunities to commit crime through entering traditionally male workplaces. Adler considered that the emancipation of women had largely been achieved by the mid-1970s and that females are now behaving more like males. On the other hand, Simon (1975), rather than emphasising the similarities between men and women, highlighted the greater opportunities that have opened up for women, particularly in the business world and education. In her view, these have led to a reduction in women's levels of frustration. As a consequence of the growth in such opportunities, there would be a decrease in violent behaviour by women and an increase in property crimes. Simon did not see women as turning to crime through trying to emulate men.

If these views are valid, the female crime rate should have been rising since the 1960s, when the women's movement started to become more influential. This is a very difficult assessment to make, not only because of the problems of interpreting criminal statistics (see Chapter 3), but also because all types of crime for both sexes have been increasing steadily throughout this period. In her book, Adler looked at female crime rates in the USA, Europe, India and New Zealand between 1960 and 1972. In the USA, she discovered an increase of 277 per cent for robbery and 168 per cent for burglary. The corresponding increases for men were 69 per cent and 63 per cent, respectively. Even greater increases were found for female juvenile offenders. The other countries she considered also showed disproportionate rises in female crime rates. However, as these are at a low level anyway, any increase can appear greatly magnified when expressed in percentage terms. Crites (1976), for example, pointed out that the 450 per cent increase in negligent manslaughter committed by girls in the USA during this period represents an actual increase from two cases to eleven!

Smart (1979) took a closer look at the criminal statistics for England and Wales. She found that the rate of increase in all categories of female crime was higher than that of male crime between 1965 and 1975. However, the point made by Crites was well-illustrated by the 500 per cent rise in murders committed by females during that period, which represented an actual increase from one case to five. The most significant points to emerge from Smart's study were that, first, there was a greater increase in the number of female crimes before the effects of the women's movement would have come into play than there was after—for example, female crime rose sharply between 1935 and 1946—and, second, that the distribution of crimes between men and women remained relatively stable throughout that period. These findings cast doubt on the theory that women's crime has increased as a result of their emancipation. A similar conclusion was drawn from an analysis of American crime figures (Steffensmeier 1981). On the other hand, Austin (1981) criticised Smart's statistical analysis, claiming that there had been a significant change in the female percentage of all offenders between 1970 and 1975.

Support for Smart's conclusion can be found in an even more detailed analysis of the crime statistics for England and Wales carried out by Steven Box and Chris Hale (1983). They considered that arguments relying on criminal statistics as evidence of an increase in female crime during the emergent period of women's liberation were fundamentally flawed because of an inadequate evaluation of the figures. It was simply not sufficient to rely on an increase in female crime during a period designated as one of greater freedom for women. For example, no concern had been shown for changes in the population levels of men and women. Nor had any attempt been made to assess other variables which might influence the figures, such as changes in the criminal justice system, the recording of statistics, or even in the law itself. Self-report studies contain different problems from those of official statistics (see Chapter 3). They tend to suggest a smaller gap between the levels of male and female offending. In a Home Office self-report study of girls, Riley (1986) observed that:

> Given equal opportunities, sex differences in crime participation by young people—as offenders or victims—are minimal.

Nor do self-report studies always indicate the seriousness of the offences. An attempt to deal with this problem was made in a study of schoolchildren in Edinburgh (Anderson *et al.* 1991), in which the children were asked to list the crimes they had committed in order of perceived seriousness. The results showed that between three and four times as many boys admitted to serious crimes of dishonesty and violence. For drug-related and less serious crimes, the difference between the sexes was much narrower, with the ratios for unruly behaviour, shoplifting and vandalism being particularly close.

There are further problems in assessing whether the women's movement has had any impact on levels of female crime. If, as Smart (1979) suggested, one of its consequences is that women have greater opportunity to offend in the workplace, one would expect a larger increase in female property crime than female violent crime. Yet, according to the figures, the opposite has been the case. This may not be all that surprising. Most of the increase in women's employment has been among the working class, who have always featured most prominently in the criminal statistics. This work has typically been of a low-level and part-time nature, and provides relatively little opportunity or incentive for acquisitive crime. Nevertheless, it is difficult to claim that the increase in employment prospects for women in itself provides any evidence of their greater involvement of crime. Carlen (1990) considered that the impoverishment and marginalisation of women provides a more plausible explanation for their increased criminality than the views put forward by Adler and Simon.

Box and Hale (1983) analysed female crime statistics from 1951 to 1979 with reference to four factors which they took to indicate the measure of women's independence in society: the level of fertility; the number of single or other unattached women; the number of women attending university; and the number of women entering employment. No statistical relationship could be found between the overall level of female crime and any of these factors. Any changes in the number of convictions for violent offences were attributed to 'labelling'. The increase in female property offending was caused by economic marginality. Box and Hale also discovered a relationship between the female crime rate and the number of women police officers. They took this to mean that women officers were uncovering more female crime than their male predecessors. The authors cautioned that they had not made any allowance for age in their analysis, and it is possible that young women in particular are strongly influenced by the effects of the women's movement.

Another type of research study was carried out in America by Josefina Figueira-McDonough (1984). By administering a questionnaire to both male and female high school students from varied backgrounds, she sought to test three different theories concerning the criminal activities of women. These were the view of Adler and Simon (above) that women's ambitions have heightened simply as a result of their greater involvement in the male world; that women have gained a stronger resolve through their failure to make greater progress; and that women have become more competitive. In addition to questions about their criminal activity, the students were asked about their school and social lives, their opinions on a wide variety of matters, including women's issues, and their hopes for their own lives. Although Figueira-McDonough found some correlation between girls inclined to feminism and a number of positive attributes, such as higher ambitions and better school performance, no significant relationship was discovered between a feminist orientation and a propensity to engage in criminal behaviour. Delinquency was most strongly linked with deprivation. Self-report studies are prone to unreliability, particularly when they are carried out on juveniles, but the evidence taken at face value is a further challenge to the hypothesis that female crime has increased because of the growing freedom gained by women.

Radical feminism

Radical feminists take a much stronger view of the position of women in what they consider to be a patriarchal society. As with control theory and radical criminology, power is the key issue, but here it is not power based on interest groups or class, but the power exercised by men over women. Radical feminists consider that no study of female crime can possibly be valid unless it is conducted within this context.

There are different 'feminisms' within criminological study (Walk-late 2004). They have in common the placing of the spotlight on to women, an adoption of methodologies which are sympathetic to womens' issues, and an antipathy to positivism. Broadly speaking, the 'feminisms' are reflected in the work of two groups of writers: those who do not wish to ally themselves to mainstream criminology, and those who are prepared to carry out research into a range of women's issues within a criminological perspective. Maureen Cain (1989) and Carol Smart (1990) fall into the first group. For them, the seeking of explanations for female crime within a conventional framework is only serving to reinforce stereotypes held by the male élite. Criminology is viewed as a discipline which could never be capable of protecting women's interests. Smart (1990) has commented that criminology needs feminism more than feminism needs criminology.

Most feminists, however, do not go this far, and direct their attentions to illustrating the particular problems that women encounter in the criminal justice system. Carlen (1992) is critical of feminist explanations of criminal behaviour. She has argued that there cannot be a true 'feminist criminology' because, other than patriarchy, there are no innately feminist theoretical concepts: men and women often commit crimes for the same reasons. In general, feminist issues ultimately break down into broader questions, such as class, racism and poverty. Carlen herself is one of several female criminologists who have carried out research in this area (for example, Carlen 1983, 1985, 1988). Particular attention has been paid to women as victims of crime, especially in relation to violent and sexual offences. Writers such as Dobash and Dobash (1979) have suggested that measures should be taken to control men who offend against women, rather than support being given to the prevalent view that the onus is on women to take precautionary action, such as not venturing on to the streets at night.

Conclusion

It is undoubtedly the case that, traditionally, writers on the sociology of crime and deviance made few, if any, specific references to female law-breaking. Feminist criminologists maintain that this omission is a reflection of women's subordinate and even oppressed role in a patriarchal society. The earlier biological explanations of female criminality, such as that of Lombroso, have rightly been criticised. Nevertheless, constitutional explanations of crime have not been confined to women. In Chapter 14, it is shown that there has been no shortage of biological explanations of male criminality.

Some sociological explanations of criminality, such as control theory, have the potential to apply to women just as much as men, even if they were not originally so presented. Women are not the only omissions from the history of criminological research. For many years criminology also overlooked issues such as the significance of power in society, the position of ethnic minority groups and the effects of colonisation (Gelsthorpe 1989). Nevertheless, as Wootton (1959) commented (with an acceptable degree of hyperbole):

> The relative rarity of women offenders . . . has for the most part been tacitly ignored by students of criminology . . . Yet if men behaved like women, the courts would be idle and the prisons empty.

It has been argued that mainstream (or, as Scraton (1990) called it, 'malestream') criminological writing followed the most 'visible' crimes and those were—and still are—crimes committed by young males. This contains an element of truth, but it is also clear that male criminologists have preferred to poke into some of the darkest recesses to study male deviance rather than turn their attentions to the activities of women. However, feminist studies have served a valuable role in emphasising that female criminality cannot be ignored or simply written off as being pathological. In future, there will be no excuse for any writer to ignore the criminal behaviour of half the population.

Postscript: masculinities and crime

It was stated earlier in the chapter that feminist and other writers have pointed out that it is more appropriate to consider gender, which is a socio-cultural concept, than sex which, as a biological category, was mistakenly the focus of concentration for theorists such as Lombroso and Ferrero. Following on from this, it has also been suggested that criminologists should be more interested in why men commit so many crimes rather than why, relatively speaking, women commit so few. Of course, the feminist critique of most criminological theories is precisely that they concentrate almost exclusively on men. However, this does not mean that these theories pay sufficient attention to the roles of male gender—or masculinities—in the commission of crime.

There have been several prominent contributions in this area, but the person who has written most specifically about crime is James W Messerschmidt. In his book *Masculinities and Crime* (1993), Messerschmidt attempted to construct a sociology of masculinity which could explain crime and delinquency. Having considered the deficiencies in criminological and sex-role theories, Messerschmidt was also critical of radical feminism for its essentialism—the assertion by some of its proponents that all men are violent and all women are victims. His theory of gendered crime is based on ideas of hegemonic and subordinated masculinities which derive from Connell's book *Gender and Power* (1987), and the work of West and Zimmerman (1987). The use of the term 'hegemony' is taken from the writings of Antonio Gramsci (1971) and refers to the assumption of power within a society without the use of force. Following Connell's analysis, Messerschmidt stated that there are three particular social elements underlying gender relations: the gender division of labour; the gender relations of power; and sexuality. These are variable elements but, considered together at any particular time, they demonstrate the conditions within which gender identities are created.

Hegemonic masculinity was defined by Messerschmidt as a form of masculinity which 'emphasises . . . authority, control, competitive individualism, independence, aggressiveness, and the capacity for violence'. Men utilise the resources available to them to assert their gender—to demonstrate they are 'manly'. In contrast, subordinated masculinities are, in Connell's terms, 'discredited or oppressed (such as homosexual masculinity in our culture)'. If other masculine outlets are unavailable, crime may be a suitable means of 'doing gender'. This is more likely to happen where circumstances demand an extra show of masculinity. West and Zimmerman's writings on 'doing gender' saw gender as a 'situated accomplishment'; a status that comes to be achieved as a result of others' expectations and attitudes, in addition to the subject's own actions.

Messerschmidt suggested that different masculinities can result in different patterns of crime. White middle-class boys generally conform at school, which accommodates masculinity, but outside school may take part in opposing masculinities involving non-violent forms of crime. White working-class boys will indulge in opposing masculinities, both in and out of school. Members of poorer and ethnic minority groups, who can see no connection between school and obtaining a job, seek alternative ways of accomplishing gender. For these boys, 'doing masculinity necessitates extra effort' because they have fewer resources, and they may therefore be more likely to create 'a physically violent opposition masculinity'. All of this is in contrast to a sex-role explanation of crime, which is founded on the basic assumption that boys behave in this manner because 'that's the way they are'.

Adult masculinities resulting in criminality were distinguished by Messerschmidt in accordance with their locality. He used the example of the workplace to illustrate the different forms that men's crime can take. Men on the shop floor assert their masculinity by humiliating women, whereas their bosses may expect a variety of services, including sex, from their female assistants and secretaries. The nature of property crime will also vary: the men on the shop floor may steal to impress their male colleagues, whereas managers and executives may resort to white-collar crime when profitability is endangered and their reputation (or masculine status) as successful businessmen is under threat.

In a later book, *Crime as Structured Action* (1997), Messerschmidt incorporated considerations of race and class into his discussion of gender. None of these three elements should be considered in absolute terms; the significance of each will vary according to the social setting and overall context of the situation. Messerschmidt asserted the interdependence of structure and action within society: 'Social structures are realised only through social action and social action requires structure as its condition'. He thought that less common forms of research, such as the study of ethnographies, life-histories and historical documents, are particularly appropriate to understand the interplay of gender, race and class in a 'structured-action' theory of criminal behaviour. In this book, Messerschmidt selected four examples to illustrate these methodologies: lynching; the life of the black power leader, Malcolm X; female gangs; and the problems of hegemonic masculinity which led to the explosion in the space shuttle *Challenger*. Rather than viewing gender as the cause of crime, Messerschmidt considered crime to be a device that can be used to reinforce gender, albeit one which generally translates into reinforcing masculinity.

Bourgois (1996) studied a group of Puerto Rican crack dealers in New York. Their parents and grandparents had occupied a traditional patriarchal role in the rural settings of their homeland. Having been attracted to America by the prospect of plentiful (if low paid) employment, they had arrived just in time to find the work disappear. Although their wives and daughters had been prepared to adapt to the new circumstances by taking the more readily available employment in the service and retail sectors, the men and their sons considered this to be 'women's work'. Finding themselves unable to support economically, or exercise control over, their women and children, who had gained their own measure of independence, a growing number of the men reacted to this crisis of masculinity by joining the drug economy whose subcultural norms included gang rape, sexual conquest and the abandonment of their families. Bourgois considered that such actions enabled the men—mindful of their father's and grandfather's former power—to attain a level of masculine dignity.

An increasing amount of literature suggests that a consideration of competing masculinities can provide a better explanation of crime than the more common accounts, including those based purely on the sex of the offender. Kersten (1996) studied sexual assault in Australia, Germany and Japan. Both official and self-report data show Australia as having a far higher level of such incidents than the other two countries: by a factor of more than twenty over Japan, and three times the number recorded in Germany. Such assaults are rapidly increasing in Australia, are growing since unification in Germany, but are declining in Japan. Although sexual offences have a higher media profile and are generally more visible in Australia, it is unlikely that these disparities have been greatly influenced by differences in the levels of reporting.

Kersten considered the usual explanations for the relatively low crime rate in Japan to be inadequate. Although the Japanese police have greater powers than their Australian or German counterparts, formal crime control is less efficient than in those countries. The existence of the 'shaming' culture as identified by Braithwaite (see Chapter 9) has been challenged by some writers (for example, Buruma 1994). There is a lower level of job equality and a higher level of pornography readership in Japan than the other two countries. Japanese men make frequent recourse to prostitution.

Messerschmidt (1993) cited public displays of toughness as a particular form of masculinity associated with violence. However, Kersten maintained that such activities in Japan would only be performed by members of the underworld, and that street fights are rare. Japanese men routinely express caring values and displays of emotion in front of other men. 'Real manhood' is also demonstrated in devotion to group membership and, in particular, the work place, which is still largely male-controlled and perhaps offers less of a challenge to masculinity. In contrast, Kersten viewed the Australian hegemonic masculinity as the celebration of physical prowess which can both perpetrate sexual assaults on women (and other 'inferior' individuals) and provide protection against such assaults by others. It is possible that this could compensate for the decline in other traditional forms of showing masculinity, such as manual farm labour.

Masculinities and crime: problems

According to Collier (1998), the sex–gender distinction and the notion of hegemonic masculinity are both problematic. His own view was that hegemonic masculinity is always contested and never finally resolved. Writings have generally associated hegemonic masculinity with negative characteristics such as uncaring, unemotional and violent. However, this seems particularly ethnocentric: both anthropological and cross-cultural studies have shown that the concept of masculinity is either unknown in some societies, or is associated with positive qualities such as nurture and concern. The assumption that 'real' men are oppressive fails to consider what determines whether a particular attribute is 'masculine' or 'feminine' in any particular context. In addition, from a woman's point of view, there may even be ambivalence as to the characteristics she wants to see in a man. As Walklate (2004) put it, '. . . do women really want their men to be "wimps" '?

Collier also viewed the sex–gender (or 'body–mind') distinction as invalid. He considered it misleading to speak of the 'body' in the traditional biological sense. Collier preferred the concept of the 'sexed body': for instance, a male 'body' may have incorporated characteristics which, under hegemonic masculinity, would be considered as 'female'. A subjective approach allowing for the study of individual differences would render unnecessary the need to make assumptions as to what constitutes any particular form of masculinity. Gender would now be 'performative'—a series of subjectivities repeated over a period of time.

Hearn (1996) claimed that there has been a failure to explain adequately what is meant by the term 'masculinity'. Sometimes the term is used to describe a general form of culture (an ideal to which all 'real' men should aspire), but on other occasions it is represented as something that can vary both within and between cultures. It is also unclear at what point of a male's life masculinity can be related to crime. Is it at birth (a biological given) or later on? This question is relevant to the widely-held view (supported by official statistics) that men eventually 'grow out of' crime. The fact that the meanings of masculinity can vary throughout a male's life has remained a largely unexplained area, as the masculinities and crime debate has concentrated on the dangerous aspects of young men's behaviour.

On the basis of her research into girl gangs, Miller (2002) has questioned whether Messerschmidt's analysis of 'doing gender' is adequate to explain female participation in what is essentially considered 'masculine' crime. Although Messerschmidt has suggested that involvement in gang activities, such as violence, can be seen as enacting an appropriate form of femininity in the social context of the gang, Miller claimed that the fact that some of the women concealed their gender from their victims showed that they are more concerned about contravening normative beliefs than with 'accomplishing femininity' through their actions.

There is arguably a subjective, or motivational element missing in Messerschmidt's analysis. In his enthusiasm to highlight the important role of gender, Messerschmidt has failed to consider fully why some men assert their masculinity in the form of criminal or deviant behaviour, whereas others choose different routes, such as playing sport. The mere assertion that there is a variety of possible masculinities that can be adopted does not completely answer this question. After all, most men do not participate in the corporate thefts, rapes and lynchings he has described. Hood-Williams (2001) argued that Messerschmidt's theory is tautologous and only provides a list of some things that some men do. Walklate (2004) claimed that 'the maleness of crime . . . also becomes the source of its explanation'. As it stands, it is open to the same charge as much of the earlier criminological writing: that it over-predicts the amount of crime that is committed.

Jefferson (1996a) has attempted to provide what he views as the missing element in Messerschmidt's work—a greater emphasis on individual identity and subjectivity—by considering later writings in the psychoanalytical tradition. Freud made a crucial distinction between the conscious, or rational mind and the unconscious mind, which is a repository for a range of repressed desires of a socially unacceptable nature. An individual's emergent personality or identity is a product of the conflicts that arise between these two competing forces (see Chapter 16). Although this explanation removes human motivation from the determinist clutches of the social environment, Jefferson considered that traditional Freudian theory only serves to replace structural determinism with biological determinism. He has sought to deal with this by drawing from the work of other psycho-analytic writers to indicate the importance of the ways in which certain aspects of the child's identity develop and, in particular, the impact this has on the way the child deals with its unconscious desires.

To assist his search to discover what underlies the development of the true 'male psyche', Jefferson has studied the boxer Mike Tyson, a man who is widely assumed to epitomise conventional definitions of 'hyper-masculinity', but who has also been in trouble for violence and rape. For Jefferson, any explanation of Tyson's behaviour based solely on his race and social background (brought up in poverty in the ghetto) is inadequate. Jefferson turned to the psychoanalytic writings of Melanie Klein (1988) and adopted modified versions of her notions of 'ambivalence', 'recognition' and 'anxiety'. For an infant, ambivalence first arises in extreme feelings of pleasure and frustration (as exemplified by the presence or absence of the breast for feeding). These will develop into strong feelings of love and hate, and the inherent contradiction between them will prove a source of anxiety for the growing child. One way of dealing with this anxiety is by striving to keep the feelings apart ('splitting'). Klein considered that, in extreme cases, this could lead to the viewing of everything and everyone as either 'good' or 'bad' and the development of paranoia or depression. Jefferson (1996b) claimed to have identified several instances of such 'splitting' in Tyson's life, including the facts that he was bullied as a child and that he once broke down in tears before a fight. Using the example of the My Lai massacre in Vietnam, Jefferson (2002) has suggested that such an analysis could also usefully be applied to wartime atrocities.

Although this account of ambivalence is not gender-specific, Jefferson (1998) has argued that it is possible to explain the notion of 'anxiety' as something which is more likely to affect boys. The distance a boy has to place between himself and his mother in order to develop his own masculinity could result in the necessary conditions for 'splitting', which could involve the development of feelings of anxiety and hatred towards women. On the other hand, Hood-Williams (2001) has claimed that girls will encounter far higher levels of anxiety on their way to achieving femininity.

The study of masculinities and crime is one of the more interesting recent developments in criminological theory, and there is a growing body of work examining the full implications of this perspective (for example, Newburn and Stanko (eds) 1994). This is an area still very much at the stage of development and it is likely that further insights will emerge.

Part 3

Biological and psychological aspects of crime

14

Biological factors and crime

Constitutional factors

The idea that criminals can be distinguished from the rest of the population by some unusual physical or biological characteristic which renders them inferior individuals goes back hundreds of years. It can be seen in Egyptian writings and in the Bible. According to Havelock Ellis, there was a law in medieval England which stated that 'If two persons fell under suspicion of crime, the uglier or more deformed was to be regarded as more probably guilty'. When Socrates was on trial, a study of his face conducted by a physiognomist was ordered; this showed that he was cruel and inclined to drunkenness. Physiognomy, which is the assessment of character from facial features, was later referred to in Cesare Beccaria's book *On Crimes and Punishments* (1764), but a fuller statement can be found in the lesser-known *Physiognomical Fragments* (1775) by Johan Lavater. Here, the reader was warned about bearded women, weak chins, 'arrogant' noses and 'shifty' eyes. Physiognomy in due course gave way to the more structured theory of phrenology, which has come to be associated with an anatomist, Franz Joseph Gall (1758–1828), although he was not the originator of the idea. Phrenology held that the workings of the mind are related to the shape of the brain and skull, and that measurement of bumps on the skull can provide an indication of personal characteristics. Thus, criminals could be identified by a particular series of bumps. However, the theory still allowed for hope of a cure, as it claimed that appropriate training could strengthen those parts of the brain that gave rise to 'desirable' characteristics.

Phrenology began to lose any remaining credibility by the early nineteenth century. It was clearly unprovable but, more importantly, it was seen as being entirely deterministic. People such as teachers and, in particular, priests were worried by the idea that individuals might think that there was no point in trying to lead a better life as their destiny was fixed at birth. Charles Darwin's book *On the Origin of*

Species by Means of Natural Selection was still half a century away. It was the publication of that work in 1859 and then his book *Descent of Man* in 1871 that was to provide the next impetus to criminal anthropology in the work of Cesare Lombroso.

(a) Cesare Lombroso

Some of the more risible claims of Lombroso tend to mask work which was seen, at the beginning of the twentieth century, as a major landmark in the study of criminals and which, for better or worse, has been influential up to the present day. Lombroso, who was familiar with Darwin's theories, viewed criminals as suffering from a depravity caused by an atavistic reversion: in other words, through a regression to the earlier form of life found in humans' ape-like ancestors. In 1870 Lombroso's early ideas were apparently confirmed when, conducting an autopsy on a famous bandit, he found that the man's brain had characteristics which are usually identified with lower primates. Lombroso provided a list of physical characteristics that would indicate such a reversion. These included an asymmetrical face; unusual ears; a nose upturned or flattened in thieves and aquiline (beak-like) in murderers; fleshy lips; receding chin; excessively long arms; and too many fingers or toes.

In a study of 383 Italian criminals, Lombroso discovered that 21 per cent of the sample had one such characteristic and 43 per cent had five or more. It was this that led him to conclude that five or more such stigmata would indicate a 'born criminal'. The stigmata were present far less frequently in a control group of 'non-criminal' (that is, unconvicted) Italian soldiers. Lombroso also found that significant numbers of anarchists had the stigmata (between 30 per cent and 40 per cent) whereas in other extreme political groups the figure was less than 12 per cent. Lombroso's research provided one of the earliest examples of the use of control groups and statistical techniques in the study of crime. However, his use of these was poor: many of his 'criminals' were Sicilians, who are known for their swarthy and stocky appearance. Moreover, a number of them appear to have been mentally ill, which itself might have affected their appearance.

(b) Charles Goring

In an attempt to challenge Lombroso's findings, a more sophisticated study was conducted in England by a group of researchers led by Charles Buckman Goring and published in 1913 as *The English Convict:*

a Statistical Study. The research compared more than 3,000 English recidivist prisoners with large groups of 'non-criminals' over an eight-year period. The non-criminals comprised Oxford and Cambridge undergraduates, hospital patients and soldiers. Goring's methodology was based entirely on objective assessments of physical and mental characteristics. Lombroso had earlier dismissed this process as involving differences that would be too small to measure and which could only be spotted by a trained observer. Goring, who compared criminals convicted of different offences with the non-criminals on the basis of thirty-seven physical characteristics, claimed that he did not find any significant difference between the prisoners and the control group:

> In fact, both with regard to measurements and the presence of physical anomalies in criminals, our statistics present a startling conformity with similar statistics of the law-abiding class. Our inevitable conclusion must be that there is no such thing as a physical criminal type.

The only exception to this conclusion was that the criminals were on average two inches shorter than the non-criminals and weighed between three and seven pounds less. Goring considered that this supported his claim—which was also based on assessments of mental ability—that criminals had a general inherited inferiority. However, this did not mean that criminals were throwbacks to an earlier stage of development, as Lombroso had thought. For Goring, the criminal was 'a selected class of normal man'. Although he asserted that Lombroso's work lacked a proper scientific basis, it has subsequently been suggested that, in his intense desire to discredit his writings, Goring suppressed findings that appeared to support Lombroso's thesis.

(c) Earnest Hooton

Goring's dismissal of Lombroso's work remained unchallenged for twenty-five years until the publication of Earnest A Hooton's book *The American Criminal: an Anthropological Study* (1939). Hooton, an anthropologist at Harvard University, surveyed 13,873 prisoners from ten different states and compared them with a control group of 3,203 people. He discovered that in nineteen out of thirty-three measurements, including all the body measurement tests, the criminals were inferior to the control group. Hooton listed various physical characteristics commonly identified among his prisoners which are reminiscent of Lombroso's 'findings': low and sloping foreheads; 'compressed jaws'; and unusual ears. As Lombroso had claimed earlier, Hooton found that tattoos were more common among criminals. The basic reason for the inferiority of criminals is heredity 'and not . . . situation or circumstance'. Hooton devoted much of his book to comparing groups of criminals on the basis of their offences. He concluded that murderers and robbers are likely to be tall and thin; tall, heavy people commit fraud; short, heavy people commit assault, rape and sexual offences; and small people are thieves and burglars.

Hooton's work was immediately controversial. His control group, while impressive in size, seems hardly representative. It included a large number of firemen from Nashville, Tennessee; patrons of a bath house; outpatients from Massachusetts General Hospital; and a group of officers of the Massachusetts militia. Hooton also ignored significant differences that his researchers had discovered among sections of the control group—differences which in some cases were greater than those between the prisoners and the members of the control group. The circular nature of Hooton's argument has also been pointed out. He ascribed physical differences between criminals and non-criminals to inferiority in the criminals, but he then used this inferiority to account for criminality. Although Hooton claimed that physical inferiority was inherited, he never provided any evidence of this. An alternative—and more plausible—explanation for physical inferiority is one based on social and environmental factors. Most convicted offenders are poor and in the 1930s many such people were undernourished. Moreover, the prison diet at that time would be relatively meagre and likely to lead to further emaciation. Nor does Hooton's analysis of different types of criminal stand up to close scrutiny. He overlooked the fact that half his criminals had been in prison before and, in many cases, for an offence different from the one for which they were now being punished.

In general, then, these theories can be criticised for almost totally ignoring the social environment and particularly the effects of poor nutrition. They also overlooked the fact that individuals of frightening appearance were liable to a greater risk of apprehension. Many such individuals may also have been mentally handicapped. Nowadays, these people would be found in hospitals, but in Lombroso's day they were more likely to end up in prison.

(d) William Sheldon and body types

A later attempt to link criminal behaviour with physical characteristics can be seen in the claim that there is a high correlation between an individual's bodily build and temperament. Its first major proponent was William H Sheldon, although he was not the originator of the idea. In his book *Varieties of Delinquent Youth* (1949), Sheldon applied his basic thesis to a sample of offenders. The human embryo has three layers of tissue: an inner layer (endoderm), a middle layer (mesoderm) and an outer layer (ectoderm). In the emerging person the endoderm is associated with the digestive system; the mesoderm with bones and muscles; and the ectoderm with the skin and nervous system. Sheldon prepared a typology matching temperamental characteristics with each of these physical aspects. An endomorphic physique has soft, rounded contours and is associated with a person who likes relaxation and comfort. A mesomorphic physique is large and muscular and is associated with action and aggression. An ectomorphic physique will be lean with prominent bones and is associated with a nervous and sensitive temperament. Everyone possesses these characteristics in varying degrees. Sheldon devised a system to measure each of them on a scale from 1 to 7. A well-balanced individual would receive a score of 4–4–4 whereas, for example, a person with a score of 4–2–7 will be strongly ectomorphic, with an average amount of endomorphic characteristics and few mesomorphic characteristics.

Sheldon compared 200 young males who had been to a small rehabilitation home in Boston at some time between 1939 and 1949 with 200 college boys believed to be non-delinquent. He found that the delinquent youths rated far higher in mesomorphy and lower in ectomorphy than the college youths, who presented a more balanced picture. One problem with Sheldon's analysis is that he did not use a strictly legal definition of delinquent, but a far more subjective assessment. However, when Sutherland (1951) re-analysed the data in accordance with legal criteria, the results still showed that the most delinquent youths obtained the highest rating for mesomorphy.

These findings were subsequently replicated in a study by the Gluecks, who compared 500 delinquent youths attending two correctional schools in Massachusetts with 500 non-delinquent youths from state schools in Boston (S Glueck and E Glueck 1956). The groups were matched for age, intelligence, race and area of residence. Photographs were used to determine body types. The findings revealed that about 60 per cent of the delinquents, but only 31 per cent of the non-delinquents, were mesomorphs. Also, the delinquent group contained less than half as many ectomorphs as the control group (14.4 per cent compared with 39.6 per cent). The research also included a study of sixty-seven personality traits and forty-two socio-cultural factors to ascertain which of these were related to delinquency.

The mesomorphs showed stronger traits related to physical aggression and insensitivity and were less inhibited by feelings of inadequacy.

However, mesomorphs who became delinquent were also more prone to emotional instability, and their upbringing was strongly linked to three factors: poor household routine, lack of family group activities and scarcity of play facilities in the home. On the other hand, factors commonly associated with the onset of delinquency, such as lack of self-control and delinquency among other members of the family, were much the same for all three types of physique.

Both the Sheldon and Glueck research has been criticised on the grounds that it does not allow for the changes in body shape that take place in adolescence; that the use of photographs is too imprecise for a scientific assessment; and that the definition of delinquency was confined to youths placed in institutions.

Juan B Cortés (1972) attempted to deal with these problems. He adopted precise techniques to assess the physique of 100 delinquents, of whom seventy were in an institution and thirty were subject to a suspended sentence or on probation. The same assessment was used to form a control group of 100 high-school children with no criminal record and a further group of twenty imprisoned adults. Cortés discovered that 57 per cent of the delinquents had a high mesomorphy rating, compared with only 19 per cent of the non-delinquents. In an attempt to ascertain if there is a link between body type and temperament, Cortés studied seventy-three boys who had a strong rating for any of the three body types to see if they described themselves in accordance with the traits usually associated with that type. He found that such a link existed, and this continued to be the case when applied to 100 college girls and the twenty imprisoned adults.

However, there are also problems with the methodology used by Cortés. The differences in physique between the groups in his study could have been due to differences in social class rather than criminality, as his non-delinquent group was drawn from a private school, whereas his delinquent group is likely to have come from the lower class. Cortés did not attempt to measure the temperaments of his subjects; he simply asked them for their own self-evaluation. Crucially, no direct link was established between criminality and temperament. At best, criminality was linked to mesomorphy, and mesomorphy was associated with certain forms of temperament. Nevertheless, Cortés did not rule out the significance of environmental factors, commenting that 'It is not, therefore, and should not be, heredity under or over environment, but only and always heredity *and* environment'.

The evidence remains unclear. When Hartl *et al.* (1982) conducted a thirty-year follow up of Sheldon's delinquents using the same body classification, they found that the original analysis still maintained, with the criminal group showing greater signs of mesomorphy. However, in the longitudinal Cambridge Study in Delinquent Development (West 1982) there was no evidence that delinquents were in any way distinctive in their physique. Sampson and Laub (1997) found that mesomorphy was a weak predictor of adult arrests for any crime.

Even if the methodological difficulties could be overcome, one fundamental problem would remain with this type of research. The finding that people of large muscular build engage in aggressive acts to get their own way more often than short puny types can be explained on the common-sense ground that they discovered at an early age that their greater physical strength enabled them to do this successfully. Research by Raine et al. (1998) discovered that three-year-old children (boys or girls), who were just half an inch taller than their peers, had a greater than average chance of becoming classroom bullies and ultimately violent criminals.

The researchers alleged that the differences could not be explained by any socio-economic factors such as family income or parental education. Similarly, these large individuals may be targeted for membership of youthful gangs. In this regard, it would be useful to know if offences that do not require physical strength, such as fraud, are committed disproportionately by mesomorphs. Any researcher undertaking this task could also enquire whether the alleged association between mesomorphy and juvenile delinquency becomes less strong with a reduction in the age of the delinquent sample.

Genetic factors

Before the development of proper research into genetic transmission, early attempts to consider the possibility of hereditary influence in criminality centred on the study of family trees. The best-known example of this was carried out by Richard Dugdale (1877) into the background of an infamous New York family he called 'The Jukes'. Having come across six members of this family in prison in 1874, Dugdale set about tracing their ancestry over 200 years. He discovered a history of poverty, prostitution and crime, which he attributed to the 'degenerate' nature of the family. Although there was no possible scientific basis for such a conclusion in Dugdale's work, and an environmental explanation seemed far more likely, the book was very influential at the time.

However, by the end of the nineteenth century, scientific theories of heredity had become more developed, as had statistical techniques. In 1901, Hugo de Vries published the first volume of his work *The Mutation Theory* in which he claimed that any living thing—plant or animal—is a mosaic of independent variable characteristics. New varieties and subspecies of life emerge by mutation as breeding occurs, and parents transmit to their offspring both desirable and undesirable characteristics, including congenital defects and diseases. In 1883, the English anthropologist Francis Galton had coined the word 'eugenics' to describe his theory for limiting hereditary defects through planned breeding.

With the help of a thorough statistical analysis, Charles Goring (1913) decided that criminal behaviour could be inherited in the same way as ordinary physical features. He discovered that long-term prisoners and those frequently incarcerated were both physically smaller and mentally inferior to other people. Goring also found a high correlation between the criminality of each parent, between the criminality of parents and their children, and between the criminality of brothers. He rejected the argument that these similarities could have resulted from shared social and environmental factors, because he could find little if any correlation between crime and conditions such as poverty, a broken home or poor education. Goring also denied that the criminality of one spouse could be induced by that of the other, as his research showed that most of them were committing offences before they married. Likewise, children could not have learned crime from their parents. This was, first, because the correlation for stealing was almost the same as for sex crimes, which parents would conceal from them and, second, because children removed from their parents in early childhood subsequently committed crimes at least as frequently as those removed later. Having excluded the influence of environmental factors, Goring felt able to attribute crime to hereditary characteristics. He considered that criminal behaviour could be controlled eugenically by reducing the reproduction of families which exhibited traits such as 'feeblemindedness, epilepsy, insanity and defective social instincts'.

Goring's methodology was not as thorough as he appeared to believe. The ease with which he felt able to discount environmental variables was scarcely justified. Goring only considered eight environmental factors and these were assessed very imprecisely. Other possible environmental influences were ignored. Goring's argument that children could not learn to commit crimes from their parents because of the improbability that parents would provide instruction on how to commit sexual offences assumed that only specific criminal techniques can be learned, rather than immoral values in general. Nor did Goring explain why, in his own research, the ratio of brothers to sisters in prison was 102 to 6. Nowhere did Goring suggest that the hereditary characteristics of criminals could vary according to sex; indeed, his thesis was based entirely on mental and physical inferiority.

(a) Twin studies

Despite the shortcomings of his methodology, Goring had realised the necessity to eliminate the possible effects of environmental factors in his research into heredity and crime. He chose to do this by the use of statistics, but another method is by the study of twins. There are two types of twins. Monozygotic (MZ) twins come from a single fertilised egg that has divided. These twins, commonly (though inaccurately) known as identical, are of the same sex, very similar in appearance, and have the same genetic structure. Dizygotic (DZ) twins result from the simultaneous fertilisation of two eggs and have no closer genetic relationship than any two siblings. If MZ twins act in the same way—such as committing crimes—this could be attributable to a common genetic factor. On the other hand, if crime is related predominantly to the environment, then all sets of twins—MZ and DZ—will have more similar levels of offending. One difficulty is, of course, that any similarity in crime rates between each twin may be a result of their common upbringing. The ideal study would be of MZ twins brought up in different families. However, there are not many twins available to study. Only one in every seventy to ninety births results in twins and, of these, only about one in four results in MZ twins. Nevertheless, the possibility of a hereditary link in criminal behaviour has encouraged researchers to investigate twins in some detail.

One of the earliest studies of criminal twins was carried out by the German physiologist Johannes Lange (1931). He discovered that in thirteen pairs of adult male MZ twins, where one twin had a prison record, the other had a similar record in 77 per cent of the cases (this is referred to as the concordance rate). However, in a group of seventeen DZ twins, the concordance rate was only 12 per cent. Lange compared these findings with a control group of 214 pairs of brothers. A similar prison record was found in only 8 per cent of cases. Other small-scale studies have found similar differences between MZ and DZ twins.

The early studies were open to two basic methodological objections. First, the classification of twins as either MZ or DZ was based purely on visual impression, and there is a possibility that some DZ twins were classified as MZ, which would have distorted the findings. Nowadays, DNA testing will reduce this risk. Also, many of the twins in the research studies were identified from psychiatric clinics, which not only provided an unrepresentative sample, but could also have encouraged the attribution of criminality when there had been no criminal conviction.

In an attempt to overcome such possible biases, Christiansen (1968) obtained from the official Danish twins register a list of the 6,000 or so pairs of twins born between 1881 and 1910 who had lived until at least the age of fifteen. He then used the official records to ascertain whether either or both of the twins had a criminal conviction. For male MZ twins he found that in 35.8 per cent of cases both had a criminal record, whereas this was only the case for 12.3 per cent of the male DZ twins. For female MZ twins the figure was 21.4 per cent, while for female DZ twins it was only 4.3 per cent. When Christiansen (1974) distinguished between offences punishable with imprisonment and lesser offences, he found that the former were even more strongly linked to genetics. There was also a higher concordance for MZ than DZ pairs among the middle class and for those born in rural districts. Christiansen believed that this fitted in with the higher crime rates routinely found among the urban working class, as the relative importance of environmental factors is increased. Nevertheless, he was aware of the difficulties in distinguishing between environmental and hereditary influences, and was not prepared to claim that his research had successfully overcome this problem.

Christiansen (1977) also studied the complete twin population of 3,586 pairs from the Danish islands. The concordance rates among the males who were convicted of crimes were 35 per cent for MZ twins and 13 per cent for DZ twins: for females, the figures were 21 per cent and 8 per cent, respectively.

Dalgaard and Kringlen (1976) studied all the male twins born in Norway between 1921 and 1930 (139 pairs). Whereas most researchers in this area have simply relied on official records, they tried to interview all pairs in which at least one twin had a criminal conviction. Dalgaard and Kringlen found a concordance rate for crime of 25.8 per cent for MZ twins, but only 14.9 per cent for DZ twins. Like Christiansen, they thought that this difference might be accounted for by upbringing, so they decided to test this by ranking the pairs of twins on the basis of mutual psychological closeness. They found that more of the MZ twins were close than the DZ twins, and thus concluded that the basis for hereditary influence disappeared. Their own research was subsequently re-interpreted by Cloninger and

Gottesman (1987), who claimed that, on this argument, psychologically close MZ twins should have had a higher concordance level than psychologically remote MZ twins. However, the research had not shown this. It would have been more appropriate to use a test of closeness in early home environment than psychological closeness. Yet, Dalgaard and Kringlen's data also failed to support that test, as there was no evidence that MZ twins brought up in a close home environment were more concordant than MZ twins brought up in other environments.

Rowe and Rodgers (1989) conducted the Ohio Twin Study, in which they compiled data from self-report questionnaires administered to 265 sets of same-sex twins and forty-three sets of different-sex twins in Ohio schools. The questionnaire sought to elicit information on temperament, view of home environment, delinquency, and delinquent friends. The effects of other siblings on twins' behaviour was also considered. Rowe and Rodgers found that, although genetic factors could influence the behaviour of MZ and same-sex twins, sibling and twin relationships also played a significant part. According to Rowe (1990), the Ohio Twin Study indicated that people consciously seek out the most favourable environment in accordance with their genetically-based personality. Therefore, MZ twins in particular are likely to choose similar friends and engage in similar activities, including anti-social ones. The research thus provided evidence of a genetic influence in crime, but only one which explains the high concordance levels in delinquent behaviour amongst MZ twins.

O'Connor et al. (1998) studied the co-occurrence of depressive symptoms and anti-social behaviour (including violence) in a sample of 720 same-sex adolescent siblings, including ninety-three pairs of MZ and ninety-nine pairs of DZ twins. The researchers found that about half the variability could be attributed to genetic factors. In a study of male twins who had served in the American military between 1965 and 1975, Lyons et al. (1995) discovered that shared environmental factors may have a stronger influence on anti-social behaviour for juvenile offenders than for adults. In a study of 1,116 sets of twins, Kim-Cohen et al. (2004) found that an ability to overcome the effects of poverty (which can include an increased likelihood of anti-social behaviour) was partly explainable by genetic endowment.

(b) Adoption studies

A further way of investigating the impact of heredity on crime is to study the behaviour of adoptees. If a child adopted soon after birth comes to resemble its biological more than its adoptive parent in a particular attribute, there is clear (although not conclusive) evidence of genetic influence. Thus, if an adoptee is removed from its 'criminal' parent at an early age, placed in a non-criminal home, and then grows up to become a delinquent, this provides evidence of a link between criminality and genetics. Adoption studies appear to provide a better control of possible environmental influences than other research methods, such as twin studies.

Crowe (1972) examined the cases of fifty-two babies born to forty-one female offenders, who were given up for adoption in Iowa between 1925 and 1956. They were matched with a control group of adopted children from parents without criminal convictions on the basis of age, sex, race, and age at adoption. According to the records, eight of the children with 'criminal' mothers were arrested and five of these served prison sentences, whereas only two of the control group were ever arrested and neither of them was convicted. Although a hereditary link is suggested, the numbers involved were very small and it is possible that the police paid special attention to the children of known offenders.

Hutchings and Mednick (1977) examined the cases of all male adoptions in Copenhagen between 1927 and 1941 where the adoptive parents were unrelated to the child. Almost half the boys who themselves were convicted of crimes had biological fathers with criminal records. Of the boys who had no criminal convictions, just under a third had biological fathers with criminal records. Hutchings and Mednick also considered the interrelation between the criminality of the biological and adoptive fathers. The effect of both being criminal was stronger than the effect of only one, although the criminality of the adoptive father had less impact than that of the biological father. These findings also suggest that some genetic predisposition to criminal behaviour may exist (the biological father), but that crime is more likely to occur in certain environmental conditions (the adoptive father).

In 1984 the research was widened to cover all adoptions in Denmark between 1924 and 1947 and dealt with a total of 14,427 cases (Mednick et al. (eds) 1987). The results and conclusions drawn were similar, with the additional finding that the correlation between the criminality of biological parents and their adoptive children (women had by now been included) was strongest in the case of persistent offenders. The Danish research has been supported by a large study in Sweden (Bohman et al. 1982). The conclusions, based on an analysis of 862 adopted males, were practically the same and there was an even clearer indication of genetic influence on criminality in the case of the 913 adopted females.

Although the evidence from adoption studies appears to suggest a genetic involvement in criminal behaviour, the influence of environmental factors is also present and it is unclear how strong a role such considerations play. Nowadays, efforts are made to place adopted children in settings with which they are familiar, and no real change in environment may occur. It is unlikely that so much attention was paid to this in the Denmark of sixty years ago. The research of Mednick and his colleagues has also been criticised by Gottfredson and Hirschi (1990) on the basis that the 1984 study, which showed a slight reduction in the correlations, should have shown an increase, as it was based on a larger sample and extended to include mothers and daughters. It is also apparent that some of the adoptive parents had criminal convictions, although this was against the principle of the Danish agencies at the time.

Other research findings are supportive of a relationship between crime, heredity and the environment. Bohman (1978) found evidence of a genetic transmission of a susceptibility to alcoholism, which itself can lead to an increased likelihood of involvement in crime. Cadoret et al. (1983) investigated the effects of a range of genetic variables—such as the criminality of a biological parent—and environmental factors—such as a disturbed adoptive sibling—on the growth of anti-social behaviour in a group of adopted children. Their conclusions suggested that the environmental factors were more significant, but that the strongest correlations occurred when the child was subjected to both genetic and environmental influences favourable to criminality.

Rhee and Waldman (2002) conducted a meta-analysis of fifty-one twin and adoption studies. They concluded that there is moderate evidence of both genetic and environmental influences in anti-social behaviour. The findings of twin studies and sibling adoption studies are more similar than those of twin studies and parent-offspring adoption studies. The twin and sibling adoption studies show a higher level of familial influence than the parent-offspring adoption studies. Although methodological issues account for variations in the results, there is no statistically significant difference between males and females in the studies that consider both sexes.

Therefore, whatever the influence of genes, it appears that the environment cannot be ignored (Rutter and Silberg 2002). As Walsh (2000) put it:

Just as a rose will express its fullest genetic potential planted in an English garden and wither in the Nevada desert, human beings will realise their genetic potential to the fullest when reared in positive environments and fall short of doing so when reared in negative environments.

(c) Chromosome abnormalities

Chromosomes, which are found in both plant and animal cells, contain genes which govern the individual characteristics of the organism. There are 23 pairs of chromosomes in each human cell.

(i) Sex chromosomes

One pair is the sex chromosomes, which determine an individual's sexual characteristics. A normal female has sex chromosomes of a similar size which are referred to as XX (after their shape). A normal male's pair of sex chromosomes contains one of a different size and shape, so they are referred to as XY. At conception, a sperm and egg combine to form a single cell which develops into an embryo. Very rarely, an abnormal cell division takes place before conception so the resultant embryo will contain an unusual number of sex chromosomes.

Until 1961, studies were mostly concentrated on individuals with an XXY sex chromosome complement. This condition, known as Klinefelter's Syndrome, is claimed by some to be associated with small testes, sterility, mild retardation, alcoholism and homosexuality. Milder forms of this condition can be treated by male hormone replacement. More severe examples are found in hospitals. Then, in 1961 Sandberg *et al.* discovered cases of XYY sex chromosome constitution in their patients. Since the extra Y chromosome is a sign of extra 'maleness', speculation began to increase that a man with this complement might show greater signs of aggression and be more involved in violent crime. The first study designed to test this was conducted by Jacobs *et al.* (1965) at Carstairs maximum security hospital in Scotland. She found that twelve of the 196 men on the subnormal wing had chromosomal abnormalities, including seven with an XYY sex chromosome constitution. Two more XYY males were later found in the 119 men on the mental illness wing (Price *et al.* 1966). As estimates have placed the number of XYY males in the general population at no more than 1.5 per 1,000 (Shah and Roth 1974), this research suggested that they are more commonly found in institutions.

The most notable physical characteristic of XYY men is that they are extremely tall, with a mean height of 6 ft 1 in, compared with a mean height of the other patients of 5 ft 7 in. Other distinguishing factors are well-developed genitals and a tendency to mild acne. The increased likelihood of XYY men's being found in institutions is perhaps what encouraged Jacobs *et al.* to describe them as being dangerous and prone to violence. This view has come to enjoy a level of popular approval, fuelled by media reports of sensational crimes allegedly committed by XYY males. However, more recent research has cast considerable doubt on this view. A further study of the original group of XYY inmates at Carstairs hospital compared them with a group of chromosomally normal patients there (Price and Whatmore 1967). Not only did the control group have a higher average number of convictions, but 21.9 per cent of them were for offences against the person, compared with only 8.7 per cent of the convictions of the XYY inmates.

Given these figures, the question arises as to why XYY males are statistically over-represented in institutions. Hunter (1966) suggested that their considerable height and build might incline psychiatrists to recommend to courts that they should be confined in hospitals for the safety of the public. This tendency could be exacerbated by the apparent intellectual inferiority of XYY males. It is possible that some XYY males are confined in institutions for behaviour which would be unlikely to result in imprisonment for other males. There has also been a claim that chromosomal abnormalities are more likely to be found in lower-class families because of their more arduous living conditions, and that members of these families form the majority of inmates in almost any institution (Kessler and Moos 1970).

Witkin *et al.* (1976) attempted to resolve this matter. Having obtained blood samples from 4,591 men born in Copenhagen between 1944 and 1947, and at least 184 centimetres in height, they found twelve XYY and sixteen XXY men in the group. Five of the XYY males (41 per cent) and three of the XXY males (19 per cent) had been convicted of a crime, compared with 9.3 per cent of the ordinary XY males. However, the crimes of the XYY males were all minor property offences, and they were no more likely to commit crimes against the person than the normal XY males. Witkin *et al.* did not find any support for the argument that class or height might account for the statistical over-representation of XYY males in institutions, but they did discover evidence suggesting that their mild degree of mental retardation could be a significant factor. However, in a review of the Witkin research, Theilgard (1983) argued that the behavioural differences between the XYYs and the controls were small, and that there was little support for the view that XYY males are particularly aggressive. Chorover (1979) has estimated that 96 per cent of XYY males lead ordinary lives.

The conclusion, therefore, must be that a study of XYY males does not in itself provide strong evidence of genetic transmission of violent or anti-social behavioural tendencies. Even if it did, it would not offer a significant explanation of criminality, given the extremely small number of men born with this particular chromosomal abnormality.

It is widely accepted that many children who are abused—especially boys—will become delinquent or adult criminals. Research has shown that maltreatment in early life can have a lasting neurochemical impact (De Bellis 2001). However, the fact that most such children do not take this path appeared to preclude a straightforward biological explanation. This view has changed with the publication of findings from the Dunedin Multidisciplinary Health and Development Study (Caspi *et al.* 2002). Based on a long-term study of 442 New Zealand men born in 1972, the researchers' conclusions showed that those who were abused as children and became criminal or anti-social adults were very likely to have a particular gene variant on their X chromosome. The gene is responsible for making an enzyme, monoamine oxidase (MAOA), which breaks down certain brain chemicals linked to displays of aggression. Men with a 'low activity' version of the gene were highly prone to react badly to childhood abuse; they were nine times more likely to indulge in anti-social behaviour such as fighting than those with a 'high activity' version. The fact that the gene is on the X chromosome—of which men have one but women two—could explain why women are less likely to behave in an anti-social way, as they have an increased chance of possessing at least one 'high activity' version of the gene.

(ii) Other chromosomes

Smalley *et al.* (2002) collected clinical, cognitive and genetic data from 203 families where there were at least two children suffering from Attention Deficit Hyperactivity Disorder (ADHD), a condition which can lead to anti-social behaviour. They discovered that there was a particular area of chromosome 16 (covering between 100 and 150 genes) which showed evidence of a 'risk gene' shared by the siblings, at a higher rate than the 50 per cent that would be expected from their degree of relationship. This gene could contribute as much as 30 per cent of the underlying genetic cause of ADHD.

Biochemical factors

Interest in the chemical structure of the human body began to develop around the middle of the nineteenth century when the secretions of the endocrine glands (hormones) started to be identified. It was later discovered that some of these secretions could be synthetically produced in laboratories, providing the same effects as the functioning of the real glands. Speculation began to increase about the consequences of hormonal imbalance on human behaviour. In 1928 Max G Schlapp and Edward H Smith published a book entitled *The New Criminology* (not to be confused with the book of the same name by Taylor *et al.* 1973), which claimed that crime resulted from emotional disturbance caused by hormonal imbalance. The authors, however, produced no clear evidence for this, simply assuming that some general findings from biochemistry would be directly applicable to criminal behaviour.

A more scientific approach was adopted by Louis Berman (1921 and 1938), who conducted biochemical research on a group of 250 inmates of New York state prison, with a control group of 250 non-criminal males from New York City. He discovered that the prisoners revealed a rate of glandular defects and disturbances two to three times greater than in the control group. The study also included a comparison between a group of juvenile delinquents and a group of non-delinquents, and this showed similar results. However, Berman did not provide any information on how the study was conducted and later researchers, such as Shah and Roth (1974), have failed to find evidence to support his conclusions.

(a) Neurotransmitters

Current research into biology and crime is concentrating on the role played by neurotransmitters. These are chemicals through which the electrical impulses within the brain pass. As this is the process by which the brain deals with information, neurotransmitters are of fundamental importance in the origins of all human behaviour. Evidence began to emerge suggesting that the levels of three particular neurotransmitters may be related to anti-social behaviour, particularly involving violence. The studies were analysed by Raine (1993). His main finding was that people prone to such behaviour have lower levels of the neurotransmitter serotonin than other people. Virkkunen and Linnoila (1993) have also identified a relationship between impulsive violent behaviour and considerably lower levels of sero-tonin than are found in non-violent people.

(b) Hormones

While neurotransmitters, which are very fast messengers, only work within the brain and spinal chord, hormones, which operate much more slowly, are chemical messengers which are distributed through-out the whole body. Biochemical research has indicated that an imbalance in hormonal levels may have adverse consequences on human behaviour.

(i) Pre-menstrual tension

Attention has been focused on the time of menstruation, when there is a wide variation in hormonal levels. Dalton (1961) found that, in a sample of 156 female prisoners who had offended during the twenty-eight days before their interview, 49 per cent had committed their crime during the eight days before or during menstruation, whereas the figure expected by chance was 29 per cent. The highest percentage was among those claiming to be suffering from pre-menstrual tension (PMT), a condition associated with symptoms such as tiredness, depression, irritability and headaches (Dalton, with Holton 1999). Although Fishbein (1992), after studying the research findings, con-cluded that a small percentage of women become more hostile during fluctuation in their hormonal levels, Dougherty et al. (1998) could find no support for an association between the menstrual cycle and aggression in two groups of women. In any case, as Shah and Roth (1974) have pointed out, pre-menstrual or menstrual tension can hardly be said to 'cause' crime. It has been estimated that between 20 per cent and 40 per cent of women suffer from severe PMT symp-toms, but no-one has suggested that four out of ten women commit criminal offences as a direct consequence.

(ii) Testosterone

PMT is not allowed as a specific defence in English criminal courts, although it has been successfully raised in diminished responsibility cases and used as a mitigating factor in sentencing (Widom and Ames 1988). On the other hand, no such mitigation of sentence is generally permitted for men who have an unusually high level of the male sex hormone, testosterone. There is a widely-held belief that this is at least in part responsible for the fact that men commonly appear to be more aggressive than women. The argument then proceeds that some men have an abnormally high level of testosterone and are thus more likely to be involved in violent crimes such as rape and murder. Experiments have also shown that female monkeys implanted with testosterone act more aggressively and develop a greater interest in sex.

Although the testosterone hormone is present in males, there are always considerable difficulties in assuming that the results of research on animals are equally applicable to humans. The higher level of intelligence in humans enables environmental considerations to play a far more significant role in their behaviour. Nor do the studies on monkeys differentiate between forms of aggression. Many people who would never instigate an aggressive act would be prepared to use violence to protect themselves or their families. Humans can also use verbal aggression, a phenomenon which is difficult to measure in animals. There is also the possibility that certain forms of aggressive behaviour may lead to an increase in testosterone levels (Brain 1994).

Olweus (1987) studied the effects of testosterone on a group of young men. He found a distinction between provoked aggressive conduct—which was usually a verbal response to another's threatening behaviour—and unprovoked aggressive conduct. The provoked aggression appeared to be clearly related to the levels of testosterone, which suggests the additional requirement of a specific environmental setting. Olweus discovered another important factor—low frustration tolerance. This can be related to specific factors relevant to upbringing, such as parental (and particularly maternal) use and tolerance of aggression. In early childhood, low frustration tolerance does not seem to be related to aggressive behaviour, but the increased testosterone level resulting from the onset of puberty has a marked effect. Such boys become far more touchy and intolerant and consequently more easily provoked.

The findings of Schalling (1987) are broadly in agreement with those of Olweus. She too concluded that high testosterone levels in young men are related to verbal rather than physical aggression. Schalling equated the possession of a high testosterone level with an extrovert, active and care-free approach, thus depicting an individual who is easily bored, but also easily aroused to anger. Ellis and Coontz (1990) pointed out that the peak age for offending in males throughout almost the whole world corresponds to the time of highest testosterone levels. Given the wide range of cultures, this phenomenon cannot be explained by social and environmental factors. Ellis and Coontz claimed that high testosterone levels can account for both property offences and offences against the person.

In a study by van Goozen et al. (1994), observation was made of a group of female to male transsexuals, who required a large dose of male sex hormones as part of their sex change process. The researchers discovered that, although the androgens did increase anger prone-ness, they did not have a direct effect on aggression.

Raine (1993) has claimed that any association between increased testosterone level and violence does not prove the direction of a causal link: it may be the aggressive behaviour itself which causes the increase. Research by Bjorkqvist *et al.* (1994) found that, if individuals expect a substance to make them more aggressive, it generally has that effect, even when the substance is a placebo.

What of the common belief that links high testosterone levels with sexual offences? The evidence is only supportive in the most extreme cases; for example, Rada *et al.* (1983) found high levels in extremely violent rapists. Although this does not prove a causal connection, treatment is still administered to sex offenders in the form of drugs designed to suppress the effects of the hormone. It appears that the drugs, when administered in high doses, can be effective in the most severe cases, although Bradford (1985) discovered that their use did not influence non-sexual aggression. Mazur (1983) suggested that testosterone is more related to dominance than to aggression.

(iii) Adrenalin

Studies have also been carried out into the relationship between adrenalin and aggressive behaviour. Adrenalin—a word often heard in sports commentaries—is a hormone, the level of which is greatly increased when an individual feels under stress. This is reflected in cortical arousal, which is a psychological reaction, and is outwardly manifested by a moistening of the skin and a heightened level of alertness. Research has indicated that convicted offenders, when faced with the threat of pain, show fewer signs of stress and less cortical arousal than non-offenders (Hare 1982). Olweus (1986) dis-covered that aggressive behaviour on the part of persistent bullies was unaccompanied by an increase in adrenalin. He also found that adrenalin levels in conditions of mild stress were lower in non-anxious extroverts (see below) and individuals considered liable to unprovoked aggression. Magnusson (1988) reached a similar conclusion in a study of hyperactive boys.

These findings suggest that violent offenders may take stronger stimuli to arouse them than is required for other people. Mednick *et al.* (1982) claimed that violent offenders, once aroused, take longer to return to their normal levels of adrenalin. This was attributed to their greater difficulty in learning from unpleasant stimuli. It is possible that individuals who are not easily aroused quickly become bored and need to resort to particularly exciting activities. These need not necessarily involve crime—sport is an example of a legitimate outlet—but may well do so, particularly if there are unfavourable environmental or social conditions present. Perhaps this idea was behind the popular belief that potential or actual juvenile delinquents (often in deprived areas) should be encouraged to join boxing clubs or participate in 'outward bound' courses.

John Baldwin (1990) considered that cortical arousability together with other biological factors could provide at least part of the explanation as to why criminality peaks at a particular age. Young children are initially frightened by many stimuli which they come to accept and even enjoy as they grow older. As adolescents, they will seek out even stronger stimuli. At the same time, the children will be learning what forms of behaviour are acceptable in society. Baldwin thought that children feel a biological urge towards seeking ever greater forms of excitement, and are socialised to channel these desires into acceptable activities such as sport. By the time young people enter their twenties, they no longer have such an urge to seek new stimuli, and perhaps not even the fitness to engage in new types of activity. With increasing age, burglary may well be replaced by bowls (or beer, or both). Baldwin appears to have suggested that the production of adrenalin and level of arousal can be affected by environmental factors. If this were the case, it would diminish the argument that adrenalin is linked to crime and instead provide support for the view that both adrenalin and crime are linked to environmental factors.

(iv) Cortisol

McBurnett *et al.* (2000) claimed that violent behaviour in male children and adolescents may be associated with low saliva levels of the stress hormone cortisol. In clinical and peer evaluations of the behaviour of thirty-eight boys, the researchers found that those with low cortisol concentrations were identified as three times more likely to show aggressive symptoms.

In experiments using rats, Kruk *et al.* (2004) discovered that increasing the stress hormone corticosterone (which is similar to cortisol) reduced the threshold for aggression, and that aggression raised the level of corticosterone. This loop, if applicable to humans, could explain why an aggressive incident can so easily escalate and become difficult to stop.

(c) Nutrition and hypoglycaemia

Since the nineteenth century there have been suggestions that a tendency to anti-social behaviour can result from a biochemical imbalance arising from nutrition. There was little scientific basis for such assertions, with the exception of experiments on animals which, although supportive, seem even less relevant here than usual. However, it has been claimed recently that food additives (Bateman *et al.* 2004) and a generally unbalanced diet (Demmig-Adams and Adams 2002) can be related to hyperactivity in children, which in itself can lead to their engaging in delinquency. Similar claims have been made with regard to substances such as monosodium glutamate, caffeine and certain chemicals found in chocolate (Curran and Renzetti 2001). A shortage of vitamin B has also been associated with both crime and hyperactivity (Lesser 1980).

Gesch *et al.* (2002) looked at 230 young offenders held in custody over an eighteen-month period, and found that those who received a vitamin and mineral supplement were placed on governor's report for anti-social behaviour less often (with a reduction of 40 per cent for serious offences, including violence). In the Mauritius Child Health Project, Raine *et al.* (2003) found that children who were assigned to 'an enrichment programme' between the ages of three and five were less likely to have behaved anti-socially at seventeen and committed an offence at twenty-three than members of a control group who did not undertake the programme. In addition to physical exercise and special educational activities, the children subject to the programme were given a particularly nutritious diet. The most beneficial effects of the intervention were experienced by the children who had shown signs of malnutrition at the age of three.

Some research has linked violent behaviour to hypoglycaemia, or low blood sugar level. Virkkunen (1987) compared three groups: violent, anti-social men; violent men without other personality problems; and non-violent, non-criminal men. Each man was deprived of food and then given a dose of glucose. In the violent and anti-social group the blood glucose level became very low and remained that way for significantly longer than the smaller decreases experienced by the other two groups. Virkunnen has also found links between hypoglycaemia and other 'problem' areas, such as truancy, minor theft and large consumption of alcohol. Extensive alcoholic intake without food preceded criminal acts in many cases, and Virkunnen (1988) has speculated that such individuals may be particularly prone to enhanced insulin secretion.

(d) The environment

It has been suggested that there may be a relationship between high levels of lead and violent behaviour. A study of lead levels in bones by Needleman *et al.* (1996) found a significant correlation between the concentration of lead and violence. However, it is possible that such findings are influenced by environmental factors: the fact that higher levels of lead are found in boys than girls (Taylor 1991) could be explained by the fact that boys tend to play outside more frequently.

Central nervous system

The central nervous system is situated in the brain and spine, and concerns conscious thought and voluntary physical movements. Electrochemical processes in the brain can be measured with a device called an electroencephalograph or, as it is commonly referred to, EEG. It is claimed that this instrument can measure particular brain wave patterns which can be associated with abnormal behaviour. Many early EEG studies found that between 25 per cent and 50 per cent of offenders had abnormal brain patterns—even higher in cases of violence—as compared with between 5 per cent and 20 per cent of non-criminal subjects. However, these studies did not clarify whether offenders do not have fully-developed brains, or simply have a low level of cortical stimulation, which is unlikely to be aroused in an experimental setting.

Mednick *et al.* (1981) sought to answer this question. They took EEG recordings from a group of non-delinquent Danish boys aged between ten and thirteen. After six years, the EEGs of boys who had subsequently committed delinquent acts were compared with those of the boys who had not. The EEGs for the boys who had been arrested on two or more occasions revealed a large amount of slow brain wave activity. Mednick claimed that this provided support for the low cortical stimulation theory as opposed to the brain immaturity theory. Petersen *et al.* (1982) measured the EEGs of nearly 600 Swedish children under fifteen, both when they were asleep and when they awoke. Twelve years later about 10 per cent had at least one criminal conviction. It was found that the offenders had slower brain wave rhythms.

Volavka (1987) compared two pieces of research on brain wave patterns, one from Denmark and the other from Sweden. Both pieces of research showed a clear link between slow brain wave activity and property offences, thus challenging the earlier view that EEG abnormalities were specific to violent offenders. As the Swedish study had excluded anyone with head or brain damage, Volavka considered that there was more support for the low cortical stimulation hypothesis. On the other hand, a study by Hsu *et al.* (1985) found the same reduced brain wave activity in groups of delinquents and adolescent psychiatric patients. This suggests that EEG abnormalities may be related to an increased risk of social problems in general and not just to anti-social behaviour.

A study by Giancola and Zeichner (1994) found that a low score on a neuropsychological frontal lobe test predicted aggressiveness among seventy-two males. Using EEG recordings, Bauer and Hesselbrock (2002) discovered that parts of the pre-frontal brain concerned with decision-making, judgement and planning were different in a sample of teenagers with conduct problems.

Technological advances in recent years—particularly in the development of computers—have led to the introduction of what is called 'brain imaging'. It is claimed that this process can identify abnormalities in both the physical structure and working of the brain. Research using brain imaging has also supported the view that some violent and sex offenders may be suffering from some form of brain dysfunction (Raine 1993).

(a) Epilepsy

Another aspect of the operation of the central nervous system that has been studied in relation to criminality is epilepsy. About one-third of sufferers manifest psychological problems (Parsons and Hart 1984) which may reflect the stigmatising of their condition, and epilepsy is correlated with socio-economic status. However, neither of these facts establishes a link with crime. It has been estimated that about 0.5 per cent of the population suffer from epilepsy.

Lombroso, without the benefit of any research, considered there was a link between crime and epilepsy, and anyone who has witnessed an epileptic seizure will have noted the uncontrolled movement of limbs. This fuels the belief that violence can occur and, consequently, some people assume that epilepsy may be related to violent crime. Yet, manifestations of violence during epileptic seizures are very rare. Cases where crime has been related to an epileptic seizure are likely to have resulted from the state of confusion which can follow such attacks (Fenwick 1990). There is some evidence that epileptics are over-represented in prison populations; Whitman *et al.* (1984) found that 2.4 per cent of males admitted to an American prison had a history of seizures. However, such findings may in part be due to dubious claims made by defence lawyers in an attempt to mitigate punishment. In addition, Gunn and Fenton (1971) discovered that only thirteen of 187 offenders with epilepsy had committed their crimes near to a seizure.

Most research in this area has been conducted into temporal lobe epilepsy (TLE) or psychomotor seizures, which are less severe forms in which the subject does not lose consciousness, but acts in a mechanical fashion and experiences greater fear and anxiety. Although some of the research supports a link between epilepsy and crime, other studies have failed to find any connection (Shah and Roth 1974). It is therefore impossible to draw any firm conclusion on this question.

(b) Brain damage and dysfunction

A further area of central nervous system operation that could be associated with criminal behaviour concerns various forms of brain damage or dysfunction. In a review of the research and literature, Buikhuisen (1987) noted the common finding that delinquents performed worse in tests for such dysfunction than control groups of non-delinquents. The delinquents experienced problems in the comprehension and organisation of material, in recalling facts or events, and in maintaining concentration. Many of the problems were traced to the frontal lobes. This is the area of the brain that governs a person's assessment and organisation of action and reaction. Damage is likely to restrict the individual's ability to appraise actions and learn through experience. There may also be a tendency to impulsivity, a lack of self-control and an increased sensitivity to alcohol. Offenders who suffer from such problems are unlikely to plan their crimes in any great detail. They will not be affected by punishment and so are likely to become recidivists.

Best *et al.* (2002) have suggested that people who are prone to aggressive or violent outbursts as a result of suffering from Intermittent Explosive Disorder (IED) could be experiencing a mild form of brain dysfunction. The researchers studied twenty-four IED patients together with twenty-two control subjects. They were given a range of tests to evaluate functioning of the orbital/medial cortex circuit, which is linked to the processing of emotions and control of impulses. The IED subjects were more likely to make choices involving disadvantageous decisions. In facial recognition tests, they were poorer at recognising expressions of anger, disgust and surprise.

Some childhood behaviour disorders are thought to be caused by brain dysfunction resulting from complications in pregnancy, birth or early childhood. O'Connor *et al.* (2002) found that women who reported feeling extremely anxious half way through their pregnancy were more likely to give birth to children who suffered from behavioural or emotional problems. The researchers considered that the mother's anxiety might directly influence the brain development of the foetuses.

A mild form of dysfunction which has been discussed in recent years is attention deficit disorder. This is sometimes identified in conjunction with hyperactivity. The symptoms include behavioural problems and poor cognitive responses. Mannuzza *et al.* (1989) tested a sample for hyperactivity both in childhood and then again in young adulthood. They found that a significantly greater number of hyperactive children than controls had been arrested, convicted and imprisoned. However, the difference could be explained almost entirely by the presence of an anti-social conduct disorder in young adulthood; hyperactivity alone could not be held responsible for the later criminal behaviour.

In the Cambridge Study in Delinquent Development, Farrington *et al.* (1990) tested a cohort of males at regular intervals from the age of eight. Information was collected on attention deficit, hyperactivity, home background and delinquency. The researchers discovered that both attention deficit and behavioural problems were associated with high rates of offending. The problems from attention deficit could be linked to low IQ, an early record of delinquency, coming from a large family, and criminal parents. The behavioural problems were connected to deficient parenting. Nevertheless, Farrington *et al.* considered that the connection between attention deficit and crime was not necessarily a biological one; there were important environmental and social factors which could have been influential. Having conducted a meta-analysis of the research, Pratt *et al.* (2002) found a 'fairly strong' relationship between attention deficit hyperactivity disorder and delinquency.

Certain learning disabilities, allegedly arising from a dysfunction in the central nervous system, have also been linked to delinquency. The best-known of these disabilities is dyslexia (reading difficulties), but they also include problems with speech and arithmetic. There is a problem here in determining whether such disabilities arise as a result of biological or social factors. It is easy to see how children with learning disabilities could be perceived as being disruptive or lazy at school. Their inappropriate behaviour may also serve to alienate potential friends, with the result that they feel rejected and isolated. They may drop out of school and start to mix with other disaffected young people.

The US Law Enforcement Assistance Administration commissioned a report to review the literature on the relationship between learning disabilities and crime, and to make recommendations. Charles Murray (1976) found six empirical studies from which a calculation could be made of the level of learning disabilities among delinquents. Estimates ranged from 22 per cent to 90 per cent, the differences mostly reflecting a variety of definitions of learning disability. In two other studies identified by Murray, a comparison was made between institutionalised delinquent groups and non-delinquent groups on their performance in eighteen tasks related to learning disability. The non-delinquent groups clearly performed better in ten of the tasks and the delinquent groups did not significantly out-perform them in any of the others. Murray concluded that 'the evidence for a causal link is feeble' and attributed this to the poor design of many of the studies.

There is no suggestion in the research that brain dysfunction alone is responsible for criminality. The problem results largely from the lack of skills an affected individual will possess in a world which seems to grow more complex by the day. Two hundred years ago such a person would have generally encountered less frustration and, with the reduced opportunities for offending, would have come to the attention of the public far less frequently. However, in today's increasingly competitive society, there is a danger that a child with brain dysfunction will grow up with a poor self-image as a result of parental frustration and rejection at school. Delinquency may provide a means both to obtain stimulation and an enhanced self-esteem.

Autonomic nervous system

This is a part of the nervous system of all mammals that governs many of the body's involuntary functions. It prepares the body for maximum efficiency by adjusting the heart rate, controlling the flow of blood, regulating the temperature, increasing the respiratory rate and stimulating the sweat glands. These variations are most commonly recorded by a polygraph (lie-detector) which is able to record changes in the sweat glands and thus, according to its supporters, is able to tell whether the subject is lying. This is because most people have been conditioned to expect disapproval or punishment when they tell a lie, and so their heart and respiratory rates increase and the extra sweat they produce more easily conducts electricity in the skin. The polygraph then detects this.

The operation of the autonomic nervous system is an excellent indicator of a person's involuntary reaction to external events. It is also viewed by some people as a vital component in the social training of children. They are conditioned by their parents to expect punishment in certain situations and will feel anxiety if they seriously contemplate placing themselves in those situations. As this feeling of anxiety is a response of the autonomic nervous system, the ease with which a child will be socialised may depend partly on the functioning of the system. If the autonomic system is slow to activate, or to deactivate when circumstances change, then a child may prove difficult to socialise.

This question was discussed by Hans Eysenck (1964), who adopted Jung's notions of introversion and extroversion as the main features of the personality. (Eysenck's views are considered in greater detail in Chapter 16.) Introverts are cautious, serious, reliable, and more concerned with their own inner world. Extroverts are considered impulsive, care-free, spontaneous, and more concerned with the external world. Eysenck also employed Pavlov's ideas of excitation and inhibition. Excitation occurs when the stimulus has passed through the autonomic nervous system and registered in the cortex. This is an essential requirement for all learning and behaviour. Inhibition refers to the slowing down of conditionability after a period of time due to something akin to fatigue in the cortex. After a 'rest period', conditioning will resume at an even higher level. Eysenck thought that there is a connection between introversion/extroversion and excitation/inhibition. Introverts have higher levels of inhibition and/or lower levels of excitement; extroverts are the reverse. Introverts therefore have a greater fear of punishment; they experience considerable anxiety in such situations and seek to avoid them. Extroverts feel less anxiety because they are less sensitive to pain. They are also more likely to seek out prohibited activities in their quest for stimulation.

Autonomic nervous system functioning has also been studied by measuring some of the functions that are usually monitored by a lie detector. Mednick (1977) claimed that the rate at which anxiety in anticipation of a punishment is reduced following the removal of the threatening situation is of considerable importance, as fear reduction is the strongest reinforcer known to psychology. If fear disappears quickly, the individual is greatly reinforced for avoiding punishment and conditioning is far more likely to occur. Mednick considered that the rate at which fear disappears can be gauged by measuring the rate of skin conductance response (SCR) recovery between the peak and return to normal level. Having reviewed the research in this area, Siddle *et al.* (1976) concluded that offenders displayed significantly slower rates of SCR recovery than matched control groups. Raine (1993), while generally supporting this finding, has pointed out that there has been little research in the area since the early 1980s.

There is some evidence that delinquents have lower heart rates when under stress. In one study (Wadsworth 1976) pulse rates were recorded among a large sample of English schoolchildren while they waited for a medical check-up. Those who later became delinquent were found to have had a significantly lower pulse rate than the non-delinquents. Raine and Venables (1984) discovered that a group of adolescent boys manifesting anti-social behaviour had lower heart rates than controls, and Maliphant *et al.* (1990) found the same result in a group of primary school boys described as disruptive by their teachers. The argument is that low heart rate may be associated with low cortical arousal, which itself may be associated with delinquency. Nevertheless, as with nearly all these biological factors, the evidence makes it almost impossible to exclude totally the influence of environmental and social factors.

Alcohol and drugs

In terms of its psychopharmacological effects, alcohol is a drug, but its separate consideration here is in keeping with the approach adopted by most researchers.

(a) Alcohol

It used to be assumed that drinking loosens moral restraints and that people who drink lose personal control and are consequently liable to behave in an anti-social way. Therefore, when researchers first began to look at the relationship between alcohol and crime, they started from the widely-held view that the pharmacological effects of alcohol directly affect the brain in such a way as to loosen inhibitions. However, it now seems that the situation is not so straightforward. A large amount of empirical evidence shows that many offenders have been drinking at the time of the offence. This is particularly the case when the crime involved violence, although there is also evidence that considerable numbers of non-violent offenders claim to have been drinking before offending (Collins 1989). Rada (1975) discovered that half his sample of convicted rapists had been drinking when they offended. From an analysis of several studies, Collins (1986) concluded that prisoners with drinking problems had committed more assaults than those without such problems. In a study of homicides in Sweden, Lindqvist (1986) found that two-thirds of the offenders were intoxicated when they killed.

A survey by the US Department of Justice revealed that 64 per cent of state prisoners convicted of violent offences claimed that either they, their victims, or both, were under the influence of drugs or alcohol at the time of the offence (US Department of Justice 1990). The National Bureau of Economic Research has found a relationship between the price of alcohol and level of spousal assault in several American states (Markowitz 1999). An analysis of data from the 1989 British Crime Survey by Mott (1990) showed that young men who had been drinking heavily were more likely than moderate drinkers to be involved in offences of minor violence.

There are, however, difficulties in assuming a direct causal relationship between the use of alcohol and crime. Alcohol does not have the same pharmacological effect on everyone; factors such as body weight, build and even race can be important. For instance, Native Americans and Eskimos metabolise alcohol more slowly than whites. There is research suggesting that a proneness to become an alcoholic can be genetically transmitted (Goodwin *et al.* 1973). Any drug—including alcohol—can worsen psychological symptoms in individuals who are already mentally disturbed. The situation of people suffering from paranoia could deteriorate following the consumption of alcohol, and they may resort to violence in the belief that they are defending themselves against some imagined threat. In any assessment, it is necessary to make allowance for the lifestyles of heavy alcohol users, which may be of greater relevance to their criminal activity (Ramsay 1996). Troubled individuals may take to drinking to increase their feelings of power. Different drinking patterns can also affect the way people respond to alcohol. For example, America not only has a high level of alcohol consumption, but its citizens tend to drink heavily during short periods of time, whereas inhabitants of other countries (such as France) spread their alcohol intake more evenly throughout the course of a day (Bartol 1991). It must also be remembered that large amounts of alcohol are consumed by people (particularly in their own homes) who do not proceed to break the law at all. This only serves to emphasise the importance of situational factors in the development of criminal incidents. In a study of more than 30,000 male US Army soldiers, Bell *et al.* (2004) discovered that, although heavy drinking did increase the risk of spousal abuse, the abuse often continued after the level of drinking had reduced.

However, in a study of over 1,000 New Zealand young people from the ages of fifteen to twenty-one, Fergusson and Horwood (2000) found evidence of a causal connection between excessive use of alcohol and both violent and property crime, which was present even after the possible influence of other factors had been controlled.

It appears that victims of crime are also likely to have been drinking. In Britain, Gottfredson (1984) discovered that the chances of being victimised increased from 5 per cent among non-drinkers to 15 per cent among heavy drinkers. This remained the case when controls were introduced for age and area of residence, although the connection was strongest for the young. In research by Hodge (1993), two-thirds of a sample of assailants and 50 per cent of their victims said they had been drinking immediately before the offence. The 1996 British Crime Survey found that victims of domestic violence had far higher levels of alcohol consumption than non-victims (Mirrlees-Black 1999). An analysis of data from the 2000 British Crime Survey by Budd (2003) showed that people who drank on three or four days a week were at the greatest risk of being the victims of alcohol-related assault. It may be that offenders realise that people who have been drinking are easy targets. It is also possible that drinkers are less careful about protecting themselves from attack or have a greater tendency to promote arguments. However, an observation of 2,365 police–citizen encounters in America found clear evidence that suspects were considerably more likely than victims to be intoxicated (McClelland and Teplin 2001).

The clearest physiological effect of alcohol consumption is that it slows a person's reaction time. It has been claimed that this contributes to drinkers' experiencing difficulty in noticing inhibitory cues, thus increasing the likelihood of conflict (Pernanen 1991). High levels of alcohol intake are likely to exacerbate the problem and various studies have shown that significant levels of prisoners have a drink problem (for example, McMurran and Hollin 1989). Evidence suggests that alcohol users are more likely than other offenders to be arrested (Petersilia *et al.* 1978). This seems hardly surprising— inebriation is unlikely to assist a swift escape—but it should be remembered when research based on samples of convicted offenders is considered. Some offenders take alcohol before committing their crime to calm their nerves. A causal link between alcohol and crime is thus established but, being of an entirely voluntary nature, it is wholly different from that which is usually assumed. Coid (1982) has suggested that, rather than alcoholism being related to violence, some alcoholics suffer from a personality disorder which increases the likelihood of their acting aggressively.

There has been a growing realisation that factors other than the purely physiological effects of alcohol are important in influencing the behaviour of an individual who has been drinking. Laboratory experiments have shown that people act more aggressively when they think they have consumed alcohol, even though they have been given a placebo (Lang *et al.* 1975). Research also indicates that people's expectations greatly influence the effects of alcohol on aggressive behaviour (Koss and Gaines 1993). Social conventions can affect the way people act after drinking and this can vary among different societies (MacAndrew and Edgerton 1969): there are particular periods, such as festivals, when drinking is considered far more acceptable (and even encouraged) than others. On the basis of a study of group drinking in the Sydney area over a twelve-month period, Tomsen (1997) concluded that much of the violence he observed was related to the assertion of masculine identity and issues of male honour. In a study of the homicide rates of fourteen European countries between 1950 and 1995, Rossow (2001) discovered a relationship between the level of homicide and alcohol sales, particularly in northern Europe where cultural practices are more likely to include heavy drinking sessions. There is also a widespread belief, especially among people working in the criminal justice system, that some offenders use the fact they have been drinking as an excuse for their crimes.

(b) Drugs

Goldstein (1985) has suggested that there is a relationship between drugs and crime at three different levels: the psychopharmacological; the economic compulsive; and the systemic.

The 'psychopharmacological' level considers whether some people behave violently following the ingestion of certain substances. Some research indicates that, whereas the use of cannabis, amphetamines or hallucinogens (such as LSD) is not related to physical aggression, cocaine or opiate usage may result in violence in certain situations (Taylor and Hulsizer 1998). However, a study of 427 New York City male adolescents found that, although cocaine usage and crime rates were similarly high, the ingestion of cocaine was unrelated to any particular type of crime (Kang *et al.* 1994). Withdrawal symptoms from severely dependent drugs can involve an irritability which may result in attacks on treatment programme workers (Mednick *et al.* 1982). It is now generally believed that the psychopharmacological effects of alcohol are more likely to be related to violence than those of drugs (MacCoun *et al.* 2003).

Environmental factors cannot be ignored. Particular drugs gain reputations for having a certain type of impact, and the expectation accompanying their use may serve to enhance the perceived effect. A drug may be taken in order to provide courage to commit a crime, or even to furnish an excuse in the case of apprehension.

The 'economic compulsive' level suggests that some drug users commit crimes to obtain the funds to support their drug use. The difference here is that the crime is not a direct consequence of ingesting the drug, which is purely instrumental to a particular purpose. Heroin and cocaine users have been regarded as the most frequent offenders, as their drugs have traditionally been the most expensive. Violence is not inevitable: research by Johnson *et al.* (1985) into heroin addicts in Harlem found that they usually avoid it where other means are available, such as drug-selling, prostitution or theft. It also emerged that many of the victims were drug users themselves or involved in other illegal activities in the area. Parker and Bottomley (1996) discovered that most crack-cocaine and heroin users gained their income from acquisitive crime and their state benefits. On the other hand, findings from the 1998–99 Youth Lifestyles Survey (see Chapter 3) showed that most people who became drug users had a history of truancy or crime (Pudney 2002).

The third of Goldstein's levels is the 'systemic'. This views crime as an inevitable part of the pattern of distribution and use of illegal drugs. It will result from the operation of rivals; disputes over territory; problems arising from the supply of adulterated or imitation drugs; the failure to pay debts; and the entrepreneurial activities of street dealers lower down the supply chain. Such crimes can be traced at least as far back as the liquor rackets of Al Capone. However, the large increase in illicit drugs circulating in many major cities nowadays has caused a considerable escalation in these types of activity.

Even where a connection is suggested between crime and drug use, it does not necessarily mean that the two are causally related. In research for the Home Office, Mott and Taylor (1974) found that a high percentage of heroin users were already involved in criminal activities before they started taking drugs. Coid *et al.* (2000) also discovered that previous offending by members of a group of opiate users attending a clinic had not always been to fund their drug-taking. On the other hand, 42 per cent of a sample of arrestees who claimed to have used at least one drug during the previous twelve months believed that there was a connection between their drug use and crime. The reason most commonly mentioned was the need for money to purchase the drugs (Bennett 2000).

Conclusion

At the height of the popularity of deviance theory in the 1960s and 1970s, constitutional and biological explanations of crime were either dismissed as the most extreme form of the much-derided positivism, or held up to ridicule as merely variations on the more ludicrous of Lombroso's views. It may seem surprising to some that criminological books pay any attention at all to Lombroso and some of his immediate successors, but it is important to remember that they wrote on the basis of the state of scientific knowledge and research techniques at the time. It is difficult to imagine nowadays the impact that must have resulted from the publication of Darwin's works. Moreover, no-one has seriously suggested that these researchers were either acting in bad faith or shared the motivations of certain politicians, who clearly had an agenda of policies aimed at 'racial purity' such as mass sterilisation and, ultimately, genocide.

The views of writers such as Lombroso, Goring and Sheldon are easy to challenge on the grounds of fundamental methodological weaknesses, particularly in their use of unrepresentative samples and inadequate control groups. It is now widely accepted that there is no strong evidence linking the shape of a body with a propensity to criminality. In any case, what evidence exists tends to link size with acts of aggression. Most people are familiar with large youths throwing their weight around, but this may simply occur because the youths have discovered that they are physically strong enough to get away with it! Research on genetics has, to a large extent, replaced this approach. However, Troy Duster (2003) has cautioned against confusing the *behavioural* genetics applied in the twin and adoption studies with the *molecular* genetics which is nowadays causing so much excitement as a result of scientists' increasing ability to measure DNA. The former has largely been concerned with comparing the frequency of various forms of human behaviour between related members of different groups (such as offenders and non-offenders). The latter has considered biological factors—traditionally with a view to eradicating disease—and has not concerned itself with questions of complex behaviour. According to Duster, this division has begun to break down, and some molecular biologists have started to make claims which go beyond the scope of their enterprise. He has offered as an illustration the New Zealand research (discussed above) into the MAOA enzyme by Caspi *et al.* (2002), where definitions such as 'anti-social' and 'maltreatment' are not fully explored.

Bearing this proviso in mind, it is clear that research is increasingly pointing towards the importance of a combination of hereditary and socio-environmental features as predictors of anti-social behaviour. Much the same is true of hormonal and other biochemical research. The physical constitution appears to be a factor of some significance, but the level of significance is greatly enhanced when the environmental setting is considered (Fishbein 1990).

Even if the evidence clearly showed that constitutional or biological factors were significant in an individual's recourse to criminality, a difficult question would then arise: what should society do about it? Extreme measures would include lengthy or even unlimited periods of incarceration, sterilisation, or perhaps even some form of genetic engineering. To some extent, this has already happened in America. Between 1911 and 1930 over thirty states enacted laws which allowed for the sterilisation of individuals manifesting anti-social and undesirable traits which were thought to have been genetically transmitted. As a result, more than 64,000 people were sterilised (Beckwith 1985). This was still occurring in the 1970s: between 1927 and 1972 more than 8,000 people were sterilised in Virginia on the grounds of feeble-mindedness (Katz and Abel 1984). At one stage, thirty-four states forbade marriage between blacks and whites, and some also made it illegal for whites to marry orientals. The American state of Arkansas only voted to abolish the law forbidding inter-racial marriages in 2000 (although it had long since fallen into disuse). It has emerged that Sweden—a country hitherto regarded as particularly progressive over such issues—had a compulsory sterilisation policy as part of a 'social and racial hygiene programme' from 1921 to 1976 (*The Guardian*, 6 March 1999). There were about 63,000 victims.

There has been a long-running debate on whether it is justifiable to lock up potentially dangerous offenders for a longer period than would be justified by their criminal record. This is technically possible for crimes where the indeterminate sentence of life imprisonment is available, such as rape or murder, but this basis of sentencing does not have the approval of the Court of Appeal. However, not only is there disagreement over what constitutes 'dangerous' criminal propensities (Floud and Young 1981) but, even if defined, it is highly unlikely that society could find a reliable method of predicting them. In recent years, there has been growing alarm at the release of paedophiles who, as a group, are statistically very likely to reoffend. So far, the response has been limited to compiling a register of their addresses, to which interested parties are given access (see Chapter 9).

It has also been suggested that people who are considered to pose a threat of dangerous behaviour should be incarcerated, even if they have not committed a crime. A report in 2002 by the Nuffield Council on Bioethics recommended that the predictive use of genetic information used in isolation in the case of people who had not acted in an anti-social manner would be unjustified because of its unreliability.

Less extreme forms of intervention could include drug therapy. Leaving aside the ethical considerations in making such intervention compulsory, there is the additional question of whether such drastic courses of action are called for when, in relation to both a link between biology and crime and the efficacy of such treatments, the evidence is inconclusive. However, it is arguable that such courses of action are unnecessary. If the evidence set out in this chapter that constitutional and biological factors are far more significant in particular environmental settings were accepted, then steps could be taken to identify types of social intervention which might help to lessen the effects of the physical problems.

15

Intelligence, mental disorder and crime

In the previous chapter there was discussion of possible physiological influences in criminal behaviour. In this perspective, a person's conduct is affected, at least in part, by some physiological or organic problem, such as a genetic predisposition or a biochemical imbalance. In contrast, the idea behind the concept of mental disorder is that the underlying causes are not physical in nature, but are due to the workings of the 'mind'. This will be addressed later in the chapter. First, however, consideration will be given to whether differences in individuals' cognitive capacity—or, as it is usually called, intelligence—can have any bearing on the likelihood of their acting in an anti-social manner.

Intelligence and crime

(a) Background

Among the first objective tests of human intelligence were those devised by Francis Galton between 1860 and 1880 and the German, H Ebinghaus. The latter's important development in 1880 was to create a way of recording a person's ability to memorise on a numerical scale. However, tests such as these never progressed beyond the science laboratory and came to be replaced with one created at the Sorbonne in Paris in 1905 by a psychologist, Alfred Binet. He had developed his test on Parisian schoolchildren and it was designed to identify those who required special assistance. In a 1908 revision, Binet and Theodore Simon related each task in the test to a 'mental age': the harder the tasks performed, the higher the mental age of the individual. In view of later controversies surrounding intelligence testing, it is worth noting that Binet thought his test was inappropriate to measure high intelligence among children. Indeed, he was concerned that such an enterprise would only prove to be at the expense of helping slower children. Binet also considered that intelligence is not a fixed entity, but can be increased through teaching.

After a series of revisions, Binet's test was taken up in the USA during the early years of the twentieth century and soon became very popular. Lewis M Terman of Stanford University published the most widely-used version, the 'Stanford Revision and Extension of the Binet Scale'. This extended Binet's fifty-four tests, arranged in order of difficulty, to ninety. Terman (1916) and other American psychologists clearly thought that intelligence is a fixed entity and should be measured, partly to indicate those who are 'feeble-minded', who can then be isolated (or, perhaps, sterilised), and partly to predict who will perform best in the educational system. Tests were administered to reformatory inmates by Henry H Goddard (1914). As they appeared to show that about half the offenders were feeble-minded, it was not surprising that the assumption grew that low intelligence directly contributes to criminal behaviour. However, the crudeness of this test was later revealed when Carl Murchison (1926) demonstrated that inmates of an American prison had a higher IQ than men enlisted during World War I. This was clearly unacceptable to the military leaders. The pass mark was revised downwards and the revision was maintained in the testing of civilians. Such modifications to the IQ test, including the standardisation of an IQ score of seventy, as the 'cut off' point (the score for the 'average' person is taken as 100), soon led to a reduction in the number of people categorised as what is now termed 'mentally handicapped'.

The legal classification of such individuals in England and Wales is now found in section 1 of the Mental Health Act 1983. The terminology defines mentally handicapped individuals as suffering from a state of arrested or incomplete development of the mind, which includes (severe) impairment of intelligence and social functioning, and is associated with abnormally aggressive or seriously irresponsible conduct on the individual's part. The purpose of this definition is that such a finding in either a civil application or a criminal case enables a court to make one of several orders, including a supervision order or a committal to a hospital. The corresponding provision in the previous law, the Mental Health Act 1959, referred to subnormality and severe subnormality, which included people of low intelligence who were considered unable to look after themselves outside an institution. The present law seems to place a greater emphasis on potential harm to others, and thus strengthens the link between low intelligence and crime. However, despite the use of the word intelligence in these provisions, there has never been any requirement under the law that the use of IQ tests should be a necessary condition for the establishment of this (or any other) mental condition.

(b) Intelligence and crime

In a 1931 article Edwin Sutherland predicted that, as the differences in IQ scores between criminals and the general public were diminishing with the improvement of testing procedures, it was only a matter of time before remaining differences disappeared altogether. According to Herrnstein and Murray (1994), this proved to be 'an article that effectively put an end to the study of IQ and crime for half a century'. The issue was not fully resurrected until an article by Hirschi and Hindelang in 1977. Having reviewed a number of studies comparing delinquents with non-delinquents, they found that the average IQ of juvenile delinquents was about ninety-two (eight points below the mean) and that this did not significantly vary in relation to race or social class. Hirschi and Hindelang accepted that IQ is not entirely related to heredity and may be influenced by environmental factors. They considered that IQ had been ignored in criminology partly because of its treatment by early writers such as Goddard (see above), and partly because of the growing influence of sociologists, who wished to emphasise the significance of social, rather than individual, factors in the causation of crime.

There is also some evidence that, not only is there an IQ gap between offenders and non-offenders, but that a disproportionate amount of crime is committed by people at the lower end of the intelligence scale. In a twenty-year longitudinal study of more than 500 boys in Sweden, Reichel and Magnusson (1988) discovered that 30 per cent of those arrested by the age of thirty were from the 6 per cent whose IQ was below seventy-seven. Further support for the link between intelligence and crime has come from the Cambridge Study in Delinquent Development (West 1982). This found that 39 per cent of those who became delinquent had an IQ of less than ninety at the age of eight, compared with only 22 per cent of the non-delinquents. The fact that the study also discovered a correlation between self-reported delinquency and low IQ is evidence that the relationship does not merely result from the inability of less intelligent offenders to avoid detection.

It is important to distinguish standard IQ testing devices from tests for social functioning. For example, Denkowski and Denkowski (1985) found that about 2.5 per cent of the prison population in twenty American states had an IQ score lower than seventy. However, in the five states where mental handicap was measured by a combination of both IQ and social functioning tests, the percentage of inmates suffering from a mental handicap was lower, and in line with the level of mental handicap found in the population as a whole.

Nowadays, IQ is measurable on both verbal and performance tests and the gap between delinquents and non-delinquents appears to be far greater on the verbal measurements. Quay (1987) has estimated that about two-thirds of delinquents are deficient in verbal ability. He considered that this may be a direct cause of anti-social behaviour in situations of conflict. However, other psychologists take the view that an indirect relationship is more likely. For example, Hirschi and Hindelang (1977) suggested that such verbal difficulties will have a marked effect on school performance. Failure at school can lead to the adoption of alternative, perhaps criminal, methods to obtain success. The implication of this view is that a low IQ will not be correlated with adult criminality. On the other hand, McMichael (1979) thought that anti-social behaviour at school precedes, rather than follows, reading difficulties. Support for this opinion came from a study by Richman *et al.* (1982), which found that a link between low IQ and behavioural problems existed in three-year-olds. Moreover, a longitudinal study by Tremblay *et al.* (1992) discovered that academic achievement was not a significant factor in later delinquency.

Findings from the Mauritius Child Health Project (see Chapter 14) have shown that poor nutrition in early childhood was related to both lower IQ ratings and an increased likelihood of anti-social behaviour at the age of 17 (Liu *et al.* 2004).

Some types of crime, such as white-collar and corporate offending, may require a higher than average IQ level, particularly on the verbal tests. Relatively little research has been conducted into this, but a Danish study by Kandel *et al.* (1988) of 1,500 boys born in Copenhagen between 1936 and 1938 discovered that men who had a father with a prison record, and who were therefore themselves considered at great risk of becoming career criminals, were able to avoid criminal convictions if they had a high IQ. No significant correlation was found in the study between IQ and socio-economic status. A study by Sutton *et al.* (1999) into bullying in English primary schools found that the bullies scored higher in social cognition tests than their 'followers', victims and defenders of the victims.

It is apparent from the research that, even allowing for methodological shortcomings, there is still a small, but clear, correlation between IQ ratings and juvenile delinquency. The real argument seems to be over what IQ tests actually measure.

(c) Race, intelligence and crime

A controversial and often heated argument has continued (particularly in America) for more than thirty years about the possible relationship between race, intelligence and crime. Studies suggest that, on average, whites have an IQ score about fifteen points higher than blacks, and East Asians (Chinese, Japanese and Koreans) obtain a score which is slightly higher still (Herrnstein and Murray 1994). Some writers have sought to use this finding to explain why blacks are over-represented in crime statistics in proportion to their numbers in the population. The problems with official criminal statistics have already been considered (see Chapter 3), but the figures—especially in America—are particularly striking. In that country, homicide is the main cause of death among black youths; blacks account for one-third of all arrests and one-half of all imprisonments; and about one-fifth of black males aged sixteen to thirty-four are subject to some form of supervision (Hagan and Peterson 1994).

In 1967, a Nobel Prize winner, William Shockley, suggested that the difference in IQ levels between blacks and whites should be investigated to see if it had any connection with poverty and crime levels. His challenge was taken up by Arthur Jensen (1969), who claimed that remedial education programmes were destined to fail as about 80 per cent of individual differences on IQ scores were caused by genetic rather than environmental factors. From this, Robert Gordon (1976) proceeded to argue that variations in delinquency rates can best be accounted for by considering IQ scores. He agreed with Jensen that IQ is largely determined by biological factors. Gordon thought that the increasing spread of urban development does not cause delinquency. In cities with populations over a certain size (Gordon claimed 44,000 inhabitants), delinquency rates stay fairly constant for both black and white offenders. However, the rates for blacks are consistently higher than those for whites. For Gordon, therefore, the extensive amount of crime in large cities can be explained by the high proportion of blacks who live there rather than by any environmental factors. He claimed that levels of delinquency among other racial groups are also related to IQ. Chinese, Japanese and Jews, who are said to have higher IQs than whites, commit relatively little crime despite their minority position in Western societies.

The principal criticism that has been made of Gordon's analysis concerns the fundamental question surrounding the whole idea of IQ testing: what is meant by intelligence? Supporters of the tests argue that they provide a valid indicator of intelligence based on an ability to solve abstract problems. Their opponents deny this and assert that IQ is not a valid test of any ability, but a measure of certain qualities which are determined by the dominant culture (Mercer 1972). In North America and Europe this is the white middle class. Alternatively, IQ tests may assess ability but, contrary to the view of Gordon, this may not be genetically determined but instead result from an individual's environment.

Loehlin et al. (1975) tested the IQs of a group of white children living in a deprived area and compared them with those of a matched black group living in a similar area. The differences in IQ scores were small and, according to the researchers, could be explained by the discrimination suffered by the black children. Simons (1978) identified studies of twins brought up separately in different environments who had been measured as having different IQs. He claimed that the questions on verbal intelligence tests were very similar to those used in tests of reading comprehension, and that such tests showed that middle-class black children increased their reading comprehension scores far more than lower-class black children. Simons argued that this suggests that the lower-class children are held back more by their experience at school than by their intelligence. A study of three special pre-school education schemes revealed that the mean IQ of the children rose during the first year of the programme from seventy-eight to 105 (Schweinhart et al. 1986).

Further support for Simons's argument has come in a report for the Office for Standards in Education (OFSTED) which revealed that one English local education authority found Afro-Caribbean students starting school as the highest achieving group, but leaving as the group least likely to have obtained five good GCSE passes (Gillborn and Safia Mirza 2000).

As the heritability of intelligence has been at the heart of the controversy over IQ testing, the question assumes a considerable importance. Hirschi and Hindelang (1977) admitted that environmental factors could be relevant in determining the level of IQ. Even such enthusiastic supporters of IQ testing as Herrnstein and Murray (1994), in conceding that the gap between blacks and whites is very gradually narrowing, said that this is because of improvements in the provision of education and social facilities for blacks. These authors considered that, on an optimum projection, the SAT scores (American school 'aptitude' or intelligence tests) of blacks and whites could fully converge 'sometime in the middle of the twenty-first century'. The American Psychological Association (Neisser et al. 1996) has also stated that there is a continuing narrowing of the IQ gap between different races and social classes. Between 1942 and 2002, the average IQ test score in the UK rose by 27 points. This is too short a period for the increase to be attributed solely to genetic factors.

Gould (1997) criticised writers who contend that there is a fixed, measurable notion of intelligence which is transmitted through generations in some immutable form, and can be used to rank individuals. He pointed out that the difference between heritability and inevitability is often overlooked: 'Millions of Americans see normally through lenses that correct innate deficiencies of vision'. Gould also highlighted the fallacy of assuming that, just because heredity can explain a certain variation among individuals within a group, it can also account for differences between different groups—for example, between whites and blacks. Dickens and Flynn (2001) have argued that people's IQs are influenced by those of others with whom they come into contact.

The term 'race' has also come to be viewed as problematic. As work continues on the Human Genome Project, it is increasingly clear that, in common usage, 'race' is a socio-political construct relating more to physical appearance and cultural identity than to similarity in genetic structure (Keita *et al.* 2004). For example, people with an African ancestry are likely to have a greater genetic variation among themselves than they have with people from a European lineage.

Moreover, it is usually members of immigrant and minority populations—as opposed to any one racial group—who are over-represented in measurements of delinquency (Tonry 1997). Perhaps the best known exposition of this was by the Chicago Ecologists (see Chapter 6). Writers such as Shaw and McKay (1942) showed that in Chicago it was the people who lived in the 'zone of transition' who were the most frequent offenders. From the early days of Chicago, the Polish and Italians came to replace the Germans and Irish in this area, and they in turn were replaced by blacks and Hispanics. It was the location that was said to determine the level of offending and, as a generation of immigrants became more established, it would generally move out to the suburbs to be replaced by a new wave. In the 1920s, concern that the overall IQ level of Americans would be diminished by the continued immigration of 'inferior' Southern and Eastern Europeans was fuelled by several studies which showed Italian-American children as having an IQ averaging sixteen points below the American average (Pinter 1923). This was partly responsible for the enactment of the Immigration Restriction Act 1924, which was designed to restrict the flow of such people into the country.

(d) Conclusion

It seems undeniable that there are—and probably always have been—people who are considered 'cleverer', 'sharper' or 'quicker' than others and, correspondingly, people who appear 'duller', 'dimmer' or 'slower'. The suggestion that this latter group may commit more offences than the former is hardly a surprising one and could be explained on several grounds. However, the claim that these characteristics can be measured; that they are largely (if not entirely) inherited; and that they are more likely to appear in certain racial groupings was always likely to be controversial.

On this analysis, once blacks and Hispanics—who seem to have replaced Irish and Italians as the 'troublesome' people of America—are fully integrated into that society, they should cease to dominate the crime rates as they do at present. The same result should also eventually occur in Britain, where widespread immigration is still a relatively recent phenomenon, dating back only about half a century.

Mental disorder and crime

Any consideration of 'disorders of the mind' begs the question as to what is meant by 'mind'. This is a problem which philosophers have considered for centuries. Although the study of physiological disease may sometimes appear imprecise, it is generally possible to locate a physical cause. The mind, however, cannot be studied in this way. Ultimately, the attribution of mental disorder is a subjective assessment, although one which nowadays is, in most countries, made within a given structure of medical and legal definitions.

This conceptual uncertainty surrounding mental disorder was partly responsible for the development of the 'anti-psychiatry' movement revolving around Laing (1967) and Szasz (1961, 1970). These writers tried to shift the debate away from psychiatric assessment into the area of social control and the potential dangers of attributing the label 'mad'. Writers such as Szasz were also concerned about the classification of particular mental states as 'illnesses', on the basis that this implied distinct forms of cerebral pathology and recognised forms of treatment. This is one of the reasons why 'disorder' is now the preferred generic term in psychiatry.

For centuries, people have associated mental disorder with crime and, in particular, violent crime. This view is still propagated by the media. Taylor (1993a) mentioned two pieces of American research: one indicated that, in prime time American television, the mentally disordered are portrayed as violent almost twice as often as the mentally healthy; and the other showed that 86 per cent of all newspaper stories about former mental patients are based on their having committed a violent crime.

The current legal definitions of mental disorder are contained in the Mental Health Act 1983. The Act is broadly divided into two parts. The first provides measures to deal with individuals duly certified as suffering from a mental disorder who have not been convicted of an offence (that is civil cases). The second concerns measures which may be ordered by a criminal court in relation to a mentally disordered individual who has been convicted of a criminal offence (other than murder, which carries a mandatory sentence of life imprisonment). There is an overlap between some of the orders a court can make in civil and criminal cases, such as the hospital order. There are also legal defences to criminal charges—such as insanity or diminished responsibility—which, if successful, will either remove or reduce actual liability for the crime (although, paradoxically, a finding of 'not guilty by reason of insanity' can still lead to a medical disposition). These issues are outside the scope of this book, although it is important to note that the vast majority of mentally disordered offenders are considered legally responsible for their crimes.

Is there a relationship between crime and mental disorder? Some early criminologists, particularly in Britain, took the view that crime itself is a symptom of mental disorder. The problem with this assessment is that, because most people commit crimes at some point in their life, this is tantamount to claiming that most of the population is psychologically disturbed. Alternatively, it may be the case that some offenders are mentally disordered—just as some non-offenders are—and there is no causal relationship.

Evidence has been found that people who are mentally ill are at greater risk of arrest. In an American study, Teplin (1984, 1985) observed 1,382 encounters between police and citizens. Of the 506 persons suspected of a crime, thirty manifested signs of mental illness and a significantly higher proportion of these was arrested than other suspects (47 per cent against 28 per cent). The crimes they were suspected of having committed were not particularly different from those of other suspects. A bias towards arresting the mentally ill was therefore indicated, either because of the lack of alternative dispositions or because they acted disrespectfully towards the police (what Reiner (2000) has referred to as 'contempt of cop'). The research, however, did not suggest that the mentally ill are more prone to criminal behaviour. In an extensive review of recent studies, Bonta *et al.* (1998) claimed that mentally disordered offenders were no more likely to commit crimes than offenders without a mental disorder. It must also be remembered that Britain and many other countries nowadays allow people to live in the community, whose mental disorder is such that, less than fifty years ago, they would have been detained in hospital. It is, therefore, hardly surprising that such people feature more prominently in criminal statistics.

In attempting to investigate a link between crime and mental disorder, consideration can be given both to the level of mental disorder in a population of known criminals and to the level of criminal behaviour among psychiatric patients.

(a) Mental disorder in criminals

Most studies of 'known criminals' have been based on prison populations. Coid (1984) could identify only two studies of court samples, both from America, and the more recent one as long ago as the 1940s. They indicated relatively low rates of disorder, although the criteria employed were considerably narrower than those used nowadays. Many disordered offenders are filtered out of the criminal justice system at an early stage.

Although the figures from different studies vary, it is clear that psychological problems are common in prison populations. Gunn *et al.* (1991) surveyed a 5 per cent random sample of sentenced male prisoners in England serving six months or more. They found that 37 per cent were suffering from some sort of psychological disorder, although this term was very widely defined. Of this figure, 2 per cent were described as psychotic. This research was essentially a rerun of an earlier project (Gunn *et al.* 1978) which had found similar percentages—31 per cent and 2 per cent, respectively. It is estimated that about 14 per cent of the general population consult their doctors about psychological problems. The 1991 study revealed fairly high percentages of alcohol and drug abuse, and the status of these conditions as mental disorders is controversial in psychiatry. On the other hand, in a study of both male and female life-sentence inmates in London prisons, Pamela Taylor (1986) discovered that up to 10 per cent were psychotic, most of whom suffered from schizophrenia. Teplin (1990) claimed that studies indicated a level of severe mental illness in the prison population of between 4 per cent and 12 per cent.

In a study of remand prisoners at Durham prison, Birmingham *et al.*

(1996) found that 26 per cent suffered from one or more current mental disorders, excluding substance abuse. Of this total, 4 per cent were diagnosed as psychotic. Brooke *et al.* (1996) studied remand prisoners in thirteen adult prisons and three young offender institutions in England. This sample represented 9.4 per cent of the male unsentenced population. Although there was a high rate of refusal to cooperate (18 per cent), the researchers discovered that 63 per cent were suffering from some form of psychological disorder, including substance abuse. The figure of 5 per cent diagnosed as psychotic was estimated at between four and five times the level found in the general population. Singleton *et al.* (1998) also discovered evidence of extensive mental disorder in a large sample of inmates from the entire prison population. Clinical assessment showed that 63 per cent of male remand prisoners had an anti-social personality disorder, and 14 per cent of female prisoners were psychotic. A similar situation can be found in other countries. Fazel and Danesh (2002) looked at sixty-two surveys of unselected prison populations which included diagnoses of mental disorders. These showed that 3.7 per cent of men had psychotic illnesses, 10 per cent suffered from major depression, and 65 per cent had a personality disorder. Gosden *et al.* (2003) found that 69 per cent of a sample of male adolescent remand prisoners in Denmark had suffered from a mental disorder during the previous twelve months.

These figures might even be an underestimate. Birmingham *et al.* (2000) found that the routine health screening on reception into prison often failed to detect mental disorder.

Nevertheless, such findings do not provide conclusive proof of a link between mental disorder and crime. Other explanations are possible: for example, mentally disordered offenders may simply be more inept in their criminality, and thus are more likely to be caught; the police may have a greater inclination to charge such people, as they consider a conviction to be the best guarantee of their obtaining treatment; or guilty pleas may be more common, again with a view to obtaining treatment (Feldman 1977). It might also be the case that the mental disorder developed subsequent to the offending, perhaps even as a result of conditions in prison (Wormith 1984).

(b) Criminal behaviour in mentally disordered populations

An alternative way of investigating a link between crime and mental disorder is to look at the crime rate among psychiatric patients. Brennan *et al.* (2000) discovered that the major mental disorders in a sample drawn from a Danish birth cohort were related to a greater likelihood of arrest for violence. A number of studies have shown that the chance of such people offending on release from hospital is significantly related to their arrest record prior to entry. In a nineteen-month follow-up study of discharged patients, Steadman *et al.* (1978) found that those whose arrest rates after release were higher than those of the general population had a significant history of earlier arrests. In contrast, those patients who had not previously been arrested had lower arrest rates following release than the population at large. The authors concluded that offending by psychiatric patients is more related to the factors which serve as general predictors of crime—such as age, gender, ethnicity and class—than to any form of mental disorder. However, it is unclear to what extent the individuals in their sample were still affected by their earlier condition on release. Toch and Adams (1989) discovered that the previous offences of mentally disordered prisoners usually occurred at times when they were suffering considerable psychological disturbance.

Attention has usually been focused on the relationship between mental disorder and violent crime, and relatively little research has been conducted into other offences. Among the minority of mentally disordered offenders convicted of shoplifting, there is an over-representation of depressives (Gibbens 1981). Taylor and Gunn (1984) discovered that over 60 per cent of remand prisoners either charged with or convicted of arson or criminal damage showed symptoms of mental disorder; in half the cases a psychosis was suggested.

The relationship between mental disorder and dangerousness was promoted by nineteenth century psychiatrists to account for serious crimes for which they could find no obvious reason (Foucault 1978). Although the study of psychiatry has drastically changed over a century, there is still a view among sections of the public that the mentally disordered are particularly prone to acts of violence. To what extent does the evidence support this belief?

Information from the Criminal Statistics suggests that about a fifth of the people found to have killed unlawfully in England and Wales successfully plead diminished responsibility and are therefore convicted of manslaughter. However, this is an unreliable indicator of mental disorder among killers, as there are several factors (including plea bargaining) which may underlie such a finding. The legal defence of insanity, dating from 1843, is hardly ever used and bears little relationship to modern concepts of mental disorder. In a study of remand prisoners either charged with or convicted of a homicide offence, Taylor and Gunn (1984) found that 9.3 per cent showed symptoms of schizophrenia, 1.9 per cent of affective psychosis, and 26 per cent of 'mixed disorders'. This finding, which was similar to that of Häfner and Böker's 1982 German research, suggests that schizophrenia is the form of mental disorder most clearly connected with serious violence, although still—it should be emphasised—to a very small degree (about 0.05 per cent of schizophrenics).

There is also evidence that people considered to be suffering from psychopathic disorder are prone to violence. The main problem with this finding is in the very classification of psychopathy itself: it is a circular definition which is to a large extent based on a tendency to violent outbursts. Black and Spinks (1985) discovered that psychopaths are likely to commit more violent crimes after their release than those classified as mentally ill, but that the association largely disappeared when previous offending was taken into account. However, other research has suggested a link. Hare et al. (1988) found higher recidivism rates for most crimes among psychopaths than non-psychopaths. A study of discharged patients from the three English special (high security) hospitals by Jamieson and Taylor (2004) revealed that two-thirds of those classified under the legal category of psychopathic disorder reoffended within two years.

There is some research evidence that post-traumatic stress disorder (PTSD) can be related to violence. Solursh (1989) studied a sample of 100 American Vietnam War veterans suffering from PTSD. He discovered in 94 per cent of the sample a pattern of 'combat addiction', where nightmares or flashbacks experienced as a 'high' would alternate with periods of severe depression. Although it also emerged that 97 per cent were classified as explosive and irritable, and 81 per cent engaged in combat-style activities such as keeping a loaded weapon and hunting, it was not recorded if any of the veterans subsequently committed criminal offences involving violence. Collins and Bailey (1990) found a relationship between PTSD and violent crime unrelated to armed combat in a prison sample of 1,140 males. The 2.3 per cent of the group who satisfied strict testing for PTSD were significantly more likely to have been arrested or imprisoned for a violent offence, and in most cases there was evidence that the symptoms preceded the crime.

Nevertheless, it remains the case that, on an analysis of both mental disorder in convicted offenders and offending rates in psychiatric populations, it is difficult to establish a firm relationship between mental disorder and crime. There are some exceptions. Schizophrenia is the psychosis most associated with violence, although the actual numbers involved are very small, and there is also an established link with psychopathy, although that seems to be incorporated in the definition of the disorder.

The legal definition

The broad term 'mental disorder' is given a legal definition in the Mental Health Act 1983. It is divided into four categories: mental illness; arrested or incomplete development of the mind; psychopathic disorder; and any other disorder or disability of mind (section 1(2)). 'Mental illness' is not defined in the Act. The term covers diagnoses of psychoses (such as schizophrenia), anxiety states, affective disorders (such as depression) and hysteria. Psychosis may be defined as a serious mental disorder which causes considerable disruption to the practical functioning, mood and reasoning processes of the person affected. The commonest form of mentally disordered offender appears to be the schizophrenic, followed by the depressive.

(a) Mental illness

(i) Schizophrenia

This is generally indicated by one or more (but not all) of a number of disturbances. There may be difficulty in associating different thoughts. Hallucinations in the form of hearing voices may occur. The individual may experience strong and inappropriate emotional responses, such as sudden amusement at another's misfortune. There may be disturbances in motor behaviour, such as continual gesturing and forming odd facial expressions. The cause of schizophrenia—believed to affect 1 per cent of the general population—is unclear, although it is increasingly believed to be a combination of genetic, biochemical and social factors. There is some evidence of a link between schizophrenia and crime. Taylor (1986) found a high level of schizophrenia among life-sentence prisoners in London. Green (1981) discovered that three-quarters of a sample of fifty-eight mentally disordered men who had killed their mothers were suffering from schizophrenia. There may be a relationship between paranoid schizophrenia and violence, where the victim is the subject of the schizophrenic's delusion. It has been suggested that Peter Sutcliffe, the so-called 'Yorkshire Ripper', may have suffered from paranoid schizophrenia (Prins 1986).

Lindqvist and Allebeck (1990) conducted a longitudinal study of the subsequent offending levels of 644 schizophrenic patients who had been discharged from Swedish hospitals in 1971. The rate of offending among the men was about the same as in the general population. (The rate for the women was higher, but the numbers were too low to draw reliable conclusions.) Although most of the crimes were property offences, the rate for violent crime was four times higher than in the general population. Nevertheless, most of the violence was for minor assaults and there were no killings. Taylor (1993b) agreed with the view that psychotics are unlikely to commit serious violent offences. Appleby *et al.* (2001) discovered that only 5 per cent of the homicides in England and Wales between April 1996 and March 2000 were committed by people who had suffered from schizophrenia.

An Australian study has found that increased rates of offending by schizophrenics were consistent with changes in criminal patterns in the general community (Mullen *et al.* 2000). It appears, however, that the public is still sceptical. Angermeyer and Matschinger (1996) found that there was a marked increase in desired social distance from mentally ill people following the publicity given to violent attacks by two schizophrenics against prominent politicians in Germany.

The most extreme forms of violence perpetrated by schizophrenics are generally aimed at themselves, through self-mutilation, or at members of their family and their friends (Taylor 1982). Planned attacks of violence assume a degree of calculation not usually found in psychotic patients and violent acts usually occur during delusions, particularly those of extreme jealousy or infidelity. Violent incidents among psychiatric patients in hospitals are sometimes blamed on the mental state of the aggressors, but there is a body of evidence which shows that most such events result from the sort of day-to-day arguments that commonly arise among institutionalised populations (for example, Pearson *et al.* 1986).

Other research has indicated that it is difficult to ignore additional factors. From a study of 121 psychotic offenders, Taylor (1985) concluded that about 20 per cent clearly offended as a direct result of their illness and a further 26 per cent may have done so. However, if social factors (such as homelessness) were taken into account, the figure would rise to over 80 per cent. Arseneault *et al.* (2000) found that schizophrenics in a sample of New Zealand young adults were more likely to act violently if they were also alcohol or marijuana abusers.

(ii) Depression

Many people describe themselves as depressed at some time in their life, but in more extreme forms depression can be diagnosed as a mental illness. There are two basic forms: major depression and bipolar disorder, which is often referred to as a 'manic-depressive' condition. Major depression is associated with feelings of considerable unhappiness and guilt, problems with appetite and sleep, and thoughts of suicide. Bipolar disorder involves a fluctuation between manic periods, which are characterised by high levels of activity and exaggerated views of self-importance, and spells of depression. Major depression is the more common: it is estimated that between 8 per cent and 11 per cent of men and 18 per cent and 23 per cent of women will be clinically depressed at least once in their life.

There are particular problems in connecting depression with crime, as there is a distinct possibility that the depression may be triggered by the consequences of offending or conviction. Depression has been linked with shoplifting (Lawson 1984) and offences of violence, particularly aimed at relatives (Häfner and Böker 1982). Researchers are now suggesting that there may be a link between depression and teenage crime, especially involving girls (Obeidallah and Earls 1999). There is also the situation of depressed individuals who kill the rest of their family before committing suicide. West (1965) found that almost a third of his sample of seventy-eight cases of murder followed by suicide were clinically depressed at the time of the offence. This is an interesting finding, as it appears that in hospital depressive patients show no more signs of violence than members of the general population (Feldman 1993). Such incidents are perhaps precipitated by social conditions. Manic depression does not appear to feature much in crime, although a study by Gunderson (1974) suggested that it might be statistically over-represented among arsonists.

(iii) Neurosis

Although there is disagreement among psychologists as to whether neuroses should be classified as a less severe form of psychosis or a disorder in their own right, there is a general consensus that little evidence exists of any relationship between neuroses and crime. Certain extreme forms of obsessive-compulsive disorder may lead to kleptomania, which is a compulsive and virtually irresistible desire to steal. The classification of neurosis is of significance because, as it is so pervasive in society, describing it as a mental illness is coming close to labelling a majority of the population as mentally disordered.

(b) Mental handicap

Following psychoses and anxiety states, the next category of mental disorder referred to in the Mental Health Act 1983 is 'arrested or incomplete development of the mind', which includes mental impairment and severe mental impairment. These in turn include impairment (or severe impairment) of intelligence and social functioning, associated with abnormally aggressive or seriously irresponsible conduct on the part of the person concerned. The people covered by these classifications are referred to as mentally handicapped. This is a continuing condition, unlike mental illness which usually manifests itself in the intermittent disturbance of what otherwise appears to be normal mental functioning. The level of handicap is usually measured for clinical (but not legal) purposes by an intelligence quotient (IQ) test, the origins of which date back to 1908 and which is still the subject of some controversy (see above).

Individuals at the lower end of the IQ scale may be suffering from an impairment arising from circumstances relating to their family (including genetic factors) or from a number of general environmental influences such as inadequate schooling. They can usually function sufficiently to support themselves. On the other hand, those at the very bottom (below 50 on an IQ test) will need some degree of assistance, depending on the level of their impairment. In their case, it is generally possible to identify the particular cause of their impairment: they may have been damaged at birth; they may have an abnormality such as Down's Syndrome; they may have received a head injury; or they may have suffered from a serious disease during childhood.

With regard to the offending levels of mentally handicapped individuals, the evidence suggests that they commit a similar range of offences to other people, with the exception of sexual offences, which appear more frequently. Tutt (1971) found that in a sample of hospitalised mentally handicapped individuals about 16 per cent had been convicted of a sexual offence prior to admission (the level for offenders in general is about 3 per cent). Robertson (1981) studied the subsequent offending of 300 mentally handicapped offenders who had received a hospital order and had eventually been released into the community. About 12 per cent of the sample were later convicted of offences involving sexual indecency and 1 per cent for rape. Robertson also compared his sample with a group of male, mentally ill offenders. The handicapped offenders were considerably younger, less likely to have been married and had fewer hospital admissions than the mentally ill offenders. Although the mentally ill had more court appearances and had spent longer in prison, the handicapped had received their first conviction at a younger age and had committed more offences as juveniles. The level of theft was similar in both groups, but the mentally ill had committed more violent offences. Robertson commented that, apart from the greater incidence of sexual offences, the mentally handicapped's model of offending was similar to that of the general criminal population. The mentally ill, on the other hand, offended rarely as juveniles and usually committed their crimes following periods of severe illness.

There are strong reasons why mentally handicapped individuals are more likely to be criminalised than other people. Everyone breaks the rules at some stage, but the mentally handicapped will probably do it less efficiently and more visibly. They are more likely to be led on by other more calculating individuals and, indeed, may not appreciate that what they are doing is wrong. Their general clumsiness may result in friendly approaches being misinterpreted as being hostile, and this may explain their higher than average conviction rate for offences involving sexual indecency (Craft and Craft 1978).

(c) Psychopathic disorder

The concept of psychopathy is one of the most problematic notions in the field of modern psychiatry. The term, which literally translates into a 'psychologically damaged' person, was first used in an Austrian psychiatry textbook in 1845 and was then taken up by German psychiatrists. It was subsequently adopted in Britain and the USA, but its original usage in Germany appears to have been misunderstood (Rafter 1997). In Britain, the term came to be associated with the nineteenth century idea of 'moral insanity' and was given statutory recognition as the category of 'moral imbecile' in the Mental Deficiency Act 1913. This was replaced by the category 'psychopathic disorder' in the Mental Health Act 1959, which was similar to the definition now contained in the Mental Health Act 1983. Although this troublesome term is still employed in Britain, American psychiatrists are more wary of it, and the word is now used interchangeably with the term 'sociopath' in the USA. Indeed, the American Psychiatric Association's Diagnostic and Statistical Manual, which is probably the most authoritative classification of mental disorders, does not include the term psychopath at all, and instead uses a wider category called 'anti-social personality disorders'.

Psychopathy is not helped by the dramatic—and often inaccurate— images that the notion has come to convey to the public as a result of its usage by the media and in films. As Rafter (1997) has stated, ' "psychopaths" is a metaphor for "those who are not like us" '. In fact, the 1975 Report of the Butler Committee on Mentally Abnormal

Offenders (Home Office and DHSS) recommended that the term should be removed from both legal and diagnostic terminology. The Committee also preferred the expression 'personality disorder', which should then be followed by a description of the main features of the disorder which affected the particular individual. However, this was not included in the Mental Health Act 1983, which provides the legal definition of psychopathic disorder as 'a persistent disorder or disability of mind (whether or not including significant impairment of intelligence) which results in abnormally aggressive or seriously irresponsible conduct' (section 1(2)). It has been estimated that this particular categorisation covers about a quarter of the patients in the English maximum security hospitals.

The definition of psychopathic disorder is hardly satisfactory. As with the others in section 1 of the Mental Health Act, it is circular, in that the disorder is assumed from the behaviour, which is then in turn used to explain the behaviour (Ashworth and Gostin 1985). This is a particularly telling point for psychopathy, as it is unusual to find civil commitments to hospital for psychopaths under the Act. In effect, psychopathic behaviour is criminal behaviour.

Walters (2004) has criticised the concept of psychopathy on several other grounds. As it has been largely constructed on the basis of medical pathology and personality traits, it is deficient in its consideration of situational factors. The attribution of the label 'psychopath' is extremely damaging to an individual, a particularly salient point given that testing produces a high number of false-positive predictions. There is also a problem of directionality—the deficits which researchers identify in a psychopath might be a consequence rather than a cause of criminality.

Various researchers have tried to identify the typical characteristics of a psychopath. There appears to be a widespread approval of the six key elements described by Cleckley (1964): (1) a lack of guilt or remorse; (2) an inability to learn from experience; (3) an inability to delay gratification; (4) an inability to form enduring emotional ties; (5) the constant seeking of stimulation; and (6) a superficial charm. It is the inability of psychopaths to trust people that renders them unsuitable for psychoanalysis and psychotherapy, and their disruptiveness that makes them difficult to treat in conventional hospital settings. Hare (2003) has provided a 'psychopathy checklist', which includes indicators such as superficial charm, grandiose sense of self-worth, proneness to boredom, pathological lying, lack of realistic long-term plans, and impulsivity. The list also suggests that psychopaths commit a variety of offences—a finding contrary to the general public perception, which identifies psychopathy with serious violence. An operational guide for practitioners was provided by the DHSS and Home Office in 1986:

> The consensus view is that psychopathic disorder is not a description of a single clinical disorder but a convenient label to describe a severe personality disorder which may show itself in a variety of attitudinal, emotional and inter-personal behaviour problems. The core problem is the impairment in the capacity to relate to others—to take account of their feelings and to act in ways consistent with their safety and convenience.

Having achieved a working definition, researchers have proceeded to investigate the possible causes of psychopathy. In the previous chapter it was shown that there is some evidence in adoption and twin studies that psychopathy can be genetically transmitted (Cadoret 1986). Psychoanalytic theory sees psychopathy as representing problems in the development of the superego. Fenichel (1945) claimed that the extreme form is the 'narcissistic psychopath' who has no superego and is able to act without any consideration for others. However, most psychopaths have an incomplete and thus ineffective superego. Family influences and early childhood behavioural problems will have been significant factors. The typical background is that of a loveless home and variable environmental influences. In addition to poor development of the superego, the resolution of the Oedipus complex, which involves the child coming to identify with the parent of the same sex, will be incomplete. This explains why psychopaths feel no guilt for their aggressive behaviour and are able to manipulate other people through indifference to their feelings (see Chapter 16). Research by Marshall and Cooke (1999) has supported the view that lack of parental abuse and lack of affection could be relevant, and a study by Seagrave and Grisso (2002) found that adult psychopaths generally had a childhood history of anti-social behaviour. However, these factors apply to many people who manifest a whole range of behavioural disorders later in life, so they do not provide much information about any distinctive features of psychopathy. Hare *et al.* (1988) found that psychopaths commit far fewer offences after the age of forty. The reasons for this are not clear.

Research conducted by Widom (1976) showed that the way in which psychopaths react in situations is particularly dependent on how the other actor is perceived. Set the task of playing a game in a hospital, pairings of psychopaths performed equally as well as pairings of nurses. However, when a psychopath was paired with a person considered to be normal, the level of cooperation diminished. Howells

(1983) argued that psychopaths assume that any person with whom they are dealing has negative views towards them and, instead of waiting to appraise a situation, they may resort to violence first.

Further evidence can be found in studies investigating physiological characteristics of psychopaths. There appear to be clear differences based on tests of autonomic nervous system functioning. Hare (1978) discovered that psychopaths, when resting, have very low levels of electrodermal reactivity, but when under stress have unusually high levels of cardiac reactivity. The fast heart rate is a reflection of lower cortical arousal, which means that the body is ignoring unpleasant environmental stimuli. An association between brain damage and anti-social personality or psychopathic disorder has recently been claimed (Raine et al. 2000).

Whatever the cause, the inability to learn from experience and thus see the consequences of anti-social behaviour is widely believed to be one of the fundamental characteristics of a psychopathic condition. Some researchers have tested this by what is termed 'passive avoidance learning'. In this process, the subject learns to respond to certain cues to avoid an unpleasant consequence, which in laboratory experiments is usually an electric shock. Psychopaths perform badly on such tests; they are usually found to be in a low state of autonomic nervous system arousal (Chesno and Kilmann 1975). However, when the unpleasant consequence was a threatened financial penalty, the psychopaths performed better than the control group (Schmauk 1970). It may be that the cognitive element in this consequence provided a different sort of stimulus: perhaps psychopaths do not respond to punishments that they register as meaningless. On the other hand, once the learning task in experiments becomes more complicated, psychopaths consistently perform worse than control groups, even if there is a financial element involved. Newman et al. (1987) conducted an experiment in which money could be acquired or lost. Whereas the controls were able to alter their performance to take account of the possibility of losing, the psychopaths found this too complicated and consistently lost. When a five-second delay was introduced between making responses, the gap in performance between the psychopaths and the controls narrowed.

The difficulties in learning experienced by psychopaths are not necessarily the result of physiological factors; they may be a consequence of very poor socialisation in childhood. Psychopaths can refuse to follow rules in virtually any setting. Hospital nurses often consider psychopaths to be more threatening and disobedient than any other group of patients.

Conclusion

Although there is clear evidence that certain forms of mental disorder are *associated* with criminality, it is by no means certain that, in many of these cases, the offending occurred *as a result of* the mental disorder. For example, the mental disorder may have been associated with social problems which themselves precipitated the offending. Even where a causal link appears to be established, the mental disorder may have developed as a result of environmental factors rather than through some organic cause. In a study of admissions to psychiatric hospitals in Massachusetts between 1994 and 2000, Hudson (2005) found that poor socio-economic conditions were correlated with a risk of mental illness. Long-term inhabitants of custodial institutions may become mentally ill as a result of their internment.

The involvement of the law in the legal definitions and punishment of mental disorder has also been problematic. Law, of necessity, requires precise definitions and categorisations but, in order to have any practical significance for psychiatrists, key provisions of the Mental Health Act have been framed in vague and tautologous statements which do not satisfy practitioners in either discipline. The law reflects society's (perceived) reluctance to allow offenders to avoid the consequences of their acts on grounds of a mental disorder, which most people do not understand and suspect may be spurious. The main changes in the Mental Health Act 1983 from its predecessor, the Mental Health Act 1959, had the effect of strengthening the control of courts over the mentally disordered at the expense of psychiatric assessments.

Nevertheless, the evidence does sometimes point clearly to an organic cause of anti-social behaviour. It is difficult to assess the usefulness of thinking of such behaviour as 'crime'. In extreme cases there may be a legal defence or, more likely, a civil committal to hospital rather than a prosecution. However, concern is expressed about the growing number of mentally disordered people who, because of the closing of hospital wards, receive little, if any, in-patient treatment. The streets of most large cities contain a growing number of such individuals, often acting bizarrely, but seldom committing more than minor public order offences. Steadman *et al.* (1998) concluded that the risk of attack from offenders recently discharged into the community from psychiatric hospitals is extremely small. Nor is it easy to make an accurate prediction as to which ones pose the greatest threat. Monahan *et al.* (2001) studied 1,000 patients discharged from civil psychiatric hospitals over a period of twelve months. The patients had earlier been measured on 134 factors designed to assess the risk of their acting aggressively. No single factor proved to be a significant predictor of violent behaviour.

At the micro (that is, individual) level of explanation, mental disorder undoubtedly accounts for a certain amount of offending. However, when looking for a macro (that is, wider societal) explanation as to why large numbers of people commit particular types of crime, mental disorder can hardly provide the answer. As Hodkins (1992) said of America (but could also have said of Britain): 'given the large amount of crime . . . the crimes of those with major psychiatric disorders and intellectual handicaps seem insignificant in comparison'.

16

Personality theories

The term 'personality' is used to describe an individual's temperamental and emotional attributes that are relatively consistent and that will influence behaviour. This chapter considers the extent to which the leading psychological explanations of personality development can be related to criminal behaviour. Psychologists use different classifications: some might include considerations of biological factors or aspects of mental disorder such as psychopathy within the category of personality. However, as these are substantial areas of interest in their own right, they have been dealt with separately in other chapters.

The search for 'criminal' traits

Psychologists refer to a persistent or stable personality characteristic as a trait. For many years they have devised tests aimed at measuring personality traits in an attempt to test the hypothesis that people who are prone to act in an anti-social way are distinguishable from 'normal' people. Some form of questionnaire is often adopted: either a multivariate inventory, which measures several different dimensions, or a univariate inventory, which simply measures one.

Perhaps the best known multivariate inventory is the impressively-named Minnesota Multiphasic Personality Inventory (MMPI). Individuals taking the test are presented with a list of 550 statements and must decide which are true or false in relation to themselves. Scores are given to ten different scales, which are considered to measure different aspects of the personality. The scales are not specifically designed to identify offenders and some of them are inappropriate for such a purpose. Waldo and Dinitz (1967) found that the most useful one for distinguishing offenders was Scale 4, which measures psychopathy. However, closer inspection reveals that the answers to certain questions will be far more predictable for delinquents; for example, one asking if the subject had ever been 'in trouble with the law'. Waldo and Dinitz discovered that the outcome of the studies where personality differences between delinquents and non-delinquents were found hinged on the answers to four out of fifty questions. Another problem with the psychopathy scale is that it has also proved particularly useful in identifying non-delinquent traits, such as non-conformity and family conflict (Hawk and Peterson 1974).

Schuessler and Cressey (1950) surveyed twenty-five years' worth of studies which, in comparing the personalities of delinquents and non-delinquents, had measured scores based on objective tests. They stated that the doubtful validity of much of the research prevented their finding that criminality and personality are linked. Many years (and studies) later, and despite greater sophistication in the methodology, Arbuthnot *et al.* (1987) conducted a similar exercise and came to the same conclusion for both multivariate and univariate inventories. No major differences could be found between offenders and controls in the degree of sensation-seeking, a trait often attributed to delinquents. Although there is some evidence that offenders have a poorer self-concept (another such trait), it is not clear whether this is the cause or result of the delinquent label. Impulsivity is a trait widely attributed to offenders, and officially-processed delinquents appear to be more impulsive than controls. However, it is possible that this is more related to their being apprehended than to their offending: impulsive criminals are likely to commit their offences in what, for them, are wholly inappropriate circumstances.

The outcome, therefore, is that personality tests have not been able to show with any large degree of certainty that delinquents have personality traits which are significantly different from those of non-delinquents. Even where such links are suggested—such as between criminality and assertiveness, lack of respect for authority, or psychopathy—there are difficulties. In Chapter 3 it was shown that there are far more delinquents than those officially recorded and many alleged non-delinquents have probably committed criminal offences. Moreover, it may be questioned whether personality traits describe anything more than how individuals are prone to react in certain situations. For example, individuals are never disrespectful to everyone they meet.

The main personality theories which seem particularly relevant to delinquent behaviour are psychoanalytic explanations and the learning theories.

Psychoanalytic explanations of crime

The origins of modern psychoanalysis can be found in the writings of Sigmund Freud (1856–1939), who practised psychiatry for many years in Vienna and published a large number of essays during the first third of the twentieth century. Like Marx, Freud wrote little specifically on crime, but his theories deal with the development of the personality and have been used by some of his followers to explain how individuals can turn to anti-social or criminal acts. Freudian theory was neatly summarised by Lazarus (1980) when he said that people suffer distress and are unable to cope properly because they carry with them a childhood agenda which interferes with adult good sense. Psychoanalysis is very complex and has been further developed by a number of writers. In this chapter, the central aspects of Freud's theory will be considered in outline.

(a) The Freudian personality

Freud's best-known contribution to psychology is the emphasis he placed on the part played in people's mental functioning by the unconscious mind. The unconscious, which contains instinctive urges and repressed memories, has been likened to 'the submerged, invisible part of the iceberg' (Hollitscher 1947). This constitutes the largest and, in some respects, most powerful section of the mind. It originates from traumatic incidents in early childhood, some of which may have been consciously experienced and others not.

In his analysis of the personality, Freud started from the position that individuals are biologically provided with selfish pleasure-seeking and destructive tendencies. These basic drives or instincts, such as to eat, be comfortable and obtain sexual pleasure, derive from the unconscious part of the mind and are expressed in a psychic energy which Freud referred to as the id. They demand instant gratification and are only subject to 'the pleasure principle'. For psychoanalysts, the most interesting forms of this psychic energy are the instincts of sex and aggression. An instinct is different from an external stimulus because it arises within the body and, unlike a stimulus, a person cannot escape from it. It is obvious that this psychic energy needs to be controlled in some way to enable the individual to live in a society, and this control is carried out by both the ego and the superego. The purpose of the ego is to restrict the urges of the id by demonstrating the reality of what will happen if it is left uncontrolled.

For example, a child's id may require a sweet but, if it is punished on taking one, the child will come to learn through the operation of the ego that it is not worth the trouble. Equally, the ego can serve the id in a positive manner: a baby will quickly learn that it if it cries it is likely to be fed.

In controlling the drives of the id, the ego is guided by the superego, which reflects the internalisation of parental or societal standards. Formerly thought of as an unconscious element, the superego is now widely regarded as part of the conscious mind (Nass 1966). It comprises two components: the conscience and the ego-ideal. The conscience is formed from moral rules and any challenges by unwelcome impulses are prevented from reaching consciousness by the ego's defences. To use the same illustration, if the child wants to take a sweet and there is no-one else present, a well-formed superego would cause the child to admonish itself if it tried to do so. The ego-ideal reflects the standards to which the individual aspires and furnishes the ego with positive goals.

To summarise, in the psychodynamic system the id creates energies which, if they are not channelled or neutralised, will emerge into consciousness or action. The nature of these energies is such that, if they remain unchecked, they will make it difficult for the individual to live alongside other people. The ego and superego act as counter-balancing agents: the superego turns the powerful energies of the id on to the ego in the form of feelings of guilt. The ego will control behaviour as required by the superego in order to avoid the pain caused by the guilt. If the id is strong and the superego weak, the ego will be unable to function properly. An individual will be aware of the dangers of being apprehended and punished, but the pleasure obtained from a criminal act (as felt through the id) will overcome any restraint from the ego. Warburton (1965) identified intelligent prisoners convicted of serious offences who claimed that the rewards of their criminal activities adequately compensated for the punishment they received. This also explains why severe punishments are assumed by the 'non-criminal' population—who, in effect, are ruled by their egos—to be an effective deterrent to crime, whereas many criminals appear not to be influenced by such punishments at all (Kline 1987).

There are, therefore, three basic psychological processes in potential or actual conflict with each other, and an individual can only lead a steady life if, in Feldman's (1964) phrase, some sort of 'balance of power' can be established between them.

(b) Phases of personality development

There are five identifiable phases of development of the instincts. The first is the oral phase, which lasts for about the first year of life. As the name suggests, the mouth is the key area of the body from which the baby obtains pleasure (sucking), conveys its feelings (crying) and, eventually, starts to show aggression (biting). The next phase is the anal-sadistic, which lasts from about the age of one to three and a half. The anus replaces the mouth in importance, and particularly as a source of auto-erotic pleasure. The child will hold back excreta and then like to play with it. This is not so obvious because of environmental influences. The child will also develop a strong emotional bond with its mother—perhaps as strong as any feelings of love it will ever experience—and enjoy being touched and cuddled. Strongly aggressive instincts may develop; small children can attack each other (and animals) without showing any apparent remorse.

The third phase is the phallic, which lasts from about the age of three and a half to five. The child starts to become interested in genitals and engages in masturbation. It will be possessive of its same-sex parent and jealous of siblings. The instinctive urges are by now coming into opposition with the desires of the developing personality. The fourth phase, the latency period, lasts from five until the onset of puberty. The instinctive urges for the most part recede into the background. The fifth and final phase is the pubertal, where the instinctive urges re-emerge. Until Freud, it was generally believed that this was when human sexuality first manifested itself. The form that the particular instincts now take (for example, kissing—or sado-masochism) will largely depend on what has occurred in the first four phases. It is only after puberty that the aim of the sexual drive is settled. In the oral and anal-sadistic phases it settles on the child's own body or the mother. In early puberty it may settle on someone of the same sex.

(c) Methods of dealing with instinctual urges

The ego has the difficult task of serving both the id and the superego. If the ego functions properly, the desires of the id will be controlled in such a way as to be acceptable to the superego. In other words, the young child will have to be trained to deal with its instinctual urges in a socially acceptable manner. This can be achieved in three main ways. The id's urges may be displaced on to another object; for example breast-suckling can be replaced by bottle-feeding. Sublimation can divert the instinct from its original aim to one which is new and more socially acceptable. Aggression can be channelled into sports such as boxing, and destructive tendencies, such as pulling legs off spiders, can be redirected at dismantling and reassembling appropriate types of toy. A reaction formation can occur which inverts the force of the original instinct into the opposite direction. For instance, a young child likes instinctively to play with dirt. Seeing its mother's displeasure, the child can use the energy behind the impulse to be dirty to subdue that impulse and strengthen the opposing tendency to be clean. On the other hand, an excessively strong reaction formation to dirt can lead to later obsessive cleanliness.

According to Freud, for any of these three mechanisms to take place properly, the process should occur slowly. Otherwise, the instinct—such as aggression—may be repressed into the unconscious mind only to appear years later at a time of crisis. Alternatively, such a personal crisis may result in a regression to a fixation point: an earlier stage of development, probably one which was not properly negotiated at the time. For example, a conflict at the anal-sadistic phase may lead to later acts of sadism in situations where obedience is in issue. Psychoanalysts refer to the disturbances in personality which may arise from such unresolved conflicts as neuroses.

(d) Resolution of the Oedipus complex

The formation of the superego is dependent not only on the role of the ego, but also on the growing child's relations with its parents and, in particular, the resolution of what Freud termed the Oedipus complex for boys at about the age of five (the corresponding process for girls is the resolution of the Electra complex: this is discussed in Chapter 13). According to Freud, the phallic stage of development brings with it incestuous desires for the parent of the opposite sex and hostility to the same-sex parent. For boys, this results from their fear of castration and for girls the concern is for loss of paternal love. The Oedipus (or, for women, Electra) complex is resolved by a defensive identification with the threatening parent, whose attributes (real or imagined) are internalised. This serves to strengthen the ego-ideal component of the superego. Once the opposite-sex parent is no longer considered an object of personal possession, the child can return to the former narcissism of its infancy, which will result in an increase in self-esteem and more frequent journeying into the world of dreams and fantasy. Freud's own writings suggested that the superego was formed at this stage, but later psychoanalysts considered that superego development continues through adolescence. However, if the Oedipus complex is not fully resolved, it may prove difficult for the superego to complete its proper development later on.

(e) Later problems with the superego

The psychic energy system needs to be carefully balanced to operate properly and an unsatisfactory development at any stage can result in problems later in life. Of course, these problems do not all result in criminal or deviant behaviour. People who are over-inhibited (perhaps with an overdeveloped superego) are particularly unlikely to break the rules. Nevertheless, psychoanalysts claim that their theory can provide explanations for criminal behaviour in three main respects, which involve an overdeveloped, weak or deviant superego.

An overdeveloped, harsh superego results from identification with a very strict parent at the Oedipal stage (around the age of five). This can lead to the repression of an unconscious conflict and consequently result in strong feelings of guilt and neurosis. For most people, this would cause adverse changes to their daily functioning not involving criminality—such as obsessive behaviour patterns—but for some the neurosis may precipitate behaviour which is anti-social or criminal. Damage might be caused to property which has a symbolic value for the offender, perhaps because it is associated with certain people on whom the individual wishes to take revenge (Glover 1949). In certain types of theft, the very act of stealing or the nature of the object stolen may indicate the nature of the conflict. Sometimes, a neurotic offender may be suffering from a harsh superego and feel extreme guilt over repressed infantile desires. The acting-out of this desire (for example, the theft of women's underwear from clothes lines) may be a way of inviting punishment to alleviate overwhelming feelings of guilt arising from unconscious, and poorly sublimated, incestuous urges. From the offender's point of view, the real crime requiring punishment is the incestuous desire, but some relief can be obtained from being punished for the actual offence. Here, there is a reversal of the usual situation: guilt precedes crime.

In their book *Roots of Crime* (1935), Alexander and Healy considered seven cases of theft that had arisen in their psychiatric practices. They concluded that there were four unconscious motives behind the thieves' stealing: overcompensation for a sense of inferiority; an attempt to relieve a sense of guilt; a spiteful reaction towards the mother; and a direct gratification of dependent tendencies in the 'carefree, vegetative existence' of the prison environment.

In other cases, crime may represent a compensatory means of obtaining desires and needs which are not provided by the family. Security, status and acceptance are examples of requirements which are usually satisfied in family life, but may not have been for the offender. Healy and Bronner (1936) conducted a study in three American cities of 105 families with two sons where one was a persistent criminal and the other was a non-offender. They discovered that the offending brother was more likely to have been frustrated and rejected by his parents and to have turned to delinquency to find a substitute satisfaction for his thwarted desires. Status can also be sought in activities such as gang membership. In an observation of Glasgow delinquents, Stott (1982) considered that their activities could be classified as reactions to family stress and the seeking of exciting activities to alleviate that stress.

However, it is more common to find a weak or unformed superego held up as an underlying cause of anti-social behaviour. Crime, particularly of a serious nature, is by no means inevitable: many individuals with weak superegos simply develop a general contempt for rules which is unlikely to lead to more than minor infringements of the law. Nevertheless, seriously disruptive conduct has been attributed to poor superego development.

An early example of this can be seen in the book *Wayward Youth* (1925) by August Aichhorn, who was a supervisor in an institution for juvenile delinquents. Aichhorn found that many of the children in his care had an underdeveloped superego. He concentrated on twelve adolescent boys who were particularly violent and had not responded to the usual forms of treatment. Aichhorn considered that they suffered from defective superego and ego development and had regressed to the anal-sadistic stage. According to Freudian theory, they needed to be 're-educated' in order to develop proper superegos. Aichhorn first allowed the boys to give full vent to their impulses; this involved the destruction of their living quarters. However, after this their behaviour slowly began to improve and eventually they were able to resist their violent impulses and re-enter the outside world. Friedlander (1951) pointed out the importance of Aichhorn's ignoring their destructive behaviour. The lack of punishment meant that the boys could not rationalise their feelings of hatred, and eventually they began to feel guilt. From that stage, work could be done to develop the boys' superego in accordance with their emotional, rather than their actual age.

Aichhorn considered that the failure to attain a properly-formed superego is generally attributable to unloving or absent parents. In more extreme forms a weak superego is associated with the self-centred, unfeeling and guiltless individual who is termed a psychopath (see Chapter 15). Many psychoanalysts consider psychopaths to have fixations arising from the pre-genital phase or an unresolved Oedipus complex. This results in hostility to both parents, and aggressive and sadistic tendencies. If these characteristics are combined with parents who fail to nurture the child properly, the consequence may be a strong narcissistic fixation (Akhtar and Thomson 1982). Frustrations at the oral and anal-sadistic phases increase the psychopath's tendency to sadism, as the growing child internalises the hostility it feels towards the rejecting parent. Aichhorn also discussed how what he termed 'latent delinquency' could arise when the superego and ego are weak during the latency period. Environmental circumstances help to determine whether the child commits delinquent acts at that stage. This may explain why those who do offend are likely to come from the lower classes (Kline 1987).

Glover (1960) argued that, as poor relationships may be confined to one parent or a problem may occur at one particular stage of development, the superego may be only partly deficient and a person's acting in an anti-social way may be restricted to very specific circumstances. A similar point had been made earlier by Hewitt and Jenkins (1946) in their study of American juvenile delinquents. Some of the boys were identified as having an overdeveloped superego and others as having an underdeveloped one. Others again, who were members of delinquent gangs, showed a normal superego in relation to gang rules, but an underdeveloped superego when it came to obeying the rules of society. This indicates that individuals other than parents, groups or environmental factors can have a significant impact on superego development (Friedlander 1947).

The third way in which superego development can affect criminal behaviour is where the superego develops normally, but the standards that are instilled by the parents are deviant ones. The behaviour of the growing child may then indicate an absence of guilt, but this would not be on account of any abnormality: the deviant behaviour would simply not be viewed by the child as wrong. Alternatively, the child may come to realise that such activities are disapproved of by society, but consider that the parents will be gratified by them.

(f) Maternal deprivation and crime

There has long been a common belief that much juvenile delinquency results from a broken home. If this were the case, the psychoanalytic explanation would be that the young child had been unable to form the necessary parental attachments and consequently had an inadequately-formed superego. The popularity of this view, particularly throughout the 1950s and 1960s, has been attributed to the writings of John Bowlby.

Problems arising from the lack of proper attachment bonds between mother and child were identified in a study by Bowlby in 1944. He compared forty-four juvenile thieves who had been referred to the Tavistock Clinic in London between 1936 and 1939 with a control group of forty-four 'non-criminal' children who had also been seen at the clinic. Whereas seventeen of the forty-four thieves had been separated completely from their mothers for a period of at least six months during the first five years of their life, only two members of the control group had undergone such a separation. Bowlby therefore concluded that maternal deprivation involving a lengthy period of separation could be a significant cause of delinquency. On preparing a report for the World Health Organization (Bowlby 1951), he discovered that other scholars working independently had reached similar conclusions.

Bowlby's views had an immediate impact and struck a chord with many people who were looking for an explanation for the post-war increase in juvenile delinquency. The expression 'broken home' entered into common usage. If the implications of his analysis were put into practice, crime could be, so to speak, nipped in the bud. Sluckin *et al.* (1983) have pointed out that the wide publicity given to Bowlby's writings had both good and bad immediate effects. On the positive side, children's hospital wards were opened up to visitors to a far greater extent than before. However, pre-school nurseries, established during the World War II, were closed down during the 1950s, often leading to less satisfactory child-minding arrangements.

Predictably, Bowlby's thesis came under attack. It was criticised by writers who were unable to replicate his findings (Little 1965); who pointed out the unrepresentative nature of his samples and the poor matching of the control group (Feldman 1977); and who challenged the theory itself. Wootton (1959), for example, pointed out that there was no evidence that any damage caused from separation was irreversible, and that the 'affectionless character' found in fourteen of the seventeen separated thieves formed only a small minority of the delinquent population. In addition, the growing women's movement in the 1960s did not take kindly to a theory that, in the eyes of some people, questioned the use of the nanny and suggested that mothers should spend as much time as possible in the company of their young children.

In 1972, Michael Rutter carried out a review of all the literature and stated that Bowlby's views had often been misrepresented: he had never suggested that only constant caring by the same person was necessary. Rutter drew a distinction between privation, which here refers to the lack of a crucial ingredient in the parenting relationship, and deprivation, which refers to actual separation. He concluded that the former is far more significant in child rearing than the latter. Nor was there any evidence that a child would suffer if it were not brought up by its natural mother. Rutter considered that 'multiple-mothering' by up to four or five individuals would have no adverse effects. Subsequently, research such as the longitudinal Cambridge Study in Delinquent Development (West 1982) has supported the argument that the family influences which may affect delinquency are far more complicated than maternal deprivation alone.

However, it seems that public opinion has not been fully deflected from considering broken homes as a significant cause of crime (Furnham and Henderson 1983). There is also still a debate as to whether a young child's development can be harmed by its mother's going out to work. Although Belsky (1988) found that infants who were cared for by a child-minder for more than twenty hours a week were more disobedient and aggressive between the ages of three and eight, Harvey (1999) discovered that early parental employment had no significant effect on a child's behaviour or self-esteem.

In an analysis of data from the Cambridge Study in Delinquent Development, Juby and Farrington (2001) made a number of interesting findings about the effects of family disruption on delinquency. The views of writers such as Bowlby were reinforced by the discovery that boys separated from their mothers were more likely to be delinquent than boys parted from their fathers. Moreover, boys who continued living with their mothers had similar delinquency levels to boys living in a harmonious relationship with both parents. The researchers also found that disruptions caused by parental conflict were more damaging than those caused by parental death.

Research has also suggested that the proliferation of part-time employment may be detrimental to child development. An American study by Han (2005) found that the employment of mothers during non-standard hours appeared to have an adverse effect on the cognitive development of their children aged up to thirty-six months. The authors suggested that one reason for this might be that the increased probability of the mothers' being tired and depressed would contribute to a less supportive home environment. Another could be the greater likelihood of inappropriate childcare arrangements being in place.

(g) Evaluation

Psychoanalytic explanations in essence claim that young children must internalise society's rules to be fully socialised; that problems in the parent–child relationship can lead to criminal behaviour in later life; and that some crimes result from earlier conflicts which are stored in the unconscious mind. It is this last element that sets this approach aside from other explanations. However, it is also the most difficult to test. A person who, according to Freud, should act in a particular way might behave quite differently. However, the hypothesis can still be verified on the basis that the conflict underlying the anticipated behaviour has been repressed. Techniques such as hypnosis, dream analysis and verbal association are ultimately subjective, and psychoanalysts do not agree on how to use them. Kline (1987) claimed that there are subliminal stimulation techniques available, based on research by Silverman (1983), which can indicate the presence of conflict, but their validity has been questioned (Balay and Shevrin 1988). It has also been suggested that neurotic conflict can be a consequence, just as much as a cause, of crime (Feldman 1964).

These problems with psychoanalytic research are well-illustrated in a study by Stott (1980). He asserted that children's main psychic needs were coping with reality, being valued by peers, and receiving care and affection from an adult. Stott's research was based on 102 youths aged fifteen to eighteen in English institutions for young offenders. He interviewed each youth personally, and his findings were not checked for reliability. No standardised questionnaires were adopted. This study is not untypical of the genre.

Kline (1987) has pointed out that psychoanalysts do not claim that they can explain all types of offending. Many property crimes, for example, involve perfectly rational targets and are the culmination of much careful planning. According to Kline, it is therefore likely that psychoanalysis is particularly relevant to seemingly irrational crimes— the types associated with psychopaths and extreme neurotics. However, there are still problems with this more restrictive explanation. Although psychoanalysis can throw some light on the increase in crime during puberty (a resurgence of earlier conflicts at the end of the latency period), as with many other explanations it does not account for its discontinuance in late adolescence (assuming that these offenders have not all undergone therapy successfully).

Moreover, Freud's claim that females have weaker superegos than males, as their resolution of the Electra complex is said to be often incomplete, should lead to far more female criminality than appears to be the case (Hoffmann 1977).

(h) Conclusion

Psychoanalysis is unfashionable in academic circles and nowadays seldom receives much more than a passing mention in books about crime. To some extent, this may be because the hold that the approach had on British criminology in the 1930s and 1940s made it a prime target for the anti-positivist reaction that started some thirty years later. Positivism itself has subsequently had to retrench and ensure that its methodology stands up to the most rigorous scrutiny. Psycho-analysis cannot even make a reasonable stab at passing this test: it is a description of inner processes which are hardly amenable to empirical testing. It could be argued that this provides the approach with a uniqueness which excuses it from the scrutiny accorded to other psychological explanations of behaviour, but such a view is unlikely to impress the critics.

Many Freudian terms are now widely used in everyday speech. In addition, millions of people throughout the world seek counselling or therapy for psychological problems and it is striking, particularly in Western societies, how many of these end up receiving treatment which is based on some form of psychoanalytic model. Of course, neither of these points validates the approach, and cognitive-behavioural techniques are making rapid inroads into dealing with a wide range of such problems. Yet, psychoanalysis does not deserve the ridicule that is sometimes heaped on it. It has the advantage of providing an explanation of all behaviour, not just that which is deviant or criminal. Psychologists of all persuasions accept the importance of the unconscious mind, and most parents nowadays will confirm mani-festations of sexuality in the behaviour of young children—something which was unthinkable before the writings of Freud.

In recent years, psychoanalytic concepts have been (re)visited by some criminologists in their study of the role that different types of masculinity can play in the commission of crime. Freud's view of the inevitability of the competing forces within the human personality is considered as an interesting alternative perspective to the more com-mon psychological approach which concentrates on observable 'dif-ferences' from 'the normal' individual. This is discussed in more detail in Chapter 13. Social psychologists are also paying more attention to

Freud's ideas. In a review of empirical studies which (without necessarily acknowledging the fact) related to Freudian defence mechanisms, Baumeister *et al.* (1998) found 'substantial support' for several of them.

Learning theories

According to learning theorists, little human action is automatic or instinctive; most of it is based on learned experiences. It is therefore arguable that this applies just as much to actions that are anti-social or criminal as to any other type of action. On this analysis, criminal behaviour could be described as normal, learned behaviour. The Greek philosopher Aristotle went so far as to argue that all behaviour is learned by association and that none results from innate characteristics. He claimed that sensory experiences are associated with each other in the mind because they occur in relationship to each other on every occasion the individual interacts with the outside world. 'Associationism' became the pre-eminent form of learning theory. It was considered by philosophers such as Hobbes and Locke and formed the basis of the first experiments on animal learning conducted by Thorndike in 1898, and on human memory carried out by Ebinghaus. It was adopted by adherents to the developing behaviourist approach, who merely substituted observable stimuli for the mental images that had been relied on previously.

The main division in learning theories nowadays is between such behavioural theorists and cognitive theorists, who still adhere to Aristotle's original belief that learning occurs through the association of ideas and factual knowledge. Behaviourists claim that people learn by trial and error through associating stimuli with responses: cognitive theorists believe that people learn through associating memories and ideas as part of a problem-solving process.

(a) Classical conditioning

There are three main explanations as to how individuals learn by way of association. The simplest method is classical conditioning, which was described by Ivan Pavlov in 1927. Relying on the fact that dogs salivate when presented with meat, Pavlov gave meat to dogs accompanied by some other stimulus, such as the ringing of a bell. After a while, he simply rang the bell without presenting the food. Many of the dogs still salivated. Pavlov argued that learning can therefore take place by association in circumstances where the subjects (here, the dogs) are purely passive and simply learn from the environment. In his experiment, the dogs came to associate the sound of the bell with the provision of meat. However, it is this very passivity that renders the process of limited value, as learning can apparently only take place in fixed environmental conditions. The feeling of fear is an example of a response which often results from conditioned responses to pain felt in early life. From the point of view of crime and punishment, classical conditioning is of little significance, as it is very rarely in society that punishment immediately follows the forbidden act.

(b) Operant learning

The second method of learning by association is known as operant learning and is usually identified with the work of Burrhus F Skinner (1938). Skinner's writing has had a major impact on the development of behavioural psychology. Operant learning is a far more useful learning device than classical conditioning, as the subject is active and, by the use of rewards and punishments, has to learn how to obtain what it wants from the environment. Experiments with rats showed that, by being rewarded with food for pushing a lever and punished with an electric shock for failing to push the lever, the rats soon learned how to operate the lever. Skinner argued that principles of behaviour should be established in accordance with the regularities between stimulus and response as observable in the laboratory. There is no place for 'intervening variables'. Skinner rejected theories and formal hypotheses and even disliked the use of the word 'cause', as it refers to a concept that is not directly observable. Instead, he referred to 'the functional analysis of behaviour'.

Although Skinner believed that people's potential for learning is influenced by their genes, it remains an essential element of his theory that individuals' behaviour patterns are largely explicable in accordance with their own learning experiences. Behaviour which results in desirable consequences will increase in frequency, in which case it is being reinforced: behaviour which produces unwanted consequences will decrease in frequency and is described as being punished. With positive reinforcement, behaviour leads to a rewarding consequence: with negative reinforcement, the behaviour avoids an unpleasant consequence. Language is considered to be verbal behaviour and is also subject to the principles of operant conditioning.

Nowadays, operant learning is of far greater interest to psychologists than classical conditioning. It is of much wider applicability, as subjects have to learn to react to competing stimuli in such a way as to maximise the attainment of their desires. Subjects do not merely react to their immediate environment; they can alter that environment for their own benefit. Unlike psychoanalytic explanations of behaviour, the determinants of behaviour come from outside the person. The theory assumes that individuals will act to maximise pleasure and minimise pain. It is not concerned with stating what should be considered pleasurable, which may, of course, vary from one individual to another. Nor did Skinner have much time for subjective influences such as intentions or expectations, which he described as 'early stages of behaviour', and went on to assert that 'No creative or initiating function is to be assigned to them'. They may be interesting in their own right, but they are unobservable and cannot be the causes of behaviour. The strictness of Skinner's approach has led to its being called 'radical behaviourism'. He has set out his position as follows (1974):

> What is felt or introspectively observed is not some nonphysical world of consciousness, mind, or mental life but the observer's own body . . . An organism behaves as it does because of its current structure, but most of this is out of reach of introspection. At the moment we must content ourselves . . . with a person's genetic and environmental histories. What are introspectively observed are certain collateral products of those histories.

Clarence Ray Jeffery (1965) suggested that criminal behaviour is operant behaviour which is reinforced by the changes it produces in the environment. Offences against property are positively reinforced by the material gain of the items: offences against the person are negatively reinforced by the removal of an enemy. Criminal behaviour is thus largely determined by an absence of aversive consequences.

(c) Social learning theory

Neither classical nor operant learning theories are dependent on subjects' having any understanding of the process in which they are engaged. A third explanation of learning by association, known as modelling or social learning theory, combines operant learning with aspects of cognitive psychology. Social learning theory claims that behaviour is reinforced not only by rewards and punishments, as in operant learning, but also by observing the behaviour of others—by using others as models. The reinforcement of behaviour creates expectations of particular outcomes and does not function merely as an automatic shaper of conduct. It is, in effect, a theory of imitation: not simply by re-enacting behaviour observed in others, but by using what has been seen in accordance with one's own goals and within the requirements of the situation. This cognitive learning will include an understanding of how people interact with others and all the processes that are necessary to facilitate this within a society. These include learning how to control impulsive desires, learning how to make rational decisions, and the development of interpersonal skills. Unlike operant learning theory, social learning theory maintains that knowledge can exert control over behaviour: people create their own environments.

One of the leading advocates of social learning theory is the American psychologist Albert Bandura. He argued that there are three main aspects to the theory: external reinforcement, which is the basis of operant conditioning; vicarious reinforcement; and self-reinforcement. Vicarious reinforcement is gained from the observation of other people's behaviour being reinforced or punished. Self-reinforcement relates to feelings of pride and achievement in one's own behaviour; this will encourage people to behave in a similar way in the future.

Perhaps Bandura's best-known experiment is the one which involved a 'Bobo doll' (Bandura and Huston 1961). While a child played in a room, an adult would enter and start to hit and kick the doll. In order to frustrate the child, it would be told it could not play with other toys that were present. The child would then be led into another room, where there would be several toys and another Bobo doll. Children who had seen the adult attack the Bobo doll would be more likely to attack the doll than others who had also been frustrated, but had not witnessed the adult's attack.

According to Bandura, the physical skills which are necessary for the commission of a crime are learned either from observing or being taught by others. The nature of this learning, together with the physical attributes of the offender, determines the type of crime that is carried out. As offenders become more skilled, they will be able to select more appropriate targets, where they are likely to be successful and avoid detection. For example, physically weak individuals learn that the best way to commit robberies successfully is to arm themselves with weapons. People develop social skills involving communicating with and understanding the actions of others. There is some research linking criminality with a low level of social skills. Although much of it has been carried out in relation to young offenders and the findings are far from conclusive, there is strong evidence of a connection between a lack of social skills and child sexual abuse (Hollin 1992).

Offenders must have particular attitudes in order to commit crimes. They must have a stance on the morality of their action and they must have views about the other people involved, such as their victims. These attitudes have been learned from others and, the greater the admiration they have for the others, the more likely they are to adopt their attitudes. However, such views of morality and other attitudes do not need to remain fixed. They can be altered by cognitive processes, and formerly disapproved practices can become morally acceptable, perhaps through a greater exposure to new models of persuasive influence. For persistent offenders, the periodic reinforcement of their values by other criminals has been sufficient to outweigh the inhibitory effects of punishment.

Nor is criminality inevitably linked with an absence of morality from the offender's point of view. Terrorists, for example, may have been brought up to believe that their crimes, which appear horrendous in the eyes of others, are a perfectly moral response to a set of socio-political circumstances. Indeed, they may consider that they will be rewarded in heaven for their deeds.

Even less highly-principled offenders may adopt the moral position that they are merely small-fry when compared with far more serious offenders. Many people who would claim to be strongly opposed to theft learn to have no moral objection to keeping quiet if they are given too much change in a shop. Euphemisms are also adopted to mask the implications of what would otherwise be considered immoral behaviour (Bandura 1986): 'perks', such as office stationery, can be taken from the place of employment. Bandura (1976) stated that learning mainly occurs in three contexts: in the family, in a subculture, and through cultural settings such as television, cinema and books. He also accepted that genetic factors could affect an individual's capacity to learn: 'Both experiential and physiological factors interact, often in intricate ways, to determine behaviour' (1986).

Bandura and his associates (for example, Bandura and Walters 1959) have generally placed great emphasis on the failure of socialisation in childhood. Feldman (1977), on the other hand, thought that adolescence and adulthood are more significant periods. He considered that classical conditioning is important in dealing with infant aggression, but that offences against property are dependent on particular models and skills which are more common after early childhood.

(d) Rational choice theory

An apparent development of social learning theory which emerged during the 1980s is rational choice theory. Based on the deterrence theories of writers such as Jeremy Bentham (see Chapter 5) and an economic utility model (Heineke (ed) 1978), the theory argues that would-be criminals make a rational assessment of the possible consequences of their actions and take the opportunity to commit a crime only if the economic advantages would outweigh the disadvantages— or, as Akers (1990) put it, would 'maximise payoff and minimise costs'. Some rational choice models of crime have been expanded to include moral judgements and family and peer group influences (Paternoster 1989). Cornish and Clarke (1987) thought that not only can rational choice theory explain why a crime was committed, but it can also account for the choice of crime and the selection of the time and place of its execution. The decisions that need to be taken will vary for different criminal offences and at the different stages involved in the commission of any particular offence. Their edited book *The Reasoning Criminal* (1986) contains rational choice empirical studies, most of which deal with economic crimes. Clarke and Cornish (1985) have also provided a detailed model of how rational choice theory could apply to a residential burglary in a middle-class area. This contains a wide range of elements that have to be considered, including: personal and background factors relating to the defendant (such as temperament, intelligence level and home background); needs (such as money, status or excitement); perceived solution (legitimate—such as work—or illegitimate); and readiness to commit the crime. The addition of the dimension of locality to rational choice theory provides the routine opportunities theory (Cohen and Felson 1979), which is discussed in Chapter 6. However, as a result of interviews with young Amsterdam street robbers, de Haan and Vos (2003) concluded that rational choice theory failed to account for notions such as impulsiveness, expressivity, moral ambiguity and shame, which are involved in this type of behaviour.

Ronald L Akers (1994) noticed that rational choice and deterrent theorists have not acknowledged their debt to social learning theory. He felt that neither of these approaches adds anything new to social learning theory, which already allows for the adoption of rational decision-making processes in considering whether to commit a crime. For Akers, social learning theory includes learning responses to rewards and punishments, and to anticipate the consequences of present and future actions. Cognitive learning goes hand in hand with choice. Even Cornish and Clarke (1987), who are generally thought of as the main exponents of a rational choice explanation of crime, accepted that there can be constraints and limitations on rationality, such as the time available, the amount and quality of information to hand, and the offender's own cognitive abilities. The question of deterrence is also important, as it is unclear whether some people are more easily deterred from criminal activity than others. On the basis of data from the Dunedin longitudinal study, Wright *et al.* (2004) found that viewing crime as risky had the greatest deterrent effect on people who were low in self-control and high in self-perceived criminality.

The various definitions of 'rational choice' provided by the theory's proponents seem to be vague and allow for almost any form of behaviour except the most extreme pathological variety. Gibbs (1989) summed it up when he wrote 'if rational behaviour is defined as simply goal-oriented behaviour ... then virtually all of human behaviour is rational and the rational–irrational distinction has no real consequences'.

(e) TV and film violence

Bandura (1973) took the view that people can learn from visual images in just the same way as they learn from personal interaction. He therefore considered that aggressive behaviour and violent individuals depicted on TV and in films can provide a model which viewers, particularly young people, may try to emulate:

> People who watch television for any length of time will learn a number
> of tactics of violence and murder. Television is a superb tutor.

Others, however, deny that such a link exists. This debate has been going on for many years, and has gradually intensified with the growing use of violent imagery by the makers of films, television programmes and computer games. There is evidence to support both sides of the argument. In the 'Rip Van Winkle Study' started in 1960, researchers checked the level of aggressiveness in subjects after watching television programmes at the age of eight and then at two intervals of ten years. The main findings were that early signs of aggression accurately predicted later aggression, particularly in boys; the most aggressive children watched the most television; children with a low IQ tended to be aggressive; and the correlation between watching television and violence held independently of father's occupation, parental discord, measurement of IQ, and the amount of television watched (Huesmann 1986). The study was criticised on the ground that the longitudinal effects were only found in boys. However, a more recent study by the same research team found that exposure to violence on TV predicted aggressive behaviour for both males and females (Huesmann *et al.* 2003).

In Britain, Bailey (1993), who interviewed 40 violent young offenders and 200 young sex offenders, found that 25 per cent had seen violent TV programmes, films and videos. She considered that this was a significant causal factor in their offending. Sims and Gray (1993), in evidence to the House of Lords' Broadcasting Group, identified over 1,000 pieces of research which purported to find a connection between exposure to violence in the media and aggression.

A study of primary-age children in California discovered that, following a reduction in access to television sets, there was a decrease in the amount of both verbal and physical aggression observed in the playground (although the finding for physical aggression was not statistically significant) (Robinson *et al.* 2001).

On the other hand, Freedman (1984) challenged the findings of research in this area, arguing that laboratory-based studies in particular are inappropriate. He thought that the correlation between the viewing of TV violence and measures of aggressiveness could be explained by other variables or the selection of violent programmes by viewers already disposed to violence. This view was supported by Wilson and Herrnstein (1985). They claimed that the only firm conclusion which can be drawn from the evidence was that aggressive children with low IQs who frequently watch violent programmes on television may be encouraged to commit further aggressive acts. Browne and Pennell (1998) discovered that offenders watch more violence on video than non-offenders. Violent offenders are more likely than non-violent offenders to prefer violent films. Sonia Livingstone (1996), after reviewing the research studies, could only conclude that the question of detrimental effects on the viewers of violence has to stay unresolved. Even some researchers who think that a relationship exists, such as Smith and Donnerstein (1998), have conceded that such exposure is only one factor among many others.

Charlton and Gunter (1999) studied the behaviour of children prior to, and following, the introduction of television on the island of St Helena in 1995. Although the amount of violence contained in the programmes was slightly higher than in the UK, the researchers found no increase in violent or anti-social behaviour on the part of the children.

It would be ridiculous to claim that no-one can ever be affected by watching depictions of violence on television or film. The real issue is whether such exposure can, in itself, play a significant causative role in subsequent violent behaviour by the individuals concerned (Buckingham 2000). It is not only the artificiality of the laboratory setting that makes this almost impossible to test. Everyone is subject to a wide range of experiences and stimuli. People's perceptions and interpretations of the same 'event' can be completely different. On balance, the situation which emerges from the psychological research is that exposure to depictions of violence can result in a short-term arousal in aggressiveness, which may be stronger in individuals who are already violently inclined. The fact that violence in films and TV programmes is generally portrayed in a social context makes it arguable that they are as much the product as the producer of contemporary society.

Despite periodic claims in the popular press, there is no firm evidence that individual acts of violence result from the modelling of violent solutions to conflict on the part of film or TV watchers, or indeed give rise to 'copycat' incidents. There is some evidence that exposure to violent depictions can lead to short-term feelings of heightened aggression in some individuals, but this does not begin to translate into their going on to commit violent crimes. Carey (1993) has summed up the situation:

> The only possible conclusion which can be drawn from a thorough review of the huge number of scientific studies designed to test such theories gives victory to neither those who believe that mass media violence does harm nor to those who believe it does not.

Following the 1993 murder conviction of two ten-year-old boys for the killing of the child James Bulger, several newspapers reported that the boys had previously watched a violent video, *Child's Play 3*. There was no clear evidence of this, let alone any proven link with the murder. *The Sun* newspaper launched a campaign to have all copies of the video burned, even though a TV channel owned by its proprietor had previously shown the film (Schubart 1995). There have subsequently been numerous claims of 'copycat' killings: for example, in America following the 1994 film *Natural Born Killers* and in Britain following the 2000 murder conviction of three teenage boys in Liverpool, who were said to have re-enacted a scene from the film *Reservoir Dogs*. The interest of several MPs was aroused by the Bulger case and the Criminal Justice and Public Order Act 1994 inserted a new provision in the Video Recordings Act 1984 (section 4A). The effect of this is that the British Board of Film Censors must consider the 'harm' (which is undefined) that may be caused to viewers by exposure to crime, drug-use, violence, horror or sex when they classify videos.

Well-intentioned TV programmes about violence and crime can also have their problems. In 1997, one of two boys who, together with their father, were convicted of murdering their mother claimed that he had decided on the means of killing her after watching a crime reconstruction on *Crimewatch UK* (*The Independent*, 12 February 1997). Gill's study of imprisoned commercial robbers (see Chapter 6) found one interviewee who claimed to have watched *Crimewatch UK* on frequent occasions and thought 'Well, if they can do it, I can do it' (Gill 2000).

(f) Differential association theory

This theory, devised by the American sociologist Edwin Sutherland in 1939, has obvious connections with learning theory. However, in this book differential association is discussed in Chapter 6, which deals with the Chicago School of Criminology, as it arose out of the writings in that tradition.

Eysenck's theory of criminality

Hans Eysenck, who was perhaps best known among the general public for his books on popular psychology, developed his theory of personality for about half a century. His first major publication relating to crime was the book *Crime and Personality* (1964), and his ideas were subsequently developed, sometimes in collaboration with other authors (and, in particular, with his wife Sybil). Although it embraces various approaches to behaviour, including an element of control theory (see Chapter 12), the analysis is based in part on learning and so it is convenient to consider it here.

The essence of Eysenck's theory is that some people are born with cortical and autonomic nervous systems which affect their ability to be conditioned by environmental stimuli. Behaviour, influenced by both biological and social factors, is taken to define an individual's personality. Eysenck sought to determine the characteristics of personality in accordance with three sets of criteria. First, he related differences in human temperament to an individual's placing on three independent dimensions: neuroticism–stability (N), psychoticism–superego (P), and extraversion–introversion (E). Each of these dimensions is seen as a continuum and most people fall within the middle range. Second, Eysenck proposed a biological basis of personality which claims that levels of N, E and P are determined by genetic influences. Third, the theory relies on socialisation. Compliance to rules is enforced through Pavlovian classical conditioning methods whereby punishment is inflicted by parents or others (Bartol 1991).

Temptation to indulge in previously-punished behaviour will result in the arousal of a conditioned anxiety response: as Eysenck put it, 'conscience is indeed a conditioned reflex'. Extroverts, who are cortically underaroused, are constantly seeking stimulation to ensure a high level of arousal. This results in impulsive behaviour and a continual search for excitement. They will, therefore, not condition as well as introverts—who are cortically overaroused—as they are more resistant to the pain of punishment. Introverts are characterised by a reserved and quiet nature (see Chapter 14).

It is an essential element of Eysenck's theory that people who engage in anti-social behaviour are more likely to be extrovert as, through poor conditionability, they will have failed to develop a proper 'conscience' as children. Moreover, he predicted that the habitual elements of neurosis, when combined with the force of extroversion, are even more likely to lead to such behaviour. Criminals, therefore, should also have a high N score. Eysenck's later addition of the P dimension (H Eysenck and S Eysenck 1968) was based on research evidence that both criminality and psychopathy are particularly common among the relatives of psychotic patients.

To summarise, therefore, the likely success of conditioning, according to Eysenck, will be as follows:

(1) stable introverts (low N, low E) = easy to condition;

(2) stable extroverts (low N, high E) and neurotic introverts (high N, low E) = less easy to condition, but present few problems;

(3) neurotic extroverts (high N, high E) = difficult to condition;

(4) neurotic extroverts with a high P rating (high N, high E, high P) = the most difficult to condition.

Each of Eysenck's criteria will now be considered in turn.

(a) Structure of personality

The concepts that Eysenck relied on at the heart of his theory are all problematic. The introversion–extroversion continuum was taken from the writings of the psychologist Carl Jung. The extrovert is described as both sociable and impulsive whereas the introvert, who tries to avoid stimulation, has a preference for being alone and only acting after due consideration. However, although extroverted personalities can easily be found among inmate populations, any visit to a prison would soon reveal large numbers of inmates with an anxious or introverted temperament. It has also been argued that extroversion is simply a label attached to behaviour that other people consider to be undesirable. Taylor *et al.* (1973) pointed out the similarity between the extroversion–introversion continuum and the distinction made by Matza and Sykes between formal values and subterranean values (see Chapter 8). Matza and Sykes argued that everyone holds subterranean values—such as spontaneity and desire for excitement and new experiences—but, for most people, they are only expressed in leisure activities. Juvenile delinquents, however, tend to adopt these values at times when other people are adopting the formal values of the steady home life or the workplace.

'Neuroticism' (N) is a psychoanalytic term and, arguably, has no real meaning outside such an explanation of behaviour (see above). Eysenck thought that neuroticism is related to the operation of the autonomic nervous system. This means that individuals at the top of the scale will experience strong reactions to any painful or unpleasant stimuli. Self-report personality questionnaires have shown a high level of the characteristics that Eysenck considered make up the N rating, such as anxiety, depression and low self-esteem. These are certainly not confined to 'neurotic' patients and can be associated with a variety of personality disorders. Moreover, it seems somewhat strange that criminality should be linked with both a high E rating, which relates to difficulty in conditioning, and a high N rating, which relates to comparative ease of conditioning.

There is also a difficulty with the precise meaning of the P scale, which is supposed to measure attributes such as hostility, a preference for solitude and a lack of feeling for others. No evidence is provided that it measures any kind of genetic transmission of psychosis (Howarth 1986). Indeed, the Eysencks subsequently suggested that, although originally intended to distinguish the psychotic personality from the neurotic, it might be a better test of psychopathy than psychoticism (S Eysenck and H Eysenck 1972). In one of his last publications, Eysenck (1996) stated that high levels of testosterone coupled with low levels of monoamine oxidase (MAOA) and serotonin (see Chapter 14) might play a significant role in the creation of psychoticism.

Evidence has been provided both for and against Eysenck's use of E, N and P. McGurk and McDougall (1981) analysed the E, N and P scores of 100 delinquent and 100 non-delinquent college pupils. The clusters predicted to be related to criminality—High E–High N, and High E–High N–High P—were only found in the delinquent group; whereas the Low E–Low N cluster was, as predicted, only found among the non-delinquents. Yet, other research has reached different conclusions. In a study of three borstal training institutions, Little (1963) showed that neither the timing of the release nor the recidivism rates of the inmates was related to extroversion or introversion. Hoghughi and Forrest (1970) found a significantly high level of introversion in a sample of approved school boys, which is completely the opposite of what would be predicted from Eysenck's theory.

Although far less popular nowadays, Eysenck's theory is still being used by researchers. An analysis of data from thirty-seven countries by Kirkcaldy and Brown (2000) found that extroversion was related to the crime rate. However, there was no significant correlation between crime and psychoticism. In a Brazilian study, Labato (2000) discovered that extroverts were more likely to use 'dramatic' weapons, such as firearms, when committing a crime, whereas introverts were more likely to use less dramatic weapons, such as knives.

(b) The biological basis of personality

Eysenck was in broad agreement with Sheldon's research on 'body types' which is considered in Chapter 14. Eysenck thought that a mesomorphic physique, where muscle and bone predominate, will be the hardest type to condition. A critique of this research can also be found in Chapter 14.

A central part of Eysenck's theory related extraversion to low cortical arousal (see Chapter 15). Yet, the evidence does not generally reveal any differences in this regard between introverts and extroverts (Gale and Edwards 1983). Eysenck also argued that extroverts require more stimulation than introverts to achieve a particular response. Delinquents (who, on this analysis, are extroverts) easily become bored and seek excitement by taking risks. Therefore, it follows—according to Eysenck—that they must have a higher optimal level of stimulation. According to this view, there is a generally-agreed appropriate level of stimulation, against which any increase can be measured. However, as no such consensus exists, the claim is difficult to verify. Zuckerman (1984) considered that there is no evidence linking optimal level of stimulation with low arousal.

One study even suggested that sensation-seekers have a more excitable central nervous system than usual (Smith *et al.* 1989).

(c) Socialisation

Eysenck's reliance on the conditioning of children by arousing anxiety or fear is criticised by many social learning theorists, who argue that the reinforcement of behaviour which is clearly contrary to that which is disapproved of (that is, desired behaviour) is just as necessary. His views have also been attacked for having made too great assumptions for human development from studies of animals in laboratories (Passingham 1972). Claims that introverts condition more easily than other people are usually based on eye-blink or electrodermal tests. Yet, as Passingham (1972) pointed out, it is doubtful whether the circumstances shown to favour conditioning in introverts (such as short intervals between the stimulus) are likely to be confronted in everyday life. In any event, the evidence appears to suggest that introverts are better conditioned by aversive stimuli; it is by no means clear that they react better to positive reinforcements (Gray 1981).

(d) Gordon Trasler

In his book *The Explanation of Criminality* (1962), Gordon Trasler set out a rather different theory of socialisation to that of Eysenck. Like Eysenck, Trasler accepted that people have a differential ability to be conditioned, which is genetically influenced and based on an individual's placing on the extraversion–introversion scale. However, Trasler placed more emphasis on the differential quality of the conditioning a child receives, and gave more weight to the withdrawal of approval than to physical punishment. The anticipation of the loss of approval was viewed as equivalent to the anticipation of pain. Trasler considered that it is better for parents to use a few well-defined principles than to try to deal with each prohibition separately. Unlike Eysenck, who thought that verbal reinforcement can have at best a subsidiary role, Trasler regarded it as a primary form of socialisation.

Trasler thought that, as the middle class provide a better quality of conditioning than the working class, the prevalence of crime among the working class can be seen as a result of lax and permissive child-rearing practices. As it is genetically-based, extroversion is equally distributed throughout the population and cannot be the cause of the different levels of crime between the classes. However, as the middle class have received more efficient social training, those who turn to crime are more likely to be extroverts and, therefore, harder to condition. Psychopaths provide a general exception to all this, as they generally lack proper mechanisms to learn social prohibitions.

(e) Evaluation

Eysenck's analysis attempted to incorporate sociological, biological and environmental ideas about criminal behaviour. Despite the views of some psychologists (for example, Feldman 1977) that Eysenck's views would be influential in developing a scientific explanation of the 'anti-social personality', criticisms have been directed at the very heart of the theory. It has been suggested that the vital link between classical conditioning and socialisation has not been adequately established (Raine and Venables 1981). Several researchers have discovered personality traits other than ones identified by Eysenck which are related to criminal behaviour (McGurk *et al.* 1981). Other writers have been unconvinced about the idea of assessing personality through such traits at all (Phares 1984).

Eysenck's theory of crime and personality has received a vast amount of empirical testing, much of it by Eysenck and his associates. As new criticisms have emerged, Eysenck retreated from earlier positions and modifications were made. He conceded that many of the early studies of the theory were inadequate because they examined personality traits individually rather than in combination, and rarely controlled for the type of crime (Eysenck and Gudjonsson 1989). In his later writings, Eysenck sought to emphasise that he was describing *anti-social* behaviour and that many crimes, such as those which are politically motivated, do not come within his analysis of this term (Eysenck 1984). In one of the later manifestations of the theory (Eysenck and Gudjonsson 1989), it was stated that it is centred on 'the actively anti-social, psychopathic criminal' and excludes 'inadequate' offenders. This relatively narrow definition does not appear to have been emphasised in the early statements of Eysenck's views.

One of the biggest problems that emerges from the copious psychological studies is the weak or even non-existent correlation between extroversion (E) and delinquency. Although this still leaves open the possibility of a relationship between crime, neuroticism (N) and psychoticism (P)—and there is evidence linking P with criminality (Furnham 1984)—it is apparent that not only are N and P questionable concepts, but that extroversion is a crucial component of the theory. Farrington *et al.* (1982) considered sixteen comparisons of convicted offenders with control groups. In most of them, offenders rated higher on N and P, but not on E. Some self-report studies indicated a correlation between E and criminality but, as these were seldom borne out by records of official convictions, the researchers concluded that extroverted youths are prone to exaggerate their misconduct. There are, however, consistent findings of a relationship between P and both self-report and official records of crime. Yet, Blackburn (1987) found that, in a study of mentally disordered offenders, high P scores were obtained by what he termed secondary psychopaths, who are more introverted than primary psychopaths.

Although Eysenck sought to explain the apparently poor relationship between extroversion and offending, his explanations are not entirely convincing. For example, he claimed that the sociability scores of prisoners may be depressed because of the restrictions placed on their behaviour. However, the evidence suggests that short-term prisoners are no more likely to be extroverted than those serving long sentences (Burgess 1972). Eysenck also stated that extroversion is mainly significant in youthful delinquency. Yet, in one of his own studies (S Eysenck and H Eysenck 1977) an E rating was only discovered more commonly in offenders aged over forty. He has also suggested that extroversion could be divided into tests for sociability and impulsiveness, with only the latter relating to offending (S Eysenck and H Eysenck 1971). A study by S Eysenck and McGurk (1980) found a sample of offenders scoring higher than non-offenders on measures of impulsiveness, with no difference between the two samples on sociability.

Conclusion

Learning theorists have not produced an individual theory of criminality, but they have highlighted the important processes by which particular environmental influences can become translated into criminal behaviour. However, it must be remembered that their analyses depend on the application of a few basic principles to the complex variety of human behaviour (Nietzel 1979). Experiments in both operant conditioning and social learning theory usually relate to specific learning tasks which are unlikely to be replicated in day-to-day living. The fact that pigeons may react to a certain stimulus in a laboratory setting does not mean they would do so in their natural environment. Nor do learning theorists pay any real attention to the variables of sex and age. Crucially, there is little consideration of differences among individuals. Eysenck attempted to deal with this, but his explanations are open to criticism. Individual differences are portrayed as deficiencies in the ability to learn how to gain rewards. This is at the expense of any consideration of individual aims, beliefs, expectations or, indeed, any other form of social stimulus. It almost seems as if the learning process is portrayed as taking place in a vacuum, without an appreciation that it involves an interaction with other human beings. Learning theories can also be criticised for failing to account for the fact that large numbers of offenders abandon persistent criminality in early adulthood.

Laboratory experiments usually involve the use of noxious stimuli on animals, but evidence suggests that verbal reasoning or statements of rules are more effective than such stimuli in affecting the behaviour of young children (Parke 1974). In the real world, it is generally impossible for the punishment to coincide with the forbidden act. Moreover, as punishment is based on a moral evaluation of particular behaviour, its efficacy is likely to depend on whether the recipient perceives it as legitimate (Zillman 1979).

It is commonly argued that, at an operational level, learning theories offer a mechanism for dominant or powerful groups in a society to impose their will on others in accordance with their own ideology. Images of George Orwell's 'thought police' in his book *Nineteen Eighty-Four* are sometimes invoked. Many psychologists appear to assume that such conditioning would only ever be exercised in a benign manner in democratic societies, such as in common child-rearing practices (although a comparison with the Victorian era shows how even these can change). In Eysenck's writings, 'the good' that should be reinforced can usually be found somewhere near the surface, as is shown in his comment 'The permissive society is earning the rewards it deserves' (Eysenck and Gudjonsson 1989).

However, it is necessary to treat this criticism with a certain amount of caution. As Ions (1977) has pointed out, 'education is itself a form of social engineering'. The question of the existence of a process which enables people to learn behaviour patterns and attitudes must be distinguished from the use (or manipulation) of that process by a society for its own ends. If such a process does indeed occur, it is important that society recognises the fact. Otherwise, the abuse which is rightly feared will become a more realistic prospect.

17

Violent, aggressive and sexual offences

Although psychological explanations have been used to explain various types of criminal or deviant behaviour, it is violent and sexual offences that are most frequently subjected to such an analysis. There are several reasons for this. It is shown in Chapter 2 that many crimes involve behaviour which was formerly considered perfectly acceptable, but which society has subsequently decided to criminalise. However, psychological theories are particularly suitable for explaining unusual behaviour which often appears aggressive and is likely to be deprecated in most countries. There is also the question of comprehension. The vast majority of people spend most of their life acting in a physically non-aggressive manner. Some may indulge in a range of criminal offences which many people find easy to understand, if not condone: crimes against property—which make up the bulk of recorded criminal offences—perhaps provide the best example of this. However, excessively violent and sexual crimes seem far more difficult to comprehend. People who may imagine circumstances in which they could act fraudulently or perhaps even commit a burglary cannot understand what drives certain individuals to mutilate their victims with an axe or sexually abuse young children. There is more likely to be a feeling that 'something must be wrong with them' and the opinions of doctors and psychologists may be sought to provide 'the answer'.

Violent and aggressive offences

The words 'violence' and 'aggression' do not have standard definitions. Indeed, neither is a term of art in the main criminal offences, which use technical words with their own particular definitions, such as assault; battery; actual bodily harm; wounding; and grievous bodily harm. Violence usually refers to the infliction of injury by force. If the word were taken to include behaviour which was not intended, but resulted from reckless or negligent conduct or omission, then the range of situations covered would be considerably extended to include, for example, accidents at the workplace and non-criminal behaviour. As this chapter concentrates on the psychology of violence, unintentional acts will not be considered (although some psychologists would deny that consequences can ever be 'accidental').

Aggression, a wider and more interesting term, is believed by many, including psychoanalysts (see Chapter 16), to be a basic human instinct which needs to be channelled into constructive activity during early childhood. In common parlance, aggression is often referred to as an attribute particularly in sport and even in business, with references to practices such as 'aggressive sales techniques'. Such usage may seem far removed from physical attacks, but it is important to realise that not only are aggressive tendencies present in everyone, but that in some social settings they are expected or encouraged. Moreover, in certain situations the use of violence is legitimised. Non-consensual violence may be inflicted in time of war, in reasonable self-defence, and in the corporal punishment of children by their parents. Consensual violence may be used (up to a certain degree of harm) in boxing and sado-masochistic activity. On the other hand, in some religious communities any form of physical violence is forbidden.

Van Eyken (1987) pointed out that, in order to amount to a criminal offence, aggression must refer to the causing of harm which is unjustified from an observer's perspective. Blumenthal *et al.* (1971) found that, whereas most of their respondents considered that student demonstrations against the Vietnam War constituted violent behaviour, few thought that violence had been perpetrated when the police hit the demonstrators. It seems impossible to separate aggression from its moral context.

A working definition of aggression for psychologists has been provided by Zillman (1979), who referred to actions which aim to inflict injury or harm on a person who is motivated to avoid it. This does not distinguish between legal and illegal behaviour, but does exclude harm which was sought by the recipient and emphasises the importance of intention on the part of the perpetrator. The definition also covers a wide range of conduct from verbal abuse to homicide.

(a) Frequency of violent offences

Homicides have a very high clear-up rate, both because the police devote a lot of resources to their investigation and because the killers were often acquainted with their victims. The mystique surrounding homicide at least partly accounts for its being the subject of much research. Although rates have increased throughout the world since the late 1960s, it is still a comparatively rare occurrence. Central and South American countries have the highest homicide rates, and England and Wales has one of the lowest. About one-third of killers are usually judged to be suffering from a mental disorder and, until the 1960s, a similar number committed suicide. Nowadays, this figure is about 8 per cent, possibly because of the abolition of the death penalty, or because the increased frequency of homicide has led to its being perceived as less reprehensible. Not surprisingly, the evidence shows that homicides and serious assaults occur most frequently in public places at weekends. Block (1977) considered that most homicides result from intended assaults that end up going too far. Robbery is an unusual form of violent crime as it involves the planned use of force, not usually accompanied by anger, with a particular purpose other than harming the victim. The legal definition of robbery in England and Wales involves 'the use or threat of force' and most robberies do not result in any physical injury to the victim.

In recent years a growing amount of attention has been paid to violence between members of a family. This has largely resulted from information obtained from small-scale victim surveys, such as those in Islington and on Merseyside (see Chapter 3). However, it is clear that, however sensitive the enquiry, many people are still unwilling to admit to being the victims of domestic violence. It was lawful in Britain for a husband to beat his wife as recently as the nineteenth century and it is still lawful for parents to beat their children, provided that only 'reasonable force' is used. Moreover, opinion polls suggest that many parents consider they should retain this right. It is for this reason that the much-used term 'abuse' is problematic with regard to physical violence against children. With adults, the legal situation is clear: an assault on a spouse or partner is just as much a crime as one committed on a total stranger. Such violence is generally perceived as being committed by men against women, but research by Straus (1993) showed that American wives reported instigating aggression against their husbands in a substantial number of cases.

(b) Explanations of violent offending

(i) Biological aspects

Explanations from a purely biological perspective are founded on the belief that the brain and muscular coordination which leads to aggressive behaviour is governed by specific neurochemical factors which operate in a similar fashion in both humans and animals. On such an analysis, the voluntary control of behaviour is always subject to the operation of internal physiological reactions. A well-known proponent of this approach was Lorenz (1966), who considered that there is a common aggressive instinct which functions to ensure the survival of the fittest for reproduction and leadership. Humans, therefore, have to organise their lives to allow for the release of aggressive energy; sport and militaristic displays are examples of such socially permissible outlets. However, Lorenz provided no clear evidence for his views. More recent writers, such as Burgess and Draper (1989), have offered accounts based on genetic influences, whereby human evolution has required the possibility of an aggressive reaction to combat threats to its survival. Furthermore, a study of twins by Rushton *et al.* (1986) based on self-reported aggressiveness suggested that a tendency to violent behaviour could be inherited.

This general approach has been widely criticised by many biologists and social scientists (American Psychological Association 1990). They have pointed out that there is no evidence for physiological mechanisms specific to aggression in animals, let alone in humans. In any event, such an analysis takes a wide view of aggression, equating action in the protection of territory, response to danger and conflicts over hierarchy. There is little similarity between animal aggression, which is usually either defensive or predatory in search of food, and human aggression, which generally arises either from anger or for instrumental purposes, such as the commission of a robbery or a revenge attack. This last form of aggression is peculiar to humans and must surely arise from cultural factors. A further problem with the biological approach is its assumption of the inevitability of human aggression. The fact that evolutionary development has prepared humans to attack in certain situations only serves to enable such a response, which will still be dependent on cultural and situational factors. It is now believed that prehistoric humans had little recourse to violence and that organised aggression has only developed during the past 10,000 years (Turner *et al.* 1976). Nor is there any strong biological evidence for sex differences in levels of aggression. Any relevant biological differences are only likely to be significant in conjunction with cultural and gender-role factors (see Chapter 13).

There is some research indicating a significant relationship between aggression and low intelligence. Huesmann *et al.* (1987) discovered a negative correlation between aggression and IQ over a period of twenty-two years, although the researchers considered that the strongest influence occurred during childhood.

(ii) Learning theories

It has been suggested that the expression of violent behaviour is related to either the experience or observation of aggression. However, there is dispute among psychologists as to what particular aspects of aggression provide the reinforcement. Some argue that aggression arising from anger is negatively reinforced by the consequential reduction of the anger, and that instrumental aggression (for example, for robbery) is positively reinforced by the attainment of the sought-after reward. Zillman (1979) reported that signs of injury or pain served as inhibitors to aggression. Berkowitz (1989) is one of several people who have claimed that the frustration of an individual's efforts is a key trigger to aggression. This may be true in some situations, but it is also the case that frustration by no means inevitably leads to aggression, and aggression can be caused by an insult or an attack.

Other learning theorists prefer to give more weight to cognitive aspects of the process. The best-known writer in this tradition is Albert Bandura, whose work is discussed in Chapter 16. Bandura claimed that most learning takes place through observation. Individuals become able to anticipate the likely effectiveness of different types of behaviour in attaining desired goals. Bandura considered that aggression is simply one means of achieving such goals; others include attempting to solve or even the avoidance of problems. Continued resort to aggression may ensue either from the reinforcement of such behaviour, or from a failure to learn alternative means of achieving desired aims or dealing with aversive events. Other research by social cognitive theorists has suggested that children who act aggressively at school and are consequently rejected by their peers have difficulty in interpreting others' intentions, and are more likely to anticipate hostility in situations that are perceived as mildly threatening (Dodge and Somberg 1987).

Longitudinal studies of delinquents and aggressive children have indicated that their behaviour is related to high levels of criminality and marital conflict on the part of their parents. Becker *et al.* (2004) observed a group of more than 350 battered women and one of their children over ten years. The women were asked periodically about their life and their child's behaviour. The researchers found that children from violent homes were 2.3 times more likely to be cruel to animals and 2.4 times more likely to start fires than those from non-violent homes.

Violent adults generally report a childhood of experiencing physical abuse and witnessing violence among others. Association with delinquent peers can also form part of the learning process.

There is no clear relationship between anger and physical aggression, and Averill (1982) has pointed out that the expression of anger can have constructive consequences in the development of relationships. However, at the other extreme the arousal of intense anger can lead to attempts to injure the instigator. Beck (1976) concluded that anger follows an assessment of an unwarranted violation of an individual's territory, both personal and physical. Assessments may also include a moral consideration as to whether the violation was intentional or justified, and what ought to have happened. It also seems likely that threats to self-esteem can lead to violent reactions in some men. Hans Toch (1969) thought that threats to masculine self-image and 'reputation' were behind many violent confrontations between police and delinquents. He also found that police officers who made the most frequent use of violence in the course of their duties had often used strong (as opposed to gentle) verbal threats early in confrontations, thus ensuring a recourse to violence more quickly than was necessary. It is possible that certain individuals with a low self-esteem consider that the only way they can influence people is through violence (Tedeschi 1983).

There is some evidence of a relationship between psychopathy and violence (see Chapter 15). According to Carney (1978), violent offenders have difficulty in trusting and empathising with others. Serin (1991) found that high ratings of psychopathy among prisoners were associated with violent offending, together with high self-reported levels of impulsivity and aggressiveness. In contrast to the emphasis on individual factors as sources of aggression, some psychologists maintain that violence can only be properly considered in its social context. For example, aggression may be necessary as a means of maintaining status in, or ensuring dominance over, a group. Violence can even be controlled by subcultural norms which provide for when it is, or is not, appropriate. In a study of accounts presented by the participants, Marsh et al. (1978) evaluated 'football hooliganism' and concluded that much of the behaviour amounts to little more than ritualised gesturing and taunting between rival supporters, often based on well-established local and regional rivalries. Both sides understand the rules, and actual violence, although reported at length by the media, is comparatively rare. Marsh et al. argued that such confrontations are functional in both providing excitement and containing aggression.

(iii) Psychoanalytic explanations

Freud maintained that aggression is an instinct and, although some-times disagreeing over the detailed implications of this, most psycho-analysts consider it to be a core principle of their approach. Aggressive energy is constantly created and can be released in violent outbursts unless properly controlled by the superego. Where normal develop-ment does not occur, fixation at certain stages can result, particularly at the oral and anal-sadistic phases. This may only be revealed in later years, for example in outbursts of sadistic violent behaviour. Even relatively minor sadistic (and masochistic) activity can result from such a fixation. The urge to kill a woman can be a reaction formation to an Oedipal desire. External factors can certainly trigger such events, but the vital aggressive drive comes from within. Psychoanalytic explanations claim that aggression can also be displaced on to other, more acceptable (or less harmful) pursuits, such as sport.

(c) Factors precipitating violence

There is a body of evidence suggesting that levels of violence are higher in hotter areas, and that rates can generally fluctuate in accordance with the temperature throughout the year. This is claimed to be the case even after allowances are made for cultural factors and increased opportunities for greater social contact during warm weather. In a study of 10,000 assaults in Dallas in 1980 and 1981, Harries and Stadler (1988) discovered a marked increase during periods of high temperature. Michael and Zumpe (1983) reported a similar finding for rape. Sivarajasingam and Shepherd (2001) looked at a sample of assault victims reporting to thirty-three hospital accident and emergency units in England and Wales between 1995 and 1998. They found that the number of assaults was significantly higher between July and September. Anderson (1989) considered that people probably blame others for the discomfort they are suffering, which is actually caused by the heat. Some researchers have suggested that infringements of, or perceived threats to, 'personal space' can also trigger aggressive behaviour. O'Neal *et al.* (1979) found that feelings of anger lead to a desire to maintain a greater interpersonal distance. It is tempting to compare this with the importance of territoriality for some types of animal, but any relationship is unclear.

Findings which link aggression with environmental factors such as noise levels are not that surprising. Perhaps more interesting is the discovery of Lieber and Sherin (1972) that the peak homicide rates in two American counties occurred during periods when there was a full moon. The authors speculated that there could be a connection between gravitational forces and emotional state. This would be in keeping with former beliefs associating lunar activity with mental disturbance.

(d) The aggressive personality

The foregoing explanation of how aggressive behaviour can originate did not distinguish between individuals who commit isolated acts of violence and those who are habitually aggressive. Research in America has indicated that violent offenders have longer criminal careers than property offenders (Blumstein *et al.* 1986). In the longitudinal Cambridge Study in Delinquent Development, Farrington (1989) found that ratings of aggression between the ages of eight and ten showed a significant correlation with self-reported aggression later in life. Nevertheless, although many aggressive adults were aggressive as children, the majority of children who fight and commit other acts of violence do not proceed to commit seriously aggressive acts in adulthood. It is possible, however, that they may have aggressive tendencies which manifest themselves in other ways.

Researchers have identified both the under-controlled violent offender, who has weak inhibitions, engages in violence on a fairly regular basis, and in an extreme form is identified with psychopathy; and the over-controlled violent offender, who has strong inhibitions against aggression and therefore, when moved to resort to it (which will be rare), will do so in an extremely violent manner. This is consistent with unaggressive individuals who are continually provoked over a period of time, ruminate over their grievances, and then finally erupt into a frenzy of violence following a single act of provocation (Zillmann 1979). The so-called 'battered woman syndrome' may provide an illustration of this.

Two regular forms of violence, which have received increasing publicity in recent years, will now be considered. They are abuse between spouses or partners and child abuse.

(e) Spouse or partner abuse

In Britain, violence in the home is generally referred to as domestic violence, although some feminist writers argue that the term 'domestic' is misleading, as it implies that the private nature of the abuse is more important than its gendered nature. The advent of victim surveys and Left Realist research led to a greater appreciation of the extent of this abuse, and both psychologists and sociologists have considered factors which may underlie such behaviour.

Various estimates of the extent of this type of abuse have been made. Mooney (1993) discovered that one in three of a sample of north London women reported having experienced domestic violence (including rape) at some time in their life, and one in ten claimed to have suffered during the previous twelve months. Using data from the National Survey of Wives in Great Britain, Painter and Farrington (1998) found that 28 per cent of wives claimed to have been 'hit' by their husbands. Nor is domestic violence confined to poor or lower-class households; Painter and Farrington also discovered that about 16 per cent of middle- and upper-middle-class wives claimed to have been hit by their husbands.

Information provided by battered women suggests that most abuse occurs in the home between 10 p.m. and 2 a.m. at weekends, and often in the presence of children or relatives. The woman will have typically felt increasingly coerced in the relationship. Violence is most likely to take place in homes where the traditional male–female role division is particularly rigid. Most such events begin with arguments based on four general themes: men's jealousy and possessiveness; disagreements about domestic work and resources; men's thinking they have the right to punish 'their' women for perceived wrongdoing; and the importance to men of retaining or exercising their power and authority. Men usually consider that their partners were responsible for the arguments and the resulting violence (Dobash and Dobash 1998). It also appears that the majority of battered women have been raped by their husbands or partners (Walker 1988).

(i) Psychological explanations

One of the clearest findings to emerge from both controlled studies and clinical surveys is that a majority of abusers have either experienced violence in childhood or witnessed violence between their parents. This is supportive of the view that abusive patterns of behaviour are passed on through social learning mechanisms. It has been suggested that abused women carry some sort of expectancy of an abusive and dependent relationship into adulthood, with their compliant response only reinforcing the abuser's physical aggression (Walker 1988). It has even been hypothesised that abused women may look for relationships similar to those of their mothers (Hanks and Rosenbaum 1977). However, most feminists would reject these arguments and ask why there are not far more cases where women abused in childhood assault their male partners. The abusers are likely to experience problems with alcohol and have a criminal record. Some will have learned a 'traditional' attitude of the subservient role of women from their fathers. There is evidence that abusers suffer from low esteem, perhaps resulting from having been abused as a child (Johnston 1988).

There is some evidence that levels of family violence are affected by levels of violence in society as a whole (Parke 1977). With the increasing strain on the provision of social services, there is a growing likelihood that abusive families will not receive the help and support they need.

(ii) Sociological explanations

Most, but not all, of the research relates to the more common occurrence of violent males physically abusing their wives or female partners. Although relatively few psychological studies have been conducted in this area, there has been an extensive contribution from sociologists. Some of these are dismissive of attempts to provide psychological explanations, arguing that such approaches seek to absolve violent men of blame and shift the focus away from the patriarchal nature of society. However, further investigation seems justified. Cultural factors alone cannot easily account for variations in the levels of abusiveness among individuals, and mere reliance on the patriarchal nature of society would considerably over-predict the amount of male violence that occurs.

Indeed, patriarchy is a key term in sociologists' explanations of domestic violence. Feminists consider most societies to be patriarchal, in that they establish and maintain the power of men over women. Traditionally, societies have been based around the family, which was viewed as an essential institution for the smooth functioning of day-to-day life. The husband and wife, although having different roles, were portrayed as broadly equal in status and jointly concerned with the bringing up of their children. Violence would be largely confined to poor or 'problem' families, and either the husband or wife could be responsible. If the violence escalated or was seen as a problem, the parties could separate.

Feminists contend that such a view of family life does not accord with reality. Although some researchers (for example, Moffitt *et al.* 2001) have pointed out that there is a significant amount of violence perpetrated by women against men, the preponderance of evidence shows that most violent acts in intimate relationships are committed by men and that, when women do resort to violence against their male partners, it differs from male violence in 'nature, frequency, intention, intensity, physical injury and emotional impact' (Dobash and Dobash 2004).

This immediately raises a query about the notion of equality. The fact that most women in relationships are dependent on men for their financial support explains why many do not readily leave their violent partners. The fate of the children can also be a complicating factor. Some women may believe the negative comments their partner makes about them. Others may be prepared to 'give him one more chance' in the belief that they can do something to stop him hitting them.

Domestic and other forms of abuse can have a particularly harmful effect on women. One result can be that they may be propelled into various forms of crime. Research on women in prison has revealed that about half of them have been abused by their husband or partner.

(f) Child abuse

Fortunately, there are few examples of severe physical harm being inflicted by parents on their children. This means that, in practice, the definition of child abuse is something of a grey area. There is some difficulty in determining at what point lawful corporal punishment becomes unlawful physical abuse. Most societies accept the right of parents to inflict 'reasonable' physical punishment on their own children, although more severe forms of beating are increasingly being considered unreasonable, and the provisions of the European Convention on Human Rights (now enshrined in domestic law in the Human Rights Act 1998) have been successfully invoked in defence of the child (see, for example, *A v United Kingdom* (1999) 27 European Human Rights Reports 611). The effect of section 58 of the Children Act 2004 is that any injury of the level of actual bodily harm or worse would not be considered reasonable punishment.

Wherever the legal line is drawn, there is no reason to believe that it will correspond to any change in the effect of the beating. For the purpose of this discussion, a distinction between abuse and punishment will be made although, in terms of the psychological impact, it may be an arbitrary one.

(i) Physical abuse

Traditionally, most people assumed that the justification for the use of physical force against children arose from a mixture of Biblical dictate ('spare the rod and spoil the child') and an understanding that parents sometimes lose their temper with a difficult child. In more recent years, however, the growing appreciation that the physical abuse of children is a genuine problem has resulted in a closer look at the dynamics of the parent–child relationship where violence has occurred. Such abuse of children is not inevitably committed by men: it has been claimed that American mothers were the aggressors in well over half the abuse cases reported to the child protective services (Straus and Gelles (eds) 1990).

Some researchers have pointed to the frequency of child physical abuse at the hands of teenage mothers, and concluded that it is their inflexibility and general deficiency in parenting skills which underlie their recourse to violence (Haskett *et al.* 1994). However, others have asserted that it is not the age of the mothers, but their lack of financial resources and social isolation that place them under considerable stress (Frude 1989, Buchholz and Korn-Bursztyn 1993). Abusive parents may have a general view of life which legitimises the use of physical aggression. In one experiment, mothers considered at low risk for child abuse displayed considerable empathy when shown a picture of a distressed child, whereas mothers considered at high risk failed to show empathy on seeing the same picture (Milner *et al.* 1995).

Herrenkohl and Russo (2001) found that differences in the developmental stage at which children experience harsh childrearing or maltreatment can be significant for later outcomes. In their study, the use of such practices by mothers at preschool age—but not school age—was associated with aggression at school. On the other hand, although the severity of maternal physical discipline at school age was associated with aggression at that age, there was no such relationship with the use of such discipline at preschool age. Herrenkohl and Russo suggested that it is the failure of a child to form a proper attachment with its mother at the preschool age which has the most powerful impact.

There is also evidence linking alcohol and drug abuse to child physical abuse. However, just as with other areas of crime, it would be wrong to conclude that this is a simple, direct causal relationship. It is likely that other problems experienced by the family often result in both substance and child abuse. Research on a sample of prisoners by Sheridan (1995) found that the level of family functioning and extent of offending were linked to both forms of abuse.

Studies of delinquent and aggressive children have shown that their behaviour can be related to the use of violence by their parents, both on each other and on their children. A survey of research findings by the Gulbenkian Foundation (1995) discovered an overwhelming relationship between harsh discipline and the development of anti-social behaviour. In a study of 900 abused children in Indianapolis, it emerged that children who had been physically abused up to the age of eleven were significantly likely to commit violent offences during the next fifteen years (Maxfield and Widom 1996).

Many abusing parents will themselves have been abused as children. Having been thus deprived of affection, they may look to their children to satisfy their emotional needs, and become frustrated when this does not happen. Personality disorders may also be present. Evidence suggests that such parents may also be suffering from depression or experiencing difficulty in controlling aggressive urges. There is no evidence to support earlier claims that significant numbers of abusing parents have a mental disorder; this is more likely to be found in cases of child neglect. Abused children have been found to manifest a greater level of mental retardation and physical handicap than samples of non-abused children, and there is an increased likelihood of their parents viewing them as 'different' (Friedrich and Boriskin 1976). However, it is unclear whether these characteristics are causally or consequentially related to the abuse. Research by McGuigan et al. (2000) showed that the holding of negative views about their children by parents is a stronger indicator of child abuse than the nature of the parents' own relationship.

Studies of physically abused children have revealed the extent of the psychological harm they have suffered. Delays in the development of speech, mistrust of, and aggressive behaviour towards, peers and poor performance on intelligence tests are common. Fortunately, such damage is not necessarily irreversible (Egeland et al. 1988). Nor does it inevitably lead to violent criminal behaviour in later life: Widom's review of the literature (1989) revealed that only a minority of abused children become violent offenders.

(ii) Corporal punishment

A large amount of research has been conducted into the relationship between corporal punishment and violent behaviour. Some of the findings—particularly those trying to ascertain the frequency of corporal punishment—come from self-report studies or surveys based on distant recollections. In America, for example, it has been consistently shown that, whereas over 90 per cent of people claim to have received some form of corporal punishment, a far smaller proportion of adults admit to having administered it.

An alternative form of data-gathering involves contacting children directly in an attempt to find a connection between their current exposure to corporal punishment and levels of aggressive or violent behaviour. Straus, who is one of the leading researchers in this area, maintains that there is a causal connection between the use of physical punishment by parents and the commission of violent crime by their children in later life. In a national study of several thousand American schoolchildren and their parents, Straus (1983) found that 15 per cent of those who did not receive corporal punishment repeatedly committed severe attacks against a sibling, compared with 40 per cent of those who were physically punished, and 76 per cent of those who were consistently abused. In addition, Straus showed that parents who professed a belief in physical punishment were more likely to assault their children. The same children were likely to hit their siblings and were significantly more likely to commit street crime. The more one parent used physical punishment, the greater was the probability that the parent would also assault the other parent (Straus 1991).

Learning theorists generally attribute crime to the failure of socialisation in childhood. Although many people would equate this with a lack of discipline, Bandura (1973) pointed out that violent crime can be learned from excessive or inappropriate use of physical punishment. A child who has been beaten will realise that the use of force, especially by a stronger person against a weaker one, can be an effective means to get one's own way. If this message comes from the parents, the learning process is even more likely to be reinforced. The child may develop anti-social behavioural patterns which lead to rejection by its friends, and result either in the child joining a deviant subculture or living in social isolation.

The inconsistent use of punishment also appears to be a contributory factor. It is likely to result in greater resistance on the part of the child and a decline in the parents' ability to regulate behaviour by positive reinforcement. Parents may then use increasingly severe forms of discipline that can culminate in physical violence (Patterson 1982).

An analysis by Gershoff (2002) of eighty-eight studies dating back some fifty years found strong evidence that corporal punishment was associated with one positive outcome—immediate compliance—and a range of negative ones, including aggression, reduced levels of moral internalisation, and mental health problems.

However, most of these studies are based on retrospective accounts given by the perpetrators or victims, and do not preclude the possible explanation that children who are violent for some other reason are more likely to receive corporal punishment. Nor are they able to ascertain whether childhood aggression develops into adult violence. For these reasons, longitudinal studies, where samples can be monitored over a period of years, would be preferable. The Cambridge Study in Delinquent Development (Farrington 1978) found that harsh discipline of boys (including severe physical punishment) at the age of eight was a predictor of violence up to the age of twenty-one. McCord (1979) observed 253 boys over a twenty-year period. At the outset, parents were classified as 'aggressive' or 'nonaggressive' towards their sons. After twenty years, McCord obtained the men's conviction and prison records, and discovered that parental aggression twenty years earlier predicted the commission of violent crimes.

In answer to the question as to why, given its extensive use, relatively few of the children who receive corporal punishment experience these negative outcomes. Straus (2001) referred to the medical analogy of smoking and lung cancer: although the relationship is clearly established, only about one-third of smokers die from the practice.

Sexual offences

A sexual practice which is considered acceptable at one time and in one place may well be abhorred as deviant or perverted in another. The pharaohs of ancient Egypt committed incest. In certain states in the USA mouth–genital contact has been illegal as a crime against nature. Male homosexuality in England was totally illegal until the Sexual Offences Act 1967 and is still a criminal offence if either participant is under sixteen or the act is committed in a public place. It will therefore be apparent that the category of sexual offence can encompass victimless crimes and even acts between consenting married partners. 'Sexual normality' is based on a combination of religious dictates and the heterosexual behaviour of couples in a family unit. Other sexual acts may be considered as deviant, but not amount to criminal offences. These include fetishism (the use of an inanimate object, such as leather, as a source of sexual arousal), mild sadomasochism between consenting parties, and transvestism (a male's obtaining sexual arousal by dressing in women's clothing). Self-report questionnaires indicate that the incidence of some of these activities is sufficiently common to raise the question of whether it is appropriate to describe them as deviant at all (Gosselin and Wilson 1980). In this chapter, discussion is confined to sexual offences involving victims.

(a) Frequency of sexual offences

In England there is no direct relationship between what are classified as sexual offences and clinical definitions of sexual deviation. For example, 'unlawful sexual intercourse with a girl under sixteen' does not necessarily indicate that the perpetrator is a paedophile (he could be a sixteen-year-old boy). Indecent exposure (exhibitionism) is prosecuted under section 4 of the Vagrancy Act 1824, and there must be intent to insult a female. There is no specific offence covering voyeurism, and 'peeping Toms' are usually charged with the common law offence of conduct likely to cause a breach of the peace. Legal definitions of offences change. Since the case of *R v R* [1992] 1 AC 599, rape can occur in a cohabiting married relationship, and following the Criminal Justice and Public Order Act 1994 it is possible for a man to be raped by another man. The Sexual Offences Act 2003 has extended the definition of rape even further to include penetration of the mouth.

Despite the large amount of publicity they receive, sexual offences form only about 0.7 per cent of notifiable offences in England and Wales and account for fewer than 2 per cent of convicted offenders. With the exception of rape—which more than tripled between 1985 and 1996 (Harris and Grace 1999)—the rate of increase in reported sexual offences has been less than for other types of crime. However, official crime statistics are an unreliable indicator of the amount of crime that occurs, and this is particularly the case in relation to sexual crimes, where the victim may be too scared or embarrassed to report the incident. At least part of the increase in the number of reported rapes in England and Wales may be the result of police changes in their procedure for dealing with rape victims, which are now designed to make the environment of the police station appear less hostile and encourage more victims to come forward. Nevertheless, the British Crime Survey 1988 estimated that the police recorded less than one-fifth of indecent assaults and rapes (Mayhew *et al.* 1989). Victim surveys themselves are likely to uncover more incidents, but they do not reveal the full picture as they usually exclude young children and, unless conducted with extreme sensitivity, are unlikely to lead to complete disclosure.

American victim surveys show considerable discrepancies in the percentage of women claiming to have been victims of rape or attempted rape, ranging from 9 per cent (Kilpatrick *et al.* 1985) to 44 per cent (Russell 1984). The same applies to victims of child sexual abuse, with estimates of 6 per cent to 62 per cent for women and 3 per cent to 31 per cent for men (Finkelhor 1986). The discrepancies may be due in part to the definitions adopted by the researchers (attempted rape may cause some difficulties) and the way in which respondents interpret them. Self-report studies also suggest a higher level of victimisation than is revealed in the official statistics and, in the area of sexual offences, the scope for under-reporting is quite considerable. A survey of imprisoned rapists and child molesters admitted to between two and five times more crimes than those for which they had been convicted (Groth *et al.* 1982). An American study by Koss *et al.* (1987) has claimed that 8 per cent of male students admitted to rape or attempted rape. However, the researchers' methodology has been criticised (Sommers 1994) and the whole question of 'date rape' on American campuses has proved to be controversial (Muehlenhard and Hollabaugh 1988).

Sex offenders as identified in official statistics are almost entirely male, with fewer than 2 per cent of those convicted being women, most of whom were implicated (perhaps as accomplices) in child sex abuse cases. They are more likely than property offenders to be over twenty-one, but adolescents are still significantly involved in child sex abuse cases (Perkins 1987). There is little reliable demographic information about sex offenders. A study by Alder (1985) found no relationship between self-reported sexual aggression and class, level of education or prestige of occupation. Nor is there clear evidence as to whether sex offenders are more likely to commit further sexual offences than other types of offender. Soothill and Gibbens (1978) conducted a long-term follow-up study of sex offenders in England and found that almost a quarter had reoffended by the end of their twenty-second year at risk. This is a considerably longer period than most follow up studies of offenders. It appears that sex offenders usually specialise in their particular type of sex crime. On the other hand, there is also evidence indicating that some categories of sex offender are likely to engage in non-sex crimes as well. In their sample of imprisoned offenders, Hall and Proctor (1987) discovered that, although sexual offences against adults proved a good predictor of later non-sexual offences, this was not the case when the sexual offences had been committed against children.

(b) Explanations of sexual offending

(i) Biological aspects

There is a widely-held belief that sex offenders suffer from an excessively high sexual drive which they are unable to control. This would be a conveniently simple explanation, but unfortunately it does not accord with reality. Certain hormones are necessary for the existence of sexual arousal in males, but there is no evidence that hormones can influence the quality or nature of sexual arousal. Most researchers now agree that some form of learning is necessary. It is, however, conceivable that this process could be affected by inherited genetic factors. Quinsey (1984) has drawn attention to animal studies showing a close link between the nerve centres of aggression and sexual arousal, and has suggested that this may be an evolutionary consequence of the advantages of forced mating.

(ii) Learning theories

These attribute sexual deviance to the learning of attachments to inappropriate stimuli. McGuire *et al.* (1965) considered that an arousing experience can lead to masturbatory fantasies. Laws and Marshall (1990) claimed that some stimuli can more easily function as conditioning agents for sexual arousal because of their evolutionary importance, and that fantasies may become behaviour on account of role models or other forms of reinforcement. Men who experience difficulty in their social dealings with women may find it easier to succumb to deviant temptations, particularly as they may involve less anxiety. Some evidence suggests that sexual arousal can be conditioned, but this in itself does not provide a satisfactory explanation as to why a particular form of deviance was selected in the first place. As with other areas of learning theories, it seems clear that situational and environmental factors cannot be overlooked.

(iii) Psychoanalytic explanations

Freud's explanation of sexual deviance centres on an unresolved Oedipus complex and a regression to earlier fixation points. Failure to identify with the father may result in incestuous desires for the mother. A continuing fear of castration may preclude normal heterosexual relationships. Homosexual paedophiles, who are often narcissistic, look for immature sexual partners whom they see as being like themselves and treat them in the way that they themselves wanted to be treated by their mother. Fenichel (1945) considered that heterosexual paedophilia can be explained in a similar way. The narcissistic males become attracted to little girls they see as being like them. They too will treat the girls in the way they wish their mother had treated them. Others suffer from a castration complex and think of young girls as less threatening. Rapists, who are ambivalent towards their mother, may regress to the anal-sadistic phase under stress and displace their hostility on to women. According to Kline (1987), degradation of women can be indicative of a reaction formation against incestuous desires, and anal fixation may explain the use of buggery in some sadistic assaults.

(iv) Cultural explanations

The cultural acceptance of both the use of force in sex between adults and sex between adults and children in earlier societies has led some writers to suggest that such activity is predominantly regulated by cultural considerations. Feminists see rape as an inevitable culmination of the exercise of power by men over women. Perhaps the most extreme manifestation of this is the statement by Susan Brownmiller (1975) that rape is 'nothing more or less than a conscious process of intimidation by which *all* men keep *all* women in a state of fear' (emphasis in original). Even allowing for the under-reporting of rapes, this view seems to overestimate considerably the extent to which the crime occurs.

The three offences that will be considered in the remainder of this chapter are indecent exposure, sexual offences against children and rape.

(c) Indecent exposure

This legal term describes what psychologists refer to as exhibitionism. Although it is one of the commonest sexual offences, there has been relatively little research into its causes and few definite findings have emerged. Psychoanalysts view exhibitionism as a repudiation of castration anxiety and a symbolic means of warding off forbidden urges towards the mother. Some learning theorists think that the behaviour may have originated in parental reinforcement of childhood genital exposure.

Researchers have concluded that, in general, exhibitionism does not involve any physical contact with the victim or lead to any more serious form of sexual offending, such as rape (for example, Rooth 1973). However, Freund (1990) claimed that up to a quarter of the exhibitionists in his study may have committed rape, and that about a third of them admitted to voyeurism or frottage (surreptitiously rubbing the genitals against another person). In a review of the literature, Blair and Lanyon (1981) could find very few studies comparing exhibitionists with non-deviant control groups. The evidence indicated that exhibitionists suffer stress in early adulthood and that most are married, although few have a satisfactory sexual relationship. In a comparison between exhibitionists and paedophiles in Australia, Myers and Berah (1983) discovered that the exhibitionists had significantly better relationships with their parents, a better record in both education and work, and a relatively low level of alcoholic involvement in their offending. Rader (1977) found that exhibitionists had less serious psychological and social problems than sexual assaulters or rapists. On the other hand, Blair and Lanyon discovered that most exhibitionists were timid and generally lacking in social skills. Many of them also had convictions for non-sexual offences.

(d) Sexual offences against children

People who commit sexual offences against children form a wide-ranging group, varying as to the nature and extent of social contact involved, the preferred age and sex of their victims, and the type of relationship they have with them. Not all such offenders have an exclusive preference for children. The criminal offences are defined in terms of age of the victim, and the offender may have no particular preference for a victim of a particular age. Consent is no defence to these charges in criminal law, and in any event apparent consent may well have been obtained by threats, coercion or simply by the authority of adult persuasive powers. The 'discovery' by the mass media of child sexual abuse in the Western world in recent years and a number of celebrated cases (for example, in Belgium in 1996) have had two particular consequences. The first has been the overshadowing of the fact that, in some societies in earlier times, sexual relations and indeed cohabitation between adult males and pubescent girls was considered perfectly acceptable. Even today, the age of consent in South Korea is thirteen. The second is that the increased publicity, together with the activities of (not always scrupulous) psychotherapists, has 'uncovered' a large amount of childhood sexual abuse, which had allegedly been repressed into the unconscious mind. Allegations that most of these findings are unsustainable have been supported by a committee set up by the Royal College of Psychiatrists (Brandon *et al.* 1998).

Sexual offences against children are more likely to involve genital fondling than vaginal or anal penetration. Nevertheless, force is used in some cases. A sexual preference for children is more common in men who offend exclusively against boys (homosexual paedophiles). This group accounts for about a quarter of known offenders. Only a relatively small minority seek out both male and female victims. Most child sexual abuse is committed by men, but women are responsible for a significant amount. Finkelhor and Russell (1984) considered that, at the lowest estimate, women were the abusers in 14 per cent of the cases involving boys and 6 per cent of those involving girls.

Child sexual abuse remains largely unreported to the authorities and it is the increasing use and sophistication of victim surveys which has brought its likely extent to the attention of the public. The surveys do not adopt a standard approach: some include verbal propositions and others extend the definition of childhood to eighteen. However, many researchers would agree with the view of Mullen (1990) that about 10 per cent to 15 per cent of women have experienced sexual abuse in childhood. For about half, this involved a single experience. Women are more likely to be abused by someone known to them. Finkelhor (1986) found that abused girls are most vulnerable between the ages ten and twelve; they are more likely to live with their natural fathers or stepfathers; they will have witnessed parental conflict; and they will have a poor relationship with one of their parents. These factors are likely to contribute to the girl's emotional vulnerability.

Psychological damage can result to victims of paedophiles, both in the short and the long term. Finkelhor noted that initial effects in more than half the victims included fear, hostility and guilt, and behavioural problems such as leaving home, eating disorders, problems at school and prostitution. In the longer term, victims may show signs of depression, anxiety, low self-esteem and lack of trust. Swanston *et al.* (2003) found that a history of child sexual abuse predicted criminal and aggressive behaviour. There may be problems with the development of sexuality (Noll *et al.* 2003). However, long-term effects are by no means inevitable and serious damage is estimated to occur in no more than about 20 per cent of victims. The worst cases are likely to reveal a combination of abuse and a dysfunctional family.

Investigations into the reasons why adults sexually abuse children often start with a consideration of why sexual relations with a child are fulfilling for the abuser. Psychoanalytic explanations suggest that many child molesters have not fully developed, feel inadequate, and consequently see sexual relations with children as less threatening and providing scope for the exercise of power. Support for this view is found in a study by Howells (1979), which showed that a sample of paedophiles viewed adults as imposing and children non-dominant.

Wilson and Cox (1983) administered questionnaires to members of an English paedophile club, who were found to be sensitive, shy, depressed, lonely and humourless. The attraction of a child to a paedophile may be narcissistic; abusers may see in children an image of themselves at that age. Alternatively, child sexual abuse may be an attempt to deal with the trauma of personal abuse in childhood. The problem with this explanation, as Finkelhor (1986) has pointed out, is that it would predict that most sexual abuse should be committed by women. On the other hand, research suggests that male heterosexual paedophiles in particular are likely to have been abused in their childhood (Freund and Kuban 1994).

On the question of why some people are sexually aroused by children, learning theorists suggest that perhaps they are conditioned through masturbatory fantasies, but there is no clear evidence to support this. However, it appears that sex offenders had their first consenting sexual experience with adults at a younger age than the average person, and it is possible that this led to earlier sexual experimentation. There is also a view that some child sexual abusers only seek out children because they are inhibited in forming adult heterosexual relationships, and are therefore not attracted by any intrinsic quality of the child. This would particularly apply to incest, where the child might fill the role of partner during marital stress or separation.

Researchers have also expressed interest in why paedophiles do not possess the usual inhibitions against sex with children. Paedophiles often state that what they do is not wrong, and this has to be the starting point of any treatment. They frequently claim that lack of resistance on the part of the child implies enjoyment (Ward and Keenan 1999). Although there is no clear scientific evidence for an association between paedophilia and mental illness, research into imprisoned child sexual abusers suggests that they suffer from deficient socialisation. However, this is a characteristic that also applies to other types of offender. Incestuous fathers are often found to have poor bonding with the abused child (Williams and Finkelhor 1990) and the greater risk of abuse for girls from their stepfathers suggests that there may be some significant causal factors in the relationship. In a comparison between paedophiles, rapists and non-offender control groups, the paedophiles were more likely to try to shift the blame from themselves on to their victims (Stermac and Segal 1989).

(e) Rape

Rape in English law is now defined in terms of a penis entering either a vagina, an anus or a mouth. There is relatively little information available on the extent of male rape—men would find it as least as embarrassing as women to report such incidents to the authorities—but it appears to be far less common than male–female attacks. It probably occurs more often in institutions, such as prisons, where heterosexual intercourse is unavailable. The research cited below is all based on the traditional definition of vaginal penetration.

Although earlier studies of rape suggested that many were committed by two or more assailants, it appears that this is now less common. Wright and West (1981), who examined all reported cases of rape in six English counties between 1972 and 1976, discovered that only 13 per cent involved multiple attackers. In such cases, about two-thirds of the offenders were under twenty-one and they had fewer previous convictions for sexual offences or manifested less psychological disturbance than solitary rapists. Group dynamics provided a better explanation than individual pathology. However, more recent research into rape convictions in England showed a larger proportion of solitary rapists, and fewer offenders and victims under twenty-one (Lloyd and Walmsley 1989). Contrary to widely-held opinion, rapists are often known to their victims. Out of 100 women who replied to a questionnaire, twenty had been raped by men with whom they had previously had consensual sexual intercourse; forty-six had been raped by acquaintances; and twenty had been raped by men whom they had met within the previous twenty-four hours (Lees 1996). Statistics for violent offences recorded by the police between 1990 and 1994 revealed that nearly two-thirds of rape victims knew their attackers beforehand and two-thirds of the attacks occurred at the home of the victim or suspect (Watson 1996). Painter and Farrington (1998) discovered that 13 per cent of wives claimed to have been coerced into having sexual intercourse with their husband against their will. Findings from the 1998 and 2000 British Crime Surveys showed that strangers were responsible for only 8 per cent of the rapes that were mentioned in the self-completion questionnaires (Myhill and Allen 2002). Rapes are rarely accompanied by serious physical injury—only 6 per cent of cases in Wright and West's research—but the psychological consequences may be far more severe. Kilpatrick et al. (1985) discovered that 19 per cent of rape victims reported attempting suicide, compared with 2 per cent of non-victimised women.

One of the central issues that emerges from research into rape is whether the crime is based on a primary desire for forcible sex or whether it is essentially motivated by needs for control and power. This latter view was taken by Groth and Burgess (1977), who divided rapes into power rapes, where the offender is seeking power either to express virility or resolve doubts over masculinity; and anger rapes, which are an expression of hatred, contempt and anger for women. In general, anger rapists do not confine their violence to sexual assault; they are likely to beat their victims severely, often causing serious injury. The offender is usually aware that he is attacking through anger, and wishes to displace his feelings on to anyone who is available. Sexual assault accompanies the physical violence because he believes this will be particularly hurtful to his victim. Violent rapes can also occur between spouses or partners. Finkelhor and Yllö (1985) found that these can result from a desire by the husband to dominate, punish and humiliate his wife, rather than as a consequence of any sexual difficulties within the marriage. To back their argument, Groth and Burgess pointed out that 75 per cent of an imprisoned sample related sexual failure during rape. Groth (1979) estimated that about 40 per cent of his sample were anger rapists.

In contrast, power rapes only involve as much force as is necessary to carry out the offence. The research of Finkelhor and Yllö (1985) showed that these were generally committed by educated middle-class men, whose problems with their wives centred around sexual dysfunction. A power rape is designed to demonstrate to both the man himself and his wife that he was in control. Otherwise, power rapes may be committed on strangers to establish the man's sense of dominance.

This analysis is not universally accepted. Felson (1993) considered that most rapists have a strong desire for sexual intercourse and view themselves as sexually deprived. Although they would rather have consensual intercourse, they are prepared to use coercion where necessary. Researchers in Switzerland compared the explanations of a small number of undetected rapists with those of an imprisoned sample (Godenzi 1994). The undetected group generally attributed their actions to sexual motives. However, most of the convicted rapists said that their actions were an expression of violence. Godenzi thought that the imprisoned men did not want to be thought of as sex offenders, or people who needed to resort to violence in order to have intercourse. Feminist writers deny that rape is a result of individual pathology, and claim that it is an inevitable consequence of the power differentials between men and women. However, even people who consider that psychological explanations downplay the significance of the social context of sexual violence between partners might accept that they could provide a plausible explanation of 'blitz rapes' on strangers (Levi 1997).

It has been suggested that rapists have similar family backgrounds to other aggressive offenders and that parental cruelty was common. Christie *et al.* (1979) found that 50 per cent of a sample of rapists had previous convictions for non-sexual assault, many of which were serious enough to attract long prison sentences. There is often evidence of sexual abuse, but with less frequency than for paedophiles. In a study of sex offenders in South East London, Craissati and Beech (2004) discovered that 51 per cent of the child sexual abusers had themselves been abused, compared with a figure of 27 per cent for rapists. There does seem to be a strong relationship between rape and anger. Van Ness (1984) found that 86 per cent of a sample of adolescent rapists reported having an argument with someone between two and six hours prior to the offence. It is also the case that extreme anger heightens autonomic arousal, which is likely to interfere with sexual arousal. This probably explains Groth and Burgess's finding, referred to above, that three-quarters of a sample of imprisoned rapists reported sexual dysfunction during the attack.

Rapists often claim that they were intoxicated at the time of their attack. Although this assertion is frequently dismissed as just a form of denying culpability for the crime, some reports point to high levels of drinking prior to the rape. Rada (1978) discovered that half the rapists he questioned had been drinking at the time of the rape, and a third had an alcohol problem. Amir (1971) noted that both victim and offender had been drinking in over 60 per cent of cases. Koss and Gaines (1993) found that, in their research, alcohol was a strong predictor of sexual aggression. Alcohol has also been related to other offences, particularly those which involve violence, and is likely to lead to a misreading of cues from another person.

Gove and Wilmoth (1990) have asserted that many rapists experience an 'intense neurological high' which, together with a need for dominance and control, reinforces the risky and sometimes difficult nature of the crime.

Another argument which has continued for many years is whether rapists are encouraged to commit their crimes by exposure to pornography. The British popular press encourages the view that such a connection clearly exists. Feminists consider that pornography dehumanises women and thus facilitates rape (Brownmiller 1975).

Bandura (1986) has concluded that extensive exposure to violent erotica reinforces the myth that women want to be raped. However, the evidence is not clearly supportive of such views. Two national commissions in the USA have reached opposite conclusions. The word 'pornography' is not a legal term and opinions differ as to whether it connotes merely an erotic depiction of pleasure between consenting adults, or whether it should be confined to the more 'hard core' portrayals involving domination, cruelty, and acts with children or animals. The liberalisation of the pornography laws in Denmark was not accompanied by any increase in sexual offences. However, Court (1984) argued that violent pornography has a 'ripple effect' in that it gradually comes to influence attitudes towards women. Court also considered that the Danish findings are of less significance now-adays, as aggressive pornography has been increasingly available since the 1970s.

There have been no longitudinal studies of the impact of porn-ography on sexual behaviour. Sex offenders are known to make considerable use of pornography, but non-offenders do as well. Carter *et al.* (1987) discovered that child sexual abusers were more likely than rapists to have had recourse to pornography both before and during their offences. In contrast, Quinsey (1984) found that sex offenders had received less exposure to pornography than non-offenders during their adolescence. It is possible that aggressive pornography may increase negative reactions to women in those men who are already predisposed to sexual aggression.

Attempts have been made to ascertain whether rapists can be dis-tinguished from other people on the basis of personal, social or sexual characteristics. As a group, rapists do not show signs of mental illness, and comparisons with other offenders on personality tests do not reveal significant distinctions. However, some psychological tests indicate that imprisoned rapists have more in common with violent offenders than with other sex offenders (Rader 1977). Unlike paedo-philes, there is little evidence that rapists are any more deficient in heterosexual skills than other offenders. Stermac and Quinsey (1986), in a comparison of rapists, non-sex offenders and non-offender control groups, found that the two offender groups were less skilled in conversation, role play and on a self-report assessment of social inter-action. The only difference between them was that the rapists described themselves as less assertive. Yet, Lipton *et al.* (1987) dis-covered that rapists had more difficulty than other offenders in detect-ing cues of affection from women in simulations of a first date. As many rapists are married or have regular sexual outlets, this finding could be significant. Lack of empathy with the victim appears to be a common feature among rapists. In a study by Rice *et al.* (1994), fourteen non-rapists, on being presented with an account of a rape where the victim was suffering, showed significantly more empathy with the victim than fourteen rapists.

One particular type of rapist that has received special attention from researchers is the so-called 'sadistic rapist', whose attacks often result in death. Brittain (1970) provided an early description of a typical sadistic murderer. He is likely to be a solitary and introspective individual with feelings of inferiority, particularly in his sexuality, and a difficulty in relating to women. At the same time, he will often be both prudish and religious. A key feature in his activities is a desire for power and he will seek employment where control over others can be exercised. His fantasy world will be based on cruelty and he is likely to be a devotee of sadistic literature. Offending may follow a challenge to his masculinity, and both the planning and committing of the crime will help to restore his feelings of self-esteem. His sexual drive and desire for power will result in the use of considerable violence in the killing, but intercourse will not necessarily occur and may be substituted by masturbation.

Brittain's view has generally been supported by later research findings. MacCulloch *et al.* (1983) discovered that sadistic masturbatory fantasies involving sexual violence and control were common in 80 per cent of a sample of hospital patients who had committed sadistic murders or assaults. The fantasy had been maintained by acts such as stalking the victim, and had climaxed in the commission of the crime. The patients had all experienced problems in forming relationships with women. Prentky *et al.* (1989) compared twenty-five multiple with seventeen single sexual killers. Fantasies involving rape and murder had been indulged in by 86 per cent of the multiple killers, but only by 23 per cent of the single killers.

There is evidence that some sexual sadists may suffer from brain disorders. Hucker *et al.* (1988) found temporal lobe abnormalities in a group of sadists, and Money (1990) has suggested that in such cases the brain may be simultaneously transmitting messages of sexual arousal and attack. However, the fact that most sadistic assaults appear to be premeditated suggests that this explanation can only apply to a small number of cases. Another explanation—that sexual attackers were abused in their childhood—must also be treated with caution as, taken alone, it does not explain why women, who are far more likely to have been abused, do not indulge in such activity.

Feminist criminology has not only highlighted the neglect of women's criminality by male criminologists: the growing interest in women as victims has emphasised the 'maleness' of much crime. Several writers have claimed that its frequency belies any notion of rape being an activity committed only by abnormal males. For example, it would be difficult to attribute the widespread use of rape in war to a small number of disturbed individuals.

The view which denies that rape is a result of individual pathology has some support. Anthropologists have discovered that rape is not an inevitable feature of organised society. Sanday (1981) reviewed information on 156 tribal groups studied by anthropologists and divided them into rape-free societies, rape-prone societies, and those for which there was insufficient information. In the 47 per cent which she classified as rape-free societies, Sanday observed a high degree of sexual equality and low levels of violence. In the 18 per cent which were rape-prone societies, she noticed that the women had little status or power, and that the societies themselves favoured male toughness and tolerated physical violence. There is also some evidence that sizeable percentages of men believe that women have an unconscious desire to be raped, or that women's attire or demeanour may invite such an attack. A study of 264 university students by Forbes *et al.* (2004) found that sexist attitudes and rape-supporting beliefs were related to aggression and sexual coercion in relationships. However, some studies have been unable to confirm that imprisoned rapists are more accepting of myths about rape or hold negative views about women. Nor do self-report studies of sexual aggression towards women provide a clearer picture. Alder (1985) could find no correlation with beliefs favourable to the sexual victimisation of women.

A distinction between physical and sexual abuse is not always clear. Men's violence towards women can be viewed as a form of control (Dobash and Dobash 1979). It involves the exercise of proprietorial 'rights' to domestic and sexual services. Scully (1990), who interviewed convicted American rapists, considered that they thought rape to be a low-risk, high-reward crime. The rapists had generally been driven by a hatred of women, which was encouraged by cultural values. Lees (1996) has argued that rape may be used to foster a sense of 'manhood', which is under threat from rising male unemployment and the growing number of women entering the workforce.

On the other hand, reliance on the notion of patriarchy can be taken too far. The idea of *all* men oppressing *all* women overlooks differences between individuals, factors such as race or class, and social relationships in general (Messerschmidt 1993; Jefferson 1996).

No proper explanation is provided of the rape-free societies described by Sanday (see above). Some feminist writers have rejected the view of women as inevitable victims who are powerless to respond to the behaviour of men (for example, Tong 1989). Nor do extreme statements of the inevitable consequences of patriarchy make the feminists' case more plausible: for example, Andrea Dworkin (1987) has argued that female subordination is an unavoidable result of heterosexual relationships.

Conclusion

This chapter has concentrated on explanations for violent and sexually aggressive behaviour which have been offered by psychologists. Such accounts are often derided by sociologists and feminists for at least implying that the perpetrators are 'atypical' and 'have something wrong with them'. Yet, the main basis of the objection—that this somehow excuses the actors—seems to miss the point. It is perfectly reasonable to enquire into why people act in a certain way. The question of punishment or excuse is for another day. It is true that some psychologists have understated the prevalence of violence and ignored important social and environmental considerations. However, many sociologists, in their distrust of psychology, have refused to accept that disturbed cognitive processes can underlie violent and sexual attacks.

Everyone has recourse to some form of violent behaviour during their life, even if it is merely a temper tantrum. Some degree of aggression is socially acceptable—and even encouraged—in certain settings, particularly involving sport. However, what distinguishes these sort of occurrences from violent incidents where the perpetrator ends up in a criminal court is partly the question of the 'victim's' consent (as in sport), but more particularly the degree of harm caused (Jones 2000). Many people are probably incapable of causing serious bodily harm intentionally (other than, perhaps, as a defensive measure) unless they are suffering from some form of psychological disorder.

As sex offenders are generally aware that they are the most reviled group among the criminal population, their own attempts to explain their conduct are likely to be self-serving, and to accord with general stereotypes. Nevertheless, psychologists are aware of this, and it is claimed that carefully-devised interviewing techniques can minimise the risks of fabrication. What emerges from the more reliable of sex offenders' own accounts varies to some extent with the nature of their behaviour. Exhibitionists show relatively few psychological abnormalities and are often married men with unfulfilling sexual lives. Many paedophiles appear to lack confidence, particularly in their ability to form sexual relationships with adult women. They often come from cold and unloving home backgrounds. Children either appear as accepting and unquestioning sexual objects, or as people on whom the love and affection which paedophiles lacked in their own childhood can be lavished. These can be held as genuine beliefs: of all sex offenders, paedophiles as a group show the greatest resistance to suggestions that what they have done is wrong.

Rapists, however, tend to convey a far less inadequate image than exhibitionists or paedophiles. Although rape is officially classified as a sexual offence, it is now widely accepted that it is more about violence. The research literature reveals frequent references to terms such as 'power' and 'anger'. In the eyes of feminists, women are the obvious victims of these emotions in patriarchal societies. However, this view does not explain why the vast majority of men do not commit rape. It appears that many violent rapists have difficulties in obtaining consensual sexual fulfilment with women, who consequently have to be punished and humiliated.

And finally . . .

In this book, consideration has been given to various theories which have been put forward as to why people commit crimes. Some of these explanations claim that they can account for all criminality; others are more modest in their ambition. Some theories locate the primary source of criminality within the individual; others consider that aspects of the organisation of society are mainly responsible. The theories have been fully discussed in the main body of the book and there is no need to summarise them here. In recent years, some criminologists, especially in America, have been trying to create integrated theories, combining both individual and societal explanations (for example, Bernard and Snipes 1996).

However, by the late twentieth century an interest in examining the various reasons why people commit crimes had become unfashionable. Why did this occur?

Recorded crime increased relentlessly throughout most of the Western world from the 1950s to the 1990s. The various measures tried by governments to deal with this phenomenon were largely unsuccessful. Politicians realised that voters wanted 'something done about crime'. Although criminologists and feminists have highlighted the plight of victims, it has been the popular press—which increasingly sets the political agenda—that has played the major role in sensitising the public to crime. Recorded levels of most types of crime are now declining, but the public appears unwilling to believe this. The New Labour government is ambivalent: on the one hand it is prepared to herald the reducing levels of crime shown in the British Crime Survey, but on the other hand it maintains that crime and anti-social behaviour are continuing major social problems. It also takes the view that too much attention has been paid to the offender and not enough to the victim. While the second part of this belief might be correct, there is no reason why it has to be one or the other: more attention could be given to both (Tonry 2004).

The relentless concentration on crime in most newspapers and the increasing focus on victims have contributed to what is a much greater concern with risk in today's society. Large sections of the population have been persuaded that crime can only be reduced by the imposition of ever harsher punishments on offenders. Many people have probably formed the impression that everything else that could be tried has been tried. The climate is now such that any action by politicians which could be portrayed as trying to 'understand' or 'excuse' the offender would risk political suicide. In the 1990s, the British public heard competing slogans from the main political parties: Tony Blair's 'tough on crime, tough on the causes of crime' and John Major's view of crime—that it was 'time to understand a little less and condemn a little more'. Governments appear to have taken the view that it is possible to look for the 'solutions' to crime without concerning themselves with the underlying 'causes'. Rather than trying to understand why people act in a certain way, an increasingly resort is made to the physical isolation of those who break the rules, whether through anti-social behaviour orders, electronic tagging, or imprisonment (Jewkes 2004).

Fewer academics are concerned with the aetiology of crime. In fairness, some criminologists never developed an interest in the first place, considering that such an approach is 'correctionalist' and, therefore, too closely allied to the political process. Others maintain that the complexity of human behaviour is so great that any attempt to isolate 'reasons' is pointless. Post-modernists think that scientific efforts to categorise or generalise human behaviour belong to the failed agenda of the old modern world, and have no place in the new post-modern era. Those criminologists whose jobs are dependent on obtaining grants for empirical research have realised that funding bodies are nowadays far more interested in situational crime prevention than in abstract theory.

The content of criminology as an academic discipline includes a fair proportion of whatever are considered to be current social problems. The focus at any particular time is usually on the areas of interest which happen to be causing most concern—or, perhaps, are simply 'in fashion'. After all, just as criminals look for different targets as a way of enriching themselves, so academics look for different targets as a way of making their mark in the field of research (and, perhaps, to enrich the rest of society). However, the difficulty with this approach is that it over-emphasises what is 'new' and creates a corresponding disregard for what was written 'in another age'. This is not only a recent problem: as long ago as 1937 Lindesmith and Levin remarked that:

> One of the sources of protection against invasion by fads, and against
> these extra-theoretical influences, of which criminology of today has not
> availed itself, is a sound appreciation of its own past.

Most of the theories that have been considered in the foregoing chapters were formulated more than twenty-five years ago, and some
were originally published in the first half of the twentieth century.
Does this longevity render them irrelevant in today's world?
Braithwaite (1989) has contended that:

> . . . the middle range theories of the fifties and sixties have survived the
> assault of the critical criminologists of the seventies and the neo-classical
> criminologists of the eighties rather more admirably than we are inclined
> to concede when we teach undergraduate criminology.

According to Downes (1998), theories such as anomie have accurately predicted more recent patterns of crime. On the other hand,
Sumner (1994) has suggested that much traditional criminological
theory was devised in the context of social democratic structures
which no longer exist. Did the widespread social and economic
changes which resulted from the Reagan–Thatcher years really go so
far as to justify this view?

There are, of course, sound criticisms that can be made—and have
been made—of these theories. Many of them are said to reduce or
even deny the role of free will and choice in guiding human action.
Crime is generally over-predicted, in that only a relatively small number of the people who are exposed to criminogenic influences or pressures go on to become persistent offenders. The question then arises
as to whether any theory which can be shown not to have general
applicability is automatically invalid. In fact, given the wide range of
behaviour that is considered anti-social or criminal, it is hardly surprising that the search for the 'holy grail' of a general theory of crime has
been unsuccessful. Yet, it is important to bear in mind that most criminological theories have not claimed to be all-embracing. In any case,
the fact that such theories—both old and new—can be shown to have
shortcomings hardly makes them completely useless. Nor does it
make an interest in theory a worthless activity.

It does appear that, at the very least, it is impossible to divorce the
commission of crime from the working of society. Even right-wing
criminologists, who are so quick to reject the possibility of societal
influences, are concerned about parental upbringing. Psychological
explanations of anti-social behaviour, as well as the development of
several forms of mental disorder, also rely on something having 'gone

wrong' in a child's early life. Indeed, most psychological research shows that societal factors cannot be ignored. Objectors to positivism on the ground that it involves the denial of freedom of choice cannot seriously contend that it makes any sense to contemplate humans' acting outside their environment. Yet, to what extent are politicians, in their concern with crime, prepared to look at the basic structures of society? Only, it seems, in a superficial way. This is exemplified by the growing interest in situational crime prevention and the spread of public surveillance. In the ethos of managerialism which is pervasive nowadays, crime too is to be managed. However, this could prove ultimately to be no more effective than trying to place a sticking plaster over a gaping wound.

Perhaps it was the belated realisation of this that led the government to broaden its crime prevention strategy to include targeting the offender as well as the offence. In 1998, £21 million was made available for the *What Works* initiative. This involves the development of programmes for the Prison and Probation Services which have been proved to be effective in reducing offending (Home Office 1999). The programmes which have so far been introduced are largely based on techniques developed in North America which involve the application of problem-solving and cognitive-behavioural principles (McGuire (ed) 1995). Any practical development to assist in the understanding of behaviour is to be welcomed, even if cautiously—the government will be well aware that these approaches attribute offending behaviour to 'faulty thought processes', and responsibility is firmly located in the individual rather than in society. Moreover, not all such interventions have proved successful. Falshaw *et al.* (2003) could find no differences in two-year reconviction rates between a sample of prisoners who had participated in cognitive skills programmes and a matched control group.

In the midst of the current preoccupation with administrative criminology, it is encouraging to see that the development of theory is still progressing, with Braithwaite's notion of reintegrative shaming and the work of Messerschmidt, Jefferson and others on masculinities and crime. Developments in this latter area have seen sociologists turn to psychoanalytic theory—something which would have been unthinkable in the 1970s. Each of these perspectives may well encounter difficulties in its development, but they represent the real way forward in the effort to understand why certain individuals in particular situations indulge in anti-social and criminal behaviour.

Finally, it may seem ironic to some people that a clarion call for politicians to consider the climate which allows criminal behaviour to continue to grow should have come from a senior judge, Sir Thomas Bingham. In the 1997 Police Foundation Lecture, Sir Thomas remarked that factors such as low intelligence, addiction to drugs or alcohol, and a family history of parental conflict, erratic discipline and physical or sexual abuse:

> . . . help to explain the commission of crime, and those who urge the imposition of ever more serious sentences as a solution . . . should pause to ask whether they are treating the symptoms rather than the disease.

Bibliography

Adler F (1975) *Sisters in Crime*. New York: McGraw-Hill

Adler F and Laufer W (eds) (1995) *The Legacy of Anomie Theory*. New Brunswick, NJ: Transaction Publishers

Advisory Council on the Misuse of Drugs (2002) *The Classification of Cannabis under the Misuse of Drugs Act 1971*. London: Home Office

Agnew R (1985) Delinquency: A longitudinal test. *Criminology*, 23, 47–59

Agnew R (1992) Foundation for a general strain theory of crime and delinquency. *Criminology*, 30, 47–87

Agnew R (1994) The techniques of neutralization and violence. *Criminology*, 32, 555–579

Agnew R and White H (1992) An empirical test of general strain theory. *Criminology*, 30, 475–499

Agnew R, Brezina T, Wright J, and Cullen F (2002) Strain, personality traits, and delinquency: Extending general strain theory. *Criminology*, 40, 43–72

Aichhorn A (1925) *Wayward Youth*. New York: Viking Press (1936)

Akers R (1967) Problems in the sociology of deviance: Social definitions and behavior. *Social Forces*, 46, 455–465

Akers R (1973) *Deviant Behavior*. Belmont, CA: Wadsworth

Akers R (1990) Rational choice, deterrence, and social learning theory in criminology: the path not taken. *The Journal of Criminal Law and Criminology*, 81, 653–675

Akers R (1991) Self-control as a general theory of crime. *Journal of Quantitative Criminology*, 7, 201–211

Akers R (1994) *Criminological Theories*. Los Angeles: Roxbury

Akers R, Krohn M, Lanza-Kaduce L, and Radosevich M (1979) Social learning and deviant behavior: A specific test of a general theory. *American Sociological Review* 44, 636–655

Akhtar S and Thomson A (1982) Overview of narcissistic personality disorder. *American Journal of Psychiatry*, 139, 12–20

Alder C (1985) An exploration of self-reported sexually aggressive behavior. *Crime and Delinquency*, 31, 306–331

Alexander F and Healy W (1935) *The Roots of Crime*. New York: Knopf

Althusser L (1971) *Lenin and Philosophy and Other Essays*. London: New Left Books

American Psychological Association (1990) The Seville statement on violence. *American Psychologist*, 45, 1167–1168

Amir M (1971) *Patterns of Forcible Rape*. Chicago: University of Chicago Press

Anderson C (1989) Temperature and aggression: Ubiquitous effects of heat on occurrence of human violence. *Psychological Bulletin*, 106, 74–96

Anderson S, Kinsey R, Loader I, and Smith C (1991) *Cautionary Tales: A Study of Young People in Edinburgh*. Edinburgh: Centre for Criminology, University of Edinburgh

Anderson S, Kinsey R, Loader I, and Smith C (1994) *Cautionary Tales: Young People, Crime and Policing in Edinburgh*, Aldershot: Avebury

Andrews D (1980) Some experimental investigations of the principles of differential association through deliberate manipulation of the structure of service symbols. *American Sociological Review*, 45, 448–462

Angermeyer M and Matschinger H (1996) The effect of violent attacks by schizophrenic persons on the attitude of the public towards the mentally ill. *Social Science and Medicine*, 43, 1721–1728

Appleby L, Shaw J, Sherratt J, Amos T, Robinson J, McDonnell R *et al.* (2001) *Safety First. Five-Year Report of the National Confidential Inquiry into Suicide and Homicide by People with Mental Illness*, London: Department of Health

Arbuthnot J, Gordon D, and Jurkovic G (1987) Personality. In H Quay (ed) *Handbook of Juvenile Delinquency*. New York: Wiley

Archer D and Gartner R (1984) *Violence and Crime in Cross-National Perspective*. New Haven, CT: Yale University Press

Armitage R (2002) *To CCTV or not to CCTV?* London: NACRO

Arneklev B, Grasmick H, Tittle C, and Bursik R (1993) Low self-control and imprudent behaviour, *Journal of Quantitative Criminology*, 9, 225–247

Aseltine R, Gore S, and Gordon J (2000) Life stress, anger and anxiety, and delinquency: An empirical test of general strain theory. *Journal of Health and Social Behavior*, 41, 256–275

Arseneault L, Moffitt T, Avshalom C, Taylor P, and Silva P (2000) Mental disorders and violence in a total birth cohort. *Archives of General Psychiatry*, 57, 979–986

Ashworth A (1993) Victim impact statements and sentencing. *Criminal Law Review*, 498–509

Ashworth A and Gostin L (1985) Mentally disordered offenders and the sentencing process. In L Gostin (ed) *Secure Provision*. London: Tavistock

Ashworth A, Gardner J, Morgan R, Smith A, von Hirsch A, and Wasik M (1998) Neighbouring on the oppressive: the government's 'Anti-Social Behaviour Order' proposals. *Criminal Justice* 16, 7–14

Association of Chief Police Officers (1993) *Your Police: The Facts*. London: ACPO

Athens L (1997) *Violent Criminal Acts and Actors Revisited*. Chicago: University of Illinois Press

Atkinson J (1978) *Discovering Suicide*. London: Macmillan

Audit Commission (2004) *Crime Recording: Improving the Quality of Crime Records in Police Authorities and Forces in England and Wales*. London: Audit Commission

Austin R (1981) Liberation and female criminality in England and Wales. *British Journal of Criminology*, 21, 371–374

Averill J (1982) *Anger and Aggression*. New York: Springer-Verlag

Bailey S (1993) Fast forward to violence: Violent visual imaging and serious juvenile crime. *Criminal Justice Matters*, 11, 6–7

Balay J and Shevrin H (1988) The subliminal psychodynamic activation method: A critical review. *American Psychologist*, 43, 161–174

Baldwin J (1990) The role of sensory stimulation in criminal behaviour, with special attention to the age peak in crime. In L Ellis and H Hoffman (eds) *Crime in Biological, Social and Moral Contexts*. New York: Praeger

Baldwin J and Bottoms A (1976) *The Urban Criminal*. London: Tavistock

Bandura A (1973) *Aggression*. New York: Prentice Hall

Bandura A (1976) Social learning analysis of aggression. In E Ribes-Inesta and A Bandura (eds) *Analysis of Delinquency and Aggression*. Hillsdale, NJ: Lawrence Erlbaum

Bandura A (1986) *Social Foundations of Thought and Action*. Englewood Cliffs, NJ: Prentice Hall

Bandura A and Huston A (1961) Identification as a process of incidental learning. *Journal of Abnormal and Social Psychology*, 63, 311–318

Bandura A and Walters R (1959) *Adolescent Aggression*. New York: Ronald Press

Banton M (1964) *The Policeman in the Community*. London: Tavistock

Barclay G and Tavares C (2003) *International Comparisons of Criminal Justice Statistics 2001*. Home Office Statistical Bulletin 12/03. London: Home Office

Barlow H (1991) Explaining crimes and analogous acts, or the unrestrained will grab at pleasure whenever they can. *Journal of Criminal Law and Criminology*, 82, 229–242

Bartol C (1991) *Criminal Behavior: A Psychosocial Approach*. Englewood Cliffs, NJ: Prentice Hall

Batchelor S, Burman M, and Brown J (2001) Discussing violence: Let's hear it for the girls. *Probation Journal*, 48, 125–134

Bateman B, Warner J, Hutchinson E, Dean T, Rowlandson P, Gant C, Grundy J, Fitzgerald C, and Stevenson J (2004) The effects of a double blind, placebo controlled, artificial food colourings and benzoate preservative challenge on hyperactivity in a general population sample of preschool children. *Archives of Disease in Childhood*, 89, 506–511

Bauer L and Hesselbrock V (2001) CSD/BEM localization of P300 sources in adolescents 'at-risk': Evidence of frontal cortex dysfunction in conduct disorder. *Biological Psychiatry*, 50, 600–608

Baumeister R, Dale K, and Sommer K (1998) Freudian defense mechanisms and empirical findings in modern social psychology: Reaction formation, projection, displacement, undoing, isolation, sublimation, and denial. *Journal of Personality*, 66, 1081–1124

Bazemore G (1985) Delinquency reform and the labeling perspective. *Criminal Justice and Behavior*, 12, 131–169

Beccaria C (1764) *On Crimes and Punishments*. Indianapolis, IN: Bobbs-Merrill

Beck A (1976) *Cognitive Therapy and the Emotional Disorders*. New York: International Universities Press

Becker H (1963) *Outsiders*. New York: Free Press

Becker H (1974) Labelling theory reconsidered. In P Rock and M McIntosh (eds) *Deviance and Social Control*. London: Tavistock

Becker K, Stuewig J, Herrera V, and McCloskey L (2004) A study of firesetting and animal cruelty in children: Family influences and adolescent outcomes. *Journal of the American Academy of Child and Adolescent Psychiatry*, 43, 905–912

Beckwith J (1985) Social and political uses of genetics in the United States: Past and present. In F Marsh and J Katz (eds) *Biology, Crime and Ethics*. Cincinnati, OH: Anderson

Beirne P (1993) *Inventing Criminology*. Albany, NY: State University of New York Press

Bell N, Harford T, McCarroll J, and Senier L (2004) Drinking and spouse abuse among US Army soldiers. *Alcoholism: Clinical and Experimental Research*, 28, 1890–1897

Belsky J (1988) The 'effects' of infant day care reconsidered. *Early Childhood Research Quarterly*, 3, 235–272

Bennett T (1986) Situational crime prevention from the offenders' perspective. In K Heal and G Laycock (eds) *Situational Crime Prevention: From Theory into Practice*. London: HMSO

Bennett T (2000) *Drugs and Crime: The Results of the Second Developmental Stage of the NEW-ADAM Programme*. Home Office Research Study No 205. London: Home Office

Bennett T and Holloway K (2004) Gang membership, drugs and crime in the UK. *British Journal of Criminology*, 44, 305–323

Benson M and Moore E (1992) Are white-collar offenders and common criminals the same? An empirical and theoretical critique of a recently proposed general theory of crime. *Journal of Research in Crime and Delinquency*, 29, 251–272

Bentham J (1789) *An Introduction to the Principles of Morals and Legislation*. New York: Hafner (1948)

Ben-Yehuda N (1985) *Deviance and Moral Boundaries*. Chicago: University of Chicago Press

Berger P and Luckmann T (1966) *The Social Construction of Reality*. Garden City, NY: Anchor

Berk R, Braskman H, and Lesser S (1977) *A Measure of Justice*. New York: Academic Press

Berkowitz L (1989) Frustration-aggression hypothesis: Examination and reformulation. *Psychological Bulletin*, 106, 59–73

Berman L (1921) *The Glands Regulating Personality*. New York: Macmillan

Berman L (1938) *New Creations in Human Beings*. New York: Doubleday, Doran

Bernard T (1984) Control criticisms of strain theories: An assessment of theoretical and empirical adequacy. *Journal of Research in Crime and Delinquency*, 21, 353–372

Bernard T and Snipes J (1996) Theoretical integration in criminology. In M Tonry (ed) *Crime and Justice: A Review of Research*. Chicago: University of Chicago Press

Best J (1990) Review of 'Crime, Shame and Reintegration' by John Braithwaite. *Social Forces*, 69, 318–319

Best J (1999) *Random Violence: How We Talk about New Crimes and New Victims*. Berkeley: University of California Press

Best M, Williams J and Coccaro E (2002) Evidence for a dysfunctional prefrontal circuit in patients with an impulsive aggressive disorder. *Proceedings of the National Academy of Sciences USA*, 99, 8448–8453

Birmingham L, Mason D, and Grubin D (1996) Prevalence of mental disorder in remand prisoners: Consecutive case study. *British Medical Journal*, 313, 1521–1524

Birmingham L, Gray J, Mason D, and Grubin D (2000) Mental illness at reception into prison. *Criminal Behaviour and Mental Health*, 10, 77–87

Bjorkqvist K, Nygren T, Bjorklund A, and Bjorkqvist S (1994) Testosterone intake and aggressiveness: Real effect or anticipation. *Aggressive Behavior*, 20, 17–26

Black D and Spinks P (1985) Predicting outcomes of mentally disordered and dangerous offenders. In D Farrington and R Tarling (eds) *Prediction in Criminology*. Albany: State University of New York Press

Blackburn R (1987) Two scales for the assessment of personality disorder in antisocial populations. *Personality and Individual Differences*, 8, 81–93

Blackwell B (2000) Perceived sanction threats, gender, and crime: A test and elaboration of power-control theory. *Criminology*, 38, 439–488

Blagg H (1997) A just measure of shame? Aboriginal youth and conferencing in Australia. *British Journal of Criminology*, 37, 481–501

Blair C and Lanyon R (1981) Exhibitionism: Etiology and treatment. *Psychological Bulletin*, 89, 439–463

Blair I (1999) Patrolling provision. *Policing Today*, 5, 16–18

Block A and Chambliss W (1981) *Organizing Crime*. New York: Elsevier

Block R (1977) *Violent Crime*. Lexington, MA: Lexington Books

Blumenthal M, Kahn R, and Andrews F (1971) Attitudes towards violence. *Proceedings of the 79th Annual Convention of the American Psychological Association*. Washington, DC: American Psychological Association

Blumstein A, Cohen J, Roth J, and Visher C (1986) *Criminal Careers and Career Criminals*. Washington, DC: National Academy Press

Bohman M (1978) Some genetic aspects of alcoholism and criminality. *Archives of General Psychiatry*, 35, 269–276

Bohman M, Cloninger C, Sigvardsson S, and von Knorring A (1982) Predisposition to petty criminality in Swedish adoptees I: Genetic and environmental heterogeneity. *Archives of General Psychiatry*, 39, 1233–1241

Bondebjerg I (1996) Public discourse/Private fascination: Hybridization in 'true-life-story' genres. *Media, Culture and Society*, 18, 27–45

Bonger W (1916) *Criminality and Economic Conditions*. Boston: Little, Brown

Bonta J, Law M, and Hanson K (1998) The prediction of criminal and violent recidivism among mentally disordered offenders: A meta-analysis. *Psychological Bulletin*, 123, 123–142

Bottomley K and Coleman C (1981) *Understanding Crime Rates*. Farnborough: Gower

Bottomley K and Pease K (1986) *Crime and Punishment: Interpreting the Data*. Milton Keynes: Open University Press

Bottomley K, Coleman C, Dixon D, Gill M, and Wall D (1991) *The Impact of PACE: Policing in a Northern Force*, Kingston upon Hull: University of Hull Centre for Criminology and Criminal Justice

Bourgois P (1996) *In Search of Respect: Selling Crack in El Barrio*. Cambridge: Cambridge University Press

Bowlby J (1951) *Maternal Care and Mental Health*. Geneva: WHO

Box S (1971) *Deviance, Reality and Society*. London: Holt, Rinehart & Winston

Box S (1981) *Deviance, Reality and Society* 2nd ed. Eastbourne: Holt, Rinehart & Winston

Box S (1983) *Power, Crime and Mystification*. London: Tavistock

Box S (1987) *Recession, Crime and Punishment*. Basingstoke: Macmillan

Box S and Hale C (1983) Liberation and female criminality in England and Wales. *British Journal of Criminology*, 23, 35–49

Bradford J (1985) Organic treatments for the male sexual offender. *Behavioral Sciences and the Law*, 3, 355–375

Brain P (1994) Hormonal aspects of aggression and violence. In A Reiss, K Miczek, and J Roth (eds) *Understanding and Preventing Violence* vol 2. Washington, DC: National Academy Press

Braithwaite J (1979) *Inequality, Crime and Public Policy*, London: Routledge

Braithwaite J (1985) White-collar crime. *Annual Review of Sociology*, 11, 1–25

Braithwaite J (1989) *Crime, Shame and Reintegration*. Cambridge: Cambridge University Press

Braithwaite J (1995) Inequality and republican criminology. In J Hagan and R Peterson (eds) *Crime and Inequality*. Stanford, CA: Stanford University Press

Braithwaite J (1997) Charles Tittle's 'control balance' and criminological theory. *Theoretical Criminology*, 1, 77–97

Braithwaite J and Mugford S (1994) Conditions of successful reintegration ceremonies: Dealing with young offenders. *British Journal of Criminology*, 34, 139–171

Braithwaite J and Pettit P (1990) *Not Just Deserts*. Oxford: Oxford University Press

Braithwaite J, Fisse B, and Geis G (1987) Covert facilitation and crime: Restoring balance to the entrapment debate. *Journal of Social Issues*, 43, 5–41

Brandon S, Boakes J, Glaser D, and Green R (1998) Recovered memories of childhood sexual abuse. Implications for clinical practice. *British Journal of Psychiatry*, 172, 296–307

Brantingham P and Brantingham P (1981) Notes on the geometry of crime. In P Brantingham and P Brantingham (eds) *Environmental Criminology*. Beverly Hills, CA: Sage

Bratton W, with Knobler P (1998) *Turnaround: How America's Top Cop Reversed the Crime Epidemic*. New York: Random House

Brennan P, Mednick S, and Hodgins S (2000) Major mental disorders and criminal violence in a Danish birth cohort. *Archives of General Psychiatry*, 57, 494–500

Brennan T and Huizinga D (1975) *Theory Validation and Aggregate National Data*. Boulder, CO: Behavioral Research Institute

Briar A and Piliavin I (1965) Delinquency, situational inducements, and commitment to conformity. *Social Problems*, 13, 35–45

Brittain R (1970) The sadistic murderer. *Medicine, Science and the Law*, 10, 198–207

Brogden M (1977) A police authority: The denial of conflict. *Sociological Review*, 25, 325–349

Brooke D, Taylor C, Gunn J, and Maden A (1996) Point prevalence of mental disorder in unconvicted male prisoners in England and Wales. *British Medical Journal*, 313, 1524–1527

Brown D and Hogg R (1992) Law and order politics—Left realism and radical criminology: A view from Down Under. In R Matthews and J Young (eds) *Issues in Realist Criminology*. London: Sage

Brown S (1985) The class-delinquency hypothesis and juvenile justice system bias. *Sociological Inquiry*, 55, 213–223

Browne K and Pennell A (1998) *The Effect of Video Violence on Young Offenders*. Home Office Research Findings No 65. London: Home Office

Brownmiller S (1975) *Against Our Will*. New York: Bantam

Bryan J (1966) Occupational ideologies and individual attitudes of call girls. *Social Problems*, 13, 441–450

Buchholz E and Korn-Bursztyn C (1993) Children of adolescent mothers: Are they at risk for abuse? *Adolescence*, 28, 361–382.

Buckingham D (2000) *After the Death of Childhood: Growing Up in the Age of the Electronic Media*. Cambridge: Polity Press

Budd T (2003) *Alcohol-Related Assault: Findings from the British Crime Survey*. Home Office Online Report 35/03

Budd T, Sharp C, and Mayhew P (2005) *Offending in England and Wales: First Results from the 2003 Crime and Justice Survey*. Home Office Research Study No 275. London: Home Office

Buikhuisen W (1987) Cerebral dysfunctions and persistent juvenile delinquency. In S Mednick, T Moffitt, and S Stack (eds) *The Causes of Crime: New Biological Approaches*. Cambridge: Cambridge University Press

Bullock K and Tilley N (2002) *Shootings, Gangs and Violent Incidents in Manchester: Developing a Crime Reduction Strategy*. Crime Reduction Research Series, Paper 13. London: Home Office

Burgess E (1925) The growth of the city. In R Park and E Burgess *The City*. Chicago: University of Chicago Press

Burgess P (1972) Eysenck's theory of criminality: A test of some objections to disconfirmatory evidence. *British Journal of Social and Clinical Psychology*, 11, 248–256

Burgess R and Draper P (1989) The explanation of family violence: The role of biological, behavioural, and cultural selection. In L Ohlin and M Tonry (eds) *Family Violence*. Chicago: University of Chicago Press

Burrows J (1979) Closed circuit television and crime on the London Underground. In P Mayhew, R Clarke, J Burrows, J Hough, and S Winchester (eds) *Crime in Public View*. Home Office Research Study No 49. London: HMSO

Bursik R and Grasmick H (1993) *Neighbourhoods and Crime*. New York: Lexington

Burt C (1925) *The Young Delinquent*. London: University of London Press

Buruma L (1994) *The Wages of Guilt. Memories of War in Germany and Japan*. New York: Farrar Straus Giroux

Cadoret R (1978) Psychopathology in adopted-away offspring of biological parents with antisocial behaviour. *Archives of General Psychiatry*, 35, 176–184

Cadoret R (1986) Epidemiology of antisocial personality. In W Reid, D Door, J Walker, and J Bonne (eds) *Unmasking the Psychopath*. London: W W Norton

Cadoret R, Cain C, and Crowe R (1983) Evidence for gene–environment interaction in the development of adolescent antisocial behaviour. *Behaviour Genetics*, 13, 301–310

Cain M (1989) *Growing Up Good*. London: Sage

Calvin A (1981) Unemployment among black youths, demographics, and crime. *Crime and Delinquency*, 27, 234–244

Cameron M (1964) *The Booster and the Snitch*. New York: Simon & Schuster

Campbell A (1981) *Girl Delinquents*. Oxford: Blackwell

Campbell A (1984) *The Girls in the Gang*. Oxford: Blackwell

Carey S (1993) Mass media violence and aggressive behaviour. *Criminal Justice Matters*, 11, 8–9

Carlen P (1983) *Women's Imprisonment*. London: Routledge & Kegan Paul

Carlen P (1985) *Criminal Women*. Oxford: Polity Press

Carlen P (1988) *Women, Crime and Poverty*. Milton Keynes: Open University Press

Carlen P (1990) *Alternatives to Women's Imprisonment*. Milton Keynes: Open University Press

Carlen P (1992) Criminal women and criminal justice: The limits to, and potential of, feminist and left realist perspectives. In R Matthews and J Young (eds) *Issues in Realist Criminology*. London: Sage

Carney F (1978) Inpatient treatment programs. In W Reid (ed) *The Psychopath: A Comprehensive Study of Antisocial Disorders and Behaviors*. New York: Brunner/ Mazel

Carter D, Prentky R, Knight R, Vanderveer P, and Boucher R (1987) Use of pornography in the criminal and developmental histories of sex offenders. *Journal of Interpersonal Violence*, 2, 196–211

Caspi A, McClay J, Moffitt T, Mill J, Martin J, Craig I, Taylor A, and Poulton R (2002) Role of genotype in the cycle of violence in maltreated children. *Science*, 297, 851–854

Centerwall B (1989) Exposure to television as a cause of violence. In G Gomstock (ed) *Public Communication and Behavior*. New York: Academic Press

Cernkovich S and Giordano P (1979) Delinquency, opportunity, and gender. *Journal of Criminal Law and Criminology*, 70, 145–151

Cernkovich S and Giordano P (1987) Family relationships and delinquency. *Criminology*, 25, 295–321

Chaiken J, Lawless M, and Stevenson K (1974) *Impact of Police Activity on Crime: Robberies on New York City Subway Systems*. Report No R-1424, NYC. Santa Monica, CA: Rand Corporation

Chambliss W (1964) A sociological analysis of the law of vagrancy. *Social Problems*, 12, 67–77

Chambliss W (1975) Toward a political economy of crime. *Theory and Society*, 2, 149–170

Chambliss W (1978) *On the Take*. Bloomington, IN: Indiana University Press

Chambliss W (1995) Crime control and ethnic minorities: Legitimizing racial oppression by creating moral panics. In D Hawkins (ed) *Ethnicity, Race, and Crime: Perspectives across Time and Place*. Albany, NY: State University of New York Press

Chambliss W and Seidman R (1971) *Law, Order, and Power*. Reading, MA: Addison-Wesley

Charlton T and Gunter B (1999) TV-violence effects: Exceptionally vulnerable viewers. *Emotional and Behavioural Difficulties*, 4, 36–45.

Chesney-Lind M (1973) Judicial enforcement of the female sex roles: The family court and the female delinquent. *Issues in Criminology*, 8, 51–69

Chesno F and Kilmann P (1975) Effects of stimulation intensity on sociopathic avoidance learning. *Journal of Abnormal Psychology*, 84, 144–150

Chester M (2003) *Naughty*. Lytham: Milo Books

Chibnall S (1977) *Law and Order News*. London: Tavistock

Chomsky N (1988) *The Culture of Terrorism*. London: Pluto Press

Chorover S (1979) *From Genesis to Genocide*. Cambridge, MA: Massachusetts Institute of Technology Press

Choudry S (1996) *Pakistani Women's Experience of Domestic Violence in Great Britain*. Home Office Research Findings No 43. London: Home Office

Christiansen K (1968) Threshold of tolerance in various population groups illustrated by results from a Danish criminological study. In A de Rueck and R Porter (eds) *The Mentally Abnormal Offender*. Boston: Little, Brown

Christiansen K (1974) Seriousness of criminality and concordance among Danish twins. In R Hood (ed) *Crime, Criminology and Public Policy*. London: Heinemann

Christiansen K (1977) A preliminary study of criminality among twins. In S Mednick and K Christiansen (eds) *Biosocial Bases of Criminal Behavior*. New York: Gardner Press

Christie M, Marshall W, and Lanthier R (1979) A descriptive study of incarcerated rapists and pedophiles. *Report to the Solicitor General of Canada*, Ottawa

Christie N (2004) *A Suitable Amount of Crime*. London: Routledge

Cicourel A (1968) *The Social Organization of Juvenile Justice*. New York: Wiley

Clarke M (1990) The control of insurance fraud: A comparative view. *British Journal of Criminology*, 30, 1–23

Clarke R (1980) Situational crime prevention: Theory and practice. *British Journal of Criminology*, 20, 136–147

Clarke R (1983) Situational crime prevention: Its theoretical basis and practical scope. In M Tonry and N Morris (eds) *Crime and Justice: An Annual Review of Research* vol 4. Chicago: University of Chicago Press

Clarke R and Cornish D (1985) Modelling offenders' decisions: A framework for research and policy. In M Tonry and N Morris (eds) *Crime and Justice: An Annual Review of Research* vol 7. Chicago: University of Chicago Press

Clarke R and Hough M (1984) *Crime and Police Effectiveness*. London: HMSO

Cleckley H (1964) *The Mask of Sanity* 4th ed. St Louis, MO: Mosby

Clinard M (1964) *Anomie and Deviant Behavior*. New York: Free Press

Clinard M (1978) *Cities with Little Crime*. Cambridge: Cambridge University Press

Clinard M and Abbott D (1973) *Crime in Developing Countries: A Comparative Perspective*. New York: Wiley

Clinard M and Quinney R (1973) *Criminal Behavior Systems*. New York: Holt, Rinehart and Winston

Cloninger C and Gottesman I (1987) Genetic and environmental factors in antisocial behaviour disorders. In S Mednick, T Moffitt, and S Stack (eds) *The Causes of Crime: New Biological Approaches*. Cambridge: Cambridge University Press

Cloward R (1959) Illegitimate means, anomie, and deviant behavior. *American Sociological Review*, 24, 164–176

Cloward R and Ohlin L (1960) *Delinquency and Opportunity*. London: Collier Macmillan

Cohen A (1955) *Delinquent Boys*. New York: Free Press

Cohen A (1965) The sociology of the deviant act: Anomie theory and beyond. *American Sociology Review*, 30, 5–14

Cohen A (1966) *Deviance and Control*. Englewood Cliffs, NJ: Prentice Hall

Cohen L and Felson M (1979) Social change and crime rate trends: A routine activities approach. *American Sociological Review*, 44, 588–608

Cohen N (2003) 661 new crimes—and counting. *New Statesman*, 7 July 2003

Cohen P (1972) Subcultural conflict and working class community. *Working Paper in Cultural Studies*, 2, 5–52. Birmingham: Centre for Contemporary Studies, University of Birmingham

Cohen S (1970) Introduction. In S Cohen (ed) *Images of Deviance*. Harmondsworth: Penguin

Cohen S (1972) *Folk Devils and Moral Panics*. Oxford: Martin Robertson

Cohen S (1985) *Visions of Social Control*. Cambridge: Polity Press

Cohen S (1988) *Against Criminology*. New Brunswick, NJ: Transaction

Cohen S (1996) Crime and politics: Spot the difference. *British Journal of Sociology*, 47, 1–21

Cohen S (2001) *States of Denial: Knowing about Atrocities and Suffering*. Cambridge: Polity Press

Coid J (1982) Alcoholism and violence. *Drug and Alcohol Dependence*, 9, 1–13

Coid J (1984) How many psychiatric patients in prison? *British Journal of Psychiatry*, 145, 78–86

Coid J, Carvell A, Kittler Z, Healey A, and Henderson J (2000) *The Impact of Methadone Treatment on Drug Misuse and Crime*. Home Office Research Findings No 120. London: Home Office

Coleman A (1985) *Utopia on Trial*. London: Shipman

Collier R (1998) *Masculinities, Crime and Criminology*. London: Sage

Collins J (1986) The relationship of problem drinking in individual offending sequences. In A Blumstein, J Cohen, J Roth, and C Visher (eds) *Criminal Careers and 'Career Criminals'* Vol 2. Washington, DC: National Academy Press

Collins J (1989) Alcohol and interpersonal violence: Less than meets the eye. In N Weiner and M Wolfgang (eds) *Pathways to Criminal Violence*. Newbury Park, CA: Sage

Collins J and Bailey S (1990) Traumatic stress disorder and violent behavior. *Journal of Traumatic Stress*, 3, 203–220

Colvin M and Pauly J (1983) A critique of criminology: Toward an integrated structural-Marxist theory of delinquency production. *American Journal of Sociology*, 89, 513–551

Commission for Racial Equality (1992) *Cautions v Prosecutions*. London: Commission for Racial Equality

Connell R (1987) *Gender and Power*. Oxford: Polity Press

Cook D (1989) *Rich Law, Poor Law*. Buckingham: Open University Press

Cook D (1997) *Poverty, Crime and Punishment*. London: CPAG

Copes H (2003) Societal attachments, offending frequency, and techniques of neutralization. *Deviant Behavior*, 24, 101–127

Cornish D and Clarke R (1986) *The Reasoning Criminal*. New York: Springer-Verlag

Cornish D and Clarke R (1987) Understanding crime displacement: The application of rational choice theory. *Criminology*, 25, 933–947

Corrigan P (1979) *Schooling the Smash Street Kids*. London: Macmillan

Cortés J (1972) *Delinquency and Crime: A Biological Approach*. New York: Seminar Press

Cotton J (2004) *Police Complaints and Discipline England and Wales, 12 Months to March 2004*. Home Office Statistical Bulletin 17/04. London: Home Office

Court J (1984) Sex and violence: A ripple effect. In N Malamuth and E Donnerstein (eds) *Pornography and Sexual Aggression*. New York: Academic Press

Cowie J, Cowie V, and Slater E (1968) *Delinquency in Girls*. London: Heinemann

Craft M and Craft A (1978) *Sex and the Mentally Handicapped*. London: Routledge & Kegan Paul

Craissati J and Beech A (2004) The characteristics of a geographical sample of convicted rapists. *Journal of Interpersonal Violence*, 19, 371–388

Crawford A (2000) Situational crime prevention, urban governance and trust relations. In A von Hirsch, D Garland, and A Wakefield (eds) *Ethical and Social Perspectives on Situational Crime Prevention*. Oxford: Hart

Crawford A, Jones T, Woodhouse T, and Young J (1990) *Second Islington Crime Survey*. London: Middlesex Polytechnic

Cressey D (1960) Epidemiology and individual conduct: A case from criminology. *Pacific Sociological Review*, 3, 47–58

Crites L (1976) Women offenders: Myth v reality. In L Crites (ed) *The Female Offender*. Lexington, MA: Lexington Books

Cromwell P and Thurman Q (2003) The devil made me do it: Use of neutralizations by shoplifters. *Deviant Behavior*, 24, 535–550

Crowe R (1972) The adopted offspring of women criminal offenders. *Archives of General Psychiatry*, 27, 600–603

Cumberbatch G, Woods S, and Maguire A (1995) *Crime in the News: Television, Radio and Newspapers*. Birmingham: Aston University Communications Research Group

Cunneen C and White R (1995) *Juvenile Justice: An Australian Perspective*. Melbourne: Oxford University Press

Curran D and Renzetti C (2001) *Theories of Crime* 2nd ed. Boston: Allyn & Bacon

Currie E (1985) *Confronting Crime*. New York: Pantheon

Currie E (1991) The politics of crime: The American experience. In K Stenson and D Cowell (eds) *The Politics of Crime Control*. London: Sage

Curry G (1998) Review of 'Control Balance: Toward a General Theory of Deviance' by Charles R Tittle. *Social Forces*, 76, 1147–1149

Curtis L (1974) Victim precipitation and violent crime. *Social Problems*, 21, 594–605

Dahrendorf R (1958) *Class and Class Conflict in Industrial Society*. Palo Alto, CA: Stanford University Press

Dahrendorf R (1968) Toward a theory of social conflict. *Journal of Conflict Resolution*, 2, 170–183

Dahrendorf R (1985) *Law and Order*. London: Stevens

Dalgaard O and Kringlen E (1976) A Norwegian twin study of criminality. *British Journal of Criminology*, 16, 213–233

Dalton K (1961) Menstruation and crime. *British Medical Journal*, 2, 1752–1753

Dalton K, with Holton W (1999) *Once a Month* 6th ed. Alameda, CA: Hunter House

Daly K and Chesney-Lind M (1988) Feminism and criminology. *Justice Quarterly*, 5, 497–535

Darwin C (1859) *On the Origin of Species by Means of Natural Selection*. New York: Rand McNally

Darwin C (1871) *Descent of Man*. London: Murray

Davis K (1937) The sociology of prostitution. *American Sociological Review*, 2, 744–755

De Bellis M (2001) Developmental traumatology: The psychobiological development of maltreated children and its implications for research, treatment, and policy. *Development and Psychopathology*, 13, 539–564 de Haan W and Vos J (2003) A crying shame: The over-rationalised conception of man in the rational choice perspective. *Theoretical Criminology*, 7, 29–54

de Than C and Shorts E (2004) *International Criminal Law and Human Rights*. London: Sweet & Maxwell

Demmig-Adams B and Adams W (2002) Antioxidants in photosynthesis and human nutrition. *Science*, 298, 2149–2153

Denkowski G and Denkowski K (1985) The mentally retarded offender in the state prison system: Identification, prevalence, adjustment, and rehabilitation. *Criminal Justice and Behavior*, 12, 55–70

Department of Health (1998) *The Government's Response to the Children's Safeguards Review*. Cm 4105. London: The Stationery Office

Dickens W and Flynn J (2001) Heritability estimates versus large environmental effects: The IG paradox resolved. *Psychological Review*, 108, 346–369

Dickinson D (1993) *Crime and Unemployment*. Cambridge: Institute of Criminology

Ditton J (1979) *Controlology*. London: Macmillan

Ditton J (2000) Public attitudes towards open-street CCTV in Glasgow. *British Journal of Criminology*, 40, 692–709

Ditton J and Duffy J (1983) Bias in the newspaper reporting of crime news. *British Journal of Criminology*, 23, 159–165

Ditton J, Bannister J, Gilchrist E, and Farrall S (1999) Afraid or angry? Recalibrating the fear of crime. *International Review of Victimology*, 16, 83–99

Dobash R and Dobash R (1979) *Violence against Wives*. London: Open Books

Dobash R and Dobash R (1998) Violent men and violent contexts. In R Dobash and R Dobash (eds) *Rethinking Violence against Women*. Thousand Oaks, CA: Sage

Dobash R and Dobash R (2004) Women's violence to men in intimate relationships. *British Journal of Criminology*, 44, 324–349

Dodd T, Nicholas S, Povey D, and Walker A (2004) *Crime in England and Wales 2003/2004*. Home Office Statistical Bulletin 10/04. London: Home Office.

Dodge K and Somberg D (1987) Hostile attributional biases among aggressive boys are exacerbated under conditions of threats to the self. *Child Development*, 58, 213–224

Doob A and Roberts J (1988) Public punitiveness and public knowledge of the facts: Some Canadian surveys. In M Hough and N Walker (eds) *Public Attitudes to Sentencing*. Aldershot: Gower

Dorling D, Mitchell R, Shaw M, Orford S, and Davey Smith G (2001) The Ghost of Christmas Past: Health effects of poverty in London in 1896 and 1991. *British Medical Journal*, 321, 1547–1551

Dorling D and Thomas B (2004) *People and Places: A 2001 Census Atlas of the UK*. Bristol: The Policy Press

Dougherty D, Bjork J, Cherek D, Moeller F, and Huang D (1998) Effects of menstrual cycle phase on aggression measured in the laboratory. *Aggressive Behavior*, 24, 9–26

Douglas J (1967) *The Social Meanings of Suicide*. Princeton, NJ: Princeton University Press

Dowie M (1988) Pinto madness. In S Hill (ed) *Corporate Violence: Injury and Death for Profit*. Totowa, NJ: Rowman & Littlefield

Downes D (1966) *The Delinquent Solution*. London: Routledge & Kegan Paul

Downes D (1998) Back to the future: The predictive value of social theories of delinquency. In S Holdaway and P Rock (eds) *Thinking about Criminology*. London: UCL Press

Dubin R (1959) Deviant behavior and social structure: Continuities in social theory. *American Sociological Review*, 24, 147–164

Dugdale R (1877) *The Jukes*. New York: Putnam

Durkheim E (1893) *The Division of Labour in Society*. New York: MacMillan (1933)

Durkheim E (1897) *Suicide*. Glencoe, IL: Free Press (1951)

Duster T (1970) *The Legislation of Morality*. New York: Free Press

Duster T (2003) *Backdoor to Eugenics* 2nd ed. New York: Routledge

Dworkin A (1987) *Intercourse*. New York: Free Press

East W (1927) *An Introduction to Forensic Psychiatry in the Criminal Courts*. London: JA Churchill

East W (1936) *The Medical Aspects of Crime*. London: J A Churchill

Edwards S (1988) Mad, bad or pre-menstrual? *New Law Journal*, 138, 456–458

Egeland G, Jacobvitz D, and Sroufe L (1988) Breaking the cycle of abuse. *Child Development*, 59, 1080–1088

Ehrlich I (1974) Participation in illegal activities: An economic analysis. In G Becker and W Landes (eds) *Essays in the Economics of Crime and Punishment*. New York: Columbia University Press

Einstadter W and Henry S (1995) *Criminological Theory: An Analysis of its Underlying Assumptions*. Fort Worth, TX: Harcourt, Brace

Ekblom P and Tilley N (2000) Going equipped: Criminology, situational crime prevention and the resourceful offender. *British Journal of Criminology*, 40, 376–398

Elias N (1994) *The Civilizing Process*. Translated by Edmund Jephcott. Oxford: Basil Blackwell (1939)

Elliott D and Ageton S (1985) *Explaining Delinquency and Drug Use*. Beverly Hills, CA: Sage

Elliott D and Huizinga D (1989) Improving self-reported measures of delinquency. In M Klein (ed) *Cross-National Research in Self-Reported Crime and Delinquency*. Dordrecht: Kluwer

Elliott D and Voss H (1974) *Delinquency and Dropout*. Lexington, MA: D C Heath

Elliott D, Ageton S, and Canter R (1979) An integrated theoretical perspective on delinquent behavior. *Journal of Research in Crime and Delinquency*, 16, 3–27

Ellis H (1890) *The Criminal*. London: Scott

Ellis L and Coontz P (1990) Androgens, brain functioning and criminality: The neurohormonal foundations of antisociality. In L Ellis and H Hoffman (eds) *Crime in Biological, Social and Moral Contexts*. New York: Praeger

Emsley C (2005) *Crime and Society in England 1750–1900* 3rd ed. Harlow: Pearson Longman

Engels F (1845) *The Condition of the Working Class in England*. London: Allen & Unwin (1950)

Erez E (1999) Who's afraid of the big bad victim? Victim impact statements as victim empowerment *and* enhancement of justice. *Criminal Law Review*, 545–556

Ericson R (1991) Mass media, crime, law, and justice. *British Journal of Criminology*, 31, 219–249

Ericson R, Baranek P, and Chan J (1989) *Negotiating Control*. Milton Keynes: Open University Press

Ericson R, Baranek P, and Chan J (1991) *Representing Order*. Milton Keynes: Open University Press

Erikson K (1966) *Wayward Puritans*. New York: Wiley

Erlanger H (1980) The allocation of status within occupations: The case of the legal profession. *Social Forces*, 58, 882–903

Evans H (1889) The London County Council and the police. *Contemporary Review*, vol LV, 445–461

Eysenck H (1964) *Crime and Personality*. London: Routledge & Kegan Paul

Eysenck H (1984) Crime and personality. In D Muller, D Blackman, and A Chapman (eds) *Psychology and Law*. Chichester: Wiley

Eysenck H (1996) Personality and crime: Where do we stand? *Psychology, Crime & Law*, 2, 143–152

Eysenck H and Eysenck S (1968) A factorial study of psychoticism as a dimension of personality. *Multivariate Behavioural Research* (special issue), 15–31

Eysenck H and Gudjonsson G (1989) *The Causes and Cures of Criminality*. New York: Plenum Press

Eysenck S and Eysenck H (1971) Crime and personality: Item analysis of questionnaire responses. *British Journal of Criminology*, 11, 49–62

Eysenck S and Eysenck H (1972) The questionnaire measurement of psychoticism. *Psychological Medicine*, 2, 50–55

Eysenck S and Eysenck H (1977) Personality differences between prisoners and controls. *Psychological Reports*, 40, 1023–1028

Eysenck S and McGurk B (1980) Impulsiveness and venturesomeness in a detention centre population. *Psychological Reports*, 47, 1299–1306

Fagan J, Piper E, and Moore M (1986) Violent delinquents and urban youth. *Criminology* 24, 439–471

Falshaw L, Friendship C, Travers R, and Nugent F (2003) *Searching for 'What Works': An Evaluation of Cognitive Skills Programmes*. Home Office Research Findings No 206. London: Home Office

Farnworth M and Leiber M (1989) Strain theory revisited. *American Sociological Review*, 54, 263–274

Farrington D (1978) The family background of aggressive youths. In L Hersov, M Berger, and D Schaffer (eds) *Aggression and Antisocial Behaviour in Childhood and Adolescence*. Oxford: Pergamon

Farrington D (1982) Longitudinal analyses of criminal violence. In M Wolfgang and N Weiner (eds) *Criminal Violence*. Beverly Hills, CA: Sage

Farrington D (1989) Early predictors of adolescent aggression and adult violence. *Violence and Victims*, 4, 79–100

Farrington D and Burrows J (1993) Did shoplifting really decrease? *British Journal of Criminology*, 33, 57–69

Farrington D and Dowds E (1985) Disentangling criminal behaviour and police reaction. In D Farrington and J Gunn (eds) *Reactions to Crime*. Chichester: Wiley

Farrington D and Welsh B (2002) *Effects of Improved Street Lighting on Crime: A Systematic Review*. Home Office Research Study No 251. London: Home Office

Farrington D, Biron L, and Leblanc M (1982) Personality and delinquency in London and Montreal. In J Gunn and D Farrington (eds) *Abnormal Offenders, Delinquency, and the Criminal Justice System*. Chichester: Wiley

Farrington D, Loeber R, and Van Kammen W (1990) Long-term criminal outcomes of hyperactivity-impulsivity-attention deficit and conduct problems in childhood. In L Robins and M Rutter (eds) *Straight and Devious Pathways from Childhood to Adulthood*. Cambridge: Cambridge University Press

Farrington D, Gallagher B, Morley L, St Ledger R, and West D (1986) Unemployment, school leaving and crime. *British Journal of Criminology* 26, 335–356

Fattah E (1979) Some recent theoretical developments in victimology. *Victimology*, 4, 198–213

Fazel S and Danesh J (2002) Serious mental disorder in 23,000 prisoners: A systematic review of 62 surveys. *Lancet*, 359, 545–550

Federal Bureau of Investigation (2004) *Uniform Crime Reports 2003*. US Department of Justice: Washington DC

Feeley M and Little D (1991) The vanishing female: The decline of women in the criminal process. *Law and Society Review*, 25, 1–35

Feldman D (1964) Psychoanalysis and crime. In B Rosenberg, I Gerve, and F Howton (eds) *Mass Society in Crisis*. New York: Macmillan

Feldman D J (1990) Regulating treatment of suspects in police stations: Judicial interpretation of detention provisions in the Police and Criminal Evidence Act 1984. *Criminal Law Review*, 452–571

Feldman P (1977) *Criminal Behaviour*. London: Wiley

Feldman P (1993) *The Psychology of Crime*. Cambridge: Cambridge University Press

Felson R (1993) Sexual coercion: A social interactionist approach. In R Felson and J Tedeschi (eds) *Aggression and Violence*. Washington, DC: American Psychological Association

Felson R and Steadman H (1983) Situational factors in disputes leading to criminal violence. *Criminology*, 21, 59–74

Fenichel O (1945) *The Psychoanalytic Theory of Memory*. New York: Norton

Fenwick P (1990) Automatism. In R Bluglas and P Bowden (eds) *Principles and Practice of Forensic Psychiatry*. Edinburgh: Churchill Livingstone

Fergusson D and Horwood L (2000) Alcohol abuse and crime: A fixed-effects regression analysis. *Addiction,* 95, 1525–1536

Ferrell J, Hayward K, Morrison W, and Presdee M (2004) *Cultural Criminology Unleashed.* London: Glasshouse

Ferri E (1881) *Criminal Sociology.* London: Unwin (1895)

Fielding H (1751) *An Enquiry into the Causes of the Late Increase of Robbers.* London: A Millar

Figueira-McDonough J (1984) Feminism and delinquency. *British Journal of Criminology,* 24, 325–342

Finkelhor D (1986) *A Sourcebook on Child Sex Abuse.* Newbury Park, CA: Sage

Finkelhor D and Russell D (1984) Women as perpetrators: Review of the evidence. In D Finkelhor (ed) *Child Sexual Abuse: New Theory and Research.* New York: Free Press

Finkelhor D and Yllö K (1985) *License to Rape.* New York: Holt, Rinehart & Winston

Fishbein D (1990) Biological perspectives in criminology. *Criminology,* 28, 27–72

Fishbein D (1992) The psychobiology of female aggression. *Criminal Justice and Behavior,* 19, 99–126

Flood-Page C, Campbell S, Harrington V, and Miller J (2000) *Youth Crime: Findings from the 1998/99 Youth Lifestyles Survey.* Home Office Research Study No 209. London: Home Office

Floud J and Young W (1981) *Dangerousness and Criminal Justice.* London: Heinemann

Foote D (1992) The benevolent paternalism of Japanese criminal justice. *California Law Review,* 80, 317–390

Forbes G, Adams-Curtis L, and White K (2004) First- and second-generation measures of sexism, rape myths and related beliefs, and hostility toward women. *Violence against Women,* 10, 236–261

Foucault M (1978) About the concept of the dangerous individual in nineteenth century legal psychiatry. *International Journal of Law and Psychiatry,* 1, 1–18

Foucault M (1980) *Power/Knowledge.* Brighton: Harvester

Frankel M (1973) *Criminal Sentences.* New York: Hill and Wang

Frayn M (1973) Unit headline language. In S Cohen and J Young (eds) *The Manufacture of News.* London: Constable

Freedman J (1984) Effects of television on aggressiveness. *Psychological Bulletin,* 96, 227–246

Freud S (1925) Some psychical consequences of the anatomical distinction between the sexes. *The Standard Edition of the Complete Psychological Works of Sigmund Freud* vol 19. London: Hogarth Press

Freund K (1990) Courtship disorder. In W Marshall, D Laws, and H Barbaree (eds) *Handbook of Sexual Assault.* New York: Plenum

Freund K and Kuban M (1994) The basis of the abused-abuser theory of pedophilia—a further elaboration of an earlier study. *Archives of Sexual Behavior,* 23, 553–563

480 | BIBLIOGRAPHY

Friedlander K (1951) *The Psycho-analytical Approach to Juvenile Delinquency*. London: Routledge & Kegan Paul

Friedrich W and Boriskin J (1976) The role of the child in abuse. *American Journal of Orthopsychiatry*, 46, 580–590

Frude N (1989) The physical abuse of children. In K Howells and C Hollin (eds) *Clinical Approaches to Violence*. Chichester: Wiley

Furedi F (2001) *Paranoid Parenting: Abandon Your Anxieties and Be a Good Parent*. London: Allen Lane The Penguin Press

Furnham A (1984) Personality, social skills, anomie and delinquency: A self-report study of a group of normal non-delinquent adolescents. *Journal of Child Psychology and Psychiatry*, 25, 409–20

Furnham A and Henderson M (1983) Lay theories of delinquency. *European Journal of Social Psychology*, 13, 107–120

Gale A and Edwards J (1983) EEG and human behaviour. In A Gale and J Edwards (eds) *Psychological Correlates of Human Behaviour* vol 2. New York: Academic Press

Galtung J and Ruge M (1973) Structuring and selecting news. In S Cohen and J Young (eds) *The Manufacture of News*. London: Constable

Garfinkel H (1956) Conditions of successful degradation ceremonies. *American Journal of Sociology*, 61, 420–424

Garfinkel H (1967) *Studies in Ethnomethodology*. Englewood Cliffs, NJ: Prentice Hall

Garland D (1985) *Punishment and Welfare*. Aldershot: Gower

Garland D (1988) British criminology before 1935. In P Rock (ed) *A History of British Criminology*. Oxford: Oxford University Press

Garofalo R (1914) *Criminology*. Boston: Little, Brown (1885)

Gaylord M and Galliher J (1988) *The Criminology of Edwin Sutherland*. New Brunswick, NJ: Transaction Books

Geis G (1960) Jeremy Bentham. In H Mannheim (ed) *Pioneers in Criminology*. London: Stevens

Geis G (2000) On the absence of self-control as the basis for a general theory of crime: A critique. *Theoretical Criminology*, 4, 35–53

Gelsthorpe L (1989) *Sexism and the Female Offender*. Aldershot: Gower

Genn H (1988) Multiple victimisation. In M Maguire and J Pointing (eds) *Victims of Crime*. Milton Keynes: Open University Press

Gershoff E (2002) Corporal punishment by parents and associated child behaviors and experiences: A meta-analytic and theoretical review. *Psychological Bulletin*, 128, 539–579

Gesch B, Hammond S, Hampson S, Eves A, and Crowder M (2003) Influence of supplementary vitamins, minerals and essential fatty acids on the antisocial behaviour of young adult prisoners. *British Journal of Psychiatry*, 181, 22–28

Giancola P and Zeichner A (1994) Neuropsychological performance on tests of frontal-lobe functioning and aggressive behavior in men, *Journal of Abnormal Psychology*, 103, 832–835

Gibbens T (1981) Shoplifting. *British Journal of Psychiatry*, 138, 346–347

Gibbens T and Prince J (1962) *Shoplifting*. London: ISTD

Gibbs J (1985) Review essay. *Criminology*, 23, 381–388

Gibbs J (1989) *Control: Sociology's Central Notion*. Urbana: University of Illinois Press

Giddens A (1989) *Sociology: A Brief, but Critical Introduction*. London: Macmillan

Gill M (2000) *Commercial Robbery*. London: Blackstone Press

Gill M and Spriggs A (2005) *Assessing the Impact of CCTV*. Home Office Research Study No 292. London: Home Office

Gillborn D and Safia Mirza H (2000) *Educational Inequality: Mapping Race, Class and Gender*. HMI 232. London: OFSTED

Gitlin T (1980) *The Whole World is Watching*. Berkeley, CA: University of California Press

Given J (1977) *Society and Homicide in Thirteenth Century England*. Stanford, CA: Stanford University Press

Glaser D (1956) Criminality theories and behavioral images. *American Journal of Sociology*, 61, 433–444

Glaser D and Rice K (1959) Crime, age and employment. *American Sociological Review*, 24, 679–686

Glover E (1949) *Psychoanalysis*. London: Staples Press

Glover E (1960) *The Roots of Crime*. London: Imago

Glueck S and Glueck E (1956) *Physique and Delinquency*. New York: Harper & Row

Goddard H (1914) *Feeble-mindedness: Its Causes and Consequences*. New York: Macmillan

Godenzi A (1994) What's the big deal? We are men and they are women. In T Newburn and E Stanko (eds) *Just Boys Doing Business? Men, Masculinities and Crime*. London: Routledge

Gold M (1970) *Delinquent Behaviour in an American City*. Belmont, CA: Brooks/Cole

Goldstein P (1985) The drugs/violence nexus: A tripartite conceptual framework. *Journal of Drug Issues*, 15, 493–506

Goode E and Ben-Yehuda N (1994) *Moral Panics: The Social Construction of Deviance*. Cambridge, MA: Blackwell

Goodman A, Johnson P, and Webb S (1997) *Inequality in the UK*. Oxford: Oxford University Press

Goodwin D, Schulsinger F, Hermansen L, Guze S, and Winokur G (1973) Alcohol problems in adoptees raised apart from alcoholic biological parents. *Archives of General Psychiatry*, 28, 238–243

Goold B (2004) *CCTV and Policing: Public Area Surveillance and Police Practices in Britain*. Oxford: Oxford University Press

Gordon D (1973) Capitalism, class and crime in America. *Crime and Delinquency*, 19, 163–186

Gordon R (1976) Prevalence: The rare datum in delinquency measurement and its implications for the theory of delinquency. In M Klein (ed) *The Juvenile Justice System*. Beverly Hills, CA: Sage

Goring C (1913) *The English Convict: A Statistical Study*. London: HMSO

Gosden N, Kramp P, Gabrielsen G, and Sestoft D (2003) Prevalence of mental disorders among 15–17-year-old male adolescent remand prisoners in Denmark. *Acta Psychiatrica Scandinavica*, 107, 102–110

Gosselin C and Wilson G (1980) *Sexual Variations: Fetishism, Transvestism and Sadomasochism*. London: Faber & Faber

Gottfredson M (1984) *Victims of Crime: The Dimension of Risk*. Home Office Research Study No 81. London: HMSO

Gottfredson M and Hirschi T (1990) *A General Theory of Crime*. Stanford, CA: Stanford University Press

Gould S (1997) *The Mismeasure of Man*. Harmondsworth: Penguin Books

Gouldner A (1968) The sociologist as partisan: Sociology and the welfare state. *The American Sociologist*, May, 103–116

Gouldner A (1975) *For Sociology*. Harmondsworth: Pelican

Gove W (ed) (1980) *The Labelling of Deviance: Evaluating a Perspective* 2nd ed. Beverly Hills, CA: Sage

Gove W and Wilmoth C (1990) Risk, crime, and neurophysiologic highs: A consideration of brain processes that may reinforce delinquent and criminal behavior. In L Ellis and H Hoffman (eds) *Crime in Biological, Social, and Moral Contexts*. New York: Praeger

Graber D (1980) *Crime News and the Public*. New York: Praeger

Grabiner A (2000) *The Informal Economy*. London: The Stationery Office

Graham J and Bowling B (1995) *Young People and Crime*. Home Office Research Study No 145. London: HMSO

Gramsci A (1971) *Selections from the Prison Notebooks*. London: Lawrence & Wishart

Grasmick H, Tittle C, Bursik R, and Arneklev B (1993) Testing the core empirical implications of Gottfredson and Hirschi's General Theory of Crime. *Journal of Research in Crime and Delinquency*, 30, 5–29

Gray J (1981) A critique of Eysenck's theory of personality. In H Eysenck (ed) *A Model of Personality*. New York: Springer-Verlag

Great Britain, DSS (1997) *Social Security Fraud*. London: HMSO

Green C (1981) Matricide by sons. *Medicine, Science and the Law*, 21, 207–214

Greenberg D (1976) On one-dimensional Marxist criminology. *Theory and Society*, 3, 610–621

Greenberg D (1981) *Crime and Capitalism*. Palo Alto, CA: Mayfield

Greer C (2003) *Sex Crime and the Media: Sex Offending and the Press in a Divided Society*. Cullompton: Willan

Groth A (1979) *Men Who Rape*. New York: Plenum

Groth A and Burgess A (1977) Rape: A sexual deviation. *American Journal of Orthopsychiatry*, 47, 400–406

Groth A, Longo R, and McFadin J (1982) Undetected recidivism among rapists and child molesters. *Crime and Delinquency*, 28, 450–458

Gulbenkian Foundation (1995) *Children and Violence*. London: Calouste Gulbenkian Foundation

Gunderson J (1974) Management of manic states: The problem of firesetting. *Psychiatry*, 37, 137–146

Gunn J and Fenton G (1971) Epilepsy, automatism and crime. *Lancet*, 1, 1173–1176

Gunn J, Maden A, and Swinton M (1991) Treatment needs of prisoners with psychiatric disorders. *British Medical Journal*, 303, 338–341

Gunn J, Robertson G, Dell S, and Way C (1978) *Psychiatric Aspects of Imprisonment*. London: Academic Press

Gusfield J (1963) *Symbolic Crusade*. Urbana: University of Illinois Press

Häfner H and Böker W (1982) *Crimes of Violence by Mentally Abnormal Offenders*. Cambridge: Cambridge University Press

Hagan J (1989) *Structural Criminology*. New Brunswick, NJ: Rutgers University Press

Hagan J (1994) *Crime and Disrepute*. Thousand Oaks, CA: Pine Forge Press

Hagan J and McCarthy B (1997) *Mean Streets: Youth Crime and Homelessness*. Cambridge: Cambridge University Press

Hagan J and Peterson R (eds) (1994) *Crime and Inequality*. Stanford, CA: Stanford University Press

Hagan J, Boehnke K, and Merkens H (2004) Gender differences in capitalization processes and the delinquency of siblings in Toronto and Berlin. *British Journal of Criminology*, 44, 659–676

Hagan J, Gillis A, and Simpson J (1985) The class structure of gender and delinquency: Toward a power-control theory of common delinquent behaviour. *American Journal of Sociology*, 90, 1151–1178

Hagan J, Simpson J, and Gillis A (1979) The sexual stratification of social control. *British Journal of Sociology*, 30, 25–38

Hall G and Proctor W (1987) Criminological predictors of recidivism in a sexual offender population. *Journal of Consulting and Clinical Psychology*, 55, 111–112

Hall J (1935) *Theft, Law and Society* 2nd ed. Indianapolis, IN: Bobbs-Merrill

Hall S and Jefferson T (eds) (1976) *Resistance through Rituals*. London: Hutchinson

Hall S, Critcher C, Jefferson T, Clarke J, and Roberts B (1978) *Policing the Crisis*. London: Macmillan

Han W-J (2005) Maternal nonstandard work schedules and child cognitive outcomes. *Child Development*, 76, 137–154

Hanks S and Rosenbaum C (1977) Battered women: A study of women who live with violent alcohol-abusing men. *American Journal of Orthopsychiatry*, 47, 291–306

Hanmer J and Saunders S (1984) *Well-founded Fears*. London: Macmillan

Hannon L and Defronzo J (1998) The truly disadvantaged, public assistance, and crime. *Social Problems*, 45, 383–392

Hansen K and Machin S (2002) Spatial crime patterns and the introduction of the UK minimum wage. *Oxford Bulletin of Economics and Statistics*, 64, Supplement, 677–697

Hare R (1978) Electrodermal and cardiovascular correlates of psychopathy. In

R Hare and D Schalling (eds) *Psychopathic Behaviour: Approaches to Research*. Chichester: Wiley

Hare R (1982) Psychopathy and the personality dimensions of psychoticism, extraversion and neuroticism. *Personality and Individual Differences*, 3, 35–42

Hare R (2003) *Hare Psychopathy Checklist-Revised* 2nd ed. Toronto: Multi-Media Health Systems

Hare R, McPherson L, and Forth A (1988) Male psychopaths and their criminal careers. *Journal of Consulting and Clinical Psychology*, 56, 710–714

Hargreaves D (1967) *Social Relations in a Secondary School*. London: Routledge & Kegan Paul

Harries K and Stadler S (1988) Heat and violence: New findings from Dallas field data, 1980–1981. *Journal of Applied Social Psychology*, 18, 129–138

Harris J and Grace S (1999) *A Question of Evidence? Investigating and Prosecuting Rape in the 1990s*. Home Office Research Study No 196. London: Home Office

Hart H (1983) *Essays on Bentham*. Oxford: Oxford University Press

Hartl E, Monnelly E, and Elderkin R (1982) *Physique and Delinquent Behaviour*. New York: Academic Press

Harvey E (1999) Short-term and long-term effects of early parental employment on children of the National Longitudinal Survey of Youth. *Developmental Psychology*, 35, 445–459

Harvey L, Burnham R, Kendall K, and Pease K (1992) Gender differences in criminal justice: An international comparison. *British Journal of Criminology*, 32, 208–217

Haskett M, Johnson C, and Miller J (1994) Individual differences in risk of child abuse by adolescent mothers: Assessment in the perinatal period. *Journal of Child Psychology and Psychiatry and Allied Disciplines*, 35, 461–476

Hawk S and Peterson R (1974) Do MMPI psychopathic deviancy scores reflect psychopathic deviancy or just deviancy? *Journal of Personality Assessment*, 38, 362–368

Hay C (1998) Parental sanctions and delinquent behavior: Toward clarification of Braithwaite's theory of reintegrative shaming. *Theoretical Criminology*, 2, 419–443.

Hay D (1975) Property, authority, and the criminal law. In D Hay, P Linebaugh, J Rule, E Thompson, and C Winslow (eds) *Albion's Fatal Tree*. London: Allen Lane

Haynie D (2002) Friendship networks and delinquency: The relative nature of peer delinquency. *Journal of Quantitative Criminology*, 18, 99–134

Hayward K (2004) *City Limits: Crime, Consumer Culture, and the Urban Experience*. London: Glasshouse

Healy W and Bronner A (1936) *New Light on Delinquency and its Treatment*. New Haven, CT: Yale University Press

Hearn J (1996) Is masculinity dead? A critique of the concept of masculinity. In M Mac an Ghaill (ed) *Understanding Masculinities*. Buckingham: Open University Press

Heidensohn F (1996) *Women and Crime* 2nd ed. Basingstoke: Macmillan

Heimer K and Matsueda R (1994) Role-taking, role commitment, and delinquency: A theory of differential social control. *American Sociological Review*, 59, 365–390

Heineke J (ed) (1978) *Economic Models of Criminal Behavior*. New York: North-Holland

Henry S and Milovanovic D (1996) *Constitutive Criminology: Beyond Postmodernism*. London: Sage

Herrenkohl R and Russo M (2001) Abusive early child rearing and early childhood aggression. *Child Maltreatment*, 6, 3–16

Herrnstein R and Murray C (1994) *The Bell Curve*. New York: Free Press

Hester S and Eglin P (1992) *A Sociology of Crime*. London: Routledge

Hewitt L and Jenkins R (1946) *Fundamental Patterns of Maladjustment*. Springfield: State of Illinois

Hickman Barlow M, Barlow D, and Chiricos T (1995) Economic conditions and ideologies of crime in the media: A content analysis of crime news. *Crime and Delinquency*, 41, 3–19

Hillyard P, Pantazis C, Tombs S, and Gordon D (2004) *Beyond Criminology: Taking Harm Seriously*. London: Pluto Press

Hindelang M (1973) Causes of delinquency: A partial replication and extension. *Social Problems*, 20, 471–487

Hindelang M, Gottfredson R, and Garofalo J (1978) *Victims of Personal Crime*. Cambridge, MA: Ballinger

Hirschfield A and Bowers K (1997) The development of a social, demographic and land use profiler for areas of high crime. *British Journal of Criminology*, 37, 103–120

Hirschi T (1969) *Causes of Delinquency*. Berkeley: University of California Press

Hirschi T (1975) Labeling theory and juvenile delinquency: An assessment of the evidence. In W Gove (ed) *The Labeling of Deviance*. Beverly Hills, CA: Sage

Hirschi T and Gottfredson M (1983) Age and the explanation of crime. *American Journal of Sociology*, 89, 552–584

Hirschi T and Gottfredson M (1989) The significance of white-collar crime for a general theory of crime, *Criminology*, 27, 359–371

Hirschi T and Gottfredson M (1993) Commentary: Testing the General Theory of Crime. *Journal of Research into Crime and Delinquency*, 30, 47–54

Hirschi T and Hindelang M (1977) Intelligence and delinquency: A revisionist review. *American Sociological Review*, 42, 571–586

Hirst P (1975) Marx and Engels on law, crime and morality. In I Taylor, P Walton, and J Young (eds) *Critical Criminology*. London: Routledge & Kegan Paul

Hochstetler A, Copes H, and DeLisi M (2002) Differential association in group and solo offending. *Journal of Criminal Justice*, 30, 559–566

Hodge J (1993) Alcohol and violence. In P Taylor (ed) *Violence in Society*. London: Royal College of Physicians

Hodgins S (1992) Mental disorder, intellectual deficiency, and crime. *Archives of General Psychiatry*, 49, 476–483

Hoffmann J and Miller A (1998) A latent variable analysis of general strain theory. *Journal of Quantitative Criminology*, 14, 83–110

Hoffmann J and Su S (1997) The conditional effects of stress on delinquency and drug use: A strain theory assessment of sex differences. *Journal of Research in Crime and Delinquency*, 34, 46–78

Hoffman M (1977) Moral internalisation: Current theory and research. In L Berkowitz (ed) *Advances in Experimental Social Psychology* vol 10. New York: Academic Press

Hoghughi M and Forest A (1970) Eysenck's theory of criminality: An examination of approved school boys. *British Journal of Criminology*, 10, 240–254

Holland G (1843) *Vital Statistics of Sheffield*. London

Hollin C (1992) *Criminal Behaviour*. London: The Falmer Press

Hollitscher W (1947) *Sigmund Freud: An Introduction*. London: Routledge & Kegan Paul

Home Office (1989) *Report of the Working Group on the Fear of Crime*. Standing Conference of Crime Prevention. London: HMSO

Home Office (1996) *Victim's Charter*. London: HMSO

Home Office (1999) *What Works: Reducing Re-offending: Evidence-based Practice*. London: Home Office

Home Office (2000) *Review of Crime Statistics: A Discussion Document*. London: Home Office

Home Office (2001) *Criminal Justice: The Way Ahead*. Cm 5074. London: Home Office

Home Office and DHSS (1975) *Report of the Committee on Mentally Abnormal Offenders*. Cmnd 6244. London: HMSO

Hood-Williams J (2001) Gender, masculinities and crime: From structures to psyches. *Theoretical Criminology*, 5, 37–60

Hooton E (1939) *The American Criminal*. Cambridge, MA: Harvard University Press

Horsley J (1887) *Jottings from Jail*. London: T Fisher Unwin

Hough M (1986) Victims of violent crime: Findings from the first British Crime Survey. In E Fattah (ed) *From Crime Policy to Victim Policy*. London: Macmillan

Hough M (1995) *Anxiety about Crime*. Home Office Research Study No 147. London: Home Office

Hough M and Mayhew P (1983) *The British Crime Survey*. Home Office Research Study No 76. London: HMSO

Hough M and Mayhew P (1985) *Taking Account of Crime: Findings from the Second British Crime Survey*. Home Office Research Study No 85. London: HMSO

Hough M and Roberts J (1998) *Attitudes to Punishment: Findings from the 1996 British Crime Survey*. Home Office Research Findings No 64. London: Home Office

Hough M, Jacobson J, and Millie A (2003) *The Decision to Imprison: Sentencing and the Prison Population*. London: Prison Reform Trust

Hough M, Lewis H, and Walker N (1988) Factors associated with punitiveness in

England and Wales. In M Hough and N Walker (eds) *Public Attitudes to Sentencing*. Aldershot: Gower

Howarth E (1986) What does Eysenck's psychoticism scale really measure? *British Journal of Psychology*, 77, 223–227

Howells K (1979) Some meanings of children for pedophiles. In M Cook and G Wilson (eds) *Love and Attraction*. Oxford: Pergamon

Howells K (1983) Social constructing and violent behaviour in mentally abnormal offenders. In J Hinton (ed) *Dangerousness: Problems of Assessment and Prediction*. London: Allen and Unwin

Hsu L, Wisner K, Richey E, and Goldstein C (1985) Is juvenile delinquency related to an abnormal EEG? A study of EEG abnormalities on juvenile delinquents and adolescent psychiatric inpatients. *Journal of the American Academy of Child Psychiatry*, 24, 310–315

Hucker S, Langevin R, Dickey R, Handy L, Chambers J, Wright S, Bain J, and Wortzman G (1988) Cerebral damage and dysfunction in sexually aggressive men. *Annals of Sex Research*, 1, 33–47

Hudson C (2005) Socioeconomic status and mental illness: Tests of the social causation and selection hypotheses. *American Journal of Orthopsychiatry*, 75, 3–18

Huesmann L (1986) Psychological processes promoting the relation between exposure to media violence and aggressive behaviour by the viewer. *Journal of Social Issues*, 42, 125–139

Huesmann L, Eron L, and Yarmel P (1987) Intellectual functioning and aggression. *Journal of Personality and Social Psychology*, 52, 232–240

Huesmann L, Moise-Titus J, Podolski C, and Eron L (2003) Longitudinal relations between children's exposure to TV violence and their aggressive and violent behavior in young adulthood: 1977–1992. *Developmental Psychology*, 39, 201–221

Hulsman L (1986) Critical criminology and the concept of crime. *Contemporary Crises*, 10, 63–80

Hunt A (1991) Postmodernism and critical criminology. In B MacLean and D Milovanovic (eds) *New Directions in Critical Criminology*. Vancouver: Collective Press

Hunter H (1966) XYY chromosomes and Klinefelter's Syndrome. *Lancet*, i, 984

Husain S (1988) *Neighbourhood Watch in England and Wales: A Longitudinal Analysis*. Home Office Crime Prevention Unit Paper 12. London: HMSO

Hutchings B and Mednick S (1977) Criminality in adoptees and their adoptive and biological parents: A pilot study. In S Mednick and K Christiansen (eds) *Biological Bases of Criminal Behavior*. New York: Gardner Press

Ingraham B (1979) *Political Crime in Europe*. Berkeley: University of California Press

Ions E (1977) *Against Behaviouralism*. Oxford: Blackwell

Jacobs D (1981) Inequality and Economic Crime. *Sociology and Social Research*, 66, 12–28

Jacobs P, Brunton M, and Melville M (1965) Aggressive behaviour, mental subnormality, and the XYY male. *Nature*, 208, 1351–1352

Jamieson L and Taylor P (2004) A reconviction study of special (high security) hospital patients. *British Journal of Criminology*, 44, 783–802

Jang S and Johnson B (2003) Strain, negative emotions, and deviant coping among African Americans: A test of general strain theory. *Journal of Quantitative Criminology*, 19, 79–105

Jefferson T (1996a) Introduction. In Jefferson T and Carlen P (eds) Masculinities, social relations and crime. Special Issue of the *British Journal of Criminology*, 36, 337–347

Jefferson T (1996b) From 'Little Fairy Boy' to 'The Complete Destroyer': Subjectivity and transformation in the biography of Mike Tyson. In M Mac an Ghaill (ed) *Understanding Masculinities*. Buckingham: Open University Press

Jefferson T (1998) 'Muscle', 'hard men' and 'Iron' Mike Tyson: Reflections on desire, anxiety and the embodiment of masculinity. *Body and Society*, 4, 77–98

Jefferson T (2002) For a psychosocial criminology. In K Carrington and R Hogg (eds) *Critical Criminology: Issues, Debates, Challenges*. Cullompton: Willan

Jeffery C (1960) The historical development of criminology. In H Mannheim (ed) *Pioneers in Criminology*. London: Stevens

Jeffery C (1965) Criminal behavior and learning theory. *Journal of Criminal Law, Criminology and Police Science*, 56, 294–300

Jenkins P (1998) *Moral Panic: Changing Concepts of the Child Molester in Modern America*. New Haven, CT: Yale University Press

Jensen A (1969) How much can we boost IQ and scholastic achievement? *Harvard Educational Review*, 39, 1–123

Jewkes Y (2004) *Media and Crime*. London: Sage

Joe-Laidler K and Hunt G (1997) Violence and social organization in female gangs. *Social Justice*, 24, 148–169

Johnson A (1959) Juvenile delinquency. In S Arieti (ed) *American Handbook of Psychiatry*. New York: Basic Books

Johnson B, Goldstein P, Preble E, Schmeider J, Lipton D, Spunt B, and Miller T (1985) *Taking Care of Business: The Economics of Crime by Heroin Abusers*. Lexington, MA: Lexington Books

Johnson D (2000) Prosecutor culture in Japan and the USA. In D Nelken (ed) *Contrasting Criminal Justice: Getting from Here to There*. Aldershot: Ashgate

Johnston L (1996) What is vigilantism? *British Journal of Criminology*, 36, 220–236

Johnston M (1988) Correlates of early violence experience among men who are abusive toward female mates. In G Hotaling, D Finkelhor, J Kirkpatrick, and M Straus (eds) *Family Abuse and its Consequences: New Directions in Research*. Beverly Hills, CA: Sage

Johnstone J (1983) Recruitment to a youth gang. *Youth and Society*, 14, 281–300

Jones D (1982) *Crime, Protest, Community and Police in Nineteenth-Century Britain*. London: Routledge & Kegan Paul

Jones J (1971) Federal efforts to solve social problems. In E Smigel (ed) *Handbook on the Study of Social Problems*. Chicago: Rand McNally

Jones S (2000) *Understanding Violent Crime*. Buckingham: Open University Press

Jones T, MacLean B, and Young J (1986) *The Islington Crime Survey*. Aldershot: Gower

Juby H and Farrington D (2001) Disentangling the link between disrupted families and delinquency. *British Journal of Criminology*, 41, 22–40

Junger-Tas J, Marshall I, and Ribeaud D (2003) *Delinqueny in an International Perspective: The International Self-Report Delinquency Study (ISRD)*. The Hague: Kugler

Kamin L (1985) Is crime in the genes? The answer may depend on who chooses the evidence. *Scientific American*, 22–25 April

Kandel E, Mednick S, Kirkegaard D, Sorensen L, Hutchings B, Knopf J, Rosenberg R, and Schulsinger F (1988) IQ as a protective factor for subjects at high risk for antisocial behavior. *Journal of Consulting and Clinical Psychology*, 56, 244–246

Kang S, Magura S, and Shapiro J (1994) Correlates of cocaine/crack use among inner-city incarcerated adolescents. *American Journal of Drug and Alcohol Abuse*, 20, 413–429

Katz J (1988) *Seductions of Crime*. New York: Basic Books

Katz J (1999) *How Emotions Work*. Chicago: University of Chicago Press

Katz J and Abel C (1984) The medicalization of repression: Eugenics and crime. *Contemporary Crises*, 8, 227–241

Keane C, Maxim P, and Teevan J (1993) Drinking and driving, self-control, and gender. *Journal of Research in Crime and Delinquency*, 30, 30–46

Keita S, Kittles R, Royal C, Bonney G, Furbert-Harris P, Dunston G, and Rotimi C (2004) Conceptualizing human variation. *Nature Genetics*, 36(Suppl), S17–S20

Kelling G and Coles C (1996) *Fixing Broken Windows*. New York: Free Press

Kellor F (1900) Psychological and environmental study of women criminals. *American Journal of Sociology*, 5, 527–543

Kersten J (1996) Culture, masculinities and violence against women. *British Journal of Criminology*, 36, 381–395

Kessler S and Moos R (1970) The XXY karyotype and criminality. *Journal of Psychiatric Research*, 7, 153–170

Kilpatrick D, Best C, Veronen L, Amick A, Villeponteaux L, and Ruff G (1985) Mental health correlates of criminal victimisation: A random community survey. *Journal of Consulting and Clinical Psychology*, 53, 866–873

Kim-Cohen J, Moffitt T, Caspi A, and Taylor A (2004) Genetic and environmental processes in young children's resilience and vulnerability to socioeconomic deprivation. *Child Development*, 75, 651–668

Kinsey R (1984) *Merseyside Crime Survey*. Edinburgh: Centre for Criminology, University of Edinburgh

Kinsey R, Lea J, and Young J (1986) *Losing the Fight against Crime*. Oxford: Blackwell

Kirkcaldy B and Brown J (2000) Personality, socioeconomics and crime: An international comparison. *Psychology, Crime and Law*, 6, 113–125

Kitsuse J and Cicourel A (1963) A note on the uses of official statistics. *Social Problems*, 11, 131–139

Klein D (1973) The etiology of female crime: A review of the literature. *Issues in Criminology*, 8, 3–30

Klein M (1988) *Love, Guilt and Reparation and Other Works 1921–45*. London: Virago

Klein MW (1995) *The American Street Gang: Its Nature, Prevalence, and Control*. New York: Oxford University Press

Kline P (1987) Psychoanalysis and crime. In B McGurk, D Thornton, and M Williams (eds) *Applying Psychology to Imprisonment: Theory and Practice*. London: HMSO

Koch B (1998) *The Politics of Crime Prevention*. Aldershot: Ashgate

Komiya N (1999) A cultural study of the low crime rate in Japan. *British Journal of Criminology*, 39, 369–390

Korn R and McCorkle L (1957) *Criminology and Penology*. New York: Holt

Kornhauser R (1978) *Social Sources of Delinquency*. Chicago: University of Chicago Press

Koss M and Gaines J (1993) The prediction of sexual aggression by alcohol use, athletic participation, and fraternity affiliation. *Journal of Interpersonal Violence*, 8, 94–108

Koss M, Gidycz C, and Wisniewski N (1987) The scope of rape: Incidence and prevalence of sexual aggression and victimisation in a national sample of higher education students. *Journal of Consulting and Clinical Psychology*, 55, 162–170

Kruk M, Meelis W, Halász J, and Haller J (2004) Fast positive feedback between the adrenocortical stress response and a brain mechanism involved in aggressive behavior. *Behavioral Neuroscience*, 118, 1062–1070

Labato A (2000) Criminal weapon use in Brazil: A psychological analysis. In D Canter and L Alison (eds) *Profiling Property Crimes*. Dartmouth: Ashgate

La Fontaine J (1998) *Speak of the Devil: Tales of Satanic Abuse in Contemporary England*. Cambridge: Cambridge University Press

Laing R (1967) *The Politics of Experience*. Harmondsworth: Penguin

Lamb S (1996) *The Trouble with Blame: Victims, Perpetrators and Responsibility*. Cambridge, MA: Harvard University Press

Lander B (1954) *Towards an Understanding of Juvenile Delinquency*. New York: Columbia University Press

Lang A, Goeckner D, Adesso V, and Marlatt G (1975) Effects of alcohol on aggression in male social drinkers. *Journal of Abnormal Psychology*, 84, 508–518

Lange J (1931) *Crime as Destiny*. London: Allen & Unwin

Lasley J (1988) Toward a control theory of white-collar offending. *Journal of Quantitative Criminology*, 4, 347–362

Lavater J (1792) *Essays on Physiognomy, Designed to Promote the Knowledge and Love of Mankind*. London: Murray

Laws D and Marshall W (1990) A conditioning theory of the etiology and maintenance of deviant sexual preference and behavior. In W Marshall, D Laws, and H Barbaree (eds) *Handbook of Sexual Assault*. New York: Plenum

Lawson W (1984) Depression and crime: A discursive approach. In M Craft and A Craft (eds) *Mentally Abnormal Offenders*. London: Bailliere Tindall

Laycock G (1985) *Property Marking: A Deterrent to Domestic Burglary*? Home Office Crime Prevention Unit Paper No 3. London: Home Office

Lazarus R (1980) Cognitive behavior therapy as psychodynamics. In M Mahoney (ed) *Psychotherapy Process*. New York: Plenum

Lea J (1998) Criminology and postmodernity. In P Walton and J Young (eds) *The New Criminology Revisited*. Basingstoke: Macmillan

Lea J and Young J (1982) The riots in Britain 1981: Urban violence and political marginalisation. In D Cowell, T Jones, and J Young (eds) *Policing the Riots*. London: Junction Books

Lea J and Young J (1984) *What is to be Done about Law and Order?* Harmondsworth: Penguin

Lea J and Young J (1993) *What is to be Done about Law and Order?* 2nd ed. London: Pluto Press

Lees S (1996) *Carnal Knowledge: Rape on Trial*. London: Hamish Hamilton

Leishman F, Cope S, and Starie P (1996) Reinventing and restructuring: Towards a 'new policing order'. In F Leishman, B Loveday, and S Savage (eds) *Core Issues in Policing*. London: Longman

Lemert E (1951) *Social Pathology*. New York: McGraw-Hill

Lemert E (1964) Social structure, social control, and deviation. In M Clinard (ed) *Anomie and Deviant Behavior*. New York: Free Press

Lemert E (1967) *Human Deviance, Social Problems and Social Control*. Englewood Cliffs, NJ: Prentice Hall

Leonard E (1982) *Women, Crime and Society*. London: Longman

Lesser M (1980) *Nutrition and Vitamin Therapy*. New York: Bantam

Levi M (1993) *The Investigation, Prosecution and Trial of Serious Fraud*. Royal Commission on Criminal Justice Research Study No 14. London: HMSO

Levi M (1997) Violent crime. In Maguire M, Morgan R, and Reiner R (eds) *The Oxford Handbook of Criminology*, 2nd ed. Oxford: Oxford University Press

Lewis O (1959) *Five Families*. New York: Basic Books

Liazos A (1972) The poverty of the sociology of deviance: Nuts, sluts and 'preverts'. *Social Problems*, 20, 103–20

Lieber A and Sherin C (1972) Homicides and the lunar cycle: Toward a theory of lunar influence on human emotional disturbance. *American Journal of Psychiatry*, 129, 69–74

Lindesmith A and Gagnon J (1964) Anomie and drug addiction. In M Clinard (ed) *Anomie and Deviant Behavior*. New York: Free Press

Lindesmith A and Levin Y (1937) The Lombrosian myth in criminology. *American Journal of Sociology*, 42, 653–671

Lindqvist P (1986) Criminal homicide in Northern Sweden, 1970–1981:

Alcohol intoxication, alcohol abuse and mental disease. *International Journal of Law and Psychiatry*, 8, 19–37

Lindqvist P and Allebeck P (1990) Schizophrenia and crime: A longitudinal follow-up of 644 schizophrenics in Stockholm. *British Journal of Psychiatry*, 157, 345–350

Lipton D, McDonel E, and McFall R (1987) Heterosexual perception in rapists. *Journal of Consulting and Clinical Psychology*, 55, 17–21

Liska A (1981) *Perspectives on Deviance*. Englewood Cliffs, NJ: Prentice Hall

Little A (1963) Professor Eysenck's theory of crime: An empirical test on adolescent offenders. *British Journal of Criminology*, 4, 152–163

Little A (1965) Parental deprivation, separation and crime: A test on adolescent recidivists. *British Journal of Criminology*, 5, 419–430

Livingstone S (1996) On the continuing problem of media effects. In J Curran and M Gurevitch (eds) *Mass Media and Society*. London: Arnold

Lloyd C and Walmsley R (1989) *Changes in Rape Offences and Sentencing*. Home Office Research Study No 105. London: HMSO

Loehlin J, Lindzey G, and Spuhler J (1975) *Race Differences in Intelligence*. San Francisco: WH Freeman

Loftus E and Ketcham K (1994) *The Myth of Repressed Memory: False Memories and Allegations of Sexual Abuse*. New York: St Martin's Press

Lombroso C (1876) *L'Uomo Delinquente*. Milan: Hoepli

Lombroso C and Ferrero G (1895) *The Female Offender*. London: Unwin

Longford F (ed) (1964) *Crime: A Challenge to Us All*. London: The Labour Party

Lorenz K (1966) *On Aggression*. London: Methuen

Loveday B (1985) *The Role and Effectiveness of the Merseyside Police Committee*. Liverpool: Merseyside County Council

Loveday B (2000) Managing crime: Police use of crime data as an indicator of effectiveness. *International Journal of the Sociology of Law*, 28, 215–237

Lowman J and MacLean B (eds) (1992) *Realist Criminology: Crime Control and Policing in the 1990s*. Toronto: University of Toronto Press

Lynch M (1987) Quantitative analysis and Marxist criminology: Some old answers to a dilemma in Marxist criminology. *Crime and Social Justice*, 29, 110–127

Lyons M, True W, Eisen S, Goldberg J, Meyer J, Faraone S, Eaves L, and Tsuang M (1995) Differential heritability of adult and juvenile antisocial traits. *Archives of General Psychiatry*, 52, 906–915

MacAndrew C and Edgerton R (1969) *Drunken Comportment: A Social Explanation*. Chicago: Aldine

MacCoun R, Kilmer B, and Reuter P (2003) Research on drugs-crime linkages: The next generation. *NIJ Special Report: Toward a Drug and Crime Research Agenda for the 21st Century*. Washington, DC: National Institute of Justice

MacCulloch M, Snowden P, Wood P, and Mills H (1983) Sadistic fantasy, sadistic behaviour, and offending. *British Journal of Psychiatry*, 143, 20–29

MacDonald Z (2001) Revisiting the dark figure: A microeconometric analysis of the under-reporting of property crime and its implications. *British Journal of Criminology*, 41, 127–149

Machin S and Marie O (2004) *Crime and Benefit Sanctions*. Centre for Economic Performance Discussion Paper No 645. London: London School of Economics and Political Science

Macpherson W (1999) *The Stephen Lawrence Inquiry*. Cm 4262. London: Home Office.

Magnusson D (1988) Antisocial behaviour of boys and autonomic reactivity. In T Moffitt and S Mednick (eds) *Biological Contributions to Crime Causation*. Dordrecht: Martinus Nijhoff

Mair L (1969) *Witchcraft*. New York: McGraw-Hill

Makkai T and Braithwaite J (1994) Reintegrative shaming and compliance with regulatory standards. *Criminology*, 32, 361–383

Maliphant R, Watson S, and Daniels D (1990) Disruptive behaviour in school, personality characteristics and heart rate (HR) levels in 7–9-year-old boys. *Educational Psychology*, 10, 199–205

Mannheim H (1965) *Comparative Criminology*. London: Routledge & Kegan Paul

Mannuzza S, Klein R, Konig P, and Giampino T (1989) Hyperactive boys almost grown up: IV. Criminality and its relation to psychiatric status. *Archives of General Psychiatry*, 46, 1073–1079

Marcus B (2004) Self-control in the General Theory of Crime: Theoretical implications of a measurement problem. *Theoretical Criminology*, 8, 33–55

Mares D (2001) Gangstas or lager louts? Working class street gangs in Manchester. In M Klein, H Kerner, C Maxson, and E Weitekamp (eds) *The Eurogang Paradox: Street Gangs and Youth Groups in the US and Europe*. London: Kluwer Academic Publishers

Markowitz S (1999) *The Price of Alcohol, Wife Abuse, and Husband Abuse*. NBER Working Paper No 6916. Cambridge, MA: National Bureau of Economic Research

Marks M and Kumar R (1993) Infanticide in England and Wales. *Medicine Science and the Law*, 33, 329–339

Marsh H (1991) A comparative analysis of crime coverage in newspapers in the United States and other countries from 1960 to 1989. *Journal of Criminal Justice*, 19, 67–79

Marsh P, Rosser E, and Harre R (1978) *The Rules of Disorder*. London: Routledge & Kegan Paul

Marshall L and Cooke D (1999) The childhood experiences of psychopaths: A retrospective study of familial and societal factors. *Journal of Personality Disorders*, 13, 211–225

Marshall T and Merry S (1990) *Crime and Accountability*. London: HMSO

Matthews R (1986) *Policing Prostitution: A Multi-Agency Approach*. Middlesex Polytechnic Centre for Criminology, Paper No 1. London: Middlesex Polytechnic

Matthews R (1992) Replacing 'broken windows': Crime, incivilities and urban change. In R Matthews and J Young (eds) *Issues in Realist Criminology*. London: Sage

Matza D (1964) *Delinquency and Drift*. New York: Wiley

Matza D (1969) *Becoming Deviant*. Englewood Cliffs, NJ: Prentice Hall

Matza D and Sykes G (1961) Juvenile delinquency and subterranean values. *American Sociological Review*, 26, 712–719

Maxfield M and Widom C (1996) The cycle of violence: Revisited 6 years later. *Archives of Pediatrics and Adolescent Medicine*, 150, 390–395

Maxwell G and Morris A (1994) The New Zealand model of family group conferences. In C Alder and J Wundersitz (eds) *Family Conferencing and Juvenile Justice*. Canberra: Australian Institute of Criminology

Mayhew H (1861) *London Labour and the London Poor*. London: Griffin, Bohn

Mayhew P and Maung N (1992) *Surveying Crime: Findings from the 1992 British Crime Survey*. Home Office Research Findings No 2. London: HMSO

Mayhew P, Clarke R, and Hough M (1980) Steering column locks and car theft. In R Clarke and P Mayhew (eds) *Designing Out Crime*. London: HMSO

Mayhew P, Elliott D, and Dowds L (1989) *The 1988 British Crime Survey: Third Report*. Home Office Research Study No 111. London: HMSO

Mayhew P, Aye Maung N, and Mirrlees-Black C (1993) *The 1992 British Crime Survey*. Home Office Research Study No 132. London: HMSO

Maynard D (1984) *Inside Plea Bargaining*. New York: Plenum

Mays J (1954) *Growing Up in the City*. Liverpool: University of Liverpool Press

Mazerolle P, Piquero A, and Capowich G (2003) Examining the links between strain, situational and dispositional anger, and crime: Further specifying and testing general strain theory. *Youth & Society*, 35, 131–157

Mazur A (1983) Physiology, dominance, and aggression in humans. In A Goldstein (ed) *Prevention and Control of Aggression*. New York: Pergamon

McBurnett K, Lahey B, Rathouz P, and Loeber R (2000) Low salivary cortisol and persistent aggression in boys referred for disruptive behaviour. *Archives of General Psychiatry*, 57, 38–43

McCarthy B (1996) The attitudes and actions of others: Tutelage and Sutherland's theory of differential association. *British Journal of Criminology*, 36, 135–147

McClelland G and Teplin L (2001) Alcohol intoxication and violent crime: Implications for public health policy. *American Journal on Addictions*, 10 Supplement, 70–86

McCord J (1979) Some child-rearing antecedents of criminal behavior in adult men. *Journal of Personality and Social Psychology*, 37, 1477–1486

McDonald L (1976) *The Sociology of Law and Order*. London: Faber & Faber

McDonald L (1982) Theory and evidence of rising crime in the nineteenth century. *British Journal of Sociology*, 33, 404–420

McGuigan W, Vuchinich S, and Pratt C (2000) Domestic violence, parents' view of their infant, and risk for child abuse. *Journal of Family Psychology*, 14, 613–624

McGuire J (ed) (1995) *What Works? Reducing Reoffending—Guidelines from Research and Practice*. Chichester: Wiley

McGuire R, Carlisle J, and Young B (1965) Sexual deviations as conditioned behaviour: A hypothesis. *Behaviour Research and Therapy*, 2, 185–190

McGurk B and McDougall C (1981) A new approach to Eysenck's theory of criminality. *Personality and Individual Differences*, 2, 338–340

McGurk B, McEwan A, and Graham F (1981) Personality types and recidivism among young delinquents. *British Journal of Criminology*, 21, 159–165

McMichael P (1979) The hen or the egg? Which comes first—antisocial emotional disorders or reading disability. *British Journal of Educational Psychology*, 49, 226–238

McMurran M and Hollin C (1989) Drinking and delinquency: Another look at young offenders and alcohol. *British Journal of Criminology*, 29, 386–394

McNees M, Egli D, Marshall R, and Risley T (1976) Shoplifting prevention: Providing information through signs. *Journal of Applied Behaviour Analysis*, 9, 399–406

Mednick S (1977) A biological theory of the learning of law-abiding behaviour. In S Mednick and K Christiansen (eds) *Biosocial Basis of Criminal Behavior*. New York: Gardner Press

Mednick S, Moffitt T, and Stack S (eds) (1987) *The Causes of Crime: New Biological Approaches*. New York: Cambridge University Press

Mednick S, Pollock V, Volavka J, and Gabrielli W (1982) Biology and violence. In M Wolfgang and N Weiner (eds) *Criminal Violence*. Beverly Hills, CA: Sage

Mednick S, Volavka J, Gabrielli W, and Itil T (1981) EEG as a predictor of antisocial behaviour. *Criminology*, 19, 219–229

Menard S (1995) A developmental test of Mertonian anomie theory. *Journal of Research in Crime and Delinquency*, 32, 136–174

Mercer J (1972) IQ: The lethal label. *Psychology Today*, September, 44–47

Merton R (1938) Social structure and anomie. *American Sociological Review*, 3, 672–682

Merton R (1948) The self-fulfilling prophecy. *Antioch Review*, Summer, 193–210

Merton R (1968) *Social Theory and Social Structure*. New York: Free Press

Merton R (1995) Opportunity structure: The emergence, diffusion, and differentiation of a sociological concept, 1930s–1950s. In F Adler and W Laufer (eds) *The Legacy of Anomie Theory*. New Brunswick, NJ: Transaction

Merton R (1997) Foreword. In N Passas and R Agnew (eds) *The Future of Anomie Theory*. Boston: Northeastern University Press

Messerschmidt J (1993) *Masculinities and Crime*. Lanham, MD: Rowman & Littlefield

Messerschmidt J (1997) *Crime as Structured Action*. Thousand Oaks, CA: Sage

Messner S and Rosenfeld R (1994) *Crime and the American Dream*. Belmont, CA: Wadsworth

Michael J and Adler M (1933) *Crime, Law and Social Science*. New York: Harcourt, Brace, Jovanovich

Michael R and Zumpe D (1983) Sexual violence in the United States and the role of season. *American Journal of Psychiatry*, 140, 883–886

Michalowski R (1983) Crime control in the 1980s: A progressive agenda. *Crime and Social Justice*, 19, 13–23

Miers D (1992) The responsibilities and the rights of victims of crime. *Modern Law Review*, 55, 482–505

Miles I and Irvine J (1981) The critique of official statistics. In J Irvine, I Miles, and J Evans (eds) *Demystifying Social Statistics*, 2nd imp. London: Pluto Press

Miller J (2002) The strengths and limits of 'doing gender' for understanding street crime. *Theoretical Criminology*, 6, 433–460

Miller W (1958) Lower-class culture as a generating milieu of gang delinquency. *Journal of Social Issues*, 14, 5–19

Milner J, Halsey L, and Fultz J (1995) Empathic responsiveness and affective reactivity to infant stimuli in high- and low-risk for physical child abuse mothers. *Child Abuse and Neglect*, 19, 767–780

Mirrlees-Black C (1999) *Domestic Violence: Findings from a New British Crime Survey Self Completion Questionnaire*. Home Office Research Study No 191. London: Home Office

Mirrlees-Black C, Mayhew P, and Percy A (1996) *The 1996 British Crime Survey*. Home Office Statistical Bulletin 19/96. London: Home Office

Moffitt T, Robins R, and Caspi A (2001) A couples analysis of partner abuse with implications for abuse-prevention policy. *Criminology and Public Policy*, 1, 5–36

Monahan J, Steadman H, Silver E, Appelbaum P, Robbins P, Mulvey E, Roth L, Grisso T, and Banks S (2001) *Rethinking Risk Assessment: The MacArthur Study of Mental Disorder and Violence*. New York: Oxford University Press

Money J (1990) Forensic sexology: Paraphilic serial rape (biastophilia) and lust murder (erotophonophilia). *American Journal of Psychotherapy*, 44, 26–36

Money J and Ernhardt A (1972) *Man and Woman: Boy and Girl*. Baltimore, MD: Johns Hopkins University

Mooney J (1993) *The North London Domestic Violence Survey*. Enfield: Middlesex University Centre for Criminology

Morgan R and Newburn T (1997) *The Future of Policing*. Oxford: Oxford University Press

Morgan R, McKenzie I, and Reiner R (1990) *Police Powers and Policy: A Study of Custody Officers*. London: ESRC

Morris A (1987) *Women, Crime and Criminal Justice*. Oxford: Blackwell

Morris T (1957) *The Criminal Area*. London: Routledge & Kegan Paul

Morris T (1988) British Criminology: 1935–1948. In P Rock (ed) *A History of British Criminology*. Oxford: Oxford University Press

Morris T (1989) *Crime and Criminal Justice since 1945*. Oxford: Oxford University Press

Mott J (1990) *Young People, Alcohol and Crime*. Home Office Research Bulletin (Research and Statistics Department) 28, 24–28

Mott J and Taylor M (1974) *Delinquency amongst Opiate Users*. Home Office Research Study No 23. London: HMSO

Muehlenhard C and Hollabaugh L (1988) Do women sometimes say no when they mean yes? The prevalence and correlates of women's token resistance to sex. *Journal of Personality and Social Psychology*, 54, 872–879

Mugford S and O'Malley P (1991) Heroin policy and deficit models: The limits of left realism. *Crime, Law and Social Change*, 15, 19–36

Mullen P (1990) The long-term influence of sexual assault on the mental health of victims. *Journal of Forensic Psychiatry*, 1, 13–34

Mullen P, Burgess P, Wallace C, Palmer S, and Ruschena D (2000) Community care and criminal offending in schizophrenia, *Lancet*, 355, 614–617

Murchison C (1926) *Criminal Intelligence*. Worcester, MA: Clark University

Murray C (1976) *The Link between Learning Disabilities and Juvenile Delinquency*. Washington, DC: Office of Juvenile Justice and Delinquency

Musto D (1973) *The American Disease*. New Haven, CT: Yale University Press

Myers R and Berah E (1983) Some features of Australian exhibitionists compared with paedophiles. *Archives of Sexual Behavior*, 12, 541–547

Myhill A and Allen J (2002) *Rape and Sexual Assault of Women: The Extent and Nature of the Problem*. Home Office Research Study No 237. London: Home Office

Naffine N (1987) *Female Crime: The Construction of Women in Criminology*. Sydney: Allen & Unwin

Nass M (1966) The superego and moral development in the theories of Freud and Piaget. *Psychoanalytic Study of the Child*, 21, 51–68

National Audit Office (1991–92) *National Insurance Fund Accounts 1990–91*. HC 33. London: HMSO

National Audit Office (2002–03a) *Tackling Benefit Fraud*. HC 393. London: The Stationery Office

National Audit Office (2002–03b) *Tackling Fraud against the Inland Revenue*. HC 429. London: The Stationery Office

National Audit Office (2003–04) *Tackling VAT Fraud*. HC 357. London: The Stationery Office

Naylor B (2001) Reporting violence in the British print media: Gendered stories. *Howard Journal*, 40, 180–194

Needleman H, Riess J, Tobin M, Biesecker G, and Greenhouse J (1996) Bone lead levels and delinquent behavior. *Journal of the American Medical Association*, 275, 363–369

Neisser U, Boodoo G, Bouchard T, Boykin A, Brody N, Ceci S, Halperin D, Loehlin J, Perloff R, Sternberg R, and Urbana S (1996) Intelligence: Known and unknowns. *The American Psychologist*, 51, 77–101

Newburn T and Reiner R (2004) From PC Dixon to Dixon PLC. *Criminal Law Review*, 601–618

Newburn T and Stanko E (eds) (1994) *Just Boys Doing Business*? London: Routledge

Newman J, Patterson C, and Kosson D (1987) Response preservation in psychopaths. *Journal of Abnormal Psychology*, 96, 145–148

Nicolson D and Sanghvi R (1993) Battered women and provocation. *Criminal Law Review*, 728–738

Nietzel M (1979) *Crime and its Modification: A Social Learning Perspective*. New York: Pergamon

Noll J, Trickett P, and Putnam F (2003) A prospective investigation of the impact of childhood sexual abuse on the development of sexuality. *Journal of Consulting and Clinical Psychology*, 71, 575–586

Norrie A and Adelman S (1989) 'Consensual authoritarianism' and criminal justice in Thatcher's Britain. *Journal of Law and Society*, 16, 112–128

Nuffield Council on Bioethics (2002) *Genetics and Human Behaviour: The Ethical Context*. London: Nuffield Council on Bioethics

Nye F (1958) *Family Relationships and Delinquent Behavior*. New York: Wiley

Obeidallah D and Earls F (1999) *Adolescent Girls: The Role of Depression in the Development of Delinquency*. Washington, DC: National Institute of Justice

O'Connell M and Whelan A (1996) Taking wrongs seriously: Public perceptions of crime seriousness. *British Journal of Criminology*, 36, 299–318

O'Connor T, Heron J, Golding J, Beveridge M, and Glover V (2002) Maternal antenatal anxiety and children's behavioural/emotional problems at 4 years. *British Journal of Psychiatry*, 180, 502–508

O'Connor T, McGuire S, Reiss D, Hetherington E, and Plomin R (1998) Co-occurrence of depressive symptoms and antisocial behavior in adolescence: A common genetic liability. *Journal of Abnormal Psychology*, 107, 27–37

O'Donovan K (1991) Defences for battered women who kill. *Journal of Law and Society*, 18, 219–240

Oliver I (1987) *Police, Government and Accountability*. London: Macmillan

Olweus D (1986) Aggression and hormones: Behavioral relationship with testosterone and adrenaline. In D Olweus, J Block, and M Radke-Yarrow (eds) *Development of Antisocial and Prosocial Behavior*. New York: Academic Press

Olweus D (1987) Testosterone and adrenalin: Aggressive and antisocial behaviour in normal adolescent males. In S Mednick, T Moffitt, and S Stack (eds) *The Causes of Crime: New Biological Approaches*. Cambridge: Cambridge University Press

O'Neal E, Brunault M, Marquis J, and Carifio M (1979) Anger and the body buffer zone. *Journal of Social Psychology*, 108, 135–136

Orcutt J (1970) Differential association and marijuana use: A closer look at Sutherland (with a little help from Becker). *Criminology*, 25, 341–358

O'Reilly-Fleming T (ed) (1996) *Post-Critical Criminology*. Scarborough, Canada: Prentice Hall Canada

Orme J (1994) *A Study of the Relationship between Unemployment and Recorded Crime*. Home Office Statistical Findings No 1. London: Home Office

Orrù M (1990) Merton's instrumental theory of anomie. In J Clark, C Modgil, and S Modgil (eds) *Robert K Merton: Consensus and Controversy*. London: Falmer Press

Osborn S and Shaftoe H (1995) *Safer Neighbourhoods? Successes and Failures in Crime Prevention*. London: Safe Neighbourhoods Unit

Painter K (1989) *Crime Prevention and Public Lighting with Special Focus on Women and Elderly People*. London: Middlesex Polytechnic Centre for Criminology

Painter K (1991) *Wife Rape, Marriage and the Law: Survey Report*. Manchester: University of Manchester

Painter K and Farrington D (1998) Marital violence in Great Britain and its relationship to marital and non-marital rape. *International Review of Victimology*, 5, 257–276

Painter K and Farrington D (2001) Evaluating situational crime prevention using a young people's survey. *British Journal of Criminology*, 41, 266–284

Palamara F, Cullen F, and Gersten J (1986) The effect of police and mental health intervention on juvenile deviance: Specifying contingencies in the impact of formal reaction. *Journal of Health and Social Behavior*, 27, 90–105

Palen J (1981) *The Urban World* 3rd ed. New York: McGraw-Hill

Palmer S (1988) *Police and Protest in England and Ireland 1780–1850*. Cambridge: Cambridge University Press

Paolucci H (1963) Introduction. In C Beccaria *On Crimes and Punishments*. Indianapolis, IN: Bobbs-Merrill

Parent D (1988) *Structuring Criminal Sentences*. Stoneham, MA: Butterworth Legal Publishers

Parke R (1974) Rules, roles, and resistance to deviation: Recent advances in punishment, discipline, and self control. *Minnesota Symposia on Child Psychology* 8. Minneapolis: University of Minnesota Press

Parke R (1977) Socialisation into child abuse. In J Tapp and F Levine (eds) *Law, Justice, and the Individual in Society*. New York: Rinehart and Winston

Parker H (1974) *View from the Boys*. London: David & Charles

Parker H and Bottomley T (1996) *Crack Cocaine and Drugs-Crime Careers*. Home Office Research and Statistics Directorate Paper 34. London: Home Office

Parliamentary All Party Penal Affairs Group (1996) *Increasing the Rights of Victims of Crime*. London: Parliamentary Paper

Parmalee M (1918) *Criminology*. New York: Macmillan

Parnaby P and Sacco V (2004) Fame and strain: The contributions of Mertonian deviance theory to an understanding of the relationship between celebrity and deviant behavior. *Deviant Behavior*, 25, 1–26

Parsons O and Hart R (1984) Behavioral disorders associated with central nervous dysfunction. In H Adams and P Sutker (eds) *Comprehensive Handbook of Psychopathology*. New York: Plenum

Parsons T (1937) *The Structure of Social Action*. New York: McGraw-Hill

Parsons T (1951) *The Social System*. Glencoe, IL: Free Press

Parsons T (1954) *Essays in Sociological Theory*. Glencoe, IL: Free Press

Passas N (1990) Anomie and corporate deviance. *Contemporary Crises*, 14, 157–178

Passas N and Agnew R (eds) (1997) *The Future of Anomie Theory*. Boston: Northeastern University Press

Passingham R (1972) Crime and personality: A review of Eysenck's theory. In V Nebylitsin and J Gray (eds) *Biological Bases of Individual Behaviour*. New York: Academic Press

Paternoster R (1989) Decisions to participate in and desist from four types of common delinquency: Deterrence and the rational choice perspective. *Law and Society Review*, 23, 7–40

Paternoster R and Mazerolle P (1994) General strain theory and delinquency: A replication and extension. *Journal of Research in Crime and Delinquency*, 31, 235–263

Patrick J (1973) *A Glasgow Gang Observed*. London: Methuen

Patterson G (1982) *Coercive Family Process*. Eugene, OR: Castalia

Pearce F and Tombs S (1992) Realism and corporate crime. In R Matthews and J Young (eds) *Issues in Realist Criminology*. London: Sage

Pearson G (1983) *Hooligan: A History of Respectable Fears*. London: Macmillan

Pearson M, Wilmot E, and Padi M (1986) A study of violent behaviour among in-patients in a psychiatric hospital. *British Journal of Psychiatry*, 149, 232–235

Pepinsky H and Quinney R (1991) *Criminology as Peacemaking*. Bloomington: Indiana University Press

Perkins D (1987) A psychological treatment programme for sex offenders. In B McGurk, D Thornton, and M Williams (eds) *Applying Psychology to Imprisonment: Theory and Practice*. London: HMSO

Perks Committee (1967) *Report of the Departmental Committee on the Criminal Statistics*. Cmnd 3448. London: HMSO

Pernanen K (1991) *Alcohol in Human Violence*. New York: Guilford

Perrone D, Sullivan C, Pratt T, and Margaryan S (2004) Parental efficacy, self-control, and delinquency: A test of a general theory of crime on a nationally representative sample of youth. *International Journal of Offender Therapy and Comparative Criminology*, 48, 298–312

Petersen K, Matousek M, Mednick S, Volavka J, and Pollock V (1982) EEG antecedents of thievery. *Acta Psychiatrica Scandinavica*, 65, 331–338

Petersilia J, Greenwood P, and Lavin M (1978) *Criminal Careers of Habitual Felons*. Washington, DC: US Department of Justice, National Institute of Law Enforcement and Criminal Justice

Peterson D, Miller J, and Esbensen F-A (2001) impact of sex composition on gangs and gang members delinquency. *Criminology*, 39, 411–440

Pettit P and Braithwaite J (1993) Not just deserts, even in sentencing. *Current Issues in Criminal Justice*, 4, 225–239

Pfohl S (1985) *Images of Deviance and Social Control*. New York: McGraw-Hill

Phares E (1984) *Introduction to Personality*. Columbus, OH: Charles E Merrill

Phillips D and Hensley J (1984) When violence is rewarded or punished: The impact of mass media stories on homicide. *Journal of Communication*, 34, 101–111

Piliavin I and Briar S (1964) Police encounters with juveniles. *American Journal of Sociology*, 70, 206–214

Pinter R (1923) *Intelligence Testing: Methods and Results*. New York: Holt

Platt T (1978) 'Street crime'—a view from the Left. *Crime and Social Justice*, 9, 26–34

Player E (1989) Women and crime in the city. In D Downes (ed) *Crime and the City*. Basingstoke: Macmillan

Polk K (1991) Review of 'A General Theory of Crime' by Gottfredson MR and Hirschi T. *Crime and Delinquency*, 37, 575–581

Pollak O (1950) *The Criminality of Women*. Philadelphia: University of Pennsylvania Press

Poole E and Regoli R (1979) Parental support, delinquent friends, and delinquency: A test of interaction effects. *Journal of Criminal Law and Criminology*, 70, 188–193

Potter H (1992) Crime, shame and reintegration: Review, questions and comment. *Australian and New Zealand Journal of Sociology*, 28, 224–232

Pound R (1930) *Criminal Justice in America*. New York: Holt

Povey D and Prime J (1999) *Recorded Criminal Statistics England and Wales, April 1998 to March 1999*. Home Office Statistical Bulletin 22/98. London: Home Office

Povey D and colleagues (2001) *Recorded Crime England and Wales, 12 months to September 2000*. Home Office Statistical Bulletin 1/01. London: Home Office

Power A and Tunstall R (1997) *Dangerous Disorder: Riots and Violent Disturbances in 13 Areas of Britain*. York: York Publishing Services

Pratt J (2000) The return of the wheelbarrow men; or, the arrival of postmodern penality? *British Journal of Criminology*, 40, 127–145

Pratt T and Cullen F (2000) The empirical status of Gottfredson and Hirschi's general theory of crime: A meta-analysis. *Criminology*, 38, 931–964

Pratt T, Cullen F, Blevins K, Daigle L, and Unnever J (2002) The relationship of attention deficit hyperactivity disorder to crime and delinquency: A meta-analysis. *International Journal of Police Science and Management*, 4, 344–360

Prentky R, Burgess A, Rokous F, Lee A, Hartman C, Renier R, and Douglas J (1989) The presumptive role of fantasy in serial sexual homicide. *American Journal of Psychiatry*, 146, 887–891

Price W and Whatmore P (1967) Behaviour disorders and pattern of crime identified at a maximum security hospital. *British Medical Journal*, 1, 533–536

Price W, Strong J, Whatmore P, and McClemont W (1966) Criminal patients with XYY sex-chromosome complement. *Lancet*, 1, 565–566

Prime J, White S, Liriano S, and Patel K (2001) *Criminal Careers of Those Born Between 1953 and 1978*. Home Office Statistical Bulletin 4/01. London: Home Office

Prins H (1986) *Dangerous Behaviour, the Law and Mental Disorder*. London: Tavistock

Pryce K (1979) *Endless Pressure*. Harmondsworth: Penguin

Pudney S (2002) *The Road to Ruin? Sequences of Initiation into Drug Use and Offending by Young People in Britain*. Home Office Research Study No 253. London: Home Office

Quay H (1987) Intelligence. In H Quay (ed) *Handbook of Juvenile Delinquency*. New York: Wiley

Quinney R (1969) *Crime and Justice in Society*. Boston: Little, Brown

Quinney R (1970) *The Problem of Crime*. New York: Dodd, Mead

Quinney R (1970) *The Social Reality of Crime*. Boston: Little, Brown

Quinney R (1974) *Criminal Justice in America: A Critical Understanding*. Boston: Little, Brown

Quinney R (1974) *Critique of Legal Order*. Boston: Little, Brown

Quinney R (1977) *Class, State, and Crime*. New York: McKay

Quinney R (1980) *Class, State, and Crime* 2nd ed. New York: McKay

Quinsey V (1984) Sexual aggression: Studies of offenders against women. In D Weisstub (ed) *Law and Mental Health: International Perspectives*. New York: Pergamon

Rada R (1975) Alcoholism and forcible rape. *American Journal of Psychiatry*, 132, 444–446

Rada R (1978) *Clinical Aspects of the Rapist*. New York: Grune and Stratton

Rada R, Laws D, Kellner R, Stivastave L, and Peak G (1983) Plasma androgens in violent and non-violent sex offenders. *American Academy of Psychiatry and the Law*, 11, 149–158

Rader C (1977) MMPI profile types of exposers, rapists and assaulters in a court service population. *Journal of Consulting and Clinical Psychology*, 45, 61–69

Radzinowicz L (1961) *In Search of Criminology*. London: Heinemann

Radzinowicz L (1966) *Ideology and Crime*. London: Heinemann

Radzinowicz L and Hood R (1986) *A History of the English Criminal Law and its Administration from 1750* vol 5. London: Stevens

Rafter N (1997) Psychopathy and the evolution of criminological knowledge. *Theoretical Criminology*, 1, 235–259

Raine A (1993) *The Psychopathology of Crime*. San Diego, CA: Academic Press

Raine A and Venables P (1981) Classical conditioning and socialisation—A biosocial interaction. *Personality and Individual Differences*, 2, 273–283

Raine A and Venables P (1984) Tonic heart rate level, social class and antisocial behaviour in English adolescents. *Biological Psychology*, 18, 123–132

Raine A, Lencz T, Bihrle S, LaCasse L, and Colletti P (2000) Reduced pre-frontal gray matter volume and reduced autonomic activity in antisocial personality disorder. *Archives of General Psychiatry*, 57, 119–127

Raine A, Mellingen K, Liu J, Venables P, and Mednick S (2003) Effects of environmental enrichment at ages 3–5 years on schizotypal personality and antisocial behavior at ages 17 and 23 years. *American Journal of Psychiatry*, 160, 1627–1635

Raine A, Reynolds C, Venables P, Mednick S, and Farrington D (1998) Fearlessness, stimulation-seeking, and large body size at age 3 years as early pre-dispositions to childhood aggression at age 11 years. *Archives of General Psychiatry*, 55, 745–751

Ramsay M (1996) *The Relationship between Alcohol and Crime*. Home Office Research Bulletin No 38, 37–44. London: Home Office

Rawlings P (1999) *Crime and Power: A History of Criminal Justice 1688–1998*. London: Longman

Reckless W (1950) *The Crime Problem*. New York: Appleton-Century-Crofts

Reckless W (1961) *The Crime Problem* 3rd ed. New York: Appleton-Century-Crofts

Reichel H and Magnusson D (1988) *The Relationship of Intelligence to Registered Criminality*. Reports from the Department of Psychology 676. Stockholm: University of Stockholm

Reiner R (1984) Crime, law and deviance: The Durkheim legacy. In S Fenton *Durkheim and Modern Sociology*. Cambridge: Cambridge University Press

Reiner R (1994) What should the police be doing? *Police*, 10, 151–157

Reiner R (2000) *The Politics of the Police* 3rd ed. Oxford: Oxford University Press

Reiner R, Livingstone S, and Allen J (2001) Casino culture: Media and crime in a winner–loser society. In K Stenson and R Sullivan (eds) *Crime, Risk and Justice: The Politics of Crime Control in Liberal Democracies*. Cullompton: Willan

Reiss A (1951) Delinquency as the failure of personal and social controls. *American Sociological Review*, 16, 196–207

Reiss A and Rhodes A (1964) An empirical test of differential association theory. *Journal of Research in Crime and Delinquency*, 1, 5–18

Rengert G and Wasilchick J (2000) *Suburban Burglary: A Tale of Two Suburbs* 2nd ed. Springfield, IL: Thomas

Reppetto T (1974) *Residential Crime*. Cambridge, MA: Ballinger

Rex J and Moore R (1967) *Race, Community and Conflict*. London: Oxford University Press

Reynolds C and Judge A (1968) *The Night the Police Went on Strike*. London: Weidenfeld and Nicolson

Rhee S and Waldman I (2002) Genetic and environmental influences on antisocial behavior: A meta-analysis of twin and adoption studies. *Psychological Bulletin*, 128, 490–529

Ricciuti H (1999) Single parenthood and school readiness in White, Black, and Hispanic 6- and 7- year-olds. *Journal of Family Psychology*, 13, 450–464

Rice M, Chaplin T, Harris G, and Coutts J (1994) Empathy for the victim and sexual arousal among rapists and nonrapists. *Journal of Interpersonal Violence*, 9, 435–449

Richman N, Stevenson J, and Graham P (1982) *Pre-school to School: A Behavioural Study*. London: Academic Press

Riley D (1986) *Sex Differences in Teenage Crime: The Role of Lifestyle*. Home Office Research Bulletin No 2, 34–80. London: HMSO

Robertson G (1981) The extent and pattern of crime amongst mentally handicapped offenders. *Apex*, 9, 100–103

Robins D and Cohen P (1978) *Knuckle Sandwich: Growing Up in the Working-Class City*. Harmondsworth: Penguin

Robinson T, Wilde M, Navracruz L, Haydel K, and Varady A (2001) Effects of reducing children's television and video game use on aggressive behavior. *Archives of Pediatrics and Adolescent Medicine*, 155, 17–23

Robinson W (1950) Ecological correlations and the behavior of individuals. *American Sociological Review*, 15, 351–357

Rock P (1988) The present state of criminology in Britain. In P Rock (ed) *A History of British Criminology*. Oxford: Oxford University Press

Rock P (1990) *Helping Victims of Crime*. Oxford: Oxford University Press

Rock P (1992) Foreword. In J Lowman and B MacLean (eds) *Realist Criminology: Crime Control and Policing in the 1990s*. Toronto: University of Toronto Press

Rohrer R (1982) Lost in the myths of crime. *New Statesman*, 22 January, 6–8

Rokach L (1986) *Israel's Sacred Terrorism*. Belmont, Mass: AAUG Press

Rooth G (1973) Exhibitionism, sexual violence and paedophilia. *British Journal of Psychiatry*, 122, 705–710

Rose S (1972) *The Betrayal of the Poor*. Cambridge, MA: Schenkmann

Rosenfeld R and Messner S (1997) Markets, morality, and an institutional-anomie theory of crime. In N Passas and R Agnew (eds) *The Future of Anomie Theory*. Boston: Northeastern University Press

Roshier B (1973) The selection of crime news by the press. In S Cohen and J Young (eds) *The Manufacture of News*. London: Constable

Roshier B (1977) The function of crime myth. *Sociological Review*, 25, 309–323

Roshier B (1989) *Controlling Crime: The Classical Perspective in Criminology*. Milton Keynes: Open University Press

Rossow I (2001) Alcohol and homicide: A cross-cultural comparison of the relationship in 14 European countries. *Addiction*, 96, 77–92

Rowe D (1990) Inherited dispositions toward learning delinquent and criminal behaviour: New evidence. In L Ellis and H Hoffman (eds) *Crime in Biological, Social, and Moral Contexts*. New York: Praeger

Rowe D and Rodgers J (1989) Behaviour genetics, adolescent deviance and 'd': Contributions and issues. In G Adams, R Montemayor, and T Gullotta (eds) *Advances in Adolescent Development*. Newbury Park, CA: Sage

Royal Commission on Police Powers and Procedure (1929) Report. Cmd 3297. London: HMSO

Runciman R (2000) *Drugs and the Law: Report of the Independent Inquiry into the Misuse of Drugs Act 1971*. London: Police Foundation

Rushton J, Fulker D, Neale M, Nias D, and Eysenck H (1986) Altruism and aggression: The heritability of individual differences. *Journal of Personality and Social Psychology*, 50, 1192–1198

Russell D (1984) *Sexual Exploitation: Rape, Child Sexual Abuse, and Workplace Harassment*. Beverly Hills, CA: Sage

Russell S (1998) Reintegrative shaming and the 'frozen antithesis': Braithwaite and Elias. *Journal of Sociology*, 34, 303–313

Russell S (2002) The continuing relevance of Marxism to Critical Criminology. *Critical Criminology*, 11, 113–135

Rutter M (1972) *Maternal Deprivation Reassessed*. Harmondsworth: Penguin

Rutter M and Giller H (1983) *Juvenile Delinquency*. Harmondsworth: Penguin

Rutter M and Silberg J (2002) Gene–environment interplay in relation to emotional and behavioral disturbance. *Annual Review of Psychology*, 53, 463–490

Sacco V (1995) Media constructions of crime. *Annals of the American Academy of Political and Social Science*, 539, 141–154

Salisbury H and Upson A (2004) *Ethnicity, Victimisation and Worry about Crime: Findings from the 2001/02 and 2002/03 British Crime Surveys*. Home Office Research FIndings No 237. London: Home Office

Sampson R (1986) Effects of socioeconomic context on official reaction to juvenile delinquency. *American Sociological Review*, 51, 876–885

Sampson R (1992) Review of 'A General Theory of Crime' by Gottfredson MR and Hirschi T. *Social Forces*, 71, 545–546

Sampson R and Laub J (1993) *Crime in the Making: Pathways and Turning Points through Life*. Cambridge, MA: Harvard University Press

Sampson R and Laub J (1997) Unraveling the social context of physique and delinquency: A new, long-term look at the Gluecks' classic study. In A Raine, P Brennan, D Farrington, and S Mednick (eds) *Biosocial Bases of Violence*. New York: Plenum

Sánchez-Jankowski M (1991) *Islands in the Street: Gangs in American Urban Society*. Berkeley: University of California Press

Sánchez-Jankowski M (2003) Gangs and social change. *Theoretical Criminology*, 7, 191–216

Sanday P (1981) The sociocultural context of rape. *Journal of Social Issues*, 37, 5–27

Sandberg A, Koepf G, Ishihara T, and Hauschka T (1961) An XYY human male. *Lancet*, ii, 488–489

Sanders A and Young R (2000) *Criminal Justice* 2nd ed. London: Butterworths

Sarno C (1996) The impact of closed circuit television on crime in Sutton town centre. In M Bulos and D Grant (eds) *Towards a Safer Sutton? CCTV One Year On*. Sutton: London Borough of Sutton

Savelsberg J (1996) Review of 'Control Balance: Toward a General Theory of Deviance' by Charles R Tittle. *American Journal of Sociology*, 102, 620–622

Savolainen J (2000) Inequality, welfare state, and homicide: Further support for the institutional anomie theory. *Criminology*, 38, 1021–1042

Scarman Lord (1981) *The Brixton Disorders*. Cmnd 8427. London: HMSO

Schalling D (1987) Personality correlates of plasma testosterone levels in young delinquents: An example of person–situation interaction. In S Mednick, T Moffitt, and S Stack (eds) *The Causes of Crime: New Biological Approaches*. Cambridge: Cambridge University Press

Scheff T and Retzinger S (1991) *Emotions and Violence: Shame and Rage in Destructive Conflicts*. Lexington, MA: Lexington Books

Schlapp M and Smith E (1928) *The New Criminology*. New York: Boni and Liveright

Schlesinger P and Tumber H (1994) *Reporting Crime*. Oxford: Oxford University Press

Schlesinger P, Dobash R, Dobash R, and Weaver C (1991) *Women Viewing Violence*. London: BFI

Schlossman S, Zellman G, and Shavelson R, with Sedlak M and Cobb J (1984) *Delinquency Prevention in South Chicago: A Fifty-Year Assessment of the Chicago Area Project*. Santa Monica, CA: RAND

Schmauk F (1970) Punishment, arousal and avoidance learning in sociopaths. *Journal of Abnormal Psychology*, 76, 325–335

Schrag C (1971) *Crime and Justice: American Style*. Washington, DC: Government Printing Office

Schubart R (1995) From desire to deconstruction: Horror films and audience reactions. In D Kidd-Hewitt and R Osborne (eds) *Crime and the Media*. London: Pluto Press

Schuessler K and Cressey D (1950) Personality characteristics of criminals. *American Journal of Sociology*, 5, 476–484

Schur E (1965) *Crimes without Victims*. Englewood Cliffs, NJ: Prentice Hall

Schur E (1980) Comments. In W Gove (ed) *The Labeling of Deviance* 2nd ed. Beverly Hills, CA: Sage

Schwartz M (1991) The future of critical criminology. In B MacLean and D Milovanovic (eds) *New Directions in Critical Criminology*. Vancouver: Collective Press

Schweinhart L, Weikart D, and Larner M (1986) Consequences of three preschool curriculum models through age 15. *Early Childhood Research Quarterly*, 1, 15–45

Schwendinger H and Schwendinger J (1970) Defenders of order or guardians of human rights? *Issues in Criminology*, 5, 123–157

Schwendinger H and Schwendinger J (1985) *Adolescent Subcultures and Delinquency*. New York: Praeger

Scraton P (1990) Scientific knowledge or masculine discourses? Challenging patriarchy in criminology. In L Gelsthorpe and A Morris (eds) *Feminist Perspectives in Criminology*. Buckingham: Open University Press

Scully D (1990) *Understanding Sexual Violence*. London: Harper Collins

Seagrave D and Grisso T (2002) Adolescent development and measurement of juvenile psychopathy. *Law and Human Behavior*, 26, 219–239

Sellin T (1938) *Culture Conflict and Crime*. New York: Social Science Research Council

Sellin T (1939) The negro and the problem of law observance and administration in the light of social research. In C Johnson (ed) *The Negro in American Civilization*: *A Study of Negro Life and Race Relations in the Light of Social Research*. New York: Holt

Serin R (1991) Psychopathy and violence in criminals. *Journal of Interpersonal Violence*, 6, 423–431

Shah R and Pease K (1992) Crime, race and reporting to the police. *Howard Journal*, 31, 192–199

Shah S and Roth L (1974) Biological and psychophysiological factors in criminality. In D Glaser (ed) *Handbook of Criminology*. Chicago: Rand McNally

Shaw C (1938) *Brothers in Crime*. Chicago: University of Chicago Press

Shaw C and McKay H (1931) *Social Factors in Juvenile Delinquency*. Washington, DC: Government Printing Office

Shaw C and McKay H (1942) *Juvenile Delinquency and Urban Areas*. Chicago: University of Chicago Press

Sheldon W (1949) *Varieties of Delinquent Youth*. New York: Harper

Sheridan M (1995) A proposed intergenerational model of substance abuse, family functioning, and abuse/neglect. *Child Abuse and Neglect*, 19, 519–530

Short J and Nye F (1958) Extent of unrecorded juvenile delinquency. *Journal of Criminal Law, Criminology and Police Science*, 49, 296–302

Short J and Strodtbeck F (1965) *Group Process and Gang Delinquency*. Chicago: University of Chicago Press

Siddle D, Mednick S, Nicol A, and Foggit R (1976) Skin conductance recovery in antisocial adolescents. *British Journal of Social and Clinical Psychology*, 15, 425–428

Silverman L (1983) Subliminal psychodynamic activation. In J Masling (ed) *Empirical Studies of Psychoanalytic Theories*. Hillsdale, NJ: The Analytic Press

Simon R (1975) *Women and Crime*. Toronto: Lexington Books

Simons R (1978) The meaning of the IQ-delinquency relationship. *American Sociological Review*, 43, 268–270

Sims A and Gray P (1993) *The Media, Violence and Vulnerable Viewers*. Evidence presented to the Broadcasting Group, House of Lords

Sims L and Myhill A (2001) *Policing and the Public: Findings from the 2000 British Crime Survey*. Home Office Research Findings No 136. London: Home Office

Singer S (1997) Review of 'Control Balance: Toward a General Theory of Deviance' by Charles R Tittle. *Contemporary Sociology—A Journal of Reviews*, 26, 492–493

Singleton N, Meltzer H, and Gatward R, with Coid J and Deasy D (1998) *Psychiatric Morbidity among Prisoners in England and Wales*. London: The Stationery Office.

Sivarajasingam V and Shepherd J (1999) Effect of closed circuit television on urban violence. *Journal of Accident and Emergency Medicine*, 16, 255–257

Sivarajasingam V and Shepherd J (2001) Trends in community violence in England and Wales 1995–1998: An accident and emergency department perspective. *Emergency Medicine Journal*, 18, 105–109

Skinner B (1938) *The Behavior of Organisms*. New York: Appleton-Century-Crofts

Skinner B (1974) *About Behaviourism*. London: Cape

Skogan W (1986) Methodological issues in the study of victimization. In E Fattah (ed) *From Crime Policy to Victim Policy*. London: Macmillan

Slapper G (1999) *Blood in the Bank: Social and Legal Aspects of Death at Work*. Aldershot: Ashgate

Sluckin W, Herbert M, and Sluckin A (1983) *Maternal Bonding*. Oxford: Blackwell

Smalley S, Kustanovich V, Minassian S, Stone J, Ogdie M, McGough J, McCracken J, MacPhie I, Francks C, Fisher S, Cantor R, Monaco A, and Nelson S (2002) Genetic linkage of attention-deficit/hyperactivity disorder on chromosome 16p13, in a region implicated in autism. *American Journal of Human Genetics*, 71, 959–963

Smart C (1976) *Women, Crime and Criminology*. London: Routledge & Kegan Paul

Smart C (1979) The new female criminal: Reality or myth? *British Journal of Criminology*, 19, 50–51

Smart C (1990) Feminist approaches to criminology, or postmodern woman meets atavistic man. In L Gelsthorpe and A Morris (eds) *Feminist Perspectives in Criminology*. London: Routledge & Kegan Paul

Smith B, Davidson R, Smith D, Goldstein H, and Perlstein W (1989) Sensation-seeking and arousal: Effects of strong stimulation on electrodermal and memory task performance. *Personality and Individual Differences*, 10, 671–679

Smith S (1984) Crime in the news. *British Journal of Criminology*, 24, 289–295

Smith S and Donnerstein E (1998) Harmful effects of exposure to media violence: Learning of aggression, emotional desensitization, and fear. In R Geen and E Donnerstein (eds) *Human Aggression: Theories, Research, and Implications for Social Policy*. San Diego, CA: Academic Press

Snodgrass J (1976) Clifford R Shaw and Henry D McKay: Chicago criminologists. *British Journal of Criminology*, 16, 1–19

Snyder H and Sickmund M (1995) *Juvenile Offenders and Victims*. Washington, DC: National Center for Juvenile Justice

Solursh L (1989) Combat addiction: Overview of implications in symptom maintenance and treatment planning. *Journal of Traumatic Stress*, 2, 451–462

Sommers C (1994) *Who Stole Feminism? How Women Have Betrayed Women*. New York: Simon & Schuster

Soothill K and Gibbens T (1978) Recidivism of sex offenders: A re-appraisal. *British Journal of Criminology*, 18, 267–276

Soothill K and Walby S (1991) *Sex Crime in the News*. London: Routledge

Soothill K, Francis B, and Fligelstone R (2002) *Patterns of Offending Behaviour: A New Approach*. London: Home Office

Sparks R (1992) *Television and the Drama of Crime*. Buckingham: Open University Press

Sparks RF (1981) Surveys of victimization: An optimistic assessment. In M Tonry and N Morris (eds) *Crime and Justice: An Annual Review of Research* vol 3. Chicago: University of Chicago Press

Sparks RF, Genn H, and Dodd D (1977) *Surveying Victims*. Chichester: Wiley

Spergel I (1995) *The Youth Gang Problem: A Community Approach*. New York: Oxford University Press

Spicker P (2002) *Poverty and the Welfare State: Dispelling the Myths*. London: Catalyst

Spitzer S (1975) Toward a Marxian theory of deviance. *Social Problems*, 22, 638–651

Srole L (1956) Social integration and certain corollaries: An exploratory study. *American Sociological Review*, 21, 709–716

Stack S (1983) Homicide and property crime: The relationships to anomie. *Aggressive Behaviour*, 9, 339–344

Stack S (1984) Income inequality and property crime. *Criminology*, 22, 229–257

Stanko E (1987) Typical violence, normal precaution: Men, women and interpersonal violence in England, Wales, Scotland and the USA. In J Hanmer and M Maynard (eds) *Women, Violence and Social Control*. Basingstoke: Macmillan

Steadman H, Cocozza J, and Melick M (1978) Explaining the increased arrest rate among mental patients: The changing clientele of state hospitals. *American Journal of Psychiatry*, 135, 816–820

Steadman H, Mulvey E, Monahan J, Robbins P, Appelbaum P, Grisso T, Roth L, and Silver E (1998) Violence by people discharged from acute psychiatric inpatient facilities and by others in the same neighborhoods. *Archives of General Psychiatry*, 55, 393–401

Steffensmeier D (1981) Patterns of female property crime, 1960–1978: A postscript. In L Bowker (ed) *Women and Crime in America*. New York: Macmillan

Steffensmeier D and Allan E (1991) Gender, age and crime. In J Sheley (ed) *Criminology*. Belmont, CA: Wadsworth

Steinart H (1985) The amazing New Left law and order campaign. *Contemporary Crises*, 9, 327–333

Stelfox P (1998) Policing lower levels of organised crime in England and Wales. *Howard Journal*, 37, 393–406

Stephenson-Burton A (1995) Through the looking-glass: Public images of white collar crime. In D Kidd-Hewitt and R Osborne (eds) *Crime and the Media*. London: Pluto Press

Stermac L and Quinsey V (1986) Social competence among rapists. *Behavioral Assessment*, 8, 171–185

Stermac L and Segal Z (1989) Adult sexual contact with children: An examination of cognitive factors. *Behavior Therapy*, 20, 573–584

Stott D (1980) *Delinquency and Human Nature*. London: Hodder and Stoughton

Stott D (1982) *Delinquency: The Problem and its Prevention*. London: Batsford

Straus M (1983) Ordinary violence, child abuse, and wife-beating: What do they have in common? In D Finkelhor, R Gelles, G Hotaling, and M Straus (eds) *The Dark Side of Families: Current Family Violence Research*. Beverly Hills, CA: Sage

Straus M (1991) Discipline and deviance: Physical punishment of children and violence and other crime in adulthood. *Social Problems*, 38, 133–154

Straus M (1993) Physical assaults by wives: A major social problem. In R Gelles and D Loseke (eds) *Current Controversies on Family Violence*. Newbury Park, CA: Sage

Straus M (2001) *Beating the Devil out of Them: Corporal Punishment in American Families and its Effects on Children* 2nd ed. New Brunswick, NJ: Transaction

Straus M and Gelles R (eds) (1990) *Physical Violence in American Families*. New Brunswick, NJ: Transaction

Sudnow D (1965) Normal crimes: Sociological features of the penal code in a public defender office. *Social Problems*, 12, 255–276

Sumner C (ed) (1990) *Censure, Politics and Criminal Justice*. Milton Keynes: Open University Press

Sumner C (1994) *The Sociology of Deviance: An Obituary*. Buckingham: Open University Press

Sutherland E (1931) Mental deficiency and crime. In K Young (ed) *Social Attitudes*. New York: Holt

Sutherland E (1939) *Principles of Criminology* 3rd ed. Philadelphia: Lippincott

Sutherland E (1940) White collar criminality. *American Sociological Review*, 5, 1–12

Sutherland E (1949) *White Collar Crime*. New York: Holt, Rinehart & Winston

Sutherland E (1951) Critique of Sheldon's varieties of delinquent youth. *American Sociological Review*, 16, 10–13

Sutherland E and Cressey D (1966) *Principles of Criminology* 7th ed. Philadelphia: Lippincott

Suttles G (1972) *The Social Construction of Communities*. Chicago: University of Chicago Press

Sutton J, Smith P, and Swettenham J (1999) Social cognition and bullying: Social inadequacy or skilled manipulation. *British Journal of Developmental Psychology*, 17, 435–450

Swanston H, Parkinson P, O'Toole B, Plunkett A, Shrimpton S, and Oates R (2003) Juvenile crime, aggression and delinquency after sexual abuse. *British Journal of Criminology*, 43, 729–749

Swigert V and Farrell R (1980) Corporate homicide: Definitional processes in the creation of deviance. *Law and Society Review*, 125, 161–182

Sykes C (1992) *A Nation of Victims: The Decay of the American Character*. New York: St Martin's Press

Sykes G and Matza D (1957) Techniques of neutralization: A theory of delinquency. *American Sociological Review*, 22, 664–673

Szasz T (1961) *The Myth of Mental Illness*. New York: Dell

Szasz T (1970) *The Manufacture of Madness*. New York: Dell

Tannenbaum F (1923) *Crime and the Community*. New York: Columbia University Press

Tappan P (1947) Who is the criminal? *American Sociological Review*, 12, 96–102

Tarling R (1982) *Crime and Unemployment*. Home Office Research Bulletin No 12. London: HMSO

Tarling R (1993) *Analysing Offending: Data, Models and Interpretation*. London: HMSO

Tarling R, Dowds L, and Budd T (2000) *Victim and Witness Intimidation: Findings from the British Crime Survey*. London: Home Office

Taub R, Taylor D, and Dunham J (1984) *Paths of Neighborhood Change*. Chicago: University of Chicago Press

Taylor D (1997) *The New Police in Nineteenth-Century England: Crime, Conflict and Control*. Manchester: Manchester University Press

Taylor E (1991) Toxins and allergens. In M Rutter and P Casaer (eds) *Biological Risk Factors for Psychosocial Disorders*. Cambridge: Cambridge University Press

Taylor I, Walton P, and Young J (1973) *The New Criminology*. London: Routledge & Kegan Paul

Taylor I, Walton P, and Young J (eds) (1975) *Critical Criminology*. London: Routledge & Kegan Paul

Taylor L (1971) *Deviance and Society*. London: Michael Joseph

Taylor P (1982) Schizophrenia and violence. In J Gunn and D Farrington (eds) *Abnormal Offenders, Delinquency, and the Criminal Justice System*. Chichester: Wiley

Taylor P (1985) Motives for offending among violent and psychotic men. *British Journal of Psychiatry*, 147, 491–498

Taylor P (1986) Psychiatric disorders in London's life-sentenced offenders. *British Journal of Criminology*, 26, 63–78

Taylor P (1993a) Mental illness and violence. In P Taylor (ed) *Violence in Society*. London: Royal College of Physicians

Taylor P (1993b) Schizophrenia and crime: Distinctive patterns of association. In S Hodgins (ed) *Mental Disorder and Crime*. Newbury Park, CA: Sage

Taylor P and Gunn J (1984) Risk of violence among psychotic men. *British Medical Journal*, 288, 1945–1949

Taylor R (2001) *Breaking Away from Broken Windows: Baltimore Neighborhoods and the Nationwide Fight against Crime, Grime, Fear and Decline*. Boulder, CO: Westview Press

Taylor S and Hulsizer M (1998) Psychoactive drugs and human aggression. In R Geen and E Donnerstein (eds) *Human Aggression: Theories, Research, and Implications for Social Policy*. San Diego, CA: Academic Press

Tedeschi J (1983) Social influence theory and aggression. In R Geen and E Donnerstein (eds) *Aggression: Theoretical and Empirical Reviews* 1. New York: Academic Press

Teplin L (1984) Criminalising mental disorder: The comparative arrest rate of the mentally ill. *American Psychologist*, 39, 794–803

Teplin L (1985) The criminality of the mentally ill. *American Journal of Psychiatry*, 142, 593–598

Teplin L (1990) The prevalence of severe mental disorder among urban jail detainees: Comparison with the epidemiologic catchment area program. *American Journal of Public Health*, 80, 663–669

Terman L (1916) *The Measurement of Intelligence*. Boston: Houghton Mifflin

Theilgard R (1983) Aggression and XYY personality. *International Journal of Law and Psychiatry*, 6, 413–421

Thomas W (1923) *The Unadjusted Girl*. Boston: Little, Brown

Thompson E (1975) *Whigs and Hunters*. London: Allen Lane

Thompson H (1966) *Hell's Angels*. Harmondsworth: Penguin

Thomson T (1998) Review of 'Constitutive Criminology: Beyond Postmodernism' by Henry S and Milovanovic D. *Canadian Journal of Sociology*, 23, 109–113

Thrasher F (1927) *The Gang*. Chicago: University of Chicago Press

Tittle C (1980) Labelling and crime: An empirical evaluation. In W Gove (ed) *The Labelling of Deviance—Evaluating a Perspective* 2nd ed. Beverly Hills, CA: Sage

Tittle C (1991) Review of 'A General Theory of Crime' by Gottfredson M R and Hirschi T. *American Journal of Sociology*, 96, 1609–1611

Tittle C (1995) *Control Balance: Toward a General Theory of Deviance*. Boulder, CO: Westview Press

Tittle C (2004) Refining control balance theory. *Theoretical Criminology*, 8, 395–428

Tittle C, Burke M, and Jackson E (1986) Modelling Sutherland's theory of differential association: Toward an empirical clarification. *Social Forces*, 65, 405–432

Toby J (1957) Social disorganization and stake in conformity: Complementary factors in the predatory behaviour of hoodlums. *Journal of Criminal Law, Criminology and Police Science*, 48, 12–17

Toch H (1969) *Violent Men*. Harmondsworth: Penguin

Toch H and Adams K (1989) *The Disturbed Violent Offender*. New Haven, CT: Yale University Press

Tomsen S (1997) A top night: Social protest, masculinity and the culture of drinking violence. *British Journal of Criminology*, 37, 90–102

Tong R (1989) *Feminist Thought: A Comprehensive Introduction*. London: Unwin Hyman

Tonry M (1997) Ethnicity, crime, and immigration, In M Tonry (ed) *Ethnicity, Crime, and Immigration: Comparative and Cross-National Perspectives*. Chicago: University of Chicago Press

Tonry M (2004) *Punishment and Politics: Evidence and Emulation in the Making of English Crime Control Policy*. Cullompton: Willan

Trasler G (1962) *The Explanation of Criminality*. London: Routledge & Kegan Paul

Trasler G (1986) Situational crime control and rational choice: A critique. In K Heal and G Laycock (eds) *Situational Crime Prevention: From Theory into Practice*. London: HMSO

Tremblay R, Masse B, Perron D, Leblanc M, Schwartzman A, and Ledingham J (1992) Early disruptive behavior, poor school achievement, delinquent behavior, and delinquent personality: Longitudinal analyses. *Journal of Consulting and Clinical Psychology*, 60, 64–72

Turk A (1969) *Criminality and Social Order*. Chicago: Rand McNally

Turner S, Turner J, and Fix A (1976) Throwing the beast back out: A closer look at Van Den Berghe's 'beast'. *American Sociological Review*, 41, 551–555

Tutt N (1971) The subnormal offender. *British Journal of Mental Subnormality*, 17, 42–47

US Department of Justice (1990) *Drugs and Crime Facts, 1990*. Washington, DC: US Department of Justice

Vagg J (1998) Delinquency and shame. Data from Hong Kong. *British Journal of Criminology*, 38, 247–264

Valier C (2003) Foreigners, crime and changing mobilities. *British Journal of Criminology*, 43, 1–21

Van Eyken A (1987) Aggression: Myth or model? *Journal of Applied Philosophy*, 4, 165–176

van Goozen S, van de Poll N, and Frijda N (1994) Anger and aggression in women: Influence of sports choice and testosterone administration. *Aggressive Behavior*, 20, 213–222

van Kesteren J, Mayhew P, and Nieuwbeerta P (2001) *Criminal Victimisation in Seventeen Industrialised Countries: Key Findings from the 2000 International Crime Victims Survey*. The Hague: WODC, Ministry of Justice

Van Ness S (1984) Rape as instrumental violence: A study of youthful offenders. *Journal of Offender Counselling, Service, and Rehabilitation*, 9, 161–170

Venables P (1987) Autonomic nervous system factors in criminal behaviour. In S Mednick, T Moffitt, and S Stack (eds) *The Causes of Crime: New Biological Approaches*. Cambridge: Cambridge University Press

Virkkunen M (1987) Metabolic dysfunctions among habitually violent offenders: Reactive hypoglycaemia and cholesterol levels. In S Mednick, T Moffitt, and S Stack (eds) *The Causes of Crime: New Biological Approaches*. Cambridge: Cambridge University Press

Virkkunen M (1988) Cerebrospinal fluid: Monoamine metabolites among habitually violent and impulsive offenders. In T Moffitt and S Mednick (eds) *Biological Contributions to Crime Causation*. Dordrecht: Martinus Nijhoff

Virkkunen M and Linnoila M (1993) Brain-serotonin, Type-II alcoholism and impulsive violence. *Journal of Studies on Alcohol*, S11, 163–169

Volavka J (1987) Electroencephalogram among criminals. In S Mednick, T Moffitt, and S Stack (eds) *The Causes of Crime: New Biological Approaches*. Cambridge: Cambridge University Press

Vold G (1958) *Theoretical Criminology*. New York: Oxford University Press

von Hentig H (1948) *The Criminal and his Victim*. New Haven, CT: Yale University Press

von Hirsch A (1985) *Past or Future Crimes*. New Brunswick, NJ: Rutgers University Press

Waddington P (1983) Beware the community trap. *Police*, March, 34

Waddington P (1986) Mugging as a moral panic: A question of proportion. *British Journal of Sociology*, 37, 245–259

Wadsworth M (1976) Delinquency, pulse rates and early emotional deprivation. *British Journal of Criminology*, 16, 245–256

Waldo G and Dinitz S (1967) Personality attributes of the criminal: An analysis of research studies, 1950–1965. *Journal of Research in Crime and Delinquency*, 2, 185–202

Walker L (1988) The battered woman syndrome. In G Hotaling, D Finkelhor, J Kirkpatrick, and M Straus (eds) *Family Abuse and its Consequences: New Directions in Research*. Beverly Hills, CA: Sage

Walker M (ed) (1995) *Interpreting Crime Statistics*. Oxford: Oxford University Press

Walklate S (1989) *Victimology: The Victim and the Criminal Justice Process*. London: Unwin Hyman

Walklate S (1997) Risk and criminal victimization. *British Journal of Criminology*, 37, 35–45

Walklate S (2004) *Gender, Crime and Criminal Justice* 2nd ed. Cullompton: Willan

Walsh A (2000) Behavior genetics and anomie/strain theory. *Criminology*, 38, 1075–1107

Walters G (2004) The trouble with psychopathy as a general theory of crime. *International Journal of Offender Therapy and Comparative Criminology*, 48, 133–148

Warburton F (1965) Observations on a sample of psychopathic, American criminals. *Behaviour Research and Therapy*, 3, 129–135

Ward T and Keenan T (1999) Child molesters' implicit theories. *Journal of Interpersonal Violence*, 14, 821–838

Waring E, Weisburd D, and Chayet E (1995) White-collar crime and anomie. In F Adler and W Laufer (eds) *The Legacy of Anomie Theory*. New Brunswick, NJ: Transaction

Watson L (1996) *Victims of Violent Crime Recorded by the Police in England and Wales 1990–94*. London: HMSO

Weisburd D, Waring E, and Wheeler S (1990) Class, status and the punishment of white-collar criminals. *Law and Social Inquiry*, 15, 223–246

West C and Zimmerman D (1987) Doing gender. *Gender and Society*, 1, 125–151

West D (1965) *Murder Followed by Suicide*. London: Heinemann

West D (1982) *Delinquency: Its Roots, Careers, and Prospects*. London: Heinemann

West D and Farrington D (1977) *The Delinquent Way of Life*. London: Heinemann

White D (1950) The gatekeeper: A case study in the selection of news. *Journalism Quarterly*, 27, 383–390

White R (1996) Target hardening: Crime and the perception of the risk. *Arena Magazine*, 25, 32–33

White R and van der Velden J (1995) Class and criminality. *Social Justice*, 22, 51–74

Whitehead J and Lab S (1990) *Juvenile Justice: An Introduction*. Cincinnati, OH: Anderson

Whitman S, Coleman T, Patmon C, Desai B, Cohen R, and King L (1984) Epilepsy in prison: Elevated prevalence and no relationship to violence. *Neurology*, 34, 774–782

Whyte W (1943) *Street Corner Society*. Chicago: University of Chicago Press

Whyte W (1957) *The Organization Man*. New York: McGraw

Wiatrowski M, Griswold D, and Roberts M (1981) Social control theory and delinquency. *American Sociological Review*, 46, 525–541

Widom C (1976) Interpersonal conflict and co-operation in psychopaths. *Journal of Abnormal Psychology*, 85, 330–334

Widom C (1989) Does violence beget violence? A critical examination of the literature. *Psychological Bulletin*, 106, 3–28

Widom C and Ames A (1988) Biology and female crime. In T Moffitt and S Mednick (eds) *Biological Contributions to Crime Causation*. Dordrecht: Martinus Nijhoff

Wikström P-O (1991) *Urban Crime, Criminals and Victims*. New York: Springer-Verlag

Wikström P-O and Loeber R (2000) Do disadvantaged neighborhoods cause well-adjusted children to become adolescent delinquents? A study of male serious juvenile offending, individual risk and protective factors, and neighborhood context. *Criminology*, 38, 1109–1142

Wilczynski A and Morris A (1993) Parents who kill their children. *Criminal Law Review*, 31–36

Wiles P and Costello A (2000) *The 'Road to Nowhere': The Evidence for Travelling Criminals*. Home Office Research Study No 207. London: Home Office

Wilkins L (1964) *Social Deviance*. London: Tavistock

Williams L and Finkelhor D (1990) The characteristics of incestuous fathers: A review of recent studies. In W Marshall, D Laws, and H Barbaree (eds) *Handbook of Sexual Assault*. New York: Plenum

Williams P and Dickinson J (1993) Fear of crime: Read all about it? *British Journal of Criminology*, 33, 33–56

Willis P (1977) *Learning to Labour*. London: Saxon House

Wilson G and Cox D (1983) Personality of pedophile club members. *Personality and Individual Differences*, 4, 323–329

Wilson H (1980) Parental supervision: A neglected aspect of delinquency. *British Journal of Criminology*, 20, 203–235

Wilson H and Herbert G (1978) *Parents and Children in the Inner City*. London: Routledge & Kegan Paul

Wilson J and Herrnstein R (1985) *Crime and Human Nature*. New York: Simon & Schuster

Wilson J and Kelling G (1982) Broken windows. *The Atlantic Monthly*, March, 29–38

Wilson J and Kelling G (1989) Making neighborhoods safe. *The Atlantic Monthly*, February, 46–52

Wilson S (1980) Vandalism and defensible space on London housing estates. In R Clarke and P Mayhew (eds) *Designing Out Crime*. London: HMSO

Wilson W (1987) *The Truly Disadvantaged: The Inner City, the Underclass, and Public Policy*. Chicago: University of Chicago Press

Wilson W (1996) *When Work Disappears: The World of the New Urban Poor*. New York: Alfred Knopf

Wirth L (1931) Clinical sociology. *American Journal of Sociology*, 37, 49–66

Witkin H, Mednick S, Schulsinger F, Bakkestrom E, Christiansen K, Goodenough D, Hirschhorn K, Lundsteen C, Owen D, Philip J, Rubin D, and Stocking M (1976) Criminality in XYY and XXY men. *Science*, 193, 547–555

Witt R, Clarke A, and Fielding N (1998) Crime, earnings inequality and unemployment in England and Wales. *Applied Economics Letters*, 5, 265–267

Wober J and Gunter B (1990) *Crime Reconstruction Programmes*. London: IBA Research Department

Wolfgang M (1958) *Patterns in Criminal Homicide*. Philadelphia: University of Pennsylvania Press

Wolfgang M and Ferracuti F (1967) *The Subculture of Violence*. Beverly Hills, CA: Sage

Wood M (2004) *Perceptions and Experience of Antisocial Behaviour: Findings from the British Crime Survey 2003/04*. Home Office Online Report 49/04

Wootton B (1959) *Social Science and Social Pathology*. London: Allen & Unwin

Wormith J (1984) The controversy over the effects of long-term incarceration. *Canadian Journal of Criminology*, 26, 423–437

Wright B, Caspi A, Moffitt T, and Paternoster R (2004) Does the perceived risk of punishment deter criminally prone individuals? Rational choice, self-control, and crime. *Journal of Research in Crime and Delinquency*, 41, 180–213

Wright R and West D (1981) Rape: A comparison of group offences and lone assaults. *Medicine, Science and the Law*, 21, 25–30

Wrightson K (1980) Two concepts of order: Justices, constables and jurymen in seventeenth-century England. In J Brewer and J Styles (eds) *An Ungovernable People*. London: Hutchinson

Yablonsky L (1962) *The Violent Gang*. New York: Macmillan

Yeager P (1994) Law, crime and inequality. In J Hagan and R Peterson (eds) *Crime and Inequality*. Stanford, CA: Stanford University Press

Young A (1996) *Imagining Crime*. London: Sage

Young J (1971) *The Drugtakers*. London: McGibbon & Kee

Young J (1974) Mass media, drugs and deviance. In P Rock and M McIntosh (eds) *Deviance and Social Control*. London: Tavistock

Young J (1975) Working class criminology. In I Taylor, P Walton, and J Young (eds) *Critical Criminology*. London: Routledge & Kegan Paul

Young J (1999) *The Exclusive Society*. London: Sage

Young J (2003) Merton with energy, Katz with structure: The sociology of vindictiveness and the criminology of transgression. *Theoretical Criminology*, 7, 389–414

Young M (1991) *An Inside Job*. Oxford: Oxford University Press

Young R and Goold B (1999) Restorative police cautioning in Aylesbury—From degrading to reintegrative shaming ceremonies? *Criminal Law Review*, 126–138

Zedner L (1991) *Women, Crime and Custody in Victorian England*. Oxford: Oxford University Press

Zillmann D (1979) *Hostility and Aggression*. Hillsdale, NJ: Erlbaum

Zimring F (1981) Kids, groups and crime: Some implications of a well-known secret. *Journal of Criminal Law and Criminology*, 72, 867–885

Zimring F and Hawkins G (1997) *Crime is Not the Problem: Lethal Violence in America*. New York: Oxford University Press

Zuckerman M (1984) Sensation seeking: A comparative approach to a human trait. *The Behavioral and Brain Sciences*, 7, 413–471

Name Index

Subject Index

A

abortion 34
accountability of the police 20, 22–7, 270, 273–4
adoption studies 349–52
adrenalin 358–9
adult masculinities 330
affection 299, 407
age of consent 447
aggression and violence 386, 403, 428–42, 456
  and adrenalin 358–9
  and alcohol 370
  and anger 433
  biological explanations 430–2
  child physical abuse 354, 438–42
  and climate 434
  corporal punishment 429, 440–2
  definitions 428–9
  domestic violence 18, 435–6
  frequency of violent offences 429–30
  and intelligence 431–2
  Intermittent Explosive Disorder (IED) 363–4
  and learning theories 432–3
  marital conflict and aggressive children 432–3
  and noise levels 434–5
  personality types 435
  police use of violence 433
  psychoanalytic explanations 434
  psychological explanations 436–7
  and psychopathy 433
  sadistic violent behaviour 434
  sociological explanations 437–8
  and testosterone 356–8
  TV and film violence 417–20
  see also murders

alcohol consumption 351, 367–70, 369
  and aggression 370
  and child abuse 439
  drink-driving 293
  and rape 452
American Criminal: an Anthropological Study (Hooton) 341–2
American Dream 163, 173–4, 381
anal-sadistic phase of personality development 402, 406
anger and aggression 433
anger rapists 451
Anglo-Saxon society 11
anomie
  anomia scale 169
  and conformity 163–4
  Crime and the American Dream (Messner and Rosenfeld) 173
  Delinquency and Opportunity (Cloward and Ohlin) 170
  Durkheim's theory 158–60, 163, 166
  The Exclusive Society (Young) 174–5
  and female crime 318
  and innovation 164, 169
  and Left Realism 269
  Merton's theory 162–70
  and power 164
  and rebellion 165, 169
  and retreatism 165
  and ritualism 164, 169
  The Social System (Parsons) 170
  and white-collar crime 167–8
  see also strain theories
anonymity of young offenders 78, 215–16
anti-social behaviour 37–8, 141
anxiety 334
appreciative sociology 132